RETAIL MARKETING MANAGEMENT

PEARSON

At Pearson, we have a simple mission: to help people make more of their lives through learning.

We combine innovative learning technology with trusted content and educational expertise to provide engaging and effective learning experiences that serve people wherever and whenever they are learning.

From classroom to boardroom, our curriculum materials, digital learning tools and testing programmes help to educate millions of people worldwide – more than any other private enterprise.

Every day our work helps learning flourish, and wherever learning flourishes, so do people.

To learn more, please visit us at **www.pearson.com/uk**

RETAIL MARKETING MANAGEMENT

PRINCIPLES AND PRACTICE

Helen Goworek
Peter McGoldrick

Pearson Education Limited
Edinburgh Gate
Harlow CM20 2JE
United Kingdom
Tel: +44 (0)1279 623623
Web: www.pearson.com/uk

First published 2015 (print and electronic)

© Pearson Education Limited 2015 (print and electronic)

The rights of Helen Goworek and Peter McGoldrick to be identified as authors of this work have been asserted by them in accordance with the Copyright, Designs and Patents Act 1988.

The print publication is protected by copyright. Prior to any prohibited reproduction, storage in a retrieval system, distribution or transmission in any form or by any means, electronic, mechanical, recording or otherwise, permission should be obtained from the publisher or, where applicable, a licence permitting restricted copying in the United Kingdom should be obtained from the Copyright Licensing Agency Ltd, Saffron House, 6–10 Kirby Street, London EC1N 8TS.

The ePublication is protected by copyright and must not be copied, reproduced, transferred, distributed, leased, licensed or publicly performed or used in any way except as specifically permitted in writing by the publishers, as allowed under the terms and conditions under which it was purchased, or as strictly permitted by applicable copyright law. Any unauthorised distribution or use of this text may be a direct infringement of the authors' and the publisher's rights and those responsible may be liable in law accordingly.

All trademarks used herein are the property of their respective owners. The use of any trademark in this text does not vest in the authors or publisher any trademark ownership rights in such trademarks, nor does the use of such trademarks imply any affiliation with or endorsement of this book by such owners.

The screenshots in this book are reprinted by permission of Microsoft Corporation.

Pearson Education is not responsible for the content of third-party internet sites.

ISBN: 978-0-273-75874-7 (print)
         978-0-273-75878-5 (PDF)
         978-0-273-79481-3 (eText)

British Library Cataloguing-in-Publication Data
A catalogue record for the print edition is available from the British Library

Library of Congress Cataloging-in-Publication Data
Goworek, Helen.
  Retail marketing management : principles and practice / Helen Goworek & Peter McGoldrick.
     pages cm
  ISBN 978-0-273-75874-7 (print) — ISBN 978-0-273-75878-5 (PDF) — ISBN 978-0-273-79481-3 (eText)
  1. Marketing—Management. 2. Retail trade. I. McGoldrick, Peter J. II. Title.
  HF5415.13.G67 2015
  658.8'7—dc23
                              2015014031

10 9 8 7 6 5 4 3
19 18 17

Print edition typeset in 10/12 pt Sabon MT Pro by 71
Printed by CPI UK

NOTE THAT ANY PAGE CROSS REFERENCES REFER TO THE PRINT EDITION

Brief contents

xiii Preface
xiv About the authors
xv Acknowledgements

1 **CHAPTER 1**
Introduction to retail marketing management

33 **CHAPTER 2**
Retail marketing strategy

55 **CHAPTER 3**
Retail consumer behaviour and market segmentation

83 **CHAPTER 4**
Retail product and brand management

109 **CHAPTER 5**
Retail buying and merchandising

136 **CHAPTER 6**
Retail pricing

161 **CHAPTER 7**
Retail marketing communications

190 **CHAPTER 8**
Retail location

216 **CHAPTER 9**
Retail design and layout

246 **CHAPTER 10**
Retail customer service

266 **CHAPTER 11**
Multichannel retailing

289 **CHAPTER 12**
Legislation and ethics in retailing

311 **CHAPTER 13**
International retail marketing and emerging markets

331 Glossary
337 Index

Contents

xiii   Preface
xiv   About the authors
xv   Acknowledgements

1   **CHAPTER 1**
Introduction to retail marketing management

2   Introduction
2   Definitions of retailing
4   History and development of retail marketing
9   The development and scope of retail marketing theory and practice
10   Retail industry associations
11   Retailer categories
11   Retail business formats
13   Non-store retailing (home shopping)
13   Retail concepts and theories
14   The retail life cycle
18   Recent developments affecting the retail environment
24   Retailing management
26   The future of retailing
27   Studying retail marketing
27   Exercises and questions
28   References
31   Further reading
32   **Case study: Re-evaluating the store**

33   **CHAPTER 2**
Retail marketing strategy

34   Introduction
34   Retail marketing strategy
35   Retail marketing planning
36   Situation analysis
36   SWOT analysis
38   Mission statements
38   Setting goals and objectives
39   Identifying consumers
39   Developing retail strategies
40   Implementation of the marketing plan
43   Internal and external marketing audits
47   Market attractiveness
47   Value chain

48	Sources of competitive advantage
48	Market penetration and diversification
49	Portfolio analysis
49	Competitive marketing objectives
50	Marketing strategy in relation to HRM and finance strategy
50	Chapter summary
51	Exercises and questions
51	References
52	Further reading
53	**Case study: WH Smith upbeat despite sales doldrums**

55 CHAPTER 3
Retail consumer behaviour and market segmentation

56	Introduction
56	Retail consumer behaviour and attitudes
57	Consumer motivation and needs
58	Consumer decision-making
61	Experiential consumer behaviour
61	Influences on consumer purchasing behaviour
66	Customer loyalty
67	Negative consumer behaviour
72	Customer profiles
73	Retail marketing research
76	Chapter summary
76	Exercises and questions
77	References
80	Further reading
81	**Case study: Targeting the female consumer**

83 CHAPTER 4
Retail product and brand management

84	Introduction
84	New product development
86	The Product Life Cycle
91	Retail product assortment
92	The product/service continuum
93	Brand management
94	Brand names
95	Brand identity and brand image
95	Brand equity
95	Brand extensions
96	Retail brand positioning – perceptual maps
98	Rebranding
98	Branded and own-label merchandise
102	Chapter summary
103	Exercises and questions
104	References
104	Further reading
106	**Case study: GLOBAL brands – ups and downs: Consumers luxuriate in shopping on the web**

109 CHAPTER 5
Retail buying and merchandising

- 110 Introduction
- 110 Buying and merchandising roles
- 111 Centralised and decentralised buying
- 112 Organisational buying theories
- 113 Buying branded and 'designer' merchandise
- 115 Buying own-label merchandise
- 116 The retail buying cycle
- 123 Retail buying for online and mail order (home shopping) companies
- 127 Supply chain management and stock control by retailers
- 128 Retail space planning and allocation
- 129 Retail sales forecasting and budget planning
- 129 Chapter summary
- 130 Exercises and questions
- 130 References
- 132 Further reading
- 133 **Case study: Supply chain – back to the source**

136 CHAPTER 6
Retail pricing

- 137 Introduction
- 137 Retail market levels – mass market, middle market and luxury
- 139 Retail pricing – objectives and strategies
- 141 Implementing demand-based pricing strategies
- 147 Calculating retail prices
- 148 Price elasticity
- 151 The relationship between price and value
- 152 Markdowns: seasonal sales, reductions and offers
- 155 Chapter summary
- 155 Exercises and questions
- 156 References
- 158 Further reading
- 159 **Case study: Price Wars threaten to reshape landscape of supermarkets**

161 CHAPTER 7
Retail marketing communications

By Helen Goworek and Kristine Pole

- 162 Introduction
- 162 Retail marketing communication strategies
- 162 Retail advertising
- 172 Public relations
- 175 Sponsorship
- 175 Sales promotions
- 177 Direct marketing
- 177 Retail marketing communications via digital and social media
- 181 Word-of-mouth
- 181 Personal selling
- 182 Relationship marketing
- 182 Chapter summary

183	Exercises and questions
184	References
185	Further reading
187	**Case study: Marketing communications at Superdry**

190 CHAPTER 8
Retail location

By John Pal

191	Introduction
192	Why are locations important – even in the digital world?
193	A framework for location decision-making
198	What types of locations do retailers use?
203	How do retailers make location decisions?
206	Site-specific issues
209	The planning system
211	Chapter summary
212	Exercises and questions
212	References
214	**Case study: Rolling out a new breed of local discount store**

216 CHAPTER 9
Retail design and layout

217	Introduction
217	Retail store design
228	Visual merchandising
234	Retail atmosphere
238	The non-store retail selling environment
240	Chapter summary
241	Exercises and questions
242	References
243	Further reading
244	**Case study: Anthropologie moves out of London**

246 CHAPTER 10
Retail customer service

By Sheilagh Resnick

247	Introduction
248	Characteristics of services
250	Service quality models
253	The service encounter
255	Electronic service delivery
257	Service culture
259	Service recovery
261	Chapter summary
261	Exercises and questions
262	References
263	Further reading
264	**Case study 1: Customer service at Boots UK**
265	**Case study 2: Self-scan checkouts**

266 CHAPTER 11
Multichannel retailing

By Anthony Kent

- 267 Introduction
- 267 Mail order
- 271 Direct marketing
- 273 Online retailing
- 275 Consumer engagement
- 275 Long tail effect
- 276 New technology
- 277 Website design
- 281 Online communications
- 281 Fulfilment and delivery systems
- 282 Multichannel retailing
- 284 Chapter summary
- 285 Exercises and questions
- 285 References
- 287 Further reading
- 288 **Case study: Asos**

289 CHAPTER 12
Legislation and ethics in retailing

- 290 Introduction
- 290 Legislation and regulations affecting retailing
- 292 Pricing
- 292 Promotion
- 293 Product
- 294 Place (location)
- 295 Legislation and ethics within the extended marketing mix
- 296 Sustainability and corporate social responsibility
- 298 Social sustainability
- 300 Environmental sustainability
- 302 Chapter summary
- 302 Exercises and questions
- 303 References
- 306 Further reading
- 307 **Case study: Some challenges in product sourcing in global retail supply chains**

311 CHAPTER 13
International retail marketing and emerging markets

By Lisa Qixun Siebers

- 312 Introduction
- 312 Defining international retailing
- 314 International retailing and its development
- 319 The international retail environment: an emerging market perspective
- 320 Psychic distance
- 321 Infrastructure and distribution in emerging markets
- 322 Retail internationalisation strategies
- 324 Chapter summary

325 Exercises and questions
325 References
328 Further reading
329 **Case study: Indonesia's ecommerce industry awakens**

331 Glossary
337 Index

Preface

Retailing is a dynamic industry in a constant state of evolution, which both reflects and influences changes in society. As the retail industry is global in terms of the sourcing of products and their distribution to consumers, it consequently has significant impacts upon the economy, society and the environment worldwide. Retail marketing is an integral component of the retail industry that affects every part of the business. The book explains that marketing activities are not confined to the marketing department of retailers but take place throughout the company, with each element of retailing playing a part in brand image to a greater or lesser extent. There are several other Retail Marketing books available which will prove useful to studying this subject, but in recent years very few have been published that concentrate on the European market, which has many different characteristics to US markets, for example. The content of the book differs from most of its competitors by exploring in further depth the impact of product development and store design upon retailing.

The main aim of this book is to inform students, academics and practitioners about the wide range of options that are available in the implementation of Retail Marketing and the career roles that relate to this discipline, with a view to ultimately optimising retail organisations' performance and contribution to society. Readers who wish to prepare for a career in the challenging field of Retail Marketing are encouraged to gain any form of retail experience they can initially, even if this is not in the same product sector or price bracket that they would ideally like to work. Jobs that involve direct interaction with customers will provide a useful grounding as this will help to provide the awareness of consumer needs that is central to marketing. The book provides a current picture of developments in the arenas of retailing and marketing, although these are subject to such rapid change that it is important not to simply read this book in isolation but to also maintain a contemporary perspective by reading trade journals such as *Retail Week* and articles about retailing in newspapers. For this reason, supplementary online materials are available that provide updates on the topics discussed in the book.

This book is designed with various potential audiences in mind. It can be read independently by undergraduate and postgraduate students who are interested in working in retailing, by academic staff who teach a module or individual lectures on the topic, or by retail employees who wish to reflect upon current practice in the industry. Those who are employed in the various stages of the supply chain that provides retailers with its products may also wish to read it to gain insights into how retailers operate. Each chapter can form an individual lecture and together they form a comprehensive overview of the key areas of Retail Marketing from both contemporary and historical perspectives. Examples of both research and practice feature throughout the book, with interviews and quotes from people working in a broad selection of marketing-related roles in the industry, from traditional customer-facing roles in small enterprises to newer occupations such as Business Intelligence Manager and Consumer Neuroscientist in large multinational companies. Learning objectives are met through the inclusion of a variety of content including relevant theories, cases on retailers and research, supported by visual input. Chapters end with a summary of the key content and retail case studies with questions. The exercises are intended to be used to provide content for discussion in seminars that are connected to retailing lectures or to be answered by individual students. Answers to the case study questions and exercises are available to academics via the book's online content.

Helen Goworek

About the authors

Helen Goworek lectures at the University of Leicester's School of Management where she teaches marketing in consumer and business-to-business contexts. Before becoming an academic she worked in buying for retailers and as a design manager for manufacturers. She developed the UK's first Fashion Buying degree course and is currently involved in research that focuses on retailing and sustainability. Helen has worked on research projects funded by Defra relating to clothing sustainability and she is a member of the organising committee for the International Colloquium on Design, Branding and Marketing (ICDBM).

Peter J. McGoldrick is Professor of Retailing at Manchester Business School within the University of Manchester. He chaired the CRSg then CRIS (Consumer, Retail, Innovation & Service) Research Centre at MBS from 2007 to 2012 and is the Founder of the Retail Research Forum, an industry–university collaboration of fifteen years' standing. His research has attracted extensive peer-reviewed and industrial funding, including several grants from the ESRC, EPSRC, DTI, OFT, EU and other funding organisations. Peter has published over 150 books and papers, mainly within the fields of retailing and consumer behaviour.

Acknowledgements

Thanks are due to the Retail Marketers from academia and industry who generously contributed chapters and vignettes or took the time to be interviewed, all of whom are credited within the book. Many thanks go to Professor Peter McGoldrick for his extremely valuable input, especially his ability to encapsulate complex systems and relationships into clear frameworks, and it was an honour to have the opportunity to work with him. From Pearson I'd like to thank Rachel Gear for instigating the book, as well as Catharine Steers and Rufus Curnow for their support and patience. In addition, the following people kindly gave their time to review the book's content or provided useful information that helped to enhance it: Dr Ranis Cheng; Dr Andrea Davies; Stuart Harrod; Dr Matthew Higgins; Professor Peter Lund-Thomsen; Kate Malloy; Lynn Oxborrow; Julia Richards; Dr Julie Rosborough; Kathy Salisbury; Judy Taft and Professor Paul Whysall. I'd like to thank Christine Gerrard, Fiona Lambert and Alison Knox for being positive role models at the outset of my retailing career. I'd also like to thank my family for their support whilst I was writing the book.

Publisher's acknowledgements

We are grateful to the following for permission to reproduce copyright material:

Figures

Figure 1.3 adapted from *Retail Marketing*, 2nd edn, Maidenhead: McGraw-Hill (McGoldrick, P. 2002) p. 294, McGraw-Hill; Figure 1.4 adapted from *Retail Marketing*, 2nd edn, Maidenhead: McGraw-Hill (McGoldrick, P. 2002) p. 22, McGraw-Hill; Figure 1.5 after Institutional change in retailing: a review and synthesis, *European Journal of Marketing*, 21(6), pp. 5–36 (Brown, S. 1987), Emerald Publishing Group Ltd; Figure 1.6 adapted from Notes on the retail accordion, *Journal of Retailing*, 42 (Summer), pp. 29–40, 54 (Hollander, S.C. 1966), Elsevier; Figure 3.1 adapted from *Consumer Behavior*, 9th edn, South Western Publishing, Thomson Learning (Blackwell, R.D, Miniard, P.W. and Engel, J.F. 2000); Figure 4.1 adapted from *Principles and Practice of Marketing*, 6th edn, Maidenhead: McGraw-Hill (Jobber, D. 2010) p. 392, McGraw Hill; Figure 4.3 adapted from *Principles and Practice of Marketing*, 6th edn, Maidenhead: McGraw-Hill (Jobber, D. 2010) p. 355, McGraw-Hill; Figure 4.7 adapted from *Retail Marketing*, Maidenhead: McGraw-Hill (McGoldrick, P. 2002) p. 364, McGraw Hill; Figure 5.3 adapted from An investigation into retail buying roles and responsibilities for own-label clothing: A multiple case-study, *The Journal of the Textile Institute*, 105(7), pp. 760–769 (Goworek, H. 2014), Taylor and Francis; Figure 6.1 adapted from *Retail Marketing*, 2nd edn, Maidenhead: McGraw-Hill (McGoldrick, P. 2002) p. 378, McGraw-Hill; Figure 6.7 adapted from The strategy of the retail 'sales': typology, review and synthesis, *International Review of Retail, Distribution and Consumer Research*, 5(3), pp. 303–31 (Betts, E.J. and McGoldrick, P.J. 1995), Routledge/Taylor and Francis; Figure 7.1 adapted from Berman, B. and Evans, J.R., *Retail Management: A Strategic Approach*, 11th edn © 2010. Reprinted and electronically reproduced by permission of Pearson Education, Inc., New York, New York.; Figure 8.1 adapted from Toward a contemporary perspective of retail location, *International Journal of Retail and Distribution Management*, 25(2), pp. 59–69 (Clarke, I., Bennison, D. and Pal, J. 1997), Emerald Group Publishing; Figure 8.5 adapted from *Retail Marketing*, 2nd edn, McGraw Hill, London (McGoldrick, P. 2002) p. 240, McGraw-Hill; Figure 9.15

adapted from *Retail Marketing*, 2nd edn, McGraw-Hill, Maidenhead (McGoldrick, P. 2002) p. 466, McGraw-Hill; Figure 10.2 adapted from A service quality model and its marketing implications, *European Journal of Marketing*, 18(4), pp. 36–44 (Grönroos, C 1984), Emerald Group Publishing Ltd; Figure 10.3 from A multi-item scale for measuring consumer perceptions of service, *Journal of Retailing*, 64(1), pp. 12–37 (Parasuraman, A., Zeithaml, V.A. and Berry, L.L 1988), Elsevier; Figure 13.1 adapted from Introduction to International Retailing, in *International Retailing: Trends and Strategies*, Pitman (P.J. McGoldrick and G. Davies (eds) 1995) London: Pitman/Pearson.

Tables

Table 1.1 from Deloitte Global Powers of Retailing 2015, http://www2.deloitte.com/global/en/pages/consumer-business/articles/global-powers-of-retailing.html Deloitte Touche Tohmatsu Limited (DTTL); Table 3.2 from Source of population percentages: NRS, 2014b, http://www.nrs.co.uk/, *National Readership Survey*; Table 4.1 with permission from Dr Edmund O'Callaghan, Head of Department of Retail Management Studies, Dublin Institute of Technology; Table 5.3 with permission from Rosemary Varley, Subject Director: Fashion Retail and Marketing at University of the Arts (London College of Fashion), London; Table 8.2 adapted from Toward a contemporary perspective of retail location, *International Journal of Retail and Distribution Management*, 25(2), pp. 59–69 (Clarke, I., Bennison, D. and Pal, J. 1997), Emerald Group Publishing; Table 8.3 adapted from A framework for network planning, *International Journal of Retail & Distribution Management*, 22(6), pp. 6–10 (Davies, M. and Clarke, I 1994), Emerald Group Publishing; Table 8.4 adapted from The importance of context in store forecasting: The site visit in retail location decision-making, *Journal of Targeting, Measurement and Analysis for Marketing*, 2, pp. 139–155 (Wood, S. and Tasker, A. 2008), Palgrave Macmillan; Table 10.1 adapted from A multi-item scale for measuring consumer perceptions of service, *Journal of Retailing*, 64(1), pp. 12–37 (Parasuraman, A., Zeithaml, V.A. and Berry, L.L 1988), Elsevier; Table 10.2 from Customer switching behaviour in service industries: an exploratory study, *Journal of Marketing*, 59 (April), pp. 71–82 (Keaveney, S., 1995), American Marketing Association; Table 13.1 from *Retail Marketing Management*, 2nd ed., Harlow: Pearson Education Ltd. (Gilbert, D. 2003) Pearson Education.

Text

Box on pages 22–24 with permission from Alastair Sneddon, former Business Intelligence (BI) Manager of Game; Case study on page 32 from *Retail Week*, 9 September, 2011, www.retail-week.com, EMAP Publishing Ltd; Box on pages 41–43 with permission from Jonathan Solomon, Head of CRM & Insights, Vision Express; Case study on pages 53–54 adapted from WH Smith upbeat despite sales doldrums, *Financial Times*, 23/01/2014 (Robinson, D. and Sharman, A.) © The Financial Times Limited. All Rights Reserved; Box on pages 63–65 with permission from Dr Cristina de Balanzó, Consumer Neuroscience Consultant, Walnut Unlimited; Case study on pages 81–82 from © Mhairi McEwan, Chief executive and co-founder of Brand Learning, first published in Marketing magazine, March 1, 2014, http://www.marketingmagazine.co.uk/article/1283341/secret-engaging-women-theres-no-secret). Reproduced from *Marketing magazine* with the permission of the copyright owner, Haymarket Media Group Limited; Box on pages 89–90 with permission from Carol Cloughton, Senior Lecturer in Marketing, University of Huddersfield; Mini case study on pages 91–92 with permission from Christina Schmidt, co-founder of Skandium; Box on pages 99–101 with permission from Dr Edmund O'Callaghan, Head of Department of Retail Management Studies, Dublin Institute of Technology; Box on pages 101–102 with permission from Kelly Molson, Marketing Director of Creative Agency Rubber Cheese; Case study on pages 106–108 adapted from Global Brands – Ups and Downs – Consumers luxuriate in shopping on the web, *Financial Times*, 21/05/2013 (Lucas, L.) © The Financial Times Limited. All Rights Reserved; Box on pages 121–122 with permission from Sarah Deacon; Box on pages 124–125 with permission from Rosemary Varley, Subject Director, Fashion Retail and Marketing at University of the Arts (London College of Fashion), London; Case study on pages 133–134 from Butler, S. 'Supply chain – Back to the source' *Retail Week*, May 2011, http://retail-week.com, EMAP Publishing Ltd; Box on pages 149–150 with permission from James Clark, Merchandising Specialist; Case study on page 159 adapted from Grocer price skirmishes pushed to new level', *Financial Times*, 19/03/2014 (Felsted, A. and Sharman, A.) © The Financial Times Limited. All Rights Reserved; Box on pages 171–172 with permission from Daniel Dunn of dunnhumby; Box on pages 180–181 with permission from Andrew Rayner, MD, e-mphasis Internet Marketing, www.e-mphasis.com, Andrew Rayner; Box on page 206 from http://www.bmstores.co.uk/landlords (date accessed 21 May 2014), B&M Retail Limited; Box on pages 206–208 with permission from Elina Waehner; Case study on page 214 adapted from Booker rolls out new breed of local discount store, *Financial Times*, 09/07/2014 (Felsted, A.) © The Financial Times Limited. All Rights Reserved; Box on pages 221–223 with permission from Martin Knox; Box on pages 237–238 adapted from 'Shop and bop till you drop', O'Flaherty, M.C., Financial Times, 21 December 2012, http://www.ft.com/cms/s/2/35fd4fd0-3d86-11e2-9f35-00144feabdc0.html, Financial Times © The Financial Times Limited. All Rights Reserved; Case study on pages 244–245 from Store Gallery: Anthropologie moves out of London with new shop in Guildford, *Retail Week*, EMAP Publishing Limited; Box on pages 277–280 with permission from Jessica Goudkuil, www.thebeadboutique.co.uk; Box on pages 297–298 with permission from Christian Smith, www.inclusi.eu/; Box on pages 317–318 adapted from Business Life – Monday Interview – Peter Agnefjäll, Chief Executive, IKEA – The self-assembled retail boss, *Financial Times*, 02/09/2013 (Milne, R.) © The Financial Times Limited. All Rights Reserved; Box on page 318 adapted from Ikea hails recovery in consumer sentiment, *Financial Times*, 29/01/2014 (Milne, R.) © The Financial Times Limited. All Rights Reserved; Box on page 322 adapted from Russia customs rules hit online retailers, *Financial Times*, 24/01/2014 (Hille, K. and Wright, R.) © The Financial Times Limited. All Rights Reserved; Case study on pages 329–330 adapted from Indonesia's ecommerce industry awakens, *Financial Times*, 21/02/2014 (Bland, B.) © The Financial Times Limited. All Rights Reserved.

Photographs/screenshots

(Key: b-bottom; l-left; t-top)

pp. 4, 5, 88: Christina Goworek; p. 8: Margaret Chaplin; pp.12, 19: courtesy of City Dressing, citydressing.co.uk; p. 21: Alamy Images: © Photos 12; p. 22: Alistair Sneddon; p. 41: Jonathon Solomon; p. 42: Vision Express; p. 45: Asda Photo; p. 63: Dr Cristina de Balanzó; p. 64: SensoMotoric Instruments GmbH; p. 81: Shutterstock.com: © Art Allianz; p. 85: Stratasys; pp. 91, 92: Skandium; p. 102: Chaucer Foods Ltd; p. 121: Sarah Deacon; p. 143: 99p Stores; p. 146: Student Lock-In; p. 169: Seven Publishing Group; p. 171: Daniel Dunn; p. 172: People Tree; pp. 173, 174: Tamsin Brooke-Smith; p. 176: Musgrave Retail Partners GB; p. 187: SuperGroup Plc; p. 201: Intu Properties plc; p. 202: Aver; p. 205: Matthew Hopkinson; p. 218: Alamy Images: © Barry Lewis; pp. 221, 222: Martin Knox; p. 225(b): Fotolia.com: © ostap25; p. 226(t): Morplan Ltd; p. 227(t): Adel Rootstein Ltd; p. 230: Getty Images: Oli Scarff; p. 232: PlanogramBuilder, © zVisuel SA, www.planogrambuilder.com; pp. 233, 234: Catwalk Cakes; p. 249: Clare Rayner; p. 253: Rex Features: Paul Grover; p. 258: HappyOrNot Ltd; p. 264: Courtesy of Boots UK; p. 265: Alamy Images: © British Retail Photography; pp. 278, 279, 280: Jessica Goudkuil; pp. 297: Christian Smith; p. 299(l): Lush; p. 317: Alamy Images: © epa european pressphoto agency b.v.

Cover image: *front:* Andrew Meredith

In some instances we have been unable to trace the owners of copyright material, and we would appreciate any information that would enable us to do so.

CHAPTER 1

Introduction to retail marketing management

Learning objectives

The objectives of this chapter are to:

- discuss competing definitions of retailing;
- define and categorise store and non-store aspects of retailing and be able to discuss their similarities and differences;
- explain the development and scope of retail marketing theory and practice;
- evaluate theories of retail change.

Introduction

This chapter introduces key themes which will be expanded upon in later sections. It offers an overview of the history of retailing and the development of retail marketing theory, then categorises types of retailer and retail business formats before specifying recent trends which have impacted upon retailing. Retail marketing has achieved an accelerated rate of change in recent years, with **multichannel retailing** and **Corporate Social Responsibility (CSR)** at the forefront of this change (Berman and Evans, 2010; Freestone and McGoldrick, 2008). Additionally, new retail formats are developing, responding to the demands of increasingly sophisticated consumers in highly segmented markets and in emerging economies. These factors are counterbalanced by the need for retailers in various parts of the world to deal with the ongoing repercussions of the global economic crisis which began in 2008. Retail sales form a significant part of the economy, with the global retail market being valued at US$10,500 billion in 2010, groceries being worth 63 per cent of the retail sector (Datamonitor, 2011). In recent decades, several large retailers have become more powerful than the manufacturers and brands that supply them with products (McGoldrick, 2002). Furthermore, the annual financial turnover of the world's largest retailer, Walmart, is greater than the gross domestic product (GDP) of most countries, as it generated revenue worth $476,294 million in 2013 and employs over two million staff worldwide (Walmart, 2014) (see Table 1.1). Walmart's financial turnover is currently close in size to the GDP of Norway at $417 billion and Saudia Arabia at $435 billion in the same year (World Bank, 2012). Although most retailers operate on a small scale, they form a high proportion of the market and the retail sector is very significant to the world's economy. Walmart itself began as a small family store in 1962. Consequently, it is useful to be aware of the operation of the many small-to-medium enterprises (SMEs), as they form the majority of the retail sector in most countries and some of them may become dominant retailers in the future.

Definitions of retailing

Gilbert (2003) defines retail as 'any business that directs its marketing efforts towards satisfying the final consumer based upon the organisation of selling goods and services as a means of distribution' (p. 6). This typifies the traditional perspective on retailing as an exclusively business-based enterprise. However, Lusch *et al.* (2011) offer a slightly different perspective, stating that retailing 'consists of the final activities and steps needed either to place a product in the hands of the consumer or to provide a service to the consumer . . . the last step in a supply chain that may stretch from Europe or Asia to your hometown. Therefore, any firm that sells a product or provides a service to the final consumer is performing the retailing function' (p. 4). Both of the definitions offered here indicate that the scope of retailing incorporates companies selling services directly to consumers via their businesses. Retailers can be seen to comprise banks and petrol stations through to firms in the leisure sector, such as restaurants, gyms and hairdressers. Definitions of retailing have traditionally been reliant on the notion of retailing being confined to **business-to-consumer (B2C)** markets. However, retailing is an activity that is not restricted to taking place within the business sector, as charities and other not-for-profit organisations also engage in retailing to support their income. The advent of sales transactions via the internet on websites such as eBay has also resulted in the increasing power of the **consumer-to-consumer (C2C)** market. It would be useful to think about this situation from your own viewpoint, considering to what extent, if at all, you, your friends and family have moved towards buying in C2C markets in recent years.

Table 1.1 Top 20 global retailers

Retail revenue rank (FY13)	Name of company	Country of origin	2013 net retail revenue (US$m)	2013 parent company/group revenue (US$m)	2013 parent company/group net income (US$m)	Dominant operational format 2013	# countries of operation 2013	2008–2013 retail revenue CAGR
1	Wal-Mart Stores, Inc.	U.S.	476,294	476,294	16,695	Hypermarket/Supercenter/Superstore	28	3.3%
2	Costco Wholesale Corporation	U.S.	105,156	105,156	2,061	Cash & Carry/Warehouse Club	9	7.7%
3	Carrefour S.A.	France	98,688	101,844	1,812	Hypermarket/Supercenter/Superstore	33	−3.0%
4	Schwarz Unternehmens Treuhand KG	Germany	98,662	98,662	n/a	Discount Store	26	6.5%
5	Tesco PLC	U.K.	98,631	100,213	1,529	Hypermarket/Supercenter/Superstore	13	2.9%
6	The Kroger Co.	U.S.	98,375	98,375	1,531	Supermarket	1	5.3%
7	Metro Ag	Germany	86,393	86,393	588	Cash & Carry/Warehouse Club	32	−0.9%
8	Aldi Einkauf GmbH & Co. oHG	Germany	81,090	81,090	n/a	Discount Store	17	5.5%
9	The Home Depot, Inc.	U.S.	78,812	78,812	5,385	Home Improvement	4	2.0%
10	Target Corporation	U.S.	72,596	72,596	1,971	Discount Department Store	2	2.9%
11	Walgreen Co.	U.S.	72,217	72,217	2,450	Drug Store/Pharmacy	2	4.1%
12	CVS Caremark Corporation	U.S.	65,618	126,761	4,592	Drug Store/Pharmacy	3	6.0%
13	Casino Guichard-Perrachon S.A.	France	63,468	64,613	2,023	Hypermarket/Supercenter/Superstore	29	11.1%
14	Groupe Auchan SA	France	62,444	63,859	1,109	Hypermarket/Supercenter/Superstore	13	4.0%
15	Amazon.com, Inc.	U.S.	60,903	74,452	274	Non-Store	14	26.7%
16	Edeka Zentrale AG & Co. KG	Germany	59,704	61,399	n/a	Supermarket	1	5.9%
17	Aeon Co., Ltd.	Japan	57,986	64,271	835	Hypermarket/Supercenter/Superstore	10	3.9%
18	Woolworths Limited	Australia	54,457	55,974	2,258	Supermarket	2	4.3%
19	Seven & I Holdings Co., Ltd.	Japan	54,258	56,600	1,890	Convenience/Forecourt Store	18	−0.1%
20	Lowe's Companies, Inc.	U.S.	53,417	53,417	2,286	Home Improvement	4	2.1%

Source: Deloitte Global Powers of Retailing 2015 (available online at: http://www2.deloitte.com/global/en/pages/consumer-business/articles/global-powers-of-retailing.html)

History and development of retail marketing

Retailing has always been interconnected with consumers' lifestyles and broader historical trends. Humans have continually engaged in consumption of different kinds to meet various needs, including survival and self-esteem, and therefore they have always been consumers. Retailing is a somewhat recent intervention in consumption. While humans were initially dependent upon their own small communities for the products they consumed, retailing developed alongside improved communication and transport channels which helped to connect communities on a wider scale through trading. Consumers both influence and react to the environmental conditions in which retailing operates by making purchases which reflect and impact upon the prevailing political, economic, societal and technological factors of the time.

Retailing has developed from a primarily localised system of providing product and services, where customers often knew the tradesperson producing the goods personally. Markets have existed for thousands of years (Evans, 2011) and in mediaeval times they became widespread, enabling producers to distribute goods regularly across a greater distance, even across continents in the case of certain products such as spices. For example in Leicester, the marketplace was established in the late 13th century and it remains in the same location in the centre of the city over 800 years later (Leicester Market, 2012). By the 14th century, Britain was dotted with market towns to which many people migrated for work, often adopting the names of their trade rather than place of birth as surnames, and retailing therefore had a major impact on society. More than a third of overseas trade in this period passed through London, reinforcing the significance of the capital city as a trade centre (Rubin, 2006). Traditional markets remain a central part of the economy and culture in many cities around the world (see Figure 1.1). The origin of language used in retailing demonstrates the close relationship between retailing and marketing. Around 1520, the word 'shopkeeper' entered the English language, signifying a seller, rather than a tradesperson, followed by a new verb in the mid-16th century, 'marketing', to mean 'the act of buying and selling in a central place' (Byrne Paquet, 2003:19).

Figure 1.1 Valencia indoor market

Source: with permission from Christina Goworek

Figure 1.1 (*continued*)

Ultimately, traditional methods of selling have developed into a sophisticated, global network for the exchange of goods and services. The Industrial Revolution began in the 18th century with the introduction of machinery utilised for mass production. Additionally, swifter transport via railways in the 19th century led to easier transportation of goods, helping to facilitate the development of larger-scale retailing. Key retailing innovations have been introduced in different decades, some of which have proceeded to dominate the retail market. For example, in the 1940s, the supermarket was an innovative retail format which was destined to eventually take over from local specialist shops in the Western world (Blythman, 2004; Byrne Paquet, 2003).

Businesses can adopt either a production orientation or a marketing orientation. A production orientation tends to have an internal focus, prioritising the technical aspects of products and manufacturing processes, with marketing being viewed mainly as a way of divesting the company of the resulting goods, with the emphasis on selling. The development of marketing has been entwined with the progress of retailing. Marketing's origins lie in the Industrial Revolution, when manufacturing became increasingly productive due to the widespread use of machinery. This resulted in a higher availability of products and a wider need for **advertising** and distribution channels to deliver them to consumers. Organisations with a marketing orientation take the reverse approach to a production orientation in that they are outward-looking and consider consumers' needs first before seeking potential opportunities to develop products and services to meet those needs. As Blythe (2009:8) states: 'The idea of placing customers at the centre of everything the company does is basic to marketing thought: this idea of customer centrality is the key concept in marketing'. Retailing is generally far more aligned with a marketing orientation than a production orientation in that retail organisations very rarely manufacture the products that they sell and their business is to regularly deal with consumers.

The traditional supply chain starts with manufacturers producing goods then selling them on to retailers, who in turn sell to consumers. Sometimes intermediaries could be involved, such as **wholesalers** who 'break bulk' by buying in large quantities and selling in smaller quantities at a slightly higher price to make it worthwhile for them to offer this service to small retailers. In effect, brands operate as wholesalers as they mainly have their products made by manufacturers and then supply it to retailers. However, unlike wholesalers brands provide added value by being responsible for the design and promotion of their products, thus offering enhanced products and services. Many well-known brands also have store chains as an opportunity to offer their whole range to customers in a retail environment where they have control of the **brand identity**, with the opportunity to promote the brand to consumers through their presence on the High Street. Wholesale companies have become less prevalent in recent years and the dual factors of globalisation and the internet now challenge the traditional supply chain to create new ways of doing business.

Globalisation and disparities in the cost of living around the world have meant that much of the manufacture of products sold in the West has moved mainly to the East. Consequently, companies that used to manufacture in the West have tended to either close or to become suppliers who still provide a design and **product development** service to retailers but arrange their manufacture offshore, rather than being responsible for production themselves. Suppliers are now more likely to be intermediaries with retailers than wholesalers are, particularly in the case of medium and large retailers. Furthermore, the internet has reduced barriers between brands and consumers, so customers can now quite easily find and order the brands they like online and buy from them directly, without the intervention of a retailer. Additionally, consumers can now quite easily sell products to each other that they have made or bought elsewhere, creating a thriving consumer-to-consumer (C2C) market facilitated by websites such as eBay.

A brief history of retail developments in the UK

A recent history of retail developments is outlined here. The Centre for the History of Retailing and Distribution provides some useful links on this topic for further investigation (CHORD, 2014). There is a well-worn phrase that Britain is 'a nation of shopkeepers' and the reasons for this are explored by Ugolini and Benson (2002) in their book of this name, which provides a detailed review of the history of retailing since the 16th century.

1950s	In the UK, post-World War II rationing[1] was in place at the start of the decade, with growing economic prosperity towards the end. Retailers were mostly small-scale local stores. Manufacturers had more power than retailers, owing to the Resale Price Maintenance Act (Gilbert, 2003), allowing manufacturers to control retail prices. Department stores in urban areas were the major store groups, selling a broad selection of **branded products**, targeting the growing groups of consumers with disposable income.
1960s	The Resale Price Maintenance Act was repealed in 1964, allowing retailers to gain more power in relationships with suppliers. A strong economy allowed consumers to have more disposable income, thereby increasing discretionary spending power, particularly in the new category of the 'teenage consumer'. Improved transport systems facilitated the wider distribution of products both nationally and internationally. Boutique fashion shops gained popularity and several expanded into store chains.
1970s	Supermarkets flourished and **own-label** retailers opened branches throughout the UK, particularly in the clothing, homeware and electrical sectors. Mail order catalogues thrived by offering a wide range of products to consumers on a 'buy now, pay later' basis. Stores offered consumers access to large electrical products such as fridges and colour TVs through conveniently spreading out payments in rental or hire-purchase arrangements.
1980s	Company mergers and acquisitions led to store groups dominating sectors within the UK mass market, e.g. Kingfisher, Storehouse and the Burton Group. Small-scale retailers declined accordingly (Blythman, 2004; Gilbert, 2003). **Market segmentation** became used increasingly by retailers, with menswear store Hepworth being transformed into Next in 1982, aimed mainly at a demographic of women in their 30s. Out-of-town retail parks were constructed throughout the UK. Electronic point-of-sale technology was introduced in stores, speeding up customer queues and the transfer of sales data to retail head offices.

1990s	Supermarkets became more acquisitive, buying up smaller competitors to expand their numbers of outlets and extending their product ranges. The internet was commercialised in 1990, thus enabling the introduction of online retailing. A financial recession took place from 1990–1991 in the US and from 1990–1992 in the UK (Hall, 1993; Taylor and Bradley, 1994), affecting retailers adversely. Chain stores increasingly dominated the mass market. Store opening times were extended due to pressure from supermarkets and Sunday opening became legal, although typically limited to six hours. US retailer Walmart entered the UK market through the acquisition of supermarket chain Asda in 1999.
2000s	Supermarkets expanded into the convenience store sector and small-scale stores continued to decline. By the end of the decade, the groceries sector was led by 'the big four': Tesco, Asda, Sainsbury's and Morrisons. Internet retailing became an established distribution channel. Sustainability became more of a priority for UK retailers, with many companies adopting CSR policies. Own-label retailers continued to dominate, Marks & Spencer (M&S) being the market leader in clothing. Low-price 'value retailers' expanded, benefitting from the economic downturn which began in 2008, whereas several long-standing High Street retail chains closed down, e.g. Woolworth, Dolcis footwear and MFI furniture,[2] which had opened in the UK in 1909, 1920 and 1964, respectively.
2010s	Social and environmental responsibility have become increasingly significant issues for retailers. M&S's wide-ranging CSR policies are influencing competitors to adopt CSR strategies as standard practice. The economic downturn appears likely to have a longer term impact, resulting in consumers spending more cautiously and several other well-established retail chains faced closure in the first half of the decade. Fast-changing digital technology affects the ways in which retailers acquire, sell and promote their products.

[1] Rationing was enforced until 1954 by using coupons to restrict the amount of goods such as food, clothing and fuel that UK citizens could buy, in order to save the country's resources.
[2] It is notable that MFI was revived in 2011 as an internet-only retailer (Centre for Retail Research, 2012) thereby suggesting that this channel could be more financially viable for a furniture company than using bricks-and-mortar outlets.

RETAIL MARKETING CAREERS
Margaret Chaplin, owner of an independent retailer

Chaplin's butcher's shop has been located in Groby, Leicestershire, since Victorian times. Margaret Chaplin and her brother now own the shop that was set up by their great-grandfather and grandfather. The shop is at the heart of the old village, which has a very long and famous heritage, having been the home of two former queens of England, Elizabeth Woodville ('The White Queen') and Lady Jane Grey ('The Nine Days Queen'). The building was originally a house rented by the Chaplins from Lord Stamford, who owned the village, until it was bought by the family in the 1920s for around £500, when it was partially converted into a shop. Margaret began working in the business in the 1970s when it was owned by her father, alongside other family members. At that time the shop was thriving and Margaret delivered meat to people in local villages in a van, especially to farms. The business also employed a boy to deliver meat on a bike, until around 1990. When demand reduced and regulations changed so that vans needed to be refrigerated to deliver meat, Chaplin's stopped offering a delivery service. Margaret says 'it's come full circle now that the big supermarkets deliver to customers at home' and she feels that these companies 'have had a massive effect because you can't compete with them on price'. A Co-operative store has also been based in Groby for over 100 years and recently moved into new larger premises next to Chaplin's, which has impacted upon the butcher's sales.

New housing developments have seen the village grow substantially since the 1980s, along with supermarkets to cater for the growing population. Margaret has noticed how the changes in women's lifestyles have affected the way in which they shop over the years. She says 'women work now and are not in the village during

Chaplin's shop in the 1920s and the present day
Source: with permission from Margaret Chaplin

the day, whereas my mother didn't work when she got married, except to help my Dad, and that was what the majority of women did. They tend to shop at one place now rather than walking to different shops and don't usually take their children into the shop, whereas this used to be commonplace. Our hours are getting less and less because there are just not the people around and it's gradually declined'.

Chaplin's was originally a vertically integrated business in that they raised some of their own animals and slaughtered meat on the premises until the 1970s. They also sold meat from animals bought from the cattle market in Leicester, as well as making their own sausages. However, when regulations about slaughtering meat changed the amount of work needed to alter the premises meant it was no longer viable to do so and it became more economical to buy meat from abattoirs in the area. Things have now changed to the extent that the meat is bought wholesale from an abattoir in Staffordshire, as it's now difficult to find in Leicestershire. The business also buys cheese from a wholesaler in Leicester and used to sell a range of international cheeses that were popular because they weren't available at other shops in the village. However, Margaret has found that the demand has reduced since the NHS began to advise people against eating products such as cheese that are considered to be high in cholesterol. Margaret also cooks fresh pies and pasties in the shop and she required a training certificate to be allowed to do this.

For anyone considering setting up a butcher's shop Margaret says there are several different areas to consider. First, she says 'it's necessary to understand what the meat is and how to cut it the right way'. Margaret learnt by example from her father, who was trained as a master butcher and she learnt how to pluck poultry such as partridges and pheasants as a child. Second, she says 'you've got to have something that attracts people into the shop, especially if you're not established there'. Margaret acknowledges the importance of brand heritage when she says 'we're lucky that we run on a name that our grandparents started for us and we try to keep up that tradition of being old-fashioned. I'm not sure that it's always worked but we have tried to alter things slightly, like setting out meat on trays in the shop. If we have too much meat cut though, it starts to go dark and people don't want it, even if it's okay. We can end up wasting it because customers have been indoctrinated into expecting bright red coloured meat in supermarkets, although it isn't what it would naturally look like'. Third, Margaret says that 'a shop needs to have an image and keep it up, especially when it's in a small community, and preferably something that's not already there, or else you can upset all of the other shops. Then the community goes, people don't talk to each other as much and a whole way of life seems to disappear. It's already happening. If you go in a big supermarket you don't get the personal touch you get in a small shop where people will say "hello, how are you?". Customers still talk a lot to us and you become a person they can confide in. You should try and make friends with customers and enjoy what you're doing, otherwise there's no point doing this sort of business, or any other sort. Unless you want to work with people in your community, setting up a shop won't work'.

The development and scope of retail marketing theory and practice

Retail marketing is defined by Fernie *et al*. (2003: 105) as 'the application of marketing concepts, theories and actions within the context of retail organisations'. Retail marketing has evolved as a discipline alongside the development of marketing theory and it is possible for marketing principles to be applied throughout the retail sector. Nevertheless, retailing has some of its own unique systems that differ from marketing in other sectors, for example in its usage of distribution and logistics. The **marketing mix** is a classic marketing model, also known as the **4Ps**: Product, Price, Promotion, Place. Since the 1960s, when the model was developed, these four elements have been viewed as the key areas on which marketers should focus, ensuring that they are blended effectively to communicate a consistent message to consumers. However, the marketing mix's dominant position in marketing theory has been challenged, as the significance of building positive relationships with customers has been at the forefront of marketing theory and practice in recent years, via **Relationship Marketing** and **Service Dominant Logic**, in which services take priority over products (Vargo and Lusch, 2004).

There is obviously a great deal of emphasis on the 'place' element within the retail marketing mix, since the physical location of stores has long been the focus of retailing. However, this is beginning to change somewhat since the advent of electronic retailing (etailing). Consequently, the marketing mix requires adaptation to make it suitable for the retail sector; for example, the display of products within stores may have a greater impact than an advertising campaign could. Whereas a high advertising spend is well suited to manufacturer brands in order for them to communicate a **brand image** directly to consumers, advertising is generally utilised less by retailers because the presence of their stores ensures that customers are frequently reminded of their existence. In 2011, 24 per cent of the UK's top 100 advertisers were retailers and 6 per cent were banks, with 42 per cent being manufacturer brands (Nielsen Media Research, 2011). In 2013, fast-moving consumer goods (FMCG) group Procter and Gamble gained second place on the list with an annual advertising spend of £177 million and the highest spending retailer was Tesco at £116 million (Nielsen Ad Dynamix, 2013). Retailers that sell manufacturer brands benefit from the brands conducting their own promotional campaigns to encourage sales of their products.

Many authors have argued for an **extended marketing mix** or **7Ps**, developed to apply more effectively to service organisations. This extended mix adds people, physical evidence and process and could be said to be more suited to the retail sector than the traditional 4Ps (Blythe, 2009). Retail marketing theory and practice have been highly influenced by the widespread development and implementation of marketing strategies and techniques in the late 20th and early 21st century. In recent years there has been a drive towards Relationship Marketing, which has been accompanied by increasing criticism of the marketing mix by academics, owing to its product-centred perspective (discussed further in Chapter 7). The move towards the Relationship Marketing paradigm potentially lends itself well to retail marketing, since retailing typically consists of numerous and repeated individual customer–retailer transactions (McGoldrick, 2002).

Retail marketing theory is published primarily within marketing and retailing journals, with a surprisingly limited selection of books being available on this topic, despite its significance to the global economy. Academic journals are therefore the best locations in which to find the widest variety of retail marketing literature. The topic of retailing also extends outside the arena of marketing to be discussed in several other academic disciplines, sometimes under the guises of consumer culture or shopping, emphasising its importance as a social and leisure activity. Anthropologists and geographers have taken an interest in the social impact of shopping centres (Miller *et al*., 1998) and retailing has also been discussed from the perspectives of architecture (Luna, 2005), history (Stobart, 2008) and sociology (Lury, 1996), among others. These subjects relate in particular to retail consumption, architecture and planning, each of which will be covered later within this book.

Retail industry associations

The British Retail Consortium (BRC) is the main trade association for UK retailers, covering all product sectors, and its mission is 'to make a positive difference by advancing vibrant and consumer-focused retail' (BRC, 2014). Most of the major High Street retailers are members of the BRC and they fund the organisation by contributing a fee based on the size and turnover of the company. The BRC runs conferences, roundtable discussions, webinars and training, as well as producing publications about the sector, many of which can be accessed for free from their website. Another key function of the BRC is to lobby government on behalf of the sector.

Retail Trust is another industry-wide body that was founded in 1832. Retail Trust comprises various charitable initiatives, one of the most well-known being Cottage Homes, which can support former retail industry workers with accommodation in their retirement. Other initiatives include retailCORe, which helps people develop careers and opportunities in retail and retailRIGHT, a project to help develop future retail leaders with pre-employment training and work experience (see www.retailtrust.org.uk). Richard Boland, Chief Executive of the Retail Trust, explains how this charity operates and offers his views on the industry as a whole:

> It's the longest established and largest charity servicing the industry. Our mission is to improve the lives of all of those involved in retail: yesterday, today and tomorrow, including all of those supplying retailers, so it's not just those employed in shops, it's also the support services. Retail is the biggest single employment group in the UK and the nearest equivalent to it would be the National Health Service (NHS). However, retailing can be quite fragmented and one in four people working in retail work in small, family-type businesses, so it cuts across the spectrum, ranging from some of the largest to some of the smallest companies, which makes it unique.
>
> This is an industry with a high element of young workers. A quarter of 16–24-year-olds who are working are employed in retail, so this industry has strong links with young people. Historically the Retail Trust has been more known for our retirement homes and now we're focusing more on younger people. Retail is often students' first ever experience of working life and I don't think we recognise this enough in the UK and think about how it might affect our views on employment. We need to think how to make students feel this industry is something worth staying in, rather than something they just view transiently while they're being educated. It's an industry where you can start as a shelf-stacker when you're 16 and end up being the CEO. The only way you understand the customer is by being on the shop floor. Knowing how to serve the customer is more important than academic prowess, so it's quite a democratic industry. We can support those who want to get into retail and can offer benefits such as bursaries and grants. We could do a lot more of that kind of work if only students would make themselves known to us. We're available to support them but they may not even realise that.

Various other industry bodies are available to serve the retail sector. The British Independent Retailers' Association focuses on supporting smaller retailers (see www.bira.co.uk). The IMRG was set up over 20 years ago to cater for online retailing (see www.imrg.org). There are also industry bodies concentrating on specific retail sectors, such as the National Farmers' Retail and Markets Association (see www.farma.org.uk). As well as providing useful information and various other forms of support, all of these retail trade associations can be viewed as potential employers for those interested in a career that can impact upon many different companies in the retail sector.

Retailer categories

Retail stores can be categorised as described in Table 1.2. Evans (2011) believes that modern retailing formats such as those listed below have evolved from previous versions, rather than being completely new innovations. To emphasise this, Evans (2011:9) states that 'modern retailing is the accumulation of incremental steps over time'.

Retail business formats

Retailers can be categorised by the business format in which they operate, alongside the categories of retailers mentioned above. It is viable for a store to fit into more than one category in Table 1.3. For example, a store could be both a multiple and a specialist, such

Table 1.2 Retailer categories

Retail format	Description
Specialist store	Offers a narrow line of products, e.g. groceries or electricals
Department store	Offers several product lines of mainly manufacturer branded goods, located in separate departments
Variety chain	Sells a variety of product lines, but unlike the department store, these are mostly under the store's own label
Supermarket	Self-service store selling groceries and household products
Superstore/hypermarket	Large self-service store selling groceries and/or other products
Convenience store	Small store selling groceries and household products, traditionally located in residential areas
Catalogue store	Offers a wide selection of goods at competitive prices, stocked in a warehouse and collected by customers from the store
Discount store	Offers a discount on standard prices, either by stocking in high volume or to sell off discontinued products
Outlet store	Sells discounted merchandise, usually from previous seasons, outlet stores are often grouped together in an outlet village
Market trader/stallholder	Individual rented stall, usually selling a narrow range of merchandise at low prices

Table 1.3 Retail business formats

Business format	Description
Chain store/multiple	Two or more outlets under the same name, product buying usually centralised
Independent store	Individual store or small chain of stores which does not belong to another company
Retail co-operative	A retailer which is owned by its members and has centralised buying
Franchise	A franchisee runs a store via a contract to sell the franchisor's goods or services, under the name of the franchisor's company
Concession	A retailer which rents a proportion of space within another retailer's store

as sports footwear chain 'Foot Locker'. While chain stores and independent stores are mutually exclusive, co-operatives are usually chain stores and independent retailers with a small number of outlets can be chain stores.

A recent development in retailing has been the use of temporary or 'pop-up' shops (see Figure 1.2). This is when a store is rented on a short-term basis, often for the purpose of promoting a specific brand which does not ordinarily have its own stores. Pop-up shops became popularised in the mid 2000s and fashion brands in Japan were early adopters of

Figure 1.2 Pop-up store
Source: with permission from City Dressing, www.citydressing.co.uk

this trend. The wider availability of retail premises, owing to the financial climate and store closures, has made this a viable option to gain brand recognition or as a trial run for opening a permanent store (Dean, 2012).

Non-store retailing (home shopping)

Non-store retailing via **home shopping** was heading into decline (Mintel, 2009) until online retailing began to revive the notion that shopping does not need to be confined to bricks-and-mortar retailers. Methods of non-store retailing can often fit more conveniently with consumers' lifestyles and, in the case of party plan, can be combined with the customer's social life.

Mail order catalogue retailing is based on purchasing products from a catalogue which is posted to the customer or which is distributed via local agents who make a commission on sales.

Direct mail is a method of targeting specific customers. Brochures featuring the company's products are posted directly to potential customers via a mailing list or products can be purchased from an advertisement in newspapers or magazines which appeal to the retailer's target customers.

Etailing *(online retailing)* takes place via transactional websites of multichannel retailers (i.e. those which also have bricks-and-mortar stores and/or catalogues) or **pure players** (who only offer their product range online).

TV retailing includes sales via specialist sales channels such as QVC and 'infomercials' which sell products directly from advertisements.

Party plan and door-to-door selling involves **personal selling** via an agent for the retailer, e.g. Tupperware, Ann Summers, Avon and Amway.

Consumer-to-consumer retailing covers informal methods of retailing, where the seller and purchaser engage in events including car boot sales, yard sales and jumble sales or sell via classified advertisements in the press. This can also include informal etailing such as auctioning products on eBay.

Automatic vending refers to convenience and snack products being sold via vending machines, often bought by customers on impulse.

Retail concepts and theories

Retailing literature has relatively few academic models in comparison to other elements of marketing, since its emphasis has been on more practical considerations. The retailing theories which are widely published are from previous eras and may be less applicable to today's dynamic retailing environment, which has been influenced by recent rapid developments in technology, amongst other factors. These theories are included here largely to illustrate the historical background and development of the academic study of retailing. However, as with all models and theories they can offer food for thought to influence your thinking about retail development and change. There is no one correct answer, theory or interpretation; some ideas are more persuasive than others. A major impediment in accounting for retail change is that retailing has not traditionally been a very theoretical area of marketing. Three cyclical theories are discussed here: the retail life cycle, the wheel of retailing and the retail accordion, which are then followed by conflict theory. There is much scope for new models to be introduced in the retailing literature to relate to the ways in which the industry currently functions and how it will operate in the future. By reviewing established theories of retailing the opportunity is for you to identify where the models seem less relevant and could be amended. If possible, you should think about how you would improve and update the models.

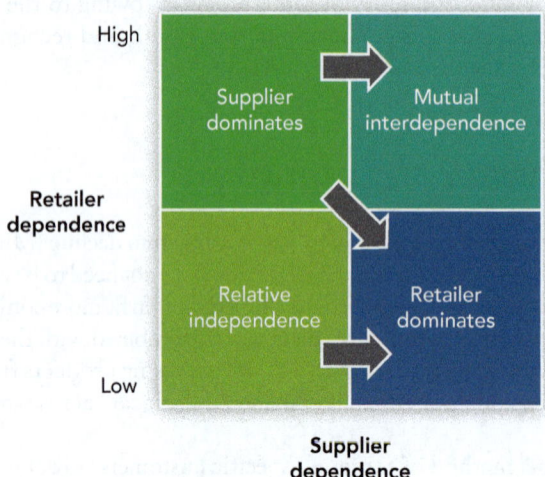

Figure 1.3 Dependence and power in retailer–supplier relationships
Source: adapted from McGoldrick, P. (2002), *Retail Marketing*, 2nd edn, based upon Hogarth-Scott and Parkinson, 1993 and Kumar, 1996. © 2002. Reproduced with the kind permission of McGraw-Hill Education. All rights reserved.

Retailer power

During the 19th and early 20th century manufacturers were usually viewed as being dominant over retailers, due to the power they achieved through their relatively large scale in comparison to retailers. This has changed more recently, as retailers have increased in size, with many being among the largest organisations in the world and the balance has therefore shifted in some cases. However, the retail industry has companies of a variety of sizes and this is a key factor that determines the power of the retailer in its relationships with suppliers. Another important factor is status, so for example a supplier or retailer that is viewed as particularly innovative or upmarket in its field can be relatively powerful without having a high financial turnover, since it may have a high level of influence. Retailers and suppliers are mutually dependent to differing extents and this is reflected in the four different quadrants of Figure 1.3 that can vary from the supplier or retailer dominating the relationship. In between these two extremes, retailers and suppliers can either be relatively independent of each other or be mutually interdependent.

The retail life cycle

The retail life cycle (RLC) (see Figure 1.4) is similar in style to the product life cycle (see Chapter 4 Retail product and brand management), based on the theory that retailers progress through four different stages from introduction to decline.

- *Introduction*: at this stage, retailers require a unique selling proposition which differentiates them from the competition, such as an exclusive product range or an offering similar to competitors but sold at lower prices or with better **customer service**. For example, Japanese retailer Uniqlo sells a mix of classic and fashionable clothing in numerous colours, with similar products and store display to its more expensive US competitor 'Gap'.
- *Growth*: this is the stage when retailers increase their sales volume and aim to become profitable; for example, Amazon.com was in business for several years before it grew sufficiently to enter this stage and became a profitable enterprise.
- *Maturity*: after growth, retail sales can level off and reach a plateau. This can be a long stage for successful retailers which implement effective marketing planning. Originally

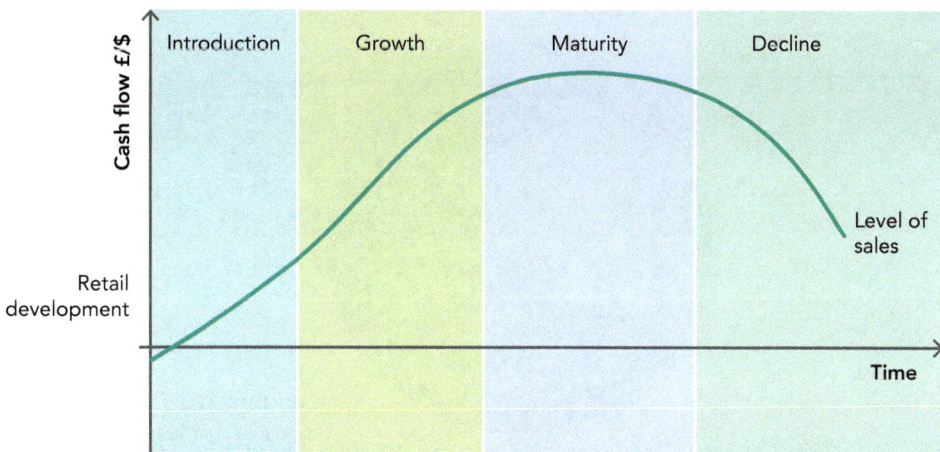

Figure 1.4 The Retail Life Cycle
Source: adapted from McGoldrick, P. (2002), *Retail Marketing*, 2nd edn © 2002. Reproduced with the kind permission of McGraw-Hill Education. *All rights reserved.*

introduced in the 1930s in the US (Byrne Paquet, 2003) self-service supermarkets currently fall into this category and mobile phone retailers have reached this stage in the UK within three decades.

- *Decline*: once retail sales begin to drop and profitability is low, the company heads into the decline stage. For some retailers, this can be a very sudden process with stores closing for good, as happened with the Woolworth chain in 2008, despite having traded in the UK for 99 years. More often, the decline can be gradual, taking place over a number of years, resulting in branch closures and a reduction of the product lines on offer.

After retailers reach the decline stage it is possible that they will become popular again and start again at the introduction stage. For example, the pawnbroker was a very traditional form of shop, offering consumers loans secured against second-hand goods. Pawnbrokers had virtually disappeared from the High Street but have now resurfaced in the UK in a new, updated form, buoyed by the recent recession. Coffee shops were originally popular during the 1950s but were considered unfashionable from the 1970s until chains such as Starbucks and Caffè Nero became widespread in the late 1990s. A criticism of the RLC could be that it presumes that retailers will inevitably follow the pattern within the model. However, retailers in a certain market sector may reduce the number of outlets they operate during an economic recession and open more a later time, when conditions are more favourable. Also, there is no indication with the RLC of the time span for each stage, since this is clearly very difficult to predict. Therefore, if two retailers launch simultaneously, one may reach decline whilst the other remains in the growth phase. It is also possible for sales to level off or reduce at any phase, then take off again, resulting in a stepped pattern to the RLC, rather than a smooth curve. Such criticisms have also been made of the Product Life Cycle model. However, an advantage of using the RLC can serve the purpose of indicating the current stage at which a retailer finds itself and to allow it to develop appropriate retail strategies for that stage.

The wheel of retailing

The wheel of retailing (Figure 1.5) is another cyclical theory which proposes that retailers pass through three stages of development after their introduction into the market

Figure 1.5 The wheel of retailing
Source: after McNair, 1958 and Brown, 1988

(McNair, 1958). In the entry phase, the wheel of retailing suggests that the retailer combines low prices with a limited product offering before trading up to become a more traditional retailer with better services and products at higher price levels. This second stage has been referred to as the 'big middle' (Levy *et al.*, 2005), as many US and European retailers fit into this category. In the final phase of the wheel, vulnerability, retailers reach maturity, characterised by conservative attitudes and declining returns on investment (Brown, 1990).

The wheel of retailing is a logical theory, yet it does not always apply in practice and is therefore open to criticism. Brown (1990: 143) is one of its major critics, pointing out its 'lack of universality' and its limited scope on price and quality, describing the theory as 'a marketing enigma, revered and reviled in almost equal measure'. However, there are various cases which support this theory. For example, M&S started out as a low-price retailer on a market stall in Leeds, England in 1884, set up by a Polish refugee named Michael Marks (Marks & Spencer, 2014). The stall initially had a sign stating 'Don't ask the price, it's a penny', and M&S has since traded up to become a traditional retailer which has led the UK clothing sector for several years (Mintel, 2010). The theory can also be applied successfully to supermarkets Tesco and Aldi, both of which initially traded at low prices and have moved into selling more upmarket products in recent years. However, many other examples contradict the wheel of retailing theory, since upmarket retailers, including jewellers, fashion retailers and delicatessens, frequently enter the market as start-up businesses. Moreover, large traditional stores such as Walmart can sell products at low prices, with the advantage of economies of scale. It is also possible for retailers to revert to an earlier stage of the wheel in certain respects. For example, whilst in the trading-up stage, UK supermarkets Tesco and Waitrose, amongst others, introduced low-price food ranges ('Value' and 'Essentials' respectively) which are more representative of the entry phase in this model.

Retail accordion

The retail accordion theory (see Figure 1.6) was developed in the 1960s by Hollander (1966) and suggests that retailers alternate their product offering, starting with a wide range then narrowing it down to a more specialised selection. Like the wheel of retailing theory, this may have had relevance at the time it was introduced. However, the retail accordion is rarely useful as a predictive model since many retailers do not follow this

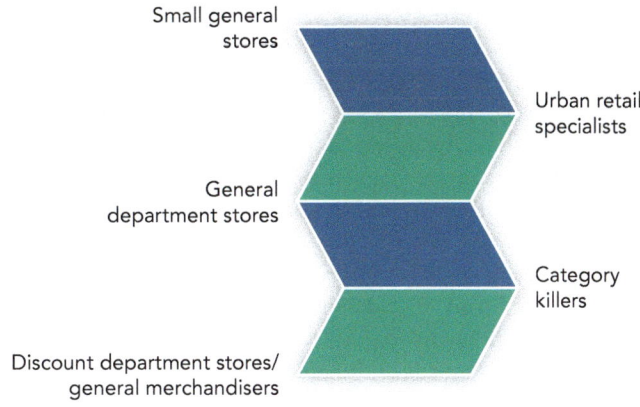

Figure 1.6 Retail accordion theory
Source: adapted from Hollander, 1966

pattern of development. For example, Amazon.com started out in 1995 with a narrow product range, as an online book retailer and has since moved on to stock many different products, as diverse as electronics and toiletries. While US retailers historically started as general stores before tending to specialise in certain product types, nowadays many retailers have never offered a broad range of goods and remain niche retailers, such as joy-ofsocks.com, which sells only socks and tights. Traditional retailers requiring specialist skills such as bakeries or confectioners also usually start as niche retailers (see Figure 1.7). The rise of etailing offers increased opportunities for specialist start-up businesses, since a niche product range can now cover a wide geographical area at a fraction of the cost of setting up bricks-and-mortar stores with the same coverage. Etailers can also offer a broad product range.

Figure 1.7 Sweet shops and bakeries are examples of traditional niche retailers
Source: authors' own photographs

Conflict theory

There has often been conflict between different types of retail innovations, ranging from competitive to anti-competitive practices. It is therefore not surprising to find that much of the terminology used within retailing and marketing is derived from military terms, such as 'strategy' and 'campaign'. Brown (1987) suggests that innovations in particular can lead to conflict where existing retailers progress through the four stages of shock, defensive retreat, acknowledgement and assessment, then adaptation. Despite appearing to apply only to negative situations, conflict can be credited with generating new forms of retailing which bridge the gap between one type of retailer and another. This happens when retailers operating in an established retail format react to the threat of newcomers in the market by adopting an aspect of the competitors' advantage over them. For example, when supermarket chains began to gain market share, traditional independent grocers formed alliances and voluntary groups to increase their buying power, as well as adopting the supermarkets' self-service strategy (Gilbert, 2003). After German discount supermarket Aldi began to increase its UK market share in 2007 (Hall, 2008), market leader Tesco hit back by copying its competitor's branding strategy. Instead of using its name on its own-label products, Aldi uses different names that mimic the presentation of manufacturer brands but are exclusive to its stores, e.g. 'Oakhurst' meat and 'Holly Lane' cakes. Tesco has adopted a similar approach, selling products exclusively under brand names such as 'Nutricat' pet food, which goes as far as having its own website (www.nutricat.com) providing veterinary advice in order to imitate branded catfood.

Some of the retail theories discussed here are potentially compatible with each other and all have tangible examples of how they can work in practice. However, none of them can be said to apply to the whole retailing sector, since each one has numerous exceptions. It would appear that an overarching retailing theory which can be applied universally has yet to be devised. Since each of these theories is organisation-centred, this calls for the introduction of a more consumer-focused retailing model in the future, which can be applied in various product sectors and in different countries. You are recommended to keep up-to-date with developments in retailing theory in academic journals, particularly the *Journal of Retailing*, as newer theories may be introduced by the time you read this book.

Recent developments affecting the retail environment

Retailing operates within the context of society and the environment in which it takes place and it is therefore influenced and affected by a variety of trends. Datamonitor (2011) estimates that by 2015, the global retailing industry will increase in value to more than $13,000 billion, an increase of around 26 per cent since 2010. This projected increase can be explained in part by demographic changes, since the world population reached 7 billion in 2011. An additional factor is that ageing populations have been on the rise in many countries (African Development Bank, 2011; Ashford, 2007; UK National Statistics, 2012) where average lifespans have been extended by improved living standards and healthcare. Retailers will need to respond to this ageing demographic, taking a more inclusive approach to age and reducing the traditional emphasis on appealing mainly to younger consumers (Lusch *et al.*, 2011).

Developments in technology, particularly the increasingly widespread use of computers, have had a significant impact on retailing. This impact began when computers started to be used by retailers for recording sales data using **electronic point-of-sale (EPoS)** systems and to communicate with suppliers. These technological developments speeded up communication channels from stores to the retail head office and from the retailer to suppliers, enabling companies to respond more quickly to consumer demand. The internet was initially used by retailers mainly as a promotional tool but retailing via transactional websites has become standard practice for large retailers in the US and Europe. It also offers small retailers the opportunity to start or expand their businesses, often at a lower cost than investing in retail premises. Internet retailing was expected to take off in the late 1990s with the so-called 'dotcom boom' but the growth of online sales stalled temporarily when major internet retailers such as boo.com went out of business. Despite this initial setback, online retailing has expanded in recent years, accounting for approximately 70 per cent of home shopping in 2008, overtaking catalogue sales at this point (Mintel, 2009).

Retail premises vacancies stood at around 14 per cent in the UK in 2013 (BCSC, 2014) a situation that has led retail landlords to adopt new strategies such as offering initial low rents or posting images on vacant properties to improve their appearance. For example, City Dressing produces virtual graphics that make empty outlets more attractive to potential new tenants and can have an interactive function, using Quick Response (QR) codes that can be read by digital devices to promote competitions or streaming live music and local information (see Figure 1.8). Jeremy Rucker, Managing Director of City Dressing, states that the company aims to make the stores look more animated by using imagery of local objects, quotes and people.

The expansion of the social networking aspect of the internet is sometimes referred to as 'Web 2.0', comprising websites such as Facebook (launched in 2004) and Twitter (available since 2006), as well as blogs. Social media have been utilised increasingly

Figure 1.8 Virtual shop windows

Source: with permission from City Dressing, www.citydressing.co.uk

by retailers as novel and cost-effective promotional tools (see Chapter 7 Retail marketing communications). Consumer feedback websites with user-generated content (e.g. www.tripadvisor.com) and consumer product reviews on retailers' websites, along with price comparison websites have enabled consumers to have more power in their purchase decision-making. This suggests a need for an increased focus on product quality and customer service, amongst other factors, by retail organisations. Radio Frequency Identification (RFID) is another form of technology which has been adopted by retailers, largely to enable tracking of merchandise from a distance using radio waves. Placing RFID processors on products can reduce labour costs in distribution, warehousing and stores with the added benefit of reducing theft. However, this technology is somewhat costly at the present time and has therefore been relatively slow to take off, though its use is now becoming more widespread in the retail sector, with Asda adopting it in 2014 to improve the accuracy of its clothing stock (Berman and Evans, 2010; Thomson, 2014).

The economic downturn, which began in 2008 and led to an almost global recession, directly affected retailers in various ways, notably being a factor in the closure of a series of well-established store chains in the UK and a raft of branch closures amongst surviving retail chains. For example, clothing group Arcadia planned to close around 10 per cent of its branches between 2011 to 2014 as leases came up for renewal (Harrison, 2011). Although technically the UK and US economies emerged from recession in late 2009, consumer confidence has been eroded. Unemployment figures rose and banks introduced more stringent lending criteria, resulting in greater restrictions on consumer spending power. Nonetheless, some retailers could be said to have benefitted from the recession, 'value retailers' being ideally placed to cater for consumers who were trading down and consequently allowing stores such as Poundstretcher and the 99p store to expand their outlets in the UK (Holland, 2012; Lalani, 2011). This has led to widespread price competition amongst retailers as a survival strategy and deflation of prices in certain product sectors. However, the luxury end of the market appears to have remained largely stable during the economic crisis, with upmarket stores competing with each other through innovative store design (see Figure 1.9).

Globalisation relates to retailing in terms of two main dimensions: the expansion of store chains in overseas markets and offshore sourcing. International retail expansion is considered to have reached saturation point in the US and Europe and Western retailers have therefore begun to expand into developing markets. The list of the world's top 10 retailers is dominated by Western companies, with just one company from the East included, Japanese retailer 'Seven and i Holdings' (Badillo, 2009). This scenario is likely to change during the next decade as emerging economies (often referred to as the 'BRIC' countries, i.e. Brazil, Russia, India and China) continue to expand. Globalisation affords retailers opportunities for retail growth caused by improving economies of scale and buying power, thus making pricing more competitive (see Figure 1.10). The globalisation of retailing has another, contrasting side to it. Since consumers have become increasingly distanced from the sources of the products they buy, many have acquired an interest in the conditions in which their purchases are manufactured, triggering requests for more transparent information about sources from retailers. It has become standard practice for retailers to develop CSR policies, for example H&M and Morrisons (H&M, 2014; Morrisons, 2014). It is possible that this practice has developed in response to such consumer interest in social and environmental sustainability and to the campaigns of pressure groups which publicise these major issues (see for example: Adbusters, 2012; Clean Clothes Campaign, 2012).

Figure 1.9 La Patisserie des Rêves, Marylebone High Street, London

Source: © Photos 12/Alamy Images

Figure 1.10 Retailers' potential growth cycle
Source: adapted from McGoldrick, P. (2002) *Retail Marketing*, 2nd edn © 2002. Reproduced with the kind permission of McGraw-Hill Education. All rights reserved.

RETAIL MARKETING CAREERS
Alastair Sneddon, Business Intelligence Manager

Alastair is the former Business Intelligence (BI) Manager of Game, a leading retailer of video games and game consoles, with a market share of over 30 per cent in the UK and Spain (Game, 2014). Alastair gained a BSc (Hons) Audio Technology from Anglia Ruskin University, then completed an MA Information Systems Management at Bournemouth University. His first job was as an Analyst Developer for Vivista and he says he fell into BI by accident as this was part of the graduate rotation scheme there, which he enjoyed and stayed in. He found he was good at it and had been interested in this area on his MA, looking at direct actions and happenings and being able to show a direct correlation. Alastair then worked at Game for seven years and progressed to become BI Manager, before leaving in 2014 to perform a similar role for The Consortium, a supplier of products and services to the education sector. Alastair has been trained in various software packages such as SQL (Structured Query Language) and he studied a project management course in his own time. Alastair says 'the meaning of BI very much depends on which industry and which job you're in, it's different things to different people. I would say that you shouldn't have anything that isn't digitisable in some way or format in your core information; that is, if someone's walking around with bits of paper, then you're not likely to be as accurate or timely'.

Source: with permission from Alastair Sneddon

Alastair described his main responsibilities at Game as 'ensuring that all core business reporting was delivered on time, was accurate and was able to provide the business with insight to allow them to make decisions which provide competitive advantage for the retail space that the business is in. That was the functional responsibility and the development and insight responsibility was more about gathering requirements, understanding the business and producing insight reporting'. In this role he reported directly to the Chief Financial Officer. Because Game works in a very reactive market, competing with supermarkets which can change prices quickly, Alastair needed to understand the impact that matching certain promotions or certain patterns would result in for the business. He therefore needed to drill down into data within the business to see the effect that changes would make.

At Game, BI covers every business function, so this included the analysis of sales data, financially driven data and customer-driven data. BI at Game included evaluating how customers' behaviour at tills or online shows in the transactional database and feeds into the MI (marketing intelligence) systems. Game has a popular customer loyalty scheme with a large number of records and Alastair was very involved in understanding consumer behaviour over time. 'Insight reporting' was part of his job there, which covers a broad base. Alastair explains 'for example, it can mean understanding the geographic spread of products, such as looking at Xbox 360 or PlayStation and finding out that there is a predominant leaning towards 360s the further North past Birmingham you go, as trade-ins are more prevalent further North so that people are able to get more money off the next game'. If there was a store where PlayStation products were the bestsellers then this insight would allow the marketing team, the buying team and the allocations team to be able to stock those stores accurately, market correctly to the customers who might be associated with that store and provide the right in-store advertising for that shop.

The nature of Alastair's job at Game was very cross-functional, so on a daily basis he interacted with the finance teams and if there seemed to be a problem with profit margin on products they would ask him to investigate this. He also worked alongside the marketing teams, buyers and allocations teams and he says 'on a day-to-day basis you never quite knew what the curveball would be that someone would throw at you, while you were working on the monthly development schedule. The nature of gaming is something that is constantly developing and we were always trying to get one jump ahead, being aware of new products like smartphones and tablets'.

In order to work in BI for a retailer Alastair says that people need to be 'really quite sharp in terms of analytics, taking a problem at a high level, breaking it down into its constituent parts, rebuilding it and representing it in a way that people understand'. For example, at Game 'attachment' means analysing which stores are attaching the most of certain types of products to other leading products; that is, noting where they're being bought by the same customer and understanding the transactional level of the data. This makes it possible to assess where particular stores perform well in terms of attachment around these products but less well with regard to other ones. Models could be used to assess data, but as these could not always be applied in practice, Alastair says 'you need to work rapidly around exceptions, so you have to be able very much to think on your feet and be very agile'.

Much of the data used by Game, such as weekly trading information, were generated automatically rather than manually. Areas of data that Alastair analysed included sales performance compared to targets such as profit margin and sales by turnover and volume, through stores and online. When products were out of stock in store a web order could be placed for customers to receive products by post. Alastair could assess how that system was performing and how each of the new week's releases or the previous month's releases were selling. He also collaborated closely with key suppliers such as EA, Ubisoft and Microsoft, to provide them with information from Game's BI systems, to enable the companies to support each other and maximise performance.

Alastair describes working on a 'top-down analytics model', so there was a level of appropriateness of information, depending on where people were in the business. The directors wanted summary information that allowed them to make decisions based on a balanced scorecard (a measurable set of objectives that are derived from business's **mission statement**). However, the heads of department, at the next level, wanted to understand how the information was reflected in their functional area. Alastair's role at Game involved integrating new systems and designing new business data models, assessing how information could be processed and used in various data systems, an area which is known as data architecture.

Though the appraisal system at Game was relatively informal, in effect, Alastair's performance was assessed constantly through Service Level Agreements, which meant that everyone in the business who needed them could access reports when required, an area in which he achieved 100 per cent consistently for three years. Alastair states 'it's important to note that you're only ever as good as your last failure. In the MI world it's very much a case of the only time people will really want to talk to you is when they find a problem and it's your fault until you prove it otherwise!'. Despite this, Alastair very much enjoyed his job, due largely to its broad scope and never knowing what he was going to come into in the morning from any area of the business, even a Sunday-morning phone call from the CEO.

Alastair had a team of three to four BI analysts or intelligence developers until the company went into administration in 2012, after which it was bought by its current owner, private investor OpCapita. Alastair says that graduates who want to work in BI or as data analysts would usually start at a junior or assistant level and work their way up. They would be expected to have strong numeracy skills, probably being qualified in a numerate discipline, such as science, accountancy or possibly business. Employers recruiting for BI roles would normally put people through numeracy and logical reasoning tests. Alastair also believes that the ability to be a creative thinker is important as information could be distributed to anyone within the business and it therefore needs to be tailored to the audience that will consume it.

Within a BI role, Alastair considers communication skills to be very important, with the ability to listen and not just to talk, as well as being a translator between the business functions and the IT functions. He thinks that self-motivation is equally vital, along with being interested in the job, as well as the patience and discipline to stick with something when it's not necessarily going as you expect. He feels it's important to take a scientific approach towards BI, as preconceived ideas may not be borne out by the results of the analytics. Alastair says 'for example, someone in the company could say "we're seeing more sales with gift cards this year" and when you analyse the numbers you find that people are not buying more with gift cards, strictly speaking. People are trading in products and receiving gift cards, then using that to buy more games, so there's a difference between received opinion and analysed, comprehended information'. Though planning can be useful, Alastair says 'you need the ability to be reactive, because you don't want to plan everything out and not have any time left for ad hoc stuff . . . from the MI side of things means you have to plan for the unexpected'. He advises graduate recruits not to be 'too much of a purist', as data and the way businesses work are not necessarily structured in an ideal academic way, so they need to be prepared for exceptions, which can involve working much more quickly than they've learnt to expect.

www.game.co.uk; www.gamedigitalplc.com; https://twitter.com/GAMEdigital

Reference

Game (2014) *Game overview* (available online at: http://www.gamedigitalplc.com/about-game/overview.aspx)

Retailing management

Retailing management covers a wide range of roles which are not limited to store management, covering Head Office-based roles, supply chain and distribution. The key Head Office function in relation to this book is the marketing department, though as you will see, marketing activity is not confined to a single department and takes place in all areas of a marketing-orientated retailer. The marketing director or manager would typically be responsible for compiling and implementing the marketing strategy, in conjunction with his or her team. Retail chains usually centralise most of their management functions at a Head Office location. This is cost-effective, although inevitably it distances Head Office personnel from customers and sales staff. In a small retailer, the company is unlikely to be large enough to employ specialists in each of these areas, so one person may have several responsibilities; for example, the owner may be in charge of HR, buying and marketing. Retailers' management functions can vary depending on the product sector. For example, M&S has the following Head Office departments (Marks & Spencer, 2014):

- Human Resources (HR)
- Information Technology (IT)
- Logistics
- Buying
- Marketing
- **Merchandising**
- Product Technology
- Food Technology
- Food Product Development
- Fashion Design
- **Ecommerce**.

The range of departments at M&S reflects the fact that the company's main product areas are clothing and food. As in most business sectors, there are variations in the terminology used to describe job roles and in the responsibilities of jobs in different retailers. Retailers can also have other management departments such as legal, imports, design, **visual merchandising** and customer service. Certain functions can be decentralised by store chains; for example, retail buying can take place separately in each branch, so that the merchandise is selected to specifically meet the different requirements of customers in each location. Management of retail outlets is decentralised and store managers are usually overseen by regional/area managers who report to a **Retail Operations** director at Head Office (see Figure 1.11).

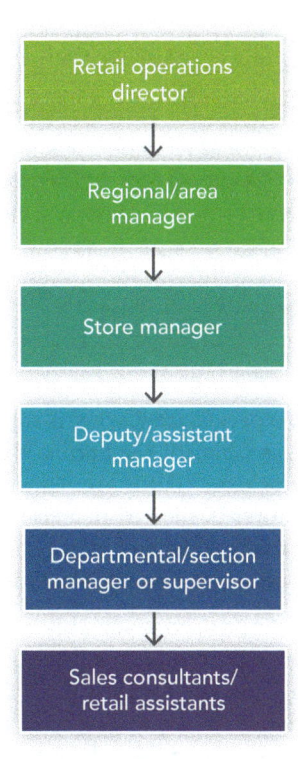

Retail operations director
↓
Regional/area manager
↓
Store manager
↓
Deputy/assistant manager
↓
Departmental/section manager or supervisor
↓
Sales consultants/retail assistants

Figure 1.11 An example of typical store management personnel structure

Additional retail-related roles can be conducted independently of the retailers themselves. Such roles include retail analysts and market researchers, who may be employed by retailers on a consultancy basis or provide marketing reports which cover a broader area of the sector. There are numerous potentially lucrative career prospects in the retail sector for those who are versatile, decisive, analytical and industrious. Several of these roles have been taken by contributors to this book who draw from their experience to explain how retail marketing works in practice.

The future of retailing

As this chapter has explained, retailing is a sector in a state of constant change. Political, economic, societal, technological, ecological and legal factors converge to impact upon this dynamic industry. Predictions for the future of retailing have been made in various publications and at retail events. For example, as we have become accustomed to the many facilities offered to the retail sector by the internet, new technical innovations such as wearable technology are being introduced that could be utilised by retail staff to enable retailing to increase its efficiency and scope (*Drapers*, 2014). Retail specialists who were interviewed about their roles for this book were asked for their opinions on the future of retailing. Business Intelligence Manager Alastair Sneddon's view is that 'the High Street won't die completely but it will turn into a showroom as opposed to a stockroom front, like Apple and Currys that just have display and it's more about style. This could be any product except maybe for clothing. I also think shops are going to start targeting demographics very specifically. You might see a shop front change from town-to-town depending on what they're consuming there'. Retail design expert Kelly Molson comments are compatible with this view, as she believes that 'omnichannel retailing seems to be the future . . . consumers want to use all channels simultaneously, from bricks-and-mortar stores, mobile, radio, direct mail etc., creating a more knowledgeable consumer'. Alternatively, branding design and business development consultant Martin Knox offers the following opinion:

> In the future, for retail to survive across any number of new channels that will emerge, we have to be thinking about the abstracts of multichannels, so for example, developing community around a shop is an abstract of what that shop is and can contribute and generate income in other ways. This is a global readjustment, something we've never seen the like of before. Growth is not sustainable. The only way for capitalism and commerce to work with the limited resources we've got is boom and bust and I don't think it'll happen like that again. We're making do, we're being creative and using our imagination . . . We have to take responsibility and we can find it incredibly empowering.

Retail expert Clare Rayner is supportive of small businesses in her view of the future. Speaking as Chair of the Future High Street Summit 2014, Clare explained that whilst many major store chains are reducing the number of their outlets, the quantity of independent stores in the UK increased every year between 2009 and 2013. Clare also discussed the new consumer engagement model of customers focusing on social, local and mobile aspects of shopping, i.e. 'So-Lo-Mo', stating:

> Physicality of presence still matters – consumers spend more, more often, with brands who have physical AND digital presence. A physical location supplements online Click and Collect, local delivery and the ability to deliver a more personal experience. Multiple points of presence increase reach, engagement and loyalty. The internet is only a threat if you ignore it so small retailers need to embrace technology; be where their customers are; bring the online/digital experience to stores; reward loyalty and make time in town a pleasure, not a chore!

Studying retail marketing

A key piece of advice for studying retail marketing effectively is to go beyond academic textbooks and articles to assess retailers' current practice first hand by observational research in stores and online. Additionally, it can be beneficial to read a broad range of industry sources and speak directly to customers whom you know, to gain their viewpoints about retailers. Retail marketing has been a field of academic study for several decades and a qualification in this area can lead to a career in the retail sector. Retail marketing career vignettes throughout the book give a taste of the varied job opportunities available in both large-scale and smaller independent retailers. Each chapter has a series of objectives that the content will address, as well as reflective questions and exercises for you to consider at the end, to test your understanding. These exercises will reinforce your learning and may form the basis of issues to debate with students in seminar groups or informal discussions. Alternatively, you can prepare answers to the questions yourself.

The major academic journals suited to the study of retail marketing are the *Journal of Retailing* and the *Journal of Marketing*. There are also many other journals with articles on retail marketing issues (see Chapter 3 Retail consumer behaviour and market segmentation). There are many excellent articles on retailing found in other journals too, which you can subscribe to or pay to download individual articles. Many journals can be accessed online for free by academics and students via university libraries or through requesting an inter-library loan. Employers can also subscribe to relevant academic journals. Marketing databases and trade journals, such as Mintel and *Retail Week*, as well as high-quality newspapers, retail trade associations and retailers' websites, are also good sources of current information on retailing. Gaining work experience, a more formal placement or working part-time in retailing should be considered as part of your studies and will obviously be an asset on your CV alongside qualifications when applying for jobs.

EXERCISES AND QUESTIONS

1. Which are your favourite and least favourite retailers? Explain the reasons for your choices. Consider ways in which your least popular retailer could improve in order to meet your needs as a customer more effectively.

2. Having read Table 1.1, you should write down some examples of retailers within each category from your own area and from other regions or countries you have visited.

3. Research into some of the key historical developments in retail marketing. What can we learn from the history of retail marketing that could be applied to contemporary retailing? The following sources could be useful for your research. A special issue of the journal *Business History* offers insights into the emergence of modern retailing between 1750–1950 (Alexander and Akehurst, 1998). For a review of retailing in the UK from 1990–2010 you are also recommended to read Burt (2010) 'Retailing in Europe: 20 years on', *International Review of Retail, Distribution and Consumer Research*, 20(1), 9–27.

4. After reading the retail marketing careers sections in this chapter compare the traditional independent shopkeeper's role with the contemporary job of a business intelligence manager. What elements do the two jobs have in common? What are the key differences in the two roles?

5. Consider the types of non-store retailing which are popular in the area where you live. Suggest which additional non-store retailing techniques have the most potential for expansion in this location and why you believe this to be the case. Which types of products do you suggest should be sold via the techniques you have chosen?

6. The rate of adoption of developments in retailing can vary from one location to another. For international readers, plot a timeline of developments in retailing in your own country and compare this with the UK (mentioned earlier in this chapter). You can draw from a variety of sources, e.g. your own experience, asking friends and family and seeking online resources. Locate and examine important structural changes that shape retail development, e.g. technology, legislation and market entry by overseas retailers. Place these changes at appropriate points in the timeline.

7. Reading the following article will allow you to gain a more comprehensive overview of the historical background to retailing:

    Evans, J.R. (2011) Retailing in perspective: the past is a prologue to the future, *International Review of Retail, Distribution and Consumer Research*, 21(1), 1–31.

    Its purpose is to assess historical events in retailing to help to forecast the future of the retail sector. Note in the conclusion the eight key principles that Evans recommends that retailers should follow and consider whether or not you agree with his suggestions.

8. Consider the information on the future of retailing in this chapter and discuss how this could affect retailers in the area where you live.

9. Read some of the job descriptions on the website of a recruitment agency that covers the retail sector to review the responsibilities of retail management roles. For example:

    www.retailchoice.com
    www.retailweekjobs.com/
    www.michaelpageinternational.com/Pages/Home/International-Presence
    jobs.marketingweek.co.uk/jobs/retail/

    Select job descriptions for at least three management-level positions with different retailers. Identify similarities between the responsibilities within these roles. Write down the aspects of the jobs which are specific to retailing, as opposed to general marketing roles. Assess one of the job descriptions in detail, assessing whether each responsibility is strategic (long-term planning) or operational (day-to-day management).

REFERENCES

Adbusters (2012) *Environmental Spoof Ads* (available online at: www.adbusters.org/spoofads/environmental).

African Development Bank (2011) *More and More Africans are Growing Old but Face Uncertain Future, Reports AfDB* (available online at: www.afdb.org/en/news-and-events/article/more-and-more-africans-are-growing-old-but-face-uncertain-future-reports-afdb-8568/).

Alexander, N. and Akehurst, G. (1998) Introduction: the emergence of modern retailing, 1750–1950, *Business History*, 40(4), 1–15.

Ashford, L.S. (2007) *Africa's Youthful Population: Risk or Opportunity?* Washington DC: Population Reference Bureau (available online at: www.prb.org/pdf07/africayouth.pdf).

Badillo, F. (2009) *Strategic Focus: Top Global Retailers*, Columbus, OH: Kantar Retail.

BCSC (2014) *Future High Street Summit,* conference presentation by Michael Green, Chief Executive of the British Council of Shopping Centres, Leicester, April 2014.

Berman, B. and Evans, J.R. (2010) *Retailing Management: A Strategic Approach*, 11th edn, Upper Saddle River, NJ: Pearson.

Blythe, J. (2009) *Principles and Practice of Marketing,* Thomson Cengage Learning.

Blythman, J. (2004) *Shopped: The Shocking Power of the British Supermarkets*, London: Harper Collins.

BRC (2014) *British Retail Consortium* (available online at: http://www.brc.org.uk/brc_home.asp).

Brown, S. (1987) Institutional change in retailing: a review and synthesis, *European Journal of Marketing*, 21(6), 5–36.

Brown, S. (1990) Innovation and evolution in UK retailing: the retail warehouse, *European Journal of Marketing*, 24(9), 39–54.

Brown, S. (1991) Variations on a marketing enigma: the wheel of retailing theory, *Journal of Marketing Management,* 7, 131–155.

Byrne Paquet, L. (2003) *The Urge to Splurge: A Social History of Shopping,* Toronto: ECW Press.

Centre for Retail Research (2012) *Who's gone bust in retailing?* (available online at: http://www.retailresearch.org/whosgonebust_previous.php).

CHORD (2014) *CHORD: Useful Links* (available online at: www.wlv.ac.uk/default.aspx?page=22691).

Clean Clothes Campaign (2012) *Improving Working Conditions in the Global Garment Industry* (available online at: http://www.cleanclothes.org/).

Datamonitor (2011) *Global Retailing Industry Profile*, New York: Datamonitor.

Dean, W. (2012) The pop-up paradigm: They may not last for long but temporary shops are here to stay, *The Independent,* 26 January 2012 (available online at: http://www.independent.co.uk/news/uk/this-britain/the-popup-paradigm-they-may-not-last-for-long-but-temporary-shops-are-here-to-stay-6294576.html).

Drapers (2014) Wearable technology market to reach £11.4bn by 2018, *Drapers,* 13 March (available online at: http://www.drapersonline.com/news/ecommerce/wearable-technology-market-to-reach-114bn-by-2018Ö5058334.article).

Evans, J.R. (2011) Retailing in perspective: the past is a prologue to the future, *International Review of Retail, Distribution and Consumer Research*, 21(1), 1–31.

Fernie, J., Fernie, S. and Moore, C. (2003) *Principles of Retailing*, Oxford: Butterworth Heinemann.

Freestone, O.M. and McGoldrick, P.J. (2008) Motivations of the ethical consumer, *Journal of Business Ethics*, 79(4), 445–467.

Gilbert, D. (2003) *Retail Marketing Management,* Harlow: Financial Times/Prentice Hall.

Hall, J. (2008) Tesco moves to counter Aldi and Lidl, *The Telegraph,* 7 January (available online at: http://www.telegraph.co.uk/finance/newsbysector/retailandconsumer/2782156/Tesco-moves-to-counter-Aldi-and-Lidl.html).

Hall, R.E. (1993) Macro theory and the recession of 1990–1991, *American Economics Association Papers and Proceedings*, 83(2), 275–289.

Harrison, N. (2011) Arcadia profits fall as Sir Philip Green confirms mass store closures, *Retail Week,* 23 November (available online at: www.retail-week.com/sectors/fashion/arcadia-profits-fall-as-sir-philip-green-confirms-mass-store-closures/5031426.article).

H&M (2014) *Sustainability* (available online at: about.hm.com/content/hm/AboutSection/en/About/Sustainability.html\#cm-footer).

Holland, T. (2012) Poundstretcher: has the value retailer made the right moves to take advantage of the gap left by Woolworths?, *Retail Week*, 16 March 2012, p. 16.

Hollander, S. (1966) Notes on the retail accordion, *Journal of Retailing*, 42(2), 29.

Lalani, H. (2011) 99p Stores presentation, *The Retail Conference*, London, November.

Leicester Market (2012) *Leicester Market History* (available online at: http://www.leicestermarket.co.uk/about/history/).

Levy, M., Grewal, D., Peterson, R.A. and Connolly, B. (2005) The concept of the 'Big Middle', *Journal of Retailing*, 81, 83–88.

Luna, I. (2005) *Retail Architecture and Shopping*, New York: Rizzoli/Universal.

Lury, C. (1996) *Consumer Culture*, Oxford: Polity Press.

Lusch, R.F., Dunne, P.M. and Carver, J.R. (2011) *Introduction to Retailing*, International/7th edn, Stamford, CT: South-Western Cengage Learning.

Marks & Spencer (2014) *M&S Head Office Careers* (available online at: careers.marksandspencer.com/careers-at-m-and-s/head-office)

McGoldrick, P. (2002) *Retail Marketing*, 2nd edn, Maidenhead: McGraw-Hill.

McNair, M.P. (1958) Significant trends and developments in the post war period, in A.B. Smith (ed.), *Competitive Distribution in a Free High Level Economy and its Implications for the University*, Pittsburgh, PA: University of Pittsburgh Press, 1–25.

Miller, D., Jackson, P., Thrift, N., Holbrook, B. and Rowlands, M. (1998) *Shopping, Place and Identity*, London: Routledge.

Mintel (2009) *Home Shopping – UK*, London: Mintel.

Mintel (2010) *Clothing Retailing – UK*, London: Mintel.

Morrisons (2014) *Morrisons Corporate Social Responsibility* (available online at: www.morrisons.co.uk/Corporate-Old2/Corporate-Social-Responsibility/Morrisons-Corporate-Social-Responsibility/).

Nielsen Ad Dynamix (2014) Top 100 UK advertisers, in *Marketing Week*, 11 April 2014 (available online at: www.marketingmagazine.co.uk/article/1289560/top-100-uk-advertisers-bskyb-increases-lead-p-g-bt-unilever-reduce-adspend).

Nielsen Media Research (2011) *Marketing's Top 100 Advertisers* (available online at: http://www.rankingthebrands.com/The-Brand-Rankings.aspx?rankingID=39&year=291).

Rubin, M. (2006) *The Hollow Crown: A History of Britain in the Late Middle Ages*, London: Penguin.

Stobart, J. (2008) *Spend, Spend, Spend: A Social History of Shopping*, Stroud: The History Press.

Taylor, J. and Bradley, S. (1994) Spatial disparities in the impact of the 1990–92 recession: an analysis of UK counties, *Oxford Bulletin of Economics and Statistics*, 56(4), 367–382.

Thomson, R. (2014) Asda rolls out RFID technology on George stock, *Retail Week*, 20 January (available online at: www.retail-week.com/technology/asda-rolls-out-rfid-technology-on-george-stock/5056707.article).

Ugolini, L. and Benson, J. (2002) *A Nation of Shopkeepers: Retailing in Britain 1550–2000*, London: I.B. Tauris.

UK National Statistics (2012) *Population* (available online at: http://www.statistics.gov.uk/hub/population/population-change/population-estimates/index.html).

Vargo, S.L. and Lusch, R.F. (2004) Evolving to a new dominant logic for marketing, *Journal of Marketing*, 68(1), 1–17.

Walmart (2014) *Fact Sheets* (available online at: www.walmartstores.com/pressroom/FactSheets/).

World Bank (2012) *Countries and Economies* (available online at: data.worldbank.org/country).

FURTHER READING

Burt, S. (2010) Retailing in Europe: 20 years on, *International Review of Retail, Distribution and Consumer Research*, 20(1), 9–27.

CEBR (2014) *Britain's Pop-Up Retail Economy,* Centre for Economics and Business Research (available online at: ee.co.uk/content/dam/everything-everywhere/documents/Pop-p%20business%20PDFs/EE%20Pop-Up_Retail_Economy_Report.pdf).

Clarke, I. and Banga, S. (2010) The economic and social role of small stores: a review of UK evidence, *International Review of Retail, Distribution and Consumer Research*, 20(2), 187–215.

Dawson, J., Findlay, A. and Sparks, L. (2008) *The Retailing Reader,* Abingdon: Routledge.

Deloitte (2014) *Global Powers of Retailing* (available online at: www2.deloitte.com/global/en/pages/consumer-business/articles/global-powers-of-retailing-2014.html).

Rayner, C. (2012) *The Retail Champion: 10 Steps to Retail Success,* London: Kogan Page.

Rettie, R., Burchell, K. and Barnham, C. (2014) Social normalisation: using marketing to make green normal, *Journal of Consumer Behaviour*, 13(1), 9–17.

Roberts, D., Hughes, M. and Kertbo, K. (2014) Exploring consumers' motivations to engage in innovation through co-creation activities, *European Journal of Marketing*, 48(1/2), 147–169.

Marketing Magazine

Marketing Week

Retail Week

www.brc.org.uk

Case study

Re-evaluating the store

By Richard Hyman, Strategic Retail Adviser to Deloitte

Five years ago, a typical non-food prime site retailer starting out and looking to reach its optimum market might have targeted as many as 200 sites to trade from. Three years ago, that figure would have reduced to between 100 and 150. Today, the figure is shrinking again. For such a retailer, it is increasingly difficult to justify each successive location beyond 75 stores, while anecdotal evidence suggests that for a growing number of retailers it is closer to 50. This reflects just how far and how fast retailing is changing and how the development of additional routes to market has not only changed the competitive landscape but the economics of the marketplace. As a result, the nature of the store of the future must necessarily be very different to that which we are used to today. Stores will become much more of a showcase for product and the experience of visiting a store will be more about shopping than simply buying.

A store geared to people buying will carry more product options whereas a store geared to shopping will be about inspiration and aspiration and much more about customer engagement. The store of the future will carry fewer products but its offer will need to have far more relevance to its target market. The customer experience is changing as consumers evolve and become more connected. Consumers are constantly connected to the internet through smart, portable and highly usable devices, they are in control of the technology they use and demand the latest technology from retailers. In this market, it will be vital that there is a seamless, joined up operating model that unites all the channels through which the retailer addresses its market. There is more to multichannel retailing than just having stores and a website. Changes will be required to support this model. Retailers will need to re-evaluate key areas of the business including range and inventory, marketing and customer services. Retail will become much more about the brand and how the retailer can truly differentiate by adding value to the customer. In a market where there are increasingly too many mouths to feed, being distinctive and having the ability to communicate this in a compelling way will be prerequisites of success.

The store remains a vital channel for retailers. A recent survey by Deloitte found that 78 per cent of customers bought their last item of clothing and accessories in-store, but rising retail stars are already operating to the new model and for many established players we expect significant downsizing of store portfolios in the medium to long term. The solution will not be the same for every retailer, but those who fail to realise the fundamental transformation required may struggle to survive. Economic conditions might be accelerating this process but they are not the driving force. This is a structural change in retail for which there is no reverse gear.

Source: Hyman, R. (2011) Re-evaluating the store, *Retail Week*, 9 September.

DISCUSSION QUESTIONS

1 What are the key changes to bricks-and-mortar stores that the article suggests will happen in the future?
2 Which factors have caused these changes?
3 What effects do you believe these changes will have on consumers?

CHAPTER 2

Retail marketing strategy

Learning objectives

The objectives of this chapter are to:

- explain the significance of strategic planning for retailers;
- explain the stages of marketing planning;
- examine how the macro-environment and micro-environment impact upon strategic decisions;
- assess how marketing strategy can help retailers to gain competitive advantage;
- explore the theory and implementation of management strategy in the retail sector.

Introduction

This chapter focuses on how retailers' management teams can develop a marketing plan from the firm's corporate strategy, its mission, goals and objectives, as well as the benefits of this approach. Key models are covered that can be used to guide marketing strategy with the aim of creating competitive advantage. The marketing planning process is discussed, beginning with an environmental audit of internal and external factors that impact upon the retailer. Marketing strategies can then be created to anticipate and adapt to changes in the retailing environment. The implementation of marketing strategies is then covered in subsequent chapters.

Retail marketing strategy

Academics have offered a range of different interpretations of strategy (e.g. Ansoff, 1984; Whittington, 2001). Strategies are broad, long-term decisions that are usually instigated by senior management and reviewed on a regular basis. The company's strategy is the plan specifically designed to achieve the objectives that have been set by the retailer (Lusch et al., 2011). To achieve an objective to increase market share, for example, a retailer may devise a strategy to attract or retain customers. Core strategy is central to the organisation and can be translated into marketing mix decisions by the marketing team and their colleagues. As well as strategies that subsequently affect the regular, day-to-day running of the business, retailers can devise longer-term strategies that impact upon the structure of the company. Such long-term strategies include diversifying into new product areas, mergers or acquisitions of other businesses and moving into new domestic or overseas markets.

Corporate strategy is usually created at the most senior level of the company, largely relating to the selection of products and markets that the business enters or exits (Gilligan and Wilson, 2007). In a stable environment, strategy may remain the same from year to year when it is considered to be meeting objectives and working effectively, but it can still be advantageous to review strategy periodically, typically on an annual basis. According to Berman and Evans (2010: 58) strategic planning is beneficial for retailers in that it:

- provides a thorough analysis of the requirements for doing business for different types of retailers;
- outlines retailer goals;
- allows retailers to determine how to differentiate themselves from competitors;
- enables firms to develop an offering that appeals to a particular group of customers;
- creates an opportunity to study the legal, economic, and competitive environment;
- allows the firm's total efforts to be co-ordinated;
- enables crises to be anticipated and avoided.

Strategic analysis may merely confirm that the present strategy remains suitable for current market conditions, or it may suggest that amendments should be made; for example, setting a target of a 25 per cent market share rather than a 23 per cent share, as a competitor has gone out of business. Parallels can be drawn with Darwin's theory of evolution, in line with evolutionary strategy, with retailers needing to adapt to survive (Ries and Ries, 2006). In a changeable external environment, such as the economic downturn which began in the US and Europe in 2008, it is advisable to review strategy more frequently than usual, in response to frequent changes in conditions. During a recession, it may be more realistic to aim to maintain the retailer's current annual financial turnover and staffing, rather than to increase them (CIPD, 2012).

Marketing strategy is described by Ferrell and Hartline (2011: 19) as 'a plan for how the organisation will use its strengths and capabilities to match the needs and requirements of the market'. Changes to the retailer's target market may become necessary in reaction to prevailing economic trends. A shift in targeting a particular income bracket or location may be required which can impact upon the marketing mix. For example, in the wake of the financial crisis, 'Migato' is one of several Greek retailers which has expanded overseas into more financially stable markets such as the UK and Egypt (Lebessi and Giannarou, 2012). High property costs and consumers' increased ownership of computers could jointly lead to a change in a retailer's distribution channel strategy through the closure of some of its bricks-and-mortar outlets and the expansion of its online product offering. A strategy to improve customer retention could result in a decision to enhance the quality of a bestselling product range, while retaining competitive prices. This could necessitate collaboration between marketing executives and colleagues in design and quality control, as well as liaison with suppliers of the products involved. When strategies have been implemented they can be monitored and controlled to ensure that they are working effectively and to keep them on track.

Retail marketing planning

Hollensen (2006: 4) defines marketing planning as 'the structured process of researching and analysing marketing situations, developing and documenting marketing objectives, strategies and programmes, and implementing, evaluating and controlling activities to achieve the objectives'.

The retail sector utilises the same tools and theories as conventional marketing planning, a component of strategic planning that aims to utilise an organisation's resources effectively in response to the changing market environment. Strategic planning is generally the responsibility of a company's board of directors or senior management team and marketing planning is a key responsibility for a marketing manager within the retail sector. Retail marketing planning is described by Lusch et al. (2011: 40) as 'the anticipation and organisation of what needs to be done to reach an objective'. The authors also state that 'a well-defined plan of action can mean the difference between success and failure' (*ibid.*). Gilbert (2003: 233) offers a more detailed description:

> Planning is the most important activity of marketing management. Retailers need to plan for merchandise, inventory control, logistics development, pricing, promotional campaigns, store location and layout, positioning of the business, branding, growth and development of the business – and other functional activities. The plan, which needs to ensure that the previous areas are considered, should provide a common structure and act as a focus for all of the company's management activities.

Gilbert (2003: 236) goes on to state that the purpose of a retailer's marketing plan is: 'to provide clear direction to the overall retailing operation based upon a systematic, written approach to planning and action'. Distributing the marketing plan to a retailer's employees within relevant departments allows them to adopt a consistent approach to implementing the company's strategy. Retailers may also consider sharing the plan with key suppliers, since they have the mutual aim of meeting customers' needs effectively. Hollensen (2006) describes the benefits of the marketing planning process as: consistency; responsibility; communication and commitment. Strategic planning can give a firm the advantage of implementing consistent strategies throughout the organisation, resulting in a more coherent brand image, thereby potentially boosting its competitive advantage and, ultimately, its profitability. However, in certain fast-moving sectors of retailing, marketing strategies may need to be implemented quickly, meaning that it may not be viable to progress through such rational and sometimes lengthy procedures.

Strategic planning of this kind is standard content in most of the key textbooks on retailing (see, for example, Gilbert, 2003; McGoldrick, 2002). However, these are not definitive rules that have to be followed and they represent a distinctly Westernised view of how management can operate (Whittington, 2001). Even in the West, many companies do not appear to follow a formal strategic planning process, since fewer than 60 per cent of businesses compile mission statements (Lusch *et al.*, 2011). In addition to this classical, Western view of strategy, which is dominant in mainstream literature, Whittington (2001) critiques three alternative perspectives: evolutionary, processual and systemic approaches to strategy. Evolutionary strategy follows the Darwinian theory of natural selection, where managers respond to changes in the market in order for the company to survive. These different types of management strategy are particularly pertinent to certain variations in the organisational cultures of retailers from different countries.

Situation analysis

Ferrell and Hartline (2011: 18) define **situation analysis** as 'the overall process of collecting and interpreting internal, competitive, and environmental information'. An effective situation analysis investigates the retailer's current position and establishes its potential future direction, by analysing internal and external factors. Jobber (2010: 39) proposes that the following key questions should be asked in strategic planning.

1. Where are we now?
2. How did we get here?
3. Where are we heading?
4. Where would we like to be?
5. How do we get there?
6. Are we on course?

The first three questions can be answered by means of a marketing audit and a **SWOT analysis** (see below). Marketing objectives can be set in response to question 4. To establish how to get there, a core marketing strategy needs to be devised, followed by the planning of an appropriate marketing mix and the implementation of the strategy. Finally, to keep the strategy on course the control phase involves evaluating and adjusting the company's marketing approach.

SWOT analysis

A SWOT analysis can be undertaken as part of the business situation analysis to identify the retailer's key strengths, weaknesses, opportunities and threats (see Figure 2.1). This assists in specifying the key issues for further examination. When a SWOT analysis is conducted effectively Hollensen (2006: 11) states that it can:

- match strengths to opportunities;
- convert weaknesses to strengths;
- convert threats to opportunities;
- minimise, if not avoid, weaknesses and threats.

Figure 2.2 gives an example of how a SWOT analysis could be applied to an established independent restaurant in a city centre location, thus allowing its management to anticipate threats and take advantage of new opportunities.

Figure 2.1 The SWOT analysis matrix

Strengths
- Receives good press reviews and customer feedback
- Good location with high footfall
- No cashflow problems
- Friendly, experienced staff

Weaknesses
- High rent in the city centre
- Premises and décor require renovation
- Limited menu range

Opportunities
- Open a second branch
- Increase promotion to bring in new customers and convert passers-by into customers
- Appeal to new market segments
- Offer an updated menu with a wider choice
- Redecorate

Threats
- Challenges from national restaurant chains opening nearby
- High concentration of take-away restaurants in the area

Figure 2.2 SWOT analysis for an independent small-scale restaurant

The information that contributes towards a SWOT analysis can be gleaned from both internal and external sources. Internal data are vital to establish the retailer's strengths and weaknesses and this can be found in sales figures, information from the firm's employees and market research conducted for the company. Market research can be compiled by the retailer's in-house market researchers or by engaging a specialist consultancy such as Retailmap. External information can also be gathered from market research and from the media. Market reports and the trade press are usually the most focused information sources for retailers, as they are the most suited to their needs. Major market research firms such as Mintel, Euromonitor, Datamonitor and Key Note provide reports on specific retail and product sectors. The financial press or the business and finance pages of newspapers are useful sources to enable retailers to keep up-to-date with local, national or international issues that can create opportunities or threats. The trade press offers frequent updates on the retail sector in publications including *Retail Week*, *The Grocer* and *Drapers*. Online subscriptions to the *Retail Bulletin* and *Retail Gazette* supply regularly updated information via email.

Mission statements

Strategic planning typically begins by composing a mission statement that sums up the company's values and reflects the interests of stakeholders in the organisation. This is normally followed by setting goals or objectives at senior management level, then devising a marketing plan. In the case of retailers, stakeholders include those who own or hold shares in the company, the customers, the employees, the local communities around the location of the company's outlets or offices and the retailer's suppliers of products and services. The mission statement should summarise concisely what the retailer hopes to achieve through the operation of its business. Berman and Evans (2010: 59) define the business's mission as 'commitment to a type of business and to a distinctive role in the marketplace', whereas Hollensen (2006: 7) states 'an organisation's mission is an expression of its purpose; it states what the organisation hopes to accomplish and how it plans to achieve this goal'. The mission statement does not need to be renewed annually but it is useful to review it at regular intervals in case changes in circumstances warrant a change in direction. The examples in Table 2.1 show mission statements from retailers in different countries and product/service sectors. Consider to what extent you think these statements truly reflect the companies. It is suggested that you look at the websites of those retailers that are not familiar to you and also look for the mission statements of retailers where you regularly shop to see how appropriate you think they are. (You may wish to use Google Translate in some cases by searching for them on Google and clicking on 'translate this page' on the list of results.)

Setting goals and objectives

Goals and objectives are the guidelines which show how the company intends to accomplish its mission. Aims or goals give an overall view of what the organisation is setting out to achieve. Objectives are more specific, detailed directives give the retailer a practical

Table 2.1 Examples of retailers' mission statements

Mission statement	Company/website
'We seek to be Earth's most customer-centric company for three primary customer sets: consumer customers, seller customers and developer customers.'	Amazon www.amazon.com
'All of our restaurants make the food we serve by hand and use only the best quality, freshest ingredients.'	Handmade Burger Co. handmadeburger.co.uk
'To maintain its leading position in the market of cosmetics and fashion, and be extended to cities with a particular business interest. The main goal should be the constant satisfying of the needs of modern consumers, offering a unique experience of shopping.'	Hondos Center www.hondoscenter.gr
'A Great European bank acknowledged for its people, creating superior value for customers and shareholders.'	Nordea Bank www.nordea.com
'A Chinese brand whose mission is to take Chinese chic to the Western world.'	Shanghai Tang www.shanghaitang.com
'We are committed to excellence in the art of hairdressing. We are passionately dedicated to providing clients with the highest level of skills, service and products in an enjoyable, friendly salon environment.'	Toni & Guy www.toniandguy.com

framework to follow, thus enabling it to implement strategies. Objectives can be set at corporate and divisional levels. The company performance can later be reviewed in comparison to these objectives either during or at the end of the financial year. Objectives can be set either for the short term or for the longer term. It is possible for retailers to use long-range planning, setting objectives for five years or more ahead, although they may review these plans annually. Effective objectives are usually 'SMART', i.e. Specific, Measurable, Realistic and on Time. They may be measurable in different ways; for example, by the percentage of improvement in terms of market share or position in comparison to competitors, such as progressing from being fourth biggest to third biggest retailer within a specific sector. Financial performance can be calculated in terms of increased annual or quarterly turnover and profitability is frequently assessed through **net profit margin**; that is, profit after tax (Berman and Evans, 2010). Adopting a more socially responsible and environmentally sustainable approach is also becoming increasingly important for many retailers. This may involve setting targets which relate to, for example, increasing diversity in recruitment, offering a more environmentally friendly product range, improving recycling within the company and sponsoring schools for the children of those employed by suppliers in developing countries.

Identifying consumers

The retailer needs to identify the type of consumers at which it targets its merchandise. This enables the company to establish the target customers' needs and wants and to offer merchandise at suitable prices and locations to meet these needs. Retailers can adopt a mass marketing approach, aiming at a broad range of customer categories, or target a smaller niche of customers. The main type of customer targeted by a retailer is referred to as the 'core customer' and they form the largest proportion, if not most of the company's clientele. They can be specified in market segments by demographic characteristics such as age group or by aspects of their lifestyle. The retailer will also probably attract customers in other categories, e.g. those who are older or younger than the core customer, but these additional customers are likely to identify with people of the core customer's age. After identifying the most suitable market segments to target, retailers can then decide on how they would like their market position in comparison to competitors to be perceived by consumers, a process known as Segmentation, Targeting and Positioning (STP) (see Chapter 3 Retail consumer behaviour and market segmentation).

Developing retail strategies

In order to develop retail strategies, retailers need to take into account controllable and uncontrollable variables. Controllable variables are those factors which are managed by the retailer, whereas uncontrollable variables are those over which the retailer does not have influence. For example, the retailer can select store locations, the merchandise it stocks and the media in which it communicates with customers. However, the retailer cannot decide where consumers choose to shop or control changes in the macro-environment such as legislation and the state of the economy.

The economic crisis combined with the impact of online retailing has led certain retailers to adopt a downsizing strategy by closing less profitable stores. Multichannel retailer Argos took the decision in 2013 to close many of its branches; however, it has the advantage of having a growing online channel. Another option that can help to strengthen a business in certain circumstances is to form a merger with another company to enable cost savings and to share facilities and expertise. Alternatively, diversification is an option for a retailer that is in a position to expand its product offering.

Maximum viable share	Grow market share	Existing markets	Adapted formats	New formats
New market segments	Related market segments	Formats Segments Trade areas Channels	National expansion	International expansion
New products, services	Related products, services	Products Services	Additional channel	Multi/omni channel

Increasing investment risks

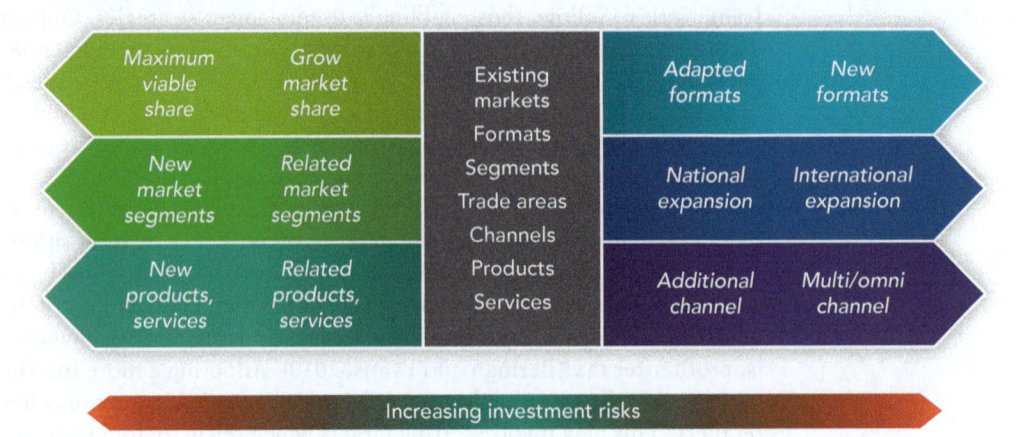

Figure 2.3 Directions for strategic retail growth
Source: developed from: Ansoff, 1988; McGoldrick, 2002

McGoldrick (2002) highlights the variety of retailers' options for strategic growth in Figure 2.3, including existing markets, formats, segments, trade areas, channels, products and services. However, investment risks increase if retailers push their boundaries far from their existing markets, for example by moving beyond related market segments or products into new areas.

Implementation of the marketing plan

Marketing plans are usually compiled in the form of a report to be shared with relevant employees (see vignette on Jonathan Solomon in this chapter). According to Hollensen (2006: 17), a marketing plan can be implemented in three main ways.

1. *Top-down planning*: top management sets both the goals and plan for lower-level management.
2. *Bottom-up planning*: organisational units create their own goals and plans, for approval by higher-level management.
3. *Goals-down-plans-up planning*: top management set the goals, but the various units create their own plans to meet these goals.

Option 1 could be considered as the traditional approach, where senior management retains the responsibility for generating ideas and making decisions about strategy. Retailers with a more contemporary and egalitarian approach allow responsibility for strategic decision-making to be shared by the units who are involved in the implementation of the strategy. Approaches 2 and 3 therefore have the advantage of team members 'buying in' to the strategic plan and potentially increasing their motivation to make it succeed, as they have been involved in its formulation. However, the involvement of various levels of staff in strategic decision-making is likely to be more time-consuming. Top-down planning by senior management is therefore likely to be quicker and more consistent, since it involves a smaller number of people, and this can be more appropriate in certain situations, particularly when problems need to be resolved urgently.

RETAIL MARKETING CAREERS
Jonathan Solomon, Head of CRM & Insights

Source: with permission from Jonathan Solomon

Jonathan Solomon is Head of CRM & Insights at the Support Office of Vision Express, a UK-based chain of opticians with 390 outlets. Jonathan studied BSc Environmental Science and MRes Marine and Coastal Ecology before embarking on a marketing career. As he needed to pay off the loan for his MRes quickly, he took an office job with an electricity company and worked his way up from there. Jonathan says 'sometimes it's just best to get your way into the company, then it's easier to prove your worth and move up. I applied for a job in market research and I didn't get it the first time but they remembered me the next time a post came up and I got it'. (Jonathan didn't mind about missing out on the initial job too much, since the person they appointed later became his wife.) Jonathan moved to Retail Strategy and then Retail Segment Manager within energy company E.ON, before working for credit card company 'Egg' as Activation and Retention Portfolio Manager. He has also gained Chartered Institute of Marketing (CIM), Strategic Decisions Group (SDG) and Market Research Society (MRS) qualifications through part-time study while working. Although his degree topics were in another discipline his transferable skills have been beneficial in his marketing work, particularly in terms of research.

Jonathan's work is split into two main areas. Firstly, he is the manager of a team of eight people, three of whom report directly to him. Jonathan has weekly one-to-one meetings with his direct reports and regularly reviews their progress, as well as helping with any requests they have. Secondly, he carries out his own tasks, which include planning ahead for his departments, developing and managing direct marketing communications, research and liaising with corporate clients. The company has over 500 corporate clients for which it runs schemes offering discounts at Vision Express to employees, including John Lewis and the NHS. Jonathan's marketing-related tasks include responsibility for all direct mail, all pure market research and all market and competitor intelligence. Jonathan's role involves dealing with people within the company and externally, such as suppliers or service providers. He deals directly with external agencies including print and postage for the creation and provision of mailshots or emails and his closest internal colleagues are the Customer Database team.

In terms of his responsibility for CRM (Customer Relationship Management), Jonathan considers it to be very important to know how often customers are going to repurchase: 'You need to look at points when you can talk to them in that repurchase cycle. It needs to be timely, personal and relevant, specific and tailored, so you need great data. I know who's coming up for an eye test, age and gender, where they live. If it's a man aged 20–50 who bought Oakley glasses before and we have some new styles in, I can ask the Database guys to provide me the data so I can contact them. You also need to know why customers purchase from you. My main advice about CRM is that if you can't measure it, don't do it. It's my responsibility to spend Vision Express's budgets of millions of pounds as efficiently as possible, so if I can't measure it I can't spend it. We use control groups, with mailshots to one group and not to another so we can compare the effect of our **direct marketing**. A lot of marketing is about understanding data and maths and **Return on Investment (ROI)**. It's quite easy to measure, if you keep on testing and alter your campaigns and check the details. If you have a good campaign you shouldn't rest on your laurels.'

Jonathan's role also involves devising strategy and implementing marketing planning. He states that 'the

Source: with permission from Vision Express

higher up the ladder you go the more you should be thinking about what you're doing longer-term and what you need to put in place to make it happen'. He has the authority to independently make certain strategic decisions, dependent upon the size of the decision, and he reports to the company's Marketing Director (who reports to the CEO). Jonathan uses marketing models such as SWOT analysis, PESTEL analysis and the Boston Consulting Group (BCG) matrix, to help devise marketing plans. Jonathan believes it makes good business sense to put a strategic plan in place on a three-year and annual basis, with annual targets for profit and turnover. However, he says 'you don't want to be planning so much you never get on with doing'. He says 'strategy is about what you will and won't do . . . every business is different in terms of how they set their strategies out and how prescriptive they are'. The company mainly uses a top-down approach to strategy which is imparted to staff at an annual conference attended by Vision Express's different divisions, joint venture partners and all store managers. There is also an element of input into corporate strategy from employees via the employee satisfaction survey, to be taken on board as part of the 'softer' elements of strategy relating to Human Resources and training (as opposed to products and finance).

When employing someone in his department, Jonathan looks for proof of key capabilities that he can match someone against, which doesn't necessarily have to be paid employment, such as a placement or work for an external body through a university. He says that general transferable skills, such as communication and the ability to meet deadlines, are important for marketers, as well as IT skills, particularly the use of spreadsheets and PowerPoint®. He also says it's important for marketing students to learn about financial terms such as ROI, net margin and **gross margin**. He believes that 'marketing should be the liveliest part of any business, they're the ones driving what the brand stands for, so they should have a spark and drive, not just competence, and we want someone who can fit in well with the team and challenge people'. In order to begin a career as a marketer, Jonathan states 'you've just got to stand out. If someone's thinking about hiring someone internally they need to think who'd be good for this role and look around. You should always be thinking about where is the next place I'd want to be and who would I need to impress, not necessarily about doing more hours, but making the difference you're making clear, so you should tell someone about it'.

Internal and external marketing audits

Companies conduct marketing audits to enable them to examine the external and internal environments in which they operate, i.e. the **macro-environment** and **micro-environment**, thus enabling them to devise appropriate marketing strategies to reflect these environments (see Figure 2.4). Key components of a marketing audit are:

- establishing the market size;
- identifying target customers;
- assessing the viability of distribution channels through which their products are made available to consumers;
- examining competitors in the same market.

Retailers can compile a marketing audit checklist to establish whether they have covered sufficient information to prepare them fully before finalising and implementing strategic plans. Observing the performance of competitors is a key part of the external marketing audit, specifying direct competitors and assessing their strengths and weaknesses. The retailer needs to discover its own market share and those of its close competitors, if one of its goals is to change or maintain its ranking in this respect. To assess the external factors that impact upon a retailer's marketing strategy, the retailer requires information about the macro-environment in a process which can be known as environmental scanning.

Figure 2.4 The macro- and micro-environments in relation to the product or service

The macro-environment

The macro-environment can be scanned by examining relevant issues often referred to as 'PESTEL' (and sometimes adapted as 'PEST' or 'SLEPT' factors):

- Political
- Economic
- Societal
- Technological
- Ethical (or environmental)
- Legal

Political

Political factors relate to the implementation of policies by local or national government bodies, such as the imposition of taxes. Political factors are also closely connected to legal factors (see below), as governments are responsible for changes in legislation. Retailers benefit from being aware of political parties' manifestos because a change of government can lead to a range of new policies that could affect their business. Other bodies can also impact upon retailers for political reasons, often in opposition to government plans. For example, British postal workers went on strike in 2013 in protest at the privatisation of the Post Office, echoing the Royal Mail strike of 1988 that disrupted deliveries for several weeks. This situation can have a significant effect on retailers that operate websites or catalogues and in 1988 this led to some retailers establishing their own courier systems to avoid relying on Royal Mail.

Economic

Economic factors relate to the present and future state of the economy on a local, national and international basis. The global economic crisis that began in 2008 led to financial recessions in many countries. While this may have appeared to be bad news for all retailers, the grocery, take-away food and cinema sectors in the UK found that sales figures improved, apparently as a consequence of consumers seeking relatively inexpensive ways of treating themselves. Employment levels and interest rates are also key economic factors affecting retailers. Certain elements of the economy can have wide-ranging consequences. Increases in fuel taxes and crude oil prices led petrol prices to triple in the UK between 1991 and 2011 (BBC News, 2011). Subsequently, this has impacted upon more than just retailers that operate petrol stations, as the expense of transporting products to stores has risen, contributing to higher selling prices for products, as well as increasing costs for customers travelling to stores. Petrol prices can therefore affect all retail product sectors. However, in terms of sustainability rising fuel prices could be viewed from a positive perspective, since this may encourage retailers and consumers to adopt more environmentally friendly practices. (See Chapter 6 Retail pricing.)

Societal

Retailers need to remain aware of societal changes that affect customers' requirements, so they need to consider overarching changes in consumers' lifestyles and values. Demographic changes such as age distribution in the population influence the sales of products and services. For example, the trend towards healthier living, improved nutrition and developments in healthcare has contributed to an ageing population in the UK, where people live to be 80 years old on average (*CIA World Factbook,* CIA, 2014). Conversely, there are also increasing levels of obesity in the Western world which present dangers to health. Such factors impact significantly upon grocery retailers (and vice versa). Lifestyle trends and cultural factors also affect customers. As well as varying from one country to another, different ethnicities and subcultures in the same country sometimes have different requirements. For example, many food retailers in the UK have responded to an increased proportion of the population originating from Eastern Europe by offering ranges of food from this region.

Technological

Many new technological developments in products and processes, such as innovations in store design, distribution and marketing channels can affect the ways in which retailers operate. They may also sell new forms of technology that impact upon their sales figures and profitability. Some of the most recent retailing innovations include interactive in-store and online technologies (see Chapter 9 Retail design and layout) and software for retailing systems. In 2014, Asda supermarkets began to offer a technological innovation to their customers by trialling a three-dimensional (3D) printing service, a new system which had previously been confined largely to business-to-business markets (see Figure 2.5). Retailers can keep up-to-date with new technical developments that could be utilised in their businesses by attending trade fairs, reading trade and technical magazines, gathering information from suppliers and accessing websites such as retail-innovation.com.

Ethical

Ethical factors comprise a wide variety of social and ecological issues. Environmental and social sustainability are major issues that have begun to achieve mainstream recognition, particularly in terms of climate change (see Chapter 12 Legislation and ethics in retailing). The conservation of non-renewable resources as well as flora and fauna can be impacted upon by the large-scale usage of raw materials and manufacturing for the products that they sell. Disposal of products can also create pollution. While laws can intervene to

Figure 2.5 The Asda 3D printing service uses scanning equipment to produce scale models

Source: with permission from Asda Photo

improve these problematic areas, retailers' voluntary ethical behaviour can go beyond legislative requirements to benefit society in many ways, such as charitable donations and community support. A key method of behaving ethically is for retailers to compile and implement a Corporate Social Responsibility (CSR) policy.

Legal

Legal factors include the introduction of laws that either affect retailers indirectly or that regulate the retail environment directly. For example, planning regulations can have a direct impact on a retailer's ability to build new outlets (see Chapter 12 Legislation and ethics in retailing). Regulations also impact upon pricing and promotion to ensure that they are fair and retailers' products need to comply with safety regulations and the Trade Descriptions Act. Additionally, retail staff have employment rights and their customers have consumer protection rights (see www.gov.uk).

The micro-environment

The micro-environment covers factors which are more directly connected to the company, particularly internal issues within the retailer, its customers and direct competitors. Internally, the key areas that the retailer needs to assess are its existing strategies, objectives, resources and performance. Externally, the company is directly connected to its customers through transactions, and with its competitors through being part of the same market sector. Marketing intermediaries such as advertising agencies can also be considered to be part of the micro-environment owing to their close connection, carrying out activities on behalf of the retailer.

The retailer's marketing division operates within the larger environment of the company and its other divisions, as indicated in the example shown in Figure 2.6. In a small retailer, various responsibilities may fall to one person whereas in a large retailer the

Figure 2.6 The retail internal environment

responsibilities can be divided between numerous employees with specialist skills in their areas. Sole traders with independent stores are therefore likely to find themselves in charge of all aspects of retailing, from product buying and promotion through to managing staff and compiling financial information, thus requiring a versatile set of skills (see case study on Bead Boutique in Chapter 11). In order to examine the micro-environment fully and to embed strategy within the firm, strengths and weaknesses of the departments, assets and processes within the company need to be assessed.

Market attractiveness

When analysing the retailer's micro-environment, market attractiveness can be assessed by using Porter's (1980) Five Forces model, which analyses the competitive industry structure in which businesses operate. An industry consists of companies that offer products of a similar type. At the centre of this model, the firms within an industry are viewed as competing for position, governed by the impact of four external forces: the threat of potential market entrants and substitute products and the bargaining power of buyers and suppliers.

When the forces in the four outer boxes are strong, then industry performance is liable to be weak, whereas if the forces are milder, this can lead to above-average industry performance (Jobber, 2010). The model can therefore enable a retailer to assess the attractiveness of entering a new market or staying in an existing one. Some industries have high entry barriers but as part of a service industry, retailers often have low barriers to market entry, in comparison to heavy manufacturing industries for example. Financial investment and economies of scale are key entry barriers which would make it much more viable to set up a small greengrocer than a computer brand. Potential new entrants to a market therefore need to recognise their capacities in terms of scale and finance before entering this market. Barriers to entry are also high in a market where there is a unique element of design or manufacture that is protected by intellectual property law or in which research and development are particularly expensive.

When suppliers have high bargaining power, perhaps because their products are in scarce supply, their prices are liable to be high. Conversely, when there are many suppliers of the same type of product, buyers usually have the stronger bargaining power. The availability of substitute products can affect a market's attractiveness. Therefore a competitor offering a different item that serves the same purpose in order to meet consumer needs, such as keeping warm or quenching their thirst, can pose a threat to the retailer. Central to Porter's Five Forces is the intensity of rivalry between competitors. This has been demonstrated in the UK grocery industry with Asda and Sainsbury's vying for second place in this highly competitive marketplace. Sainsbury's returned to achieving the second largest market share in 2012 with 35 consecutive quarters of sales growth, overtaking Asda which had taken this position for several years (Withnall, 2013), despite Sainsbury's selling higher-priced merchandise than Asda on average. Sainsbury's success in this respect may have been attributable, at least in part, to its differentiation strategy and stronger brand image, whereas rival Asda could be said to have adopted a cost leadership strategy, in line with its parent company Walmart (see 'Sources of competitive advantage' below).

Value chain

Another concept initiated by Porter (1985) is value chain analysis, which breaks down the major activities of a company into stages and assesses how costs and differentiation can affect value at each stage.

Porter (1985) suggests that a company could be viewed as a collection of primary and support activities. Porter's model represents the contribution of central functions of the organisation horizontally and operational components vertically, acknowledging that each area can add value to the company by being run more cost-effectively or being differentiated from its competitors. McGoldrick (2002: 147) states that '(a) particular merit of the value chain concept is in helping to highlight the specific components, their relative contributions to the value creation process, and their relative costs'. It is important to view added value from the target customer's viewpoint, rather than solely from the retailer's perspective, since perceptions of the value offered by retailers can affect their purchase decisions. Commissioning market research that measures levels of customer satisfaction can therefore assist in analysing the value chain.

Sources of competitive advantage

Successful retailers need to gain a competitive advantage over rival companies. This can be achieved by adopting one of three generic strategies: differentiation, cost leadership or focus (Porter, 1980). Retailers aiming to differentiate themselves from the competition can offer an emphasis on one or more elements of the marketing mix which appeal strongly to the target customer and exceed those of their rivals, such as high quality or unique design in their products or services. Those aiming for cost leadership adopt a low-price, no frills approach. For example, the economy airlines benefit from the economies of scale achieved through selling to the mass market. A focused product or service offering targets a specific market segment or a niche product area, e.g. lingerie chain Victoria's Secret. However, there is a danger in limiting the market and product type as competitors can target the same types of consumer and product trends can change.

Market penetration and diversification

Ansoff's product–market matrix is a model that maps opportunities for companies to stay in existing markets or move into new ones. It offers four strategic options from which retailers can select.

1 **Market penetration** (for an existing product in an existing market) – retailers aim to achieve a larger share of an existing market by gaining sales from competitors, for example through a targeted communications campaign (Dibb and Simkin, 2008).
2 **Product development** (for a new product for an existing market) – retailers can expand upon existing product ranges by updating the previous range or introducing a new product line. This has become standard practice for most brands and retailers of electronics and fashion products.
3 **Market development** (for a new market for an existing product) – retailers maintain the same types of product but aim them at new markets, by promoting a different function or targeting different locations or market segments.
4 **Diversification** (for a new product in a new market) – retailers can seek new markets by expanding into new products or services, either through design and development within the company or acquisition.

The selection of which of these options to follow should be influenced by the marketing audit. For example, if the retailer finds that an existing market is already saturated with established retailers in this field then it may be preferable to adopt a diversification strategy.

Portfolio analysis

An analysis of the portfolio of a retailer's strategic business units (SBUs) can be conducted using the market growth–market share matrix originally developed by the Boston Consulting Group (BCG). SBUs can be positioned on the matrix with one axis denoting market share in relation to competitors and the other axis representing annual market growth in the industry (see Figure 2.7). Stars are those products which are gaining a high percentage of growth to reach a high market share. Question marks are SBUs which are in a high growth market but have not yet achieved a high market share. The company can investigate question marks' potential to become stars, for example through increased investment in promotion, or to leave them to decline into a low market share when they become dogs. Cash cows are those products or brands which have attained high market share but which have low growth, possibly owing to market saturation and maturity. Products are likely to move from one section of the grid to another over time and retailers need to introduce new merchandise regularly to become tomorrow's stars and cash cows. Marketing strategies can be adopted to divest dogs or question marks and to put the company's finances to better use for products which can potentially achieve better performance.

Competitive marketing objectives

After a situation analysis has been conducted, **strategic objectives** can be set, for the retailer to build, hold, harvest or divest of SBUs, product ranges or individual products or subbrands within the organisation (Dibb and Simkin, 2008). This is particularly pertinent to the retail sector, where each of these four alternatives can be applied to the volume of products that are stocked within a certain timescale. For example, when products are new to the company the objective could be to build up investment in this type of merchandise. In 2010 retailers selling electronic products began to build up stocks of tablet computers that were new innovations at that time, in anticipation of increasing demand from consumers. However, for more established products, it can sometimes be advisable to maintain the same sales figures as the previous year by using a 'hold' strategy. There are parallels between 'build' objectives and the 'growth' stage of the Product Lifecycle (see Chapter 4 Retail product and brand management). Similarly, the 'hold' objective is defensive to maintain market share. It can relate to products that have reached the 'maturity' stage and therefore sales figures have reached a plateau.

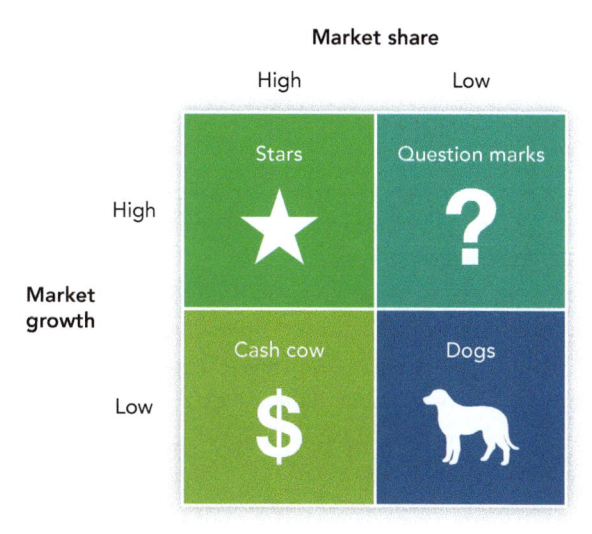

Figure 2.7 The BCG Portfolio Analysis matrix

Implementing a build objective for such a product could result in surplus stock that needs to be marked down. Maximising profit margins in the short-term while sales of a product are declining and thus losing market share, is known as 'harvesting'. When products move towards the end of the decline phase it is time for divestment, allowing stocks to dwindle gradually or to dispose of them more quickly with markdowns, to retract from this market and make way for products which are in higher demand.

Marketing strategy in relation to HRM and finance strategy

All divisions of the company must carry out the corporate strategy effectively if the retailer is to achieve the optimum level of success. As well as marketing strategies, retailers need to develop compatible Human Resources Management (HRM) and finance strategies, for example, that are consistent with the retailer's overall strategy. People are central to the services marketing mix and HRM can support them by recruiting, training and helping to keep suitable employees within the business. Retailers' HRM policies need to cater for an industry that is characterised by high numbers of part-time staff, who are relatively young on average and many of whom work temporarily over the Christmas season.

Finance is also clearly required to implement the marketing plan and to pay staff's wages, one of the retailer's major outgoings. It should be borne in mind that marketing strategies have financial implications that can impact upon other areas of the business, so marketing objectives need to be in keeping with an organisation's financial objectives. Marketing and finance departments need to maintain clear lines of communication to achieve this aim. It is usual for retailers to set objectives to achieve a certain level of profitability or financial turnover and these can be used as measures of success for the marketing department or the retailer in general. However, during challenging economic times, or in not-for-profit retail organisations such as charity stores and museum shops, aiming to reach break-even point may be a satisfactory target. Goals measured in sales volume (rather than turnover) or customer satisfaction can apply equally well to the for-profit or not-for-profit sectors.

CHAPTER SUMMARY

This chapter focused on the development of retailers' marketing strategies, comprising the following key areas.

- The firm's corporate strategy is devised via the compilation of a mission statement, goals and objectives.
- A situation analysis specifies the strengths and weaknesses of the company and its external opportunities and threats.
- Audits of the micro-environment (political, economic, societal, technological, ethical and legal factors) and macro-environment within which the retailer operates enable it to tailor its strategy accordingly.
- Various key theories can be used to guide marketing strategy, including Porter's Five Forces, the BCG matrix, Ansoff's product–market matrix and the value chain.
- Competitive advantage over rival companies can be achieved by adopting one of three generic strategies: differentiation, cost leadership or focus (Porter, 1980).
- Retail marketing strategy needs to be compatible with strategy in other areas of the business including HRM and finance.

EXERCISES AND QUESTIONS

1. Select a retail sector for a particular product type (e.g. electronics or toys) and conduct a PESTEL analysis to assess the macro-environment that affects this sector. Which are the main issues that you believe would impact upon a small independent store selling this product type?
2. Find the mission statements for three retailers. Which one of the three do you think is most in line with your own perceptions of the retailer? How could the other two be amended, if at all, to make them more suited to the retailers concerned?
3. Watch the following video featuring Michael Porter explaining the importance of strategy to an organisation. Make a note of the key points he mentions and discuss why they are relevant to retailers. http://www.youtube.com/watch?v=DViVtgD0xwE
4. Select ten retailers that are located in your nearest town or city. Assess which one of the following generic strategies each of these retailers are following: cost leadership, differentiation or focus.
5. Research Ansoff's product–market matrix online and apply it to a selection of different retailers or brands in a particular product sector, placing them in the appropriate sections.
6. Why is it important to align marketing strategy with the strategies used in other areas of the company, such as HRM and finance?

REFERENCES

Ansoff, H.I. (1984) *Implementing Strategic Management*, Harlow: Prentice-Hall.

Ansoff, H.I. (1988) *Corporate Strategy*, Harmondsworth: Penguin.

BBC News (2011) *MPs urge ministers to scrap a planned rise in fuel duty*, BBC News, 15 November (available online at: http://www.bbc.co.uk/news/uk-politics-15730087).

Berman, B. and Evans, J.R. (2010) *Retailing Management: A Strategic Approach*, 11th edn, Upper Saddle River, NJ: Pearson.

CIA (2014) *CIA World Factbook: United Kingdom* (available online at: www.cia.gov/library/publications/the-world-factbook/geos/uk.html).

CIPD (2012) *Human Resources in the Recession: Managing and Representing People at Work in Ireland. Executive Summary*, Dublin: Chartered Institute for Personnel and Development (available online at: http://www.cipd.co.uk/global/europe/ireland/resources/useful-publications/human-resources-recession.aspx).

Dibb, S. and Simkin, R. (2008) *Marketing Planning: A Workbook for Marketing Managers*, London: South-Western Cengage Learning.

Ferrell, O.C. and Hartline, M.D. (2011) *Marketing Management Strategies*, International/5th edn, South-Western Cengage Learning.

Gilbert, D. (2003) *Retail Marketing Management*, Harlow: Financial Times/Prentice Hall.

Gilligan, C. and Wilson, M.S. (2007) *Strategic Marketing Planning*, 2nd edn, Oxford: Butterworth Heinemann.

Hollensen, S. (2006) *Marketing Planning: A Global Perspective*, Maidenhead: McGraw-Hill.

Jobber, D. (2010) *Principles and Practice of Marketing*, 6th edn, Maidenhead: McGraw-Hill.

Lebessi, M. and Giannarou, L. (2012) Greek retail firms try their luck abroad, *Ekathimerini*, 30 January (available online at: http://www.ekathimerini.com/4dcgi/_w_articles_wsite2_1_30/01/2012_425143).

Lusch, R.F., Dunne, P.M. and Carver, J.R. (2011) *Introduction to Retailing*, International/7th edn, Stamford, CT: South-Western Cengage Learning.

McGoldrick, P. (2002) *Retail Marketing*, 2nd edn, Maidenhead: McGraw-Hill.

Porter, M.E. (1980) *Competitive Strategy: Techniques for Analyzing Industries and Competitors*, New York: Free Press.

Porter, M.E. (1985) *Competitive Advantage*, New York: Free Press.

Ries, A. and Ries, L. (2006) *The Origin of Brands*, New York: Harper Collins.

Whittington, R. (2001) *What is Strategy – and Does it Matter?* 2nd edn, London: Thomson.

Withnall, A. (2013) Sainsbury's overtakes Asda to become second-largest UK supermarket as profits soar 9%, *The Independent*, 13 November (available online at: http://www.independent.co.uk/news/business/news/sainsburys-overtakes-asda-to-become-secondlargest-uk-supermarket-as-profits-soar-9-8936616.html).

FURTHER READING

Cuthbertson, C. and Reynolds, J. (2004) *Retail Strategy: The View From the Bridge*, Oxford: Elsevier.

Gauri, D.K., Trivedi, M. and Grewal, D. (2008) Understanding the determinants of retail strategy: an empirical analysis, *Journal of Retailing*, 84, 256–267.

Levy, M., Grewal, D., Peterson, R.A. and Connolly, B. (2005) 'The concept of the big middle', *Journal of Retailing*, 8(2), 83–88.

Porter, M.E. (1996) What is strategy? *Harvard Business Review*, 74(6), 61–78.

Warnaby, G. and Woodruffe, H. (1995) Cost effective differentiation: an application of strategic concepts to retailing, *International Review of Retail, Distribution and Consumer Research*, 5(13), 253–269.

Case study

WH Smith upbeat despite sales doldrums

By Duncan Robinson and Andy Sharman

Shares in [stationery and book retailer] WH Smith hit an all-time high in January 2014, despite a slump in sales as the retailer showcased its ability to maintain profits in spite of a falling top-line.

The rally, which sent shares up 3 per cent to £10.43, came in spite of a 4 per cent drop in total sales for the 20 weeks to January 18.

Sales on the High Street continued to decline sharply, with like-for-like sales down 6 per cent in the division, but an improved performance in its travel unit helped pep up the group's shares.

The performance highlights the strategy that has helped WH Smith increase underlying earnings every year, despite falling sales, for almost a decade.

Kate Swann, the newsagent's formidable former chief executive, cut costs relentlessly to maintain profitability. She also shifted the group's estate so that it had less exposure to the high street and far more to railways and airports.

Her successor Steve Clarke, who used to run WH Smith's High Street division, has been clear that he is following the same strategy. This year WH Smith will add about 60 stores to its travel division – half in the UK, and half internationally.

Airports, both in the UK and increasingly abroad, have proved particularly profitable for the group.

"When you have proved yourself in Heathrow, which is one of the most expensive in the world, you have a lot of

Source: WHSmith plc

experience," said Kate Calvert, analyst at Investec, "From an airport perspective, the retailer that gets the contract is the one that gets the most revenue for the landlord."

Sales in the retailer's travel division benefited from a recovery in airport passenger numbers for the 20 weeks to January 18th, with like-for-like growth in the latter half of the period.

"The trend [in passenger numbers] is definitely improving," said Mr Clarke, "we are still a long way below 2008 levels."

The focus on transport hubs was a return to the newsagent's origins. William Henry Smith launched the first WH Smith store in Euston station in 1848.

. . . Mr Clarke has won round investors by outlining plans to strip even more costs from the group. Some retail observers question whether the group's estate can handle more cuts.

[WH Smith sales stem mainly from its bricks-and-mortar outlets, as it derives only a tiny fraction of its sales from the web.]

A Twitter account dedicated to retweeting pictures of threadbare carpets in WH Smith stores has nearly 4,000 followers.

But Mr Clarke hopes that installing more self-service checkouts, and making warehouse staff wear hands-free headsets to help them pick items quicker, will further reduce costs. The continued emphasis on boosting margin has convinced some previously sceptical financial analysts.

The shares have rallied 60 per cent [in the year to January 2014].

. . . "Consistency is what we love about it," said Ms Calvert of Investec. WH Smith has not had a major profit warning in the best part of a decade.

But not all are won over. While the strategy works in the short term, it is not a model that can work forever without top-line growth, said John Stevenson, an analyst at Peel Hunt, "WH Smith is about cost saving and margin growth, but that can't continue in perpetuity."

Source: Robinson, D. and Sharman, A. (2014) *Financial Times*, 23 January.
© The Financial Times Limited 2014. All Rights Reserved.

DISCUSSION QUESTIONS

1 Which strategies has WH Smith used that have resulted in a substantial rise in share prices without increasing sales?

2 Why does the analyst suggest that some of these strategies are not financially sustainable in the future?

3 What are the main PESTEL factors that currently affect the stationery and books retail sector?

4 After visiting the company's website www.whsmith.co.uk or one of its branches to examine the retail layout and range of merchandise WH Smith offers, propose two key potential strategies that you would recommend them to implement during the next three years.

CHAPTER 3

Retail consumer behaviour and market segmentation

Learning objectives

The objectives of this chapter are to:

- evaluate explanations for consumer motives for shopping;
- apply consumer behaviour theory to retailing;
- evaluate market segmentation theory and techniques;
- demonstrate how market research enables retailers to understand consumer behaviour;
- explain how consumer behaviour impacts upon retail marketing decisions.

Introduction

As satisfying customers' needs and wants is central to the marketing concept, it is important for retailers to understand the behaviour and attitudes of their customers in order to make effective marketing decisions. To enable them to satisfy their customers' needs, first retailers need to identify them. This can be achieved by categorising customers into groups with similar characteristics using market segmentation. To be able to understand their customers' behaviour and to categorise them, retailers can utilise a variety of marketing research techniques. Understanding the process of consumer decision-making and the various factors that influence consumption decisions are key aspects of Consumer Behaviour (CB) theory. This chapter refers to the behaviour of private consumers who purchase for personal or household use (organisational retail buying is covered in Chapter 5).

Retail consumer behaviour and attitudes

Retailers can aim to understand their customers more effectively by researching into CB, investigating who buys products or services and how, when, where and why they buy them (Jobber, 2010). Increasing freedom of choice in product consumption for the general public since the 1950s has made it appropriate for firms to study the behaviour of consumers in order to explain consumer preferences (Antonides and van Raaij, 1998). CB, defined by Solomon *et al.* (2006: 6) as 'the study of the processes involved when individuals or groups select, purchase, use or dispose of products, services, ideas or experiences to satisfy needs and desires' and its theories have evolved largely from the fields of psychology and sociology, as it involves the study of human behaviour. Sociologists understandably view CB from more of a social than a business perspective and they use the term 'consumer culture', described by Lury (1996: 4) as 'a specific form of material culture in contemporary Euro-American societies'. A more recent development in the study of CB from a psychology viewpoint is the introduction of neuro-marketing, the application of neuroscience to provide a deeper understanding of the physiological aspects of consumer decision-making, thus allowing marketers to intervene more effectively in the decision-making process (Yoon *et al.*, 2012). Jobber and Fahy (2009: 56) state that consumer neuroscience 'allows us to examine precisely which part of the brain responds to stimuli, and from this we can infer how the consumer is likely to react . . . it can get beyond the expressed behaviour of consumers to reveal their true emotions'. Consumer neuroscience uses fMRI (functional magnetic resonance imaging) and electroencephalograph (EEG) technology to track brain responses alongside other neurophysiological techniques (see Retail Marketing career vignette, below).

Consumers' attitudes relate to their opinions regarding products and brands. According to the Theory of Planned Behaviour (Ajzen, 2005), beliefs, attitudes, social pressures and ability to act combine to shape consumers' intentions to purchase and ultimately affect their consumer behaviour. It is useful for retailers to know whether consumers' attitudes are positive, negative or neutral towards them and their merchandise, so that they can address any issues accordingly. Consumers hold attitudes towards their enjoyment of shopping in itself and retailers can respond to this by offering an environment which will be enjoyed by their core customers. Consumers' opinions, preferences and behaviour are constantly changing in response to the economy, politics, the environment and societal issues, among other factors. Consumers' perceptions can vary and this can lead to differing interpretations of the information delivered by and about retailers; for example, through their store environments, marketing communications or media coverage. The same message can therefore be interpreted differently by separate market segments or individual consumers, dependent upon their beliefs and feelings. Consumers' perceptions can influence to what extent they pay attention to the information to which they are exposed, leading them to filter out messages which do not resonate with their own opinions and beliefs. The perceptual process starts with stimuli that are sensed by the consumer via sight, hearing, touch, smell and taste. People consequently interpret these sensations as having particular meanings, resulting in perceptions (Solomon *et al.*, 2006). This perceptual process enables consumers to perceive attributes of specific products or services in relation to each other, which can then be positioned on a perceptual map (see Chapter 4).

Monitoring consumer preferences for products and services is no easy task, but it is facilitated by acquiring and analysing market research and relevant internal company data. Information about CB can be useful to all of the departments within retailers; for example, visual merchandisers responsible for in-store displays can use data on customers' behaviour within the store to display products more effectively, with the intention of increasing sales volume. CB theory recognises that purchase choices are often not made by individuals in isolation and that more than one person can influence the purchase decision. Blackwell *et al.* (2000) suggest that consumers can adopt one or more of the following five roles when purchasing products or services:

- *initiator:* begins the purchase decision-making process;
- *influencer:* persuades others to make a certain product or service choice;
- *decider:* has the power or money to select a product or service;
- *buyer:* makes the retail transaction;
- *user:* the person who uses or consumes the product or service.

This theory is exemplified by family members acting as initiators and influencers in the purchase of a holiday, with one or both of the parents being likely to take the role of the final decision-maker and buyer and the whole family going on the holiday. The knowledge that younger family members participate in the decision can impact upon the choice of holidays offered by a travel agency or tour operator and the way in which they are promoted via advertisements, brochures and websites. The influence of peer group pressure when consumers select products or services also needs to be taken into account by marketers, with teenagers being particularly prone to influence by their peers when making purchase decisions. Equally, consumers can choose to reject particular products or retailers to dissociate themselves from certain peer groups (Bannister and Hogg, 2001).

Consumer motivation and needs

Since meeting consumer needs is a key tenet of the marketing concept, it is important to have an understanding of the needs that provide consumers with the motivation to purchase goods and services. Maslow's hierarchy states that there are five stages of need, starting with basic survival needs and progressing to security and safety, then social needs and self-esteem. The fifth stage is self-actualisation, which it can be argued that very few, if any, actually reach, leaving people constantly striving to achieve it. According to Maslow's theory, when a person satisfies one of the five levels, the next level of the hierarchy is in sight and becomes a key source of motivation. For example, consumers who earn enough to have a reasonable standard of living and social life may seek ways in which to heighten their self-esteem, through acquiring prestige brands. Many may feel that to reach the self-actualisation level they need to achieve a certain level of consumption, although for others this state may be attained through more philanthropic or spiritual means.

Consumption needs can be split into two main areas: utilitarian and hedonic (Blythe, 2013). Utilitarian needs are more functional and work-based, tending to correspond with the lower levels of Maslow's hierarchy, whereas hedonic needs are centred more on enjoyment and relate to the higher two levels. Most retailers aim to attain a balance between consumers' utilitarian and hedonic needs, e.g. by offering both a low-priced generic product range and a selection of more luxurious ready meals. Alternatively, hedonic needs may be met by offering a stimulating store environment, particularly appealing to a range of senses (see Chapter 9 Retail design and layout). Retailers can also display products prominently in stores or online to act as a stimulus for customers to recognise needs; for example, by locating complementary products together to encourage multiple purchases to be made.

Consumer decision-making

Understanding how consumers arrive at purchase decisions is central to CB theory and it aims to explain why and how customers buy products and services. The consumer decision process (CDP) model, shown in Figure 3.1 (Blackwell *et al.*, 2000) is a widely used academic model regarding consumer behaviour in relation to purchasing. This model was originally developed with five stages and was referred to as the 'EKB model', named after its initial authors: Engel, Kollat and Blackwell. It has since been expanded to the seven-stage model shown here with the addition of stages 5 and 7. These additional stages reflect a growing awareness in society of the environmental and social impacts of the consumption and disposal of products.

1. Need recognition
2. Information search
3. Pre-purchase evaluation of alternatives
4. Purchase
5. Consumption
6. Post-consumption evaluation
7. Divestment

Figure 3.1 The consumer decision process model
Source: adapted from Blackwell *et al.*, 2000

Need recognition

The model starts with the recognition of a consumer's need or problem, which may be due to a replacement product being required or the desire for a new product or service, often driven by a stimulus from promotional activity or seeing new products belonging to members of the consumer's peer group. Retailers can provide this stimulus through advertising or other forms of promotion to set in motion the chain of events leading to the purchase. When customers are already in stores or looking at etailers' websites, point-of-sale material or online promotion can provide the stimulus for customers to make unplanned purchases. According to Neff (2008), 29 per cent of consumers buy products in categories they hadn't initially intended to buy, so retailers can take advantage of this opportunity to increase sales. Having anticipated consumers' needs, retailers can identify ways in which their products and distribution channels can meet them. Key methods for established retailers to identify their customers' needs are to conduct market research with customers and to evaluate sales data to assess which products have been successful. Retailers can then aim to fulfil the same needs which those products met with updated merchandise.

Information search

Having recognised a need, the consumer is likely to seek information about products or services that could satisfy that need. Some may rely on memories of past purchases and promotions by recalling an 'evoked set' of alternative items (Blythe, 2013). Consumers have the options of looking for products in stores or online and seeking information in magazines, newspapers and other media. **Word-of-mouth (WoM)** recommendations from friends can be particularly influential, as they are often viewed as more authentic and reliable than paid-for promotion, and user reviews online ('eWoM') can also be persuasive. Retailers can facilitate the information search by providing help from sales staff as well as written details, photographs and user reviews online, even if the retailer's website is non-transactional.

Shopping trips may not always entail making purchases and can sometimes be used by consumers simply to search for information instead ('window shopping') in order to minimise the risk involved in making a purchase. Expensive products such as cars and electronic equipment are therefore likely to involve a lengthy information search, which could be spread over a period of weeks or months, as there is a high perceived risk with such purchases. This longer-than-average decision-making process for buying high risk, relatively expensive goods, is known as extended problem-solving. More straightforward decisions with less risk attached involve a limited problem-solving approach. Even more basic is the habitual or routine decision, which requires little thought on the part of the customer and is therefore swift and repetitive. For example, regularly buying the same brand of cereal is so habitual that it can be hard to alter and retailers may therefore need a strong stimulus to prompt customers to consider changing brands, e.g. via prominent point-of-purchase promotions or substantially lower prices. The information search usually results in a range of alternative solutions to meet the consumer's need. This can be facilitated by the use of price comparison websites such as comparethemarket.com, reading consumer magazines such as *Which?* or by using a product comparison facility on a retailer's website. Consumer product reviews on websites can be a powerful influence, since customers may consider them to be independent because their authors are not paid for writing them. However, such reviews' objectivity and provenance can sometimes be questionable.

Pre-purchase evaluation of alternatives

Choice criteria are those attributes used by consumers to enable them to make decisions on purchasing particular products or brands. Consumers' choice criteria can change depending on their position within the family lifecycle. Whereas low price and a fashionable make could possibly be the most significant criteria for car-buyers in their early 20s, when they reach their late 30s their priorities may have changed to make safety and space to accommodate children the key choice criteria, the car's price being less of an issue. When choosing a retailer, consumers may evaluate the group of attributes that the retailer possesses (Lutz and Bettman, 1977); for example, the convenience of buying online may be outweighed by the time taken for product delivery.

For low-price products a purchase decision generally requires low involvement and may consist of a very swift review of the alternative brands and variations of a product on a supermarket's shelves before a decision is reached. If the consumer has decided to buy a branded product the decision can involve consideration of which retailer and from which of their branches to make the purchase. Increasingly, a further decision may need to be made: whether to buy the product in a shop to receive it quickly or to purchase it online, delaying delivery but saving a trip to the store. In stores, sales staff can help customers with the information search, although it has become rarer nowadays for sales staff to be available for advice. Exceptions are upmarket stores or those which sell products with detailed technical features. For example, PC World offers customers a 'Knowhow' service for advice during the purchase and post-purchase stages. Websites have the advantage of being able to provide detailed written information about their products. Bricks-and-mortar shops are beginning to harness technology to help bridge this gap. Mobile technology is now allowing stores to utilise the internet via the use of quick response (QR) codes on products which can be scanned with smartphones to provide detailed information to assist in purchase decisions.

Purchase

The purchase stage involves the consumer deciding whether or not to buy the product or service, when to purchase it, in which location and by which payment method. The selling environment and service can have a significant influence at the purchase decision stage and factors such as store or web design and service quality must be considered carefully by retailers (see Chapter 9 Retail design and layout). Retailers can influence the timing of a consumer's purchase with the use of promotions such as a discount or free gift within a limited timescale (see Chapter 7 Retail marketing communications).

Post-consumption evaluation

During consumption of the product or service, the consumer forms a view of its performance, which is likely to influence the choice of making a repeat purchase of the product or brand. Retailers can help to overcome consumers' dissatisfaction with a purchase decision (cognitive dissonance) by offering money back or an exchange for products. Although this may look as if it would have a potentially negative effect on the store's turnover, it can reduce risk for consumers and make them more inclined to shop with the retailer again. Also, customers who are dissatisfied with purchases are more likely to tell their friends than the retailer, so minimising negative WoM through good service recovery is worthwhile. A positive post-consumption evaluation can benefit retailers not only through store loyalty, but also through word-of-mouth, so that customers have opportunities to post positive online reviews.

Divestment

Finally, when a product is worn out or is no longer required, the consumer has to select a method of discarding or recycling it. This may be affected by laws or regulations to which consumers and retailers must adhere. For example, there are regulations in the European Union (EU) for disposing of items such as batteries and electrical goods, as these items can harm the environment (see Chapter 12 for further discussion on this topic). Consumers are not expected to be consciously aware of having gone through all of the stages in the CDP model and when making routine purchases or impulse buying, the first three stages can be bypassed. Customers who purchase groceries online have the opportunity to skip the decision-making process on a regular basis, owing to the facility to store lists of favourite products and select a whole shopping list with one click. Although this model is widely used, it has been criticised for its assumption that consumers always make rational decisions (Solomon *et al.*, 2006).

Experiential consumer behaviour

The CDP model presumes a negative situation at the outset of the buying process: in contrast to this, **experiential consumer behaviour** views purchasing as more of an enjoyable experience, based on hedonistic, emotional values rather than rational thinking. Instead of viewing the consumer in a problem-solving scenario, experiential CB takes into account the holistic shopping experience, relating to the enjoyment of the purchasing process and the surroundings in which it occurs (Holbrook and Hirschman, 1982). More recently, Chang *et al.* (2011) investigated the impact of the store environment on customers' emotions and found that hedonic motivation affected the respondents' subsequent purchasing behaviour by increasing their impulse purchases. They therefore recommend that retailers with a high number of hedonically motivated customers should provide store layout and customer service to provide an enhanced social experience (Chang *et al.*, 2011). As a shopping experience can be more difficult to achieve via the internet than in a store, bricks-and-mortar retailers have a distinct advantage in this respect. Online retailers can ensure that they address the experiential perspective of CB, to minimise this potential disadvantage.

Influences on consumer purchasing behaviour

CB is influenced by a combination of consumers' personal characteristics and social factors. Consumers' personalities incorporate the values that motivate their purchases (Blackwell *et al.*, 2006) and it is therefore useful for retailers to understand more about their customers through market research techniques such as **focus groups** and **ethnography** (see Market Research below). Social influences are culture, subcultures and reference groups, whose traditions or trends consumers follow to conform to group norms, thereby engendering a sense of belonging. Culture is defined by Blythe (2013: 189–190) as 'the set of shared beliefs, attitudes and behaviours associated with a large and distinct group of people . . . culture is one of the main drives of behaviour and influences almost everything we do, including (of course) our consumption behaviour'. Culture can be associated with particular geographic locations, religion and language and has its own overarching set of norms and conventional behaviour. Understanding culture is especially significant for retailers seeking to expand overseas or to appeal to market segments from different cultures. For example, Bicester Village's outlets provide advice and signage in Chinese to accommodate a growing number of visitors from China (see Chapter 6 Retail pricing).

Consumers can be influenced by different reference groups depending on the purchasing situation; for example, when shopping for work clothes they are usually influenced by the way their colleagues dress and the social norms which prevail in the workplace. However, friends and peer groups' styles are likely to be more influential when purchasing casual clothing. Reference groups can often include people whom consumers have never met, but whose lifestyle or image they aspire to, such as pop stars or members of fashionable subcultures. Clothing retailers can identify those reference groups which are influential to their customers and thus predict clothing trends which will be acceptable to their target market. For example, Swedish fashion retailer H&M has sold clothing ranges modelled by Lana del Rey or endorsed by Madonna, and River Island has developed a Rihanna fashion range, to profit from their aspirational influence on customers.

Gender is another demographic factor which can affect CB. Research by Bakewell and Mitchell (2004) investigated men's reputation as reluctant shoppers, since they exhibit different approaches to shopping than women (as you may also have found from your own experience). Because men are now generally more involved in shopping than they have been traditionally, their decision-making styles are of particular interest to the retailers which serve them. Men were found on the whole to prefer to conserve time and energy when shopping, usually making purchase decisions quickly (Bakewell and Mitchell, 2004). In contrast, women have been found to view shopping as an enjoyable activity, although this does not apply in all cases of course. To a certain extent, it may depend on what type of products they are buying or where they are shopping. Despite changes in legislation and society regarding equality, 82 per cent of grocery shoppers are women, according to the CEO of Waitrose (quoted in Grainger, 2014). Even if this figure is limited to this relatively expensive supermarket, it is a figure which has implications for other grocery retailers in terms of appealing to female consumers and understanding their shopping habits. This statistic also suggests that, despite societal and legal changes in relation to equality, shopping duties can still conform to traditional gender roles.

The complexity of shopping behaviour in relation to gender is illustrated by Tai (2005) who investigated the purchasing behaviour of female Chinese consumers. Her research resulted in the compilation of 15 shopping style dimensions including brand consciousness and green consciousness. An alternative method of learning about female shopping habits is suggested by Brown (1995: 770), who asserts that 'it is arguable that much the most interesting – or contemporary if nothing else – depictions of consumer behaviour are to be found in works of romantic fiction', a theory which he supports with an analysis of two popular 'sex and shopping' novels about a fictional retailing dynasty. Retail research firm Shoppercentric also found differences between male and female shopping behaviour, concluding that men 'love having bought something. They just don't like the process. It's a subtle difference, but an important one' (Hardie, 2012: 32). In their survey, Shoppercentric discovered that 31 per cent of men often bought from the first shop they visited, in comparison to 23 per cent of women, suggesting that women shop around more before making purchase decisions (*ibid.*).

Opinion leaders and the diffusion of innovation

Opinion leaders are those who influence others to purchase through WoM recommendations or more tacit behaviour. Opinion leaders actively seek out new innovations and are willing to go out of their way and spend more than most to acquire them. Influential opinion leaders include journalists and bloggers who review products or retailers and are usually perceived by consumers as being independent, objective authorities on particular market sectors, who can also be referred to as 'mavens'. The term 'market maven' is used for a consumer who is influential in setting trends in terms of purchasing products and enjoys shopping (Solomon *et al.*, 2006). Clothing companies such as Puma employ

RETAIL MARKETING CAREERS
Dr Cristina de Balanzó, Consumer Neuroscience Consultant, Walnut Unlimited

Source: with permission from Dr Cristina de Balanzó

Cristina de Balanzó is the founder and director of Walnut Unlimited, a consumer neuroscience consultancy founded in London in 2013 and which since 2014 has belonged to the market research company Marketing Sciences Unlimited, part of Creston group. The name Walnut was chosen because it's a memorable word that can be used as a metaphor for the brain. Cristina describes her job title and role as 'the main nut'. Walnut Unlimited uses the latest research techniques, especially advances in neuroscience, to understand consumers and shoppers.

Walnut Unlimited remit comprises communications and product testing, in-store and shopper marketing, brand identity development and workshops that link different areas of brand interaction. The company's clients include retailers and brands such as KFC and Heineken. Cristina is involved in all aspects of the company, from arranging consumer neuroscience workshops and delivering outcomes to clients, to organising the website. She liaises with each client to obtain the brief to be fulfilled, and then briefs this to the delivery team. Cristina then manages the project and acts as the main consultant, ensuring that she and her colleagues follow the ethics codes of the NMSBA and ESOMAR. She plans to hire more project managers as the company expands.

Cristina's previous roles include being Global Head of Neuroscience for the research company Taylor Nelson Sofres (TNS) and working as a Strategic Planner then as an Account Manager at advertising agency McCann Erickson for nine years. Cristina is well qualified to work in this field, having gained a first degree in Sociology and a PhD with a thesis investigating how to improve advertising effectiveness and consumer insight using a cognitive neuroscience approach. She manages to achieve a balance between working as both a consultant and academic, as she is also a visiting speaker at Ramon Llull University in Spain and Renmin University in China, where she lectures in neuroscience to postgraduate students. A recent paper that she co-wrote was based on research that evaluated the ability of EEG and eye-tracking to predict the effect of advertising on consumers (Calvert et al., 2012). Cristina has written several publications about consumer neuroscience and she has been a speaker on this topic at conferences throughout the world (see https://app.box.com/shared/y8md1r64c8). She also combines her academic and industrial knowledge by running consumer neuroscience training workshops in various countries (see http://walnutunlimited.com/web/live/neurosciencemasterclass/).

Cristina states that neuroscience is needed to help understand consumer behaviour, rather than just using traditional consumer research techniques because 'consumers can't always articulate why they buy something, they just do it'. Her research has demonstrated retail customers' attachment to brands, revealing that price is not the only filter that they use when making purchase decisions, as demonstrated by the activation of neural networks during brain tracking. The Walnut Unlimited team combine neuroscience with behavioural tasks and qualitative research such as in-depth interviews to produce their final recommendations and to tailor the research design to the client's brief. Cristina explains the significance of consumer neuroscience further in this extract from her PhD thesis:

> The marketing community, market researchers, advertisers and, especially, those who are dedicated to brand creation, need the tools that provide them with a deep knowledge of consumers to ensure the success of their communication. This success must be achieved in the context of a complex market, where there has been a massive increase in products and brands, saturation advertising, and where the customers have taken control. This is why, now more than ever, attaining a privileged position in consumers' minds represents a huge challenge for brands. It also obliges the sector to redefine its working methods in order to discover new paradigms of knowledge that deepen understanding of how decisions about purchases are made. Consumer insights are the answer about how a brand can attain a privileged position in the mind of the consumer. This concept covers all the wisdom of this universal truth of human nature which can lead the brand and/or product to connect with the consumer and exert influence on their behaviour. In other words, it succeeds in persuading them. Advances in cognitive neuroscience bring new knowledge to the emerging area of neuromarketing.

Source: with permission from SensoMotoric Instruments GmbH

The use of consumer neuroscience is not widespread at the time of writing. However, Cristina predicts that it 'will probably be implemented more widely in a couple of years', as mobile EEG technology has become available and technological improvements are leading to the generation of 'cleaner' data from the equipment which can prevent the required information from being contaminated by other activity in the brain. Another contributing factor is the formation of the Neuromarketing Science and Business Association, which helps to spread awareness of this field, having launched the

'Neurotalent' award for students in 2013. Cristina contends that consumer neuroscience offers a valuable alternative and an additional insight into traditional market research techniques as 'it gives insights into behavioural patterns' and 'it will give clues about how to optimise web design and targeting'. Cristina considers having her ideas commissioned to be the best aspect of her job, as she says she 'enjoys translating insights into action'. In order to become a consumer neuroscientist Cristina believes 'you have to be really passionate about it, you need to read a lot of scientific papers without needing a specific science background and you need to have a general interest in how the brain works . . . you need to be brave and to be able to break the rules'.

For case studies on Walnut Unlimited's work with clients see: http://walnutunlimited.com/web/case-studies/

Selected publications by Dr Cristina de Balanzó

Calvert, G., de Balanzó, C. and Watkins, S. (2012) 'Opening the black box: an academic evaluation of the ability of electroencephalography (EEG) and Eye Tracking (ET) to predict advertising effectiveness', ESOMAR (available online at: http://www.esomar.org/web/research_papers/Advertising-Research_2397_Opening-the-Black-Box.php).

De Balanzó, C., Serrano, N. and Scamell-Katz, S. (2010) 'Damasio: a starting point for integrating neuroscience findings into retail research', ESOMAR World Research Conference, *Odyssey 2010: The Changing Face of Market Research: Congress Papers*. Amsterdam: ESOMAR, pp. 465–483.

De Balanzó, C. (2011) *Consumer Insights and Neuroscience. The Relationship Between Neurobiological Measures and Advertising Effectiveness*, PhD thesis.

Serrano, N. and de Balanzó, C. (2011) 'Neuroscience and communication strategy: redefining the role of the unconscious', *Trípodos*.

Serrano, N. and de Balanzó, C. (2012) 'Neuromarketing y memoria: implicaciones para la comunicación publicitaria', *Pensar la Publicidad*, 6(2), 297–313.

professional opinion leaders to seek out trends which are likely to appeal to their customers. This is a process known as 'coolhunting', which involves observing and talking to consumers who are perceived as being influential to their peers.

The 'diffusion of innovations' theory categorises consumers into groups of people who influence others to buy new products and services, resulting in trends for these innovations diffusing throughout the population (Rogers, 1962). This model was originally developed in the context of a study of agricultural markets in the US over 50 years ago, so the percentages may not relate directly to the contemporary retailing. However, the terms used are still applicable today, so retailers can assess where their customers fit into this model and who will influence them. The opinion leaders who set new trends are referred to within the model as 'innovators'. Although they are estimated to form only a small proportion of the population they are socially active, and in some cases may be famous, and therefore have the opportunity to influence large numbers of people. Increasingly, ordinary members of the public are able to have a wider impact via social media and blogs. Retailers may therefore be persuaded to pay them to review or promote merchandise online. For example, bloggers such as Susie Lau are invited to fashion designers' catwalk shows in London and Paris to encourage them to write online reviews of the shows (BBC, 2012; Style Bubble, 2012).

'Early adopters' are influential at more of a local level, buying innovations when they are still relatively new, often under the influence of innovators. The 'early majority' adopt innovations a little later than early adopters, but before the late majority, who wait until new products or services are widely socially accepted before investing in them. Laggards are those who take a very long time to adopt innovations, if at all, with a tendency to be in older age brackets and lower-income groups than people in the previous categories. This can therefore restrict their ability to invest in new products. Consumers may not consistently fit into the same category; for example, they may behave as early adopters in relation to one product type, but be in the late majority with regard to another. Rogers estimated the percentages of types of adopter that existed as 2.5 per cent innovators, 13.5 per cent early adopters, 34 per cent each for early and late majority and 16 per cent laggards. However, bear in mind that this model was developed in the 1960s. The proportions of each category may vary today owing to changes in society and they may also vary dependent upon the market sector. However, defining customers within these five categories can allow retailers to identify more easily which products are likely to appeal to their target market.

Customer loyalty

Retail customers can be segmented by behavioural characteristics, especially in their level of usage of a product or brand. Consumers can be loyal to certain retail brands because they relate closely to a brand's values, to the extent that they form a personal attachment that becomes part of their own identity. De Chernatony and McDonald (2003: 439) describe brand loyalty as 'a measure of a consumer's attachment to a specific brand and (this) is a function of several factors such as the perceived quality of the brand, its perceived value, its image, the trust placed in the brand, and the commitment the consumer feels towards it'. In the retail domain, this can be referred to as store loyalty (Gilbert, 2003). Loyal consumers may have a set of brands to which they are attached. They may feel discomfort in selecting other brands which are less familiar to them, or which they feel are not compatible with the image they wish to project. Gilbert (2003: 309) proposes the following method of segmenting consumers who exhibit brand loyalty or store loyalty:

- hard-core loyals have undivided loyalty to one brand;
- soft-core loyals are loyal to two or three competing brands;
- shifting loyals are loyal to one brand for a time before moving their loyalty to another brand;
- switchers do not show loyalty to any particular brand and can often be tempted to switch by promotions and discounts.

Brand loyalty can be a result of various factors, including: force of habit; lower risk in switching brands; convenience; lack of choice; and the influence of the media and reference groups (*ibid.*; McGoldrick, 2002). Information about brand-loyal customers is of interest to retailers owing to these customers' high spend with the company and positive WoM recommendations about the brand to other consumers. When writing **customer profiles**, retailers usually describe their 'core' or 'target' customers who exhibit strong loyalty towards the brand. Loyal customers' spending patterns and demographics can be identified via loyalty card or store card usage, providing valuable information for retailers. Loyalty may be engendered by the availability of loyalty cards to a certain extent, e.g. by a smartcard or more basic stamp per purchase format. However, consumers are likely to obtain cards for several stores in practice, making the cards potentially more useful for data gathering by retailers than for encouraging genuine loyalty. Vlachos and Vrechopoulos (2012) even go so far as to propose that a state of consumer–retailer love and attachment exists, which they claim can be positively linked to store image, perceived value and Corporate Social Responsibility (CSR).

Retailers can aim to build relationships with customers via Relationship Marketing (RM) with the aim of reinforcing or increasing their customers' loyalty by sending them preview information, offers and other communications. For example, retailers can send preview catalogues or emails to loyal customers so that they have the advantage of seeing new products prior to their launch. Feedback from customers on these previews can benefit the company by offering advance information on the popularity of the new products, helping them to anticipate sales figures and thereby allowing them to order appropriate quantities to satisfy demand. The term Customer Relationship Management (CRM) can also be used to describe retailers' direct communications with consumers to encourage repeat purchasing. A method of gauging the level of customers' loyalty to a retailer is to assess its 'net promoter score'. This loyalty metric uses responses about customers' willingness to recommend a brand to others on a scale of 1–10, with those rating it 9–10 being termed promoters and those selecting 1–6 being detractors, the rest being passive. To calculate a net promoter score, the total percentage of detractors is subtracted from the total percentage of promoters (Satmetrix, 2014). Although the net promoter score is claimed to be a predictor of a company's growth potential, it has been criticised by academics for not being tested rigorously (Keiningham *et al.*, 2007).

Negative consumer behaviour

Much of the research into CB in the retailing and marketing literature focuses on fulfilment of customer needs, with sparse coverage of consumption's more negative aspects. For example, widely accessible consumer credit encourages people to buy goods that they cannot afford and is likely to have contributed to the global economic downturn in 2008, leading to criticism of the banks which offer it. Negative CB, including compulsive and compensatory consumption, can also be referred to as 'consumer misbehaviour' (Tonglet, 2002). (The same term is used by McGoldrick and André [1997] to describe supermarket customers who defect to competitors.) Impulse buying takes place when customers cannot resist the urge to buy goods or services that they did not initially plan to buy. A study of 4,200 consumers found that 68 per cent made unplanned purchases during major shopping trips (Inman and Winer, 1998), thus offering retailers a broad scope to persuade consumers to buy at the point-of-sale. Retailers exploit the tendency for customers to buy on impulse by locating products in tempting positions, such as in the payment area where customers have to wait for a short time and where it is easier to get their attention. However, compulsive buyers behave addictively, rather than just making the occasional impulse buy. Research has shown that compulsive shopping is more likely to be a female trait (Dittmar and Drury, 2000). Another study found that compulsive buyers were more price-conscious and brand-aware than non-compulsive shoppers (Kukar-Kinney *et al.*, 2012).

Another form of consumer misbehaviour is shoplifting, which is clearly a significant issue within the retail sector. Retail crime cost UK retailers an estimated £511 million in 2012–2013, with theft by customers accounting for 82 per cent and theft by employees 5.3 per cent (BRC, 2014). Retailers benefit from being familiar with criminal behaviour in order to install suitable security measures to avoid thefts. The fact that the number of burglaries in UK stores between 2012–2013 declined by 49 per cent is positive news, probably helped by retailers' expenditure on security. Goods displayed near the entrances of stores to attract customers are obviously at risk and retailers need to take this into account when devising store layout. Although it is not quite as extreme as consumer crime, a study on 'consumer rage' identified different forms of reaction to customer service encounters such as 'retaliatory rage' (McColl-Kennedy *et al.*, 2009). This is also useful for retailers to be aware of, both to protect their customer staff and to prevent customers from being antagonised by staff's behaviour.

Retail market segmentation

Market segmentation is defined as 'the process of identifying groups of people who behave in similar ways to each other, but somewhat differently than other groups' by Blackwell *et al.* (2006: 41), with the purpose of improving customers' satisfaction and retailers' profitability. This enables retailers to aim their products more effectively towards the target market in terms of matching product or service design, quality, price, promotion and distribution channel to consumers' different needs and preferences. The four main methods used to segment markets are: **demographic, geographic, psychographic** and **behavioural segmentation**. Additionally, geo-demographic methods can be used, that merge two of these main methods, to provide a broad range of consumer categories (see below). After deciding on their market segmentation strategy, retailers can assess how to target those segments and to establish its position in relation to competitors in the market, a process known as Segmentation, Targeting and Positioning (STP) (see Chapter 2 Retail marketing strategy). It is not always essential to segment markets, as products or services with a broad appeal across many segments of the population can use mass marketing, but this has become somewhat rare (Blythe, 2013).

Demographic and geographic segmentation

Demographic factors are described by Solomon *et al*. (2006: 9) as 'statistics that measure observable aspects of a population', including: age; gender; occupation; income; marital status; ethnic group and religion. Knowing the demographic characteristics of a given population can be beneficial to retailers in various situations, e.g. for defining target segments or selecting appropriate store locations. Family lifecycle (FLC) stages were devised by Wells and Gubar (1966) to sum up consumers' demographic characteristics. FLC categories provide a range of descriptive groups in which consumers can be placed. These groups vary from bachelors through to newly married couples, full nesters, empty nesters and 'solitary survivors', based on the notion that needs change along with family situation. Although the FLC stages are still mostly relevant, they are not entirely consistent with societal changes which have occurred since the 1960s, since they are based on age, marital status and number of children. When describing ages for target customers it is best to define specific age groups (such as 35–44) rather than using relative terms such as 'younger' or 'older' which can be vague and misinterpreted. For example, students might perceive people in their 30s as being older, whereas tutors may view them as still being young!

It is important to keep up-to-date with demographic trends, as they are constantly in a state of change. Societal changes have led to 35 per cent of the adult population of England and Wales in 2011 never having been married, up from 30 per cent of the population in 2001. The introduction of UK legislation permitting same-sex marriage in 2014 could be likely to affect this statistic in future years. There has been an increase in the average age of the UK population in recent years, due to a combination of the birth rate and longer life expectancy. It has been projected that around a third of babies born in 2013 could live to be 100 years old (ONS, 2013a). Retailers therefore have an opportunity to cater more effectively for a market that is characterised by an ageing population. The lowest ever infant mortality rate was achieved in 2012, yet fewer children are being born, so the birth rate is slowing down. The average age of a woman having a first child is now 28, which has generally increased since the 1970s, due in part to increased participation in education and employment (ONS, 2013b). Young adults are tending to wait longer to move away from the parental home, with 26 per cent of 20–34-year-olds in the UK, mostly males, still living with their parents (ONS, 2014). This is consistent with the increase in the average age at which people in the UK first marry, which was 30 years old for women and 32 for men in 2011 (ONS, 2013c). Key demographic statistics about the UK population are featured in Table 3.1.

Geographic segmentation groups consumers by country or region, e.g. the UK can be split into counties or larger regions. This is particularly apt for retailers since their outlets are based in specific locations; hence this information is significant for site selection of stores. Geodemographic segmentation places people into groups according to the type of

Table 3.1 UK population statistics (based on figures from ONS, 2014)

Demographic aspect	Statistics
UK population	63.2 million (2011 census)
Gender	Female 51%; Male 49% (2011)
Life expectancy at birth	Female 82.6 years; Male 78.7 years (2010/12)
Average number of children per family	1.7
Ethnicity	White British 80.6%; the rest of the population being mainly of 'Asian/Asian British', 'Other White' or 'Black/African/Caribbean/Black British' origin

neighbourhood in which they live, in the expectation that consumers who live there have similar traits. There are various systems for classifying consumers geodemographically. For example, ACORN (A Classification of Residential Neighbourhoods) categorises the whole of the UK into six main categories.

1 Affluent achievers
2 Rising prosperity
3 Comfortable communities
4 Financially stretched
5 Urban adversity
6 Not private households

These six types of household are categorised into 17 groups, including 'lavish lifestyles', 'steady neighbourhoods' and 'struggling estates', which are further subdivided into 59 specific types of consumer based mainly on accommodation (CACI, 2014). The full ACORN 2014 classifications can be downloaded from: acorn.caci.co.uk/downloads/Acorn-User-guide.pdf. Note that student accommodation is classified as type 34. 'Mosaic' is an alternative geodemographic method of classifying consumers (Experian, 2012).

Socio-economic groups are used to categorise customers into six key groups, based around their income bracket and occupation (see Table 3.2). Although they are not much more detailed than the vague and dated notions of working, middle and upper classes, they give marketers more specific options to define their customers and are widely used in the industry and media. Initially developed in the 1960s, the groups attempt to merge social and economic factors to group together various occupations. The ranking of the socio-economic groups works more effectively in social than in economic terms in the present day, as income levels have changed in comparison to each other in the decades since the system was introduced. For example, in some cases skilled tradesmen (in the C2 category) have the capacity to earn more than their C1, or even group B counterparts. Socio-economic groups are used by the National Readership Survey (NRS) for print media to specify their typical readership, alongside the volume of readers, with the aim of attracting advertisers who target these groups (NRS, 2014a). The groups are often merged, e.g. ABC1, to show that a publication appeals to the most affluent population segments. Information compiled by the NRS shows the increasing affluence in the UK, with C2DE consumers reducing from 65 per cent of the population in 1968 to 45 per cent in 2008, with a corresponding rise in ABC1 groups (Ipsos Mori, 2009).

Household members, including students living at home, are usually classified based on the income of the household's main earner. University students are often surprised to find that technically they fall into the C1 category if they are living away from home, even though they don't have a full-time income, as they are generally preparing for a

Table 3.2 Social grading system using socio-economic groups

Socio-economic group	Description and examples of occupations	Percentage of population 2012–2013*
A	Higher managerial and professional, e.g. managing director, surgeon, barrister	4
B	Managerial or professional, e.g. accountant, lecturer, departmental manager	22
C1	Supervisory or clerical, junior managerial, e.g. retail supervisor, office administrator, foreman	27
C2	Skilled manual workers, e.g. plumber, hairdresser, builder	22
D	Semi-skilled and unskilled manual workers, e.g. driver, cleaner, shop assistant	16
E	No income or subsistence level, e.g. state pensioner, casual labourer, unemployed	9

(*Source of population percentages: NRS, 2014b)

management-level career. Another method of segmenting the population in a socio-economic framework is the National Statistics Socio-Economic Classification (NS-SEC). This system was developed by the UK government to classify the population in the 2001 census into 17 employment categories which can be grouped into three main classifications:

- higher managerial, administrative and professional
- intermediate
- routine and manual.

Psychographic segmentation

Although demographic and geographic categorisations can be useful for segmenting retailers' customers in many cases, they are not always the best ways of defining customers. Consumers' lifestyle characteristics, personality and attitudes (i.e. psychographics) can be used to describe them in detail and can be more appropriate than segmentation by demographic factors, as consumers in the same age groups and regions can often have different lifestyles and values. Psychographic segmentation is a particularly apt method for retailers to use since consumers will purchase items to enable them to pursue their chosen lifestyles. Being aware of customers' typical holiday destinations, the type of cars they drive and where they spend their leisure time can enable retailers to build up a much clearer picture of whom they intend to target with their products. Certain retailers post collages to illustrate their typical customers' lifestyles on the wall of the buying office as a permanent reminder to their buyers of who will be buying and using their products. Being aware of which magazines and newspapers customers read, their favourite TV channels, radio stations, social media and websites, will allow retailers to select appropriate media in which to advertise or gain PR exposure (see Chapter 7 Retail marketing communications). Identifying their customers' favourite musical genres, films and TV programmes can enable retailers to assess the most suitable types of music to play in stores and which celebrities, songs and cultural references to feature in promotional campaigns. To help target specific groups of consumers, advertising agencies sometimes devise their own market segments based largely on psychographic traits, for clients such as retailers and brands. Becoming familiar with consumers' personalities through finding out about their attitudes, interests and opinions, can also assist retailers in selecting appropriate products and advertising techniques which will appeal to their customers. Retailers can conduct qualitative research such as focus groups with customers in order to discover their psychographic characteristics. However, there is still a risk of stereotyping consumers through the use of psychographics, since they are clearly all different individuals who are similar in some attitudinal respects and different in others.

Behavioural segmentation

Behavioural segmentation relates to customers' usage of a product, e.g. if they are highly loyal, regular or infrequent users of a product or service. A loyal customer may buy most of a certain type of product at a particular retailer, whereas others may only shop there occasionally, thus affecting their patterns of behaviour. Another form of behavioural segmentation is when a product is used by customers for different purposes; for example, a group may buy musical instruments to use for their work, whereas consumers will play them in their own leisure time. Different customers can also derive different benefits from the same product, such as buying a DVD either for entertainment or for educational purposes. The purchase occasion can also differ, so a consumer might visit a florist to buy a gift or for him/herself, in which case the presentation requirements and choice of flowers can vary.

Arnold and Reynolds (2003) investigated shopping behaviour from the perspective of consumers' motives and revealed six key motivations for shopping:

- seeking adventure
- socialising
- seeking gratification
- searching for ideas
- buying for others
- searching for value.

These dimensions were assessed in relation to different clusters of shoppers who were categorised into a taxonomy summarised in Table 3.3. These five segments can prove particularly useful to retailers as an alternative to demographic segmentation, by identifying the shopper types in their target market and designing stores to fit their behavioural patterns.

Table 3.3 Shopping motivation groups

Shopper segments	Shopper characteristics
Minimalists	Mainly male, high proportion over 25 years and over, lacking hedonic motivation
Gatherers	Mainly male, high proportion under 25 years old, looking for ideas and buying for others
Providers	Mainly female, high proportion over 25 years and over, looking for value and buying for others
Enthusiasts	Mainly female, high proportion under 25 years old, with high level of hedonic motivation
Traditionalists	Slightly more females than males, fairly even spread between age groups, with moderate hedonic motivation

Source: categories from Arnold and Reynolds, 2003

The seven population segments

Segment willingness and ability

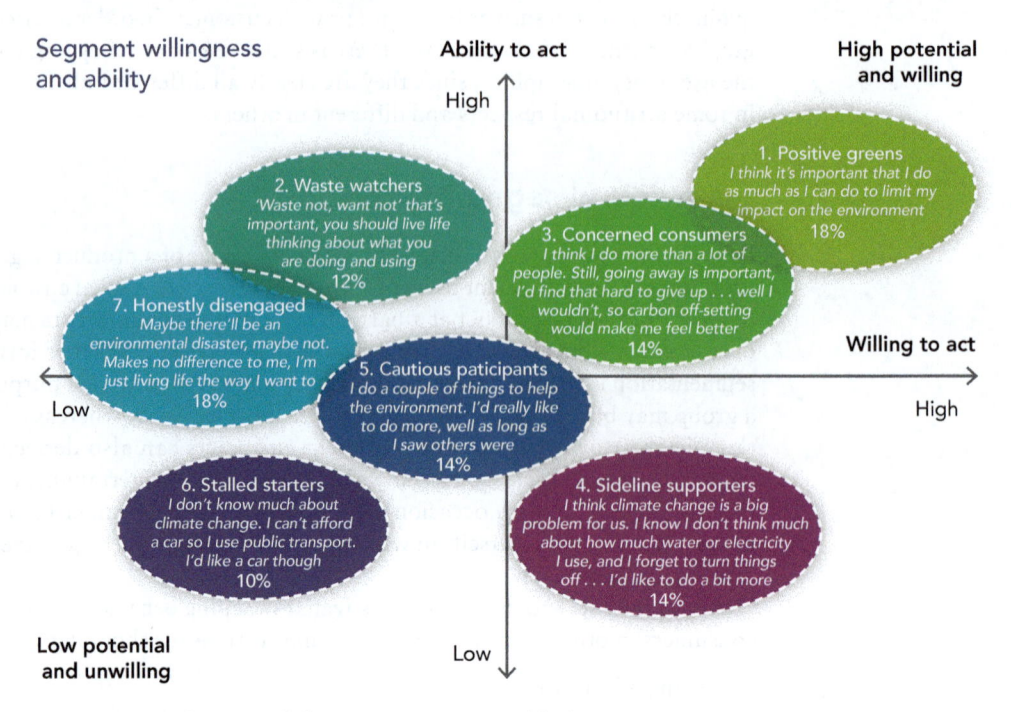

Positioning map axes: Ability to act (High / Low, vertical) × Willing to act (Low / High, horizontal). Quadrants labelled "High potential and willing" (top right) and "Low potential and unwilling" (bottom left).

- **1. Positive greens** — *I think it's important that I do as much as I can do to limit my impact on the environment* — 18%
- **2. Waste watchers** — *'Waste not, want not' that's important, you should live life thinking about what you are doing and using* — 12%
- **3. Concerned consumers** — *I think I do more than a lot of people. Still, going away is important, I'd find that hard to give up . . . well I wouldn't, so carbon off-setting would make me feel better* — 14%
- **4. Sideline supporters** — *I think climate change is a big problem for us. I know I don't think much about how much water or electricity I use, and I forget to turn things off . . . I'd like to do a bit more* — 14%
- **5. Cautious participants** — *I do a couple of things to help the environment. I'd really like to do more, well as long as I saw others were* — 14%
- **6. Stalled starters** — *I don't know much about climate change. I can't afford a car so I use public transport. I'd like a car though* — 10%
- **7. Honestly disengaged** — *Maybe there'll be an environmental disaster, maybe not. Makes no difference to me, I'm just living life the way I want to* — 18%

Figure 3.2 A framework for pro-environmental behaviours
Source: Defra, 2008 (available online at: http://archive.defra.gov.uk/evidence/social/behaviour/documents/behaviours-jan08-report.pdf, with permission from Defra)

Another example of a classification for behavioural segmentation is the Framework for Environmental Behaviours developed for Defra (see Figure 3.2), which categorises consumers based on the impact of their consumption on the environment. The categories range from 'Positive greens' to 'Honestly disengaged', each of these polarised groups being estimated to cover 18 per cent of the population (see also Chapter 12 Legislation and ethics in retailing).

Displayed within a positioning map comparing willingness and ability to act, categories 1–5 exhibit differing levels of engagement with sustainable behaviour. Group 6 'stalled starters' may behave in environmentally ways unintentionally, being driven more by economy, e.g. using public transport because it is cheaper, and group 7 express no interest in behaving sustainably. Retailers can use market research to identify the proportions of their customers that fall into these categories and offer them appropriate sustainable products to respond to or even influence their preferences.

Customer profiles

Details of the lifestyle of a retailer's typical 'target customer' can be compiled to provide a customer profile or 'pen portrait' of the people at whom the retailer's products or services are aimed. The customer profile could cover a range of different target customers or be narrowed down to a description of a single individual, viewed as a typical (although fictitious) customer, who may be given a name and a detailed lifestyle. Customer profiles can be either written or visual, typically containing descriptions or a collage of target customers' choices of accommodation, workplace, holiday destinations, media preferences and leisure pursuits etc., often incorporating both psychographic and demographic factors.

They can be shared with the retailer's staff, thereby enabling buyers who are selecting merchandise, marketers who are choosing suitable promotional material and designers who are developing store interiors to build up a realistic picture of the target market (Arnold and Reynolds, 2003). For example, fashion retailer Miss Selfridge aims to target 'stylish and self-assured customers aged 18 to 24' (Arcadia, 2011). Below is an example of a customer profile from another company in the Arcadia group, menswear retailer Burton. Since it is from the retailer's website (Burton, 2014) and therefore available to the public, it is written using informal terms to communicate directly with consumers or job applicants:

> Next time you're down the pub, have a look round at any groups of guys drinking together. For every ten guys in a round, if most of them are dressed pretty conservatively while two or three are slightly more fashion conscious than the others, you've found the perfect Burton customer profile. There are two core Burton customers: Mainstream quiet – the guy who wants nice, better quality but safe and accessible pieces. Mainstream loud – a fashion follower, who is willing to take a few more risks than his quiet counterpart. Burton's product reflects the type of clothes these blokes want to buy. The product is of good quality, safe styles, and has a few hints towards trends. Our customer wants to feel comfortable in the clothes he wears. He wants to be the average guy down the pub and not stand out too much, unless he is trying to impress on a night out.

Here is an example of a more formal, albeit brief, demographic customer profile aimed at a business audience in a report by Mintel (2012):

> Relative to the average department store shopper, House of Fraser customers show a bias to the under 45s shopper. They are also especially well represented among the AB socio-economic group. Regionally its relative strength lies with consumers in Yorkshire/North East and London. The company now also attracts an above-average number of C1 shoppers, which it didn't a few years ago.

Retail marketing research

Marketing research is defined by Zikmund and Babin (2010: 5) as 'the application of the scientific method in searching for the truth about marketing phenomena', so that objective conclusions can be reached. Retailers have a variety of marketing research methods at their disposal to investigate CB or to assess other aspects of the market, such as their competitors. There are two main options available: **primary research**, which is conducted for a specific organisation, and **secondary research**, which has already been compiled. It is advisable to conduct secondary research first, because the information that the company is seeking may have already been published, thus saving the company the time and expense of investing in their own exclusive research.

Secondary research

Secondary research is also known as 'desk research' and this refers to information that has previously been published, usually in print or digital form. Most of the sources that will prove useful have a cost attached but this would normally be far cheaper than the cost of an individual retailer carrying out the research themselves. There are also numerous useful sources that are available free, particularly from government or industry bodies. It is obviously advisable to check the reliability of secondary sources though, particularly online, and it is essential to ensure that information is from a trusted and valid organisation, as opposed to online encyclopaedias using wikis, for example, since anyone would be free to insert incorrect information. Publications that are relevant to retailing include market reports, academic journals, trade journals, textbooks and government reports. University and college students often have the advantage of gaining free access to market reports, academic journals and trade journals via their institution's library resources or through requesting an inter-library loan. Retailers can subscribe to relevant journals or purchase individual articles online and brief abstracts outlining the main research findings are freely available on journals' websites. Academic assignments about retailing (and consequently marks) can be enhanced by referring knowledgeably and accurately to previous studies published in journals such as: *Journal of Retailing*; *International Journal of Retail and Distribution Management*; *International Review of Retail, Distribution and Consumer Research*; and *Journal of Services Marketing*.

There are also many articles that are pertinent to retailing found in more generic marketing or business journals and some have 'special issues' on retailing. These are collections of articles on a particular theme, or in commemoration of an event, such as an academic conference. For example, there is a special issue on etailing and e-shopping in the *European Journal of Marketing* (2009, edition 43, 9/10). Marketing databases such as Mintel, Key Note and Datamonitor can be useful sources to supplement journal articles by providing market reports with background information on the retailing industry. Datamonitor produces a Global Retailing Industry Profile that gives an overview of leading companies and market forecasts. Datamonitor also produce Retail Industry Profiles on specific product sectors in particular locations, e.g. food retailing in Denmark and apparel retailing in China.

Articles from high-quality newspapers can also be useful and reliable sources to be used to supplement journal articles, since they provide information about very current developments in retailing. Many newspapers have business sections which refer to retailing news in brief, as well as in-depth articles on certain companies, usually providing a more independent viewpoint than the company's own publicity. For example, *The Times* has a section on retailing in the business pages of each edition and other useful sources to access online are *The Independent, The Telegraph, The Guardian, Financial Times,* the *Wall Street Journal* and *China Daily*. Trade journals are particularly relevant for retailers, providing timely and concise retail news, in-depth industry insights and advertising for services and recruitment, through hard copies or online subscriptions. The *Retail Bulletin* and *Retail Gazette* provide free regular retail industry updates online. Additionally, *Marketing Magazine, Marketing Week* and *Retail Week* are very useful trade magazines available in hard copies and online, as well as those for specific retail sectors including *The Grocer* and *Drapers*.

Primary research

Primary research can be conducted by a retailer's own marketing team or a specialist market research agency can be commissioned to produce it on behalf of the retailer, such as JRA Research and QRS Research. There are two key types of market research: quantitative and qualitative. Figure 3.3 outlines some of the options for market research techniques. Quantitative research is usually carried out in the form of a survey with a questionnaire as the research tool, resulting in statistical outcomes. Qualitative research deals with verbal or written outputs from respondents and is usually more suited to investigating people's opinions and attitudes. This can take the form of discussions such as interviews or focus groups. For example, clothing retailers can bring together a panel of typical customers for a focus group to discover their views on a new range of garments. Primary research studies can also use mixed methods by combining both quantitative and qualitative techniques. There are many similarities between the methods and terminology used in market research and academic research.

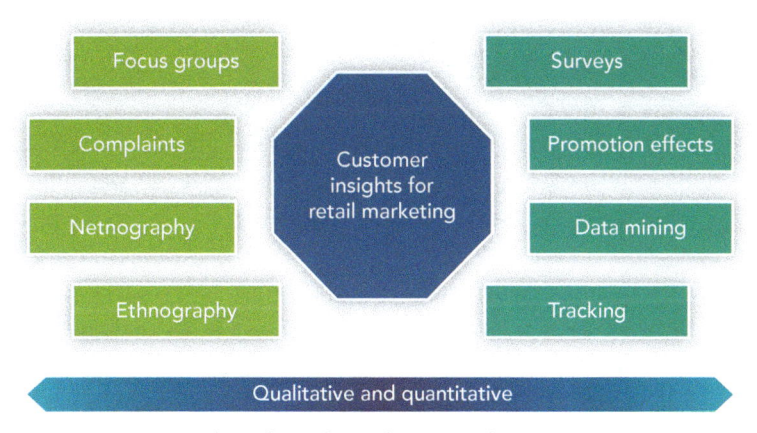

Figure 3.3 Examples of retail insight research
Source: Peter McGoldrick

Retailers can also use data mining techniques by analysing existing information about their customers, such as their purchase patterns which have been recorded via the use of customers' loyalty cards. Observational research is a technique which can be used by retailers such as supermarkets, enabling them to observe the ways in which consumers navigate stores and select products. Specialist companies such as Envirosell, who operate in the US, Thailand, Japan, India, Mexico and Brazil, can be commissioned by retailers to conduct research on their behalf. Details of Envirosell's projects can be viewed at www.envirosell.com. Envirosell has found that the longer shoppers spend in stores, predictably the more they will buy and the time they spend there depends on the quality of the retail experience (Underhill, 2009). Envirosell's founder, Paco Underhill (2009: 40) states: 'the overarching lesson we've learnt from the science of shopping is this: amenability and profitability are inextricably linked. Take care of the former, in all of its guises, and the latter is assured'. Therefore, retailers can encourage customers to stay in the store through providing a positive experience and this can have positive effect on profitability. Observation can be conducted by retailers to view patterns of CB so that store design and service can be optimised to meet consumer needs. TNS Magasin (a division of the global market research company Taylor Nelson Sofres) uses eye-tracking technology, where an infra-red light is used to track the wearer's eye movements, as another method to observe consumers, providing detailed data (see Chapter 9 Retail design and layout).

Ethnography is another, more in-depth, observation-based form of research which was originally developed for use by sociologists and anthropologists. Ethnography is defined by Bryman and Bell (2011) as: 'a research method in which the researcher immerses him- or herself in a social setting for an extended period of time, observing behaviour, listening to what is said in conversations between others and with the fieldworker, and asking questions'. Retailers can employ ethnographers to reveal detailed aspects of consumers' shopping behaviour and usage of products. Kozinets *et al*. (2010) also introduced the term 'netnography' to describe marketing research which involves observations of online communications to reveal consumers' views of products and services. Netnography is facilitated by the increased use of social media. Information which consumers post on social media websites, such as Facebook, can be viewed freely by retailers, giving a personal and comprehensive view of customers' activities and interests. Social media website Pinterest was launched in 2010, allowing users to share favourite images by 'pinning' them to virtual notice boards (Thompson, 2012). Pinterest offers retailers the opportunity to observe consumers' visual interests, in the form of both visual and virtual ethnography (Bryman and Bell, 2011).

CHAPTER SUMMARY

Understanding the behaviour and attitudes of their customers can enable retailers to make more effective marketing decisions. This understanding of behaviour patterns and the roles that consumers play can be gained through implementing marketing research and market segmentation.

- Consumers can play various roles in purchase decision-making: initiator; influencer; decider; buyer or user; and sometimes a combination of these roles.
- Consumers are motivated to purchase by the five levels in Maslow's Hierarchy of Needs: from basic survival to security and safety, social needs, self-esteem and self-actualisation. Alternatively, needs can be categorised into two groups: utilitarian (based around functionality) and hedonic (centred on enjoyment).
- The CDP presumes that consumers make rational decisions, proceeding through seven stages: need recognition; information search; pre-purchase evaluation of alternatives; purchase; consumption; post-consumption evaluation; divestment. However, experiential CB proposes an alternative view, that shopping is motivated by hedonistic values rather than rational thinking.
- Consumer neuroscience is a recent innovation in marketing research that uses fMRI and EEG technology to track customers' brain responses to shopping.
- Consumers' cultures, subcultures, personalities and reference groups affect their beliefs, attitudes and values and therefore impact upon their purchasing behaviour.
- Research findings indicate differences in patterns of male and female purchasing behaviour, suggesting that women engage in shopping more enthusiastically than men.
- Store loyalty can be encouraged via the use of loyalty cards and Relationship Marketing. Loyalty can be quantified using a net promoter score.
- Negative aspects of CB include compulsive shopping and shoplifting.

EXERCISES AND QUESTIONS

1 Apply the first four stages of the CDP model to two purchases you have made within the last month, one for a high-cost and the other for a low-cost product or service. Compare the total time you spent making decisions about purchasing these items. Secondly, apply stages 5, 6 and 7 of the CDP model to a high cost item you bought last year. Consider whether or not you would buy this product or brand again or recommend it to a friend.

2 Describe occasions where you have acted in the following roles, but you were not the person who paid for the purchase: (a) initiator, (b) influencer, (c) decider, (d) user.

3 Watch the following video, then discuss the reasons why a knowledge of consumer neuroscience can be useful to retail marketers: vimeo.com/64050513.

4 What are the advantages to retailers of developing customer profiles? This blog from industry experts The Whole Brain Group and this information from Mintel may give you some ideas and help you to specify the demographic details of your customers: blog.thewholebraingroup.com/steps-to-creating-an-ideal-customer-profile; oxygen.mintel.com/methodology/1/

5 Devise a 300–500 word customer profile for a retailer of your choice using the technique of describing a hypothetical typical customer, featuring both demographic and

psychographic characteristics. You may wish to base this on someone you know who is a loyal customer of the retailer. You can compile the customer profile in either a visual or written format, or a combination of both.

6 Read the article by Arnold and Reynolds (2003) on 'hedonic shopping motivations'. Note the categories in which they place consumers – Minimalists, Gatherers, Providers, Enthusiasts and Traditionalists – and consider people you know who may fit into some of these groups. You should also decide which category best describes your own shopping behaviour.

7 Look at the websites for two market research agencies, e.g. qrs-research.co.uk/ and www.jraresearch.com, and compare the companies' services for quantitative and qualitative research. Based on the information available on their websites, assess which of the two companies you would recommend a supermarket chain with 30 outlets to use for primary research into its customers' requirements for:
   - a quantitative study
   - a qualitative study.

   Explain your reasoning for each choice.

8 The stages of the Family Lifecycle were compiled by Wells and Gubar (1966) and were re-addressed by Gilly and Enis (1982) (see http://www.acrwebsite.org/search/view-conference-proceedings.aspx?Id=6007). The FLC classification can be criticised for its lack of relevance to contemporary society, since lifestyles and values in many countries have changed in the intervening decades. How would you revise and rename the categories to make them more relevant for market segmentation by contemporary retailers?

9 Firstly, you should download and read this brief guide to social grades A-E published by Ipsos MORI: www.ipsos-mori.com/DownloadPublication/1285_MediaCT_thoughtpiece_Social_Grade_July09_V3_WEB.pdf

   Now select three retailers in your nearest town or city and for each store assess which are the main socio-economic groups that shop there. Explain the reasoning behind your choices.

REFERENCES

Ajzen, I. (2005) *Attitudes, Personality and Behaviour*, 2nd edn, Milton Keynes: Open University Press.

Antonides, G. and van Raaij, W. (1998) *Consumer Behaviour: a European Perspective*, Chichester: John Wiley and Sons.

Arcadia (2011) *Arcadia Responsibility Report: Fashioning a Brighter Future* (available online at: http://www.arcadiagroup.co.uk/fashionfootprint/responsibilty-report-2011)

Arnold, M.J. and Reynolds, K.E. (2003) Hedonic shopping motivations, *Journal of Retailing*, 79, 77–95.

Bakewell, C. and Mitchell, V.W. (2004) Male consumer decision-making styles, *International Review of Retail, Distribution and Consumer Research*, 14(2), 223–240.

Bannister, E. and Hogg, M. (2001) Consumers and their negative selves, and the implications for fashion marketing, in Hines, T. and Bruce, M. (eds), *Fashion Marketing: Contemporary Issues*, London: Butterworth Heinemann, pp. 190–202.

BBC (2012) *Women's Hour: London Fashion Week*, BBC Radio 4, 20 February (available online at: http://www.bbc.co.uk/programmes/b01c7lk2).

Blackwell, R.D., Miniard, P.W. and Engel, J.F. (2006) *Consumer Behavior*, 10th edn, Mason: South-Western.

Blythe, J. (2013) *Consumer Behaviour*, 2nd edn, London: Sage.

British Retail Consortium (2014) *Retail Crime Survey 2013* (available online at: http://www.brc.org.uk/brc_policy_content.asp?iCat=48&iSubCat=646&sPolicy=Retail+Crime).

Brown, S. (1995) Sex and shopping: a 'novel' approach to consumer research, *Journal of Marketing Management*, 11, 769–783.

Bryman, A. and Bell, E. (2011) *Business Research Methods*, 3rd edn, Oxford: Oxford University Press.

Burton (2014) *The Customer* (available online at: www.burton.co.uk/careers/thecustomer.html).

CACI (2014) *A Classification of Residential Neighbourhoods* (available online at: http://acorn.caci.co.uk/downloads/Acorn-User-guide.pdf).

Calvert, G., de Balanzó, C. and Watkins, S. (2012) Opening the black box: an academic evaluation of the ability of electroencephalography (EEG) and Eye Tracking (ET) to predict advertising effectiveness, ESOMAR (available online at: http://www.esomar.org/web/research_papers/Advertising-Research_2397_Opening-the-Black-Box.php).

Chang, H.J., Eckman, M. and Yan, R.N. (2011) Application of the Stimulus-Organism-Response model to the retail environment: the role of hedonic motivation in impulse buying behavior, *International Review of Retail, Distribution and Consumer Research*, 21(3), 233–249.

De Chernatony, L. and McDonald, M. (2003) *Creating Powerful Brands*, 3rd edn, Oxford: Elsevier/Butterworth Heinemann.

Dittmar, H. and Drury, J. (2000) Self-image – is it in the bag? A qualitative comparison between 'ordinary' and 'excessive' consumers, *Journal of Economic Psychology*, 21(2), 109–142.

Experian (2012) *Mosaic Classifications* (available online at: http://www.experian.co.uk/business-strategies/mosaic-uk-2009.html).

Gilbert, D. (2003) *Retail Marketing Management*, 2nd edn, Harlow: Financial Times/Prentice Hall.

Gilly, M.C. and Enis, B.M. (1982) Recycling the family life cycle: a proposal for redefinition, *Advances in Consumer Research*, 9, 271–276.

Grainger, L. (2014) Food issue: what supermarket bosses buy, in *The Times Magazine*, 24 May (available online at: http://www.thetimes.co.uk/tto/magazine/article4094940.ece).

Hardie, C. (2012) How men shop, *Retail Week*, 17 February, pp. 32–33.

Holbrook, M. and Hirschman, E. (1982) The experiential aspects of consumption: consumer fantasies, feelings and fun, *Journal of Consumer Research*, 9(2), 132–140.

Inman, J.J. and Winer, R.S. (1998) Where the rubber meets the road: a model of in-store consumer decision making, *Marketing Science Institute*, 98–122 (available online at: http://www.msi.org/reports/where-the-rubber-meets-the-road-a-model-of-in-store-consumer-decision-makin/).

Ipsos Mori (2009) *Social Grade: A Classification Tool* (available online at: www.ipsos-mori.com/DownloadPublication/1285_MediaCT_thoughtpiece_Social_Grade_July09_V3_WEB.pdf).

Jobber, D. and Fahy, J. (2009) *Foundations of Marketing*, Maidenhead: McGraw-Hill.

Jobber, D. (2010) *Principles and Practice of Marketing*, 6th edn, Maidenhead: McGraw-Hill.

Keiningham, T.L., Cooil, B., Andreassen, T.W. and Aksoy, L. (2007) A longitudinal examination of net promoter and firm revenue growth, *Journal of Marketing*, 71(3), 39–51.

Kozinets, R.V., de Valck, K., Wojnicki, A.C. and Wilner, S.J.S. (2010) Networked narratives: understanding word-of-mouth marketing in online communities, *Journal of Marketing*, 74(2), 71–89.

Kukar-Kinney, M., Ridgway, N.M. and Monroe, K.B. (2012) The role of price in the behavior and purchase decisions of compulsive buyers, *Journal of Retailing*, 88(1), 63–71.

Lury, C. (1996) *Consumer Culture*, Oxford: Polity Press.

Lutz, R.J. and Bettman, J.R. (1977) Multi-attribute models in marketing: a Bicentennial review, in Woodside, A.G., Sheth, J.N. and Bennett, P.D. (eds), *Consumer and Industrial Buying Behavior*, New York: Elsevier/North-Holland.

McColl-Kennedy, J.R., Patterson, P.G., Smith, A.K. and Brady, M.K. (2009) Customer rage episodes: emotions, expressions and behaviors, *Journal of Retailing*, 85(2), 222–237.

McGoldrick, P. (2002) *Retail Marketing*, 2nd edn, Maidenhead: McGraw-Hill.

McGoldrick, P.J. and Andre, E. (1997) Consumer misbehaviour: promiscuity or loyalty in grocery retailing, *Journal of Retailing and Consumer Services*, 4(2), 73–81.

Mintel (2012) *Department Store Retailing – UK* (available online at: store.mintel.com/department-store-retailing-uk-march-2012.html).

Neff, J. (2008) Pick a product: 40% of public decide in store, *Advertising Age*, 28 July, pp. 1, 31.

NRS (2014a) *What We Do* (available online at: www.nrs.co.uk/what-we-do/).

NRS (2014b) *Social Grade – Definitions and Discriminatory Power* (available online at: www.nrs.co.uk/lifestyle-data/).

ONS (2013a) *One Third of Babies Born in 2013 are Expected to Live to 100*, Fareham: Office for National Statistics (available online at: http://www.ons.gov.uk/ons/rel/lifetables/historic-and-projected-data-from-the-period-and-cohort-life-tables/2012-based/sty-babies-living-to-100.html).

ONS (2013b) *Live Births in England and Wales by Characteristics of Mother 1 2012*, Fareham: Office for National Statistics (available online at: www.ons.gov.uk/ons/dcp171778_330664.pdf).

ONS (2013c) *Marriages in England and Wales (provisional) 2011*, Fareham: Office for National Statistics (available online at: http://www.ons.gov.uk/ons/dcp171778_315549.pdf).

ONS (2014) *Large Increase in 20- to 34-year-olds Living with Parents since 1996*, Fareham: Office for National Statistics (available online at: http://www.ons.gov.uk/ons/rel/family-demography/young-adults-living-with-parents/2013/sty-young-adults.html).

Rogers, E.M. (1962) *Diffusion of Innovations*, New York: Free Press.

Satmetrix (2014) *The Net Promoter Score and System* (available online at: www.netpromoter.com/Home).

Solomon, M., Bamossy, G., Askegaard, S. and Hogg, M.K. (2006) *Consumer Behaviour: A European Perspective*, 3rd edn, Harlow: Financial Times/Prentice Hall.

Style Bubble (2012) *About Me* (available online at: http://www.stylebubble.co.uk/style_bubble/about-me.html).

Tai, S.H.C. (2005) Shopping styles of working Chinese females, *Journal of Retailing and Consumer Services*, 12, 191–203.

Thompson, V. (2012) Need to know: Pinterest, *Retail Week*, 9 March, p. 25.

Tonglet, M. (2002) Consumer misbehaviour: an exploratory study of shoplifting, *Journal of Consumer Behaviour*, 1(4), 336–354.

Underhill, P. (2009) *Why We Buy: The Science of Shopping*, London: Simon and Schuster Paperbacks.

Vlachos, P.A. and Vrechopoulos, A.P. (2012) Consumer-retailer love and attachment: antecedents and personality moderators, *Journal of Retailing and Consumer Services*, 19, 218–228.

Wells, W. and Gubar, G. (1966) Life cycle concepts in marketing research, *Journal of Marketing Research*, November, 355–363.

Yoon, C., Gonzalez, R., Bechara, A., Berns, G.S., Dagher, A.A., Dubé, L., Huettel, S.A., Kable, J.W., Liberzon, I., Plassmann, H., Smidts, A. and Spence, C. (2012) Decision neuroscience and consumer decision making, *Marketing Letters*, 23, 473–485.

Zikmund, W.G. and Babin, B.J. (2010) *Exploring Marketing Research*, International/10th edn, Mason, Ohio: South-Western Cengage.

FURTHER READING

Arnold, M.J. and Reynolds, K.E. (2003) Hedonic shopping motivations, *Journal of Retailing*, 79, 77–95.

Kobrak, H. (2012) How to avoid five common mistakes in market segmentation, *Advertising Age*, 20 February (available online at: adage.com/article/cmo-strategy/avoid-common-mistakes-market-segmentation/232796/).

Puccinelli, N.M., Goodstein, R.C., Grewal, D., Price, R., Raghubir, P. and Stewart, D. (2009) Customer experience management in retailing: understanding the buying process, *Journal of Retailing*, 85(1), 15–30.

Robinson, D. (2014) Web shopping – online stores think local to grow global, *Financial Times*, 25 January 2014 (available online at: http://www.ft.com/cms/s/0/6d338714-84f0-11e3-8968-00144feab7de.html#axzz2ufYYSfur).

Shukla, P., Banerjee, M. and Adidam, P. T. (2013) The moderating influence of socio-demographic factors on the relationship between consumer psychographics and the attitude towards private label brands, *Journal of Consumer Behaviour*, 12(6), 423–435.

Yoon, C., Gonzalez, R., Bechara, A., Berns, G.S., Dagher, A.A., Dubé, L., Huettel, S.A., Kable, J.W., Liberzon, I., Plassmann, H., Smidts, A. and Spence, C. (2012) Decision neuroscience and consumer decision making, *Marketing Letters*, 23, 473–485.

Case study

Targeting the female consumer

Source: with permission from Shutterstock.com/© Art Allianz

For brands seeking to engage with women, the secret is that there really is no secret; the key is simply to know your audience and what it wants. Given that good marketing involves segmentation and targeting, at its worst, it sometimes also becomes about caricature and stereotyping. Nowhere is that more evident than when brands try to engage with women. A lot of this marketing is about pigeonholing: the housewife (recently referred to as 'chief household officers') or 'soccer mom', the urban professional and so on. But more than ever, women don't fit into those neat little niches. Just look at technology. For years it was assumed that being a tech geek was a guy thing, but 65 per cent of women now buy online, and women like Meg Whitman lead huge tech companies such as HP and eBay. Women are becoming what Carol Bekkedahl, senior vice-president, digital sales, at Meredith National Media, calls 'the biggest tech geeks out there'.

In an interview with WARC, Bekkedahl – who publishes the titles *Better Homes & Gardens* and *Ladies' Home Journal* – noted: 'All of the new innovation happening in technology today is supercharged by women's activity. Look at the rise of Pinterest, Instagram, Vine, Snapchat: all fuelled predominantly by women's activity.' So what are the lessons marketers need to learn about female consumers?

Don't fall for the caricature

See them as a whole person. Avoid the tendency in female targeting to pigeonhole people – 'young professional', 'beauty-obsessed' – as people rarely fit neat labels. As with any marketing, you need to have a deep understanding of your audience; spend quality time with them and understand their lives. Don't assume you can target women with a tablet computer or car just by making it pink – the same applies to pens, as Bic discovered when its launch of the 'Cristal for Her' line was met with outrage from Amazon reviewers.

Be honest

In the past, a lot of marketing to women has been about painting a glossed-over picture. Now, however, we are seeing how insight allows marketers to know when and how to be confident and honest in their communication, leading to some great results. Just look at Dove, for one. Similarly, John Frieda blazed a trail by talking openly about hair 'frizz' and Olay no longer avoids the word 'wrinkles'.

Women are social creatures

Whether in online or offline social networks, they both influence and are influenced in turn. Know the neuroscience behind how women think and what drives their behaviour, and understand how to get into those networks of influence. For example, research shows that women remember more than, and in different ways from, men; marketers need to connect to both women's emotional and rational sides, and be very aware of their strong attention to detail.

You don't need to be radical

It's about the right creative and media choices. Fiat's 'Motherhood rap' spread virally online and seems to have rung true with many.

Inform, don't patronise

There are products and services that women undoubtedly will need – for example, a garage or car-dealership network could target single and newly divorced women with a free vehicle-maintenance service – but don't be sexist or patronising.

Women have a lot of money to spend and can be a brand's most loyal and engaged customers, if they are targeted appropriately and relevantly. As with any audience, the key is to know who they really are and what they really want.

Source: Mhairi McEwan, chief executive and co-founder of brand learning, first published in Marketing magazine, 1 March, 2014 (article can be found at: http://www.marketingmagazine.co.uk/article/1283341/secret-engaging-women-theres-no-secret). Reproduced from Marketing magazine with the permission of the copyright owner, Haymarket Media Group limited.

DISCUSSION QUESTIONS

1 Based on reading the article and from examples that you have seen, what problems are created when marketers use stereotyped perceptions of women?

2 Advertisers can also be considered guilty of stereotyping male consumers. What lessons do marketers need to learn about male consumers to avoid this happening? How do these lessons differ from those mentioned in this article about female consumers?

3 What would be your advice for advertisers to enable them to target female consumers effectively, based on the information in this article?

4 Which of the market research methods discussed in this chapter could be used to investigate the shopping behaviour of supermarket customers? From these, select the most suitable market research method for investigating the behaviour of female consumers in a supermarket of your choice.

CHAPTER 4

Retail product and brand management

Learning objectives

The objectives of this chapter are to:

- explain the key functions and processes involved in product management;
- assess the place of product and brand management within the retail marketing mix;
- explain the product development process;
- discuss the main concepts of branding and their application to the retail sector.

Introduction

The purpose of this chapter is to show the reader the significance of effective product and brand management. Selling products is central to retailing and therefore an understanding of the nature of products and brands and the ways in which they are developed is beneficial to those wishing to learn about this sector. Retail organisations very rarely own the factories which manufacture the products that they sell and this chapter explains how retailers work in collaboration with suppliers to develop merchandise to appeal to target consumers. Retailers have two main choices in the branding of their products: to offer an 'own label' which is exclusive to the store (called a 'private brand' in the US) or to sell merchandise from other companies' brands that are also available in competing stores ('manufacturer brands' or 'national brands' in the US). A fundamental component of any brand is its choice of name. Effective brand names are clear, easy to remember, distinctive and can be transferred easily to brand extensions.

New product development

Ferrell and Hartline (2011: 198) state that 'the development and commercialization of new products is a vital part of a firm's efforts to sustain growth and profits over time. The success of new products depends on the product's fit with the firm's strengths and a defined market opportunity'. New Product Development (NPD) refers to the process through which products are designed, prepared and produced prior to becoming commercially available to customers. The stages of the NPD process are outlined here (see also Figure 4.1).

1 **Idea generation** is normally the responsibility of designers but ideas may also be initiated by retail buyers and can be inspired by sources such as research into trends, suppliers, new technical innovations, suggestions from within the retailer and customer feedback.

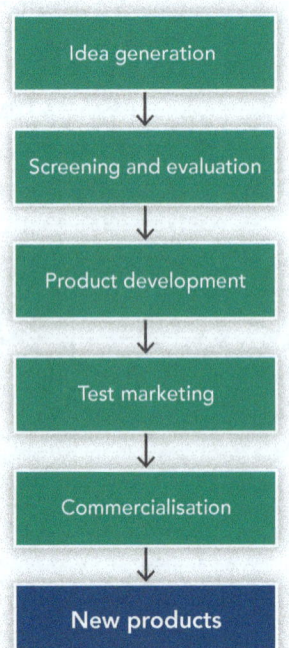

Figure 4.1 The New Product Development (NPD) process
Source: adapted from Jobber, D. (2010) *Principles and Practice of Marketing*, © 2010. Reproduced with the kind permission of McGraw-Hill Education. All rights reserved.

2. **Screening and evaluation** take place so that the numerous ideas generated by designers are filtered down into those with the most potential to meet the retailer's customers' needs. At this stage the ideas probably exist as drawings or computer-aided designs (CAD) produced by designers using software such as SolidWorks or Autodesk. To test their viability and market potential some of the concepts can be made into samples that act as working models, e.g. by manufacturing a one-off prototype or using a 3D printer (see Figure 4.2). Making samples can also assist in estimating the costs and technical requirements involved in manufacturing the item. For own-label merchandise, suppliers can then present these samples to retail buyers (and sometimes designers and merchandisers) so that they can evaluate whether to proceed with manufacturing them in bulk quantities. A business analysis can also be conducted to investigate the commercial viability of the product.

3. **Product development** involves finalising its specifications and a test batch may be produced. For example, a sample of a dress may have been made in a size 12, but garments in the full size range can be constructed and tried on by models at the development stage, to ensure a good fit for final consumers. The plan for the product launch can also be prepared during this phase.

4. **Test marketing** can take various forms. For certain products it can be a trial run, being sold in a small number of the retailer's stores to assess customers' reaction to it. While the advantage of a product trial is that feedback from customers can be acquired before the retailer invests in a large quantity of merchandise, it can delay the full launch of the product to the market and could mean that the retailer misses out on the peak timing for a product trend. Many retailers therefore leave out this stage and go straight to stocking a bulk quantity. Another option for test marketing is to organise a focus group of some of the retailers' customers and ask for their feedback on the product before the order quantities are decided.

5. **Commercialisation** is the stage during which the product is manufactured and becomes available to consumers, usually managed by buyers, merchandisers, technologists and marketers in the retail sector. The product launch may be accompanied by a promotional campaign to create awareness among consumers.

Figure 4.2 Mojo 3D printer from Stratasys
Source: with permission from Stratasys

To assist in the NPD process buyers, merchandisers and other retail employees at management level usually conduct **comparative shopping** trips at regular intervals. These trips are undertaken to observe comparable merchandise sold in the outlets of competing retailers as well as noting price ranges. Comparative shopping may be done informally with a visit to retail outlets in a particular location or viewing competing websites. Sometimes the information can be recorded in a report to distribute among colleagues. (This can also be known as 'competitor shopping' and is often abbreviated to 'comp. shopping'.) Alternatively, retailers can commission a specialist company to produce a comparative shopping report. Its purpose is to analyse how competitors' product and price ranges compare to those sold by a particular retailer, and to enable the buyer to gain a shopping experience from the same perspective as the company's target customers.

Directional shopping is the term used for travelling with the aim of gaining an awareness of future trends for a specific type of merchandise, mainly by viewing products from more expensive trend-setting stores or websites (Goworek, 2006). Buyers may visit cities such as Paris, London and New York, depending on the company's location and travel budget, for directional shopping trips. They can also visit trade fairs in different countries to view manufacturers' or brands' product ranges. Buyers of branded merchandise may make some of their buying decisions at such trade fairs (see Chapter 5 Retail buying and merchandising).

The Product Life Cycle

The Product Life Cycle (PLC) is a classic marketing model and is similar in format to the Retail Life Cycle (see Chapter 2 Retail marketing strategy). The PLC model can help retailers to estimate the life stage and the potential future sales pattern for a particular product by comparing its sales turnover to timespan (see Figure 4.3). The model assumes that products progress from introduction to a phase of sales growth, after which sales reach a plateau at the maturity stage before finally heading into decline. The Marketing Mix can be adapted as the product progresses through the different stages as explained below. However, the PLC is open to criticism as it may not always follow this smooth shape and sales may sometimes begin to decline then take off again, e.g. owing to increased publicity, changes in the weather or season. Seasonal products such as umbrellas, sun cream, Christmas decorations and pumpkins are prone to variations in the standard PLC shape. Furthermore, it is easier to use this model retrospectively as it is very difficult to predict a product's future sales and the length of time that it will spend in each stage. For example, classic products such as Heinz ketchup and Levi's jeans have

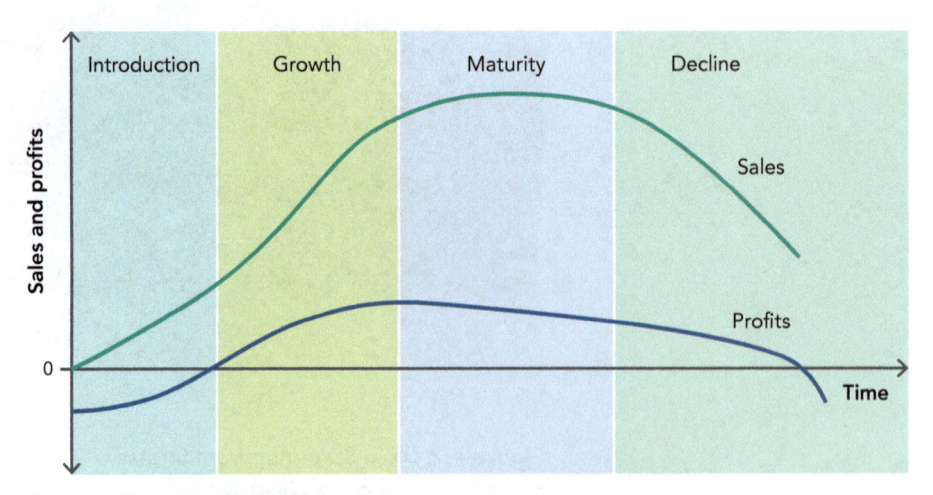

Figure 4.3 Product Life Cycle

Source: adapted from Jobber, D (2010) *Principles and Practice of Marketing*, © 2010. Reproduced with the kind permission of McGraw-Hill Education. All rights reserved.

extensive maturity phases, whereas short-lived fads can be highly popular with a swift growth stage and a sharp decline. Despite this, most retailers will have gained experience of sales patterns with previous products that will make them better able to predict a new product's PLC performance.

Introduction

At the introduction stage a product should usually have a high level of promotion to create awareness of its availability to consumers. The product itself is likely to be an initial, basic version, since it has not yet been tried out in the market and it is as yet unknown whether it is worthwhile financially to develop different versions. Products start out by making a loss in effect, as the NPD costs inevitably have to be paid up front, before the product can be manufactured and launched. The number of retailers distributing the new product is initially limited and it would typically be stocked by relatively expensive stores within the market level. The company that has developed the product needs to recoup the expense of NPD costs and to take advantage of its uniqueness the price of a new product is often fairly expensive (price skimming). Alternatively, a retailer can sell the product at a low price initially to achieve market penetration, which can enable it to move quickly into the growth stage (see Chapter 6 Retail pricing).

Growth

In the growth phase, the quantities of the product sold increase and there is a possibility it may begin to break even, although its success is dependent on various elements of the marketing mix. The level of promotion should be maintained to improve awareness and encourage customers to continue to buy it. With increased demand, distribution channels are likely to widen, with larger chains being able to selling the product at lower prices than in the previous stage. Even with reduced prices, the product may be able to attain a higher profit margin than during the introduction phase, as all or most of the NPD costs may have been covered and due to economies of scale for larger production quantities.

Maturity

The aim in the maturity stage is to maintain sales of the product and to extend this phase as long as reasonably possible. This can be encouraged through reminder advertising, which does need to be as extensive as during the previous two stages. Prices may be lowered to appeal to the mass market and new versions of the product may have been introduced. Competitors may have copied the product at this stage or earlier, and since they didn't need to spend so much time or money on research and development as the original company did, they can possibly sell it at a cheaper price. The company that originated the item therefore needs to compete by differentiating its product from the competition; for example, by offering different colours and materials or new features.

Decline

In the decline stage, sales begin to trail off, as the product may have become obsolete and replaced by newer, more functional or more stylish products. The aim is generally to harvest, i.e. for the retailer to gain a profit on the product while it still can. Sometimes, the product may be reduced in price to remove it from stock quickly before it is completely obsolete. As competitors leave the market whilst the product is in decline, there may be less competition around, allowing the original company to charge more. Once it has reached the decline stage and is in short supply, the exclusivity that this affords a product can rejuvenate interest in it. For example, innovators (see Chapter 3) often use second-hand/vintage stores as a source of inspiration and once they begin to wear these styles the broader population may also adopt the same fashion. In this case, the PLC will take the form of a 'fashion swing' where it moves back into the introduction stage immediately after its decline, sometimes before it has entirely disappeared from the market. For example, records have achieved a revival in recent years after a steep decline, with a resurgence of interest in vinyl that saw sales reach their highest level for 15 years in the UK in 2013, spurred on by the publicity and events associated with 'Record Store Day' (Ahluwalia, 2014). Record players and cassettes still have some demand as many customers have retained record collections with which they have a strong emotional bond as they trace the pathway of their lives, and new equipment may be needed to replace worn-out hi-fi systems. An adaptation to many of the new wave of turntables has allowed them to record music digitally via a USB connection, to make them compatible with contemporary music consumption.

Deciding on the right point at which to reintroduce products after a decline is crucial and they have the advantage of appealing both to customers who have nostalgic memories of them, yet looking novel to younger consumers who may be seeing them for the first time (see Figure 4.4). Offering products inspired by a previous era can be described as

Figure 4.4 In-store display of retrobrand products

Source: with permission from Christina Goworek

retrobranding, defined by Brown *et al.* (2003: 20) as 'the revival or relaunch of a product or service brand from a prior historical period, which is usually but not always updated to contemporary standards of performance, functioning, or taste', seeing retro goods as 'brand-new, old-fashioned offerings'.

PRODUCT TRENDS AND THE DIFFUSION OF INNOVATION
By Carol Cloughton, Senior Lecturer in Marketing, University of Huddersfield

Trend can be defined as the way in which things deviate away from the norm. The focus in retail is on identifying change and how it will affect the mainstream (Vejlgaard, 2008), how this will reflect in the attitudes and behaviours of consumers and how you effectively predict and apply these changes in time for the mainstream in a particular market sector (Higham, 2009). Trend identification and implementation offers opportunities for retailers to not only develop new products, but to adapt existing products, develop new sales and communication channels or even refocus their service offers in line with the changing nature of their target market. Vejlgaard (2008: 7) states that 'a trend is not something that *has* happened, but rather a *prediction* of something that is *going to* happen in a certain way – specifically, something that will be accepted by the average person'.

How new ideas and products shift through society was the basis of the Diffusion of Innovations (Rogers, 1962). The four main elements of the diffusion process as defined by Rogers (2003: 11) follow the stages, '(1) an *innovation* (2) is *communicated* through certain *channels* (3) *over time* (4) among the members of a *social system*'. Critically it's important to understand that if an idea is new to an individual, it is classed as an innovation (*ibid.*). His work on diffusion is at the core of diffusion theory and discussion. Since the first edition in 1962, the number of publications about the topic rose from 405 to an estimated 5,200 by 2003 when the fifth edition was launched (Rogers, 2003). Studies on trends have been conducted in the fields of rural sociology, medical sociology, education, anthropology, geography, communication and marketing (Kinnunen, 1996). The mapping of a trend therefore has been accepted in many disciplines, and Rogers's outline of typologies is utilised today in areas of marketing.

There are triggers that alter attitudes towards past or present behaviours, and there are certain types of individuals that are likely to respond to these changes ahead of others. The types of adopters Rogers identified were Innovators, Early Adopters, Early Majority, Late Majority and Laggards and the influence that each typology had on the other. Rogers defined Innovators as venturesome individuals who look for ideas outside of the local peer network and are likely to communicate with other innovators in varied geographical distances and are critical in launching an idea into the community. Early Adopters are respected and well integrated within a social system, held in high esteem which they maintain by introducing and evaluating new ideas. The Early Majority deliberate and the Late Majority are sceptical and rely on the reassurances given to them by others that the new idea adheres to social norms. Laggards have traditional values so only accept an idea that has previously been accepted by the majority (Rogers, 2003).

Trends are driven by changes in the market environment that affect the attitudes and behaviours of consumers. Shifts in the socio-cultural, economic, political and technological environment initiate trends, and it's these changes that will impact on the consumers. Mapping the shifts in the market environment helps to identify whether the consumer will or will not adapt or react to their influence in the social context in which they live. Although it is recognised that anticipating and effectively implementing trends in industry sectors is difficult to anticipate due to the unpredictability of the macro environment (Higham, 2009; Vejlgaard, 2008), this is nonetheless the route that the trend forecaster must take. Critically, for a trend to be worthy of investment in any industry sector, particularly if the investment in resources is significant, the trend must have a long-term benefit for the consumer groups who are, or will be, adopting the trend. Not only is the nature of the new idea or product key, but how the individuals contribute to the diffusion process is also important. Spatial proximity plays a significant role, but the value of the innovation is paramount so must be considered against their economic situation, personal characteristics and position within the community or culture the individual is part of (Wejnert, 2002). We have developed a large, complex communication network system. The spread of the internet in particular has resulted in greater opportunities for influence as it reduces the spatial distance between influencers and their potential audience. This can enhance the diffusion process as it provides a much wider spread of influence sources on the adoption rate.

Early adopters are the peers in a social system whose subjective evaluations will influence the decision-making process through either planned or spontaneous spreading of the new idea (Rogers, 2003). It is their influence that ensures a new idea or product is introduced to the mainstream market; the early and late majority. These opinion leaders have a network of connections through which the ideas are communicated. Gladwell (2002) provided analysis of the 'tipping point', the point where an idea, change in social behaviour or even a product becomes a social epidemic. That is, it becomes of value to the majority. For these social epidemics to succeed, he identified a process that facilitated change: the Law of the Few, the Stickiness Factor and the Power of Context. 'Stickiness' is defined as a concept that has been so effectively communicated that it is at the forefront of the mind. The Law of the Few refers to influencers that utilise their social networks to transfer their views. The first is a Connector who has extensive social connections both outside and inside their own communities, Mavens provide knowledge-based evaluations of the idea to inform and persuade and are key in word-of-mouth communication, and Salesmen are persuaders utilising psychological subtleties to inform. They are also high in social ranking within societies. These are Rogers's (2003) early adopters and are defined as the opinion leaders within a community by Gladwell (2002: 203) as they are the change agents that communicate the idea: '[w]hat Mavens and Connectors and Salesmen do to an idea in order to make it contagious is to alter it in such a way that extraneous details are dropped and others are exaggerated so that the message itself comes to acquire a deeper meaning . . . he or she has to find some person or some means to translate the message of the Innovators into something the rest of us can understand'.

Both Higham (2009) and Vejlgaard (2008) recognise that opinion leaders affect the adoption of an idea or product into the mainstream, however Vejlgaard recognises that it isn't necessarily the influence of opinion leaders that can affect the rate of adoption in a society, as alongside this there has to be an available mass within that society that are ready to be influenced. As Higham (2009: 163) states: 'For a trend to be broadly accepted it should be compatible with consumers' current practices, cultural beliefs and value systems.' The core of marketing is the customer, so trend analysis has to be from their perspective with a commercial outcome within a mainstream retail environment. Higham (2009) divides why a trend can be driven from one adopter typology to another into two variables, the active and passive drivers. Active drivers are the qualities the innovation has. Simplicity has aided the adoption of technology and Higham cites the iPod as an example. Previous MP3 models were available, but did not have the simple functions that Apple offered. Visibility from one adopter group to the other will speed the rate of the adoption as well as the number of adoptions. Beauty and fashion-related products fall into this category. Less visible products such as interiors and even personal financial products have a lower communication rate alongside limited visibility to the individuals in a society so this will impede the speed of the adoption process as well as the number of adopters (Higham, 2009).

References

Gladwell, M. (2002) *The Tipping Point: How Little Things Can Make a Big Difference*, 1st edn, London: Abacus.

Higham, W. (2009) *The Next Big Thing*, 1st edn, London: Kogan Page.

Kinnunen, J. (1996) Gabriel Tarde as a founding father of innovation diffusion research, *Acta Sociologica*, 39(4), 431–442.

Rogers, M.R. (1962) *Diffusion of Innovations*, 1st edn, London: Free Press.

Rogers, M.R. (2003) *Diffusion of Innovations*, 5th edn, London: Free Press.

Vejlgaard, H. (2008) *Anatomy of a Trend*, 1st edn, New York: McGraw-Hill.

Wejnert, B. (2002) Integrating models of diffusion of innovations: a conceptual framework, *Annual Review of Sociology*, 28, 297–326.

Retail product assortment

Retailers can offer a 'narrow and deep' or 'broad and shallow' **product assortment**, which should be consistent with the rest of the company's marketing strategy. In the UK, a narrow and deep buying policy usually refers to buying a product assortment with a relatively small number of product lines in high volume, which minimises the amount of time spent on the development of different products for own-label buyers (Goworek, 2007). As this method is usually more cost-effective, it can lead to higher profits for the companies involved and/or lower prices for the store's customers. A 'broad and shallow' policy means offering a wide selection of product lines in limited quantities. The products could possibly cost more than in other retailers but the customer is offered a wider choice of products within the store (Varley, 2006). Retailers with a **scrambled assortment** of merchandise offer a selection of unrelated products, such as UK store chain The Range and Spanish retailer Ale-Hop. Retailers need to make decisions about the number of product lines offered to the consumer and the volume in which they are available. However, Hart and Rafiq (2006: 342) note the inconsistent and often ambiguous interpretation of the term 'assortment' within a retail context and they therefore propose that width should be defined as 'the number of departments or extent of different product classifications offered by the retailer' and that breadth is 'the number of product lines carried within a category' while depth is 'the number of product lines carried within a category'.

MINI CASE STUDY
An original approach to product assortment: Skandium

Source: with permission from Christina Schmidt, Skandium

London-based multichannel retailer Skandium has a varied product assortment that includes furniture, homeware, books, jewellery, watches and toys, with a unifying theme of Scandinavian modernism. Skandium was founded in 1998, opening the first store in 1999 and trades today from three stores and a shop-in-shop in Selfridges, as well as its website. The company's retail mix prioritises a discerning selection of products and strong customer service. Christina Schmidt, one of the company's three Scandinavian founders, explains the background to this unique retail concept:

> The whole concept was built from a one-bed flat in London. We saw the new Iittala table-top concept when visiting Finland in summer 1998. Kitchen and table-top items from old designs, and new editions showcasing the epitome of modernism, very functional and timeless, so we said 'Let's build a company around this idea of functionalism, including heritage and new designs. Let's do the Finns, Swedes and Danes, a collective concept'. So the direction was clear from the start, giving us a portfolio of credentials. There are so many masters in the Scandinavian school of modernism, Alvar and Aino Aalto, Arne Jacobsen, Hans Wegner, Kaj Frank, Tapio Wirkkala, Eero Saarinen and so many more. We brought them together and my partner came up with the name to give it a Scandinavian connotation.

Source: with permission from Christina Schmidt, Skandium

The whole idea of Skandium was to make it feel like a candy store . . . timeless design made 'juicy' – mixing old with new to emphasise even more on the adequacy of good design which, when executed well, is absolutely timeless.

Christina still cites good country stores selling organic produce and a brand such as Paul Smith as some of her favourite ways of retailing. She also points out that Habitat and the Conran shop were important having studied their history well. Skandium is the UK agent for some of the milestone-setting brands such as Iittala, Marimekko, Fritz Hansen, Louise Poulsen and many, many more, offering a wide selection of Scandinavian brands. Besides this, Skandium produces its own portfolio of furniture and table-top ware, with their chest of drawer series manufactured by East London furnishing company Isokon Plus. All timeless, well manufactured and always relevant.

In addition to offering a unique product assortment, providing exceptional customer service is another important component of Skandium's strategy. Christina feels that the most important element in retailing is 'to make the customer feel included' and she goes on to say '. . . good retail is to be in the DNA of the presentation, when you step through the door you get a rush of excitement . . . retail is theatre and if it's a good play on stage you'll be part of the fantasy'. Skandium's staff are from 14 different countries and Christina encourages them to engage in conversation with the customers rather than just saying 'Yes, madam'. Christina says 'the days are over where people just leave their money and when employers dish out jobs. Everyone on the shop floor needs to add something through their personality. I want good "tennis partners" to the customer on the shop floor, otherwise it does not serve the customer, nor feed the business. There is a high demand on our store crews who need to be able to memorise and handle the content of over 280 brands, not anything for the faint hearted . . .'. Christina is inspired by Pret A Manger, who she says 'set the standard for good retail', and she adopts their principle of employing staff who 'give their whole heart'.

Interview with Christina Schmidt; www.skandium.com

The product/service continuum

As there is not always a distinct line between products and services, it is better to consider them as being placed on a continuum with a pure product at one end, through to a pure service at the other. However, even a relatively pure product contains an element of service, in that a company or farm has provided the product either to a retailer or directly to the customer. Examples on this continuum can be seen in Figure 4.5. Food that has some element of preparation that saves the customer time and effort begins to move away from being solely a product. In the middle of the continuum is a service that leaves the customer with part of a physical product, e.g. fabric in the case of furniture re-upholstery, although the cost is likely to relate mostly towards the service that has been provided. With takeaway food, the service usually forms an even more significant part of the cost. Hairdressing is very much a service but it may also include some tangible elements such as product applied to customers' hair or sold on the premises. At the far end of the spectrum are pure services, usually provided by a specially trained individual, for example a fitness trainer or lecturer. Although the pure service is intangible the customer may sometimes be provided with a tangible product, such as an exercise plan or lecture handouts. It is not possible to locate all retailers on a specific part of the goods/services

Figure 4.5 The physical product/service continuum

[Basic provisions, e.g. bread, milk] → [Chilled or frozen ready meals] → [Furniture re-upholstery] → [Takeaway food] → [Hairdressing] → [Fitness trainer]

continuum, as this depends to some extent on the products they sell and the customer service they offer. For example, most stores are self-service nowadays and would therefore tend to be positioned towards the left-hand side, by supplying products with an element of service, whereas more traditional-style stores with a high level of customer service would be located towards the right, without going so far as being a pure service.

Brand management

Retail brands are often managed by employees within the retailer's marketing department. They are usually responsible for ensuring that the brand identity is used consistently and effectively throughout the company on products, packaging, stores or websites, catalogues or brochures and all forms of marketing communications. Brands that sell to retailers also generally have marketing departments which often employ people in the role of brand manager, being responsible for groups of products under the same brand. For example, French parent company L'Óreal employs brand managers to oversee its various brands such as Redken and Lancôme. Branding can be difficult to define as various authors have different opinions and brands can be viewed from the very different perspectives of companies, consumers and legislation. Branding can form a strong connection between product and marketing communications, since the brand logo can often promote the product whilst simultaneously forming part of the product through its label or packaging.

The main challenge for brand managers is to generate and maintain brand awareness amongst consumers, which can be accomplished largely through devising and implementing an appropriate marketing communications strategy (see Chapter 7 Retail marketing communications). Aaker (1991) proposes four levels of brand awareness.

1 Being unaware of a brand.
2 **Brand recognition**, where the consumer will remember the brand if prompted.
3 **Brand recall**, where the consumer remembers the brand unprompted.
4 Top of the mind.

Stage 4 would be the optimal position for a brand or retailer, where the consumer feels an emotional attachment and may exhibit strong brand loyalty or store loyalty. This is demonstrated by classic and enduring labels such as Fred Perry, Converse and Dr Martens being linked with various youth subcultures where the brand forms an integral or even essential component of participants' image and lifestyle. When brands reach stages 3 and 4 they essentially become part of the consumer's evoked set; that is, the options which they immediately recall when making purchase decisions, thus giving these brands a higher chance of being bought (see Chapter 3 Retail consumer behaviour and market segmentation). Brands that elicit a high level of both love and respect are referred to as 'lovemarks' by Kevin Roberts, CEO of Saatchi and Saatchi Ideas Company. Roberts (2006) believes that mystery, sensuality and intimacy are the qualities that set lovemarks apart from mere brands, citing Mac, Diesel, Crayola and Nutella as examples. However, the fourth stage of top of the mind recall is likely to apply only to a minority of consumers. It is therefore more realistic for marketers who work either for retailers or brands to develop marketing communications that aim mainly to convert consumers from stage 1 to 2 or from 2 to 3. Brands can also be managed at a higher, corporate level, when the parent company seeks to promote the corporate brand to stakeholders such as the media or shareholders, rather than consumers. **Corporate branding** also incorporates aspects such as employer branding, which seeks to portray a positive image of the company with the aim of recruiting strong job candidates, especially graduates. The applicants themselves can also engage in personal branding, promoting themselves as brands in relation to their careers, through their reputation and CV content. Conversely, internal branding promotes the company to existing employees, mainly via internal communications and training, thus helping to achieve the organisation's goals.

Brand names

While the choice of a brand name may be viewed as fairly important, the name itself is not the most significant element of branding. As Gilbert (2003: 318) states:

> A name cannot make or break a retailer or company. What matters is how well a retailer's stores, merchandise or services meet its customers' needs . . . The choice of a name is only one part of the overall company strategy that has to be backed up by a sophisticated and cohesive branding programme.

Traditionally, retailers often used family names for businesses (see Chaplin's case study in Chapter 1 Introduction to retail marketing management) and a person's name can still evoke a sense of a traditional company, even when the person is fictitious, e.g. Ted Baker and Jack Wills. Retailers' brand names can sometimes be abstract terms, which can make them unique and more memorable. Brand names can use relevant descriptive terms, such as JD Sports or Oak Furniture Land. FMCG's often use abstract names that are sometimes variations on real words; for example, Ariel. Words in another language are often seen as adding glamour or luxury to a brand, e.g. English retailer Marks & Spencer uses the Italian term for its subbrand Per Una whereas French retailer Monoprix calls its own-label beauty products Miss Helen. The use of a different country's alphabet can also create associations in consumers' minds between the brand and another region (see Superdry case study below). Promoting the product or retailer's country of origin can form part of an aspect of marketing known as 'place branding' or, on a larger scale 'nation branding' (Kavaratzis, 2005). Subbrands are used by retailers to give different identities to some of their product ranges, often when they are aimed at different target customers. Subbrands may retain the main brand name as a prefix or suffix, e.g. George at Asda. Subbrands can also be used to identify different levels of supermarkets' price architecture, e.g. Morrisons supermarkets use the Value brand to identify their cheapest product range.

Descriptive brand names can help them to be memorable and applicable to their product ranges, such as British Home Stores (BHS) and Jamie's Italian. However, it is important that they don't become dated or restrict the retailer's image to a particular product type, e.g. Carphone Warehouse, which appears to be ready for a new brand name. Alliteration and phonetics are some of the techniques that can be used to make brand names easier to memorise. Abbreviations and acronyms such as B&Q and Asos (formerly As Seen On Screen) can also improve memorability owing to their brevity. Fashion designers often use their initials to label their diffusion ranges (i.e. cheaper than their standard runway collections) such as CK (Calvin Klein) and DKNY (Donna Karan New York). Puns and other humorous forms of wordplay can be used by retailers to gain attention, e.g. sandwich shop Subway and hairdresser Cut & Dried have dual meanings, but it is obviously advisable to use puns with caution!

Brand identity and brand image

Kapferer (2008: 171) indicates the central role played by brand identity when he states that 'a brand is not the name of a product. It is the vision that drives the creation of product and services under that name. That vision, the key belief of the brand and its core value is called identity'. Brand identity is managed by the sender in the form of messages transmitted via the marketing mix which are subsequently received by consumers and interpreted as brand image (Kapferer, 2008). Therefore, while retailers and brands are responsible for establishing and projecting their brand identity, they do not have control over brand image, since it exists in the minds of their customers. Brand personality is a term used to represent the characteristics (e.g. fun, lively, stylish, reliable, etc.) that we perceive a brand to possess and it therefore forms a key component of brand image. Brands and their products can be copied illegally by counterfeiters which can lead to a dilution of brand image. Brands are usually registered as Trade Marks to prevent counterfeiting from happening and to enable them to take legal action if it does. Copycat brands seek to benefit from association with an established brand's identity. While it may have a different name, similarities in design and packaging can imply to customers that a copycat product has the same qualities as the original brand. Similarly, stores targeting the same market sector can adopt copycat names, such as Poundland and Poundworld, thus giving them very similar brand images.

Brand equity

Brand equity is the value of a brand to a company and its stakeholders, described by Ferrell and Hartline (2011: 204) as 'the marketing and financial value associated with a brand's position in the marketplace'. While equity implies financial assets, and profitability is indeed one of its key elements, brand equity goes beyond this to incorporate the loyalty and recognition that the brand engenders. People trust familiar brands in a similar way to trusting people whom they have known a long time. This familiarity can lead to a sense of comfort and emotional attachment that means consumers often opt to purchase a recognised brand over a cheaper, less familiar one, even when the generic product is essentially the same. For example, Tate & Lyle sugar and Saxa salt are still strong brands despite the availability of much cheaper competing products from supermarket own-labels. However, brands cannot be complacent, since customers can be tempted towards retailers' own-label products with factors such as substantial price savings or more convenience. Tate & Lyle illustrated the financial value that famous brands can attain when its sugar business was sold in 2010 to a US company for £211 million, with the right to use the brand name on its sugar products. American Sugar Refining's co-president Luis Fernandez said: 'Tate & Lyle is steeped in 130 years of tradition and consumer loyalty. We recognise the importance and history of the Tate & Lyle sugar brand and are proud to add it to our existing brand portfolio' (BBC, 2010). Retailers that sell few or no own-label products generate brand equity from the national brands that they sell and the choice of these brands therefore plays a crucial part in the image that they portray to their consumers. Lowering prices substantially can attract higher numbers of customers initially, but ultimately this strategy may devalue a retail brand and harm it in the longer term.

Brand extensions

Brand extensions afford retailers and brands the opportunity to exploit the brand equity in their existing products by applying the same brand name to a new product category. Brand extensions can therefore achieve growth for the brand by providing more goods to existing customers or by reaching new customers. Advantages of brand extensions are that there is existing public awareness of the brand name, thus potentially reducing promotional costs (Gilbert, 2003). A line extension occurs when the brand adds another product to one of its existing categories, such as Sainsbury's offering an additional flavour of potato crisps. However, when Sainsbury's first began to sell own-label crisps, this could have been considered a brand extension. The brand extension may sometimes be given its own subbrand, e.g. on the Sony PlayStation, Nintendo Wii and Microsoft Xbox, the parent brands are not emphasised, even though they are long-established and famous names. The more novel names of the consoles stand out to their target consumers, who are typically younger than those who buy the parent brands.

Brand extensions are usually carried out in a closely related area, such as the trend for ice cream versions of confectionery brands. However, when brands extend into very different fields this is known as brand stretching. For example, Virgin originally started as a music retailer and record label in the 1970s and subsequently extended into many areas, including retail ventures such as 'Virgin Brides' (wedding dresses) and 'Virgin Vie' (make-up and toiletries), though it is now most famous for its airline and media divisions. Fashion brands are well known for brand extensions that maximise the potential profitability of strong brand equity by applying their names to related product categories such as accessories and perfumes. The high costs associated with catwalk shows can result in fashion brands having low profits, but this can be offset by a brand extension which is more affordable to a larger number of consumers and that does not require investment in a fashion show.

A designer–retailer collaboration is a form of brand extension that is exclusive to the retail sector. Debenhams department store was a UK pioneer of such collaborations and at the time of writing offers womenswear collections in collaboration with 16 well-known ready-to-wear designers, including Jasper Conran, Betty Jackson, John Rocha and Matthew Williamson. The fashion designer offers adapted versions of clothing in his or her signature style that the retailer can sell much more cheaply than the designer's catwalk range, but at a higher price than the retailer's own label. The relatively low price of the garments is due largely to economies of scale due to fairly high quantities being manufactured by the retailer's suppliers, usually in more cost-effective materials than the designer's own range.

Retailers can decide not to use brand extensions, usually when they choose to expand into a more expensive market, preferring instead to expand by opening new divisions of the company that give them a fresh brand image that customers do not associate with the cheaper prices of the parent organisation. For example, Spanish company Inditex, the world's largest clothing retailer, has a portfolio of retail brands including 'Massimo Dutti' and 'Pull & Bear' that are more expensive than their more famous sister company Zara. Similarly, the second largest fashion retailer, Stockholm-based H&M, has recently opened more upmarket store chains '& Other Stories', 'Cos' and 'Cheap Monday' that consumers may not realise are part of the H&M group (Milne, 2014).

Retail brand positioning – perceptual maps

Brand positioning aims to locate a brand in a particular place in comparison to its competitors, in the mind of the consumer. Retailers can use a positioning map such as Figure 4.6, where the circles represent different retailers. In this case, one axis reflects price and the other quality, thus a high price, high quality retailer such as Harrods would be placed in the top right-hand quadrant if this map was applied to the department store sector. A positioning map can be applied to product brands, retailers or their subbrands. This can also be known as a **perceptual map** because it is based on consumers' perceptions. Retailers' marketing departments can produce positioning maps or they may commission agencies such as Retailmap which conducts research for retailers including Boots, Debenhams, Gap and River Island (Retailmap, 2014). A map can be composed from the retailer's own view of where it stands in the market or it can be collated more formally, and probably more accurately, by conducting market research to seek customers' perspectives on its market position.

RETAIL BRAND POSITIONING – PERCEPTUAL MAPS

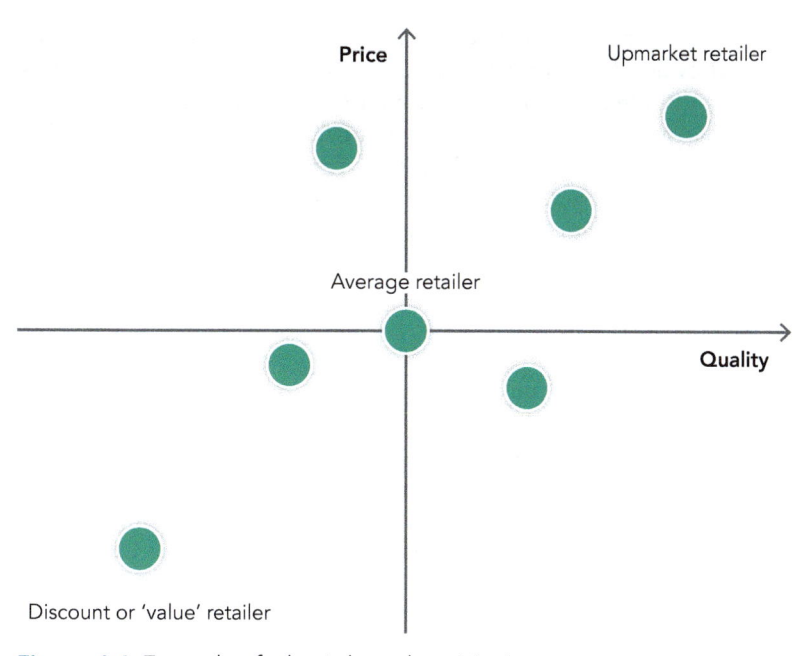

Figure 4.6 Example of a basic brand positioning map

When assessing a whole sector, as in the example in Figure 4.7, the retailer or brand perceived to be the average in the sector can be located in a central position. If the positioning map has been commissioned for a specific retailer, this retailer can be placed centrally, with its closest competitors arranged in appropriate positions around it (illustrated by the circles in Figure 4.7). This gives the retailer the opportunity to see whether it is positioned too closely to a competitor or whether there is a gap in the market. For either of these reasons, the retailer may aim to reposition itself. If a retailer is positioned very near to its competitors, it may be that the retailer is not sufficiently differentiated from

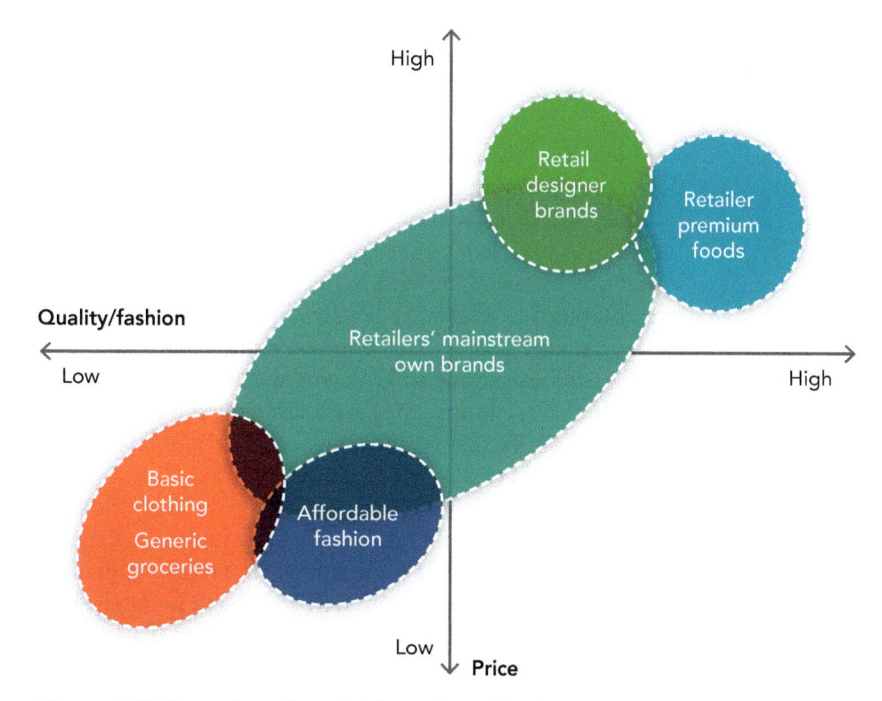

Figure 4.7 Examples of retailer brand positioning

Source: adapted from McGoldrick, P. (2002) *Retail Marketing*, 2nd edn © 2002. Reproduced with the kind permission of McGraw-Hill Education. All rights reserved.

other stores, leading to confusion for consumers, who may consequently choose to shop elsewhere for similar products. To add another dimension to a positioning map, the dots can be altered in size to indicate the size of market share for each company. A further dimension can be added by showing the map as a 3D cube, with an additional axis running from front to back. Parent companies with a portfolio of brands can use positioning maps to assess the market positions of their brands to ensure that they do not compete too closely with each other and to check whether any repositioning is required.

Rebranding

Brand names can be changed when companies decide to undergo rebranding, e.g. due to mergers and acquisitions. Rebranding can also be used to avoid negative connotations, with Kentucky Fried Chicken now being referred to as KFC. Similarly, Pizza Hut temporarily changed the name of some of its branches to Pasta Hut in 2008 to increase awareness of the introduction of more pasta dishes to its menu (Bailey, 2008). This formed part of a revamp costing £18 million, illustrating the potentially costly nature of rebranding, which can come under criticism from the media and consumers. A change of name can clearly pose other risks to a retailer because recognition and awareness of the company which may have been built up over many years can be lost. Elements of the original name can sometimes be retained to avoid this issue, e.g. former competitors Premier Lodge and Travel Inn combined to form the Premier Travel Inn hotel chain, which is now known as Premier Inn. Fashion retailer Chelsea Girl rebranded itself as River Island in the 1980s, to progress from its image as a 1960s boutique, thereby facilitating its expansion into the menswear market and later, the introduction of childrenswear. The company more recently drew on its brand heritage by using Chelsea Girl as a womenswear subbrand, consisting of garment designs from its archive which had become fashionable again. Rather than undergoing a complete rebrand a brand can be updated without changing its name, to refresh its image with the aim of increasing its sales and/or changing its brand positioning. This can range from an almost imperceptible amendment to the brand's font through to the introduction of new products or a complete redesign.

Branded and own-label merchandise

Retailers have the choice of offering products which carry another company's brand, developing own-label merchandise or, in some cases, retailers sell a combination of branded and own-label merchandise. For example, department store House of Fraser mainly sells branded products but it also offers clothing and homeware under the 'Linea' brand which is exclusive to its outlets and is developed by its in-house staff in conjunction with suppliers. Retailers that sell branded merchandise select finalised products from other companies sold under branded names that are trademarks of the brand/supplier, rather than bearing the shop's own label. Levy and Weitz (2012: 342) describe national (manufacturer) brands as being 'designed, produced, and marketed by a vendor and sold to many different retailers', whereas private-label (store) brands are developed by a retailer and sold exclusively in that retailer's outlets.

Many retailers that sell branded goods are independent retailers, for whom developing an own brand would not be viable, owing to the expense of developing the products and the inability to meet minimum manufacturing quantities, which would usually be too large for them to accommodate in a small number of stores. Department stores frequently sell branded goods, even if they are part of a national chain, as by definition they sell a wide variety of product types and working with many different brands enables them to do this. Although branded products are referred to in various texts as 'manufacturer brands' in many cases, companies supplying branded ranges concentrate on design, sales and promotion/advertising, subcontracting the production to manufacturers, often based overseas, as is the case with many renowned brands. Products can be selected from branded ranges by attending trade exhibitions, visiting brands' showrooms (i.e. stores that are only open to trade customers) and meetings with sales representatives for the brands at the retailer's office. Retail sales figures for branded merchandise can be influenced by several factors which are controlled by the brand, such as advertising and promotion campaigns and the brand's quality of service and delivery (Goworek, 2007). The provision of a promotional campaign by the brand can be beneficial to retailers by boosting sales of branded products that they sell. However, a disadvantage is that the retailer holds no sway over the content and media involved in the brand's marketing communications.

Many large retail chains sell own-label merchandise either under the retailer's name or a label exclusive to the retailer. Certain retailers sell various different own-labels that are subbrands, e.g. Sainsbury's Taste the Difference or Marks & Spencer Blue Harbour, or names that have no direct connection to the retailer's name, e.g. Papaya garments sold by Matalan. Own-labels are available in most market sectors and are usually sold alongside manufacturer brands, for example in supermarkets. Buyers for own-label retailers usually collaborate with suppliers in the product development process and the retailer therefore exerts an influence on the appearance and function of the products. Price ranges of own-label products can vary, but they are often 20–40 per cent cheaper than well-known manufacturer brands (McGoldrick, 2002). There is a trend towards retailers offering their own subbrands to appeal to different market segments. For example, Asda supermarkets offer essential grocery items at low prices under the 'Smart Price' label, standard products with the Asda label and more expensive products under the 'Extra Special' label. The logos and packaging for each of these labels are designed to be compatible with their price levels.

Branded products are normally more expensive than own-label products, sometimes owing in part to the use of better design and materials. However, branded products also have a higher price largely because there is an extended supply chain and at least three companies need to generate a profit from the products, i.e. the retailer, the branded company and the manufacturer. Retailers' own-label ranges are generally sold for lower prices, yet are often more profitable for them than selling branded merchandise, because only retailers and manufacturers profit from them and promotional costs are generally minimal. However, own-label ranges involve more time and expense for product development by the retailer's staff, in collaboration with suppliers.

INTERNAL BRAND COMMITMENT WITHIN COLLABORATIVE INDEPENDENT RETAIL NETWORKS

By Edmund O'Callaghan, Head of Department of Retail Management Studies, Dublin Institute of Technology

Internal **brand commitment** has been defined as 'the extent of psychological attachment of employees to a brand, which influences their willingness to exert extra effort towards reaching the brand's goals' (Burmann et al., 2009b: 266). The development of internal brand commitment could be regarded as a seminal activity for corporate brand building in retailing, given its potential to enhance business performance. The formation of Collaborative Independent Retail Networks (CIRNs) involves a group of independent retailers co-operating together under one corporate banner for mutual market advantage, and has been significant as a survival strategy for independent retailers in recent years. At a minimum, these CIRNs have enabled independent retailers to achieve competitive parity with the more powerful national and international multiple operators in terms of pricing and product offer. Examples of CIRNs operating in the Irish market are shown in the table below.

Table 4.1 Independent retail networks within the Irish retail sector 2011

Retail corporate brand	Collaborative network of . . .	Retail sector
Musgrave Retail Partners (SuperValu Centra, Day Break & Day Today)	Approx 800 independent retailers	Supermarkets/Convenience stores
Spar/Eurospar	Approx 452 independent retailers	Supermarkets/Convenience stores
Londis/Londis Top Shop	Approx 360 independent retailers	Supermarkets/Convenience stores
Topaz	Over 300 independent retailers	Petrol forecourt
Mace (BWG)	Approx 230 independent retailers	Supermarkets/Convenience stores
Gala	Approx 200 independent retailers	Convenience stores
Topline Hardware	100 independent retailers	Hardware
Costcutter	Approx 65 independent retailers	Convenience stores
Expert	56 independent retailers	Electrical
Euronics	47 independent retailers	Electrical
Arro Home & Garden	39 independent retailers	Hardware/Garden centre
Property Partners	38 independent retailers	Property
Toymaster	35 independent retailers	Toys
Carry Out	34 independent retailers	Off licences
Albany Home Décor	23 independent retailers	Home improvement
World of Wonder	22 independent retailers	Toys

Source: compiled by author from company websites

From a conceptual point of view, these inter-organisational relationships require an interpretation that goes beyond the transactional and rational financial lens of a supplier–retailer relationship (Coase, 1992) with an emphasis on contractual terms, to a relational interpretation, based on commitment, social exchange and organisational identification (Hunt and Morgan, 1994; Morgan and Hunt, 1994). Although the concept of commitment has been viewed as a multidimensional construct, there is little empirical evidence to validate this conceptualisation. In general, three dominant dimensions of commitment are thought to exist: affective, normative and calculative commitment. Affective commitment is linked to an individual's emotional attachment and refers to a desire to remain with an organisation. Normative commitment refers to feelings of obligation or duty, whereas calculative commitment refers to commitment that emerges from an exchange where one party offers something of value to the relationship in exchange for the promise of consistent future behaviour. A study of owner–managers within a CIRN within the Republic of Ireland found evidence of internal brand commitment as a multidimensional construct. The study concluded that, whereas calculative commitment builds organisational commitment, internal brand commitment requires an affective dimension that leads to what can be interpreted as brand citizenship behaviour (Burmann and Zeplin, 2005; Burmann et al., 2009b, Burmann et al., 2009a).

Management implications

Management need to develop strategies to move owner–managers along the relational continuum, and away from a purely transactional view of the relationship. While economic benefits build organisational commitment, and sound business rationale for network membership is always necessary, internal brand building cannot take place within this purely transactional context. After all, the owner–manager is sacrificing complete autonomy in decision making for the benefits of network membership. Management should continually formulate strategies for the development of affective commitment within a collaborative network, the key to internal brand commitment. Normative commitment is more likely to develop between owner–managers because of informal sharing of information, rather than a perceived need to reciprocate the benefits experienced as a result of network membership.

This study won the prize for best paper at the EAERCD conference in Valencia, 2013.

References

Burmann, C. and Zeplin, S. (2005) Building brand commitment: a behavioural approach to internal brand management, *Journal of Brand Management*, 12(4), 279–300.

Burmann, C., Jost-Benz, M. and Riley, N. (2009a) Towards an identity-based brand equity model, *Journal of Business Research*, (62), 390–397.

Burmann, C., Zeplin, S. and Riley, N. (2009b) Key determinants of internal brand management success: an exploratory empirical analysis, *Journal of Brand Management*, 16, 264–284.

Coase, R.H. (1992) The institutional structure of production, *American Economic Review*, 82(4), 713–719.

Hunt, S.D. and Morgan, R.M. (1994) Organizational commitment: one of many commitments or key mediating construct?, *Academy of Management Journal*, 37(6), 1568–1587.

Morgan, R.M. and Hunt, S.D. (1994) The commitment-trust theory of relationship marketing, *Journal of Marketing*, 58(3), 20–38.

RETAIL MARKETING CAREERS
Kelly Molson, Managing Director of a design agency

Kelly Molson, Managing Director of creative agency Rubber Cheese
Source: photograph with permission from Kelly Molson

Kelly Molson is Managing Director of Rubber Cheese, a creative agency working via digital, mobile, social and traditional channels. Kelly and co-founder Paul Wright (her business partner and Creative Director) launched the company in 2002. Kelly began her design career after gaining a BTEC National Diploma in Graphic Design. She worked as a designer for an advertising agency, a print studio and then a packaging company where she worked on point-of-sale items and packaging design for retailers including House of Fraser, Paperchase, BHS and Faith Shoes. Next, Kelly worked for a promotions company designing wine and champagne labels before moving to an ecommerce firm where she designed online shops. Kelly and Paul founded their company at a time when they both felt frustrated in their current job roles and wanted more client interaction and responsibility.

Kelly describes her main responsibility as 'managing the company and employees, ensuring the smooth day-to-day running of the company! It's a relatively small agency so I also share a lot of new business responsibility and account management with my business partner. I meet with clients to understand their requirements and develop specifications for projects'. She decided to take a step back from designing around five years ago to concentrate on running the business, although

Packaging design by Kelly Molson's company, Rubber Cheese.

Source: photograph with permission from Chaucer Foods Ltd

she is still involved with the creative process as she takes briefings from clients, who are mainly retailers, restaurants and food or drink brands seeking graphic or web design input. Kelly enjoys meeting new people and helping to solve problems, so she considers the excitement of a new client meeting as the best part of the job. She says 'I love the ongoing relationships we build with our existing clients and suppliers . . . However, I find the financials difficult as it's not my core skill, so we have support from people that can!'

Kelly works closely with her team, especially Paul, and she helps him to plan the workloads for their designer, Rachael, and their developer, Liam. Kelly also manages Trudy, their Marketing Assistant, who works mainly on sales with their clients. Externally, Kelly liaises with a wide range of suppliers from printers, developers and **search engine optimisation (SEO)** specialists to exhibition designers that she can call on when needed. She says that teamwork is especially key in a small team, with the team members being located near each other in the studio. Kelly says 'it's important we are all able to talk openly as we brainstorm ideas regularly, and everyone will have the opportunity to put ideas forward . . . clear communication skills are key to any project, for the team and for the client. It's the difference between a project succeeding or failing'. Planning and organisation are also important to the team so they have planning meetings twice a week and each have shared online calendars to be able to plan their workload efficiently. Creativity, self-motivation and computer skills are also key within the team.

Kelly considers 'attention to detail, an eagerness to learn, a personable outlook and a creative portfolio' to be the main qualities needed by designers. She considers qualifications to be less important than ability and personality. Despite having been accepted to study a university Higher National Diploma course, Kelly chose not to continue study at that point and went into full-time employment instead, as at that time having a degree wasn't a necessity for a junior designer role. She says 'Personally, I still don't think it should be. We've never employed people based on their qualifications, more on whether they have the practical skills required, the personality fit for us and our clients and the eagerness to learn'. Kelly believes that designers should immerse themselves in different aspects of design as things can change quickly, so it's important for them to keep up-to-date. To illustrate this, Kelly began her career as a print designer and now 70 per cent of the projects that her company takes on are digital.

www.rubbercheese.com; https://twitter.com/TheChiefCheese; https://twitter.com/RubberCheese

CHAPTER SUMMARY

Products are central to the marketing mix of the retailer and are usually purchased from suppliers and manufacturers, rather than being produced by retail companies. In the retail sector, products and brands are managed jointly by designers, buyers, merchandisers, technologists, marketers and brand managers. The key models that relate to retail product management are described below.

- New Product Development (NPD) is the process of generating and developing product concepts in preparation for production.
- The Product Life Cycle (PLC) proposes that products usually pass through the stages of introduction, growth, maturity and decline. Many products are revived after the decline stage, often in an updated form.
- The Product/Service continuum shows that there is not always a clear distinction between products and services and most retailers fall somewhere in between, as they usually offer both.

Brand management seeks to create and maintain brand awareness, largely through effective management of the different elements of the marketing mix, particularly promotional strategies. The following aspects of branding need to be considered by brand managers.

- Retailers can choose to sell products from other brands, their own-label products or a combination of both.
- Brand name is a significant component of brand identity and subbrands may also be used to signify a retailer's product offering for different target customers or price ranges.
- Brand identity is projected by companies but brand image reflects consumer's perspectives on the brand.
- Brand equity is the value of a brand to its stakeholders, going beyond financial worth to incorporate value created by brand loyalty and goodwill towards the company.
- Rebranding can be used to update or refresh brand identity.

EXERCISES AND QUESTIONS

1. Consider two different retailers of your choice, one that has a 'narrow and deep' assortment and another with a 'broad and shallow' product assortment. Write down the reasons why you believe the stores have selected these different types of product assortment. These reasons are likely to relate to their target customers, product sectors, price ranges, store size and locations, amongst other factors.

2. Select at least five stores or services from a shopping centre. Where would you position them relative to each other on the product/service continuum?

3. Compare the advantages and disadvantages for retailers and consumers of offering:
   - own-label products;
   - ranges of merchandise from other companies.

4. Based on relevant information in this chapter, generate ideas for brand names for either a small delicatessen or independent clothing retailer. Select the name that you think is most appropriate and select a suitable font for the brand name from the choices in Microsoft Word or other sources.

5. Many retailers now offer own-label subbrands (e.g. Aldi and Tesco) which do not feature the retailer's name prominently. What are the advantages of adopting this strategy?

6. For a retailer of your choice draw a positioning map with the retailer placed centrally and six or more competitors positioned around it. Use price on one axis and another relevant dimension on the other, such as product quality, service quality or fashionability. Use the map to assess who are the two closest competitors for your chosen retailer.

7. Read the following essay by Robert Kozinets and name at least three retailers or brands that engage in retrobranding: spreadablemedia.org/essays/kozinets/#.U9kgRhsg_IU
In what ways does retrobranding appeal to consumers?

REFERENCES

Aaker, D.A. (1991) *Managing Brand Equity*, San Francisco: Free Press.

Ahluwalia (2014) Vinyl to get you into the investment groove, *The Times*, 12 April (available online at: http://www.thetimes.co.uk/tto/money/article4061128.ece).

Bailey, C. (2008) Pizza Hut to become Pasta Hut, *Daily Telegraph*, 6 October 2008 (available online at: http://www.telegraph.co.uk/news/uknews/3145545/Pizza-Hut-to-become-Pasta-Hut.html).

BBC (2010) Tate & Lyle sells sugar arm to American Sugar Refining, *BBC Business News* 1 July (available online at: http://www.bbc.co.uk/news/10472258).

Brown, S., Kozinets, R.V. and Sherry, J.F. (2003) Sell me the old, old story: retromarketing management and the art of brand revival, *Journal of Customer Behavior*, 2, 85–98.

Ferrell, O.C. and Hartline, M.D. (2011) *Marketing Management Strategies*, International/5th edn, South-Western Cengage Learning.

Gilbert, D. (2003) *Retail Marketing Management*, 2nd edn, Harlow: FT Prentice Hall.

Gladwell, M. (2000) *The Tipping Point: How Little Things Can Make a Big Difference*, New York: Little, Brown.

Goworek, H. (2006) *Careers in Fashion and Textiles*, Oxford: Blackwell Publishing.

Goworek, H. (2007) *Fashion Buying*, 2nd edn, Oxford: Blackwell Publishing.

Hart, C. and Rafiq, M. (2006) The dimensions of assortment: a proposed hierarchy of assortment decision making, *International Review of Retail, Distribution and Consumer Research*, 16(3), 333–351.

Jobber, D. (2010) *Principles and Practice of Marketing*, 6th edn, Maidenhead: McGraw-Hill.

Kapferer, J.N. (2008) *The New Strategic Brand Management*, 4th edn, London: Kogan Page.

Kavaratzis, M. (2005) Place branding: a review of trends and conceptual models, *Marketing Review*, 5, 329–342.

Levy, M. and Weitz, B.A. (2012) *Retailing Management*, 8th edn, New York: McGraw-Hill Irwin.

McGoldrick, P. (2002) *Retail Marketing*, Maidenhead: McGraw-Hill.

Milne, R. (2014) H&M steps up pace of online plans, *Financial Times*, 18 June (available online at: http://www.ft.com/cms/s/0/ac28e976-f6b7-11e3-b271-00144feabdc0.html).

Retailmap (2014) *Associated Services* (available online at: http://www.retailmap.com/en/associated-services/).

Roberts, K. (2006) *The Love Marks Effect: Winning in the Consumer Revolution*, New York: PowerHouse Books.

Varley, R. (2006) *Retail Product Management*, 2nd edn, London: Routledge.

FURTHER READING

Alexander, N. and Colgate, M. (2005) Customers' responses to retail brand extensions, *Journal of Marketing Management*, 21(3–4), 393–419.

Anselmsson, J. and Johansson, U. (2013) Manufacturer brands versus private brands: Hoch's strategic framework and the Swedish food retail sector, *International Review of Retail, Distribution and Consumer Research*, 24(2), 186–212.

Bridson, K., Evans, J., Mavondo, F. and Minkiewicz, J. (2013) Retail brand orientation, positional advantage and organisational performance, *International Review of Retail, Distribution and Consumer Research*, 23(3), 245–264.

Calderwood, E. and Freathy, P. (2014) Rebranding a federation: insights from the UK co-operative movement, *Journal of Marketing Management*, 30(1–2), 90–116.

Chen, C.M., Chou, S.Y., Hsiao, L. and Wu, I.H. (2009) Private labels and new product development, *Marketing Letters*, 20(3), 227–243.

Gil-Saura, I., Ruiz-Molina, M.E., Michel, G. and Corraliza-Zapata, A. (2013) Retail brand equity: a model based on its effects, *International Review of Retail, Distribution and Consumer Research*, 23(2), 111–136.

Keller, K.L., Aperia, T. and Georgson, M. (2011) *Strategic Brand Management: A European perspective*, London: Financial Times/Prentice Hall.

Madhavaram, S., Badrinarayanan, V. and McDonald, R.E. (2005) Integrated marketing communication (IMC) and brand identity as critical components of brand equity strategy: a conceptual framework and research propositions, *Journal of Advertising*, 34(4), 69–80.

Martos-Partal, M. and Gonzaléz-Benito, Ó. (2011) Store brand and store loyalty: the moderating role of store brand positioning, *Marketing Letters*, 22(3), 297–313.

Varley, R. (2014) *Retail Product Management*, 3rd edn, London: Routledge.

Wheeler, A. (2012) *Designing Brand Identity: An essential guide for the whole branding team*, 4th edn, Hoboken, NJ: John Wiley and Sons.

Wood, L. (2004) Dimensions of brand purchasing behaviour: consumers in the 18–24 age group, *Journal of Consumer Behaviour*, 4(1), 9–24.

Design Week

Drapers

Journal of Brand Management

Journal of Product and Brand Management

You are recommended to visit the Design Museum and the Museum of Brands, Packaging and Advertising in London in person or online at: designmuseum.org and www.museumofbrands.com

Case study

GLOBAL brands – ups and downs: Consumers luxuriate in shopping on the web

By Louise Lucas

The companies whose brand values rose the most in the 2013 BrandZ rankings are all about the fun things in life: designer outfits, cheap and cheerful fashion, beer, shops and movies.

Leading the catwalk is Prada, the Italian luxury designer that was founded in 1913 and listed on the Hong Kong stock exchange in June 2011 – to join L'Occitane and Samsonite in tapping Asian investor demand for well-known Western consumer brands with a convincing China growth strategy.

Milan-based Prada raised $2.14bn when it became the first luxury brand to list in Hong Kong. Fast forward nearly two years and its brand value has pirouetted 63 per cent in the past year to $9.4bn, just ahead of the 61 per cent leap posted by Brazilian beer Brahma.

Peter Walshe, global director of BrandZ, dubs Prada "exclusivity that travels": strong brand management that it has successfully transported to the likes of China and Latin America.

Far from diluting the brand with lower price offerings, such as perfumes, it has opened entry points along the chain "allowing different people access without having to dilute the brand too much".

The same applies to Gucci, Prada's luxury fashion house stable mate, which saw its brand rise 48 per cent to $12.7bn. Gucci also holds the title of highest brand contribution in the category – as opposed to the financial component of the brand valuation. Alongside Burberry, it has the category's highest growing brand contribution. "Gucci is exceptionally good at retaining the classic look but adding the modern touch, which is what Coca-Cola does so well", says Robin Headlee, vice president for Europe at Millward Brown. "They are keeping it modern but keeping the craftsmanship and doing a lot digitally: 13 per cent of online sales come from its mobile platform".

Digital sales are blossoming in importance, for all the fancy sleek glass stores that dot the most chic streets of Shanghai, Tokyo and Paris. The trick, says Mr Walshe, is to recreate the luxury experience of super-smart stores online – and not just on bigger screens, but also on mobiles as a lot of sales are generated via phone handsets.

Steve Wilkinson, head of consumer products at Ernst & Young in the UK, says social media has created a win-win for the luxury and apparel sectors.

"Brand owners, on the one hand, are able to get more feedback from consumers more quickly, while the most loyal consumers are able to get more engaged with the apparel and luxury lifestyle, on the other", he says,

"This interaction may be nothing new, but social media have made this interaction much more frequent, and ultimately richer".

Perhaps no one platform sums up that interaction so well as eBay, where shoppers and sellers come together and buying entails more than a single click – and can, indeed, include anxious moments crouched over the computer or phone to see if you have won your quarry.

Ebay's brand value rose 40 per cent over the year, ranking it the 11th biggest riser with a brand value of $17.7bn. This put it on a par with Disney, valued at $23.9bn.

In between luxury experiences and bidding came the High Street fashion stores. The number three big riser, Zara, was up 60 per cent at $20.2bn. As a result, the Spanish fashion house has overtaken sportswear group Nike as number one in the apparel rankings. Behind it was Calvin Klein, up 52 per cent at $1.8bn.

"Zara is relevant because it is affordable fashion, being delivered very quickly and then expanding that into the wider regions", says Mr Walshe, "It's a good example of a company investing in the brand and exporting that difference to relevant segments and markets".

Also highlighting a bigger theme is the ascent of Amazon, the online retailer, which rose 34 per cent to $45.7bn, overtaking the far less virtual Walmart: a classic tale of clicks winning out over bricks.

"We saw bricks suffering but now there is the advance of the clicks" says Mr Walshe, "but also Amazon has been more fleet of foot and maybe it is easier [to move from online to physical than vice versa] because it does not already have existing infrastructure, so can create something more cost efficient in the first place".

It is the first time such a gap has opened up between Amazon and Walmart.

At $9bn, that gap is the equivalent of Aldi – the German discount store whose brand value has slipped lower even as its popularity with Europe's cash-strapped shoppers surges – that is wedged between them.

Brandz Rankings: Customer research and financial analysis produce a unique result

The BrandZ valuation methodology, used to calculate the Top 100 Global Brands, combines extensive and continuing consumer research with rigorous financial analysis. BrandZ is distinguished from other brand rankings because of the way it obtains consumer viewpoints.

WPP's BrandZ is the world's largest repository of brand equity data. Worldwide, in-depth quantitative consumer research is conducted to build-up a global picture of brands on a category-by-category and country-by-country basis.

This research covers two million consumers and more than 10,000 different brands in over 30 countries. This in-market consumer research differentiates the BrandZ methodology from valuations that rely only on a panel of "experts" or purely financial and market desk research.

Before reviewing the details of the BrandZ ranking methodology, it is worth considering these three fundamental questions: why is brand important? Why is brand valuation important? How does BrandZ work as a valuation tool?

Table 4.2 Top 10 global brands 2013

Ranking	Brand
1	Apple
2	Google
3	IBM
4	McDonald's
5	Coca-Cola
6	AT&T
7	Microsoft
8	Marlboro
9	Visa
10	China Mobile

Source: BrandZ Top 100 (available online at: www.wpp.com/wpp/marketing/brandz/brandz-2013/)

Brands provide clarity and guidance for choices made by companies, consumers, investors and other stakeholders. They embody a core promise of values and benefits consistently delivered and provide the signposts needed to make decisions.

At the heart of a brand's value is its ability to appeal to relevant and potential customers. BrandZ measures this appeal and validates it against actual sales performance. Brands that succeed in creating the greatest attraction power are those that are:

Meaningful. In any category, these brands appeal more, generate greater "love" and meet expectations and needs.

Different. These brands are unique in a positive way and "set the trends", staying ahead of the curve for the benefit of the consumer.

Salient. They come spontaneously to mind as the brand of choice for key needs.

Brand valuation is a metric that quantifies the worth of these powerful but intangible corporate assets. It enables brand owners, the investment community and others to evaluate and compare brands and make faster and better-informed decisions.

BrandZ is the only brand valuation tool that peels away all of the components of brand value and gets to the core – how much brand alone contributes to corporate value. This core, what Millward Brown Optimor, who create the ranking, call brand contribution, differentiates BrandZ. The brand value is calculated in three steps.

*First, calculating financial value. This starts with the corporation. In some cases, a corporation owns only one brand. All corporate earnings come from that brand. In other cases, a corporation owns many brands. The earnings of the corporation need to be apportioned across a portfolio of brands.

Financial information from annual reports and other sources, such as Kantar Worldpanel and Kantar Retail, is analysed to ensure the correct portion of corporate earnings is attributed to each brand.

This analysis yields a metric called the attribution rate. Corporate earnings are multiplied by the attribution rate to arrive at branded earnings, the amount of corporate earnings attributed to a particular brand. If the attribution rate of a brand is 50 per cent, for example, then half the corporate earnings are identified as coming from that brand.

What happened in the past or even today is less important than future earnings. Predicting these requires adding another component to the formula. This component, the brand multiple, assesses future earnings' prospects as a multiple of current earnings. It is similar to the calculation used by financial analysts to determine the market value of stocks.

Information supplied by Bloomberg data is used to calculate a brand multiple. Branded earnings are multiplied by the brand multiple to arrive at financial value.

*Second, calculating brand contribution. This reveals the branded business as a proportion of the total value of the corporation. To arrive at brand value, a few more layers need to be removed, such as the rational factors that influence the value of the branded business, for example, price, convenience, availability and distribution.

Because a brand exists in the mind of the consumer, the brand's uniqueness and its ability to stand out from the crowd, generate desire and cultivate loyalty that have to be assessed.

This unique factor is called brand contribution and is provided by the BrandZ study.

*Third, calculating brand value. The Financial Value is multiplied by brand contribution, which is expressed as a percentage of financial value. The result is brand value.

Brand value is the dollar amount a brand contributes to the overall value of a corporation. Isolating and measuring this intangible asset reveals an additional source of shareholder value that otherwise would not exist.

FT *Source*: Lucas, L. (2013) Global brands – ups and downs: Consumers luxuriate in shopping on the web, *Financial Times*, 21 May. © The Financial Times Limited 2013. All Rights Reserved

DISCUSSION QUESTIONS

1. Consider how brand value has been calculated in the case. What are the potential difficulties of assessing brand value by this method? Suggest other potential ways in which brand value can be analysed.

2. What are the key factors needed for a brand to have high attraction power, according to the article? What other factors do you consider to be important in this respect? Use examples of successful brands to support your answer.

3. Download the BrandZ Top 100 report for 2014 at www.wpp.com/wpp/marketing/brandz/, or for a more recent year. Compare the top 10 brands in it with those from the 2013 top 10 and assess the PEST factors that may have been responsible for any changes that you see, i.e. brands moving up, down or out of the top 10.

CHAPTER 5

Retail buying and merchandising

Learning objectives

The objectives of this chapter are to:

- assess the scope of buying and merchandising;
- explain the different stages of the buying cycle;
- outline the processes involved in the selection, development, ordering and monitoring of retail merchandise;
- discuss the issues involved in supply chain management for retailing.

Introduction

This chapter explains how buying and merchandising work together to acquire the merchandise which is so fundamental to the performance of the retail organisation. Retail buyers are responsible for overseeing the selection of merchandise of appropriate quality and style, aimed at specific types of customer and price brackets and they therefore perform a central role in retail product management and pricing. McGoldrick (2002: 279) stresses the importance of buying in the retail organisation when he states: 'Buying represents the translation of a retailer's strategic positioning statement into the overall assortment and the specific products to support that statement. The retail buyer therefore holds a pivotal role in the implementation of retail strategy . . . '. Retail merchandisers play an equally significant part in the retailer's performance, as they are responsible for managing the processes that enable the products selected by the buying team to arrive on time in the right quantities in the correct locations. **Retail buying** is a form of **organisational buyer behaviour (OBB)**, as distinct from consumer buyer behaviour. However, it differs from OBB in that retailing operates in a business-to-consumer (B2C) capacity, rather than being a solely **business-to-business (B2B)** operation. As retailing is a service industry, retailers purchase completed products to sell to consumers, rather than buying components for use in production (Johansson, 2001).

While OBB is covered in depth in academic literature, there are far fewer studies about retail buying and merchandising, despite the significance of this function to the retail sector (McGoldrick, 2002). Kline and Wagner (1994) point out that retail buyers are located in a different position within the distribution channel to industrial buyers, between suppliers and consumers, rather than between component suppliers and manufacturers or retailers. Therefore, the retail buyer often requires awareness of consumer demand more than technical knowledge. Overall, the aim of buying and merchandising (B&M) teams is to maximise the profitability of retailers, by collaborating with their colleagues and suppliers to meet customers' needs.

Buying and merchandising roles

The retail buying and merchandising literature is somewhat fragmented and with a lack of contemporary research in this field it can therefore be difficult to build up a picture of the diverse responsibilities of these roles. Most journal articles on retail buying either focus on small components of the job, such as decision-making variables (Kline and Wagner, 1994) or explore associated topics, e.g. the recruitment of buying staff (Draper, 1994; Faes *et al*., 2001). Studies by Fairhurst and Fiorito (1990) and Swindley (1992) provide holistic views of the buyer's role in the US and UK respectively, but there is currently a gap in the literature for an overview of how retail buying operates contemporarily. Recent books on retail buying mainly adopt a US perspective of this function (e.g. Clodfelter, 2008; Diamond and Pintel, 2005) which is useful to know, but which may not apply to every part of the world. Some of the books on retail marketing omit to mention retail buying and merchandising (e.g. Gilbert, 2003) but others include chapters which give valuable insights into this function by making connections between various academic studies (e.g. Dawson *et al*., 2008; McGoldrick, 2002; Levy and Weitz, 2012).

Methods of buying and merchandising products for retailers can vary between different companies and market sectors. Buyers of branded products select from finalised ranges of merchandise whereas buyers of own-label ranges develop products in collaboration with their suppliers (see Chapter 4 Retail product and brand management). In a small company buyers and merchandisers may be responsible for selecting a wide range of product types and these functions may be combined with a sales role. Large retailers usually have separate

B&M departments for different product types, such as homeware or fashion. The terminology used for the buying role can vary. For example, in the UK, buyers may be known as selectors or product developers in certain companies (Goworek, 2007), whereas they are called merchandise buyers in the US, according to the National Retail Federation (Berman and Evans, 2010). Retail buying requires a blend of creative and commercial knowledge and Jane Shepherdson, CEO of womenswear retailer Whistles and former Brand Director of Topshop, describes the buyer's role as 'a combination of being creative and taking big risks with sometimes huge amounts of money involved' (Goworek, 2007), whereas River Island buyer Helen Fahy describes retail buying as 'developing a well-balanced and profitable range . . . ensuring that developments are right for the customer' (Goworek, 2006).

B&M departments plan, select, order and monitor the progress along the supply chain of the ranges of products sold by the retailer. To achieve this, they frequently work together, as well as liaising with colleagues internally and suppliers externally. In the case of own-label ranges, buyers may also participate in product development alongside suppliers (see below). Selecting and negotiating with suppliers are core responsibilities in retail buying and management of the supply chain and product distribution are central to the merchandising role. It is important for buyers and merchandisers to collaborate with their suppliers for their mutual benefit. Consequently, buying and merchandising often involve more travel than most other retailing jobs, mainly to visit suppliers. Additionally, market awareness and commercial/financial awareness were found to be among the most important characteristics of retail buyers in a survey by Swindley (1992). Retail B&M teams may collaborate with various internal departments internally, to facilitate the purchase, development and sales of product ranges, which may include in-house design; quality; marketing; store management; visual merchandising; finance; imports/exports; publications and legal departments. This may depend to some extent on the size of the company, as larger retailers tend to have a broader range of specialist departments.

Centralised and decentralised buying

In larger retail chains it is standard practice for B&M teams to be centralised in a department based at the retailer's Head Office, with responsibility for buying subdivided into sections by product type. Fenwick, a UK chain of 11 department stores, is an exception to this in that it operates decentralised buying, thus enabling buyers in each branch to make merchandise selections tailored to the needs of customers in their particular city (see Figure 5.1). However, as a chain store, Fenwick can still benefit from the economies of scale offered by purchasing certain products in bulk for all of its stores. Certain retailers have centralised B&M that is located on a different site from the Head Office, with the advantages of proximity to the distribution centre, usually based in the Midlands, and to take advantage of cheaper office space away from major cities. For example, some of the major supermarkets locate their clothing B&M divisions separately from Head Office, such as 'George Clothing' for Asda and 'Nutmeg' childrenswear for Morrisons, both of which are based in Leicestershire whereas their Head Offices are in Yorkshire. Another way to take advantage of **centralised buying** is through selecting goods from retail buying groups known as 'symbol groups' as they incorporate the group's symbol on the store fascia. While retaining their independence, small retailers can benefit from the bulk buying power of symbol groups that have international recognition, offering own-label products and support such as management training, in exchange for an agreed payment. For example, both Spar (groceries) and Euronics (electronics) are available in 30 countries, giving them very effective economies of scale and UK-based symbol groups Numark chemists, Londis and Mace can also offer competitively priced products to independent stores. Associated Independent Stores (AIS) is another UK organisation that offers its members the opportunity to purchase its own-label fashion and homewares, as well as branded products.

Figure 5.1 Fenwick department store in Newcastle
Source: Nick Bagnall

Organisational buying theories

Models of organisational buyer decision-making (OBDM) are relevant to the retail buying decision process, even though they are largely based on research in B2B markets, rather than retailing, and were written quite some time ago. Webster and Wind (1972: 31) researched into various aspects of OBB and consequently devised the organisational decision process, which comprises the following stages:

1 identification of need;
2 establishing objectives and specifications;
3 identifying buying alternatives;
4 evaluating alternative buying actions;
5 selecting the supplier.

These five stages can be applied to buying in almost any industry and this model is therefore still in use today. It is possible to apply this decision-making framework in many situations but some of the stages may be left out for routine purchases such as rebuying basic products that do not require new specifications. However, Webster and Wind's model finishes without referring to crucial decisions made by retail buyers after the supplier selection stage, which can impact upon product quality and design. Additionally, retailing has been affected substantially by changes in society and technology in recent decades and the model therefore has the potential to be expanded upon and adapted, to be applied more directly to contemporary retail scenarios. Webster and Wind (1972: 12) proposed that their model could 'help the marketer to analyse available information about the market and to identify the need for additional information' as well as 'aid in the design of marketing strategy'. Similarly, the **buying cycle** model (see later in Figure 5.4) can be used to assist in designing buying strategy in the context of a retailer's marketing strategy.

Organisational buying decisions are frequently joint decisions, influenced by people playing various roles, a concept which has also been applied to consumer decision-making (see Chapter 3 Retail consumer behaviour and market segmentation). However, since organisational buying decisions are generally more complex and time-consuming, they are more likely to be influenced by a larger group of people than consumer decisions. The group of people influencing the organisational buying decision is referred to as the Decision Making Unit (DMU) and the group members were allocated the following roles by Webster and Wind (1972):

- Influencers
- Gatekeepers
- Deciders
- Buyers
- Users.

The role of initiator was later added for those who take the lead in the purchasing process (Bonoma, 1982). (You will notice that most of these terms have also been applied to consumer buying behaviour – see Chapter 3 Retail consumer behaviour and market segmentation.) In a retailing context, merchandisers usually initiate buying for a large retailer by making an initial plan to specify the products that need to be bought, in addition to acting as influencers of the buying decision. Suppliers can also act as influencers, as they can offer the retailer a variety of products from which to select. Gatekeepers, such as administrators within the buying team, are those who have the authority to grant suppliers access to buyers. Retail buyers take the central role of deciders in the DMU, typically at an experienced buyer or senior buyer level, with buyers at a junior level more likely to be influencers. In large retailers buyers and merchandisers may engage in the preparatory work in selecting products, but the final purchase decision is often taken by a committee that also includes technologists and senior managers or directors. The DMU buyer role is normally taken by retail buyers and/or merchandisers, with buyers deciding on the design and specification of products and either buyers or merchandisers being responsible for completing orders and contracts for suppliers.

In B2B markets the 'user' role applies to people within the organisation who use the products within the business as part of their role. However, when products are bought for resale the users, i.e. consumers, are outside the organisation, so only the initiator; influencer; gatekeeper; decider and buyer roles are relevant to retailers in this context. Nevertheless, retailers act in the same way as B2B purchasers to a certain extent, when they buy items that are solely for use in the business, rather than for resale. This can include items such as uniforms and card payment machines where the users are the retailers' employees. Products to be used within the company are usually selected by a department known as 'purchasing' or 'procurement', rather than being the responsibility of the retailers' buying teams (Buchanan, 2008). The procurement department is able to contribute to the retailer's profitability by selecting products of the right price and quality to enable the company to function efficiently and effectively.

Buying branded and 'designer' merchandise

Retailers that sell products from branded or designer ranges (see Chapter 4 Retail product and brand management) are often independent retailers or department stores, e.g. Debenhams in the UK and Åhléns in Sweden and Norway. Buyers for small independent retailers often have the opportunity to meet their customers directly by spending some of their work schedule selling in the store, thus giving the retail buyers an advantage when selecting merchandise for their market segment. Independent chains with two or more outlets may employ specialist buyers to cater for the company's different branches, e.g. the owner of footwear retailer Tin Fish acts as buyer for the company's two stores and its website (Goworek, 2007). Retail buyers of branded ranges can select their merchandise from representatives of the brand through various methods of interaction, such as visiting showrooms or exhibitions (see Figure 5.2), or meetings at the retailer's premises. At the luxury end of fashion retailing, buyers can sometimes be invited to select products at

Figure 5.2 The Premium and Green Showroom womenswear trade fairs take place during Berlin Fashion Week

Source: authors' own photographs of Berlin Fashion Week and designer Katharina Kaiser

fashion shows, followed up by meetings to view the products more closely and to specify quantities. Luxury brands often limit the number of retailers that are permitted to stock their ranges to maintain an exclusive brand image.

Trade exhibitions for specific product types often take place either annually or twice per year, allowing buyers to select new suppliers and products from a wide range of brands in their product sector. These exhibitions or trade fairs are often listed in trade journals, trade websites or the venues' websites and they are not usually open to the general public. Entry to the exhibitions is often for a nominal charge on production of a business card or free if booked in advance, as they are funded by the exhibitors who wish to promote their products to buyers. Sometimes trade fairs featuring major brands will even be selective about which retailers they permit to enter, with the aim of preventing new product concepts being leaked or copied. UK trade fairs take place at locations such as Olympia in London and the National Exhibition Centre (NEC) in Birmingham, enabling buyers to select products from international brands without the expense of travelling overseas. Trade shows often take place for more than one day and directories of the show are good sources of new suppliers to follow up afterwards. Examples of trade fairs are given in Table 5.1.

Buying own-label merchandise

Many multiple retailers sell own-label merchandise and their buying teams participate in the development of these ranges. The role of the own-label buyer has many similarities with that of the buyer for branded products. However, buying own-label merchandise involves collaboration in the product development process, making decisions about the form and content of the products prior to manufacture, whereas for branded products, the brand makes these decisions (Goworek, 2010). Own-label buyers are therefore involved in making decisions about the merchandise they buy at an earlier stage than their counterparts for branded products. Furthermore, own-label buyers usually have little involvement, if any, in monitoring deliveries and **stock control** of their products. Thus they tend to relinquish responsibility for decision-making about the range once production has been completed and quality approved, handing over control of the products to their merchandising colleagues during the trading period. The typical differences between own-label and branded product buying roles are shown on either side of Figure 5.3, with the commonalities between them being listed in the central area, based on research into buyers of clothing and accessories in various price brackets.

An experienced own-label buyer conducts a wide variety of tasks in conjunction with internal colleagues and external suppliers. Department stores and various other retail chains may have a team of buyers who purchase own-label merchandise and another group to buy branded goods. Occasionally a buyer could be responsible for buying a mix of branded and own-label products. Retail buyers' involvement in product development for

Table 5.1 A selection of European trade fairs for branded merchandise

Trade fair	Product types	Location	Timing
Spring Fair	Gifts and homeware	Birmingham	February
Maison & Objet	Interiors and homeware	Paris	January and September
Pure Womenswear	Contemporary womenswear, accessories and footwear	London	February and August
Pitti Immagine Uomo	Menswear	Florence	January and June
Pitti Immagine Bimbo	Childrenswear	Florence	January and July

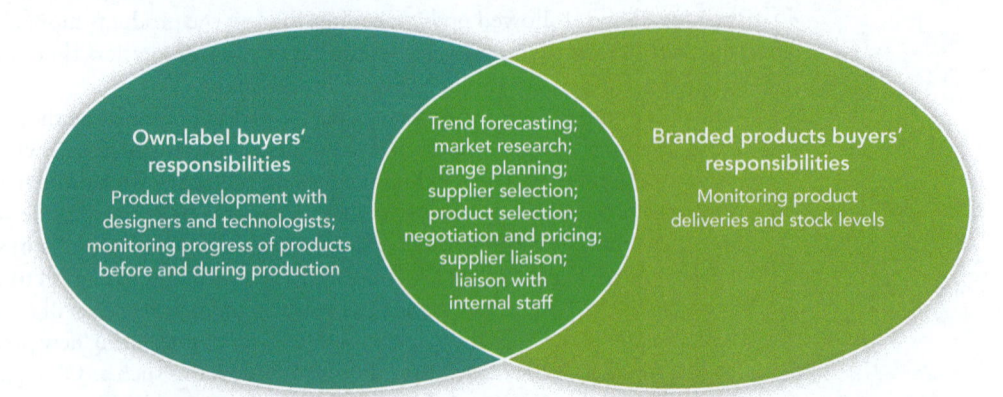

Figure 5.3 A comparison between own-label buyers' and branded product buyers' responsibilities
Source: adapted from Goworek, 2014

- Own-label buyers' responsibilities: Product development with designers and technologists; monitoring progress of products before and during production
- Shared: Trend forecasting; market research; range planning; supplier selection; product selection; negotiation and pricing; supplier liaison; liaison with internal staff
- Branded products buyers' responsibilities: Monitoring product deliveries and stock levels

own-label products can vary, depending on the retailer's buying policy, the buyer's level of seniority and the buyer's experience, e.g. a design-related qualification may enable the buyer to have a strong influence on the design of the merchandise. A study by Johansson and Burt (2004: 801) compared buying for own-label and manufacturer brands in the UK, Sweden and Italy, finding that 'private brands must engage in activities which are traditionally the domain of the manufacturer' and that '. . . involvement in private brands will mean that the buying process will be more extended, in terms of the tasks and activities performed and managed, and therefore more complex than that for manufacturer brands'.

Suppliers frequently employ their own product developers or designers and they may therefore have a lot of input into the design of own-label products. A designer employed by a supplier may work on only one or two retailers' accounts and therefore behave virtually as though they work for the retailer, despite the salary and design studio being paid for by the supplier. Since a supplier would very rarely be owned by the retailer it supplies, as it is usually a separate firm, it is important to build a level of trust between the two companies, since the supplier is also likely to be providing design ideas for competitors. Alternatively, retailers can employ their own in-house design teams, who may design some or all of the retailer's own-label products, though this is not always necessary for own-label retailers, as they can rely on this facility from their suppliers. It is not essential for own-label retail buyers to have design training, but they need to be creative and gain some awareness of the technical aspects of their products to know the scope for design. Retail buyers are likely to be involved in making decisions about features of the products such as styling, colour, materials and proportions, in collaboration with designers and technologists who specialise either in fabrics or garments. Buyers may go on directional shopping visits for inspiration when developing new ranges, sometimes alongside designers from the retailer or its suppliers (see Chapter 4 Retail product and brand management).

The retail buying cycle

The buying cycle is the term used by many UK retailers for the key events and processes that the buyers carry out in order to select a product range (Goworek, 2007). Figure 5.4 summarises the main events in the buying cycle chronologically. Not every retailer uses the buying cycle in exactly this format but it is intended to be applicable to many different retail companies and it is likely that in even the smallest retailer many of the stages will be relevant. The length of the buying cycle differs between companies and product types, but it could vary from a matter of days to more than a year from reviewing current

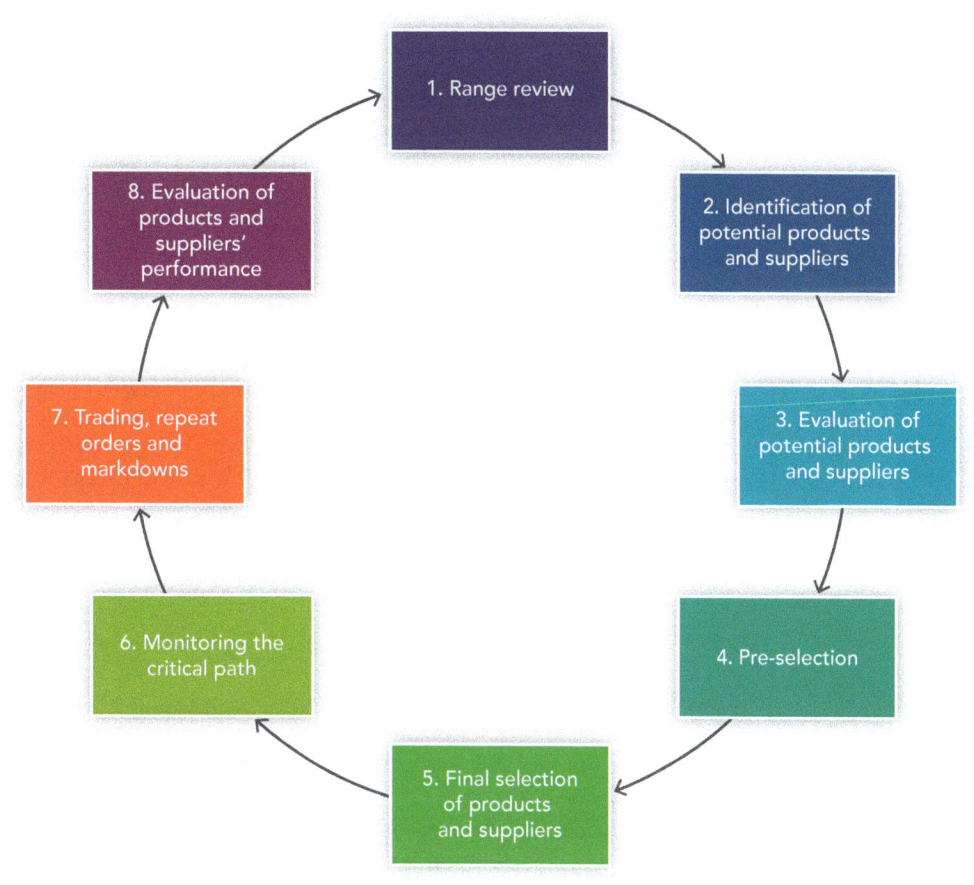

Figure 5.4 The retail buying cycle

sales up to the delivery of new products into stores. The buying cycle relates to products being sold within a specific trading period, within a particular season (of three or six months) which can be subdivided into phases when the products are delivered and sold. For example, fashion-led retailers such as H&M or Zara can have more than one delivery of new products per week, compared to a more classic clothing retailer which would be more likely to keep most of the same merchandise in stock for two to three months.

In many retailers, a range of goods usually progresses through various stages of selection, managed by buyers and, in larger companies, with the support of merchandise teams. Buying cycle stages can exchange places or be eliminated under certain circumstances, e.g. where a product is considered to meet current trends, it may be signed off by management without featuring in the 'pre-selection' meeting. The terms used for the stages or meetings can also differ between companies and it is therefore difficult to compose a model that applies precisely to all retail organisations. The retail buying cycle is a team effort, with employees in differing roles agreeing on the selection of products to be sold. The schedule is usually planned in reverse chronological order, beginning with the launch date of the range and working back to the deadlines necessary to achieve delivery on time. It is crucial that all deadlines are met, as consistent lateness by a buyer would result in merchandise not being available to customers at the required time, resulting in reduced profits for the company. Typical stages within the retail buying cycle, featured in Figure 5.4, are explained below. Buyers and merchandisers work on ranges for different seasons or phases simultaneously, since the timescale of the buying cycles overlap, so within the same day they could be working on monitoring the **critical path** for one phase, whilst selecting the products for the following phase and identifying potential suppliers for another phase.

Range review

The buying cycle begins with a review of the performance of a product range in a previous season, for example the same time in the previous year. The range's performance in terms of sales volume, quality and delivery will come under scrutiny from the B&M team. The **range review** serves the purpose of learning lessons from a prior trading period to enable realistic sales and budget forecasts to be made for a future seasons. Weak sellers can be dropped, allowing room for the introduction of new items with more sales potential, whereas bestselling products can be repurchased or updated. A brief for buying the new season's range can therefore be produced, incorporating a budget plan, essentially acting as a large-scale shopping list for the buyer. Buyers and merchandisers collaborate with the staff in the organisation who are responsible for finance in order to establish a viable budget for a trading period, forecasting key financial elements such as sales turnover and target profit margins. In certain retailers, a formal range review meeting is held where merchandisers present the key findings about a previous season to their colleagues in buying, design and technology, with a report being produced for reference.

Identification of potential products and suppliers

Sourcing is the activity whereby retailers seek new suppliers and products by investigating appropriate companies that could potentially provide items to meet their customers' needs and wants. Retail buyers are heavily involved in sourcing, which takes place before orders for products are placed. In medium to large companies sourcing is often conducted by buyers with the support of colleagues such as merchandisers and garment technologists. An own-label retailer can either give the supplier specifications of the products they wish to have manufactured or alternatively they can develop ideas for products in collaboration with the supplier. A buyer of branded merchandise can select products from suppliers' ranges.

Evaluation of potential products and suppliers (range planning)

Selecting products for the retailer requires painstaking planning and organisation of the product range by the buying team. **Range planning** involves compiling a collection of products within financial and design parameters, suitable for the target customer's taste and lifestyle (Goworek, 2007). This usually occurs several months before delivery of the products to the stores, to allow time for production and distribution to take place. The initial steps in range planning can begin more than a year ahead of the selling season, depending upon the complexity of the product design and manufacture, as well as the delivery timescale. Retailers need to plan the balance of different types of product effectively, so that consumers are offered sufficient variety in terms of price and style. For own-label products, retail buyers meet designers and sales personnel from suppliers to view design ideas for product ranges or to request samples of the retailer's own designs. At this stage it is only a plan in that orders have not yet been placed, but the retail buyer and/or merchandiser checks in advance that the suppliers are able to provide the items which they are considering including in the range. The range plan itself is usually a table or spreadsheet that shows descriptive and numerical details of the products, e.g. product description, reference number, colour, material and order quantity (see Table 5.2).

Pre-selection

Once range planning has been carried out, retail buyers and merchandisers evaluate the product prototypes they have selected to date, in the form of samples or photographs. Retailers may hold a meeting at the pre-selection stage when they can assess how all the products work together as a whole, to check that they have a workable price architecture (see Chapter 6 Retail

Table 5.2 An example range plan

| Men's T-shirts range plan 2015 ||||||||
Reference number	Product description	Supplier	Material	Colourways	Size	Quantity	Cost price	Selling price
BZ201	Basic round-neck T-shirt	Raven, China	100% cotton jersey	White Burgundy Grey Black	XS-XL	5000 3000 3000 5000	£2.40	£6.99
BZ202	V-neck T-shirt	VSJ Garments, China	98% cotton 2% elastane	White Grey Black	XS-XL	2000 1500 2500	£1.96	£6.99
BZ203	T-shirt with headphones print	Raven, China	100% cotton jersey	White Burgundy	SML	2500	£3.45	£10.99
BZ204	T-shirt with moustache print	Olympic, Greece	100% cotton jersey	White	SML	4000	£3.88	£10.99
BZ205	Long-sleeve round-neck T-shirt	Raven, China	100% cotton jersey	Burgundy Grey Black	XS-XL	4000 3000 5000	£2.84	£7.99
BZ206	Long-sleeve tie-dye T-shirt	Olympic, Greece	100% cotton jersey	Blue	SML	3000	£4.52	£12.99
BZ207	Long-sleeve music print T-shirt	BC Garments, Turkey	100% cotton jersey	Red	SML	3000	£4.28	£12.99

pricing) and offer sufficient variety to customers. Buyers may then review and renegotiate the cost prices of the products to ensure that they can meet the target profit margin whilst selling for a suitable retail price. They also need to ensure that each product order can be placed with an appropriate supplier/manufacturer with a viable delivery date. Retailers can negotiate with suppliers on price as well as other factors (Lusch et al., 2011).

After evaluating the range of merchandise and deciding which products to present at the **final selection** meeting, buyers can calculate figures such as the average selling price, average cost price and average profit margin for the range. This can be a time-consuming activity that involves the compilation of a great deal of data, which need to be collected and inputted accurately. The average selling price can be calculated fairly simply by adding together the selling price of each product in the range and dividing it by the total number of options (a mean average). However, a weighted average would be more useful, that also takes into account the quantity that has been ordered of every individual item, so if the cheaper options have been bought in higher quantities, the average selling price would be lower when using a weighted average, rather than the mean average.

Final selection

The final range selection is the key meeting for the buying function, attended by senior management such as buying and merchandising managers, when decisions are made about which products are to be sold by the retailer. The buyer is responsible for presenting the range to colleagues, usually in the form of product samples, and occasionally as drawings or computer-generated images. The merchandiser supports the buyer in this meeting with financial information about the range. Buyers at a final range selection meeting may also be asked how the average selling price compares with that of previous seasons, and a distinct increase in average selling price would need to be justified. By calculating the average margin of the range the buyer may be able to include garments which do not appear to be sufficiently profitable but are compensated for by higher margins from other garments.

Senior managers usually need to approve and sign off the range of products presented at the final range selection. After the product range has been selected, buyers and merchandisers place orders with the suppliers of the products. Amendments to products in the range may be requested by senior managers, based on their experience and knowledge of the market sector. Senior managers also have the advantage of being present at final selection meetings for ranges presented by several buyers, which can give them more insight into overall trends that affect the retailer. Following final selection, buyers continue working with suppliers to ensure that deliveries arrive at the specified time and to approve product details such as colour and size to prepare for bulk production.

Monitoring the critical path

Buyers need to work back from the delivery date to construct a critical path, which consists of the key dates in the production and delivery processes that need to be adhered to in order to meet the deadline. This allows them to check whether everything is on track to be in stores for the planned **trading** period. The retailer liaises with the suppliers on an ongoing basis to check that key deadlines are met for product manufacture and distribution to enable the merchandise to be delivered to stores on the agreed dates. For an own-label retailer the critical path is generally more complex than for a retailer that sells branded merchandise. For example, a buyer for an own-label range will usually need to approve some of the design aspects of each product in the range, such as the colour of fabrics when they are ready for bulk production, comparing them to the agreed shade that had been requested in the order. Own-label fashion buyers also need to make sure that garments fit accurately to the retailer's specifications, so they may request samples from suppliers to try on models or mannequins before the whole quantity is manufactured. If buyers are not satisfied with any of these features the manufacturer will be asked to make amendments and resubmit samples until each aspect is authorised. These monitoring procedures should ensure that the retailer's customers will be able to rely on purchasing products of the expected quality and dimensions. Colleagues in **Quality Control (QC)**/technology consequently play a key role at this stage.

Trading, repeat orders and markdowns

Managing the distribution and delivery of stock during the selling period is often referred to within the retail sector as trading. During the trading period, while products are available for sale to consumers, buyers and merchandisers monitor sales figures on a regular basis. The retailer's branches can distribute sales data via Electronic Point-of-Sale (EPOS) systems for buyers and merchandisers to analyse sales patterns. The first week's sales are particularly significant, to enable potential best-sellers to be identified. Repeat orders may be placed for products which sell more quickly than anticipated. Conversely, products with low sales volume may be reduced in price (marked down) to improve the selling rate. Buyers can arrange store visits to hear feedback from sales staff about customers' responses to the products in the range.

Evaluation of products' and suppliers' performance

Retailers assess the total sales figures of products during a specified time period. Detailed data about the sales figures and profit margins of products sold by the retailer in the past are usually compiled by merchandisers in a large retailer, or by the buyer in an independent retailer. They can also evaluate the performance of suppliers in terms of non-financial aspects such as product development, quality, delivery times and

RETAIL MARKETING CAREERS
Sarah Deacon, Junior Buyer

Sarah is a Junior Buyer at Millers, a division of Specialty Fashion Group in Sydney, Australia. Sarah gained a BA (Hons) Fashion, Marketing and Communication degree in 2007 from Nottingham Trent University and during her studies she learned about the industry through live projects, including being a finalist in the L'Oreal Branding competition. She also completed work experience as a Buyer's Administration Assistant (BAA) at Shop Direct Group and as a PR assistant with Kilpatrick PR and Apples and Pears Marketing. After graduating Sarah worked at M&S Head Office in London for six years, initially as a Production and Manufacturing Assistant, before a sideways move to become a Senior BAA for women's holiday wear.

Millers is Australia's largest women's apparel retailer with over 350 stores nationally, a further 28 stores in New Zealand and a growing online store. The company targets a 'more mature customer who still has an interest in current fashion trends' but wants a comfortable style. Sarah describes her role at Millers as developing and delivering her own product range, while supporting her Senior Buyer to range and buy two other larger product categories. In order to achieve this she works on ranges of four new stories (garment collections) per month with the Head of Buying, ensuring trends, colours and products are being adhered to, influenced by her inspiration trips and catwalk trends. Sarah describes her main responsibilities as follows.

Sarah Deacon – Junior Buyer
Source: with permission from Sarah Deacon

- Working through brand handover sheets and packages of technical information about products following range planning and selection meetings, ensuring colleagues in planning, Quality Control and design are kept informed about which items have been selected for the range.
- Working with the design team to ensure colour palettes and range plans are up-to-date with products launching by month.
- Maintaining the department's critical path by ensuring all processes within this run smoothly, allowing stock to be delivered at the right time. Sarah follows this process through from initial booking to launching the product in stores.
- Presenting best and worst sellers in Monday trade meetings and reacting to these findings by repeating and re-colouring best-selling styles within the season, or cancelling styles which become a concern.
- Liaising with suppliers on a daily basis, maintaining a close working relationship via emails and video conferences with vendors.
- Working with the marketing and visual merchandising teams to ensure product launches as planned, so that cohesive stories in stores and promotions can achieve their full potential.
- Maintaining commitment to production with manufacturers, ensuring there is enough stock in stores and open-to-buy (OTB) is filled with the correct number of options/buys per month.
- Fitting all garments on models with the garment technician, ensuring the fit of sample and production garments are right.
- Managing BAA and Assistant Buyer to ensure purchase orders are raised and samples are maintained for various events.

- Looking after all department approvals including fabric (lab dips/trim/print strike-offs), yarn approvals and production samples.
- Cross-costing and negotiating cost prices with suppliers to ensure departmental margin is achieved.
- Monitoring market activity through comparative shopping to identify trading opportunities.

Sarah reports directly to her Senior Buyer to sign off her product range before presenting it to the Head of Buying and GM. She works frequently with her Garment Technologist, fitting garment samples to check that they are the right shape and size for their customer, ensuring all comments are communicated clearly to the supplier to achieve the best possible fit. She liaises with the planning team (known as merchandisers in the UK) to ensure all product options are filled and OTB is achieved to maintain and grow the sales plan on her area, whilst ensuring she has the right stock at the right time in stores to deliver the sales plan that has been forecast. Sarah also works closely with the company's Visual Merchandising (VM) and Marketing teams to build outfits for roadshows (presentations to sales staff), window displays and point-of-sale, as well as ensuring there is enough product and stock available to drive promotional sales. She liaises with the ecommerce manager to ensure that online sales are growing for the department.

Dealing with the people who supply her product range is also a major part of Sarah's job: 'I liaise with about 25 different suppliers on a daily basis – with prices, delivery issues, booking confirmations, cross-costings, developments, approvals etc.' Sarah sources products for her range from New Zealand; China; Bangladesh; India and Cambodia. Her Senior Buyer travels on costing trips to meet the suppliers in person in China and Bangladesh or on directional shopping trips to New York, LA and London every eight weeks. Sarah has the opportunity to travel to different states in Australia twice a year to help outfit-build and run roadshows to promote Millers' fashion ranges to the company's sales staff.

Compared to buying in the UK, Sarah says that the job differs in Australia in terms of lead times and supply base, with none of the product being sourced from Europe. The Australian weather is so different from the UK that this has to be taken into consideration when buying ranges, as Sarah explains:

> Australian states have hugely different weather patterns so you need to be more savvy when building your range, ensuring there is the correct product in store at the correct time for both cold climates (Melbourne/New Zealand) and hot climates (Northern Territory/Western Australia). Trends in the UK are six months to a year ahead of Australia so certain trends will always take longer to grasp here. Millers has a separate team for Buying, Planning and Allocation, but that is very rare in Australia so you are expected to be very adaptable and be able to apply your skills to each of these areas. In the UK most Full-Service Vendor (FSV) suppliers have a UK-based office where an account manager will attend all initial product design meetings and present trend ideas before ranging. In Australia this process is very different – inspiration is taken directly from product bought by the retailer on buying trips and you have much less direction from your supply base. All product is ranged in-house, which is then fed to suppliers for sampling. I am working with many more FOB suppliers than FSV suppliers.

Sarah considers the following to be the key skills required to perform well as a retail buyer: teamwork; time management; prioritisation; communication; self-motivation; creativity; computer skills (Excel, Powerpoint and Word); technical skills; numeracy; planning and organisation. When employing buying staff the company looks for people who are motivated, professional, highly organised and creative. Sarah says:

> To work in buying you need to have a broad commercial awareness and the ability to learn quickly in challenging surroundings. They look for people who are strong team players, good at communicating and can react and adapt quickly to trends and a fast-paced working environment. To be a Junior Buyer you need to have worked your way up the buying ladder from a BAA to Assistant Buyer. Working across a variety of product areas is also a strong quality as you will have experience working with a variety of fabrics (e.g. Jersey and Wovens) and different suppliers (long and short lead-time). You need to have a strong commercial awareness of the ladies' wear market and keep up-to-date with the key fashion trends from the catwalk down to street level . . . You must be driven to deliver the very best product for the customers and the business.

Sarah's own performance is assessed through Key Performance Indicators (KPI's) set by the company. She describes her favourite part of the job as: 'building my own range from trends and inspiration I have seen on the catwalk or during inspirational shopping trips and implementing these trends/ideas in the product I buy. Successful sales and great feedback from store colleagues and customers is also a great part of the job!'. However, Sarah considers the more difficult aspects of her job to be price negotiations, dealing with late deliveries and difficult suppliers. Sarah offers the following advice to those contemplating a future career in buying:

> The best advice I could give someone is to not rush into accepting the first job that is offered to you after university if it is not the area of retail you want to build a career in. I was lucky as I managed to use my work experience in Merchandising as a positive and cross over into buying. However, it is very difficult to make this change once you have begun your career in one or the other. Make sure you do as much work experience as possible before graduating, as there will be hundreds of people going for the same job and you need to stand out from the crowd. Be prepared to start at the bottom with admin-based, less creative roles, as this is the start of a long ladder, but you will get there eventually!

www.specialtyfashiongroup.com.au/; www.millers.com.au/

communication. This information is invaluable to retail buyers as it is highly influential in the development and selection of the new range. To evaluate whether or not the range performed well the sales figures for a range can be compared to the forecast that had been predicted at the outset and also against the sales volume of the range in the same period during the previous year, known as 'This Year/Last Year' trading figures (TYLY). All of these data can be used to inform stage 1 of the buying cycle 'range review' for a subsequent trading period.

Retail buying for online and mail order (home shopping) companies

Retailers that sell products online or via mail order catalogues, known as the 'home shopping' sector, can require differences in their buying processes in comparison to bricks-and-mortar retailers. Therefore multichannel retailers (who sell through more than one distribution method, e.g. stores and a website) may need to operate slightly different buying systems for each of these channels (see also Chapter 11 Multichannel retailing). Etailers or mail order companies employ buyers and merchandisers in the same way that bricks-and-mortar retail multiples do (Goworek, 2007). Although mail order companies were significant retailers during the 19th and 20th centuries, online retailing (etailing) has clearly become prevalent in the home shopping market in the 21st century. Even former traditional mail order companies such as Grattan, which was established over 100 years ago, has now become primarily an etailer (www.grattan.co.uk). Large etailers of this kind, which sell numerous product types, act in a similar way to department stores by employing buyers who select branded merchandise or exclusive own-label ranges. As home shopping relies on selling its products via photographs, rather than physical merchandise in shops, items can look very different in an image rather than on a shelf or hanger, particularly if highly regarded photographers, stylists and models are involved. The quality of photography can therefore affect consumer demand, which buyers and merchandisers need to anticipate when specifying order quantities. Buyers for multichannel retailers may find distinct variations in the popularity of products depending on whether they are sold online or in-store.

Another difference with buying for the home shopping sector is that accurate product samples need to be available to be photographed in advance of the trading period. This can be achieved in a relatively short timescale if the product is shot in a studio but can take a lot longer if a professional photo shoot is arranged with models and stylists, taking place in an outdoor location in a different country to take advantage of the climate overseas. Buyers are then under pressure to ensure that the products that are manufactured in bulk are identical in style and colour to the sample that has been photographed, and are delivered on time in order to satisfy customers, which are issues that would be slightly less significant in a store environment.

CATEGORY MANAGEMENT
By Rosemary Varley, Subject Director, Fashion Retail and Marketing, University of the Arts (London College of Fashion), London

The process of range planning in fashion retailing is fundamentally different to that in fast-moving consumer goods (FMCG) retailing because of the need for change in the product range. Fashion assortments intrinsically vary from season to season and often change frequently during each one. It is therefore difficult to apply **category management** in fashion in its pure form. In their paper, Dewsnap and Hart (2004) advise that fashion brands should be flexible and pragmatic when applying category management as the process can be viewed as inflexible. Nevertheless, the concept of a product category playing a particular role within the overall assortment in order to make a contribution to the strategic positioning of a retail brand identity is certainly of interest to fashion retail brands.

Van der Vorst (2004, cited in Kapferer, 2008) suggests that the relationship between brands and products can be analysed using the concepts of distinctive and generic in terms of product facets, and core and peripheral in terms of brand facets. The distinctive product facets are those that strongly communicate a brand's identity, whereas the generic product facets are those features that are easily and often replicated by alternative or competitive brands; core brand facets can be considered to be those aspects of a brand that are found in all product category embodiments of a brand, while peripheral facets are those only relevant to a specific category. Combining these concepts with those of the established category management roles outlined in Table 5.3, four fashion category roles are proposed.

The iconic category maintains all major brand facets in every product and the identity of the brand is distinctive through the category, providing a strong coherence between product and brand, and consumers consider the brand to be a destination for the purchase of this product type. In order to satisfy customers a deep product assortment is recommended to ensure that most customer needs can be met, for example a variation in sizes, lengths, fabrication weight, colour and textures. Product detailing can change to ensure updated styling is incorporated, but the essential product type should be recognisable and reassuring. In the case of Burberry for example the iconic category would be trench-coats.

The aspirational or occasional category is one where particular brand facets may be included in the product design in order to maintain coherence between the brand and the products, however there is more freedom here to blend other facets that are more relevant to the specific product category rather than the brand. These facets may be innovative product features, or new styling ideas which add excitement and interest to the product ranges and the brand in general. As the relationship to the brand is apparent and shows the brand/product manifestation moving in a new and modernising direction, it is suggested that there needs to be a deep assortment in these categories to demonstrate confidence and commitment to new reincarnations of the brand. For Burberry, handbags could be the aspirational category.

An extension category would be one that is well established for the brand, and represents it in an easily understood way for the consumer, but there is no really strong coherence between the brand and the product. It is a category that existing customers will be aware of but customers new to the brand may not be. Other brands are seen to have competence and be competitive in the category. However, this type of category provides a brand with the opportunity to include products within the assortment that are on trend, or in growing

Table 5.3 Proposed category role matrix for fashion brands

		Brand	
		Core	Peripheral
Product	Distinctive	**Iconic** Maintains all major brand facets in every product within the category. The identity of the brand is distinctive through the product category. Product and brand coherence is strong. Category acts as a destination for consumer purchase of brand. A deep assortment is recommended. Strategic brand communications should feature products from this category. Visual merchandising should feature products from this category, but they should not dominate all displays.	**Aspirational/Occasional** Only some brand facets may be included, and may be blended with other facets which are more related to specific product categories. Coherence between brand and product is apparent. Category acts as excitement creator; the brand embodiment may be new, innovative and/or adds interest. A deep assortment is recommended. Strategic brand communications should feature products from this category. Visual merchandising should emphasise the category.
	Generic	**Extension** All major brand facets are present, but the product category does not have strong coherence with the brand; many other brands are competitive in this category. The category is established and may be growing in the market and/or be on trend. A shallow assortment is recommended, with the potential to deepen. Products from these categories can appear in brand communications and visual merchandising, but they should not be dominant.	**Convenience/Staple** The category may or may not have strong coherence with the brand; other brands may have stronger product coherence, or product coherence has been strong in the past. The brand offers the category as way of delivering service to the consumer. Well-established category, possibly with stagnant or declining demand. A shallow assortment is recommended. These categories should not usually feature prominently in strategic brand communications or visual merchandising although they may be used in targeted promotional activity.

Source: adapted from R. van der Vorst (2004), cited in Kapferer (2008: 285) and Varley (2006: 49)

markets to capitalise on brand loyalty and/or impulse purchasing. Some of these categories could be considered 'outfit completers' or complementary products. A shallow assortment is therefore recommended, with the potential to deepen maintained should demand grow. Continuing the example, Burberry offer jeans but only in a small number of alternatives.

Convenience or staple products are those that take the outfit completing idea further, simply being offered to prevent a customer having to go to an alternative brand to satisfy this need as other brands offer this product category, some perhaps consider them as iconic products of their own. The convenience/staple category may have been one that had stronger brand coherence and therefore offered in more depth in the past, but is now a stagnant or declining category for the brand and so a shallow assortment is recommended. For Burberry, the small accessories category has become a staple.

This interpretation of category management seems to be a logical and appropriate way to underpin the management of increasingly dynamic fashion assortments. More retail brands are now faced with international merchandise planning and it is suggested that strategic category roles based on product/brand coherence could play an important role in this.

This interpretation of category roles puts less emphasis on them as drivers of sales and profits than previous iterations in the FMCG context, and more on the appropriate management of clothing categories to bring good financial performance in the long term.

RETAIL MARKETING CAREERS
Lito Giourouki, Global Category Manager

Sparkling, exotic, international – a few words to describe the career so far of Lito Giourouki! After graduating with an MSc in Marketing from Manchester Business School, Lito joined the marketing team at Vimto, before moving on to Reckitt Benckiser. She worked on the Scholl and Durex brands for nearly three years, prior to becoming Category Marketing Manager for the Napolina brand, then International Marketing Manager for Italian Foods.

These varied supply-side responsibilities provided Lito with an excellent commercial background for her latest role as Global Category Manager with Tesco plc. While researching her excellent Masters dissertation, Lito worked with the Retail Research Forum, including Tesco; this group of senior industry executives guided and reviewed her work. Following her graduate studies and subsequent marketing roles, Lito now benefits from an excellent management development programme, including the Tesco Academy. She has exceptional flair and understanding of the critical interface between suppliers and retailers, the essence of the category manager role.

Recently travelling to Thailand and neighbouring countries sourcing exotic food and drinks, Lito loves her role at Tesco. As a 'people person', she enjoys the constant interactions, including working with top international suppliers to identify profitable opportunities across categories. 'On a daily basis my time is spent conducting analyses, generating and managing insight and meeting with internal and external stakeholders to develop global category plans'. Lito's work is not office-bound, with travel most weeks including Tesco's markets in East Europe and East Asia, sharing best practice and building relationships with local teams:

> To establish areas of future growth we take into account a variety of factors and metrics: internal sales, total market sales, consumer trends, and changes in the macro environment. We then overlay key customer metrics, such as penetration, frequency of purchase, etc. to determine where each country sits in the category development cycle.

Lito Giourouki – Global Category Manager
Source: Lito Giourouki

Data from Kantar, dunnhumby, AC Nielsen, etc. inform these decisions. Lito enjoys analysing consumer trends and understanding factors that shape customers' everyday purchasing decisions. 'This role is particularly interesting because we conduct the same analyses in all the different countries we operate and can compare shoppers' attitudes and behaviours around the world'. Cross-cultural communication and harmonisation of terminology/data across markets may sometimes be difficult, but Lito thrives on such challenges!

Interview by Peter McGoldrick

Supply chain management and stock control by retailers

As retailers do not usually manufacture the products they sell, retailers need to buy their merchandise from suppliers (or 'vendors' in the US). The retailer therefore needs to manage the suppliers to ensure that they deliver suitable products by the agreed delivery date. Most suppliers also deal with other companies that supply their materials and product components, hence the term **supply chain management** is used. The supply chain can consist of several suppliers in various countries, starting with suppliers of raw materials and ending with the retailer. Each company is therefore reliant on the previous links in the chain to be able to supply the retailer effectively.

The terms 'merchandising' and 'stock control' can sometimes be used synonymously in retailing. Merchandisers (also referred to as stock controllers or optimisers) arrange for the products selected by the buying team to be produced by suppliers and distributed via the retailer's distribution channels. However, merchandising can also be considered to be a broader role that is not limited to stock control, particularly in the larger own-label retailers, where merchandisers can be highly influential in the selection of products and suppliers (see 'Retail marketing careers' section in Chapter 6 Retail pricing). Berman and Evans (2010) describe merchandising as: 'Activities involved in acquiring particular goods/services and making them available at the places, times, prices, and quantities that enable a retailer to reach its goals'. This is relevant to the US market but it is not always the case in other countries. For example, in the UK the buying component, i.e. 'acquiring goods/services' is generally a separate function from merchandising, undertaken by specialist buyers, as explained above.

Retailers and suppliers need to communicate effectively with each other as they liaise on a regular basis and have the same common aim: to sell commercial products that appeal to their customers. The balance in the relationship between retailers and suppliers has shifted over time, so that retailers are often viewed as being the more powerful side (Fernie and Sparks, 2009). However, the reverse may be true of small independent retailers, where brands have the upper hand and can select whom they will permit to stock their merchandise. Whatever the size of the retailer or supplier, it is to the advantage of both sides to work together for mutual benefit. Traditionally, in retailer-supplier liaison, buyers often occupied a central role for the retailer, dealing directly with account managers or sales agents representing suppliers to develop a product range. Whilst this still usually occurs, it has also become common practice for other roles within retailers and suppliers to liaise with their counterparts in the other organisation, so that buyers are not the only point of contact. For example, to enable effective category management for a specific product type, the retailer's QC's may communicate directly with a manufacturer's production team.

Retailers can deal directly with manufacturers, but they are more likely to deal with an intermediary such as an overseas sourcing office or a UK-based sales and design office with offshore manufacture, since the majority of products sold by most retailers in the UK are imported, with the Far East being a particularly popular source of merchandise. For European retailers, it is rare to buy products from the domestic market as this is rarely cost-effective. However, a move back towards buying in the UK has begun in recent years, with trade exhibitions such as Pure London actively promoting the idea of buying garments that are Made In Britain and supermarkets aiming to source a higher number of locally sourced products (Lucas, 2012) (see case study at the end of this chapter). Buyers are normally responsible for selecting the countries and suppliers where the products in the range will be produced, usually from the retailer's existing supplier base, with advice from colleagues in QC and Merchandising. QC's (also known as garment technologists) ensure that the merchandise meets the standards expected by the retailer, by specifying the required quality levels for manufacturing, sometimes in the form of a written guide, and checking that samples of merchandise meet these levels specified. Products that fail to meet the required standards are likely to be rejected, thus affecting the availability of merchandise in stores in the short term and potentially impacting on the decision to use the supplier again in the longer term.

After products have been delivered by suppliers, retail merchandisers (or buyers in small retailers) often use a Weekly Sales, Stock and Intake Plan (WSSI, commonly known as 'Wizzy'), which is a computer spreadsheet or document to monitor levels of sales and stock. The WSSI allows merchandisers to monitor product sales in terms of value, units, cost and margin terms. Each product has a unique reference number known as an **SKU (stock-keeping unit)**. Merchandisers often assess the availability and performance of their stock by calculating the quantity of stock available at the beginning-of-the-month (BOM) and at the end-of-month (EOM). Specialist merchandising software is available from various companies and can be tailored to the retailer's needs. When products selling less than planned and best-sellers are identified, action can be taken to control the amount of stock. Merchandisers plan despatch from the retailer's Distribution Centre (DC), transport and arrival of the merchandise at the company's stores. For international retailers this can be on a large scale, with DC's in numerous countries.

The delivery of merchandise to stores to replace goods which have been sold during the trading period is known as replenishment. Retailers usually aim to replenish stock at the rate at which it is sold, either with repeat orders of existing items or with new products. When a product has sold out it is referred to as a **stockout**. Too little stock makes stores look sparse and limits the amount of products available for customers to buy. Too much stock causes a different problem: removing the excess products to make way for more profitable stock through promotional tactics or price reductions. Both of these problems result in reduced profitability. Allocating stock to stores can be a separate function from planning and analysis so it is carried out by allocators (or 'branch merchandisers') rather than merchandisers. Spanish fashion retailer Zara delegates some of the responsibility for allocating merchandise to store managers, who order quantities of styles from the retailer's range from Head Office, operating in a similar way to a buyer for an independent store (BBC, 2004).

Retail space planning and allocation

Retailers need to plan the space allocated to products in stores. For UK retailers, this is often the responsibility of the merchandising department. Sales and profitability vary according to the positioning of the product in store and where the space is allocated, e.g. ground floor space is more valuable than upper floors as it has higher footfall. Space allocation depends on the relationship between retail space, sales turnover and profitability. This is normally expressed in value per square metre and is referred to as the sales density. According to Varley (2006: 144), some of the main objectives of retail space management are 'to optimise both short-term and long-term returns on the investment cost of retail space' and to 'provide a logical, convenient and inspiring interface between the product range and the customer'. Retailers plan by dividing retail space into areas where specific product types will be sold and measuring it. This therefore impacts upon other aspects of retailing such as store design and profitability. It can also be worthwhile to allocate space for stock with low sales volume or margins to ensure that the customer is presented with a full array of merchandise in a product category, particularly if the store is a specialist in a product sector, rather than being a general retailer. Specific locations for products are decided on by using 2D visual representations of the store space called **planograms** or software which can recreate a realistic 3D view of the store (see Chapter 9 Retail design and layout).

Retail sales forecasting and budget planning

Retailers' sales forecasts are frequently based on sales figures for a product range at the same time in the previous year, with a percentage increase for expected growth (or decrease if necessary), taking into account predicted trends. Current sales figures are often compared to the same date/s last year, to judge relative performance, i.e. TYLY. Sales figures can be affected by various factors including time of year, retail price, celebrity endorsement and other promotional activity. The weather can be one of the most significant factors impacting upon product sales, affecting not only which products consumers decide to purchase (e.g. ice cream, umbrellas, coats etc.) but also influencing whether or not they are inclined to go shopping. Budgets are planned for product areas, deciding the amount of money which will be available to buyers and merchandisers for a range for a particular season/year. A budget is a projection of the amount of money the retailer will spend on merchandise from suppliers for the season and the expected sales turnover. Budgets are usually based on a combination of historical sales figures, mainly from the previous year and forecasts for future sales, influenced broadly by the financial performance and expansion plans of the retailer and general trend forecasting (Varley, 2006). **Open-to-buy** is a portion of the budget retained for selecting products shortly before or during the trading season, to respond more quickly to constantly changing product trends and customer needs, which is becoming an increasingly important factor in catering for today's educated consumers who have increased their expectations of retailers.

CHAPTER SUMMARY

Buying and merchandising are the functions which allow retailers to offer a suitable range of merchandise at appropriate prices to meet their customers' needs, delivered at the right time in the right quantities. Buyers may fulfil both of these functions in small independent stores and in larger retail chains the responsibilities are likely to be split into separate buyer and merchandiser roles. Retail buyers are largely responsible for selecting products, amongst many other duties, whereas merchandisers deal with more numerical and logistical tasks. Buyers and merchandisers therefore require diverse skills, blending business acumen with creative thinking. Retail buying is a form of organisational buying and it may be centralised, decentralised or performed by a retail buying group. The stages involved in retail buying take the form of a buying cycle, so called because of its cyclical nature, which follows these eight steps, with the information from the final stage feeding into the first stage of the next cycle.

- Range review.
- Identification of potential products and suppliers.
- Evaluation of potential products and suppliers.
- Pre-selection.
- Final selection of products and suppliers.
- Monitoring the critical path.
- Trading, report orders and markdowns.
- Evaluation of products' and suppliers' performance.

Buyers who work for retailers that sell own-label merchandise are likely to be involved in product development for the items that they buy, whereas buyers of branded products select items that have already been finalised by the supplier. Some of the key responsibilities in retail buying and merchandising for retailers of either own-label or branded products are:

- liaising with internal staff and external suppliers or agencies;
- sales forecasting and budget planning;
- range planning;
- negotiating prices, product features, quantities and deliveries;
- managing product distribution and retail demand;
- building effective relationships with suppliers for mutual benefit.

EXERCISES AND QUESTIONS

1. Discuss the skills and personal characteristics required to work effectively in buying and merchandising, then assess which are the three most important of these points for each job in the following types of retailer:
   a chain of ten hardware stores that only sells branded merchandise;
   b large fashion retailer that sells own-label menswear.

2. Based on the content in the chapter, name some of the other retail job roles with which buyers work internally and describe which tasks they collaborate on.

3. Assess the main differences in the buying cycle between buying branded and own-label ranges of the following product types:
   - tinned vegetables
   - men's jeans
   - bath towels.

4. What are the advantages and disadvantages of centralised buying and decentralised buying, e.g. John Lewis versus Fenwick?

5. Review the information on products for two symbol groups in the same product sector, based on the information on the companies' websites, e.g. Spar, Mace and Nisa. If you were setting up your own grocery store, which of these symbol groups would you choose to buy from and why?

6. Which ethical issues are involved in retail buying and merchandising? (See also Chapter 12 Legislation and ethics in retailing.)

REFERENCES

BBC (2004) *Store Wars: Fast Fashion*, BBC News, 9 June (available online at: http://news.bbc.co.uk/1/hi/business/3086669.stm).

Berman, B. and Evans, J.R. (2010) *Retailing Management: A Strategic Approach*, 11th edn, Upper Saddle River, NJ: Pearson.

Bonoma, T.V. (1982) Major sales: Who really does the buying?, *Harvard Business Review*, May–June, 111–119.

REFERENCES

Buchanan, M. (2008) *Profitable Buying Strategies: How to Cut Procurement Costs and Buy Your Way to Higher Profits*, London: Kogan Page.

Clodfelter, R. (2008) *Retail Buying: From Basics to Fashion*, 3rd edn, New York: Fairchild Books.

Dawson, J., Findlay, A. and Sparks, L. (2008) Chapter 3 'Merchandising and Buying', *The Retailing Reader*, Abingdon: Routledge, pp. 311–331.

Dewsnap, B. and Hart, C.A. (2004) Category management: a new approach for fashion marketing?, *European Journal of Marketing*, 38(7), 809–834.

Diamond, J. and Pintel, G. (2005) *Retail Buying*, 7th edn, Upper Saddle River, NJ: Pearson Prentice Hall.

Draper, A. (1994) Organizational buyers as workers: the key to their behaviour, *European Journal of Marketing*, 28(11), 50–62.

Faes, W., Knight, L. and Matthysens, P. (2001) Buyer profiles: an empirical investigation of changing organizational requirements, *European Journal of Purchasing & Supply Management*, 7, 197–208.

Fairhurst, A.E. and Fiorito, S.S. (1990) Retail buyers' decision-making process: an investigation of contributing variables, *International Review of Retail, Distribution and Consumer Research*, 1(1), 87–100.

Fernie, J. and Sparks, L. (2009) *Logistics and Retail Management*, London: Kogan Page.

Gilbert, D. (2003) *Retail Marketing Management*, 2nd edn, Harlow: FT Prentice Hall.

Goworek, H. (2006) *Careers in Fashion and Textiles*, Oxford: Blackwell Publishing.

Goworek, H. (2007) *Fashion Buying*, 2nd edn, Oxford: Blackwell Publishing.

Goworek, H. (2010) A Model of the Decision-Making Process for Retail Buying, Academy of Marketing Conference, Coventry University.

Goworek, H. (2014) An investigation into retail buying roles and responsibilities for own-label clothing: a multiple case-study, *Journal of the Textile Institute*, 105(7), 760–769.

Johansson, J. and Burt, S. (2004) Buying of private brands and manufacturer brands in grocery retailing: a comparative study of buying processes in the UK, Sweden and Italy, *Journal of Marketing Management*, 20, 799–824.

Johansson, U. (2001) Retail buying: Process, information and IT use: a conceptual framework, *International Review of Retail, Distribution and Consumer Research*, 11, 329–357.

Kapferer, J.N. (2008) *The New Strategic Brand Management*, 4th edn, London: Kogan Page.

Kline, B. and Wagner, J. (1994) Information sources and retail buyer decision-making: the effect of product-specific buying experience, *Journal of Retailing*, 70(1) 75–88.

Levy, M. and Weitz, B.A. (2012) *Retailing Management*, 8th edn, New York: McGraw-Hill Irwin.

Lucas, L. (2012) Buying British Campaign – shoppers prefer to save pennies over jobs, *Financial Times*, 2 June.

Lusch, R.F., Dunne, P.M. and Carver, J.R. (2011) *Introduction to Retailing*, International/7th edn, Stamford, CT: South-Western Cengage Learning.

McGoldrick, P. (2002) *Retail Marketing*, Maidenhead: McGraw-Hill.

Swindley, D.G. (1992) The role of the buyer in UK multiple retailing, *International Journal of Retail and Distribution Management*, 20, 3–15.

Van der Vorst, J. (2004) *Branding: A Systems Theoretic Perspective*, Nijmegen University, Netherlands.

Varley, R. (2006) *Retail Product Management*, 2nd edn, London: Routledge.

Webster, F. E. and Wind, Y. (1972) A general model for understanding organizational buying behaviour, *Journal of Marketing*, 36, 12–19.

FURTHER READING

Aastrup, J., Grant, D.B. and Bjerre, M. (2007) Value creation and category management through retailer–supplier relationship, *International Review of Retail, Distribution and Consumer Research*, 17(5), 523–541.

Ailawadi, K.L., Bradlow, E.T., Draganska, M., Nijs, V., Rookerkerk, R.P., Sudhir, K., Wilbur, K.C. and Zhang, J. (2010) Empirical models of manufacturer–retailer interaction: a review and agenda for future research, *Marketing Letters*, 21(3), 273–285.

Anselmsson, J. and Johansson, U. (2014) Manufacturer brands versus private brands: Hoch's strategic framework and the Swedish food retail sector, *International Review of Retail, Distribution and Consumer Research*, 24(2), 186–212.

Bruce, M. and Daly, L. (2007) Challenges of fashion buying and merchandising, in Hines, T. and Bruce, M. (eds), *Fashion Marketing: Contemporary Issues*, Oxford: Butterworth-Heinemann, pp. 54–71.

Chung, J.E., Sternquist, B. and Cheng, Z. (2006) Retailer–buyer supplier relationships: the Japanese difference, *Journal of Retailing*, 82(4), 349–355.

National Careers Service (2014) *Job Profiles: Retail Merchandiser* (available online at: https://nationalcareersservice.direct.gov.uk/advice/planning/jobprofiles/Pages/retailmerchandiser.aspx).

Tims, A. (2014) How do I become . . . a fashion buyer?, *The Guardian*, 27 February (available online at: http://www.theguardian.com/money/2014/feb/27/how-become-fashion-buyer).

Case study

Supply chain – back to the source

There is much talk about the potential for greater UK sourcing, but is it feasible and what would it mean for retailers' supply chain teams? Sarah Butler examines the pros and cons. Shop Direct, Arcadia and N Brown are all examining sourcing more goods in the UK. Food retailers, meanwhile, are boosting local sourcing in response to consumer interest in British produce and a desire to support local farmers. For clothing and general merchandise retailers, there may be some marketing mileage about flying the flag, but rising transport and labour costs mean that switching out of the Far East is becoming a genuine option. Shoppers' increasingly unpredictable behaviour is a further incentive. Some retailers emerged from the Christmas trading season with hefty stock overhangs that were difficult to clear as long lead times led to wrong buying decisions. Alan Braithwaite, chairman of supply chain consultancy LCP Consulting, says increasing market volatility means that finding sources with shorter lead times has become an imperative. Buying and merchandise director Paul Short of mail order company N Brown says that even in the home shopping specialist markets, where keeping up with fashion trends hasn't traditionally been a priority, shoppers are demanding the latest looks: 'We can see the market getting faster and faster and that's changing the business dramatically.'

Fast and loose

Deeper analysis about how fast categories sell through and how to respond to demand will become an important part of a supply chain team's work. It may mean a complete switch in strategy for retailers that have relied on selling high volumes to underpin large orders of low-cost goods from the Far East. Braithwaite says: 'If they can't predict stable demand for product then companies are prepared to accept higher costs for cutting down lead times and fulfilment in a matter of weeks.' He adds that even after transport costs there is a net margin gain of between 15 and 20 per cent on producing in Asia for high volume lines, but that doesn't take into account the risk of discounting stock if those volumes cannot be sold. After taking markdowns into account, the difference can slim down to between 5 and 10 per cent. Ongoing inflation in China, meanwhile, means that the gap continues to close.

Shop Direct chief executive Mark Newton-Jones says it has found that UK sourcing – with its shorter lead times – delivers better sell-throughs (i.e. selling items at full-price). As a result, the margin is only 5–6 per cent less than clothing sourced from the Far East and he says 'We couldn't turn this product around in any other way and so we see it as incremental sales despite the lower margin. As labour rates keep going up in the booming economies of the Far East and Near East, we can see that in a couple of years there won't be any margin degradation.' Meanwhile UK or European sourcing can mean lower inventory levels as the company doesn't need to order the same volume of goods required by Far Eastern manufacturers. This in turn means the cost of warehousing and shipping can be reduced, while expensive buying trips to the Far East can be cut back. Short says shortage of capacity in the Far East has been another issue, driving up prices and hitting reliability: 'Last year was probably the most difficult year we have experienced for many years in dealing in the Far East.'

In an attempt to find an alternative, N Brown held an away-day in Leicester for more than 50 UK-based suppliers and is in talks with 30 of those, examining the quality and quantity of what they might be able to produce. Some of those also have facilities in near-Europe countries such as Morocco and Turkey, which might offer an alternative to the Far East.

Playing catch up

N Brown's need to investigate suppliers based less than 100 miles from its head office highlights the problem for a new generation of supply chain managers in finding suitable sources of production in a much depleted UK manufacturing industry. Companies will need to build new relationships as well as expertise in sourcing components and fabrics because the backup infrastructure ubiquitous in countries such as China now barely exists in the UK. Supply chain managers will also have to examine product ranges carefully to identify how to divide up sourcing to get the most benefit.

Certain categories, such as high fashion, knitwear or hosiery are much more suited to UK production than technical, labour-intensive items such as bras or jackets.

Fashion retailers from River Island to New Look have been making high fashion ranges and repeat orders in the UK and relatively nearby countries such as Turkey for some time because of the benefits of quick response. DIY retailers, meanwhile, source heavy goods such as plasterboard locally because of the inhibitive transport costs. Fragile, short-lived product such as plants are also likely to be bought in the UK. As margin differences narrow, analysis may reveal new product areas that make sense. Braithwaite says: 'Retailers will need to go through a structured review process and identify where they can reach out and find local capacity. Then there will be a challenge to negotiate the right sort of deals.'

Supply chain managers will have to support that with better analytical and negotiation skills, while supply chain teams will need to work closely with sales and operations teams to ensure the implications of buying closer to home and from a broader array of sources are fully understood throughout the business. 'This is a new game and buying and merchandising teams haven't had to play it before', Braithwaite says. Short agrees. N Brown has teamed up with Manchester University to study the total cost implications of sourcing in the UK or Europe and surrounding countries for a selection of products against buying in the Far East. 'I can see us increasingly having dual and triple sourcing for products and we will have to do analysis to make sure we are making the right decision. We will need a lot more information than we have had in the past. Buyers have been too easily swayed by the cost price but we have to look at net margin rather than intake margin.'

Nevertheless, he admits opportunities are limited. N Brown currently makes less than 5 per cent of its clothing in the UK and Short makes clear any expansion could only work for certain categories such as knitwear, simple jersey tops and high fashion garments. Shop Direct, meanwhile, only sources about 1 per cent of its clothing in the UK at present. It is planning a significant increase for autumn/winter but even then it will still only amount to about 6 per cent. M&S has been touted as a potential returnee to UK sourcing. Its head of UK sourcing for clothing and home Garry Gordon says it is open to opportunities. It does source some clothing here, particularly in hosiery, and has a significant UK homeware sourcing operation including an eco-furniture factory in Wales. However, he sums up the view of many high street retailers: 'We are not seeing a shift in production back to the UK in any significant numbers. The clothing industry is a global industry with a global supply base.'

For most product, the margin gains still make sourcing abroad worthwhile and a greater swing towards the UK is likely to face significant capacity issues. Braithwaite says: 'There isn't the local capacity and finding suppliers or distributors who are prepared to take a risk is a challenge.' What's more, those manufacturers that have capacity will need reassurance of an ongoing relationship if they are to be persuaded to increase volume and lower prices, particularly at a time when the weak pound is driving demand from Europe. Short says N Brown might consider helping to finance the development of a supplier if it found the right partner with which it could build a long-term relationship. 'I think there will need to be Government support to get the skill set in place in the UK', he notes.

Sourcing in the UK

Benefits

- Shorter lead times allow quick response to unpredictable markets.
- Easier to meet demand for newness and high fashion and so achieve additional sales.
- Closer monitoring of factories for better quality.
- Lower inventory levels required as product can be topped up relatively quickly.
- Reduction in discounting with right product at right time.
- Avoids expensive long-distance transport costs.
- Can cut back on expensive, time-consuming buying trips.
- Supporting British industry.

Difficulties

- Manufacturing capacity in the UK is low and suppliers may require financial support to meet demand.
- Existing manufacturers want to focus on higher value items rather than volume.
- Potential competition for capacity could drive up prices.
- Even with reduction in discounting, margins are lower.

Source: Butler, S. (2011) Supply chain – back to the source, *Retail Week*, May.

DISCUSSION QUESTIONS

1 According to this article, what are the key reasons why retailers are reconsidering sourcing more merchandise in the UK?
2 What are the main potential problems for buyers and merchandisers involved with sourcing in the UK from the viewpoint of:
   a grocery retailers
   b electronics retailers
   c clothing retailers
3 What impact would sourcing more products from the domestic market (rather than overseas) have on the responsibilities of a retail buyer?
4 What can European retail buyers do in terms of sourcing to achieve a compromise between the low prices but long-lead times of the Far East and the higher prices but shorter lead times of European suppliers?

CHAPTER 6

Retail pricing

Learning objectives

The objectives of this chapter are to:

- explore the relationship between pricing and other factors within the retail marketing mix;
- explain the differences between retail market levels;
- evaluate the theories and techniques used to specify retail prices;
- examine how pricing relates to a company's profitability;
- discuss the impact of external influences on price-setting, such as competitors, consumers and suppliers;
- examine the types and effects of price markdowns.

Introduction

Pricing decisions are crucial to the profitability of retailers, as price is the major, and often only, source of their revenue. However, it is important to remember that all of the other elements of the marketing mix should help towards maximising companies' profits and that pricing should be consistent with these other elements. Price is defined by Gilbert (2003: 157) as 'the monetary value assigned by the seller to something purchased, sold or offered for sale, and on transaction by a buyer, as their willingness to pay for the benefits the product and channel service delivers'. This definition recognises that price is not simply a function of the retailer but that customers also have a part to play in that they choose whether or not to accept a selling price.

Retail price strategy is affected by five different key factors, from the retailer's overall strategic objectives through to how it is implemented and then adjusted, e.g. when marked down during a seasonal sale. The price charged by a supplier to a retailer is known as the 'cost price'. Retail prices are rarely based solely on the cost price plus retailer **mark-up**, as customers' perceptions of the value of the product or service should also be taken into account. As well as customers, suppliers and competitors also influence retail pricing and, at a broader level, government regulations and policies exert an impact (Berman and Evans, 2010). Setting lower prices than the competition is a tempting strategy to follow to increase market share, but price is arguably the easiest part of the marketing mix for competitors to copy and initiating a price war can ultimately be a dangerous strategy to adopt.

Retailers have various methods of determining selling prices for their merchandise, which are discussed below. Pricing objectives interact with decisions on several other aspects of the retail mix: merchandise; location; promotion; credit; customer service; credit and store image, in addition to legal constraints (Lusch et al., 2011). For certain retailers, pricing has become the foremost element of the marketing mix, and is therefore the key component of their brand image, such as supermarkets Asda and Lidl. Price can also be an important element for retailers at the luxury end of the market, to reinforce their exclusive status. Pricing has become a particularly significant element of the retail marketing mix since the worldwide economic crisis that began in 2008, causing many retailers to focus on delivering lower prices in response to consumers seeking better value for money. For many retailers, setting prices is the responsibility of buyers or merchandisers, therefore much of this chapter relates to tasks which form part of their roles (see also Chapter 5 Retail buying and merchandising).

Retail pricing is inherently a multidimensional function, as Figure 6.1 illustrates. In common with all price setters, retailers must have regard for demand and cost conditions, as well as the activities of their competitors. More than most forms of pricing, retail pricing is highly susceptible to change, whether fashion retailers are timing their sales around seasonal events, or supermarkets are responding to the special offers of rivals. As most shopping is still through stores, location plays a large part, as sales volume in individual retail outlets is affected by local demand and competition. Many retailers are also working with very large product assortments, providing various opportunities for **psychological pricing** to optimise the price image for the store, not just for the individual items. The following sections summarise these pricing dimensions and associated strategies.

Retail market levels – mass market, middle market and luxury

Retail markets can be split into several different levels by price bracket, with almost all stores offering their own unique assortment of prices ('pound stores' being a notable exception – see below). The 'mass market' refers to retail chains that are typically found

Figure 6.1 Facets of retail pricing

Competition
- Price positioning
- Penetration pricing
- Skimming pricing
- Price matching

Time
- Special offers
- Seasonal sales
- Everyday low prices
- Price auctions

Economics
- Costs and demand
- Price elasticity
- Retail margins

Assortment
- Leader lines
- Price lining
- Odd-even ends
- Price bundling

Locations
- Internet prices
- Local price flexibility
- Prices for store formats
- International prices

Source: adapted from McGoldrick, P. (2002) *Retail Marketing*, 2nd edn © 2002. Reproduced with the kind permission of McGraw-Hill Education. All rights reserved.

on the High Street or in shopping centres, charging relatively low prices owing to the economies of scale involved in selling large quantities of merchandise. Retailers at the cheapest end of the mass market, that sell reduced-price merchandise, are also known as discounters. At the opposite end of the price spectrum is the luxury market, with upmarket retailers selling expensive goods that are sometimes referred to as 'designer' products. The 'middle market' covers the large range of prices in between these two extremes. Additionally, retailers that sell products at the mid-level of the mass market are also often termed 'middle market' by industry and in the press, particularly Marks & Spencer (*Retail Week*, 2013).

The mass market forms such a large proportion of the retail market (especially in the UK) that it can easily be subdivided into further categories. Multiple retailers such as Neal's Yard Remedies, that stock products that are higher in price than the average in the mass market could be termed 'high-end High Street', with many of their prices crossing over with the middle market. There is no strict definition of where each of these market levels starts and finishes, especially since prices of a single international retailer can vary in the different countries in which it trades. It is consequently more realistic to view the different retail market levels as a continuum rather than as distinct price segments (see Figure 6.2).

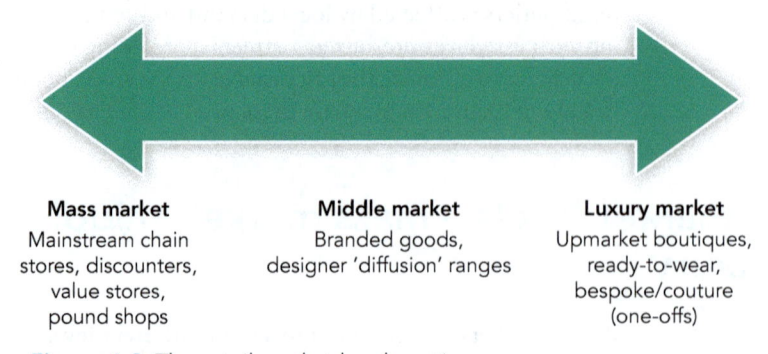

Mass market
Mainstream chain stores, discounters, value stores, pound shops

Middle market
Branded goods, designer 'diffusion' ranges

Luxury market
Upmarket boutiques, ready-to-wear, bespoke/couture (one-offs)

Figure 6.2 The retail market level continuum

Table 6.1 Examples of retailers at different market levels

Retail market levels	Mass market	Middle market	Luxury market
Examples of retailers (and countries where they are based)	Aldo (Canada) Asda (UK division of US retailer Walmart) H&M (Sweden) House of Fraser (UK) Victoria's Secret (US)	Comptoir des Cotonniers (France) Diesel (Italy) DKNY (US) Hotel Chocolat (UK) Space NK (UK)	Boodles (UK) Cartier (France) Louis Vuitton (France) Prada (Italy) Ralph Lauren (US)

Many brands in the luxury market sell their products in other retailers' stores as well as in their own outlets. At this market level, items such as clothing which are manufactured exactly to consumers' measurements or specifications are referred to as 'couture' or 'bespoke' (e.g. tailoring). As they are essentially custom-made 'one-off' pieces and are consequently labour-intensive, this is one of the main reasons why they are so expensive. Retailers from various countries illustrate different market levels in Table 6.1.

Price architecture

Once a retailer has established which price level it will adopt, the specific range of prices within this level should be decided upon. This can involve building the retailer's own **price architecture**, a term used within the industry to describe offering more than one price level in order to appeal to different types of customer or occasion. For example, many supermarkets adopt a 'good, better, best' policy, with 'good' pricing referring to their low-cost ranges of generic, everyday products, usually presented in minimal packaging. 'Better' products are generally own-label or manufacturer brands, offering a wider selection of items representing the mid-price level of the retailer. 'Best' are those products which are the most expensive in the store and they may be exclusive to the retailer or from upmarket manufacturer brands. They are targeted towards the retailer's highest income customers or aimed at more typical customers for special occasions. 'Best' products are perceived as luxury merchandise, which can be indicated by their packaging and the addition of a 'subbrand' name, e.g. 'Taste the Difference' products at Sainsbury's.

Retail pricing – objectives and strategies

Pricing objectives can often be profit-based, aiming for a specific net profit margin or an increase in average margin. Another pricing objective can be to increase market share by undercutting competitors' prices, in the hope of attracting their customers. Pricing objectives are derived from the retailer's overall strategic objectives. For example, a key business objective may be to increase market share and this could be achieved by implementing prices from a range of different techniques, as specified below. Pricing can also be affected by other corporate objectives, for example aiming to improve customer satisfaction through product quality could result in increased selling prices. Solomon *et al*. (2009: 357) propose that setting objectives should be the first step when planning prices:

- develop pricing objectives;
- estimate demand;
- determine costs;

- evaluate the pricing environment;
- choose a pricing strategy;
- develop pricing tactics.

Managers may need to develop different pricing strategies to appeal to more than one market segment. Various pricing strategies and tactics that are suitable to be implemented in a retailing context are discussed below. To set a retail price, retailers may simply multiply the cost price of the product from the manufacturer by a set percentage (**cost-orientated pricing**). Alternative strategies would be to set a price which is comparable to that of similar products sold by competitors (competition-orientated) or to estimate the amount that customers will be prepared to pay (demand-orientated). In practice, retail price-setting can often involve achieving a balance between two or three of these methods, as shown in Figure 6.3. It is important for retailers to be aware of the prices charged by competing retailers to gain a sense of where they stand in relation to the competition. Retailers can opt to charge above, below or at the same level as the average market price, depending on their market positioning. Alternatively, retailers may wish to price-match or 'benchmark' a key competitor. For example, Waitrose is viewed as a relatively expensive supermarket but it has a policy of charging the same prices as the UK market leader on many branded products. The key options for retail pricing strategies are discussed further below.

Cost-orientated pricing

Cost-orientated pricing is based on the cost of buying the products from suppliers marked up by a standard percentage by the retailer, then rounded up or down to the nearest set price point (e.g. £4.99 or £5). This can be referred to as 'cost-plus' pricing. This technique does not take into account the level of demand from consumers for the merchandise, the prices charged by competitors or the wider economic environment. It is therefore a somewhat simplistic, traditional pricing technique. Suppliers are the companies that provide the products to the retailers and they may either be manufacturers themselves or intermediaries who liaise between manufacturers and retailers. Intermediaries, such as wholesalers, take a profit margin, thus making the products more expensive if the retailer worked directly with manufacturers. However, if a retail organisation is not large enough to have high order quantities produced or lacks the sourcing knowledge, then they may find it preferable, or have no alternative but to buy a smaller quantity at a higher price from a wholesaler.

Manufacturers' prices usually need to cover the costs of making the products, as well as adding a profit margin to make transactions financially viable. Manufacturers' overheads would typically include variable costs which fluctuate depending on the quantity

Figure 6.3 The overlap between key pricing methods

of products manufactured, e.g. materials and operatives' wages. Manufacturers' costings can typically be based on the following formula:

Fixed costs + variable costs + profit margin = cost price

Manufacturers' fixed costs, such as rent for premises and management salaries, remain virtually the same whatever the size of the production quantities. Because fixed costs per item reduce as the quantity of products manufactured increases, factories can charge lower prices or make higher profits when order quantities are high. Also, operatives can become more efficient with more experience of making the same item and therefore quicker at manufacturing, up to a certain point. Furthermore, the cost of materials and components for a manufacturer can be reduced as their suppliers can also offer cheaper prices for large quantities. These contributing factors allow retailers to have better negotiating power for lowering cost prices from suppliers when purchasing products in high volume.

Competition-orientated pricing

Retailers that select prices similar to those of their competitors are engaging in competition-orientated pricing. They study their competitors' pricing carefully to benchmark close competitors, thus ensuring that they offer competitive prices for their customers. Certain retailers make competition-orientated pricing a feature of their brand image, e.g. department store John Lewis has traditionally used the phrase 'Never Knowingly Undersold' to indicate that they have set out to match the prices of their competitors. Retailers can also use a technique of undercutting the competition's prices intentionally, in order to tempt customers away from the places where they usually shop. If the price cuts are temporary then this can be termed promotional pricing (see Chapter 7 Retail marketing communications) or if they remain low this is known as everyday low pricing (EDLP) (see below). Price comparison websites such as Kelkoo and Price Runner have made it much easier for consumers to compare prices of merchandise from competing stores and websites and mobile devices have enabled people to make these comparisons whilst out shopping. Therefore, retailers need to pay more attention to their competitors' prices in the current climate than they did in previous decades.

Demand-orientated pricing

Demand-orientated pricing takes place when prices are set depending on the volume of demand from customers for products or services, rather than being based solely on the costs involved in manufacturing the product or providing a service. Demand can be affected by a wide range of different factors, many of them beyond the control of the retailer, so a PESTEL analysis can be a useful model to assess macro-environmental factors that could influence pricing strategy (see Chapter 2 Retail marketing strategy). Demand-orientated pricing has numerous variants, several of which are described below.

Implementing demand-based pricing strategies

Psychological pricing

A popular method of retail pricing is for products and services to be priced to end in odd figures such as '.99' or '.95', with the intention that the customer will perceive the cost as being cheaper than the nearest pound, dollar or other currency. There is no clear evidence to confirm that this **odd pricing** technique has the desired psychological effect, yet it has become a conventional practice in the UK since the introduction of decimalised money (i.e. 100 pence in each £ sterling) in the 1970s. Upmarket retailers often distance themselves from this practice by using round pricing, i.e. whole numbers. Perhaps surprisingly it is also becoming more common to use whole numbers in prices at the competitively priced end of the market. This technique has been adopted by supermarket Iceland, setting a trend which certain competing supermarkets have begun to follow. Iceland currently makes a feature of its prices by printing them on the packaging, whereas many of their competitors locate prices on the shelves, rather than on the products themselves. Retailers have also been known to engage in price wars by reducing price endings below 99p to 98p, with even-ended prices gaining in popularity.

Market penetration pricing and pricing skimming

Paradoxically, both **pricing skimming** (setting artificially high prices) and market penetration (where lower than market value prices are charged) can both be effective demand-orientated methods of pricing used by retailers when launching new products. A market penetration strategy is more appropriate when similar products already exist in the market and the retailer wants to gain market share quickly by charging prices below those of its competitors (Gilbert, 2003). This lower initial price may be publicised as a 'trial price' so that customers are prepared for the fact that the price will rise at a later stage and they may wish to take advantage of the current discount (Solomon et al., 2009). Pricing skimming (or market skimming) is more suited to a product that is innovative and in relatively short supply, with few direct substitutes. A high price can be charged using this tactic to maximise profits while the product is viewed as new and exclusive, before competitors have chance to offer similar merchandise. Setting high prices can occasionally increase demand for products, since it makes them appear to be more exclusive and desirable to consumers, with demand reducing when prices are lowered (Solomon et al., 2009). This situation is usually limited to products at the luxury end of the market, with customers for whom social status is particularly important. Market penetration and pricing skimming are both usually temporary measures; once they have achieved their objectives and the product has established itself in the market, retailers are then likely to pitch the product more closely in line with competitors' prices.

Price lining

If retailers always chose to add a specific margin percentage to cost prices (using cost-plus pricing) they would frequently end up with retail prices with random endings, e.g. €14.73, which consumers are not accustomed to seeing, and which are more difficult to remember than standard '.00' or '.99' endings. It is therefore usual for retailers to use **price lining** by adopting a selection of price points that meet their customers' expectations. For example, €40 may be the most popular price for a pair of trousers at a mass market retailer, so customers may expect more styling details or better quality fabric for a pair at a higher price such as €50. Retailers may have a broad range of price points, especially if they have a 'good, better, best' price architecture (see above) or a wide assortment of merchandise. In contrast, certain retailers aim for a single price throughout the store, as used by Dollar Tree in the US and Euroland in the Netherlands (see 99p case study below). Dollar$tore in Sweden also offers low prices but sells goods at a selection of different price points rounded off to '.0' in Swedish krone.

MINI CASE STUDY
99p Stores

99p stores outlet in Derby and co-founder Hussein Lalani
Source: with permission from 99p Stores

The first 99p Store was opened in 2001 in Holloway, London, by Nadir Lalani with his sons Hussein and Faisal. Since then the company has built up to a turnover in excess of £269 million in 2012 and attracts around 1.5 million customers per week. The Lalani family had previously owned a small chain of 'Whistle Stop' convenience stores in London and after selling this they invested the money in 99p Stores, inspired by the Dollar Stores they'd seen in the US. By 2012 99p Stores had over 200 branches in the UK, with rapid expansion being facilitated by taking over 70 outlets vacated by Woolworths (which exited the UK market after 99 years in 2008). The business has a new 375,000 sq. ft. distribution centre in Northampton in central England and it has also adapted its format to a lower-priced chain, €uro 50 Stores, based in the Republic of Ireland. The firm's growth is continuing, with plans to open 100 new 99p Stores in the UK between January 2014 and December 2015. Commercial director Hussein Lalani says 'we are finding that our stores work in every part of the country and up to 1 in 4 of our customers are from ABC1 groups'.

99p Stores stock a wide variety of food and household products, all sold at the same price, slightly undercutting their main competitors, Poundland and Poundworld. The chain's product ranges include toiletries, tools, books, car care, toys and accessories. As is typical in this market sector, 99p Stores mainly develop their own lines to cater for their price point and also occasionally stock end-of-line items, e.g. when a manufacturer has changed its packaging and wants to sell out of the previous version. The retailer has its own buying and merchandising teams for domestic and imported products, sourcing goods mainly from China, as well as from India, Pakistan and America. 99p Stores sell their own-label merchandise under names such as 'Delifresh' and 'Brite', as well as purchasing well-known brands. Regarding brands, Hussein states: 'If you look at the three main players in this sector, our turnover is coming up to about £1.5bn. If you're Cadbury's or Walkers crisps you can't ignore this sector of the market so they come up with bespoke products for us that fit into our price point. It's not so much end-of-line products because if we want to capture our customers and get them in every week they want some kind of predictability, so they know that product's going to be there each time they visit.'

The economic crisis that led to a recession in the UK helped to create a suitable environment in which 'pound shops' thrived, with consumers seeking highly competitive prices and continuing to do so after the end of the recession. In light of this, fresh products have become a key area of growth for 99p Stores, as Hussein states: 'like-for-like growth on our chilled section is currently above 20 per cent. We're competing with the convenience sector and supermarkets because we noticed through the recession people used to come to us to get cleaning products and toiletries, but they were going to the supermarkets to get meat, milk and other grocery products. We have chilled meats, eggs, butter and cheeses and we'd like to get our customers to do their whole shop in our store.'

Owing to their low pricing, 99p Stores pursue an everyday low pricing (EDLP) policy, without the need for seasonal sales. Their main pricing strategy is single-pricing but they also use **multiple-unit pricing** on some lines, such as three packets for 99p. Hussein states 'sometimes our sector does get criticised in the media . . . but supermarkets hike up the price then show an artificial discount. We don't, we just use simple pricing all year round, the same price, no gimmicks'.

Source: 99p Stores, 2014 and interview with Hussein Lalani. You can see BBC interviews about 99p Stores with Hussein Lalani online at: http://www.youtube.com/watch?v=PoasI35Ejcw; http://www.youtube.com/watch?v=qLgbvAF7HIE

Backward pricing and reverse auctions

Backward pricing is based on how much the retailer expects customers to be willing to pay for a product or service. The desired retail selling price is therefore established before the retailer seeks a supplier to provide items at a cost price that will enable the retailer to achieve this selling price. The formula for backward pricing is therefore:

Chosen selling price = cost price from supplier
 + retailer's standard margin (mark-up)

If the cost price charged by the supplier does not enable the retailer to make its usual profit margin then the retailer is unlikely to purchase the product. Therefore, a potential disadvantage of this pricing method is that the retailer may miss out on stocking key products that are in demand from consumers by remaining rigid about the intended selling price and mark-up. Yet products which are in high demand can be profitable for retailers due to being sold in large quantities, even if they make a lower mark-up than average per item.

Like backward pricing, **reverse auctions** are initiated by retailers. They are similar to standard auctions in that they involve bids, but the bids made by suppliers are the prices they will charge for their products, in contrast to an ordinary auction where bids are the amounts that buyers are willing to pay. In a reverse auction a retailer sets a specification for a product and suppliers tender for the business by each proposing a cost price. The suppliers would normally be unaware of the prices tendered by their competitors, so it is similar to a blind auction in this respect. The retailer is likely to select the best value price, which may either be the lowest or a competitive price with added value factors, such as better quality materials or a faster delivery date. This technique can also be described as competitive bidding (Jobber, 2010).

Multiple-unit pricing

This pricing technique can be implemented with the aim of selling products in large volumes within a relatively short period of time. Encouraging customers to buy in bulk is more cost-effective for the retailer as more products can be sold with the overheads of only a single transaction and store space can be used more efficiently if there is a quicker turnover of products purchased. Where products are sold in multiple packs retailers often specify the price per unit on the shelf. This pricing method is useful when the retailer wants to sell merchandise which is perishable or fashion-sensitive and therefore needs to be sold at a faster rate. The customer benefits by receiving a cheaper price per unit on offers such as 'Buy One Get One Free' (BOGOF). However, the downside for the customer is that they may buy more items than they will use, particularly for perishable items, thus cancelling out the benefits of the cheaper price per unit. Additionally, this can potentially harm the environment through the purchase of extra products that have unnecessarily depleted raw materials and which may be disposed of in landfill. Supermarkets have been criticised in recent years for using BOGOF offers and the estimated wastage of 15 m tons of food per year in the UK has been attributed partly to this practice in a report by a House of Lords EU Committee (Swinburne, 2014).

Price bundling is another form of multiple-unit pricing, when a reduction can be given on a different, but related product, e.g. a discount on double cream when strawberries are purchased, or a printer offered at a reduced price when bought with a laptop. The aim of price bundling is to encourage consumers to make a multiple purchase in one sales transaction.

Segmented pricing

This flexible method of pricing refers to retailers selling products or services at different prices depending on the market segment that purchases them, e.g. children, students and people of pension age receiving a discount in cinemas. Prices can also be based on time segments with reductions offered on products and services at quieter times of the day or year, to encourage more custom when there is spare capacity to be filled, such as restaurants offering a discount in the mid afternoon. A recent development in **segmented pricing** has been the introduction of 'student lock-ins' at shopping centres, to offer a discount to students at numerous outlets in a certain location, at a specific time later than the centre's usual opening hours, often supported by live music, DJs and other entertainment (Figure 6.4). Students register for the events in advance to receive discounts at the events, which have been organised by Total Students Ltd in towns and cities around the UK, including Bournemouth, Bristol, Hatfield, Leeds and Sheffield, since 2010 (Student Lock-In, 2014).

Figure 6.4 Student lock-in at Cabot Circus, Bristol
Source: with permission from Student Lock-In

Pricing second-hand goods and auctions

Traditional auctions, where products are sold to the highest bidder, are still popular for second-hand goods. Prices in auctions are not set in advance as they are derived directly from demand, but the product will not be sold if there are only demands below a reserve price, i.e. the minimum that the seller is prepared to take. Paradoxically, whilst being a preferred method of selling expensive art and antiques, auctions are also viewed as a potential way to purchase relatively cheap houses and cars.

Auctions have become used more frequently in recent years as a method of buying goods online in consumer-to-consumer markets, using eBay and other online auction websites. EBay has been instrumental in making it more widely acceptable to purchase second-hand goods, offering consumers an effective way of buying products more cheaply. Certain bricks-and-mortar retailers have also moved into offering second-hand (or 'pre-owned') goods in store, pricing them below the rate for the price of new products. This also puts consumers in the unusual position of selling products to retailers, especially in the videogame market where the product's quality is not usually diminished by being second-hand.

Geographical pricing

Prices for the same product in branches of a single retail chain can sometimes vary, depending on where the retail outlet is based (Sullivan and Adcock, 2002). If the retailer has stores overseas, prices may need to be increased in certain countries because of currency exchange rates and the costs incurred by the company in exchanging money into another currency. The widespread adoption of the euro throughout most of the European

Union has helped to avoid this expense to some extent. However, even within the same country a retailer may charge different prices for a product, depending in which region or part of town the branch is located. This can be due to higher profit margins being required to make it financially viable to operate certain outlets, owing to more expensive rents or stores being smaller and therefore less cost-efficient. The **geographical pricing** technique is sometimes used by supermarkets in the UK.

Everyday low pricing

Retailers that charge consistently low prices throughout the year, with relatively few price promotions and markdowns, practise everyday low pricing (EDLP). This technique is adopted by a minority of stores and it is used successfully by large retailers where economies of scales make low prices feasible, such as supermarkets Asda and Aldi, as well as clothing retailer Matalan. The aim of EDLP is to encourage customer loyalty from price-sensitive consumers.

Predatory pricing

Predatory pricing is an approach that can be used by large retailers to set prices below those of competitors, or even below the cost charged by their suppliers, with the aim of driving competitors out of business. Several large niche retailers have raised prices after competitors have been diminished, leading to them being accused of using predatory pricing. This is one of the many areas of pricing with the potential for unethical practice. (See Chapter 12 for further discussion of ethics and legislation in relation to pricing.)

Calculating retail prices

Many consumers would probably be surprised to discover that it is standard practice for retailers to charge consumers between twice and 3.5 times the cost price from the supplier. However, the mark-up (the difference between the retail selling price and the cost price that is retained by the retailer) is not pure profit as most, if not all, of this profit margin covers the company's costs for premises, bills and employees' wages, among other outgoings (including marketers' salaries). Each retailer has a target margin that it seeks to achieve by using a mathematical formula. For a typical High Street retailer the mark-up may constitute around two-thirds of the final selling price, so multiplying a supplier's cost price by three, then rounding up to the nearest price point is an example of a straightforward way to estimate a retail selling price. Retail buyers or merchandisers need to make a judgement about the most appropriate price whilst making a suitable profit margin, based on all of the data available to them, often influenced by previous experience (Goworek, 2007). The retailer's margin may be calculated using the following formula:

$$\text{selling price} - \text{cost price} \times 100 = \frac{\text{margin percentage}}{\text{selling price}}$$

In practice, the formula is likely to be more complex and can vary from one country to another, e.g. in the UK 20 per cent Value Added Tax (VAT) needs to be included in the price for most products at the time of writing (see Chapter 12 Legislation and ethics in retailing). This formula calculates the gross margin, i.e. the percentage of the selling price that remains after the cost price is subtracted *before* the retailer's costs have been taken into account, so it means that the margin in this case is not pure profit. The examples of margin calculations below apply to a retailer with a mark-up of three times cost price (i.e. the retailer's target margin is two-thirds or 66.67 per cent of the selling price). The percentages are rounded to two decimal places here:

(a) Selling price = £30; cost price = £10

(30 − 10) ÷ 30 × 100 = 66.67% profit margin

(b) Selling price = £30; cost price = £9

(30 − 9) ÷ 30 × 100 = 70% profit margin

This example shows the effect of a lower cost price in (b) increasing the margin percentage from 66.67 per cent (i.e. two-thirds) in (a) to 70 per cent in (b). The retailer could afford to charge £29 for the product in example (b) but this would be an unusual price point that customers are not used to seeing, so £30 or £29.99 would be more typical and the merchandise could therefore make the retailer a better margin. However, a lower margin than the target might be charged for a product if the retail buyer believes that customers will be too price-sensitive to pay a higher selling price, if the item is believed to be an important addition to the product range. Having a mix of some items with higher margins and some lower than the target percentage is a technique referred to as 'marrying margins', where the overall margin should balance out evenly on average across the product range. It is possible to calculate the average margin for the whole range, aiming to achieve the target profit margin overall, rather than for each individual item. Further examples of retail margin calculations are given below.

(c) Selling price = £45; cost price = £15

(45 − 15) ÷ 45 × 100 = 66.67%

(d) Selling price = £120; cost price = £41.20

(120 − 41.2) ÷ 120 × 100 = 65.67%

(e) Selling price = £6,499; cost price = £2,130

(6,499 − 3870) ÷ 6,499 × 100 = 67.23%

Retail buyers can use computer software to calculate profit margins but a sound understanding of the way in which the margin is calculated is important and sometimes margins may need to be estimated quickly, with or without a calculator, whilst the buyer is negotiating with suppliers. It may seem counter-intuitive, but a lower margin than average does not necessarily result in lower profitability for an item, because total profits are ultimately dependent on the quantity of items being sold. For example, if a pair of jeans has a mark-up of only 2.5 times the cost price and sells 1000 pieces, it could potentially be more profitable for the company than a pair of chinos with a selling price of 3 times the cost price that sells only 200 pieces.

Price elasticity

When the price of a product falls, demand from consumers will tend to increase and as price increases, demand will reduce; that is, price and demand are inversely related (see Figure 6.5). Moreover, the law of supply and demand dictates that a surplus of product will result in lower prices. **Price elasticity** is the degree to which changes in price affect the quantities of products purchased by customers. If customers for particular products are price-sensitive, demand is elastic and consequently small price changes will cause large changes in the quantities customers buy, i.e. lowering prices will create significant changes in demand (Gilbert, 2003).

Figure 6.5 The relationship between price and demand

RETAIL MARKETING CAREERS
James Clark, Merchandising specialist

James Clark has extensive experience in retail merchandising and he now teaches this subject as a Lecturer and International Co-ordinator at the University of the Arts. James studied BA (Hons) Business Finance before starting his retailing career as a stock clerk at Fenwick, then moving on to Debenhams where he worked for five years, progressing from an allocator's position to become an assistant merchandiser, then a junior merchandiser. His next job was in a merchandiser's role for Viyella for three years before working for House of Fraser for eight years, initially as a senior merchandiser and subsequently as Head of Merchandising. In this role, on a day-to-day basis James oversaw the management of stock flows into and out of the business by ensuring that his team drove the maximum financial benefit from the product ranges. He describes the main responsibilities of this job as 'reviewing sales and profit results with the Buying and Merchandising (B&M) teams to set the trading agenda for the week ahead, as well as assessing the implication of trading results for the remainder of the season'. As a result, James discussed changed priorities and requirements with senior colleagues from other areas of the business such as finance, retail operations and supply chain. He also worked closely with the Head of Buying and key suppliers, as well as liaising with the Board of Directors and his role involved regular travel to visit suppliers.

As Head of Merchandising James was keen to maintain the competitiveness of the company's offer compared to direct and indirect competitors. When setting prices, James considers that 'having a compelling price architecture of opening, mid and top price points relative to the industry is important as is being aware of price trends of other products that your customers may buy instead of your own, electronics for example. Prices must also deliver to the retailer's margin requirements, and I would work with the buying team to make sure that they knew about margins and supplier funding budgets, to make sure the cost prices negotiated reflect not just selling prices, but also the cost base'.

James was also responsible for agreeing suitable markdown offers with his team, to support the sell-through of products. These could be either in-season offers or the bigger end of season sale. James describes the spending of markdown as 'a necessary evil, we cannot get all of our ranges right, but it must be controlled and carefully planned'. He worked together with the finance team to go over the rationale and predicted cost of the sale and he found that receiving their approval was just as important as the customers' approval of the prices.

Describing the more strategic, longer term aspects of the role, James says 'in conjunction with the Head of Buying I was responsible for setting the medium- to long-term strategy for the product offer, identifying opportunities, planning the financial progression of the business and negotiating the required support from other stakeholders to deliver our strategy'.

James considers the following skills to be important for merchandisers: 'a strategic mind set; empathy and understanding of other roles; negotiation and persuasion', in addition to core skills such as communication, IT and planning. When appointing staff in merchandising roles James would look for highly numerate, motivated candidates with lateral thinking skills, vision and the ability to make effective decisions. Selecting the right employees for the role was a particularly important feature of the job, as James was assessed in relation to staff retention rates, as well as on his budget performance (i.e. the financial turnover and profitability of the range).

James found the most enjoyable aspects of merchandising to be seeing the trading results and achieving challenging budgets. However, he considers the more difficult features of the job to be keeping a consistent train of thought and 'resisting the flow of good ideas from the buyers that we could not afford'. He recommends that merchandisers should think carefully before acting, as the consequences of their actions can be widespread, i.e. affecting the retailer, suppliers and customers.

The demand curve in Figure 6.6 demonstrates that when the price for a product is high, the quantity sold can be relatively low and vice versa. However, the demand curve does not always follow this pattern, e.g. when demand is inelastic. When changes in price create little change in demand for merchandise and customers are not price-sensitive, this is known as inelastic demand. Products which possess unique and desirable characteristics or that are relatively limited in number may have inelastic demand.

Reducing the price of a product from €140 to €95 seems a plausible reduction of 32.1%. Under inelastic demand conditions, this 32.1% price reduction increases quantity sold only by 18% to 295 units, while under elastic demand conditions for the item, the quantity sold increases by 80% to 450 units.

The effects on revenue are that at the original price of €140 and selling 250 units, total revenue would be €35,000. After the price reduction to €95 with inelastic demand, the total revenue would decrease to €28,025, a fall of −19.9%. With elastic demand, the price decrease would result in revenue to €42,750, a rise of 22.1%.

Of course the effects on retailer margins are less straightforward, as manufacturers may be required by powerful retailers to accept lower supply prices, if retail prices need to be reduced, thereby reducing the potential negative impact on the retailer's gross margins.

The following formula can be used to calculate elasticity:

$$\text{Price elasticity} = \frac{\text{Percentage change in quantity demanded}}{\text{Percentage change in price}}$$

A coefficient of more than one shows that demand is elastic, i.e. when a price increase reduces demand significantly. A coefficient of less than one suggests inelastic demand, with a price increase having relatively little effect on demand. For example, if a retailer reduces the price of a bag of rice by 10 per cent from €1 to 90 cents and the sales quantity then increases by 17 per cent, then the coefficient for price elasticity of demand would be 1.7 (i.e. 17 per cent divided by 10 per cent). Even though the retailer's mark-up has been

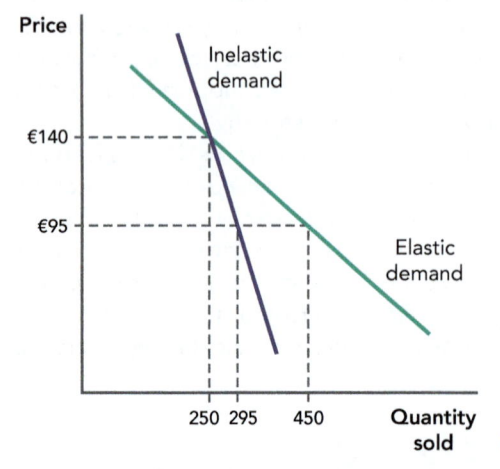

Figure 6.6 Price elasticity

reduced in this example by 10 cents per item, the increased sales quantity can more than compensate for this if sufficient quantities are sold. The difference in price elasticity can sometimes be as a result of the market segment at which the product or service is targeted and this is dependent upon demographic or psychographic characteristics of the target market (Gilbert, 2003) (see Chapter 3 Retail consumer behaviour and market segmentation).

Price elasticity is affected by price sensitivity, which indicates to what extent customers are sensitive to alterations in price. Retailers now have the ability to use software to determine price elasticities reliably using price analytic software from companies such as SAP and Oracle (Grewal et al., 2011).

Consumers are less price-sensitive if they believe that a product has unique attributes, whereas they are more price sensitive if a product can be easily substituted by a cheaper alternative. It is becoming increasingly easy for customers to compare alternative prices while shopping if they are purchasing online or checking prices on a mobile device during a store visit. Where product substitutes are not easily available, retailers can take advantage of the situation by charging higher prices than the usual market value, such as the selling price for refreshments in cinemas. In certain circumstances, increasing a product's price can improve demand, as it can imply that products are exclusive and of high quality. Demand can also be affected by price changes for different products that can be used as substitutes, e.g. if the price of cocoa beans increases then customers may buy more flowers as gifts, instead of chocolates.

The relationship between price and value

Value is defined by Ferrell and Hartline (2011: 233) as 'a customer's subjective evaluation of benefits relative to costs to determine the worth of a firm's product offering relative to other product offerings'. The term 'value' is often associated with low prices, as illustrated by the description of low-priced clothing stores such as Lidl and Matalan as 'value retailers'. However, value is dependent on other elements of the retail marketing mix, rather than pricing alone. A product with a relatively high price can therefore still be considered good value by a consumer if it serves its purpose well and possesses attributes which are not present in cheaper products in the same category. Consequently, consumers do not always perceive the lowest-priced product as being the best value. Products with expensive prices may be perceived by consumers as high-quality products, whereas lower prices can be viewed as indicators of poor quality. However, this is not always necessarily the case. High expenditure on promotional strategies, particularly mass media advertising to impart a strong brand image for products, is usually recouped by the retailer via charging a high retail price.

When products are sold in large quantities the promotional costs can be relatively small per item. However, when the products are more exclusive and are therefore sold in limited quantities, such as 'luxury' or 'designer' merchandise, the promotional costs are spread over fewer items and therefore each individual item needs to make a larger contribution to pay for the promotion. For example, identical leather bags from a branded label could be sold at two very different prices depending on the quantity being produced, as shown in Table 6.2 below. The difference in the retail prices can be attributed largely to the fixed cost of the brand's advertising being distributed over different quantities of the product. Selling in low quantities is therefore often the main reason why small-scale designers or producers need to charge high prices in order to be profitable.

This is a very simplistic calculation of how promotional costs are covered and in practice there would be other factors in addition to promotion impacting upon the selling price. Nevertheless, this gives an indication of the potential strength of the effect both quantity and promotion can have on pricing. Additionally, advertising is often used to promote a brand or retailer in general so it may not be possible to specify an exact amount of promotional budget to a particular product that it sells. However, each item

Table 6.2 The impact of quantity and promotional costs on retail selling price

100 pieces of a bag sold by a brand to a retailer	Retail selling price
100 pieces × £20 manufacturing price = £2000 + £1000 advertising costs = £3000 ÷ 100 pieces = £30 each × 2.5 (retailer's mark-up)	£75
1000 pieces of the same item sold by a brand to a retailer	
1000 pieces × £20 manufacturing price = £20,000 + £1000 advertising costs = £21,000 ÷ 1000 pieces = £21 each × 2.5 (retailer's mark-up)	£52.50

a manufacturer or retailer sells would probably be expected to make a financial contribution towards the company's promotional budget. Another key factor is that the bag manufacturer would be able to charge less per item for a higher quantity, i.e. a lower cost price, because higher quantities can create a better economy of scale, as explained above. Therefore if this example were put into practice the cost price for 1000 pieces might be around 10 per cent cheaper per item than for 100 pieces, thus creating further distance between the two selling prices. In many countries, sales taxes also need to be factored in, e.g. Value Added Tax (VAT) in the UK, at a current rate of 20 per cent for most items sold at retail (HM Revenue and Customs, 2014). (Note that certain essential items do not incur VAT, including children's clothes and many food items and businesses need to reach a certain amount of financial turnover before they need to charge VAT.)

Markdowns: seasonal sales, reductions and offers

The reasons why retailers use markdowns vary but legislation in different countries can impact upon retailers' decisions to reduce prices. For example, to avoid deceiving customers in the UK, legally the retailer has to have charged the initial higher selling price for a reasonable period before a price can be marked down (see Chapter 12 Legislation and ethics in retailing). Perishable products often require deep discounts so that they can be sold before they expire to avoid disposal, and some retailers make a feature of this by locating them together in one display unit, to attract price-conscious shoppers. DIY retailer B&Q often sells its Christmas trees at reduced prices towards the end of December and supermarkets often heavily discount products which have reached their sell-by dates. Merchandise can be marked down owing to a wide variety of reasons, including the following:

- merchandise is of poor quality;
- matching competitors' prices;
- buying too many of a product to meet demand;
- products are not well suited to the target market;
- products are perishable;
- products were displayed or promoted inadequately;
- needing to make way for new stock to be displayed.

When a product is marked down a decision needs to be taken as to how much to reduce the price. These decisions are usually taken by retailers' merchandisers or buyers. Deep discounts of 50 per cent or more may be used if the retailer is keen to dispose of the stock quickly. Alternatively, retailers may use lower percentages for price cuts initially, increasing reductions if the goods have not sold after a set time period. Selecting the right discount at the right time is an important skill for a buyer or merchandiser. Luxury brands usually avoid markdowns as they may be perceived as cheapening the brand. Instead, they can dispose of stock which has not sold at full price by sending it to designer outlet villages (see below), discount stores such as TK Maxx or discount designer websites, e.g. yoox.com. The advantage of sending markdown merchandise to other outlets is that this leaves space free in the designers' stores to sell more profitable full-price merchandise to cover the high overheads such as rent that are typically paid by upmarket stores in expensive locations. In some cases, designer brands have also been accused of destroying clothing by cutting it or sending it to landfill so that it cannot be sold at a cheaper price that dilutes the brand image (BBC Radio 4, 2010). Various options for the positioning of price reduction activities are highlighted in Figure 6.7.

Seasonal sales are the traditional time periods at which retailers discount high proportions of their stock for an extended time, typically several weeks during January and mid-summer. However, markdown events have become more frequent for many UK retailers, with certain stores having a section for reduced-price merchandise for most or all of the year. A 'blue-cross sale' is a technique employed by Debenhams department stores, amongst others, consisting of one or two days where selected merchandise is reduced temporarily. This can also be referred to as a 'sales event' and is a useful device for disposing of slow-selling items before the seasonal sales take place. In the US 'Black Friday' sales events take place on the first Friday after Thanksgiving. Notionally, this marks the first day of the year on which retailers become profitable, i.e. move 'into the black', but in practice successful retailers are likely to be in profit before this date (Lusch *et al.*, 2011). 'Cyber Monday', which takes place the following week, is so called because many consumers returned to work after a holiday and bought products online via better internet connections in the workplace, thus generating another surge in purchases.

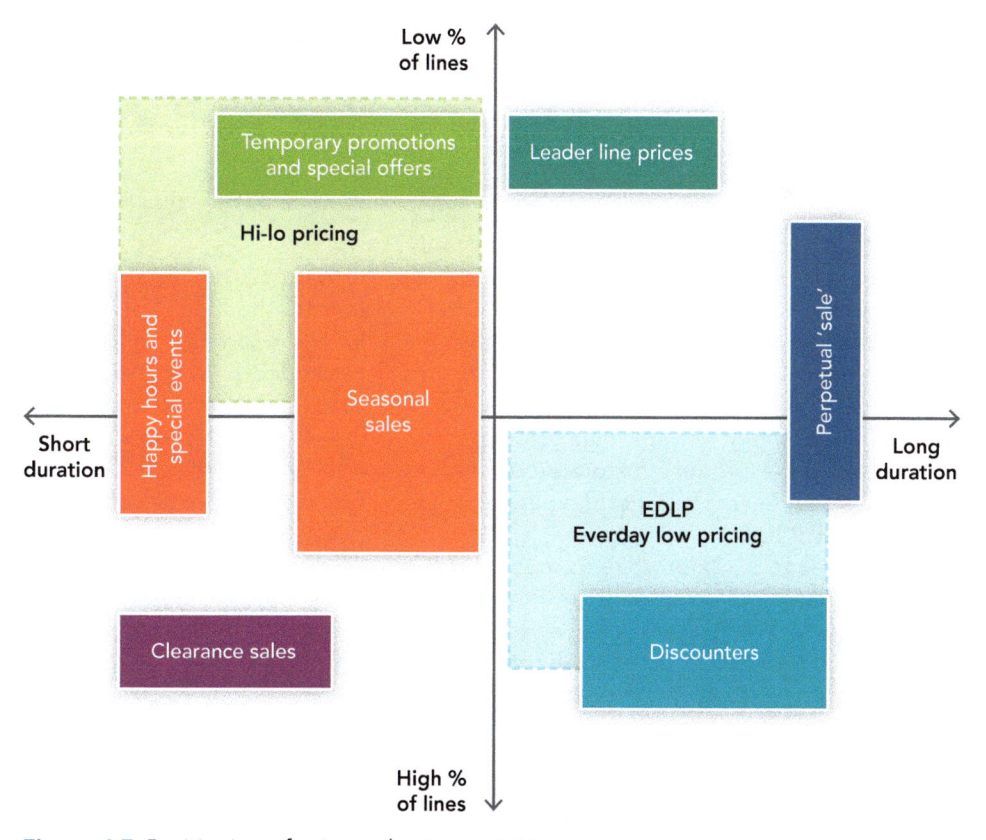

Figure 6.7 Positioning of price reduction activities
Source: adapted from Betts and McGoldrick (1995)

Discount coupons can also be used to create temporary price reductions to increase sales volume and this technique is moving increasingly from printed media to online coupons (see Chapter 7 Retail marketing communications).

A **grey market** or 'parallel market' exists where prices for branded products are relatively low, owing to being sold via an unauthorised distributor. For example, an authorised retailer could sell products that they have bought legitimately from a brand to a third-party distributor at a discount. The third party may then sell this stock to another retailer overseas, without the knowledge of the brand. Brands usually aim to restrict this practice, especially in the luxury price bracket, as it can be inconsistent with their brand image. This is a legal issue as the brand that owns the trademark has not consented to the transaction, although the law regarding the grey market and parallel imports can vary from one country to another (INTA, 2014).

THE EXPANSION OF DESIGNER OUTLET VILLAGES

The discount designer outlet sector has experienced a growth phase in recent years, gaining popularity both with brands wanting to dispose of stock and well-heeled customers seeking discounted quality merchandise. Outlet villages draw together a selection of retailers that wish to distribute merchandise from previous seasons in an attractive, purpose-built environment, usually supported by the same standard of catering facilities that can be found in a mainstream shopping centre. McArthurGlen Group, Europe's largest operator in this sector, which owns Cheshire Oaks amongst other outlets, reported a 15 per cent rise in sales overall, and a 56 per cent rise in sales of designer collections, in November to December 2012 (Leroux, 2012). Henrik Madsen, MD of McArthurGlen in Northern Europe, says that retailers' attitudes towards discount outlets have changed: '(w)e have seen a surge in our business with the designer luxury brands over the last two to three years . . . It's fair to say that the brands have started thinking much more carefully how they manage their inventory. We provide a great opportunity for them to sell product in a protected environment where they keep control of the destiny of the brand' (Leroux, 2012).

Bicester Village in Oxfordshire, owned by Value Retail and opened in 1995, is possibly the UK's most well-known outlet village. Its New England-style retail space expanded during the 2000s and alongside a wide range of designer discount stores it now provides food from celebrity chefs' restaurant chains, as well as playground facilities, to cater for family-friendly days out. In 2010 'Bicester reported sales of £1400 per square foot . . . which is three times as much as Selfridges and vastly more than smaller shopping centres', according

Bicester Village
Source: author's own photograph

to Walsh (2011a). Bicester Village has become a major tourist attraction, featuring a vast array of designer brands including Dior, Gucci, Prada and Ralph Lauren. Facilitated by the provision of a Shopping Express coach to Bicester twice daily from Oxford Street (Bicester Village, 2014; Tobin, 2012), 80 per cent of Chinese travellers visit the village while on holiday in London. Favourable VAT rules, which refund this sales tax to overseas visitors, make the prices of luxury brands very attractive in comparison to their cost in China. Sales from Chinese visitors to Bicester Village were estimated to have increased by 80 per cent in 2010 and many retailers there now employ staff who speak Chinese, as well as restaurants translating menus into Chinese (Walsh, 2011b). Consequently, Value Retail has expanded into China, opening a site in Suzhou in 2014, to be followed by another outlet village in Shanghai in 2015, in addition to owning nine outlet villages in Europe (Value Retail, 2014).

CHAPTER SUMMARY

Retail pricing is a topic with a wide variety of facets that can be categorised in terms of time, assortment, location, competition and economics. Prices should be set to achieve a balance between covering manufacturing costs and meeting customer expectations whilst achieving profitability for the retailer. Pricing is closely connected to the other elements of the retail marketing mix and needs to be compatible with product, marketing communications and location to achieve a consistent brand image and market position. The retail sector operates different levels of pricing in the mass, middle and luxury markets.

This chapter has explained a diverse range of pricing methods that can be adopted by retailers within three main categories: cost-orientated, competition-orientated and demand-based pricing. There is a wide choice of demand-orientated approaches, since they are responsive to customer needs and therefore highly compatible with marketing-orientated retailing. Retail buyers and merchandisers usually take responsibility for retail price-setting, requiring knowledge of the retailer's strategic objectives; competitors' pricing; customers' sensitivity to price and macro-environmental influences on pricing. Price elasticity is a key issue, affecting to what extent consumers will alter the amount they purchase in response to changes in price. There is a close relationship between price and value, although value can be equated with quality as well as price. Retailers have the capacity to use various markdown techniques when stock has not achieved the volume of sales that had been forecast. Overall, the chapter has shown that pricing has a significant role to play in the marketing mix of retailers.

EXERCISES AND QUESTIONS

1 Which pricing strategies mentioned in this chapter would you advise a retailer to adopt to achieve the following objectives?
   a Increasing market share.
   b Increasing profit margins.
   c Improving the company's brand image.
   d Making the retailer's merchandise more sustainable.

2 In what ways do you believe price-comparison websites such as Kelkoo affect consumer decision-making? Draw from your own experience as a consumer by considering times when your purchase choice has been influenced by information from this type of website.

3 Compare the pricing strategies of two different supermarkets. Make a note of the prices of similar basic branded and own-label products, e.g. soap and bread. Calculate the average difference between the prices of the own-label products and the branded products, expressing the difference as a percentage of the price of the branded products. Was the difference in pricing between own-label and branded products similar in both supermarkets? If not, consider possible reasons why they might differ.

(As a reminder, the average can be calculated by adding together the total sum of the prices of the products, divided by the total number of products. The percentage can be found by dividing the difference by the total price of the branded products and multiplying this by 100.)

4 Watch the following video about Euroshop in Germany: http://www.youtube.com/watch?v=s9kRRRzTLgQ.
   a Which aspects of retailing does the store manager place great importance upon?
   b How does the single pricing policy affect the staff?
   c How much is this market worth in Germany according to the YouTube clip?

5 Discuss to what extent it is viable and desirable for low-cost retailers such as pound stores to address social and environmental responsibility in the selection of their products. (See Chapter 12 Legislation and ethics in retailing.) Viewing the Corporate Social Responsibility (CSR) policies of these stores may help with your answer.

6 Assess the pricing policies of three different retailers of the same product type by visiting their stores nearby, e.g. a national or international retail chain, a smaller store chain and a one-off independent store. Make notes for each store about pricing strategies mentioned in this chapter, including markdowns, psychological pricing and price lining, adding other pricing strategies if you wish. (You will need to ask the retailer's permission if you make notes while you are in the store.) Look at specific product ranges to enable direct comparisons to be made, e.g. T-shirts, trousers and tailored jackets. Make comparisons in order to assess which store you believe has implemented the most appropriate pricing policy in relation to meeting its target market's requirements.

7 Compile three lists with examples of retailers that primarily use (a) cost-orientated, (b) competition-orientated and (c) demand-orientated pricing. Discuss whether there are any similarities between the retailers in each list, e.g. in their market level or product types.

8 Consider three products that you have bought at markdown prices, making a note of the percentage discount and where you bought them. Which of the reasons for markdowns mentioned in this chapter do you believe applied to these products? Do you consider these products to be good value? Give reasons for your answers.

9 Calculate retail margins for the products below, using the formula mentioned in this chapter. After calculating each margin, assess whether the result would be above or below the target margin for a retailer with a 3 × cost price mark-up policy. You could also try estimating this before completing the calculations.
   - Selling price = €20; cost price = €7.15
   - Selling price = €4.99; cost price = €1.66
   - Selling price = €1.25; cost price = €0.45
   - Selling price = €65; cost price = €22.30
   - Selling price = €34.99; cost price = €10.87

REFERENCES

BBC Radio 4 (2010) *You and Yours: Wasteful Disposal* (broadcast on 22/1/2010, details available online at: http://www.bbc.co.uk/radio4/youandyours/unwanted_clothes.shtml).

Berman, B. and Evans, J.R. (2010) *Retailing Management: A Strategic Approach*, 11th edn, Upper Saddle River, NJ: Pearson.

Betts, E.J. and McGoldrick, P.J. (1995) The strategy of the retail 'sales': typology, review and synthesis, *International Review of Retail, Distribution and Consumer Research*, 5(3), 303–31.

Bicester Village (2014) *Luxury Travel Service: Shopping Express* (available online at: http://www.bicestervillage.com/en/your-visit/getting-here#shopping-express).

Ferrell, O.C. and Hartline, M. (2011) *Marketing Management Strategies, 5th edition*, South-Western Cengage Learning.

Gilbert, D. (2003) *Retail Marketing Management*, 2nd edn, Harlow: FT Prentice Hall.

Goworek, H. (2007) *Fashion Buying*, 2nd edn, Oxford: Blackwell Publishing.

Grewal, D., Ailawadi, K.L., Gauri, D., Hall, K., Kopalle, P. and Robertson, J.R. (2011) Innovations in retail pricing and promotions, *Journal of Retailing*, 87(1), 43–52.

HM Revenue and Customs (2014) *VAT rates explained: standard, reduced, zero, exempt* (available online at: http://www.hmrc.gov.uk/vat/forms-rates/rates/rates.htm).

INTA (2014) *Cross-Border Topics: Parallel Imports (Gray Market Goods)* (available online at: http://www.inta.org/TrademarkBasics/FactSheets/Pages/ParallelImportsFactSheet.aspx).

Jobber, D. (2010) *Principles and Practice of Marketing*, 6th edn, Maidenhead: McGraw-Hill.

Leroux, M. (2012) Designer villages boom as top brands hold their noses, *The Times*, 14 January (available online at: http://www.thetimes.co.uk/tto/business/industries/retailing/article3286339.ece).

Lusch, R.F., Dunne, P.M. and Carver, J.R. (2011) *Introduction to Retailing*, International/7th edn, Stamford, CT: South-Western Cengage Learning.

McGoldrick, P. (2002) *Retail Marketing*, 2nd edn, Maidenhead: McGraw-Hill.

Retail Week (2013) Marks & Spencer's fourth quarter: What the analysts say, *Retail Week*, 11 April (available online at: http://www.retail-week.com/city-and-finance/marks-and-spencers-fourth-quarter-what-the-analysts-say/5048139.article).

Solomon, G.W., Marshall, E.W., Stuart, E.W., Barnes, B. and Mitchell, V.W. (2009) *Marketing: Real People, Real Decisions*, Harlow: Financial Times/Prentice Hall.

Student Lock-In (2014) *Get Involved* (available online at: http://www.studentlockin.com/index.php/page/promotional).

Sullivan, M. and Adcock, D. (2002) *Retail Marketing*, London: Thomson.

Swinburne, Z. (2014) Supermarkets urged to scrap buy-one-get-one-free as shoppers waste 222m tons of food a year, *The Independent*, 6 April (available online at: http://www.independent.co.uk/life-style/food-and-drink/news/supermarkets-urged-to-scrap-buy-onegetonefree-as-shoppers-waste-222m-tons-of-food-a-year-9241174.html).

Tobin, L. (2012) Chinese tourists pack their suitcases at Bicester, *The Independent*, 12 October (available online at: http://www.independent.co.uk/news/business/analysis-and-features/chinese-pack-their-suitcases-at-bicester-8209793.html).

Value Retail (2014) *The Villages* (available online at: http://www.valueretail.com/the-villages/the-villages).

Walsh, K. (2011a) Designer outlets lure the fashion tourists, *The Sunday Times*, 3 July (available online at: http://www.thesundaytimes.co.uk/sto/public/roadtorecovery/article661635.ece).

Walsh, K. (2011b) Retail village lured by China, *The Sunday Times*, 24 April (available online at: http://www.thesundaytimes.co.uk/sto/business/Retail_and_leisure/article611343.ece).

FURTHER READING

The following are key sources that would be useful for students to read around the topic and develop a fuller understanding of the concepts.

Broeckelmann, P. and Groeppel-Klein, A. (2008) Usage of mobile price comparison sites at the point of sale and its influence on consumers' shopping behaviour, *International Review of Retail, Distribution and Consumer Research*, 18(2), 149–166.

Chen, G.R. (2010) The risk reduction role of advertising in relation to price rigidity, *European Journal of Marketing*, 44(11/12), 1839–1855.

Grewal, D., Ailawadi, K.L., Gauri, D., Hall, K., Kopalle, P. and Robertson, J.R. (2011) Innovations in retail pricing and promotions, *Journal of Retailing*, 87(1), 43–52.

Kukar-Kinney, M., Ridgway, N.M. and Monroe, K.B. (2012) The role of price in the behavior and purchase decisions of compulsive buyers, *Journal of Retailing*, 88(1), 63–71.

Macé, S. (2012) The impact and determinants of nine-ending pricing in grocery retailing, *Journal of Retailing*, 88(1), 115–130.

Case study

Price Wars threaten to reshape landscape of supermarkets

By Andrea Felsted and Andy Sharman

When supermarket chain Morrisons announced in March 2014 that it would invest £1bn cutting prices over the following three years, it threatened to turn the regular skirmishes between Britain's big grocers into trench warfare. The big four – Tesco, Asda, Sainsbury's and Morrisons – had sparred for the previous five years, trying to win cash-strapped customers as the economy turned down and the volume of food bought fell for the first time in living memory. However, experienced supermarket watchers say this time the situation is much more serious. 'This is very, very different', says Dave McCarthy, analyst at HSBC. So far the battles have largely been fought between the big four, which together control about three-quarters of the market, but in the past five years new challengers have emerged. German discount supermarkets have not only expanded aggressively but have shed their no-frills image. New products, such as lobster tails and luxury Christmas puddings, have appealed to the squeezed consumers in the B and C1 socio-economic groups. According to Kantar Worldpanel, the consumer research group, more than half of British consumers have shopped in Aldi or Lidl.

Other value retail chains, including Poundland and B&M are expanding their grocery offer. Dalton Philips, Morrison chief executive, said last week: '[The discounters] are a growing channel. Price is extremely important in that channel'. Late in 2013 Asda said it would spend £1bn cutting prices in the following five years, and in February 2014 Tesco said it would spend £200m cutting prices of core products such as tomatoes, onions and cucumbers. Days later Tesco said it would cut the price of its own-label four-pint bottle of milk from £1.39 to £1. Its rivals quickly followed.

Unlike previous battles, which have been fought on offers largely funded by suppliers, the latest offensive is focused on cutting the prices of everyday items. This involves sacrificing some profit to drive sales, rather than passing the pain on to suppliers. 'There are some serious pledges here to reduce prices substantially on some high-profile items, which will cost tens of millions of pounds, this is real', says Mr McCarthy. Much depends on the reaction of rivals. Tesco, Asda and Sainsbury all run price-matching schemes, raising fears of contagion.

Justin King, chief executive of Sainsbury, described his rivals' price tactics as part of the 'cut and thrust of the market' and called the threat of discounters nothing new. 'We have been competing hard with them, and we will continue to', he said. Andy Clarke, chief executive of Asda, also told the *Financial Times* that 'structural change in the market is something you could see coming for some time' and that Asda had already responded by cutting prices and ditching 'gimmicks' such as money-off vouchers.

Some analysts say Tesco will be drawn into the fray. 'Tesco has the strongest margin, but this has been shrinking for several years. It may now be pushed to rethink its pricing in order to defend market share, which has come under pressure', wrote analysts at Fitch Ratings credit agency. An expert on the grocery market says price-cutting campaigns might play into the discounters' hands. Not only have Aldi and Lidl gained free publicity – they have responded on price. Concerted action by the discounters could lead to a nightmare scenario for the big four, where they erode profit, only to see little impact on sales.

FT *Source*: adapted from Felsted, A. and Sharman, A. (2014) Grocer price skirmishes pushed to new level, *Financial Times*, 19 March. © The Financial Times 2014. All Rights Reserved. Pearson Education is responsible for providing this adaptation of the original article.

DISCUSSION QUESTIONS

1 Describe the different pricing strategies that are mentioned in this case study, using the terminology discussed in this chapter. Based on the information from the case, what are the potential dangers and advantages of competing retailers using these strategies to engage in a price war?

2 Visit Aldi's and Lidl's stores or websites, noting their price architecture, product ranges and store/web design and layout. What aspects of pricing, products and retail design help to differentiate them from other supermarkets that may account for their growth in market share?

3 Search for articles about the price competition between the 'big four' UK supermarkets to assess the current situation. How have the supermarkets' pricing and relative market share changed, if at all, since this case study was written?

CHAPTER 7

Retail marketing communications

Helen Goworek and Kristine Pole

Learning objectives

The objectives of this chapter are to:

- explain the main marketing communications tools available to retail organisations;
- consider the role of integrated marketing communications and the role played by each communication channel;
- explore the differences between in-store and online promotion techniques;
- evaluate the suitability of communication methods and media within a retailing context.

Introduction

The purpose of this chapter is to provide the reader with an understanding of how marketing communications (or 'marcomms') can be implemented within the retail sector. The main communication strategies used by retailers are discussed, linked to their suitability for different types of retailer. The term **integrated marketing communications (IMC)** is often used to emphasise that different communication strategies need to be complementary and well blended. The traditional emphasis of promotion has been on winning new customers. However, retailers are now focusing more on adopting techniques that enable them to benefit from retaining existing customers, thereby placing an increasing emphasis on Relationship Marketing. It is important for retailers to take the time to evaluate the efficiency and effectiveness of promotional activity with a view to maximising the company's resources in future promotional campaigns. Retailers' marketing teams are likely to be responsible for devising and implementing marcomms strategies, often with the support of advertising agencies or marketing consultants.

Retail marketing communication strategies

The most effective communications strategies differ according to the type of retailer, e.g. own brand or branded, and their sector, e.g. electricals, clothing, fast-moving consumer goods (FMCGs) (see Table 7.1 in the following section, which shows the percentage of advertising spend by different retailers to different media). Retailers who have physical stores can also use their layout, store design and customer service to help communicate their brand. The steps in planning a retail marcomms strategy involve setting promotional objectives before establishing the budget that will be required to achieve this, then devising and implementing a suitable promotional mix within the parameters of the budget and time (Berman and Evans, 2010). It is important to review the effectiveness of the promotional mix so that this can influence future promotional campaigns (see Figure 7.1).

Note that there is a difference between long-term objectives, which focus on promoting the retailer holistically, and short-term objectives, which concentrate more on specific products and pricing. Promotional objectives should be derived from the retailer's overall strategy. It is not advisable for the retailer to simply set an objective to increase sales, as many factors other than advertising can impact upon sales turnover. It is therefore rarely possible to give direct credit to an advertising campaign for increased sales or conversely, to blame it for poor sales figures, since factors outside the scope of advertising and possibly external to the company may be the cause. Companies can implement a push strategy, a pull strategy, or a combination of both when promoting their products. A push strategy is where a brand concentrates on pushing products through distribution channels by promoting them to retailers to ensure they reach consumers, or promoting the retailer in general. On the other hand, a pull strategy is when products are promoted directly to consumers so that they are persuaded to seek them out (Gilbert, 2003). Promotional objectives are often discussed in relation to their effect on financial performance, and while this reflects the traditional view of the purpose of a business, environmental and social sustainability are also increasingly playing a part in retailers' strategies and objectives. (The topic of sustainability is covered further in Chapter 12 Legislation and ethics in retailing.)

Retail advertising

Advertising has been defined by Gilbert (2003: 179) as 'any paid form of non-personal communication through the media about a product that has an identified sponsor'. Advertising is often referred to as 'above-the-line' promotion, whereas other types of promotion

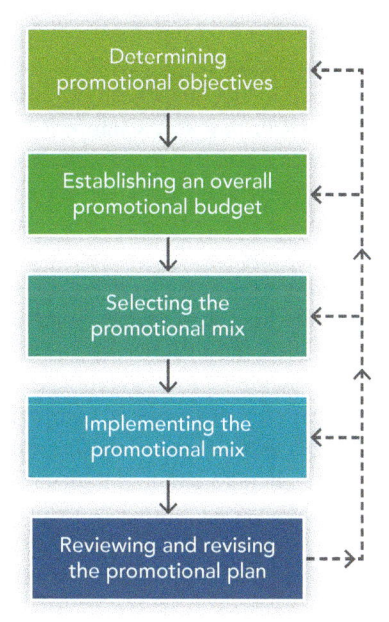

Figure 7.1 Planning a retail promotional strategy
Source: adapted from Berman and Evans (2010)

are known as 'below-the-line' methods. This term developed in the early years of advertising when invoices were divided by a horizontal line and all advertising costs were 'above the line' and the remaining activities below. For example, retailers have the capacity to communicate with their customers via store windows, catalogues or websites, but this is not considered to be advertising, according to Gilbert's definition. Today, although the terms above are still used, retailers focus on the integrated nature of the campaign and how each element of the communication mix works together to promote and reinforce the desired brand image or objective. One of the most fundamental theories for advertising is the AIDA model, which proposes that to be effective, advertising must first attract consumers' attention, then generate their interest before creating a desire for the product that leads to action by purchasing it (see Figure 7.2). This theory can assist retail marketers by reminding them to ensure that advertising prioritises gaining attention and interest, otherwise the message will be wasted. The AIDA model can also be considered relevant to other forms of promotion.

'Above-the-line' promotion (i.e. in paid-for media) is an important element of many large retailers' marketing communications campaigns, with the aim of informing,

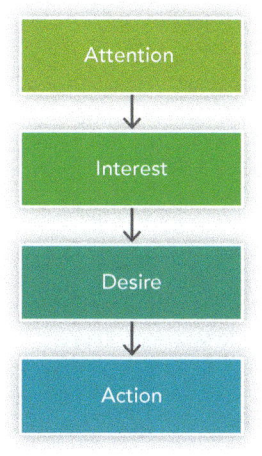

Figure 7.2 The AIDA model

persuading or reminding consumers about the company or its products. However, it should be borne in mind that advertising can play a less important part in the promotional mix for smaller retailers and in certain countries, depending on the product sector and market conditions. The concepts of 'Black Friday' (see Chapter 6) and 'Cyber Monday' relate mainly to the US market but they can also be of relevance in other regions of the world. While the concepts behind these designated days are not entirely accurate, they are used to generate publicity and extensive advertising at these times can have positive effects on retail sales figures.

In the UK, some of the major clothing and homeware retailers, such as M&S and Next, used to undertake very little above-the-line mass media advertising, usually only advertising seasonal sales and preferring instead to rely on their ubiquitous presence in the High Street and word-of-mouth promotion by loyal customers. However, during the last decade the retail market has become more saturated and competitive, and advertising is now widely used by existing competitors as well as new market entrants. It has become standard practice for many major UK retailers to conduct high-profile advertising campaigns, often at the launch of a new season's product range or prior to Christmas. Of key importance to the retailer is how to spend their advertising budget for maximum effectiveness, and to do this decisions need to be taken in relation to the cost of the medium per number of the target audience that it reaches. In Table 7.1 it is evident that different types of retailers place a different emphasis on the media channels, although TV and Press still dominate the sector.

The top ten UK retailers for advertising expenditure are shown in Table 7.2. Unsurprisingly, it is dominated by national supermarkets who take up the top three places. Furniture retailer DFS is at number 4, reflecting the fact that its marketing mix prioritises sale prices that are promoted extensively throughout broadcast media and the press. FMCG companies Procter & Gamble and Unilever invest heavily in advertising to promote their many brands in the UK, each exceeding the spending of any individual retail chains.

Depending on the size and structure of the retail organisation there are a number of ways retailers create and implement a campaign. For example, retailers can commission

Table 7.1 Comparison of retailer type by advertising medium (%)

	Clothing[*]	Electricals[†]	Supermarkets[‡]	Department stores[§]
Cinema	0.1	–	0.2	–
Direct mail	0.4	1.3	5.1	8.2
Door drops	–	0.3	2.3	0.6
Internet	4.9	2.9	4.3	7.7
Outdoor	3.8	–	4.6	6.2
Press	49.2	21.4	42.8	35.7
Radio	1.0	3.7	2.7	3.9
TV	40.6	70.3	38.0	37.8
	100	100	100	100

[*]Mintel Clothing Report (UK) October 2012.
[†]Mintel Electrical (UK) Good Retailing February 2013.
[‡]Mintel Supermarkets: More Than Just Food Retailing, (UK) November 2012.
[§]Department Store Retailing (UK) March 2012.

Table 7.2 Top 10 UK retailers by advertising expenditure 2013

Rank	Advertiser	Expenditure
1	Tesco	116,269,526
2	Asda	97,035,247
3	Morrisons	81,522,591
4	DFS	75,682,183
5	McDonald's	72,148,548
6	Sainsbury's	60,440,611
7	Aldi	56,594,569
8	Boots	56,129,214
9	Dixons Retail (Currys/PC World)	54,242,348
10	Marks & Spencer	50,710,168

Source: Marketing Magazine, 2014

agencies to develop advertising campaigns on their behalf; for example, McCann (mccann.com) who currently service IKEA's advertising. Full-service agencies provide a wider range of services such as selecting appropriate media and booking advertising space on behalf of the retailer. However, it can be more cost-effective for large retailers to have an in-house advertising department. For example, Specsavers, the market-leading UK optical retailer, has run a long-term humorous advertising campaign developed by its in-house team. This features various people finding themselves inadvertently in embarrassing situations due to poor eyesight, ending with the slogan 'Should've gone to Specsavers'. Humour is often employed in advertising campaigns, although it is important that the humour is aimed carefully at the target market, taking culture into account (Lee and Lim, 2008). Different types of media available for promotion are featured in Figure 7.3 and

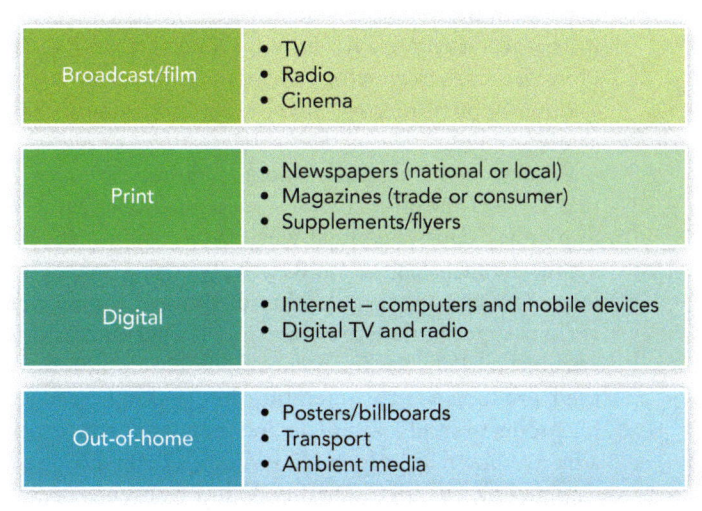

Broadcast/film	• TV • Radio • Cinema
Print	• Newspapers (national or local) • Magazines (trade or consumer) • Supplements/flyers
Digital	• Internet – computers and mobile devices • Digital TV and radio
Out-of-home	• Posters/billboards • Transport • Ambient media

Figure 7.3 Main advertising media channels

discussed below in more depth, with extra detail on the growing use of digital media by retailers for promotional purposes.

The extent of the potential audience for print media can be found from the NRS (National Readership Survey), a body funded by publishers and advertising practitioners, that collates data on 250 UK publications, including online versions since 2012, based on 36,000 interviews with readers each year (see www.nrs.co.uk). The coverage of broadcast/film media can be judged by gaining viewing or listening figures from various industry bodies, such as BARB (Broadcasters' Audience Research Board), which installs meters in thousands of participants' homes to report their viewing activity, RAJAR (Radio Joint Audience Research) and CAVIAR (Cinema and Video Industry Audience Research). The advantages and disadvantages of a variety of different advertising media are assessed in Table 7.3.

New technology, particularly in digital media, can create crossover between advertising and non-paid forms of promotion. Further information relating to adverts and products can be made available on the company's website or other online sources without paying for advertising space. Adverts can also be uploaded to YouTube and consumers may even do this without the retailer's intervention. This can be viewed by other consumers as an independent and more authentic endorsement of the advert. For example, John Lewis's 2013 Christmas TV advert 'The Bear and the Hare' has been viewed on YouTube around 13 million times at the time of writing; free coverage which would have been very costly via TV advertising. This is in contrast with avoidance behaviour by viewers, who are able to fast-forward past adverts when watching TV with systems such as Tivo or viewing programmes On Demand, on TV or digital devices. Conversely, online advertising can also permit consumers to choose to engage in more depth by participating in interactive content linked to the advert. Consumers are clearly now able to exert a greater degree of choice over whether or not they engage with broadcast advertising. The variety of different media in which retailers can choose to advertise is discussed in further depth below.

Broadcast media and film

The range of TV channels and radio stations now available via the wide reach of satellite and digital channels enables retailers to advertise to specific demographic groups of consumers. However, as consumers begin to watch programmes at their own convenience, with the ability to skip adverts, the reach of TV advertising may become reduced in the near future, with an adverse effect on its viability as an advertising option. However, cinema viewing figures have remained buoyant and product placement offers another opportunity for advertising by paying to have products and brands featured in use in films.

As new media channels emerge retailers have more outlets for their message. In particular YouTube offers retailers an opportunity for featuring adverts sometimes in addition or as exclusive content where advertising space has not been bought through other media channels, e.g. Zara. Retailers are also able to harness TV technology in different ways. Owing to the availability of slimmer, smaller and more economical TV screens, various supermarkets now broadcast adverts in-store, for example near entrances or attached to shelves at the point-of-purchase. Manufacturers can pay retailers to promote their products via this method, thus making retailers a potential advertising channel for product brands. Retailers and manufacturers can also sell directly to consumers via adverts known as 'infomercials' in breaks on TV channels or from the programmes on channels such as QVC (Quality, Value, Convenience), which broadcasts to a potential 166 million customers in the US, UK, Germany and Japan (QVC, 2012).

Table 7.3 Comparisons between the main types of advertising media

Advertising medium	Advantages	Disadvantages
TV	Wide audience coverage, dependent on TV channel and programmes chosen; TV adverts have a lot of scope to gain attention through both images and sound; repetition makes TV adverts particularly memorable; opportunities to 'sponsor' relevant programmes.	Advert production and TV channels with a large audience are expensive; much of the coverage may be wasted if channels and programmes are not sufficiently targeted at the retailer's potential customers; dwindling audiences for broadcast TV.
Radio	More economical than TV; can be more targeted to a specific audience, especially local and digital stations.	No visual input and audience may lack attention by listening while otherwise occupied.
Film	Big impact due to screen size and options for longer adverts than TV; target audience can be selected through the choice of films where adverts are shown; product placement can be used.	Limited audience size which can be difficult to predict in advance.
Newspapers and magazines	Newspapers offer wide coverage for mass market products; free local magazines funded by advertising and local newspapers are beneficial to small independent retailers; magazines are useful for targeting consumers with specific interests that relate to the retailer's product types.	Readers can skip over adverts while concentrating on editorial content; many adverts vying for readers' attention.
Supplements/flyers	Leaflets inserted as supplements in newspapers or magazines can either be included in all copies or targeted at local areas; can be kept by consumers as reminders more easily than ordinary adverts.	Supplements can easily fall out of publications or irritate purchasers and may be discarded before reading.
Internet	Banner ads and sponsored ads can be aimed at potential customers through particular websites or web searches; can be cost-efficient due to being highly targeted; moving images can be incorporated to gain attention; TV adverts can be shown before relevant YouTube videos or on-demand programmes.	It can be difficult to find consumers and gain their attention among the vast amount of information on the internet; there are many websites to choose from, with a wider selection required to gain exposure to the same quantity of viewers as traditional TV channels.
Posters	Good for very specific geographic targeting, e.g. close to a retail outlet; relatively inexpensive; can sometimes have 3D or interactive content.	In-depth decision-making required to decide on locations; posters are susceptible to fading, being torn or graffiti.
Transport	Can be noticed by commuters whilst they have little to distract their attention; useful for targeting particular locations.	Numbers of people using public transport can vary a great deal depending on region and time of year.
Ambient media	Novel ideas can capture people's attention and be remembered more easily; original concepts may go viral, being spread by consumers with no cost.	May require more maintenance than traditional media; permission may need to be sought to install them; can be vandalised.

TK MAXX PROMOTIONAL CAMPAIGN

TK Maxx has invested in a number of campaigns in recent years (Kimberley, 2012), to appeal to their 'bargain hunter' customer profile whose key behaviours include repeat visits to the store. Brown (2011) reported that TK Maxx realised that shoppers were unaware that the retailer employed experienced fashion buyers and bought some current season collections. The company therefore devised a television advert under the strapline 'Do your thing', focusing on street dancers following some of the latest trends that are available in store. Using British rapper Maverick Sabre they then supported this with brand interaction through the hashtag #doyourthing and showcased it on YouTube. They also sponsored the Channel 4 show 'Frock Me', a programme showing viewers how to create their own look from clothes they already own coupled with some of the latest fashions. It was supported by a Facebook campaign which showed behind-the-scenes footage (McEleny, 2010). The head of marketing at TK Maxx stressed how social media is integral to the brand development and will be key to all of their advertising campaigns (McEleny, 2010).

TK Maxx has a history of supporting charitable causes. In 2012 the company launched its biennial 'Give up clothes for good' campaign where customers were encouraged to bag unwanted clothes and hand them in to TK Maxx to raise money for Cancer Research UK. It also has a long-standing campaign supporting 'Comic Relief' and in 2013 sold fair trade T-shirts with a comical picture of celebrities sporting the signature red nose. The T-shirt was designed by the British fashion designer Stella McCartney reinforcing the fashionability of the brand.

Print media

Newspapers and magazines are widely used for advertising as part of an integrated campaign. For example Aldi launched the 'Like Brands only Cheaper' campaign across national newspapers, TV, Facebook and posters. Magazines have a unique position in that they are often targeted at specific interest groups, e.g. cyclists and homecrafts, and growth in online magazines is likely to offer retailers additional avenues. Print adverts frequently use photography but they can also use illustration and be inspired by different forms of art such as installations and sculpture. Retailers need to select the most appropriate type of imagery for the brand image and selecting the right illustrator or photographer requires careful consideration.

Since standard advertising can lack credibility with consumers, retailers can opt instead for 'advertorials' in magazines that take on the appearance of editorial articles, but have been specified and paid for by the retailer. Customer magazines have been helping to build brands and customer relationships, e.g. Boots *Health and Beauty*, which has a readership of over three million and *Your M&S* magazine is the fifth most read UK magazine with around 3.5 million readers (Readwood Group, 2013). The 'adzine' is a type of publication which has become particularly popular with supermarkets where it is often free or sold at a relatively low price, providing an ideal format to include recipes that use ingredients from the store. John Lewis's *Edition* magazine is produced four times per year and has been edited by a former Marie-Claire editor. As well as a print edition being available in store, *Edition* can be read online or via an app (John Lewis, 2014). *Sainsbury's magazine* offers articles and recipes to appeal to its target customers (see Figure 7.4).

Print media can also take the form of separate printed items that are not published in the media, including supplements that are inserted in magazines and newspapers. Retailers can pay for flyers to be distributed when newspapers are delivered or exchange them with other local shops, a technique used by Cow, a small multichannel vintage clothing retail chain (see www.wearecow.com).

Figure 7.4 Sainsbury's magazine
Source: with permission from Seven Publishing Group

Radio advertising

Radio adverts are relatively economical and can be more targeted at geographic market segments in comparison to TV advertising. However, this depends on the country and region. Broadcasting regulations and the market for radio can vary in different countries. Local BBC radio stations in the UK are government-funded via a licence fee and therefore do not permit advertising. Radio broadcasting has traditionally been a useful advertising medium for smaller retailers but this has changed in recent years. Local commercial radio stations tend to have a regional or city reach, e.g. Capital FM in London. Classic FM is a commercial radio station with national reach giving a retailer choices over geographic coverage. However, radio advertising for retailers remains small (see Table 7.1).

Outdoor media

Outdoor advertising channels are often referred to as 'out-of-home' media (OOH) and have exhibited steady growth in recent years (Wilson and Till, 2008). Such media as billboards and public transport are particularly suited for advertising retailers, as they can remind or inform customers about a retailer while they are in the area. Certain companies specialise in providing OOH media, such as JC Decaux and Clear Channel. 'Eye' is a company which supplies OOH media in the UK, US, Australia, New Zealand and Indonesia, such as airport signage ('Eye Fly'), shopping mall media ('Eye Shop') and roadside billboards ('Eye Drive') (see www.eyecorp.com/). New technology is being used to provide innovative outdoor media such as interactive bus stops, to take advantage of consumers' waiting time (see www.digitalsignage.net/2011/03/08/video-games-bus-stops/). Posters remain a popular advertising medium and are becoming more innovative in their style and format.

Other novel forms of OOH media are being used to gain consumers' attention. Ambient media refers to those items that are non-traditional forms of advertising media in the consumers' surroundings. Promotion through **ambient media** is often humorous or surreal and often uses large-scale items, adding another dimension to advertising. For example, the Malmö 2014 festival in Sweden was promoted via a three-dimensional advert that people could walk around or sit on, making it more like an interactive art installation than a traditional advert, although it was also photographed for a conventional poster. Guerrilla marketing is a term for promotions which are usually located outdoors but may not use official advertising space, so they may not always be quite within the law. For example, pavements can be covered in graffiti that directs customers to a particular store, or reverse graffiti is used where part of existing graffiti is cleaned off in the shape of a brand name. Such techniques are not well-suited to most retailers and can clearly create legal issues. The scope of guerrilla marketing has been extended to include non-conventional marketing techniques such as viral marketing (see below).

Implementing advertising campaigns

In advertising agencies, campaigns are implemented by art directors, who concentrate on the visual aspects of adverts, and copywriters, who are responsible for the written information, usually supervised by a creative director. The term 'creative' is used for a member of the team who devises the adverts. The advertising sector is led by several well-known agencies, including WPP and Publicis, many of whom have offices worldwide and the news in marketing trade magazines frequently contains reports of accounts they have acquired (as inevitably the agencies are good at promoting themselves).

Von Oech (2008) suggests using the following approaches when generating advertising concepts:

- adapting contexts;
- imagining different scenarios;
- reversing expectations;
- connecting unrelated ideas;
- comparing different situations;
- eliminating an element;
- parodying and other forms of humour.

Adverts can be dominated either by visual or verbal/written information and it is down to the creative team to make decisions on the specific colours, style, fonts and layout to be used. The most prominent feature of the copy is usually the headline, often the strapline or slogan of the company, which the advertiser particularly wants consumers to remember. 'More reasons to shop at Morrisons' is an example of a strapline that became memorable due to its play on words, reinforced by being played to a well-known tune in TV adverts. A print advert may also have a subheading with a little more detail, as well as body copy when the advert has a narrative or provides more information. Art directors initially sketch out plans for the layout of adverts, to estimate the position of visuals and text, with photographers or illustrators being commissioned for the final images. Arens *et al.* (2011: 382) propose several ways to select the main focus for the visual elements of press advertising:

- the package containing the product;
- the product alone;
- the product in use;

- how to use the product;
- product features;
- comparison of products;
- user benefit;
- humour;
- testimonial;
- what will happen if the product is not used.

A retailer may consistently use the same advertising agency or different agencies may be pitched against each other, all proposing concepts from which the retailer will select a favourite to implement. As well as finalising the content for an advertising campaign, advertising space needs to be selected and bought, which is the job of a media buyer. The choice of media and frequency of the adverts depends largely on the available budget, the product type and the target market.

RETAIL MARKETING CAREERS
Daniel Dunn, Brand Media Manager

A top honours degree from the highly competitive International Management with American Business Studies (IMABS) programme at Manchester Business School was an excellent launch pad for Daniel Dunn's career with dunnhumby. While the first-class degree, a year at the Schulich School of Business in Toronto, plus many personal skills caught the attention of the selectors, they were also impressed at interview by Dan's direct experience while a student at the 'sharp end' of retailing and service: replenishing shelves in a supermarket, retail banking advisor, rep work at Disney World Orlando, football club marketing intern. Dan reflects: 'Never underestimate the influence work experience can have in making your CV stand out compared to everyone else.'

From its origins in developing the analytical power for Tesco's Clubcard, dunnhumby has expanded worldwide into 36 offices with over 2400 employees. While retaining the close relationship with the world's third largest retailer, dunnhumby also services the data mining and customer insight needs of many leading suppliers and non-competing retailers, laying claim to being the World's Leading Customer Science Company. After just four years in this dynamic organisation, Dan has progressed swiftly from graduate entrant, through account manager, to Media Director for the Procter & Gamble account. Dan enjoys especially using data mining insights to create relevant and meaningful marketing communications, also rewarding customers for remaining loyal to a brand.

Source: with permission from Daniel Dunn

Dan identifies the key skills for working in dunnhumby as 'teamwork and collaboration, communication, attention to detail, autonomy, courage, planning and organisation'. 'OGSM' (Objectives,

Goals, Strategies, Measures) are defined before any internal or client meeting, achieving directness, clarity and effectiveness. Likewise, an organisation in which empowered individuals have great autonomy needs 'RACI', a similarly clear definition of who is Responsible, Accountable, important to Consult, and important to Inform. From the outset, dunnhumby look for employees who believe in putting the customer first, and who display a passion for working with loyalty marketing. Along the way, the company provides excellent training in client consulting skills, communication, and great presenting; Dan certainly demonstrates these skills when he revisits his university to share his state of the science knowledge and great enthusiasm with current retail and marketing students.

Retail marketing careers vignette by Peter McGoldrick.

www.dunnhumby.com; twitter.com/dunnhumby

Public relations

Publicity or **public relations**, commonly known as 'PR' is often described as 'free publicity'. This description gives the impression that there are no costs attached to PR, but more specifically it means that the medium in which the publicity features is not paid directly for it. In fact, it does usually require an investment on the part of the retailer to gain the publicity by employing PR specialists. Berman and Evans's (2010: 537) definition of PR is 'communication that fosters a favorable image of the retailer'. As is the case with advertising, retailers can commission agencies or appoint their own in-house staff to conduct PR campaigns. For example, department store chain House of Fraser employs an in-house PR division at its London Head Office, divided into teams specialising in different product areas.

PR generates interest and goodwill for retailers through sending press releases and photographs to appropriate media and organising events such as product launches to which the media are invited (see Figure 7.5), as well as other methods. Information about a retailer's products and suitable photos can be provided in press releases, to enable journalists to build a story incorporating the company's merchandise. New product innovations; rebranding; successes; links with celebrities; changes in personnel and financial statements are all issues that could be considered newsworthy. The fact that retailers and brands often pay for advertising space in the media in which they are seeking coverage via PR may help their chances of being featured in the editorial sections too.

Figure 7.5 Public relations campaigns by People Tree: prototype advertising campaign and founder Safia Minney at press launch for design collaboration with Zandra Rhodes 2014

Source: with permission from People Tree

'Gifting' is a PR technique used by many large or upmarket retailers, which involves giving its products away to celebrities or other opinion leaders, e.g. bloggers, in the hope that this will tempt consumers to aspire to owning these items (see Superdry case at the end of this chapter). Claire's Accessories used a PR strategy focused on social media and music using a tie-in with favourite teen band One Direction in 2013. A new website showcased social media and integrated 'How To' fashion videos for different age groups and a gift finder. They also linked up with teen blogger Abimarvel, who picks her favourite items and then blogs about them (Bacon, 2013).

Ries and Ries (2004) stress the importance of using PR, suggesting that it should take prominence over advertising. Berman and Evans (2010) concur with this view, pointing out that publicity has more credibility with consumers, though a downside is that the retailer lacks control over the message given by the media. Retailers have several options for countering negative publicity, such as contacting people who post negative comments online to explain or make amends for the problems that they have discussed, thus demonstrating to other customers that they offer good service recovery (see Chapter 11 Multichannel retailing).

RETAIL MARKETING CAREERS
Tamsin Brooke-Smith, PR specialist

Tamsin graduated with a BA (Hons) Fashion Marketing and Communication degree from Nottingham Trent University in 2004. While at university she completed work experience on the fashion desk of both *The Times Magazine* and *The Telegraph Magazine* as well as in the Next Press Office. Following university she took a work placement at a magazine in Brussels, writing articles for the lifestyle pages. Her first permanent job in PR was working at Next Head Office, where she stayed for two years, working her way up from Press Office Assistant to Junior Press Officer. She then worked for department store chain House of Fraser for five years, first as a Press Officer then as a Senior Press Officer, managing the interiors PR team. Tamsin moved on to work as a freelance Creative Project Manager in PR and Marketing for House of Fraser, Dwell and Sainsbury's, as she enjoyed the photo shoot/event management side of her job. She was then offered her current position as Senior Production and Project Manager for homewares at Sainsbury's. Tamsin describes her role as:

> . . . managing the production of photo shoots, 'look books', events and websites which are used as a PR tool by the lifestyle team in the Sainsbury's Press Office. In terms of photography, the aim of the role is to create imagery which is then issued to the media who may use the shots online or in print. Journalists may also request the product used in the imagery to use in their own fashion or interiors

Source: with permission from Tamsin Brooke-Smith

Source: with permission from Tamsin Brooke-Smith

photo shoots. I work across both fashion and homewares and spend a large chunk of my time liaising with the buying and design teams to ensure I am familiar with the product ranges in order to create effective PR materials. I have to ensure that imagery created is 'on brand' and shows off the product well but appeals enough to press for them to use the photography editorially. I also manage the production of press shows which can be large scale seasonal press shows for homewares or fashion where we unveil the new season's range ahead of its launch in store, or a smaller more targeted event such as press dinners with key journalists, which can be more of a relationship-building exercise rather than a product launch.

Tamsin liaises with stylists; photographers; retail buyers; designers; graphic designers and marketing managers, as well as other people who work in PR such as PR Assistants, Press Officers, PR Managers and the PR agencies which support Sainsbury's. In her previous roles she also worked with journalists regularly. Tamsin says that she considers teamwork to be 'essential for any project based work. I often work on projects with people from other agencies so working effectively as a team can make a big difference in terms of how successful the project is and how smoothly it runs'. She also describes communication as vital 'because in PR you are required to liaise with numerous people and communicating the correct information in the most efficient way is essential'.

As Tamsin works in lifestyle PR, being creative is important since she is constantly trying to devise interesting ways to promote products to stand out from other brands. Much of her work is office-based, so computer skills are essential, especially Excel for critical paths, PowerPoint and Word. Photoshop can also be a useful skill in PR as the job involves sending images. Budget management is a big part of Tamsin's role so it is important to be numerate and able to manage finances. She is often juggling several projects at the same time and she says 'being organised is pretty integral to getting things done and planning ahead can save a lot of time when it comes to big projects'.

When employing staff to work in PR Tamsin describes the qualities she looks for as 'confidence, bubbly personality, articulate, well organised, strong written English and great communication'. She advises candidates to 'be positive, adopt a can-do attitude and try to make friends with as many stakeholders as possible – it's always good to have people on side!'. She also recommends those looking for a career in PR to be prepared for criticism from buyers who are naturally protective of their product ranges and may not like how it ends up being used in look book photography and the press. She says 'you need to be very thick-skinned in retail PR and it's best not to dwell on criticism too much!'.

Tamsin's favourite aspect of the job is planning and art directing the interiors photo shoots. She begins by being briefed on the trends and product ranges by the retailer's buyers and designers, then looking for suitable locations for photo shoots. She plans what to shoot and where in the form of a written and visual plan. She directs the stylist and photographer at the shoot to get the photographs required for the PR look book that can then be distributed to the media. Tamsin says 'It's great to see the photography when it's all finished and I get great satisfaction when I see the images used by the media in print or online'.

tamsinloves.com; Twitter:@tamsinloves; www.sainsburyshome.co.uk

Sponsorship

Sponsorship is a promotional strategy employed by various retailers. Sporting events are key areas for sponsorship, since they offer retailers an opportunity to place company logos on sportspeople's clothing and at sites associated with the events. This allows the brands to be seen during sporting events and in the media without paying for advertising space directly. Lear *et al.* (2009) found that 20 per cent of sports endorsements were by retailers. Japanese clothing retailer Uniqlo sponsors top Japanese and European tennis players and includes its logo on the players' clothing (Uniqlo, 2012). Several retailers use sponsorship in a less overt way than this, by supporting cultural or educational initiatives related to their products or local communities. For example, shoe retailer Bata has set up a shoe museum near its headquarters in Toronto, to which it has donated a historic shoe collection (Bata, 2012). In return, the sponsors gain exposure of the brand name that stands out from above-the-line advertising and their donations can therefore have a positive longer-term effect on the retail brand image, since sponsorship is less transient than advertising. However, it is important for the sake of the company's brand image to be highly selective in the choice of people or organisations being sponsored. They need to be reliable and consistent with the brand personality, because if they receive negative publicity the connection can tarnish the retailer's image.

Sales promotions

Sales promotions are very widely used in retail settings, either in-store or online, providing customers with incentives to purchase particular products for a limited time. As the Advertising Standards Authority (ASA) states: 'A sales promotion can provide an incentive for the consumer to buy by using a range of added direct or indirect benefits, usually on a temporary basis, to make the product more attractive' (ASA, 2010: 38). As consumers are very familiar with sales promotions, retailers continue to find novel ways to implement them in order to gain attention. For example, pharmaceutical retailer Boots prints out discounts on its sales receipts to customers, stationery retailer WH Smith gives out discount cards valid for a specified period of time after purchases are made and McDonald's has discount vouchers printed on the back of bus tickets for journeys near to its outlets. Table 7.4 incorporates a range of different sales promotion techniques and their potential effects on retailers and customers (see also Chapter 6 Retail pricing.)

Point-of-purchase (POP) promotions take place in stores, where they have the opportunity to influence customers at the time of purchase decision-making, and can therefore encourage impulse buying. They can take various forms and are most typically free-standing displays supplied by the product manufacturer to attract customers' attention, often in cardboard as they may be temporary. POP displays are useful for small items such as cake decorations or spices where the retailer's usual shelving is not well suited to the products. POP promotions can also include leaflets or flyers with details of products and price offers. **Co-operative promotions** are used to promote both a retailer and brand jointly, e.g. when flyers for recipes are given away in stores with the logos of both the store and the brand (see Figure 7.6). TV screens can also be used to advertise items in store at the crucial time when the consumer is in the process of making the final choice of product. POP techniques are promoted by POPAI, a trade association that arranges conferences and seminars for retailers and brands that engage in POP (see www.popai.co.uk).

Table 7.4 Sales promotion techniques

Type of sales promotion	Effects
Coupons/Multiple buys	Discount coupons encourage customers to visit stores and stimulate sales of specific products; coupons can be costly to distribute; multiple buys can be expensive for the retailer but high sales volume can compensate by creating economies of scale; Buy One Get One Free offers can cause unnecessary waste for consumers when they are persuaded to buy more than needed; both techniques can result in customers purchasing further items while in store.
Competitions	Can create good publicity and positive WoM from customers; useful source of contact names and addresses for retailer's database; prizes and administration of the competition can be expensive for the retailer.
Sample products	Encourage customers to trial products and to interact with staff; can lead to further sales of the product; expensive to implement.
POP displays	Increase prominence for brands; persuade people to try products; can be costly and difficult to find enough space in store.
Promotional event	Promotional events such as book signings, product launches and exhibitions can create good PR opportunities but are expensive to set up and take up space in store.
Refund vouchers	Can encourage return visits by customers to cash in vouchers, e.g. when supermarkets offer a price check on brands from competitors; can make consumers perceive the store as being more expensive than competitors.
Seasonal sales	Discounts offered throughout the store can create high footfall; discounts lower retailers' profit margins but high volume of sales can compensate; sales can disrupt store layout and appearance; can dilute brand image of upmarket retailers.

Figure 7.6 Co-operative promotion by supermarket Budgens and food brand Old El Paso on an in-store recipe leaflet

Source: with permission from Musgrave Retail Partners GB and General Mills UK Ltd

Direct marketing

Direct marketing involves communicating directly with existing or potential customers to promote companies and their products. Traditionally this was done by post but increasingly it is conducted by email and other forms of digital communication. Databases can be built up through various means, of which loyalty cards are one of the most effective ways to acquire customer contact details. Competitions in-store or online can be arranged by retailers and brands with the main intention of gathering email addresses. Certain retailers ask customers to sign up if they wish to receive news and offers from the company. This technique is particularly suitable for retailers with high brand equity such as Jack Wills.

Direct marketing can also encompass direct selling, where the customer can purchase goods directly from an advert, thereby merging a distribution channel with a communication channel. Most advertising media can be used for direct selling, but magazine adverts and flyers are amongst the most popular. For example, Graze is a company selling healthy snacks that has focused its promotional strategy on inserting flyers in magazines and at cashdesks in stores such as WH Smith, as well as online banner adverts, using special offers to persuade customers to subscribe to its regular delivery service.

Retail marketing communications via digital and social media

There are three main classifications of digital media.

1 **Paid** – this type of media is bought by the retailer to target specific customers. It might include display advertising, affiliate advertising and SEM (search engine marketing). Most paid advertising remains in the hands of traditional print and TV media.

2 **Earned media** – here a retailer posts a story or image that is considered of interest to other readers so the content is posted, for free, on other digital media channels. This has strong links to PR where a good story will create conversations that appear online, in social media and in print.

3 **Owned media** – these are the digital channels that the retailer owns and the most important way is through company websites, which is the hub for all digital content. Websites can form a promotional function as well as a transactional one, with certain retailers' websites remaining solely promotional to provide information to consumers, e.g. Aldi does not currently sell online in the UK but uses its website to promote its products.

Retailers are increasingly including consumer-generated reviews on their transactional websites, which can influence other customers in their purchases, since they may be viewed as independent and objective opinions. However, it can be difficult to authenticate these reviews and there is no guarantee that they are impartial. Retailers can also drive consumers towards their websites by providing interesting or entertaining information which can be accessed for free, such as blogs and pages of information or downloads at little or no cost (Meerman-Scott, 2008). This technique is particularly effective when consumers forward links to this content to their contacts, thereby causing it to go viral if it is distributed widely via electronic word-of-mouth (eWOM). 'Groupon', a company which offers consumers substantial discounts with local retailers during a specified time period, benefits from eWOM when consumers forward emails to friends to publicise the deals being offered. Viral marketing can be very beneficial when retailers produce content that is sufficiently entertaining to encourage consumers to distribute the message themselves.

It should be noted that, although much access to the internet or social media for the purposes of promotion is free or incurs relatively minimal costs, there are also many opportunities to pay for advertising online. This is illustrated by impressive growth in online advertising revenue, which rose to an all-time high of $11.6 billion in the first quarter of 2014 in the US, up 19 per cent on the same period in the previous year (Interactive Advertising Bureau, 2014). Similarly, in the UK total online advertising was worth £6.2 billion in 2013 (full year) showing like-for-like increase of 15.2 per cent with mobile advertising accounting for 16.8 per cent of the total (Interactive Advertising Bureau, 2014). Advertising is a significant source of income for social media companies, providing Facebook with 83 per cent of its revenue (IABUK, 2012) and Twitter with 90 per cent of its revenue (Neal, 2014). Accordingly, SEM is becoming increasingly popular, as internet access becomes more widespread. Search-engine optimisation (SEO) is a process which aims to put companies' websites high on the list of answers on search engines such as Google or Yahoo. Alternatively, sponsored adverts can be paid for by retailers on search engine results pages (SERPs) to ensure they achieve a place at the top of the list. Research by Gauzente (2010) found that consumers responded more positively to sponsored adverts on search engines in comparison to banner adverts on websites (which usually appear at the top or side of the screen). Another option for retailers is to advertise on the website of a company that is not a direct competitor, paying the host site per customer clicking through onto the retailer's website in a system known as 'affiliate advertising'.

Third-party websites offer alternative ways of promoting retailers. In addition to operating their own eponymous websites, many retailers have set up their own You Tube channels to communicate directly with customers. For instance, Specsavers have their own You Tube channel (see www.youtube.com/user/SpecsaversOfficial?ob=0&feature=results_main). In addition to You Tube, retailers such as Walmart also operate corporate channels aimed at the business community (compare www.youtube.com/user/Walmart and www.youtube.com/user/WalmartCorporate?blend=2&ob=0). Another option is for retailers to pay for their products to be featured on price comparison websites such as www.kelkoo.com. Consumers can post reviews of leisure retailers such as hotels and restaurants on www.tripadvisor.com which can give companies positive free publicity. However, the retailers have no control over this **user-generated content (UGC)**, other than the ability to respond to consumers' comments and there is no guarantee that the comments are genuine. This has resulted in companies with defamatory reviews threatening legal action against the website (Cochrane, 2011).

Another form of third-party promotion on the internet is for a retailer's merchandise to be reviewed by a blogger. Blogs (an abbreviated term for 'web logs') discuss specific interests such as electronic gadgets and fashion and there are likely to be bloggers available for virtually any type of product sold by a retailer (see Figure 7.7). Bloggers perform a similar role to journalists, without usually being employed by magazines, and they may review the products entirely independently or the retailer could send them items for review (which the bloggers often get to keep afterwards). Bloggers are likely to have followers who view them as innovators or early adopters and consequently look to them for inspiration when buying new products. They can therefore be highly regarded by retailers and consumers alike, since they have a great deal of influence, and popular bloggers can now be afforded similar status to fashion magazine editors at runway shows. However, bloggers' objectivity can sometimes be called into question since they are given free products by companies. Retailers can set up blogs on their own websites, usually written by members of the marketing team, to promote their products in a more informal and engaging way than traditional advertising.

The term 'social media' is defined as 'a group of Internet-based applications that build on the ideological and technological foundations of Web 2.0 and that allow the creation and exchange of User Generated Content' by Kaplan and Haenlein (2010: 61). Retailers

STYLE BUBBLE

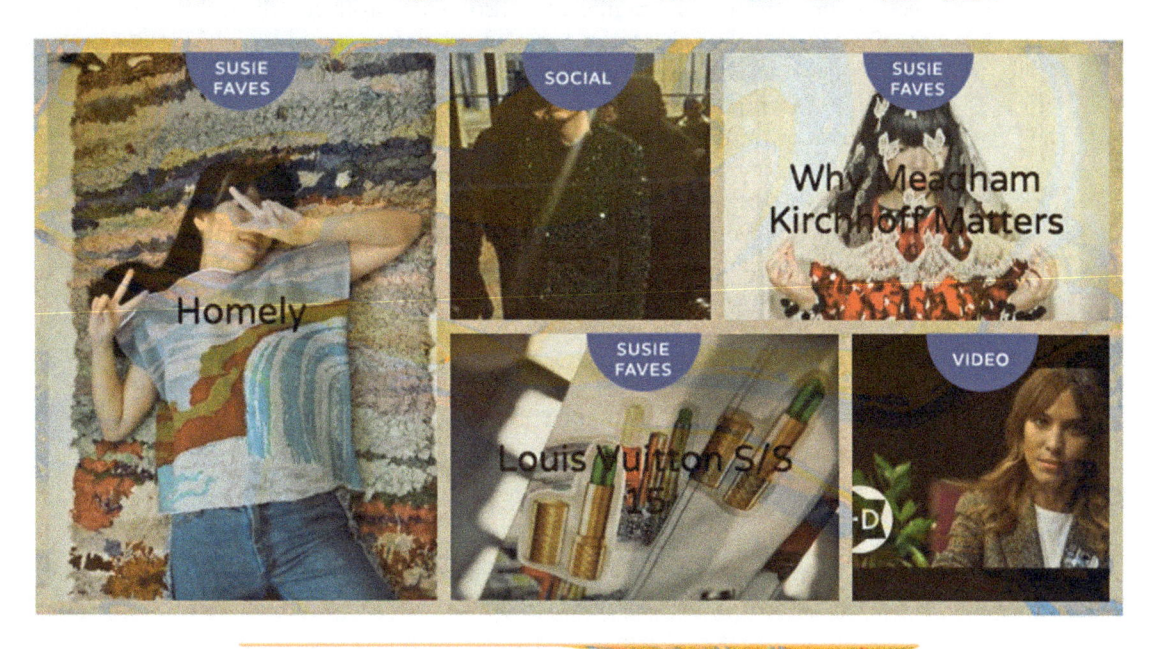

January 20, 2015
Into the Chateau

>>I never "got" the allure of the Chateau Marmont in Los Angeles until I had been given the time last weekend to properly roam its rooms, its vaguely haunted corridors and the outside cottages and bungalows. And thanks to Mulberry, I styled up their S/S 15 pieces with my own clothes and also got to poke my nose around the premises to find little nooks to do this impromptu shoot (yes that is wet brickwork you see there – evidence that it does rain in LA from time to time…). It's hard not to be seduced by all the restored details of this Hollywood haunt. The chipped away tile work and the old-fashioned 1920s ventilation in the bathrooms, the personalised stationery with that endearingly faux-Medieval font of a logo, the restored O'Keefe and Merritt hob in the kitchenette, the mirrored dressing table and the curiously high number of closets (Hollywood starlets and their unusually large trousseaus?). And then beyond its walls, the seclusion provided by the foliage even though you're technically located on Sunset Boulevard, the lemon tree (I took one – sorry – they are very juicy) and the old logo-ed lifebuoy by the pool and all the Spanish tile details to go with the accompanying bungalows. Consider me charmed by the Chateau.

Figure 7.7 Influential fashion blog www.stylebubble.co.uk
Source: Susie Lau

can utilise social media websites such as Facebook, Twitter and Pinterest by having their own pages to promote themselves through communicating with their 'friends' and 'followers'. Social media can have a more positive effect on consumers when pages are set up by fans of the retailer, rather than by the company, since this increases its credibility. A report in *Retail Week* (Thompson, 2012a: 25) about website Pinterest suggests:

> Using the social networking site is a good way to build brand presence online, introduce the retailer's product to a new audience and ultimately increase sales. Images are linked to the retailer's website, so users can click through to the transactional site. Retailers can also monitor the kinds of images being shared and searched for by users in order to keep up with trends.

Mobile-device retailing (m-tailing) has developed as internet-enabled smartphone and tablet PC usage have increased, enabling consumers to have more frequent access to social media. The ability to use retailers' applications (apps) allows consumers not only to receive information from retailers, but also to buy products whilst they are on the move, thereby blurring the boundaries between promotion and distribution. Five per cent of online sales transactions in the UK were made from mobile devices in 2012 (Thompson, 2012b). For example, 15 per cent of Net-A-Porter's traffic comes from mobile devices (Econsultancy, 2013) and the forecast growth of smartphone and tablet ownership is predicted to grow this channel significantly. This then opens the market for advertising and customer communications. Since digital technology is likely to have progressed further by the time you read this, you are advised to read the following sources to keep in touch with contemporary developments: retail trade journals; digital media magazines/websites; business sections in newspapers and academic journals such as the *Journal of Interactive Marketing*.

THE POWER OF LOCAL SEO
By Andrew Rayner, MD of e-mphasis Internet Marketing

For retail businesses Local Search Engine Optimisation (Local SEO) brings together the key benefit of search marketing, that it is targeted. Search achieves this by addressing the needs of potential consumers as they are searching for information. In Local SEO, targeting is further enhanced using location. This is because location is often an important factor in the consumer buying process, particularly where shoppers want to view the actual product before buying, providing comfort that any after sales issues can be easily addressed, and also for convenience, getting access to the product quickly, or avoiding delivery charges or delays. Local SEO takes several forms.

(a) Organic website SEO which involves placing key phrases within the content of a web page and within links to the retailer's site on other websites (inbound links). These are factors that search engines use to determine the order of web pages presented in the search engine results page (SERP). In the case of Local SEO these key phrases would include reference to the location.

(b) Optimisation of business listings such as Google+ Local or Bing Business Portal. This involves placement of key search text in the appropriate fields on business listings held by the search engines. The geographical location of these listings is understood by the search engines so that relevant searches, those that include both the target

Source: with permission from Andrew Rayner

phrase and reference to location, cause the listing to appear in search results, usually with a map. The location can be specified either by street address, town, county, postcode or even implied by the location of the device the user searches on. This technique also works for searches performed in map tools, e.g. Google places, which result in a list of local businesses that best match the search terms, based on proximity to location, search text relevance, and in some cases consumer review.

(c) Use of local directory, review or community websites which often provide a facility for business profiles. These are mostly free but in some cases incur a listing fee or offer a paid upgrade in the form of enhanced placement. Usually grouped by product offer or sector these listing pages regularly appear in the same organic search results as in 'a', providing businesses with the opportunity to get multiple placements on target SERPs. In addition, many local internet users visit these sites for social or search purposes, much like people previously used community groups or yellow pages.

Local SEO is neglected by major brands and so there is often little competition for search phrases of this type. This enables agile small businesses to dominate the market in their local area and compete with larger companies. In conclusion, Local SEO is a powerful technique for businesses that serve consumers because it offers cheap, targeted and often untapped marketing opportunities.

www.e-mphasis.com

Word-of-mouth

Word-of-mouth (WoM) refers to consumers informing each other about products, brands and retailers, making recommendations or criticisms. Positive WoM has significant advantages over other forms of promotion, since consumers may perceive their peers' views as objective, impartial and authentic and no costs are incurred for the retailer, yet it is the technique over which retailers have the least control. Many consumers have become jaded by the proliferation of advertising in their lives and they are therefore likely to consider friends, family, online reviews and bloggers as more reliable sources. It is paradoxical that WoM is a powerful method of promotion that derives its value from the very fact it is not controlled by companies. However, retailers can undoubtedly have a strong impact on the messages spread via WoM by providing an effective marketing mix with a good standard of customer service and behaving with honesty and integrity. Retailers can give customers a platform to facilitate an exchange of views, e.g. user reviews on the website or a Twitter account with tweets that actively encourage customers to offer their comments.

Personal selling

Personal selling forms part of Integrated Marketing Communications in retailing as well as being a fundamental element of customer service. For products that are expensive or highly technical, and therefore create a higher level of risk for the customer, personal selling is of particular importance and is widely used. Sales personnel perform a crucial role for retailers in a store setting, due to their direct communication with customers. Sales advisors are in the valuable position of being able to both impart information about the retailer's products to customers and to receive feedback from them. Sales staff are also significant because they have the capacity to influence customers to proceed to the purchasing stage of the consumer decision process at the point-of-sale.

Personal selling by sales staff can involve persuading customers to purchase products, sales transactions, maintaining customer satisfaction and dealing with product returns and complaints (Berman and Evans, 2010). Sales personnel can be trained to use customer-orientated sales techniques, as well as being motivated to provide high quality customer care through rewards and bonuses. Retailers usually set customer service targets to enhance performance in this area. Personal selling is a flexible and effective way to generate sales, but it is also time-intensive and expensive, and therefore retailers with low price ranges only use it to a limited extent. Etailers have the drawback of not being able to provide face-to-face communication with customers, but this can be compensated for by offering fast, efficient responses to questions online, access to staff via the phone and giving clear, detailed information about products online. Online consumer assessments of retailer customer service give retailers a strong incentive to avoid under-performance. (See also Chapter 10 Retail customer service.)

Relationship marketing

Relationship marketing (RM) can help to build long-term relationships between retailers and customers through various types of interaction. Grönroos (1994) was responsible for the academic development of the RM approach, which takes into account the lifetime value of the customer to the retailer, rather than a series of individual transactions, thereby aiming to meet the needs of both parties in the relationship. This can sometimes mean that making losses or low profits on certain transactions and offering financial incentives to customers can be worthwhile for the retailer in the long run. Although RM is sometimes described as a new marketing paradigm its roots go back to the traditional forms of retailing that were mentioned in chapter 1, where the tradesperson knew customers personally. It is rarely possible for large retailers to replicate this situation precisely in the present day, but consumers have become so accustomed to the impersonal nature of mass production and retailing that a personal touch can lead them to feel more valued. RM can encourage customers to feel an emotional connection with a retailer that leads to long-term loyalty. Independent stores have a significant asset in that they can get to know customers personally and this social interaction offers them a competitive advantage over larger chains that should not be underestimated. Many small retailers may practise RM without being conscious of it, since it is natural for them to form relationships with their customers, with whom they may often be on first-name terms.

The relationships formed between companies and their clients in business-to-business (B2B) marketing helped to inspire the development of RM between businesses and consumers (B2C). Another term similar to RM is Customer Relationship Management (CRM) and this is an apt term for large companies where a large amount of data exists about customers that has to be managed in order to meet their requirements. Direct marketing forms a key component of RM because it allows retailers to contact customers with specific offers, product news or events tailored to their needs and interests. Loyalty card schemes enable retailers to analyse patterns of purchasing by customers, anticipating their needs and allowing them to send offers that are likely to be viewed as appealing. RM is relevant to all aspects of the business that affect customers' interactions with a retailer and it can therefore be considered as more than simply a method of promotion.

CHAPTER SUMMARY

Retailers and the products that they sell can be promoted through a wide range of integrated marketing communications (IMC). Marketers use IMC strategies to set promotional objectives and a budget to help achieve them before devising and implementing a promotional mix within a set time-frame. The suitability of communication methods and media should be assessed depending on factors such as cost, company size, product sector, target market and timing. The main promotional methods available to retailers are outlined below.

- Advertising by paying for space in broadcast, print, digital or out-of-home media. Implementing advertising campaigns requires teams of art directors, copywriters managed by a creative director, as well as media buyers.
- PR, which seeks to gain 'free' publicity, although it incurs costs for the retailer through employing in-house marketing staff or independent PR agencies to arrange events, photography and press releases.
- Sponsorship to gain exposure for the retailer's brand name by offering funding to organisations such as sports teams or entertainment events.
- Sales promotions within stores, on websites or in the media, including multiple buy offers and competitions.
- Personal selling by staff talking directly to customers.
- Word-of-mouth, a very valuable form of promotion whereby consumers exchange information about companies or products with their peers, over which the retailer has very little control.

The use of digital media for communications strategies is a growth area, using paid, earned or owned media and social media websites can promote retailers at relatively low cost. Retailers can utilise search engine optimisation (SEO) to help their companies to be ranked more highly in internet searches. Direct marketing can be used by retailers to communicate personally with consumers and may form part of a Relationship Marketing (RM) strategy to build up a long-term relationship with customers.

EXERCISES AND QUESTIONS

1. Using one of von Oech's seven approaches to generating advertising ideas, as mentioned in this chapter, develop a press advert for a retailer of your choice, including copy (text). You can either draw or describe the visual elements of the advert.
2. Consider the AIDA model in relation to an existing advert for a retailer. Assess how the advert captures consumers' attention and interest.
3. Using YouTube and collecting adverts from print media, select two adverts that use humour and product features techniques. Critique the adverts and suggest potential improvements that you believe could make them more applicable to their target audience.
4. Look up the latest figures available for the top expenditure on advertising by retailers at www.marketingmagazine.co.uk. How have the top ten retailers in the list changed since 2013? What do you think are the reasons behind these changes in advertising spend for the retailers concerned?
5. What are the advantages and disadvantages of retailers using PR in comparison to advertising?
6. In which aspects of marketing communications discussed in this chapter can social media be used? Although social media accounts are usually free to set up, explain why the use of social media as a promotional tool can still incur costs for a retailer.
7. Select the most appropriate types of Out of Home media for the following types of retailer then develop some copy for a poster for a real or fictitious company in one of these sectors:
   a Pet supplies
   b DIY
   c Bakery.

You may find it useful to look at the range of media available for this exercise at www.outdoormediacentre.org.uk.

8 Select a well-known retail chain in your country or region, of which you are a customer. Compile a list of the range of methods of marketing communications used by this retailer after visiting an outlet and searching online. Consider whether there are any other promotional methods that they do not appear to be using currently which could have persuaded you to increase your purchases there. This may include, for example, using a wider variety of advertising media or different methods of promotion. You should then analyse whether or not it would be viable for the retailer to adopt your suggested tactics, or whether any factors would stop them doing so, e.g. lack of budget or conflict with brand image.

REFERENCES

Arens, W.F., Weigold, M.F. and Arens, C. (2011) *Contemporary Advertising and Integrated Marketing Communications,* 13th edn, New York: McGraw-Hill Irwin.

ASA (2010) *The CAP Code: The UK Code of Non-broadcast Advertising, Sales Promotion and Direct Marketing,* Advertising Standards Authority (available online at: http://www.cap.org.uk/The-Codes/CAP-Code.aspx).

Bata (2012) *The Bata Shoe Museum* (available online at: http://www.batashoemuseum.ca/).

Bacon, J. (2013) Meet the Fixer, *Marketing Week,* 9 May, pp. 14–18.

Berman, B. and Evans, J.R. (2010) *Retailing Management: A Strategic Approach,* 11th edn, Upper Saddle River, NJ: Pearson.

Brown, J. (2011) TK Maxx Unveils Radical New Ad Message, *Retail Week,* 21 March.

Cochrane, K. (2011) Why TripAdvisor is getting a bad review, *The Guardian,* 25 January (available online at: http://www.guardian.co.uk/travel/2011/jan/25/tripadvisor-duncan-bannatyne).

Econsultancy (2013) *How Net-A-Porter plans to build on its mobile success in 2013,* http://econsultancy.com/uk/blog/62366-how-net-a-porter-plans-to-build-on-its-mobile-success-in-2013.

Gauzente, C. (2010) The intention to click on sponsored ads: a study of the role of prior knowledge and of consumer profile, *Journal of Retailing and Consumer Services,* 17, 457–463.

Gilbert, D. (2003) *Retail Marketing Management,* 2nd edn, Harlow: Financial Times/Prentice Hall.

Grönroos, C. (1994) From marketing mix to relationship marketing: towards a paradigm shift in marketing, *Management Decision,* 32(2), 4–20.

IABUK (2012) *Online advertising accounts for 83% of Facebook's revenue,* Internet Advertising Bureau UK (available online at: http://www.iabuk.net/news/online-advertising-accounts-for-83-of-facebooks-revenue).

Interactive Advertising Bureau (2014) *At $11.6 billion in Q1 2014, Internet Advertising Revenues Hit All-Time First Quarter High* (available online at: http://www.iab.net/about_the_iab/recent_press_releases/press_release_archive/press_release/pr-061214).

John Lewis (2014) *Edition magazine* (available online at: http://www.johnlewis.com/edition-magazine/c6000190261).

Kaplan, A.M. and Haenlein, M. (2010) Users of the world, unite! The challenges and opportunities of social media, *Business Horizons,* 53, 59–68.

Kimberley, S. (2012) Ogilvy & Mather captures TK Maxx digital advertising, *Campaign*, 26 April (available online at: http://www.brandrepublic.com/news/1128898/).

Lear, K., Runyan, R.C. and Whitaker, W.H. (2009) Sports celebrity endorsements in retail products advertising, *International Journal of Retail & Distribution Management*, 37(4), 308–321.

Lee, Y.H. and Lim, E.A.C. (2008) What's funny and what's not: the moderating role of cultural orientation in ad humor, *Journal of Advertising*, 37(2), 71–84.

McEleny, C. (2010) TK Maxx takes sponsorship of Channel 4 Fashion Show onto Facebook with video app, *New Media Age*, p. 6 (available online at: web.ebscohost.com/ehost/pdfviewer/pdfviewer?sid=ce6e3a59–4a4c-4e1e-b549-b855112bdf28%40sessionmgr15&vid=5&hid=21).

Marketing Magazine (2014) Top 100 UK advertisers, *Marketing Magazine* (available online at: http://www.marketingmagazine.co.uk/article/1289560/top-100-uk-advertisers-bskyb-increases-lead-p-g-bt-unilever-reduce-adspend).

Meerman-Scott, D. (2008) *The New Rules of Advertising and PR*, Hoboken, NJ: Wiley and Sons.

Neal, R.W. (2014) Twitter (TWTR) Q1 2014 Earnings preview: slumping user growth offsets strong increase in revenue, *International Business Times*, 28 April (available online at: http://www.ibtimes.com/twitter-twtr-q1–2014-earnings-preview-slumping-user-growth-offsets-strong-increase-revenue-1577387).

QVC (2012) *QVC's global corporate facts* (available online at: http://www.qvcuk.com/ukqic/qvcapp.aspx/app.html/params.file.%7CCorporateFacts,html/walk.html.%7CCor_uk_QVCfacts,html?&cookie=set).

Ries, A. and Ries, L. (2004) *The Fall of Advertising and the Rise of PR*, London: Harper Collins.

Rose, H. (2011) New York, Paris, Milan, Cheltenham?, *The Times Magazine*, 19 March, pp. 40–47.

Thompson, V. (2012a) Need to know: Pinterest, *Retail Week*, 9 March, p. 25.

Thompson, V. (2012b) Need to know: Tablets and mobile devices, *Retail Week*, 16 March, p. 27.

Uniqlo (2012) *Sponsored Athletes* (available online at: http://www.uniqlo.com/us/company/sponsored-athletes.html).

Von Oech, R. (2008) *A Whack on the Side of the Head: How You Can Be More Creative*, New York: Business Plus.

Wilson, R.T. and Till, B.D. (2008) Airport advertising effectiveness: an exploratory field study, *Journal of Advertising*, 37(1), 59–72.

FURTHER READING

Bojei, J., Julian, C.C., Wel, C.A. B.C. and Ahmed, Z.U. (2013) The empirical link between relationship marketing tools and consumer retention in retail marketing, *Journal of Consumer Behaviour*, 12(3), 171–181.

Danaher, P.J. and Rossiter, J.R. (2011) Comparing perceptions of marketing communication channels, *European Journal of Marketing*, 45(1/2), 6–42.

Diamond, J. (2011) *Retail Advertising and Promotion,* New York: Fairchild.

Duan, W., Gu, B. and Whinston, A.B. (2008) The dynamics of online word-of-mouth and product sales: an empirical investigation of the movie industry, *Journal of Retailing,* 84(2), 233–242. (This is the journal's most cited article at the time of writing.)

Floyd, K., Freling, R., Alhoqail, S., Cho, H.Y. and Freling, T. (2014) How online product reviews affect retail sales: a meta-analysis, *Journal of Retailing,* 90(2), 217–232.

McNeill, L.S. (2012) Sales promotion in the supermarket industry: a four country case comparison, *International Review of Retail, Distribution and Consumer Research,* 22(3), 243–260.

Huang, M., Cai, F., Tsang, A.S.L. and Zhou, N. (2011) Making your online voice loud: the critical role of WOM information, *European Journal of Marketing,* 45(7/8), 1277–1297.

Smith, B.G. (2013) The public relations contribution to IMC: deriving opportunities from threats and solidifying public relations, *Public Relations Review,* 39(5), 507–513.

Taylor, D.G. and Levin, M. (2014) Predicting mobile app usage for purchasing and information-sharing, *International Journal of Retail & Distribution Management,* 42(8), 759–774.

Advertising Age adage.com

Adweek www.adweek.com

Brilliant Ads twitter.com/Brilliant_Ads

Campaign www.campaignlive.co.uk

MediaWeek www.mediaweek.co.uk

Case study

Marketing communications at Superdry

Despite its successful blend of Japanese graphic text and retro US styling, many of Superdry's customers may be surprised to find that the fashion retailer is an English company, launched in Cheltenham in 2003. Superdry's unlikely headquarters location is an industrial estate in Gloucestershire. The company's founders, Julian Dunkerton (CEO and main shareholder) and James Holder (design director), were inspired by a shopping trip to Japan when they predicted that the type of fashion branding they saw there could also be popular in the UK. This insightful prediction has netted them a reported £478 million and £188 million, respectively, and their firm now employs 3000 people (Rose, 2014). This is in stark contrast to 1985 when Julian Dunkerton set up Cult Clothing on a market stall, backed by a small weekly allowance offered by the government to people setting up new businesses at that time. The market stall's popularity allowed Cult to become a chain of stores. Meanwhile James Holder had started out designing T-shirts aimed at the skateboarding community before developing the 'Bench' brand. James met Julian in 1992 when he approached Cult about becoming a supplier.

Classic retro styling makes the clothes anti-fashion in a sense, as they can be worn from one season to the next without appearing outdated. According to Craven (2011) Julian Dunkerton describes the brand's style as 'clothes you could wear to the pub without being laughed at'. The products are of a good quality standard and since their prices are generally higher than average High Street products, the company can afford to manufacture some of its merchandise in Turkey, where it has also opened retail outlets (Ralph, 2013). Turkish production costs more, but has shorter delivery lead times than manufacturing in China and India, where some of the company's other products are made. To maintain the brand image, Superdry shops do not hold seasonal sales, preferring instead to send products to its discount outlets, including one in Bicester Village and a highly successful eBay shop that sells seconds.

Superdry has expanded through a combination of brand extensions and retail expansion, both online and offline, in the UK and overseas. It has achieved various periods of rapid growth as adoption of the brand has

Superdry press photograph shows the emphasis on branding
Source: with permission from SuperGroup plc

become increasingly widespread, e.g. 86.9 per cent growth in the year up to January 2011 (Rose, 2011). When the parent company SuperGroup floated on the stock market in 2010 its initial share price of £5 valued the company at £400 million, although share prices have fluctuated significantly since that time. The Superdry business has also grown in terms of online sales, as its products are sold on its own website, as well as by retailers including Next and Asos, leading to the opening of a larger warehouse based in Staffordshire in 2013, employing an additional 200 people (Hipwell, 2013). It also has websites in 16 different languages (Thompson, 2013).

The remaining Cult stores were replaced by the Superdry fascia in 2012, so the company no longer sells other brands such as G-Star (Leroux and Pagnamenta, 2012). The stores have a contemporary industrial style with a blend of metal, dark wood and spotlighting with a background sound track of remixed chart songs. A factor that has shaped the number of outlets the company has opened is that Superdry stores are so enticing to consumers that landlords have been known to pay them to open branches to attract more trade to their shopping centres (Finch and Wood, 2010). Having started off selling menswear, Superdry's current brand extensions include womenswear, accessories, perfume and cosmetics. They also plan to offer more sports-orientated outerwear in response to rugby players' requests and there are plans to open a trial skiwear shop in Austria (Clark, 2014). The brand is now sold in more than 100 countries (Thompson, 2013) and Germany has been pinpointed as a key country for expansion, with 13 stores planned there by the end of 2014. Superdry has recently bought out its franchise partners in Germany, Spain and Scandinavia, to facilitate its European expansion (Clark, 2014).

Superdry's marcomms strategy is somewhat unconventional in that it doesn't use advertising. However, advertising-style photography shoots of Superdry products are used for in-store posters and to distribute to the press, either to feature in fashion pages or to use alongside articles on the company in the business pages. Superdry employs a Global Social Media Manager whose responsibilities have included the development of a mobile-optimised Facebook app (Fashion United, 2012). The company uses competitions as a promotional strategy, such as offering a prize of a year's supply of Superdry T-shirts for the winner and two friends. Superdry also uses its Facebook and Twitter accounts to promote its products and offer competitions. Another way in which Superdry does not follow a typical marketing path is that it chooses not to use market segmentation, although it initially targeted 15–25-year-olds. It aims instead at an unusually broad range of demographics (Rose, 2011) so you are likely to find teenage girls queuing at the tills alongside women in their thirties and men in their forties.

PR has played a major part in the promotional mix of the Superdry brand and the company has an in-house PR team. Its most successful PR coup proved to be a key element in Superdry's early success, when David Beckham was photographed wearing a Superdry 'Osaka 6' T-shirt for the cover of his 2005 calendar, giving the brand the ultimate celebrity endorsement. Superdry follows the standard fashion business practice of sending its products as free gifts to certain celebrities and Beckham has also been pictured wearing a leather jacket that had been sent to him by the company. The brand's clothes have also been worn by many other well-known names from Jamie Oliver and Gwen Stefani to Leonardo di Caprio. Press events are essential within Superdry's PR strategy. The Spring/Summer 2014 range was launched at a cocktail party for journalists and bloggers above its central London Regent Street store (Superdry, 2014). In June 2014 Superdry showed its collection at London men's fashion week, an event which is usually exclusive to more expensive labels, and hosted a launch party attended by stars such as Tinie Tempah and Mark Ronson (Rose, 2014).

REFERENCES

Clark, A. (2014) SuperGroup dips toe in wider waters, *The Times*, 11 July (available online at: www.thetimes.co.uk/tto/business/industries/retailing/article4144494.ece).

Craven, J. (2011) Is it edgy? Is it expensive? No, it's Superdry, *The Times*, 27 July (available online at: http://www.thetimes.co.uk/tto/life/fashion/article3105941.ece).

Fashion United (2012) *Superdry looks to drive social brand* (available online at: www.fashionunited.co.uk/fashion-news/fashion/superdry-looks-to-drive-social-brand-2012101615999).

Finch, J. and Wood, Z. (2010) Superdry fashion label sees profits almost triple, *The Guardian*, 15 July (available online at: www.theguardian.com/business/2010/jul/15/superdry-profits-triple-supergroup).

Hipwell, D. (2013) The writing on the wall is in Japanese, *The Times*, 6 May (available online at: www.thetimes.co.uk/tto/business/industries/retailing/article3756994.ece).

Leroux, M. and Pagnamenta, R. (2012) SuperGroup ditches 'security blanket', *The Times,* 13 July (available online at: www.thetimes.co.uk/tto/business/industries/retailing/article3473488.ece).

Ralph, A. (2013) SuperGroup puts unrest to one side to strike deal in Turkey, *The Times,* 23 August (available online at: www.thetimes.co.uk/tto/business/industries/consumer/article3850541.ece).

Rose, H. (2011) New York, Paris, Milan, Cheltenham?, *The Times Magazine,* 19 March, pp. 40–47 (available online at: www.thetimes.co.uk/tto/magazine/article2945797.ece).

Rose, H. (2014) People have a go at us, but we are conquering the world, *The Times,* 14 June (available online at: www.thetimes.co.uk/tto/life/fashion/mensstyle/article4118520.ece).

Superdry (2014) *Superdry SS14 Press Day,* www.superdry.com/blog/tag/spring-summer-14/

Thompson, S. (2013) International sales soar for SuperGroup, *The Times,* 7 November (available online at: http://www.thetimes.co.uk/tto/business/industries/retailing/article3915610.ece).

See www.superdry.com/blog/ for information about student internships at Superdry.

DISCUSSION QUESTIONS

1. Does Superdry use a push or pull promotional strategy? Why do you believe they have chosen this promotional strategy? As their potential customers discuss whether or not you agree with this choice of strategy.

2. Superdry's promotional mix is unusual for a well-known fashion brand in that it doesn't involve advertising. Do you believe that the company should advertise its products? Provide reasons to explain your answer.

3. Using an internet search, investigate Superdry's international expansion. If you worked for a consultancy employed to advise Superdry how to amend its marketing communication strategy to enhance its expansion overseas, what recommendations would you make?

CHAPTER 8

Retail location

John Pal, Manchester Business School

Learning objectives

The objectives of this chapter are to:

- explain why retail locations are an important part of the retail marketing mix;
- describe the types of locations used by retail firms;
- explore the ways retailers make location decisions;
- identify the strategic and managerial dimensions of retailers' location decision-making;
- explain the influence of the planning system on location decisions.

Introduction

George Davies is known as a serial retail innovator and creator of Next, George at Asda and Per Una. When he was devising the Next format he focused on developing the concept and the product in particular. It appears he left the initial location decisions to his senior management team. As he states in his autobiography (Davies and Davies, 1989: 67):

> Trevor's sites were cheap, and they were cheap for two very good reasons. The first was that he had chosen the wrong towns. When I'd originally been asked where we should look for our new sites, I'd replied, 'Wherever the Tory voters are'. It may have seemed a peculiar reply . . . but the point I was making was that *you should always go where your customer is*, and not be guided solely by the rental of your shop. (Emphasis in the original)

Moreover, Davies and Davies (1989: 67) go on to explain that 'as long as you have the right town, you can do very well with an off-pitch site'. But there is a need to view Davies' analysis cautiously, given the way that retailing has changed since then.

It has often been suggested that the three most important criteria for success in retailing are 'location, location, location' and indeed Jones and Simmons (1987) had a book so titled. In addition Bennison *et al*. (1995) claimed that location was the *primus inter pares* (first amongst equals) of the retail marketing mix. Perhaps this can be linked to the then CEO of Tesco, Sir Terry Leahy, claiming that retailing is a local activity in that shoppers would frequent their nearest store. That might hold true in terms of food shopping but for other goods this might not be the case.

So how can we understand what a retail location is and why it is important? In previous research the issue of retail location has been typified as one of the Ps (place) of the marketing mix but more specifically Walters (1988) identified the trading format as an important part of the mix. This definition has been used by Burt *et al*. (2011) in examining IKEA's different approaches in three countries. In terms of the geographical research, retail location has been examined in terms of how sites can be chosen and how trading areas (or catchments) can be defined.

The way that retail location is now understood, in a very complex and fast-moving environment, is by a fusion of the marketing and the geographic approaches, first mooted by Bennison *et al*. (1995) where they also highlighted that retail locations can also be examined at various scales of analyses. These levels range from the micro-level where issues relating to a specific store are made and are generally tactical in nature; through the meso-level decisions which relate to the monadic or operational decisions specific to a site including issues relating to the catchment for a store; and, finally, the strategic decisions of coverage of a store network where the retailer has to be aware of macro-level issues.

Much of previous research prior to Clarke *et al*. (1997), which had built on the work by Bennison *et al*. (1995), had related to the technical issues of identifying new sites for stores and was based on store expansion. Retail locations can also be understood from a financial perspective in that they represent an important asset for the business. The financial risks in making the wrong location decision with a retailer saddled with a poor performing store can be vast. In general terms smaller stores are easier to site than larger ones as the latter will require more space, usually in off-centre locations. The levels of investment in retail locations can be very large. Tesco, for instance, is one of the biggest property developers in Europe and had a property portfolio worth an estimated £30 billion, representing 75 per cent of the company's enterprise value, which reportedly makes Tesco the largest property owner and manager in Europe (Leahy, 2009). To gauge the sums from a capital expenditure basis, clothing retailer Next's levels of capital expenditure are also sizeable as seen in Table 8.1.

Table 8.1 Next's levels of capital expenditure (in £m)

	2013	2014	2015 (est)
Warehouse and other	21	22	38
Store refurbishments	10	13	5
New and extended stores	51	70	72

Source: Next plc (2014)

Retail locations have also become important for the grounding of capital (Wrigley, 1998). According to Wood and Tasker (2008: 239) their experience of having worked as location specialists at Tesco and Sainsbury's respectively 'suggests that a 10 per cent variation in a sales forecast from reality for a medium-sized grocery superstore could change the affordable bid for a site by £5million'.

Why are locations important – even in the digital world?

From the humblest barrow on a street market to the grandest department store in the most expensive shopping street in the world, a major function of the location is to access customers and provide them with the right goods. But a retailer wanting to grow has to consider how to do this and one of the key ways is through adding more locations. Most of the retailers we see today started in business as a single shop and have grown either organically and/or through acquiring competing businesses. In the early stages of development major UK multiple grocers such as J Sainsbury, Morrisons and Tesco invested some of their profits in opening more stores. This can be seen as organic expansion. However, as these retailers became bigger and their profits increased they could invest ever larger sums in either more store openings and/or even acquiring competing retailers.

Increasingly the store is not only seen as a place to buy products but a location from which to collect product that may have been ordered over the internet. Marks & Spencer (M&S), for instance, uses its network of Simply Food stores as a collection point for their customers' internet-ordered products. Department store group John Lewis Partnership do the same using their network of Waitrose food stores. This 'click and collect' approach is being adopted by many retailers such as catalogue retailer Argos, House of Fraser and Next.

As a consequence customers no longer have to wait at home for the delivery of product but they can collect their product in store. In addition they can also return their product

HOUSE OF FRASER'S DOT.COM STORE

House of Fraser is a full-line department store retailer operating from 62 stores and has almost 5.5 million square feet of selling space. That makes its average store size about 62,000 square feet. Its stores are located in major towns and cities and regional shopping centres. Two of the major cities where it has not traded from until 2012 were Liverpool and Aberdeen. Finding a site large enough to accommodate the full range led the company to devise and trial its dot.com format. These stores are less than 2000 square feet but are located in prime pitch sites in the shopping centres. Customers can order product from the store via iPads and terminals. They can then collect and return product there, as well as ordering from anywhere else. An interesting feature is the presence of fitting rooms in the store. This allows customers to try on an item of clothing they had ordered and if not wanted they do not have to go through the usual returns process.

at their nearest store thereby avoiding the need to post product back to the retailer. So we can see that a retailer's location is changing in the way it is used by retailers. However, it is not just traditional retailers who are changing. Catalogue retailer N Brown, which has emerged as a powerful online operator, announced it was examining opening more retail outlets. As of May 2014 the firm had nine stores and had plans to open a further nine by the end of 2014 including a flagship on the premier UK shopping street Oxford Street in London (Insider Media, 2014).

It can be seen therefore that the number and purpose of retailer's locations is becoming an even more important decision. Sites are expensive to acquire, stores costly to build and freeholds and leaseholds can be a major cost to a retailer. As a result of this retailers are having to consider not just where to locate stores but how many to have to enable the right amount of coverage.

A framework for location decision-making

To appreciate the range and scope of location decisions that a retailer makes, a framework adapted from the work of Clarke *et al.* (1997) is presented in Figure 8.1. It is a well-worn cliché that having the 'right goods in the right place at the right price' is important to

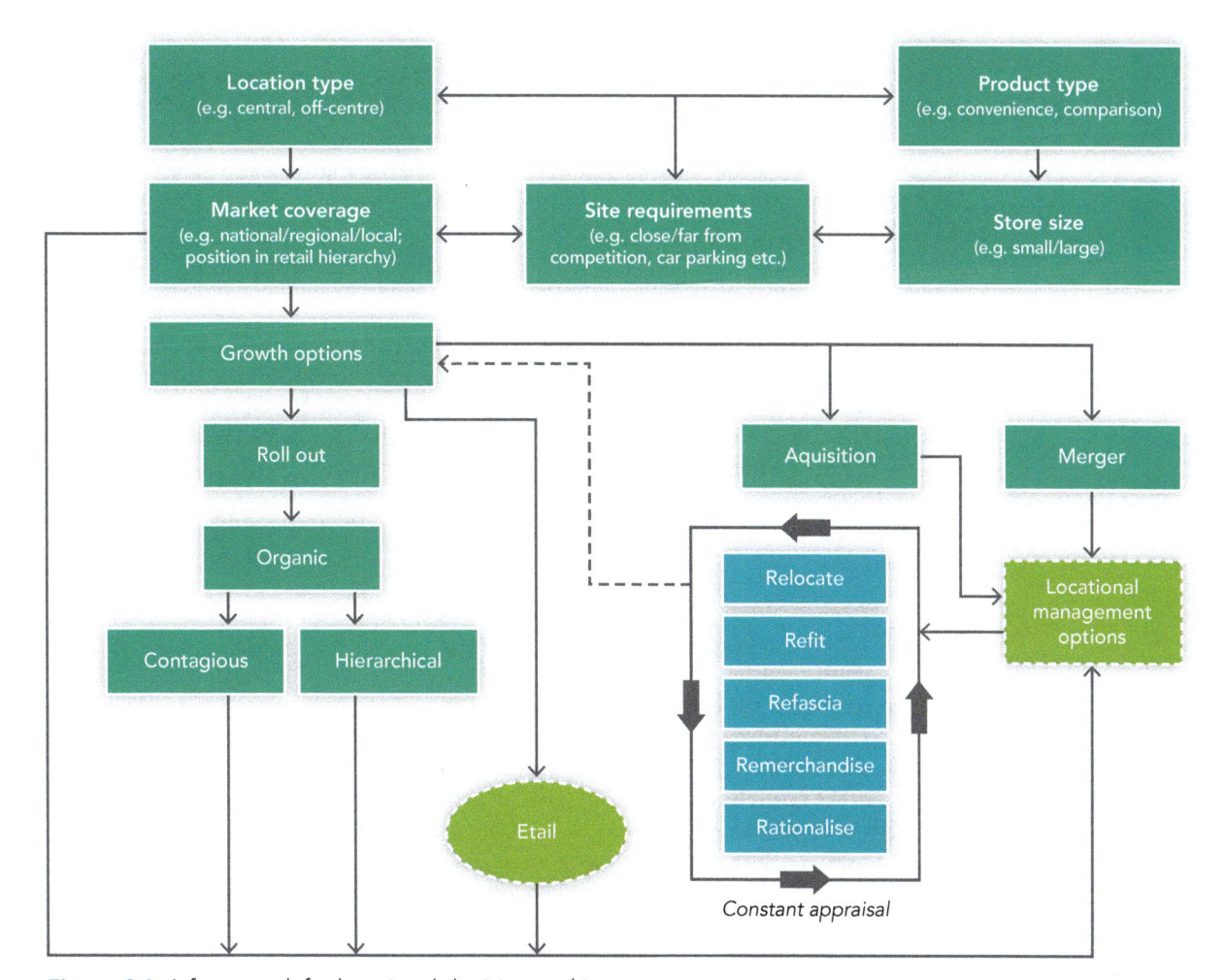

Figure 8.1 A framework for locational decision-making

Source: adapted from Clarke et al., 1997

success in retailing. Therefore matching the product with the location is critical. For instance, having a full-line department store in a small town may not be a good idea as there might not be the custom to support it. The 'right price' element also has to incorporate all the costs of the business and one of these is that related to property or the locational costs. Working through Figure 8.1 it can be seen that retailers have to choose where to trade from at a number of different 'scales'. First of all is that related to the geographic region (i.e. market coverage). That decision is also made in the context of what size a store will be and also where it will be located within a market.

Strategic dimensions

A key decision for many retailers is to decide whether to own or lease their stores. M&S has been one retailer that has adopted the use of owning the freehold on their stores or entering into long leases. More recently some retailers have been selling their stores and leasing them back to release capital to invest in other ventures or just to return money via dividends to shareholders. Next provides an interesting example of a retailer with a flexible property strategy. It appears that Next is using shorter than the typical or standard institutional lease of 25 years, as 50 per cent of leases will expire between 2013 and 2020, and 80 per cent of them by 2023 (Next plc, 2013). Next also has a major online presence through its *Directory* business and having stores is still important for the firm so as to be able to meet the demands of 'click and collect'. Next also states it is seeking better lease terms. It is interesting to note that there seems to be changing views about whether to own or lease, and the flexibility that accrues from this process. In a recent case M&S tried to manoeuvre itself out of a lease and lost a court case relating to breaking the lease early. It was suggested that the balance of power in lease negotiations was now tipping towards landlords (Somerville, 2014).

Roll out

The process of acquisitions of a retail firm or a batch of stores from a retailer can add more stores in under-represented areas. Morrison's acquisition of Safeway giving it access to the market in the South of England; Tesco's acquisitions of Yorkshire-based Hillards and Scottish-based Wm Low also gave them entry to under-represented markets. Another notable feature of these acquisitions is that they also included distribution centres that served these markets. In contrast Tesco's acquisition of over 800 stores from T&S allowed them to enter the convenience market, a market in which they had little exposure or experience.

Contagious expansion

A major reason for the constrained coverage, of some food retailers in particular, is that related to the ability to distribute to these food stores and the importance of minimising the cold chain. There are examples of successful regional chains such as Booths supermarkets in the north west of England, and Waitrose who were also originally focused on the south of England. As Waitrose expands it first has to build additional distribution centres to service the extended store network. As a consequence these two retailers have generally expanded organically and in a contagious manner. Similarly Aldi (Thompson *et al.*, 2012) has expanded contagiously.

Tesco's unprofitable Fresh & Easy concept was targeted at the west coast of the USA (Birchall, 2007a, 2007b) and despite vast amounts of research into the locations and size of stores to be opened the venture failed. Their approach was one of contagious expansion. One of the reasons for its failure was a mismatch between the products and the format devised, and with customer expectations. These strategic level decisions are the riskiest yet potentially the most lucrative. However, as Tesco reported, this venture cost the firm £1 billion (Felsted, 2013).

Hierarchical expansion

At the other extreme are retailers of comparison, or higher order goods, such as clothing and footwear. Reaching the right types of customers may be reliant on being at the right point in the retail hierarchy – the hierarchical approach to expansion. For instance a retailer such as Ted Baker is located in the largest and more prestigious centres and is not constrained by issues related to distribution.

Once the market coverage (geographical area) has been selected then a retailer needs to consider at what points in the retail hierarchy its format will be located. In essence, centres at the top of the retail hierarchy focus on comparison goods retailing, whilst lower down the retail hierarchy the emphasis is on serving much more local needs with a focus on convenience. The top 50 locations in Great Britain (out of over 800 shopping locations) by retail expenditure as of 2013 (CACI, 2013 see Figure 8.2) included London's West End, Glasgow, Manchester, Birmingham, Liverpool, Westfield London, Leeds, Nottingham, London's Knightsbridge and Bluewater Regional Shopping Centre. In these locations one would expect to see the major national chains such as those from the Arcadia Group, M&S, jewellers, an Apple store and other comparison goods retailers. At the other extreme of the retail hierarchy are neighbourhood or district centres that might be anchored by a small supermarket, and have stores such as a chemist, shoe shop, bargain store and so on. There tends to be a greater proportion of smaller, independently owned retail outlets in neighbourhood centres. The retail hierarchy has a few large centres at the top and the further down the hierarchy the smaller the centre and the more of them there are (Goodwin, 2007).

That is not to say that major multiples are not represented in smaller centres because retailers such as Boots, Superdrug and WH Smith all operate from these and in many cases also from some of the very largest centres. A key issue is that they tailor their range and store operation for a particular location. Multiple retailers will therefore develop smaller-sized formats of their overall offer and provide an edited range. In the most general terms a retailer of highly specialised comparison goods, be it fashion or high-end electronics, will expand hierarchically, picking off the biggest centres.

Locational management options

Once a retailer has a portfolio of stores the firm has to manage that and is constantly addressing a range of locational management options: these are the 6Rs identified in Table 8.2. This process is ongoing as retailers seek to make the most out of each location from which it trades.

Closing stores – rationalisation

In many cases the decisions are not just where to open but where to close with an eye on the impact on the overall business. Closing stores means the retailer can cut costs and bring the firm back to a situation of improved profitability. More pointedly there

Top 50 GB Centres

Ranked on total annual spend from residents, tourists and workers. Excluding online spend.

Rank	Name	Expenditure £m
1	London – West End	£5,080
2	Glasgow	£1,790
2	Manchester	£1,680
4	Birmingham	£1,430
5	Leeds	£1,390
6	Liverpool	£1,310
7	Westfield London	£1,270
8	London – Knightsbridge	£1,180
9	Bluewater	£1,120
10	London – Covent Garden	£1,110
11	Nottingham	£1,080
12	Westfield – Stratford City	£1,080
13	Trafford Centre	£1,050
14	Edinburgh	£1,040
15	Meadowhall	£980
16	Milton Keynes	£970
17	Kingston upon Thames	£910
18	Norwich	£890
19	Bristol	£870
20	Newcastle upon Tyne	£830
21	Leicester	£830
22	Brighton	£790
23	Reading	£710
24	Cardiff	£700
25	Gateshead – intu Metrocentre	£660
26	Aberdeen	£640
27	London – King's Road	£640
28	Croydon	£630
29	Southampton	£620
30	Bath	£620
31	Sheffield	£620
32	Brent Cross	£600
33	Cambridge	£590
34	Derby	£580
35	Dudley – Merry Hill	£570
36	Plymouth	£550
37	Cribbs Causeway	£530
38	Bicester Village	£520
39	Bromley	£520
40	Exeter	£510
41	intu Lakeside	£500
42	Watford	£500
43	Guilford	£490
44	York	£490
45	Oxford	£480
46	London – Canary Wharf	£460
47	Cheltenham	£460
48	Chesire Oaks – McArthurGlen Outlet Centre	£450
49	Ipswich	£430
50	Hull	£410

Figure 8.2 The retail hierarchy
Source: CACI, 2013, reproduced with permission, www.caci.co.uk

seems to be a search for an optimal number of stores and the cutting of a tail of stores (especially for retailers who have over-expanded) can lead to a loss of market share but an improvement in profitably (see Srinivasan *et al.*, 2013). At its zenith in the 1990s Next had almost 1000 stores in the UK across a variety of formats and in 2014 was trading from just over 500 and is an example of how it is not the number of stores *per se* that

Table 8.2 Examples of the 6Rs of location management options (adapted from Clarke et al., 1997)

Option	Example
Roll out: opening of new stores or extension of an existing one.	Original Factory Shops announces plans to open up to 500 stores. Principal criteria are towns under 20,000 population with an ideal size of 6,000–15,000 sq ft. http://www.theoriginalfactoryshop.co.uk/en-GB/Information/Useful-information/Landlords/
Relocate: close store in one part of a town or centre and open in another elsewhere. May occur when lease is due for renewal.	Ted Baker has had four different locations in Manchester city centre in the space of 20 years. It moved out of King Street and the Triangle shopping centre in the city centre and moved into two new developments: New Cathedral Street and Spinningfields.
Refit: improving the internal fabric of an existing store. May occur as part of a capital expenditure cycle but retailer has to decide sequence of refits and which locations would be best suited to this.	Argos has refitted stores as a result of the threat of the internet and has launched its digital concept store. M&S have been refitting stores and introducing 'beauty' departments.
Remerchandise: adding/deleting range (and services) in response to local needs.	Stores in student areas add student 'starter packs', e.g. cutlery, plates, bedding, at the start of the academic year. Morrisons revamped their fruit and vegetable departments.
Refascia: altering image of store by changing name or appearance. Retailer decides to change trading format or acquire a competitor and has to bring the new stores into the portfolio.	Co-op acquisition of Somerfield; Morrisons' acquisition of Safeway. Superdry refasciaed its 20 Cult stores into Superdry in 2012.
Rationalise: closure of individual units or even sell off of a division. Retailer decides to divest of stores because of poor trading and/or focus on core stores.	Monsoon Accessorize have sold a number of stores and were seeking joint sites for these two formats. KMart closed 600 under-performing stores (see Shields and Kures, 2007).

will lead to overall profitability. The idea of store closures (**rationalisation** in Table 8.2) is a key strategic decision.

Increasingly, decisions about rationalising the number of stores are becoming more prevalent, for mature retailers in particular, especially with the emergence of the internet. Moreover, the perceived saturation in grocery retailing and even in the charity sector (Alexander *et al.*, 2008) means that making a good or right decision is even more challenging.

When one retailer acquires another one a review of locations will be undertaken and where there is overlap in provision, stores may be closed or, indeed, sold on at the request of the competition authorities. When Morrisons acquired Safeway, it would have had two stores in close proximity in Southport. As a requirement of the acquisition Morrisons were compelled to sell one of the stores to a competitor so they did not have a monopoly in the town.

Retailers have also developed different-sized operations to fit in at different points of the retail hierarchy. Tesco, for instance, has Tesco Extras that offer a full range of food and non-food, through what was termed its 'conforming store format' – the 25,000 square foot superstore, and increasingly its Tesco Metro and Tesco Express formats that have a much more limited range trade in neighbourhood locations from stores of just 3000 square feet. Other retailers such as Aldi and Lidl also have a conforming store format as they know what range will fit in that size store and *vice versa* leading to Aldi identifying and publicising their locational needs as shown in the box below.

MINI CASE STUDY
Aldi – finding sites

Aldi's requirements are for sites with a 'catchment population in excess of 10,000 and ideally situated on principal roads with prominent road frontage'.

The company states it prefers to purchase freehold, in a town centre or on the edge of centre sites suitable for development (min. 0.8 acres).

However, they do appear to have some flexibility in their site requirements as they state they will consider leasing new or existing space on Retail Parks, purchasing or leasing space within District Centres, and even consider existing retail premises.

Aldi also identify specific towns that they are interested in trading from and break this down by region on their interactive map on their website.

In Scotland they were interested in the following towns and cities: Aberdeen (north & south); Arbroath; Ayr; Bearsden; Coatbridge; Crieff; Cumbernauld; Dumbarton; Dumfries (north); Dundee (south); East Kilbride (north & east); Edinburgh (all areas); Falkirk (east); Glasgow (all areas); Helensburgh; Jedburgh; Kirkintilloch; Milngavie; Peebles; Perth (north & south).

Source: adapted from https://corporate.aldi.co.uk/en/property/requirement-towns/ (accessed 12 May 2014).

There are a number of operational benefits from adopting a conforming store format and also a contagious expansion approach. These include the knowledge of the optimum range to fit in the known space and therefore not requiring a variety of tailored planograms for stores of differing size; the ability to advertise locally; the opportunity to have tight area/district managerial control of stores (as well as being able to move staff between stores without them having to relocate); and the efficiencies accruing from having a nearby distribution centre to service a network of nearby stores without exceeding maximum drivers' hours permitted under legislation.

What types of locations do retailers use?

There are many retail location types. Originally most retail outlets would have been located in a town or city centre because that was the point of greatest accessibility for the majority of the local population. This was at a time when retailing was ostensibly a local activity with customers visiting their nearest stores. But with the advent of increasing affluence and access to motor cars customers were now able to travel further for products. Not only that, but town and city centre locations were not only costly to trade from but also did not have enough space for large stores such as superstores and hypermarkets.

Retail location types can be thought of in terms of customers' needs. On the one hand there are staple items such as grocery items bought on a regular and frequent basis, and on the other hand there are more discretionary purchases such as clothing, footwear, household goods, furniture, carpets and televisions etc. One framework that has been developed to understand the types of products sold in different locations was that explained by Davies and Clarke (1994). Their framework takes the product types in terms of whether the product is convenience or comparison and plots this against the ability to carry home that product in terms of portability (see Table 8.3).

However, since Davies and Clarke's framework was devised the emergence of travel hubs such as railway stations and airports have become important locations for retailers to trade from, and do not easily fit in with their framework. A typical mainline railway

Table 8.3 A shopping location model

	Bulky purchase	Portable items
Comparison goods	Carpets Large electrical items DIY products	Clothing Footwear
Typical location	Retail park	Town or city centre Regional shopping centre Enclosed in-town shopping centre Factory outlet
Convenience goods	Weekly grocery shopping	Top-up grocery items
Typical location	Off-centre superstore	Neighbourhood centre or local parade

Source: adapted from Davies and Clarke, 1994

station may host a couple of coffee shops such as Starbucks or a Costa, a small chemist outlet of a national chain such as Boots or a Superdrug, a WH Smith and, increasingly, small convenience-sized outlets of the main grocery chains such as a Tesco Express, a Sainsbury's Local and/or an M&S Simply Food. Euston railway station in London even hosts a branch of Accessorize, Fat Face, Paperchase and shirt specialist T.M. Lewin. These mainline travel hubs are providing retailers with an 'intervening opportunity' – that is a chance to retail from a location that is between the origin and destination of a journey – which is typically a place between home and place of work.

In town and city centres the retailing of comparison goods takes precedence. And within some centres areas of specialisation can occur either by design or by organic means. In Glasgow, for example, the Argyll Arcade is focused on jewellery stores and promotes itself as 'offering the largest selection of diamond jewellery, wedding rings, and watches in a single location in Scotland' (http://argyll-arcade.com/). In Birmingham there is even a jewellery quarter with over 100 specialist retailers, designers and craftsmen located a little way off the main city centre shopping (http://www.jewelleryquarter.net/shopping/). This agglomeration of retailers enables shoppers to browse a full range of special shops in one go. Convenience goods retailers, such as grocery stores, by contrast may not want to be co-located with the direct competition.

Another location type that is changing is that of the retail park. Originally conceived as 3 to 5 large 'sheds' located in off-centre locations, such as brownfield sites, with stores of about 10,000 square feet selling space and selling bulky goods, retail parks have evolved to offer a greater range of products. Having free car parking has usually been an important part of the retail park 'offer', giving it a competitive advantage over town and city centres which have car parks but with sometimes relatively expensive parking charges. Regent Road Retail Park in Manchester, for instance, hosts a large Sainsbury's, and branches of Mothercare, Staples, Dunnes, TK Maxx, Deichmann Shoes, Boots and the Carphone Warehouse.

John Lewis Partnership, known for its full-line department stores, has developed a standalone John Lewis at Home format which offers an edited range of the full offer and focuses on electricals, household and homeware products that can trade from smaller catchments and has a smaller footprint.

Swedish retailer IKEA, once the preserve of large off-centre locations in major conurbations, has had to adapt the locations it would ideally like to trade from and has even developed a format just under a mile from Ashton town centre, on the outskirts of Manchester, which is on a joint site with M&S and a Sainsbury's store.

The days of retailers operating one format from one type of location are over. Multiple retailers now have a suite of format types that will trade from a repertoire of locations.

MARKS & SPENCER'S LOCATIONS

M&S has a history going back over 120 years, and started with a single stall in Kirkgate Market in Leeds. Now an international, multichannel, retailer M&S trades from major shopping centres, high streets, retail parks, railways stations, airports, petrol and motorway service stations. Each of the different location types offers different ranges, and the retailer defines its UK formats as:

- 'Premier' (12 stores)
- 'Major' (59)
- 'High Street' (228)
- 'Simply Food owned' (176)
- 'Simply Food franchised' (243)
- 'Outlets' (48).

Source: adapted from M&S (2014) Annual report at: http://annualreport2013.marksandspencer.com/strategic-review/our-plan-in-action/focus-on-the-uk/uk-stores/

These changes in location types and where retailers find they can trade successfully from does not mean that it is possible to trade from just anywhere. Matching the location with the product and the consumer need and motivation are all important. But not only do retailers have to consider the marketing issues of getting a location that consumers will need they also need to consider carefully the financial returns to be made from each location from which they trade. One way that they have been able to gain better returns is if they are a big enough 'draw' for, say, a shopping centre.

When new shopping centres are being developed, the management of that centre may offer rent-free periods or 'reverse premiums' whereby the shopping centre company will actually pay the retailer to take space in the centre. These incentives would normally only be offered to the largest retailers that would be used to anchor a development. Examples of anchor tenants include John Lewis, M&S, Debenhams and House of Fraser. These anchor tenants would normally be situated at either ends of an enclosed shopping centre (see Figure 8.3) to encourage shoppers to walk the full length of the centres.

A rather different approach to shopping centre layout has been that adopted by Bluewater Regional Shopping Centre, which is three-sided (see Figure 8.4).

The news that a large anchor tenant had signed to occupy a unit for a new shopping centre could then be used to entice other retailers to take space in the new development. These rent-free periods may last up to 2 years. Incentives could also include the developer paying for some, or all, of the fitting-out costs of the store. Some retailers are also able to negotiate break clauses in the lease and stop trading from the new store after a couple of years.

Also of increasing importance for some major retailers are locations in Factory Outlet Shopping Centres (see also Chapter 6 Retail pricing). Typically located away from traditional shopping locations these standalone outlet 'villages' include Cheshire Oaks (http://www.mcarthurglen.com/uk/cheshire-oaks-designer-outlet/en/), and Fleetwood Freeport (http://www.freeport-fleetwood.com/). These centres are managed and promoted as a single destination. Retailers with discounting or outlet stores in these locations include many household names such M&S, Next and Thornton's, and also internationally recognised operators such as Gap, Antler, Adidas, Lacoste and Polo Ralph Lauren. Here retailers sell their ends of lines and out of season product at large discounts. Customers enjoy large, usually free car parking. The usual agreements are that the owner of the shopping village complex will take a percentage of sales as its rental fee – an approach more prevalent in the United States.

WHAT TYPES OF LOCATIONS DO RETAILERS USE? | 201

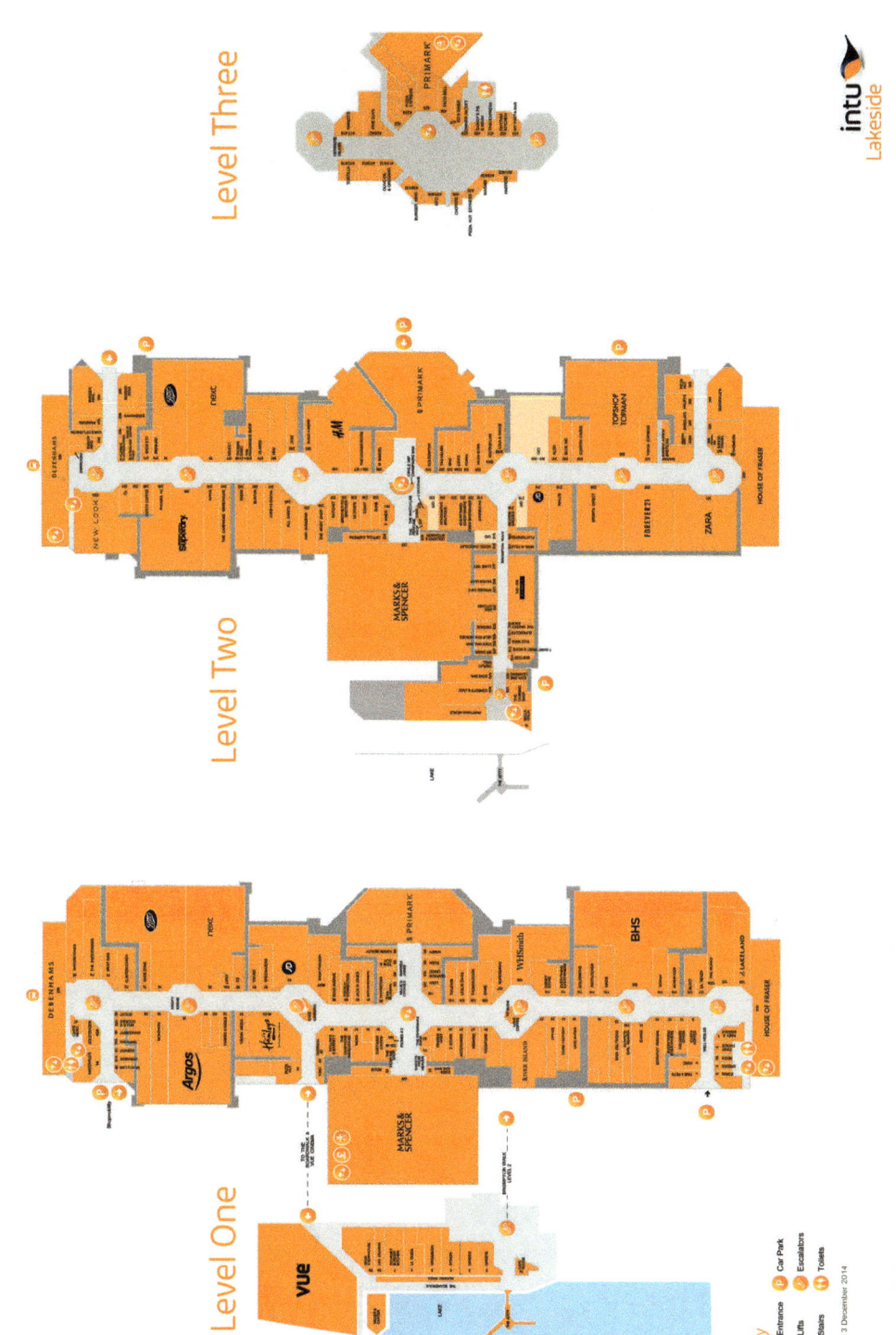

Figure 8.3 Lakeside Regional Shopping Centre
Source: reproduced with permission from Intu Properties plc

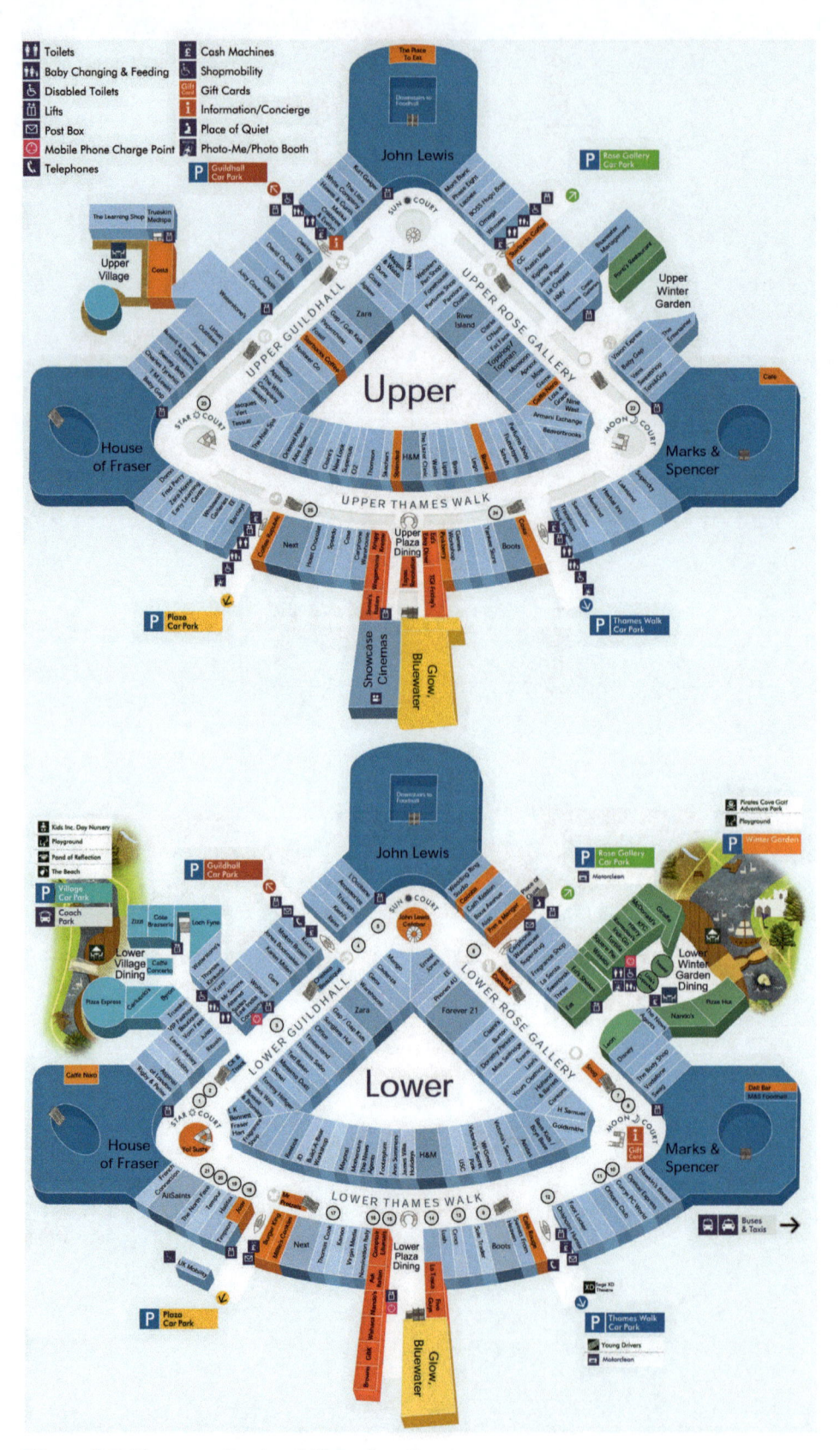

Figure 8.4 Bluewater Regional Shopping Centre
Source: reproduced with permission from Aver

How do retailers make location decisions?

Andy Street, Managing Director of John Lewis Partnership, is quoted as saying this at the opening of the firm's department store on the outskirts of York:

> This is our 41st shop – we have said publicly there are probably about 65 catchments that are big enough to take a John Lewis. This is not about looking for 125 shops. It's about where the gaps are. It's not hard to work them out frankly. [As cited in Ruddick (2014)]

Street mentions the term 'catchment', one of the key principles in store-based retailing and this refers to the area from which a retailer will draw its trade. Catchment areas can vary in size. For instance a small, convenience store may draw its custom from people within a 10 minute walk of the store. An IKEA, at the other extreme, will draw its custom from people who may live up to a 90 minute drive time away. M&S has an ambition that 80 per cent of its customers will be within a 45 minutes' drive time of one its regional stores and 90 per cent within 30 minutes of any its stores (M&S, 2014). A fuller list of factors involved in retail location decision-making is provided by McGoldrick (2002) – see Figure 8.5.

Another key determinant of defining a successful retail location is related to the threshold of a store – that is the minimum number of customers required to make a store viable. A key issue to consider then is how retailers define their catchments and thresholds.

Much of the literature on retail location decision-making is about store openings and expansion. Key techniques (see Table 8.4) used to work out where to open new stores has been reviewed by Wood and Tasker (2008).

The models are used at different scales, and the techniques can be used in combination. So 'walking the site' to actually see what is happening at a micro-level is part of sense-checking data that may be generated from a modelling process. For instance, a model may identify a good location but the site characteristics may mean that because a store is located on one side of a road or junction access to it may be problematic. A matter of a few metres may be the difference between success and failure. Moreover, managerial

Population	Accessibility	Costs	Competition
Population size Seasonal fluctuations Age profile Lifestyle characteristics Current shopping patterns Internet/store shopping Broadband penetration Income levels Disposable income/capita Occupation classifications Cultural/ethnic groupings Neighbourhood classifications Main employers Economic stability Unemployment levels Home ownership levels Housing density Household size Housing age/type Housing development plans	Pedestrian flows Pedestrian entry routes Public transport: • types • cost • ease of use Car ownership levels Road network: • conditions • driving speeds • congestion • restrictions • plans Parking: • capacity • convenience; • cost • potential Visability Access for staff Access for deliveries Access for click & collect	Purchase price Leasing terms Planning application costs Site preparation Building restrictions Building costs Development concessions Rates payable Refurbishment needs Maintenance costs Security needs/costs Staff availability Local wage rates Delivery costs Promotional media/costs Turnover loss – other branches	Existing retail competition: • direct competitors • indirect competitors • e-competitors Retail synergies: • cumulative attraction • anchor stores • compatibility Existing retail specification: • size of selling areas • turnover estimates • department/product mix • trade areas • age of outlets • standard of design Retail saturation index Competitive potential • expansion/refurbishment • repositioning • vacant sites • interception • competitors' policies

Figure 8.5 Retail location factors checklist

Source: adapted from McGoldrick, P. (2002) *Retail Marketing*, 2nd edn, © 2002. Reproduced with the kind permission of McGraw-Hill Education. All rights reserved.

Table 8.4 Summary of location techniques

Technique	Description
Experience	Can be intuitive in approach or have a few rules in place. Relies on prior knowledge. No costs involved. Only useful for low-cost operations. It is claimed that when one of the limited line foreign discounters opened in the north west of England their sites were chosen by 'counting chimney pots', i.e. areas that were densely populated. These tended to be areas of higher levels of lower income families.
Checklists	Uses a number of variables such as catchment population, costs, accessibility, and visibility of store. Can be used to compare sites. May need to include some form of weighting between variables.
Analogues	Compares a potential store location to one the firm already trades from. The sales potential for the new store is then extrapolated from the analogue store.
Multiple regression	Builds a model to establish relationship between store sales and variables that could affect store performance such as catchment characteristics, drive time, and competition.
Geographical Information Systems	Ties together marketing information such as loyalty card data with mapping software to visualise areas of under-representation (see Alexander et al., 2008; Hernandez, 2007).
Spatial interaction models	Works on the basis that people will travel further to a more attractive centre, but as costs of so doing increase the likelihood decreases. Examples of this type of model are those of Reilly and Huff (see Birkin et al., 2002). Much of the work in this area is for single product groups – whereas in reality people usually buy a 'bundle' of goods in one shopping trip.

Source: adapted from Wood and Tasker, 2008

judgement can be an important element of the retail location decision process as managers can link their intuitive insights with quantitative models such as the MIRSA Analogue-Finder system as described by Clarke *et al.* (2003). In general terms larger organisations with larger store networks or even a few large stores will pay more attention to location planning, whilst smaller retailers tend not to have the resources to commit to this activity (Alexander *et al.*, 2008), relying more on rule of thumb and intuition.

Finding the optimal location, given the very competitive nature of retailing, and the fact that the best sites tend to go first means that retailers have to make existing locations work 'better' and, for major multiples, managing a portfolio of stores becomes a key issue. This is becoming ever more critical as some retailers leverage the use of the internet and the role of the store, and indeed the need for a physical presence, comes into question.

When defining catchment areas for siting a store it has to be appreciated that many catchments overlap and can compete for the same group of customers. Wood and Browne (2007: 244) identify the range of information that can be used in determining a store's catchments and includes population data (from the Census); geodemographic data (e.g. from Experian); and, footfall and vacancy data (e.g. from Local Data Company). A good example of deriving a catchment is shown in the study about a charity (Alexander *et al.*, 2008) where the catchment, then site characteristics, were determined followed by sense-checking the site by undertaking a footfall analysis around potential locations.

Also customers do not always act rationally in accordance with simple spatial models in terms of visiting their nearest centre and factors such as ease of access or costs of car parking may be an important determinant of which centre a consumer visits. A study by Li and Liu (2012: 596) established '. . . 73% of the variation of store sales can be accounted for by the variations of these five factors: accessibility (distance), attractiveness (store size), the demographic characteristics of customers, agglomeration, and competition'.

RETAIL MARKETING CAREERS
Matthew Hopkinson, Director of a data company

Matthew Hopkinson is a director of The Local Data Company (LDC). The London-based company analyses store locations to help optimise retail performance. Here, Matthew explains in his own words the issues involved in knowledge-based location planning.

The overall costs in the opening of a shop or leisure outlet are significant from the location research, legal and agents' fees, to fitting out and stocking the unit before the first person pays a penny into the till. The rise of alternative on- and offline channels makes choosing the right unit in the right location paramount, especially when lease commitments on average stand at 15 years. In addition, if you require funding then your bank or backers need to be convinced by the evidence of your strategy.

At LDC we are the only company in the UK who physically verifies over half a million premises in over 7000 locations from small parades to high streets, shopping centres and retail parks. As such we are the 'radar' for retailers up and down the country and provide the insight and knowledge to support investment and divestment decisions.

So what should you know? Well, here is what I would say you need to know.

If you are an existing retailer – where do you perform well and where do you wish you had never opened? From this you create a portfolio risk analysis that not only tells you about the existing locations and why they might not be performing but also where are good peer locations that I could do well and where should I avoid?

How are my existing and target locations changing (e.g. vacancy rates, persistence if vacancy, quality of offer, classification mix, diversity, churn, anchor occupiers, competitor activity)?

Competitor analysis. Where are your competitors/proximity retailers opening and closing and have they changed their location or format?

Finally, when looking at a new premise, do you know the history of occupation for the last 5+ years along with how the area (say 200m radius) has changed over the last three years? Is it on the up or on the decline? Agents don't like to deliver news if it may jeopardise a deal!

Source: with permission from Matthew Hopkinson

Overlaid on the key questions above will be how the local economy (e.g. unemployment, employment, house prices) and demography (e.g. age, ethnicity, social group) has changed but this is very difficult to gauge anything concrete due to the age and lack of detail in the data available.

So in conclusion it is vital that you have a good understanding of national and regional trends and apply these to detailed local knowledge from the building to the street to the town to the out of town retail park or superstore. All of these locations compete for consumer spend and with the rise of online transactions the consumer is changing their physical shopping habits at the fastest rate in the history of retailing. Being relevant and in the right location could be more important today than ever before.

www.localdatacompany.com; Twitter:@localdataco

Site-specific issues

Retailers of different products with different target customers need different types of sites from which to trade. A high-end jeweller may not necessarily want to be in the busiest shopping centre, deciding instead to be sited in a more secluded and up-market (i.e. more expensive) site co-located with similar retailers. A more mainstream jeweller on the other hand will rely on serving a higher volume of customers as it offers rather less expensive product. There are vast varieties of retail types and potential sites from which to trade, so each retailer will need to decide what the key factors are in choosing a specific site.

Wood and Browne (2007: 245) identify the following as important variables when assessing a specific site: pedestrian flows; number and location of car parking spaces; quality and location of the competition; proximity of adjacent services that may generate more footfall; and, type and structure of residential catchment. This was echoed to a certain extent by the work of Roig-Tierno *et al.* (2013) who identified the site factors (e.g. size of sales floor and availability of parking), location characteristics (e.g. accessibility by various forms of transport, visibility and the amount of passing trade), catchment demographic composition, and the type and presence of competition as important factors in a store being viable.

There will probably never be the perfect site and a retailer may have to compromise on certain factors. For instance, a retailer may have to take a smaller store but because it has a high passing trade (or footfall) it can justify trading there. Many retailers devise different formats and can operate from different sites and from different-sized stores. B&M Bargains is an example and is shown in the box below.

'OUR VISION IS SIMPLE . . . TO BE BRITAIN'S NUMBER 1 VARIETY RETAILER'

'B&M prides itself on selling strong brands albeit at low margins. Unlike other discounters, we focus on the key brands rather than own-label or tertiary brand products.

We have two formats: B&M Bargains and B&M Homestore. The former has between 8000 and 10,000 sq ft of sales area. The extremely competitive offering attracts a high footfall, stores achieving 10,000 transactions in an average week, peaking at nearly 30,000 per week. This footfall is one of the highest enjoyed by any UK retailer. It demonstrates the crowd pleasing offer we bring to any retail destination.

Our B&M Homestore format has a bulky goods bias, and can trade up to 35,000 sq ft in good visibility Out of Town locations. Many Homestores also have a Garden Centre attached. These Homestores primarily sell Paint, Wallpaper, Furniture, Home Textiles, Furnishings, Wall Decor, Garden & Leisure products'.

Source: http://www.bmstores.co.uk/landlords (accessed 21 May 2014)

RETAILING IN BERLIN
By Elina Waehner

Retail locations often develop their own style and 'flavour' which appeal to customers who identify with a certain lifestyle evoked by the combination of retailers and attractions in the area. One such location is Berlin-Mitte, described here by Berlin resident and fashion retail specialist Elina Waehner, alongside other interesting classic and contemporary retailers in the city.

Source: Elina Waehner

Retailers in the Berlin-Mitte area

Berlin-Mitte is an area near the centre of Berlin that was originally established in 1920, as a result of boundary changes. In 2001 it was enlarged to its modern borders, uniting former Eastern and Western parts in the heart of the city. The Alexanderplatz with its TV-tower (Fernsehturm) and the Museum Island (Museumsinsel), as well as the Brandenburg Gate, Reichstag (German Parliament building) and Tiergarten are all located in Berlin-Mitte. However, there is a definite area between the Stations 'S Hackescher Markt', 'S Oranienburger Tor' and 'S Alexanderplatz' that is being considered by local citizens and by international experts as a special design area: Mitte stands for contemporary design, art and fashion. Cafés, designer stores, ateliers, restaurants and boutiques are mixed in an international blend. In Mitte you will find handmade pasta, Asian, Italian, American and British food, as well as fashion made by designers in Berlin. The key word for making retail work in this special place attractive to tourists and design-passionate people is 'authentic'. The interiors and products speak loudly to the customer about their origin, in accordance with modern European style and an ecological approach to production. These ingredients are all blended together for an affordable price to create the modern cocktail called 'design-magnet Mitte'.

Designer Lena Hoschek sells garments with a classic, retro appeal that is echoed in the store interior, reflecting the look of homes from the same era as the clothing and giving the retailer an authentic Berlin atmosphere. The Lena Hoschek store was originally located in Berlin-Mitte and in 2014 moved to larger premises in Berlin-Westend.

In contrast to Lena Hoschek, Modulor is a contemporary Berlin-based retailer that is one of the biggest creative supply stores in Germany and is known by professional creatives all around Europe. The Modulor-Material Total was founded in 1988 in Berlin as a small supply store for architects. Today it serves around 2000 customers daily and the customers are professionals as well as students who find inspiration through materials, instruments and other products available on 3000 m² divided into two floors. Modulor sells over 16,000 items sourced from over 450 different suppliers from around the world in different sectors of production – a unique mixture with all kinds of pencils, portfolio presentation tools, material, workboxes, papers, 3D architectural models, boards, lamps, books, tables and chairs for designers, etc. Their customers are anyone who has a creative project: typically an architect or product designer, but it could also be a student working on an assignment. The Modulor concept is based on the idea of shared passion. The people who source, sell and buy the products are all inspired by materials, instruments and techniques in modern design. All of the Sales Associates in the store know the features of the materials for which they are responsible and there is a Help Desk on each floor. Modulor products are also available online. Additional services are outlined below.

The material box

In addition to a printed catalogue, every customer can order a special box with a representative selection of all the materials, available in the store to have a concrete idea of how the materials feel and look, priced at €19.50 at the time of writing. The box is being updated on a regular basis. Every sample is labelled with a number. The customer can enter the number in the Modulor website search window to receive all the additional information

Lena Hoschek store in Berlin-Mitte
Source: Elina Waehner

about the material: colours, shapes, sizes, etc., as well as prices (see www.modulor.de/en/Modulor-Sample-Box/Modulor-Sample-Box.html).

Community and location

Modulor is located in the Aufbau Haus (named after the publishing house located in the same building) at Berlin's Moritzplatz in Kreuzberg. The building provides office spaces and serves as a connecting point for the creative community of the area. The immediate neighbours are small manufacturers of paints, mosaics, textiles, furnishings, the Kai Dikhas modern art gallery, photographers' and artists' studios, as well as a theatre, a night club, a performing arts studio, the Design Academy Berlin and the Create Berlin Association, uniting and representing around 350 member design organisations in the city. Modulor has rented the space in the new building since 2011 and personally approached the organisations to join it within the Aufbau Haus to create a unique service and product portfolio for the customer. The Network is called 'Planet Modulor' and consists of 30 partner organisations.

www.aufbauhaus.de; www.modulor.de; shop.lenahoscheck.de; Twitter:@lenahoscheck

The planning system

When a retailer wants to open in a new location it may acquire an existing store and change it (via refascia and refurbishment) into one of its store types. In cases where a change of use of a retail outlet is proposed then it may also be necessary to work through the planning system for a change of use.

But if a retailer wants to open a store in an area or location where no store had existed before then it is more than likely that the retailer will have to apply for planning permission to build an outlet. In many instances the applicant (who may be the developer, a retailer, or a developer acting on behalf of a retailer) will have to apply for planning permission.

When a new location has been identified by a developer (and here we take 'developer' to also include retailer as well) then it is at this point that the developer will have to apply for planning permission from a Local Planning Authority (LPA) (see Figure 8.6). When coming to its decision the LPA will have to take heed of any local planning policies in place through its development plan. In turn this local policy has to take account of any national planning policy. What is notable is that there can be a disconnect between local polices, which may be out of date, and any national policy which has been amended therefore taking precedence over any local policy.

In England and Wales the retail policy has been found in Planning Policy Guidance 6, which has been amended to Planning Policy Statement 6. In 2013 policy related to the siting of retail outlets was then incorporated into the National Planning Policy Framework.

Retail planning policy has generally been playing catch-up with retail developments as in many cases local, and indeed national, policy was not aware of new formats. As a result of the general vagueness of planning policy major retailers in particular have been

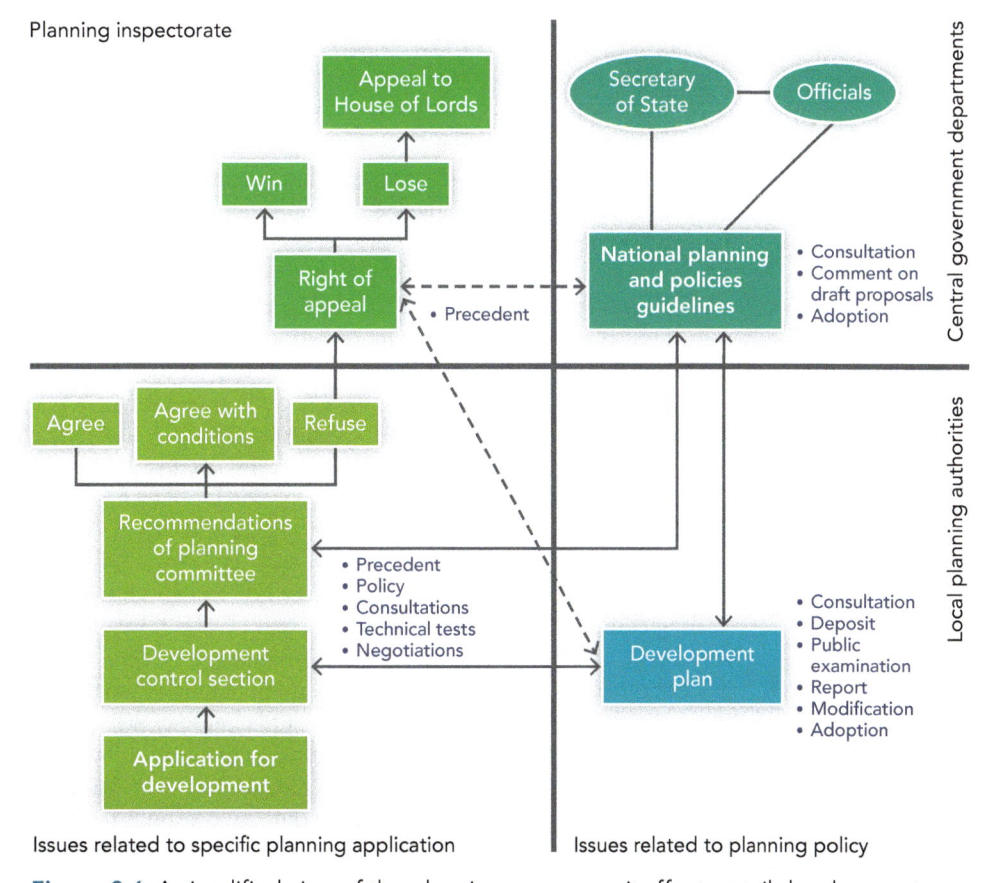

Figure 8.6 A simplified view of the planning process as it affects retail development
Source: devised by John Pal

MANCHESTER CITY COUNCIL'S RETAIL PLANNING POLICIES

In Manchester City Council's policy the overall thrust of the policy is to 'maintain the vitality and viability of its centres, provide services as locally as possible and minimise the need to travel by car'. The policy identifies three main hierarchy types.

- '. . . Manchester City Centre – top of the hierarchy with the largest centre and biggest catchment area. It forms part of the Regional Centre, is the main comparison shopping destination for the Manchester City Region and has a significant and expanding role as a key tourist destination.

- 17 District Centres. These centres will continue to develop roles as key centres providing both local food and non-food shopping, leisure facilities, community activities, employment, and local services. Mixed use development will be promoted including when higher density residential development is provided within the scheme.

- 22 Local Centres . . .'.

Source: http://manchester-consult.limehouse.co.uk/portal/planning/cs/pre-publication?pointId=1274111885342 (accessed 15 May 2014).

able to succeed in their retail proposals. In many instances these new developments have been in off-centre locations. In the mid- to late-2000s there had been a general tightening of national policy against off-centre development and the adoption of the sequential approach, first broached in the mid-1990s has been taking hold. In LPAs retail policy it is possible to discern the application of retail hierarchy which seeks to divert new retail development into specific centres (see Figure 8.6).

One of the key points to be aware of when considering the influence and impact of the planning system on retailers' location decision-making has been the interpretative nature of the various policies. It has been shown that the vagueness of policies has enabled retailers to get their developments built (see Jones, 2014; Pal et al., 2001; Pal and Medway, 2008).

There are two main levels at which major retailers in particular can get involved in the planning system. Firstly, at the local level the application for development may see powerful food retailers such as Tesco and Sainsbury's have an application for a store rejected because it does not meet the local plan policies. At this point the retailer may go to appeal, or engage in a dialogue with the LPA to establish what it could do to get its plan passed. In some instances a retailer may offer some form of planning gain. This is where the retailer may, for example, offer to build a new roundabout to help traffic flow at the proposed store, change its plan to incorporate a mixed development, e.g. some social housing, or even offer to fund a park and ride scheme.

Secondly, the major retailers have been involved in lobbying central government in the national policy-making process. The national policy has been changed in response to concerns about the decentralisation of retailing and the impact on the vitality and viability of town and city centres. This movement off-centre still remains and retailers such as Next, historically based in town or city centres (and regional shopping centres), have been opening on retail parks. Next has claimed that opening these outlets gives a better service to customers as well as creating new jobs. However, it should be pointed out that it is not the purpose of the planning system to judge the economic benefits in terms of job creation, although that is something an applicant may well promote.

In general terms the planning system in England and Wales (Scotland and Northern Ireland have similar but different systems) has been pro-development and retailers have in the main been able to see their plans come to fruition. In other instances some retailers have seen a general tightening of the planning system and therefore to get their (large) off-centre stores built they have become involved in urban regenerations schemes. Almost in parallel retailers such as Tesco have been adopting a small store policy that helps circumvent some of the restrictive nature of national planning guidance whilst also 'filling in gaps' at the micro-scale and these Express stores have almost become the de facto local shop. Indeed the Tesco acquisition of T&S stores went unchallenged by the competition authorities allowing the retailer to enter this market. As a result Tesco has stores of various sizes in different locations. The process is outlined in Figure 8.7.

Asda at Eastland's (adjacent to Manchester City's football ground) and Tesco have built large stores in deprived areas without any existing retail facilities. As part of the development the retailers guarantee to employ a proportion of their staff from the local, long-term unemployed as well as showing how a new store would provide access to a wide range of fruit and vegetables for the local populace. The UK government has a policy whereby people are encouraged to eat five pieces of fruit and vegetable a day and so a retailer can show how a new store would help meet this health policy.

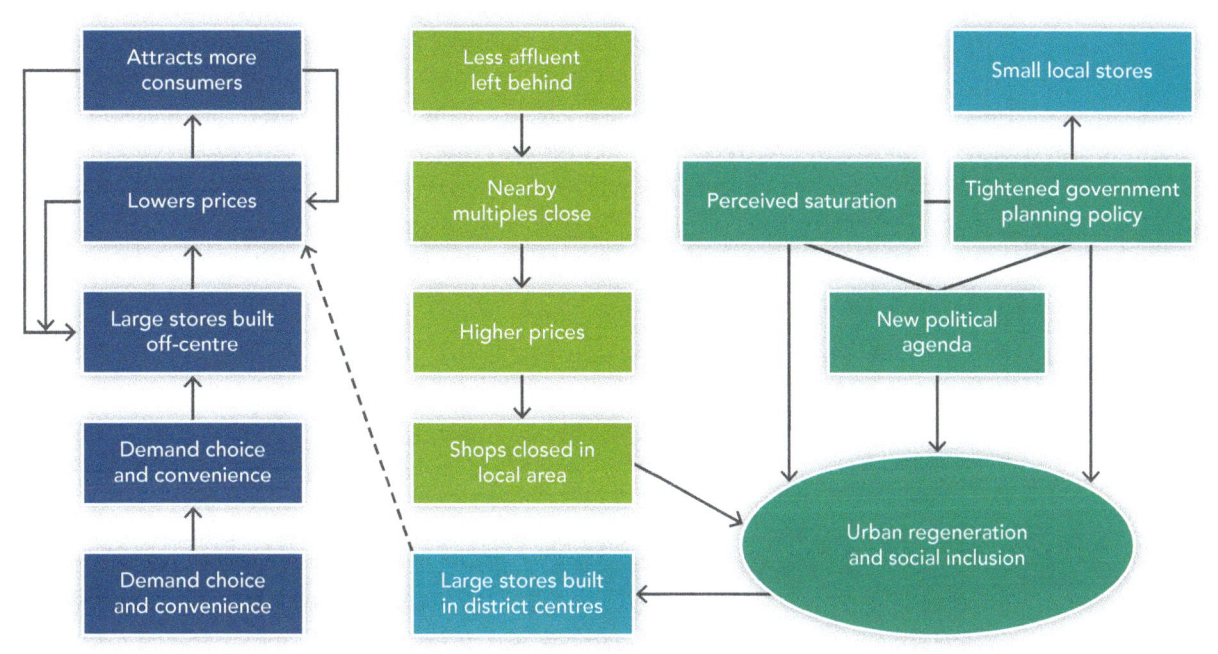

Figure 8.7 The three concurrent systems of UK retail grocery development
Source: devised by the chapter author, John Pal

CHAPTER SUMMARY

This chapter has identified the role of the retail location and even in the move to multi-channel retailing it can be seen that locations are still important. Location can represent a sizeable investment for a retailer and the decisions the firm makes varies from the strategic ones about market coverage and how to roll out stores, through to more tactical ones about tailoring and editing ranges leading to remerchandising of stores. Increasingly location decisions are about where to close stores as major retailers seek to optimise their store estate. What makes for a good location varies from one retailer to another and the way the decisions are made depend on the size of the firm and the size of the individual investment in a store. Moreover, major retailers are powerful enough to influence national and local planning such that many of their development plans come to life.

EXERCISES AND QUESTIONS

To further understand the content of this chapter, carry out the following exercises.

1. Examine a retailer's annual report and accounts for the last three years. Establish the levels of investment in location and review the key statements as to what changes the retailer has made over the last three years. What changes does the retailer intend to make to its store portfolio over the next two years – use the 6Rs to frame your analysis.
2. Visit two retailers operating in the same sector, e.g. a high-end fashion store with one that is at the value end. Describe the site of both and generate a checklist of factors on how both companies could assess any future sites.
3. Assume that you work for a retail consultancy and have been asked to advise a foreign-based food retailer. The retailer wants to develop a grocery format in the UK of about 15,000 square feet targeted at affluent customers. What advice would you give the retailer on its locational strategy and especially how it should determine its market coverage?
4. Find two major shopping centre plans – use the internet to download these. Analyse these plans and establish the anchor tenants of each.
5. Choose a major retailer and establish what types of locational management options it has been using over the last three years.
6. Find out what the local retail planning policies are for where you live. On the basis of the policies what types of retailer are likely to be able to get planning permission?

REFERENCES

Alexander, A., Cryer, D. and Wood, S. (2008) Location planning in charity retailing, *International Journal of Retail & Distribution Management*, 36(7), 536–550.

Bennison, D., Clarke, I. and Pal, J. (1995) Location decision making: an exploratory framework for analysis, *International Review of Retail, Distribution and Consumer Research*, 5(1), 1–20.

Birchall, J. (2007a) Tesco aims to fill 'grocery gap', *Financial Times*, 28 June, available from http://www.ft.com/cms/s/0Ö572440dc-2514–11dc-bf47–000b5df10621.html?siteedition=uk#axzz31tF5G0xx.

Birchall, J. (2007b) Tesco's US plans and store list, *Financial Times*, 6 November, http://www.ft.com/cms/s/0Ö707e1514–8c82–11dc-b887–0000779fd2ac.html#axzz32Abnp5az.

Birkin, M., Clarke, G. and Clarke, M. (2002) *Retail Geography and Intelligent Network Planning*, Chichester: Wiley.

Burt, S., Johansson, U. and Helander, A. (2011) Standardized marketing strategies in retailing? IKEA's marketing strategies in Sweden, the UK and China, *Journal of Retailing and Consumer Services*, 18(3), 183–193.

CACI (2013) *Retail Dimensions Report*, London: CACI. (A web search on this will give a choice of summary items that have mentioned extracts from this report.)

Clarke, I., Bennison, D. and Pal, J. (1997) Toward a contemporary perspective of retail location, *International Journal of Retail & Distribution Management*, 25(2), 59–69.

Clarke, I., Mackaness, W. and Ball, B. (2003) Modelling Intuition in Retail Site Assessment (MIRSA): making sense of retail location using retailers' intuitive judgements as a support for decision making, *International Review of Retail, Distribution and Consumer Research*, 13(2), 175–193.

Davies, G. with Davies, J. (1989) *What Next?* London: Century.

Davies, M. and Clarke, I. (1994) A framework for network planning, *International Journal of Retail & Distribution Management*, 22(6), 6–10.

Felsted, A. (2013) Tesco counts cost of failed US venture, *Financial Times*, 8 April, http://www.ft.com/cms/s/0/a4aa2fbc-a077-11e2-a6e1-00144feabdc0.html#axzz32Abnp5az.

Goodwin, A. (2007) The UK retail hierarchy: beyond the shopping centre pipeline, *Journal of Property and Leisure Research*, 6, 79–83 (http://www.palgrave-journals.com/rlp/journal/v6/n1/full/5100041a.html, accessed 15 May 2014).

Hernandez, T. (2007) Enhancing retail location decision support: the development and application of geovisualization, *Journal of Retailing and Consumer Services*, 14, 249–258.

Insider Media (2014) Store openings boost N Brown, *Insider News North West*, 1 May.

Jones, C. (2014) Land use planning policies and market forces: utopian aspirations thwarted? *Land Use Policy*, 38, 573–579

Jones, K. and Simmons, J. (1987) *Location, Location, Location*, Toronto: Methuen.

Leahy, T. (2009) *Presentation at Manchester Business School*, 25 November.

Li, Y. and Liu, L. (2012) Assessing the impact of retail location on store performance: a comparison of Wal-Mart and Kmart stores in Cincinnati, *Applied Geography*, 32, 591–600.

M&S (2014) *M&S Annual Report 2013: UK Stores* (available online at: http://annualreport2013.marksandspencer.com/strategic-review/our-plan-in-action/focus-on-the-uk/uk-stores/).

McGoldrick, P. (2002) *Retail Marketing*, London: McGraw-Hill.

Next plc (2013) Half year results (available from http://www.nextplc.co.uk/~/media/Files/N/Next-PLC/pdfs/reports-and-results/2013/hy-results-jul-2013-slides.pdf), accessed 14 May 2014.

Next plc (2014) Annual results (available from http://www.nextplc.co.uk/~/media/Files/N/Next-PLC/pdfs/reports-and-results/2014/Next%20AR2014%20web.pdf), accessed 14 May 2014.

Pal, J., Bennison, D., Clarke, I. and Byrom, J. (2001) Power, policy networks and planning: the involvement of major grocery retailers in the formulation of Planning Policy Guidance Note 6 since 1988, *International Review of Retail, Distribution and Consumer Research*, 11(3), 225–246.

Pal, J. and Medway, D. (2008) Working the system, *Environment & Planning A*, 40, 761–67.

Roig-Tierno, N., Baviera-Puig, A., Buitrago-Vera, J. and Mas-Verdu, F. (2013) The retail site location decision process using GIS and the analytical hierarchy process, *Applied Geography*, 40, 191–198.

Ruddick, G. (2014) John Lewis really believes it's better together, *Daily Telegraph*, 19 April, p. 39.

Shields, M. and Kures, M. (2007) Black out of the blue light: an analysis of Kmart store closing decisions, *Journal of Retailing and Consumer Services*, 14, 259–268.

Somerville, M. (2014) Marks and Spencer loses break lease case (http://www.retailgazette.co.uk/articles/21232-marks-and-spencer-loses-break-lease-case), accessed 14 May.

Srinivasan, R., Sridhar, S., Narayanan, S. and Sihi, D. (2013) Effects of opening and closing stores on chain retailer performance, *Journal of Retailing*, 89(2), 126–139.

Thompson, C., Clarke, G., Clarke, M. and Stillwell, J. (2012) Modelling the future opportunities for deep discount food retailing in the UK, *International Review of Retail, Distribution and Consumer Research*, 22(2), 143–170.

Walters, D. (1988) *Strategic Retailing Management*, London: Prentice Hall.

Wood, S. and Browne, S. (2007) Convenience store location planning and forecasting – a practical research agenda, *International Journal of Retail & Distribution Management*, 35(4), 233–255.

Wood, S. and Tasker, A. (2008) The importance of context in store forecasting: the site visit in retail location decision-making, *Journal of Targeting, Measurement and Analysis for Marketing*, 16, 139–155.

Wrigley, N. (1998) PPG6 and the contemporary UK food store development dynamic, *British Food Journal*, 100(3), 154–161.

Case study

Rolling out a new breed of local discount store

By Andrea Felsted

Sunita and Suresh Kanji are proudly showing off their new convenience store in the Little Hulton area of Manchester.

The couple, who live in Bolton, had previously spent five years running a convenience store across the road. But the building was council-owned, and they wanted to find a more permanent location.

When the land opposite became available, they looked at building a new store. They approached Booker, the cash-and-carry wholesaler, which supplies 3000 independent stores under the Premier banner. However, given the size of the plot, Booker suggested that the store become one of its new breed of local discount stores, known as Family Shopper.

"It's busy", says Mr Kanji, of the store that opened on May 1st. "From the previous place we were, this is a massive improvement. It has been a good move".

Charles Wilson, chief executive of Booker, says the Family Shopper stores offer value – pitched between what could be found in a hard discounter and a regular supermarket – but in a neighbourhood location, and with the longer opening hours of a convenience store.

The aim is to locate the Family Shoppers – which have their own distinctive branding – closer to where people live than the hard discounters, which require bigger sites. At 2000 sq ft, the Family Shopper compares with a typical hard discount store at about 10,000 square ft.

Booker is looking to build a chain of up to 400 discount convenience stores over the next four years, underlining the rise of discount food retailing in the UK, especially the challenge from Aldi and Lidl.

At Little Hulton, the nearest Lidl is about 2 miles away, although there is a Farm Foods, which specialises in frozen food, about 500 m away. Some 60 per cent of products are branded, with the remainder private label, under the Euro Shopper brand. This range, exclusive to Booker in the UK, is sourced through the AMS buying group, of which Ahold of the Netherlands is the largest member.

This gives Booker the buying power that comes from purchasing large volumes, enabling the Family Shopper stores to stock good quality products, but at low prices.

With 1200 core products, the Family Shopper looks more like a small supermarket than a typical local convenience store, and the value message is loud and clear. Sunblest bread is 69p; four Andrex toilet rolls are £1.99, while milk and cheese are £1.

There is also a range of £1 non-food lines, to compete with the pound shops.

Value is important because the majority of those in a 1 km radius are either of moderate means or hard pressed, according to retail analyst CACI's classification. The area has also been hit hard by benefit cuts.

For Booker, the chain provides an additional source of revenue, and bolsters its buying power across the group. Mr Wilson says it could have 300–400 Family Shopper stores in the next three to four years.

Booker supplies the store operator, on its best terms. Mr and Mrs Kanji must operate to Booker's standards, but the couple own the store, and are entitled to all the profit they generate.

The couple spent £750,000 on the project, including buying the land and building the store and three apartments above. Some £200,000 came from the bank, with the remainder from friends and family.

The finished project will be valued by the bank shortly. The couple also have planning permission for seven dwellings on the land beside the shop.

But early trading at the store has been so promising that Mr Kanji, who also owns a garage, wants to open another Family Shopper.

"It's a no-brainer," he says.

Source: Felsted, A. (2014) Booker rolls out new breed of local discount store, *Financial Times*, 9 July. © The Financial Times Limited 2014. All Rights Reserved.

DISCUSSION QUESTIONS

1 Which location technique (see Table 8.4) was primarily used to decide on the site for the store in the case?

2 Mr and Mrs Kanji opted for 'roll out' as a way of expanding their business. If they had not chosen this option, which one of the other '6Rs' (Table 8.2) would you have recommended them to pursue? Explain the reasoning behind your choice.

3 Which of the four key elements of retail location factors (Figure 8.5) was the most important in deciding on the location of the store in the case? Rank the importance of the remaining three elements in relation to this retail outlet.

4 In what ways are the product and price range of Family Shopper stores compatible with the location decision in the case?

CHAPTER 9

Retail design and layout

Learning objectives

The objectives of this chapter are to:
- explain the significance of retail store design;
- describe the different options for store layout;
- evaluate the impact of visual merchandising on consumers;
- discuss various types of retail atmospherics.

Introduction

Most retailing currently takes place in bricks-and-mortar (BM) stores, although online sales have clearly increased in recent years. UK online shoppers spent £38.8bn in 2013, with sales forecast to increase by 16 per cent to £45bn in 2014 (Internet Retailing, 2014). This section discusses the environment of both in-store and non-store retailing, assessing the similarities and differences between these methods of selling products. The BM retail selling environment essentially consists of the store itself plus its staff, in addition to atmospheric aspects such as music and aroma. This gives physical stores a distinct competitive advantage over websites, particularly for customers who value the experiential, hedonistic aspects of consumption, and view shopping as a social experience. However, online retailing has its own competitive advantages, including price and convenience, which can appeal more to the consumer's rational side.

Retail store design

In retailing, stores, websites and catalogues are the main elements of 'physical evidence' (or physical environment, as some authors prefer to call it) within the extended marketing mix (the '7Ps'). Retail store design plays a crucial role in communicating a brand image to consumers (Davies and Ward, 2005) and providing an environment that customers wish to visit. Store design and products or services need to be compatible in order to form a consistent image, as part of an effective marketing mix. As Varley (2006: 163) points out:

> If the product range and the outlet work in harmony, the retailer's positioning strategy is reinforced, but if they work in conflict, the positioning will be unclear to customers, who will become confused and disappointed.

The presentation of stores and their products or services need to appeal to the target market and to be compatible with their lifestyles if customers are to be enticed away from competitors. Store image involves both the physical, relatively permanent aspects of the store and the layout of the products within it. Academic journal articles focusing specifically on store design are somewhat limited and tend to be mostly outdated, yet in practice store retailers update store design quite frequently, resulting in new techniques, styles and technology being developed on a regular basis. However, store design is a topic of interest in a broad range of literature in other fields, including design, architecture, geography and psychology, particularly in relation to its effect on consumers (Greenland and McGoldrick, 2005; Turley and Chebat, 2002). Many leading architects have collaborated with retailers through designing stores, especially at the luxury end of the market, e.g. Rem Koolhaas for Prada, Frank Gehry for Issey Miyake stores in the US and Renzo Piano for Hermès in Japan (Luna, 2005).

Exterior store design

In Western markets, retailers normally rent their stores rather than owning them, but there is still scope for them to conduct a certain amount of exterior design. The fascia, i.e. the shop's exterior signage, is particularly significant, as it acts as a key form of communication with customers and it is essential for it to stand out among its competitors. The fascia can also be known as the 'marquee' (Berman and Evans, 2010). Colour; lettering fonts; texture; imagery and materials can all be utilised by graphic designers when devising a retail fascia. On the store exterior, windows are also important for retailers to be able to present merchandise and information to customers and to invite them inside.

Some large-scale retailers, such as IKEA, prefer not to have window displays however, thereby minimising display costs. This is particularly the case in out-of-town locations, where fewer stores compete for consumers' attention. Many modern stores of this type are designed by specialist retail architects, commissioned either by retailers or by the companies who own the retail space (Kent and Kirby, 2009). Several stores have moved beyond being simply retail spaces due to their iconic architectural design, making them landmark tourist attractions, e.g. the metal-studded Selfridges store in Birmingham, UK and the Art Nouveau-style *Au Printemps* department store in Paris.

Store entrances have an impact on enticing customers in, or sometimes deterring them from entering. Standard door entrances to stores are popular in traditional town centres, reflecting the fact that shops evolved from being tradesmen's homes in the past (see Figure 9.1). In shopping centres or purpose-built stores, open entrances are more popular, where there is a permanent, wide space for shoppers to enter during opening hours, removing any barriers (Diamond and Diamond, 1999). Variations on open entrances are the funnel entrance, where the customer walks down a small corridor past windows displaying merchandise on either side (see Figure 9.2) and the semi-open entrance where a doorway-sized entrance is kept open permanently during opening hours (see Figure 9.3). In certain countries disabled access is required by law, so this has to be accommodated by retailers, e.g. by providing ramps for steps outside store entrances.

The design and other environmental factors within a shopping centre can also influence customers to shop at a specific branch of a retailer. A major new shopping centre was launched by Westfield in September 2011 in Stratford, London, which had the advantage of being located near to the stadium of the 2012 Olympic Games. This shopping centre also gained favourable press coverage for grouping its stores by product sector, making it more convenient for shoppers to find their intended retail destinations. Although this is standard practice in some parts of the world, such as the Middle East, this layout is novel in comparison to other malls of this kind. Westfield Stratford is also notable for the use of innovative 'Pavegen' floor tiles (which were developed by graduates of Loughborough University) made from recycled materials. The tiles can harness kinetic energy

Figure 9.1 Traditional door entrance for Hatchards bookshop in London
Source: © Barry Lewis/Alamy Images

RETAIL STORE DESIGN 219

Figure 9.2 This branch of All Saints has a funnel entrance
Source: authors' own photograph

Figure 9.3 Semi-open store entrance for the North Face with open-backed window on ground level and closed-back window above
Source: authors' own photograph

Figure 9.4 Zara uses closed-back window displays

Source: authors' own photograph

from shoppers' steps, lighting up the tiles and generating electricity to help the shopping centre to achieve its sustainability targets (Loughborough University, 2011). The imaginative use of design in this way can offer shopping centres a competitive advantage, by making them stand out from competing locations, giving them the added bonus of free publicity. (Westfield Stratford shopping centre can be viewed at: http://uk.westfield.com/stratfordcity/news-and-events/opening.)

Stores often act as three-dimensional adverts for retailers on the High Street and they can therefore be considered to be part of the 'promotion' aspect of the marketing mix, as well as being the key element within 'place' in the retailing sector. Indeed, it seems likely that Apple and Niketown stores serve the purpose of promoting the company and enhancing its brand image in key locations, rather than being profitable as retail outlets because they contain relatively small volumes of stock on the shop floor. Certain store chains, such as international fashion retailer Zara, have become successful despite conducting a minimal amount of formal promotion. Zara's success can be credited to the attractive design of the stores and high-profile locations, combined with products that cater well for its customers' needs (see Figure 9.4). Channelling finances into store design and product design in preference to advertising has allowed Zara to gain a reputation for good design which consumers can communicate to each other via word-of-mouth.

RETAIL MARKETING CAREERS
Martin Knox, Brand Design Consultant

Martin Knox is a brand design business development consultant who works mainly for the retail sector. Martin describes his current role as 'going into organisations with some constructive disruption, getting people to take a bit of time to think beyond the ways they normally think and do things'. Martin's job involves store design and developing brand identity, amongst several other responsibilities. Martin's definition of business, distilled from various sources, is 'utilising the minimum of resources to create value'. However, he believes that sticking solely to that definition will not generate income, awareness or loyalty for companies.

Martin studied BA (Hons) Fine Art but he had always wanted to get involved in graphic design and was given the opportunity to do this soon after graduating. In the early 1980s he realised that there was an opportunity in the Midlands to provide a service for fashion businesses whom he felt were 'not being well served by the design community', so he says 'I saw the need for someone who could work with the fashion industry with empathy and I got very busy'. Martin was commissioned to carry out some design work for the newly formed Next stores and he was asked by George Davies (CEO at that time) to set up an in-house graphic design facility for Next on a consultancy basis, so that

Source: with permission from Martin Knox

Source: with permission from Martin Knox

he could still work with other clients. Martin says of his time at Next:

> It was fantastic and we didn't know what the rules were. We didn't know the way you should or shouldn't do things in retail marketing or shop design or graphic design. We did what we felt was right and put everything into that and it really worked. Our customers loved Next and we repaid that loyalty. Next was something new that grew with our customers. You don't see that very much anymore.

In 1989 Martin decided to move on from Next to develop a credible, wide-ranging design business, working with another designer from his former team and some freelance colleagues. Martin says:

> The people that commissioned the work still didn't have the confidence to work with new emerging design companies but they worked with me because I had the Next pedigree and we were really busy right from the start. So I worked with BHS, M&S, Sainsbury's and Boots and through the 90s we grew and grew. I wanted to grow the business into retail design and exhibition design, which we did, working for First Sport, Converse, Kangol, the Post Office, Poundland, Early Learning Centre and other clients.

By 2000 Martin's company had an annual turnover of £2.5m and 15 staff but the business had become so large that it differed from Martin's values and way of thinking. He therefore decided to work independently, in a studio with an eclectic mix of visual inspiration (see above) with a network of collaborators to call on, dependent on the type of project being worked on. Martin's job also involves travelling in the UK to meet customers and to see interesting exhibitions. In relation to his travel he says:

> The trade shows are probably really good for students because they show what's happening now and what has happened. I'm not in the business of what's happening now, I'm in the business of what's going to happen in five years' time. I get ideas from all sorts of places: Yorkshire Sculpture Park is a wonderful, magical place, the Pitt Rivers Museum in Oxford and the Sir John Soames Museum in London. When you look at the back streets you see the things that are intended to be hidden from general view, so they're not High Streets, they're not showcases, they're where hidden things go on. I look very closely, then I step back and I look at the whole. What frustrates me is what we get presented with in retail in terms of product and brand is more of the same, just a little bit different and there's never anything new . . . it's just revisiting what's already been there and the product and the ambience of the store will feel like they're trapped in a cycle.

One of Martin's recent retail projects was with Cancer Research (CR), which has around 650 shops that follow a traditional charity shop format, where stock consists of donated products. Martin was therefore commissioned to look at ways of refreshing the retail business. This was more about the purpose of the shops, their business, culture and structure, than their design. Over the years CR had been through a number of initiatives to have the shops redesigned and, although as a result they looked better, they were difficult to merchandise and expensive to fit. The shops were split into two so in one half they had the product and in the back of the shops was a customer information zone. Martin decided to start by looking at the purpose of the shops, which at the time of the brief was just to generate income by selling donated products. Martin says:

> I spent three months researching, looking at how they go about their business, talking with people who work in the stores and those who manage. I also delved into Cancer Research activities and I was staggered to discover the breadth of what CR get involved in, which was phenomenal. I gave them the idea to give the stores essentially three functions. The first function would be to sell product and generate income. The second function would be that they are vehicles to communicate the breadth of what CR get involved with. The third function was to develop, encourage and support communities around the shops. CR have fundraising groups in most towns in the UK so I illustrated ways they could use the shops, amending the shop fitting so they could use them for organised fundraising events and have meetings, a whole raft of things around creating community, going back to communicating what the charity's about. Each of those things will contribute to the other.

In terms of store design Martin reviewed elements such as lighting and decor. He discovered a white emulsion paint that reflects 92 per cent of the light that hits it, instead of 64 per cent like normal paint. He found that the shops were fairly dark and their electricity bills were high, so this was a straightforward way of helping them to simplify their lighting. Martin explains:

> This is what I mean by constructive disruption, taking what they've got, taking their thinking and shaking it a little bit. The people who know their customers and how to run the shops are the people who run them on a day-to-day basis. I added a few elements of design. I redesigned how the cash desk works. I had signposting systems so people could get a handle on what's where straight away and a number of ways of getting the CR message across from a very simple chalkboard where the manager could write the comments to quite multi-layered graphics systems. I get involved with the physicality of a brand or store or organisation, how it presents itself, but I get involved with the culture of it as well, the spirit of an organisation. The essential message for me there was how you go about retail, because it isn't good enough anymore to fill a space full of stuff and just expect it to sell . . . the stuff might be wonderful and the space might be beautiful and a lovely environment, but it isn't enough. Increasingly we're less and less interested in stuff and as consumers we're becoming more interested in what this product means to us, what's its history, where's it made, what impact is it going to have on the environment, what impact will it have on me? So the thing itself is becoming less important. Retail has to become more about the 'why' and less about the 'what'. The 'what' would be the product, the experience, the environment. The 'why' would be a sense of belonging, the provenance, a community around a shop and an organisation.

Martin was also commissioned to design a new retail business to be trialled by CR, focusing on cards and gifts. This project gives an indication of the scope of his responsibilities and how they extend beyond designing. Martin worked with colleagues to formulate a business model, name it, design its whole identity (the stores, brand, presentation materials and promotional items), oversaw product sourcing and selection, conceived merchandising, virtual merchandising (VM) internal and external marketing, as well as induction and support for staff.

Martin specifies the key qualities that people need to shine in the creative industries as: creativity; critical thinking; curiosity; spontaneity; self-awareness; self-discipline; courage; a sense of wonder; humility; humour; endurance and reliability. Martin says he is always looking to meet interesting people with creative and marketing skills. He works with a range of different types of company, such as shopfitters Resolution Interiors in Somerset. Martin has worked with them for over 20 years and describes them as 'very imaginative in the way they source product, one of the best shopfitters I've ever come across'. Martin states that his favourite aspects of the job are 'making a difference, being a positive catalyst for change and positively touching the lives of many people'. However, he finds that when clients don't take responsibility for what they would need to in order to support his work, this can make the job more difficult.

www.mknox.co.uk; Twitter:@martinknox

Interior store design

Interior store design consists of semi-permanent fixtures, such as flooring, walls, lighting and décor, which are updated periodically (see Figure 9.5). Lighting can impact upon the fittings, which are movable items that can be rearranged more frequently to update the look of the store and to accommodate new product ranges. Fittings include types of furniture made specifically for stores, including sales counters; presentation cases; racks and shelves (see Figures 9.6 and 9.7); **gondolas** (display units for the shop floor, see Figure 9.8) and tables (see Figure 9.9); as well as mannequins (shop dummies, see Figure 9.10). Mirrors are essential fittings in clothing and beauty stores, both in the store itself and in fitting rooms, yet are sometimes hard for consumers to find. The style of mirror can complement the store design and the quality of glass can affect consumers' decision-making as it can enhance the appearance of the item. A new technological development from UK company Holition is a mirror that allows customers to try on an item then use a touchscreen to view it in different colours, without the need to try them on, as used by Uniqlo in its San Francisco store (Retail Innovation, 2013).

Store layout

Two of the most commonly used layouts in retailers are the **grid layout** with rows of aisles, favoured by supermarkets, and the **freeform layout**, where merchandise is grouped into clusters around the store, so that customers can wander around the products (Lusch *et al.*, 2011). The **boutique layout** displays goods centrally, with other products typically stacked on shelves by the walls, with customers typically travelling in one direction in a clear pathway around the central area, hence its alternative name of 'racetrack' layout. Store interiors are designed strategically via collaboration between marketers and designers, so that the layout guides customers around the store in a way that is intended to

Figure 9.5 Lighting is a key feature of the store design in Schuh
Source: author's own photograph

Figure 9.6 Minimal in-store shelving and novel use of lighting in Flannels store
Source: authors' own photograph

Figure 9.7 Shelving used as a key component of store design
Source: © ostap25/fotolia.com

Figure 9.8 Slatwall double-sided gondolas
Source: with permission from Morplan Ltd

increase purchases (see Figure 9.11). For example, a store such as Asda (the UK division of Walmart) which is primarily a supermarket, locates clothing and electrical goods departments near the entrance, where customers must pass before arriving at the food section. At this point, customers have empty trolleys so the lure of low-priced non-food products can tempt them to make impulse buys and Asda's 'George' clothing range has achieved a significant share of the UK fashion market (Mintel, 2010). Sales can also be encouraged by taking advantage of 'hotspots' around stores to sell relatively small products that can be bought on impulse, typically at locations where customers pause such as checkouts and at the bottom of escalators. However, retailers should consider the moral aspects of

Figure 9.9 The Body Shop uses tables and baskets as part of its display fittings
Source: author's own photograph

Figure 9.10 Mannequins at Adel Rootstein's London showroom
Source: with permission from Adel Rootstein Ltd

enticing people to buy products that they did not intend to purchase, either because it impacts upon sustainability or health. The 'hotspot' technique has been criticised where it is used to tempt customers to buy confectionery, especially when it is at children's eye-level next to the tills. In response to this criticism and to discourage unhealthy eating, supermarkets such as Aldi have begun to remove displays of sweets from checkout areas.

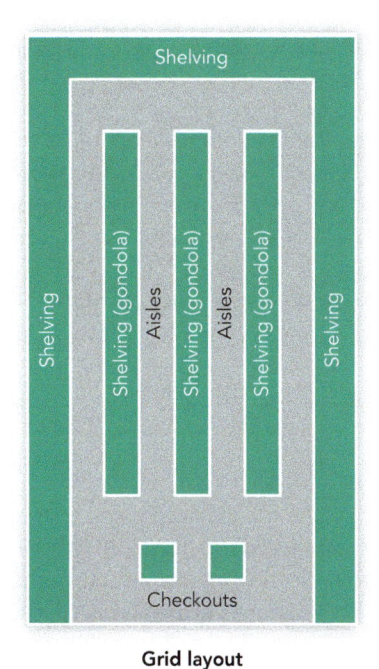

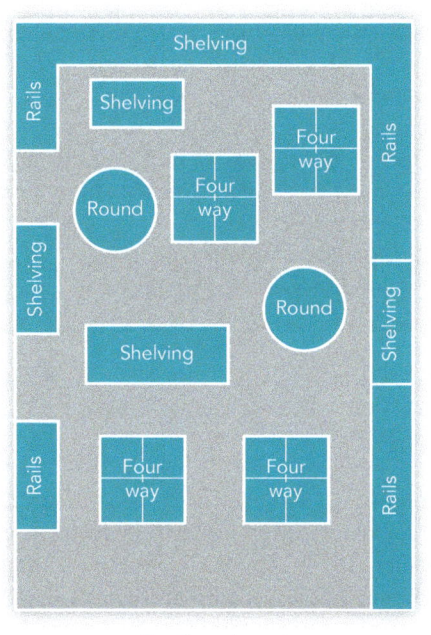

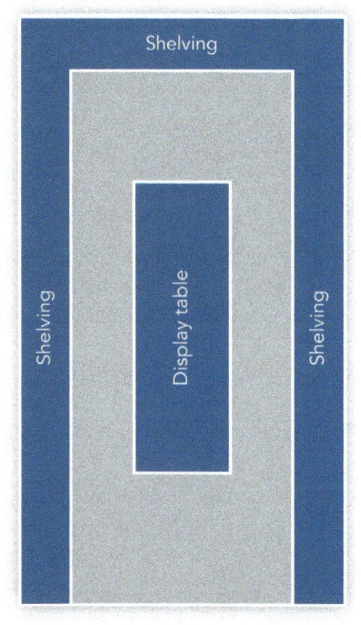

Figure 9.11 Standard options for store layouts
Source: adapted from Varley and Rafiq (2004)

USING EYE-TRACKING RESEARCH TO INVESTIGATE THE IMPACT OF RETAIL LAYOUT ON CONSUMER DECISION-MAKING

Eye-tracking is a method of conducting consumer research that is used mostly by FMCG companies, as well as by retailers of groceries, DIY and fashion. Siemon Scamell-Katz, former Global Consulting Director for Taylor Nelson Sofres (TNS), who pioneered this technique in a consumer research context, says that 'the study of shopping marries science with art'. Siemon and his colleagues set up a retail design business and wanted to conduct research that would help them to take into account customer needs when designing. After initially being involved in store design, the consumer research side eventually overtook the design side of Siemon's company and the business was later sold to TNS. The move into the field of consumer research happened after a leading supermarket asked the firm to investigate the effect of store layout on shoppers. They used 120 CCTV cameras and observed 400 shoppers, who were interviewed about their store visits afterwards.

The results of the research led Siemon to identify 'mission-based shopping' when consumers' actions vary depending on their shopping intentions, e.g. to find a little black dress or to do their top-up grocery shopping, thus determining where they go and how they behave when they're in a store. He therefore describes mission-based shopping as 'a really important fundamental', stating that 'the retailer has to plan for every mission and decide which ones to focus on . . . different missions demand different requirements from the stores'. Consumers' missions can vary depending on their location, with many US consumers bulk buying on a monthly basis for example, facilitated by large cars and houses, whereas Vietnamese shoppers might shop daily for smaller amounts owing to scooters and motorbikes being a more popular mode of transport.

When looking for new techniques to research into CB, Siemon says that it was difficult to find anyone suitable to help them in pre-internet days. However, fortunately they discovered vision scientist Dr Mark Dunne at Aston University and he helped them to use vision equipment for consumer studies. Siemon explains, 'We did some experimental work using symbols for horizontal and vertical tracking and as the equipment became more portable in the mid-'90s we used it in store. The results were amazing'. Unbeknown to Siemon at the time, other retail research pioneers were also thinking along the same lines. In the US Paco Underhill and Herb Sorensen were investigating the same type of equipment for this purpose and Georges Chetochine had developed a similar idea in France.

Siemon has noted a growth in the use of eye-tracking for consumer research in recent years: 'For some reason the US were quite slow into eye-tracking but that's absolutely boomed over the last couple of years, so it's starting to become a standard tool, particularly in FMCG.' Siemon calls for more widespread use of eye-tracking technology by retailers, as he considers that there's a significant difference between how the industry seems to think people see and how we actually see, with consumers being oblivious to around 80 per cent of the items in a store. Siemon believes that 'if we could stop propagating the myth that you can just put some cardboard in a store and it'll make people behave differently, that would be a great step forward'.

Sources: interview with Siemon Scamell-Katz and Scamell-Katz, S. (2012) *The Art of Shopping: How and Why we Buy*, London: LID.

Visual merchandising

Visual merchandising (VM) has often been described as 'the silent salesperson' because it minimises customers' need for help from sales staff (Bell and Ternus, 2006). VM is defined by Pegler (1998: 1) as 'displaying merchandise with the aim of maximising the volume of product sales'. Berman and Evans (2010: 508) offer a more detailed definition of VM: 'A proactive, integrated retail atmospherics approach aimed to create a certain look, properly display products, stimulate shopping behavior, and enhance physical behavior.' These definitions demonstrate that VM is responsible for enticing as many target customers as possible into the store through effective window displays and, once they are inside, encouraging them to purchase through the skilful layout of products in store. VM involves a flair for composition and layout, combined with an appreciation of the taste of the store's target customers. An awareness of the company's brand image is also essential in order for products to be displayed effectively.

VM takes place within retail outlets and it should not be confused with merchandising, which is the retail function responsible for ensuring that products are manufactured, transported and delivered in the right quantities to the right stores at the right time, usually based at Head Office in large store chains (see Chapter 5 Retail buying and merchandising). VM is a topic that is under-represented in academic literature (Lea-Greenwood, 1998), yet it has a significant impact at the point where customers make purchase decisions. At any given time, the main product trends are likely to be similar throughout the High Street and more than one store in a single location may sell the same products at similar prices. VM methods can therefore be used to enable a retailer's brand image and product range to be differentiated from those of its competitors, providing a Unique Selling Proposition (USP) that influences the customer's store choice decision. In large retail chains, VM is often a centralised operation, with merchandise presentation being decided at Head Office by senior VM staff and implemented in branches by in-store or regional staff. Various techniques and types of equipment are available for VM and Varley (2006: 183) states that its scope includes:

- choice of fixtures and fittings to be used;
- method of product presentation;
- construction of 'off-shelf' displays;
- choice of store layout (to encourage complementary purchases);
- use of point-of-sale material (to encourage impulse purchases);
- construction of window displays.

Window display

Window display is usually the most obvious aspect of VM to the consumer, hence the historical use of the term 'window dressing' for this retail operation. The way in which products are displayed in the window forms a powerful part of the retailer's brand image, influencing customers' current purchases and acting as a visual reminder for future purchase intentions. Eye-catching merchandise is usually placed in the window display to attract customers, though they often buy more basic products once they enter the store. Window displays can be enclosed, so that they are not seen from inside the store or they can be open-backed, so that passers-by can easily view the merchandise within the shop. The displays can be themed and changed frequently to revive customers' interest, often based upon seasonal events such as Valentine's Day, Christmas and Easter to attract attention and to indicate how the retailer can fulfil customers' current needs (see Figure 9.12).

Signage and graphics

Signage on a store window can be an effective way for retailers to notify customers of specific events such as new product launches, so windows can be used as free advertising space for the company to disperse information to passing consumers. In 2001, Marks & Spencer publicised the launch of its new fashion collection 'Per Una' with a countdown of the days to its arrival in the windows of relevant branches. The initial sales targets for this clothing range were greatly exceeded and it is possible that the anticipation created by such a promotion may have contributed to this (BBC, 2001). More recently, H&M has launched a more sustainable 'Conscious Collection' of clothing, promoted via signage in its store windows.

230 CHAPTER 9 RETAIL DESIGN AND LAYOUT

Figure 9.12 Christmas window display and preparation is complemented by interior VM in Selfridges' Oxford Street store
Source: with permission from Getty Images/Oli Scarff

In-store interiors, signage on walls, fixtures and fittings help customers to find the products they require and can persuade them to make impulse buys. Signage also provides customers with useful information such as opening times and product details and it can therefore be considered to be an aspect of customer service (see Chapter 10 Retail customer service). The use of strategically placed, informative signs can be a more economical way to improve the customer experience than employing additional staff to impart information. Consumers have become accustomed to clear signs and directions to navigate online and this could increase their expectations of the quality of signage in stores. Technology can help to improve the impact of signage. For example, digital signs showing that cashiers are available have become established fixtures in Post Offices and low-priced retailers with queuing systems, improving both efficiency and cost-effectiveness. More recently, interactive tablets in fixed positions in stores have been introduced to provide information for customers in electronics retailers. The offer of free wi-fi in stores now enables signage to extend its reach beyond the store's resources and to provide more information than traditional signs could accommodate, via consumers' own electronic devices. For example, consumers can download apps and scan QR codes in stores as digital forms of signage. Attending trade fairs such as the European Sign Expo in Munich (see www.fespa.com) and Digital Signage Expo in Las Vegas (see www.digitalsignageexpo.net) allows retailers to keep up-to-date with the latest innovations in signage.

In-store display

Well-displayed merchandise can give customers more freedom to make purchase decisions without the need for input from store staff. A balance needs to be achieved between displaying a wide range of products to offer customers a broad choice and leaving enough space to avoid the store looking cluttered. Deciding on the most appropriate balance usually depends upon the price range of the store. Upmarket stores tend to display the least amount of merchandise, with high investment in interior space and décor providing a more luxurious environment, consistent with the price of their products. At mass-market level, display opportunities in the store tend to be exploited by retailers where possible, to enable them to maximise valuable retail space (see also 'retail space allocation' in Chapter 5 Retail buying and merchandising). Point-of-purchase (POP) incorporates both store display and promotion, when visual or written information to promote specific products is displayed alongside the merchandise at the location where it is sold in-store. For example, this can take the form of separate, stand-alone shelving designed specifically for certain products or small in-store posters stating that a particular item has been featured in a magazine. POP promotion is usually intended to make a particular brand's products stand out amongst competitors at the point where the purchase decision is made. This incurs costs for the brand through providing POP materials or fittings and a payment may also need to be made to the retailer.

Retailers often use modular display systems that can be adjusted to different sizes to accommodate the size and style of current product ranges. In-store layout of merchandise can be organised by grouping products in certain colours, themes, brands or product types. However, since many retailers open seven days a week it can be difficult to find time or space to practise store layouts. This problem can be solved by constructing a replica store at the retailer's Head Office for a centralised VM team to work in, although this is an expensive investment and it is therefore not often practicable. Alternatively, the VM team can take over a retailer's flagship store to devise the layout of products, but since the advent of seven-days-per-week opening, this work may need to be done during the night (Goworek, 2006). To overcome these problems, specialist software has been developed to enable the visual layout of merchandise to be planned on a computer (Planogram Builder, 2014, see Figure 9.13). Planograms to demonstrate the in-store presentation of products can be drawn either manually or by using software. Planograms form the intersection between in-store display and merchandising as they incorporate both layout and space allocation (see Chapter 5 Retail buying and merchandising).

The overall style and layout of a store needs to be suited to the types of product it sells and its price range, to achieve a consistent store image, which forms a core component of the retailer's total brand image (see also Chapter 4 Retail product and brand management). For example, Gonalston Farm Shop is an independent retailer that has different types of layout and fittings for various product types, all of which are compatible with the brand image of a traditional, high quality store in a rural setting, offering both self-service and personal selling (see gonalstonfarmshop.co.uk/fish/).

Reconstructing the store layout can have an immediate impact on sales. Catwalk Cakes is based in North Laine in Brighton and attracts a lot of passing trade in this area known for its abundance of small, independent retailers. While the large decorated cakes in the window attracted the attention of passers-by, when smaller fresh products were moved into the window owner Janice Hansen found that sales increased substantially (see Figure 9.14).

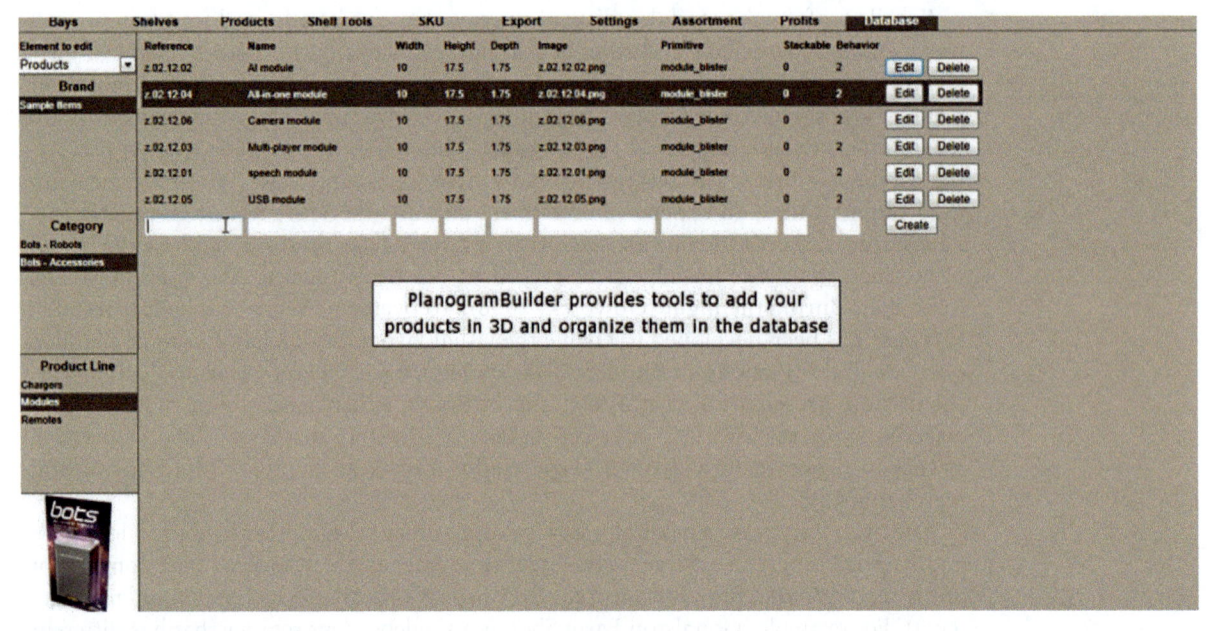

Figure 9.13 Planogram Builder Visual Merchandising software
Source: © zVisuel SA, www.planogrambuilder.com

VISUAL MERCHANDISING **233**

Figure 9.14 Catwalk Cakes window display and interior product display
Source: with permission from George Hansen, Catwalk Cakes

Figure 9.14 (*continued*)

Retail atmosphere

Retail atmosphere has a strong impact on consumers' perceptions of a retailer's brand image and it is defined by Berman and Evans (2010: 508) as 'the psychological feeling a customer gets when visiting a retailer'. The four dimensions of retail atmosphere are specified in sensory terms by McGoldrick (2002: 460) as: visual, aural, olfactory and

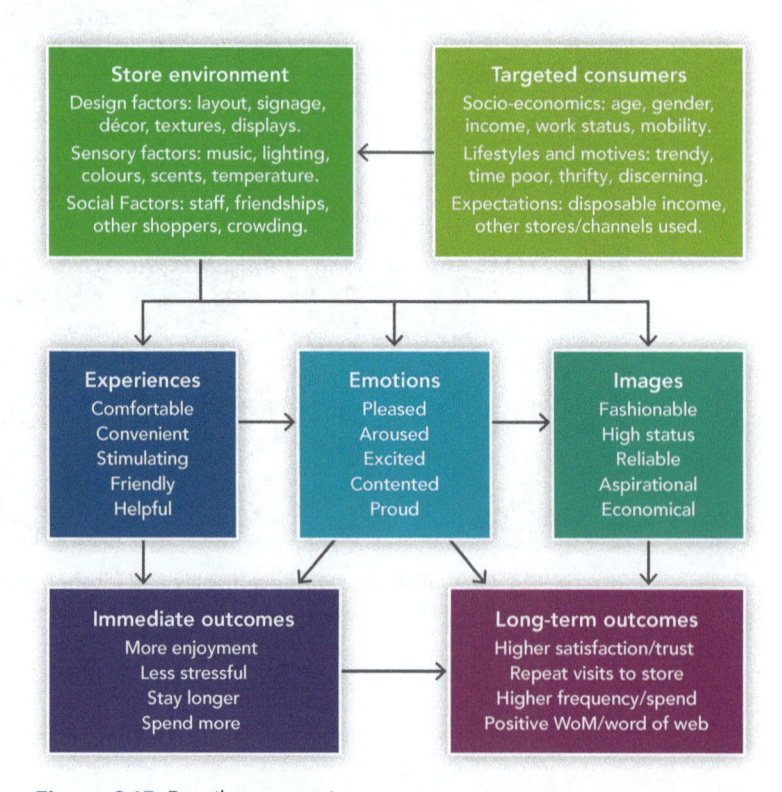

Store environment
Design factors: layout, signage, décor, textures, displays.
Sensory factors: music, lighting, colours, scents, temperature.
Social Factors: staff, friendships, other shoppers, crowding.

Targeted consumers
Socio-economics: age, gender, income, work status, mobility.
Lifestyles and motives: trendy, time poor, thrifty, discerning.
Expectations: disposable income, other stores/channels used.

Experiences
Comfortable
Convenient
Stimulating
Friendly
Helpful

Emotions
Pleased
Aroused
Excited
Contented
Proud

Images
Fashionable
High status
Reliable
Aspirational
Economical

Immediate outcomes
More enjoyment
Less stressful
Stay longer
Spend more

Long-term outcomes
Higher satisfaction/trust
Repeat visits to store
Higher frequency/spend
Positive WoM/word of web

Figure 9.15 Retail store environments

Source: adapted from McGoldrick, P. (2002) *Retail Marketing*, 2nd edn © 2002. Reproduced with the kind permission of McGraw-Hill Education. All rights reserved.

tactile (Figure 9.15). The visual dimension (i.e. sight) concerns colour, brightness, size and shapes. The aural atmosphere (sound) can vary through the use of volume, pitch and tempo. The olfactory element relates to aromas in store, whereas texture, softness and temperature are tactile elements. These are the four main points that will be discussed in this section but additionally, taste would of course be an essential sensory factor in a restaurant setting. Retail atmosphere has become increasingly important and retailers have become part of the 'third place', a term denoting environments which are neither home nor work locations, in which consumers choose to spend leisure time (Mikunda, 2004).

Visual components

Colour and lighting are the key visual components in store design. The texture of materials can also potentially be a visual element, which crosses over with tactility. Products themselves also form a major part of many retailers' visual image (see Chapter 4 Retail product and brand management). Research by Bellizzi et al. (1983) suggests that the use of warm colours such as red and yellow can attract customers, thus implying that they would be particularly useful colours for store windows and entrances. More recently, Kent (2007: 737) has also investigated colour as a factor within the retail environment:

> A characteristic of larger retail spaces, such as department stores and shopping malls, has been the promotion of vision as the key sense. Colour is used to stimulate this sense, and change the emotional state of the customer.

This demonstrates the ability of atmospherics to affect consumers' moods in a retail setting and the importance for the retailer of making appropriate decisions in this context. For example, the selection of lighting within a store can alter the appearance of the merchandise. Lighting can be chosen to mimic natural daylight or it can contain a hint of colour. (This is one of the reasons why products can sometimes appear to be a different shade of a colour at home than in store.) Stores also utilise spotlights to accentuate certain products. A study carried out in Belgium revealed that using weaker lighting than usual in stores did not affect sales volume overall, yet using spotlights could increase sales of the highlighted products (Quartier et al., 2011).

Aural components

As with other atmospheric aspects, music can influence shoppers' behaviour and their perception of the store. Fast tempo music tends to speed up shoppers' movements and slower music can have the reverse effect. This tactic can therefore be used by stores to encourage customers to move more quickly at busy periods, e.g. in restaurants at lunchtimes. Certain stores go a step further than simply playing music by running their own in-house radio stations and broadcasting promotional information between music tracks. Perhaps surprisingly, research has demonstrated that when music is played in a store, this lengthens customers' perceptions of the amount of time that they have waited in a queue, yet they feel more positive towards the company as a result, even if the music is disliked (Hui et al., 1997).

Olfactory components

Various studies have investigated the effects of olfaction (i.e. the sense of smell) on consumer behaviour. Scent is relatively cheap and easy to change in comparison to other aspects of atmospherics. New aromas can therefore be introduced regularly to avoid customers becoming de-sensitised to them. Conventional wisdom holds that piping attractive scents into stores has a positive impact on consumers. It is therefore surprising to find that Bone and Ellen (1999) dispute this widely held view. After reviewing numerous studies on the topic, they concluded that there is insufficient evidence to show that olfaction has a positive effect on customers. In contrast, more recently Parsons (2009) conducted a study in stores which are usually odourless, and consequently recommended that any scent they used should be associated with the type of store for it to have a positive effect on customers. The results of this research showed that the use of a pleasant but irrelevant scent could lead to negative responses. These results have implications for retailers in terms of selecting the right type of aroma to elicit positive behaviour from consumers. Taste is another dimension closely related to olfaction that would apply to a retailer that sells or serves food and drink.

A TRUE SENSORIAL EXPERIENCE: BOON CHOCOLATE STORE

By Ann Petermans, University of Hasselt, Belgium

The BOON chocolate store, located in the Belgian city of Hasselt, is among the best examples of experience stores in Belgium's famous chocolate confectionery (Wooliscroft and Ganglmair-Wooliscroft, 2009). Founded in 2005, it offers a broad range of home-made chocolates, as well as an annexed tearoom where hot choco-lattes, coffees and refreshing chocolate milk beverages – all prepared in artisanal style – constitute the limited but focused assortment.

BOON (www.thechocolateexperience.be) is located in a magnificent building in a street at the back of the central shopping streets of the historic city centre of Hasselt. The location of the store immediately reflects the retail branding: it appeals to features such as quality, luxury and handicraft. Entering the store shows that the retail branding continues into an appealing store interior. Although BOON as a retail environment is relatively small (circa 125 square metres), customers are being immersed in a multi-sensorial 'chocolate environment': they can see different kinds of home-made chocolates delicately presented in the counter, they can smell chocolate, see and hear how personnel carefully prepare and serve coffees and other drinks for customers, and they evidently can touch, taste and enjoy their own. While waiting at the counter for a portion of carefully packed chocolates or in the annexed tearoom for their hot drinks, consumers can have a look at BOON's in-store atelier of the chef, where all the chocolate products that are sold are being made. This atelier is covered with glass walls, so that customers can have a look at the production process. In the atelier, the transparency and openness towards the public is fortified by using the colour white. Evidently, the choice of the colour and the glass walls also helps to seemingly enlarge the work space of the chef, which is rather small.

Completely in line with the 'theme' of a chocolate experience, the interior of the store environment consistently refers to the most important chocolate colours: light and dark brown and white. While the walls have been painted in these tints, the ceilings are white. The floor is covered with dark coloured parquet. The in-store furniture consists of small wooden tables and easy chairs and seats which allow customers to sit at ease. The lighting is warm, and together with the other elements of the retail design triggers a cosy, comfortable and warm interior where customers experience a homely atmosphere. In the store, the lighting fixtures are covered with images of children tasting chocolate. This not only appeals to customers' emotions, but also emphasises the cosy in-store atmosphere.

BOON thus immediately 'catches' customers upon entering the store. The colours, the materials, the in-store aroma and general in-store atmosphere make customers feel at ease. Every element seems to fit with the retail branding and the general story the retailer and the designer want to tell. The retail design breathes quality, and articulates the quality of the handicraft of the owner. The public seems to appreciate the efforts of the concerned retailer and designer: BOON is a successful chocolate store. Since their launch in 2005, the concept has found its way to other parts of the world. In the meantime, chefs trained by the owner of BOON have opened their proper chocolate stores in Sydney (http://www.boonchocolates.com.au) and Oregon (http://www.coastalmist.com). The owners' passion for quality and the love of the product stimulates them to continue to be involved in the craftsmanship of making chocolates.

Reference

Wooliscroft, B. and Ganglmair-Wooliscroft, A. (2009) Co-production in memorable service encounters: three hot chocolates in Belgium, in A. Lindgreen, J. Vanhamme and M. Beverland (eds), *Memorable Customer Experiences. A Research Anthology*, pp. 149–158, Surrey: Gower Publishing Company.

Tactile components

Tactile aspects of stores can relate to shop fittings, fixtures and products, all of which impart messages about the environment to customers. Trying on products offers customers both visual and tactile sensations, but it can be a time-consuming process. Department store Debenhams was the first UK store to trial virtual changing rooms by offering wi-fi in its stores which allows customers to download images of themselves trying on garments (Pithers, 2011), thus removing one of the most tactile aspects of shopping in order to facilitate faster consumer decision-making. It is also now possible to download apps for Facebook to enable customers to try garments on avatars of themselves (Thompson, 2012). Many tactile components affect other aspects of atmospherics. For example, the materials used in the décor and fixtures alter the resonance of sound in a store. Additionally, retailers can use heating and air-conditioning to regulate the temperature, with the aim of extending the time customers spend in the store. However, the main tactile experience for consumers in store is through handling products and this is a major asset for most bricks-and-mortar retailers, since it cannot be replicated by websites. As retail market research consultant Paco Underhill (2009: 172) states: '. . . virtually all unplanned purchases – and many planned ones, too – come as a result of the shopper seeing, touching, smelling or tasting something that promises pleasure.'

Innovations in retail atmospherics

By Mark C. O'Flaherty

The mirrorball of online retail is spinning faster than ever – but that doesn't mean the offline retail world isn't dancing right along. Indeed, in order to differentiate the real-world shopping experience from the virtual, fashion brands are getting physical, that is, they want you to come in person to their party, club or shop, be it underground, avant-garde or classic. 'Retail has become boring,' says Armand Hadida, founder of the Paris concept store L'Eclaireur, acclaimed for its eclectic mix of cool labels and avant-garde merchandise displays. 'Everything had been duplicated. We want to develop the new concept of a lifestyle destination'. And so in summer 2011, L'Eclaireur opened Le Royal Eclaireur inside the Royal Monceau hotel; a shop styled as a penthouse suite. Aiming to fuse digital habits with a personal social touch, L'Eclaireur's suite shares an approach with the British brand Burberry and its recently opened super high-tech London flagship, with its massive video screens and central dance floor-cum-show space. 'It's about technology rather than showing loads of clothes', says Hadida. 'You pick something on screen, have lunch or a spa treatment here and then it's delivered to you right after'. Hadida is also overhauling the bar and restaurant element of another of L'Eclaireur's outposts, this one at Faubourg St Honoré, refocusing on 'haute gastronomy'.

Another example of dressed-up retailing is Miu Miu's private members' club, which touched down at the Café Royal in London for three days in 2012. It featured a bar, restaurant and late-night shopping for select invitees. The edgy, directional Dalston retailer LN-CC in north London regularly holds soirées in a nightclub space at the rear of its store. The Rose Bakery, in London boutique department store Dover Street Market, is one of the fashion industry's most cliquey dining spots. But the social aspects of the Dover Street brand are not limited to lunch. When a branch opened in Ginza, Tokyo, owner Rei Kawakubo invited Michael Costiff, mastermind of a legendary London 1990s nightclub Kinky Gerlinky, to recreate a version of the late 20th-century store World, with its eclectic ethnic jewellery, Malcolm McLaren rarities, Brazilian football shirts and Chairman Mao cushions, in the new space. Why bring back the old? Well, 'World was more than a shop', Costiff says, 'it was a meeting place, a dating agency and place to pick up club flyers'. By transplanting World into the Comme des Garçons universe, Kawakubo is effecting a hip club vibe, while making a reference to a subculture she finds inspiring, 'it's about a time when there was still an underground, before mobile phones and the internet'.

Then there are the flagship stores of Victoria's Secret, Abercrombie & Fitch (A&F) and its sibling labels Hollister and Gilly Hicks – sexually charged party spaces with blacked-out or louvred windows where shoppers are frequently forced to queue outside to gain entry. The interiors are dark and loud, with shirtless Bruce Weber muscle-boy assistants and an atmosphere pumped full of fragrance. A&F aims to echo the visual and musical atmospherics of its stores when selling online, by offering an app, images on Instagram and a download of its playlist, enabling customers to replicate the stores' atmosphere. Hollister and A&F aim at youthful consumers, mainly in their teens and 20s, with the emphasis on the 'place' and 'people' elements of the marketing mix, making them the key components of their brand identity. Much of the clothing is relatively classic and functional but the retailers' logos are placed prominently on much of the merchandise, thus acting as a status symbol for many of their customers, that communicates with their peers.

Despite being based in Ohio (rather than in Hollister City, California) Hollister portrays a relaxed, beach lifestyle (see Figure 9.16). Hollister entered the UK market in 2008 and its central London branch has a video wall with a live feed from Huntington Beach, California. A visit is bewildering for many past their teens, but for most of its impressionable target customers it's a rite of passage. After all, to sell well, a polo shirt has to differentiate itself from other polo shirts. Like clubs, brands are about identity and a collective sense of belonging. And if there's a queue outside, that makes it all the more appealing.

Figure 9.16 Hollister exterior
Source: author's own photograph

FT *Source*: adapted from O'Flaherty, M.C. (2012) Shop and bop till you drop, *Financial Times*, 21 December. © The Financial Times Limited 2012. All Rights Reserved. Pearson Education is responsible for providing this adaptation of the original article.

The non-store retail selling environment

In non-store retailing, atmospherics are more restricted than in stores, concentrating largely on the visual elements, as these retailing methods are more limited in their ability to stimulate the full range of senses. Etailers have the advantage of being able to provide a large amount of visual and aural information at relatively low cost in comparison to stores. Figure 9.17 shows an example of graphic design for in-store promotional materials and web design by design company Rubber Cheese to form a consistent online/bricks-and-mortar brand image for Cambridge-based shoe retailer Modish (see www.modishonline.co.uk). Another non-store distribution channel is via catalogues and, while this market is gradually diminishing in comparison to the rise of online sales, catalogue retailing has much in common with online sales, and is at the time of writing still a viable distribution channel. Websites and catalogues can portray products in realistic (and often idealised) settings via the medium of photography. The quality of paper and the type of binding selected for a catalogue can also be tangible, tactile cues to consumers which help to communicate the retailer's brand image. Despite their lack of premises and specialist design facilities, non-store retailers can occasionally have advantages over the store environment. For example, market stalls can sometimes create strong atmospheric retail experiences for customers, offering a sense of being part of a community.

There are various similarities between the environment in bricks-and-mortar stores and non-store retailers. Multichannel retailers need to develop the retail environment to convey a consistent brand image throughout its distribution channels. For example, multichannel

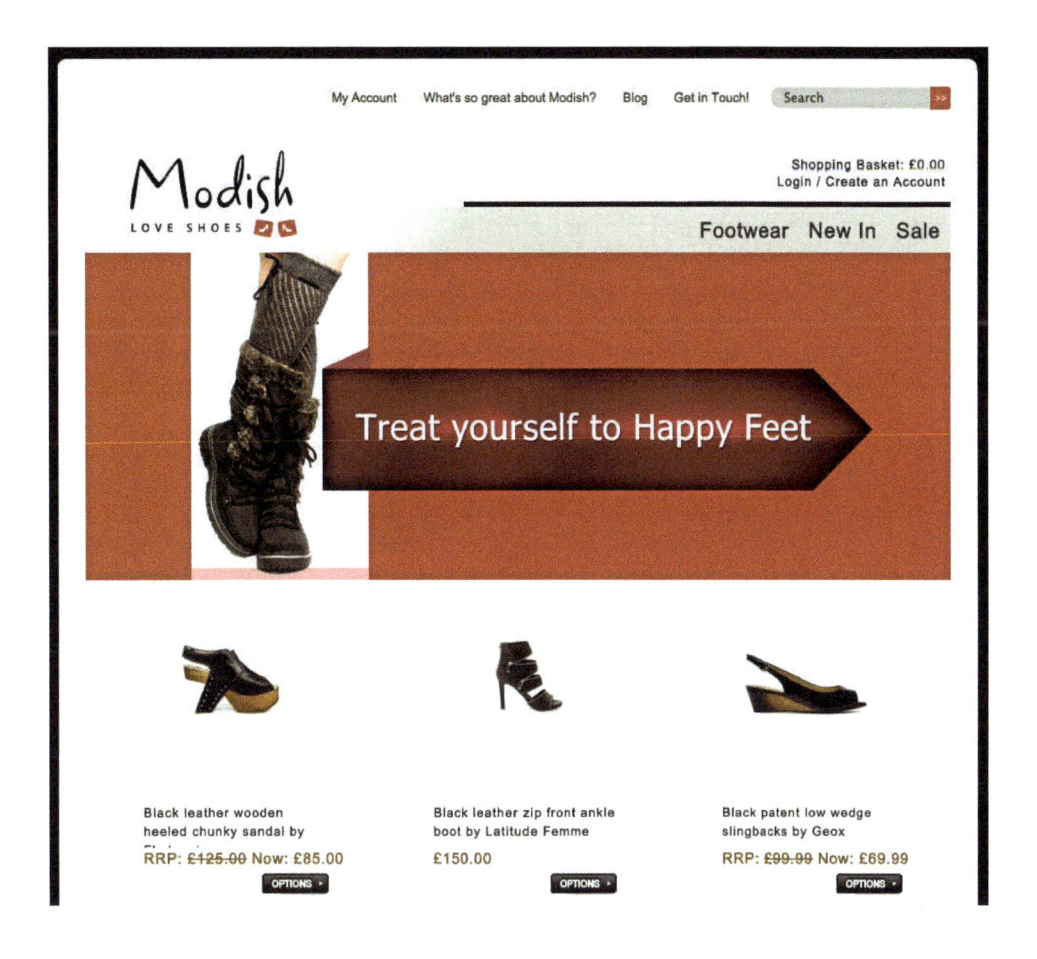

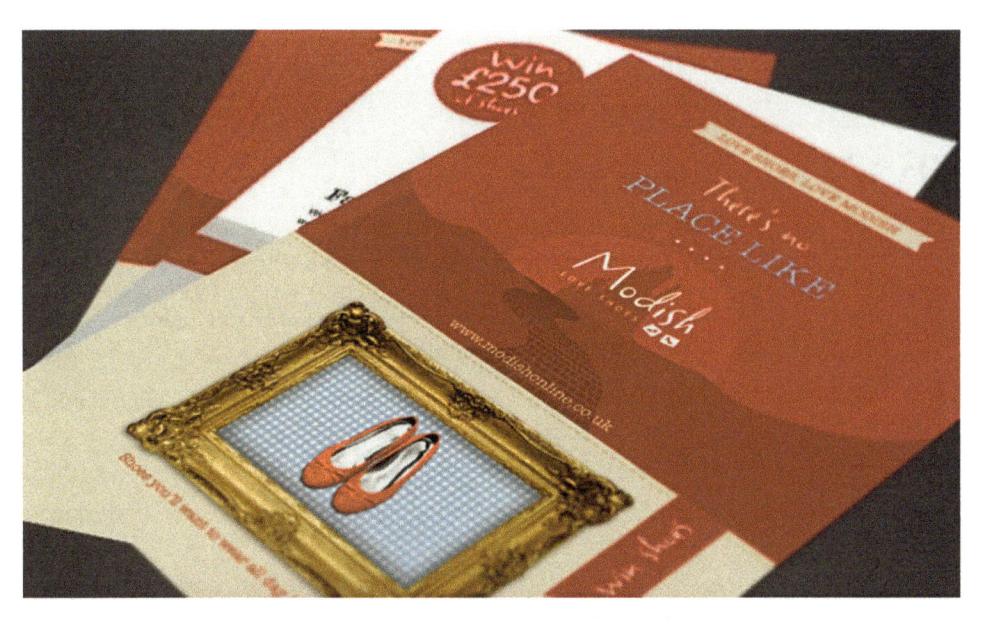

Figure 9.17 Logo, website and promotional material design for Modish Shoes
Source: Rubber Cheese Design

clothing retailer 'All Saints' uses a radio station on its website, playing the same type of music as its stores, to try to recreate the store environment online through both visual and aural techniques. Transactional websites and catalogues are both forms of home shopping (see Chapter 11 Multichannel retailing). It is important that the presentation of the website is consistent with the retailer's marketing mix and brand image. The home page or cover performs the same function as the store exterior and the standard format of the page is equivalent to the interior store design. Online VM relates to how the products are photographed and positioned on the page. The order in which products are placed on a page has a similar effect to products being positioned towards the front or back of stores, those in a more prominent position often achieving higher sales volume. Presenting two-dimensional images is similar to placing products on shelves and 3D rotations on websites allow complete views of products to be seen, in the same way as freeform layouts do in stores. Retailers employ specialist web designers to create their websites or art directors to devise catalogue layouts, who liaise with retail marketers to achieve the desired style of presentation. Clear, detailed photographs help to sell home shopping products effectively and a zoom function helps to show the texture of the materials, to compensate for the lack of tactility and minimise product return rates. Optical retailer Vision Express overcomes the drawback of not being able to try on glasses online by allowing customers to upload photos of themselves via the retailer's website, to which images of glasses can be added or a realistic view of the products (Vision Express, 2014).

Etail checkouts and catalogue order forms can be designed to make payment quick and straightforward for customers, such as using the minimum number of clicks on a website, thereby lowering barriers to purchasing. A study of VM in relation to US etailers revealed that consumers were disappointed with the presentation of products on selected websites (Khakimdjanovaa and Park, 2005). The results showed that etailers without stores make more use of 3D product images, possibly because they do not have the option of presenting their products three-dimensionally in stores, and customers were found to prefer this approach.

CHAPTER SUMMARY

Design and layout are particularly important factors in the 'place' and 'promotion' elements of the marketing mix for all types of retailers, forming part of the overall brand image. Design and layout apply to both the exterior and interior of the store, the home page and web pages of an etailer or the cover and inside pages of a catalogue.

- Stores can have a traditional, open, semi-open or funnel entrance. Store windows can be either open-backed or closed.
- The main options of store layout are grid, freeform and boutique.
- Interior design for stores includes choice of fixtures that include lighting, flooring, walls and décor.
- The main fittings used for store layout are counters, presentation cases, gondolas, tables, racks, shelves, mirrors and mannequins.
- Window display and in-store display are referred to as visual merchandising (VM).
- Signage and in-store graphics can be used to improve the customer experience in terms of information and aesthetics.

- Retail atmospherics cover four dimensions: visual, aural, olfactory and tactile. Atmospherics are becoming increasingly important, as certain bricks-and-mortar stores are seeking to differentiate themselves from etailers, to maximise the advantage of having a physical environment.
- Design and layout are also significant for non-store retailers, as the quality of images and ease of ordering affect consumers' purchase decisions.

EXERCISES AND QUESTIONS

1. Visit a shopping centre or row of shops near to where you live. Describe the interior and exterior design and layout for three to five selected stores including entrance type, fixtures and fittings. Consider the reasons behind these design and layout decisions and whether they are well suited to the types of product sold by these stores.

2. Assess which of the choices of store entrance and fittings you would consider to be most appropriate for a small-to-medium size independent store selling:
   a jewellery;
   b electrical goods;
   c men's clothing.

3. What are the advantages and disadvantages of the grid layout and the freeform layout from the perspectives of retailers and customers?

4. How can eye-tracking help retailers to improve their store design and layout? Research into the latest developments for eye-tracking and other technological innovations that could assist store design and layout.

5. Consider a bricks-and-mortar retailer with an environment which appeals to you as a consumer and that you feel is a good example of store design. Make a list of all the elements of the store that make you feel this way, grouped under the four aspects of atmospherics listed above. Which of the four aspects are the strongest in relation to this store, in your view? Explain your reasoning and consider how the other aspects could be improved to appeal to consumers more effectively.

6. Select a retail outlet or website that you feel is a bad example of retail design and/or layout. Making reference to some of the content in this chapter, offer three suggestions to improve the design or layout.

7. What are the key similarities and differences between design and layout for etailers and BM stores?

8. Select two etailers of your choice and consider how the design of their websites can encourage customers to buy. Layout; background colour; images; zoom or 3D function on photographs; product information and ease of navigation are some of the main points you should assess, but you may wish to cover other points too. You should then decide which website has been designed most effectively from a consumer perspective and list the reasons for this decision.

REFERENCES

BBC (2001) *Trouble at the Top: George, Marks and Sparks*, BBC2 TV programme broadcast on 6 December.

Bell, J. and Ternus, K. (2006) *Silent Selling*, 3rd edn, New York: Fairchild.

Bellizzi, J.A., Crowley, A.E. and Hasty, R.W. (1983) The effects of color in store design, *Journal of Retailing*, 59(1), 21–45.

Berman, B. and Evans, J.R. (2010) *Retailing Management: A Strategic Approach*, 11th edn, Upper Saddle River, NJ: Pearson.

Bone, P.F. and Ellen, P.S. (1999) Scents in the marketplace: explaining a fraction of olfaction, *Journal of Retailing*, 75(2), 243–262.

Davies, B.J. and Ward, P. (2005) Exploring the connections between visual merchandising and retail branding: an application of facet theory, *International Journal of Retail & Distribution Management*, 33(7), 505–513.

Diamond, J. and Diamond, E. (1999) *Contemporary Visual Merchandising*, New Jersey: Prentice-Hall.

Goworek, H. (2006) *Careers in Fashion and Textiles*, Oxford: Blackwell Publishing.

Greenland, S. and McGoldrick, P. (2005) Evaluating the design of retail financial service environments, *International Journal of Bank Marketing*, 23(2), 132–152.

Hui, M.K., Dube, L. and Chebat, J.C. (1997) Impact of music on consumers' reactions to waiting for services, *Journal of Retailing*, 73(1), 87–104.

Internet Retailing (2014) *UK retailers expected to make online sales of £45bn this year: study* (available online at: http://www.internetretailing.net/2014/03/uk-retailers-expected-to-make-online-sales-of-45bn-this-year-study/).

Kent, A. (2007) Creative space: design and the retail environment, *International Journal of Retail & Distribution Management*, 35(9), 734–745.

Kent, A.M. and Kirby, A.E. (2009) The design of the store and its implications for retail image, *International Review of Retail, Distribution and Consumer Research*, 19(4), 457–468.

Khakimdjanovaa, L. and Park, J. (2005) Online visual merchandising practice of apparel e-merchants, *Journal of Retailing and Consumer Services*, 12, 307–318.

Lea-Greenwood, G. (1998) Visual merchandising: a neglected area in UK fashion marketing?, *International Journal of Retail & Distribution Management*, 26(8), 324–329.

Loughborough University (2011) *Pavegen: Award-winning green graduate company celebrates major new installations*, 14 February (available online at: http://www.lboro.ac.uk/departments/lds/news/new-pavegen-installations.html).

Luna, I. (2005) *Retail Architecture and Shopping*, Rizzoli/Universal.

Lusch, R.F., Dunne, P.M. and Carver, J.R. (2011) *Introduction to Retailing*, International/7th edn, South-Western Cengage Learning.

McGoldrick, P. (2002) *Retail Marketing*, 2nd edn Maidenhead: McGraw-Hill.

Mikunda, C. (2004) *Brand Lands, Hot Spots and Cool Cases*, London: Kogan Page.

Mintel (2010) *Clothing Retailing UK*, London: Mintel.

Parsons, A.G. (2009) Use of scent in a naturally odourless store, *International Journal of Retail & Distribution Management*, 37(5), 440–452.

Pegler, M.J. (1998) *Visual Merchandising and Display*, 4th edn, New York: Fairchild Publications.

Pithers, E. (2011) Debenhams launches first virtual pop-up store in the UK, *The Telegraph*, 27 October (available online at: http://fashion.telegraph.co.uk/news-features/TMG8853548/Debenhams-launches-first-virtual-pop-up-store-in-the-UK.html).

Planogram Builder (2014) *Planogram Online Visual Merchandising and Planogram Software* (available online at: http://www.planogrambuilder.com/).

Quartier, K., Vanrie, J. and Van Cleempoel, K. (2011) Experimental retail design research: a designer's perspective with lighting as a case, *1st International Colloquium on Global Design and Marketing*, University of Lincoln, 9–10 December 2011.

Retail Innovation (2013) *Uniqlo's Magic Mirror*, Retail Innovation (available online at: http://retail-innovation.com/uniqlos-magic-mirror/).

Scamell-Katz, S. (2012) *The Art of Shopping: How and Why We Buy*, London: LID.

Thompson, V. (2012) Web Watch, *Retail Week*, 9 March, p. 26.

Turley, L.W. and Chebat, J.-C. (2002) Linking retail strategy atmospheric design and shopping behaviour, *Journal of Marketing Management*, 18, 125–44.

Underhill, P. (2009) *Why We Buy: The Science of Shopping*, New York: Simon and Schuster.

Varley, R. (2006) *Retail Product Management*, 2nd edn, London: Routledge.

Varley, R. and Rafiq, M. (2004) *Principles of Retail Management*, London: Palgrave Macmillan.

Vision Express (2014) (available online at: www.visionexpress.com).

FURTHER READING

Burrows, D. (2014) Can a store redesign increase sales? *Marketing Week*, 9 April (available online at: www.marketingweek.co.uk/analysis/marketing-tactics/retail/can-a-store-redesign-increase-sales/4009944.article).

Joy, A., Wang, J.J., Chan, T.S., Sherry Jr., J.F. and Cui, G. (2014) M(Art)Worlds: consumer perceptions of how luxury brand stores become art institutions, *Journal of Retailing* (available online 25 February 2014, DOI: 10.1016/j.jretai.2014.01.002).

Kent, A.M. and Kirby, A.E. (2009) The design of the store and its implications for retail image, *International Review of Retail, Distribution and Consumer Research*, 19(4), 457–468.

Newman, A.J. and Foxall, G.R. (2003) In-store customer behaviour in the fashion sector: some emerging methodological and theoretical directions, *International Journal of Retail & Distribution Management*, 31(11), 591–600.

Retail Innovation (website of UK-based retail expert Craig Smith) retail-innovation.com

Visual Merchandising and Store Design (US trade journal) vmsd.com.

Case study

Anthropologie moves out of London

Fashion and homewares retailer Anthropologie has opened its first English store outside London. But will its aspirational and arty ambience work away from the capital? When the first Anthropologie store opened in the UK back in 2009, the arrival of the more grown-up format from parent group URBN Inc., which also operates Urban Outfitters, was a big deal. At the time, the distinguishing point of the Regent Street store was a massive living wall of plants, which continues to 'live' in the staircase atrium. That and vintage tables acting as fixtures which could also be purchased attracted much interest. Four years on and Anthropologie has bedded down as far as London is concerned and, with a second store on the King's Road and one in Edinburgh, it has made progress – albeit perhaps not quite at the speed that was originally talked about. In April 2013, however, the retailer opened its fourth UK store in Guildford, Surrey.

Pay for the display

Located on cobbled Guildford High Street, the shop, which has a selling area of about 10,500 sq ft, is on the site of a former Habitat and trades from two floors. There is nothing to indicate the property's former occupant and in the 16 weeks that URBN chief operating officer Andrew McLean says the store has taken to create, the interior has been completely stripped out and remodelled. McLean says Habitat had actually managed to 'close down quite a lot of the selling area' and that the Anthropologie store design team, which created the template for this shop at the US headquarters, has done everything from relocating the staircase to installing new floors. It has also divided the space into rooms on the ground floor thanks to the creation of two large square arches that allow views through the space, and which also mean the shop is not a big white box.

The ground floor is predominantly about homewares, some apparel and accessories, while upstairs its clothing and a cast-iron four-poster bed in its own see-into room. All of which will be familiar to those who have visited the London stores, as will the merchandising techniques. Country manager Gisela Garcia Escuela says that the product mix in Anthropologie is 'around 60% apparel, 30% homewares and the rest is accessories'. The majority of the display fixtures are pieces of reclaimed vintage furniture that have been stripped and left untreated. They are for sale as well as the merchandise that is piled onto them. 'It's actually a very good business', says McLean, standing in front of a long, snaking Art Nouveau display cabinet in dark wood priced at £16,000. It, in fact, is the most expensive piece of furniture in the store and would require a very large house to accommodate it. It provides a focal point on the ground floor opposite the cash desk and Garcia Escuela says that she hopes it doesn't get sold because it helps to define the mid-shop area. Elsewhere on the ground floor the furniture-cum-display vehicles help to break up the space and all of them are heavily merchandised.

Art and installations

There is also the usual Anthropologie feature at the front of the shop, designed to provide a visual introduction to what lies beyond. This takes the form of a cone, created by threads that reach from a circular plate on the floor to a single point on the ceiling. It is an expensive and somewhat extravagant use of space in a store as it occupies a fair amount of the mid-shop in the prime selling area – just inside the entrance. However, given that Anthropologie is about adding value to merchandise by creating an appropriate environment with a mix of installations, artwork and a washed-out colour palette on the walls, it makes sense. The floors are worth noting too. In this store, the ground floor's zones are demarcated by a grey tiled surface, a herringbone wooden floor and then an area that is formed of reclaimed wood. Shoppers may not consciously notice the change from one area to the next, but they will probably be aware that this is a store formed of distinct zones.

The right demographic

The upper floor, where there is a lot of natural daylight, is reached via a long, dark-wood staircase. The wall to the side of the staircase has an abstract painting on it and the sense on reaching the top is of an art gallery rather than a store. The question is will the format work outside London? Garcia Escuela is clear: 'It's Surrey. It's a London customer and we know who this is'. McLean adds: 'The demographic is bang on and is exactly what we want'. He says that in the long term the view at Anthropologie is that there is room for 'around 40 stores in the UK'. The roll-out is considerably slower than was originally talked about when the retailer arrived in 2009, but McLean is quick to point out that stores will only be opened in appropriate locations as sites become available. 'If the right space presents itself, then we'll go with it', he says.

Demand for more

In spite of the distinctly aspirational nature of the product pricing in these stores, McLean says that the anticipated payback on any shop is two years. 'We've never been hurt by putting the capital into any store', he says. 'You have to invest and it has to look good. When you under-do it, she notices'. The Guildford store is almost like a London satellite, at least as far as Garcia Escuela and McLean are concerned, and it seems probable it will succeed. McLean says that one of the unintended advantages of a gradual opening programme has been pent-up desire. 'The demand for the brand across Europe is unabated', he maintains.

There will be another Anthropologie store opening before Christmas – a pop-up in Westfield London. It is to be assumed that both Westfield and Anthropologie will be aiming for it to be sufficiently robust to become a permanent part of the centre's offer – alongside the Urban Outfitters store in this location, which is also on the site of a former Habitat shop. Anthropologie is, both in terms of price and appeal, a niche offer. But to judge by the number of shoppers who had beaten a path to its door on a wet Tuesday in Guildford, it has plenty of fans.

Source: Retail Week (2013) Store Gallery: Anthropologie moves out of London with new shop in Guildford, *Retail Week*, 4 November.

DISCUSSION QUESTIONS

1 How have the four elements of retail atmosphere been applied to the store described in the case?

2 Compare the websites for Anthropologie and Urban Outfitters (or the stores if you are able to visit both of them). Which aspects of layout and product assortment do they have in common and what are the main differences between the two retailers?

3 What are the key points of Anthropologie's store design and layout that make it different to competitors such as furniture stores and department stores?

CHAPTER 10

Retail customer service

Sheilagh Resnick, Nottingham Business School

Learning objectives

After completing this chapter you should be able to:

- recognise theories relating to services;
- understand service quality models;
- recognise the role of the service encounter;
- understand the meaning of service culture and the principles of service recovery;
- examine how retail customer service will be delivered in the future.

Introduction

Retailing is a world-wide phenomenon and integral to most economies. The economic and social importance of the UK retail sector for example is undisputed; the sector is the third largest in the world and in 2012 accounted for 6 per cent of the country's Gross Domestic Product (GDP) and for employment of 10 per cent of the country's workforce. Around three million people work in retail, the largest private sector employer in the UK, accounting for 10.5 per cent of total employment. Retail employment is far more flexible than most other sectors and has a much higher proportion of part-time workers. Many members of this workforce are employed in delivering a service to customers either through face-to-face contact in shops and stores or increasingly via the phone or the internet.

The traditional 'bricks-and-mortar' retail sector now faces increasing levels of disruption from online and mobile innovations, which impact on consumer perspectives on what has been the accepted retail model of the face-to-face service encounter experience. These changes are not unique to the UK but are occurring on a global basis. Some of the key changes in retail are the rise of the technology-savvy customer; the spreading fad and fashion-consciousness, the growing importance of experimental shopping and increasing consumer assertiveness. Multichannel retailing, by which shoppers can purchase across a number of different retail channels typically online or via the physical store, is reshaping the traditional retail experience (Dugal *et al.*, 2012). In addition, an increase in the use of automated self-checkout systems in retailing and retail services now enables the customer to complete the purchase themselves, thereby reducing the need to encounter service staff or engage in a face-to-face customer service experience. These are just a few of the many changes occurring in retail that are influencing how customer service is perceived and delivered. This chapter will explore some of these changes but it is useful to look at the basic premise of retail customer service as a starting point.

The term 'Customer Service' is a broad definition that can encompass both the technical process of **service delivery** and a functional evaluation of how well the service has been delivered. Customer service is the term most commonly used within retail organisations to describe the interface between the customer and the organisation, the service provider, but is also used to describe a department whose responsibility it is to provide assistance to customers with problems or complaints. There are a number of terms used to describe the customer–organisation interface, e.g. customer relations, the customer experience or after-sales service, but in successful retail companies the responsibility for providing a service to customers should reside with every person in the organisation. Such organisations may also have a 'customer service' or 'customer relations' department but the culture of the organisation is such that everyone in the organisation is responsible for serving the customer. This may not be through direct contact with a customer but through providing a supporting service to someone who is directly serving the customer. The concept of service and service culture will be explored in this chapter but as every definition of goods and services involves a customer it may be useful to define the meaning of a customer in a retail context, which is:

- a person who buys, especially one who buys from or patronises an establishment or organisation regularly;
- any person with whom a service provider or seller has dealings.

As retail organisations have found it harder to differentiate their offering through their assortment of goods, the interaction between retail staff and customers becomes more important as it can represent the means by which retailers establish relationships with their customers. Retail organisations can distinguish their service through their customer-facing staff, which, unlike other elements of the retail marketing mix such as the product, the price or the place, cannot be easily replicated by competitors.

Retail sales staff can also exert a major influence upon retail image because in their search for information, customers draw upon their experiences with sales staff to help constitute their buying decisions.

Service staff can play an important role in influencing customers' evaluation of service quality delivery as the level of service offered, combined with other factors such as physical facilities, merchandise, post-transaction satisfaction and store atmosphere, collectively create a store's image (Lindquist, 1974). Many retail organisations have looked increasingly towards a service-led offering as the customer and service staff interaction has assumed greater prominence and a number of high profile retailers, such as John Lewis Partnership, Boots UK and Nordstrom in the US, have established and maintained a position of ongoing strength by focusing on this particular aspect of their overall retail offering and making the 'people dimension' of the marketing mix a major focus of retail competitive endeavour. In order to understand retail customer service some of the key service concepts need to be explored to understand just what is meant by services and a service delivery.

Characteristics of services

Services are very important to a country's economy and in the UK, for example, services make up almost 80 per cent of the GDP. Generally, services fall into a number of sectors such as professional services, which incorporates banking, law and insurance; social and personal services such as restaurants, childcare and hospitality; retail services, which typically are shop or goods-based services; infrastructure services such as communications and transport; and public services, which are governmental services but can also include areas such as education and healthcare. The nature of services is very complex and there are many different ways of attempting to define what is meant by the term services. A simple definition is as a process, which transforms inputs such as labour, skills, materials into outputs, services and Figure 10.1 illustrates this in a diagrammatic way.

Services are less distinct than products as they are intangible in nature and presented as an activity, analysis or action performed for someone's benefit (Kotler, 1991). Services have a number of characteristics (Parasuraman *et al.*, 1985) which distinguish them from products:

- *intangibility*: services cannot be touched or held in a physical sense;
- *simultaneous production/consumption*: the service is delivered to the customer who utilises the service at the same time;
- *time perishability*: services are performed only once and cannot be stored as an inventory;
- *variability*: delivery will vary from person to person;
- *flexibility*: services can be adjusted to individual customers;
- *customer participation*: customers frequently participate in the delivery of a service;
- *labour intensiveness*: services involve a high level of personal interaction between the service provider and the customer.

The factor that distinguishes services from goods is that they are usually people- or equipment-based and they typically require the presence and participation of a customer.

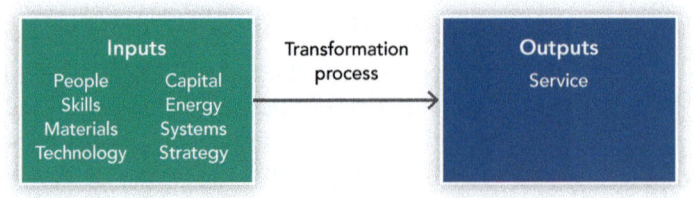

Figure 10.1 Service production as a process

One definition of a service that tries to encapsulate its many characteristics is as something which 'can be bought and sold but which you cannot drop on your foot' and it is this inability to touch or look at services before they have been consumed, which makes a service a subjective and almost abstract concept. There are many terms to describe the process of delivering a service to customers and while some are used to define processes such as the 'service encounter' or **service recovery** other definitions seek to evaluate the standard of the service being delivered. One of the core service concepts is that of service quality since, if an organisation does not deliver a service quality, customers will become dissatisfied and fail to repurchase.

CONSUMER ENGAGEMENT IN AN INDEPENDENT STORE
By Clare Rayner, retail expert, organiser of The Retail Conference and Future High Street Summit

This case demonstrates the importance of the consumer experience when it comes to attracting, converting and retaining customers and is based on Clare's experience with clients. An independent children's book shop was struggling to survive, and like many high-street retailers spiralling costs and reducing footfall were having a massive impact on their ability to trade profitably. Customers who did visit the shop did not convert their interest in products into purchases, in fact many used the shop to experience the product which they later bought online, perhaps from Amazon or other outlets. This is known as 'showrooming' and is a disaster for smaller independents who share their product knowledge but fail to secure the sale. Something had to be done. The owners, passionate about local families and aware of the importance of reading to stimulate imagination in children, took a brave decision. They decided to transform their business from being 'just another shop' to being a social hub, a place for families to come and enjoy books. In this last ditch attempt to turn around their failing business they added a small café, ran regular children's story times, colouring contests and added some toys for kids to play with in the shop, which were also made available for sale. The whole customer experience changed. The store was now an experiential, social, fun place to go and not just a book shop. There was also more for consumers to buy too, they'd added extra, high margin items to their offer (café items), a wider variety (toys) and became more of a place to go to than a just shop.

The business transformed. They'd recognised something many major high-street chains fail to recognise – the changed demands and behaviours of a

Clare Rayner, retail expert, organiser of The Retail Conference and Future High Street Summit
Source: with permission from Clare Rayner

NEW consumer. They achieved a business turnaround because they recognised that busy consumers either buy from the cheapest/ most convenient provider (in particular with items that are the same regardless of retailer – such as books, games, music etc.) or they buy from places where they have great experiences, a place they care about, a place they want to support because it offers them so much more than commodities. The fact is that when high-street retailers can't compete on price they need to compete on service and on experience. The new model of consumer engagement is either transactional (based on price) or experiential (where the proposition extends far beyond shopping and becomes social and fun.)

This children's bookshop epitomises what's needed to turn around the fortunes of ailing retailers today. Major chains are slower to respond as change is harder to implement in large, established businesses, but they can do it. Smaller, agile businesses may well lead the way, however, in transforming the high streets, giving the new consumer more of what they want, and bring a new life and vibrancy to our town centres.

www.retailchampion.co.uk; www.retailconference.co.uk; www.futurehighstreet.co.uk; Twitter:@clarerayner

Service quality models

Service quality is one of the most researched concepts of customer service as it is maintained that for retail organisations 'quality is the lifeblood that brings increased patronage, competitive advantage and long term profitability' according to Clow and Vorhies (1993: 22). Christian Gronroös was one of the first academics from the 'Nordic School of Marketing' to combine the two notions of service and quality. His model of service quality (1984), shown in Figure 10.2 is based on the premise that two components exist, technical quality, which is *what* is achieved and functional quality, which is *how* it is achieved. Service quality is the difference between the expectations and perceptions of these two processes. Gronroös defined customer expectations of service as a function of corporate image created through advertising, price and public relations. Perceptions of service were as a result of how both the functional and technical aspects of the service performed, which endorsed the quality element as being integral to the overall service delivery. An example of the relationship of technical and functional quality can be illustrated by a visit to the hairdresser. You can assess the technical quality of your haircut by the appearance

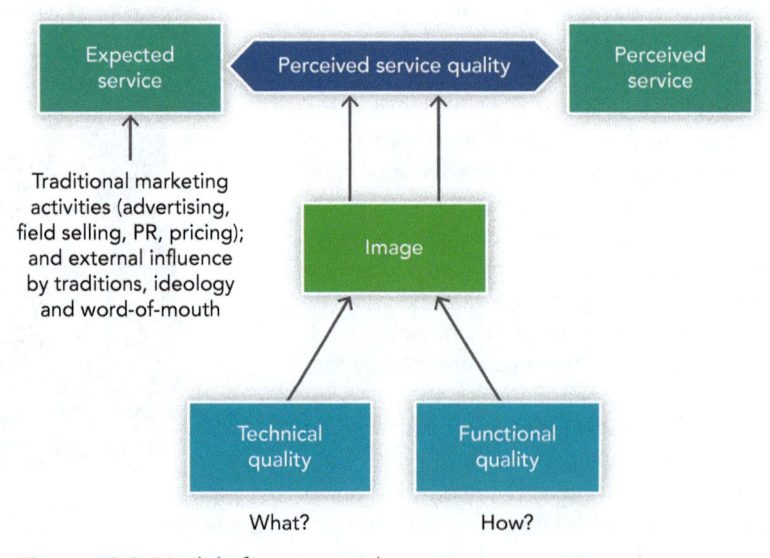

Figure 10.2 Model of service quality
Source: Gronroös (1984)

of the salon in terms of cleanliness, a pleasant environment and good range of equipment; by the way in which your hair is cut and the final result of the finished haircut. But the general attitude of the hairdresser, his/her manner and how knowledgeable and friendly he/she is towards you, are components of the functional quality of the service. For most customers both the technical and the functional delivery of a haircut need to be delivered if they are to perceive that they have received a service quality experience.

The nature of retail services infers that people on both sides of the service delivery will be heterogeneous and that service delivery will vary from provider to provider, from customer to customer and also from episode to episode (Parasuraman *et al.*, 1985). Because of this, retailers' service aspirations cannot always be guaranteed, and what the retailer hopes to achieve may be different to what the customer actually perceives is delivered. It is broadly believed, though, that a high level of retail service quality is necessary to create and sustain competitive advantage (Dabholkar *et al.*, 1996) and there is a general consensus that service quality can be conceptualised as the resultant of a comparison between expectations and perceptions of a service-related activity (Grönroos, 1984; Parasuraman *et al.*, 1985; 1988).

The idea that concepts of expectations and perceptions were intrinsic to service quality formed the basis of the service quality model of Americans Parasuraman *et al.* (1985), who defined service quality as the provision of a service in meeting or exceeding customer expectations. This premise was developed into a model, which suggests that four factors and five service quality dimensions shape customer expectations (see Figure 10.3). The service quality model is constructed around expectations and perceptions theory from research undertaken by Parasuraman *et al.* in 1985 and later refined by Zeithaml *et al.*, in 1990. Their research was undertaken across a number of retail service industries such as retail banking and insurance. Their findings suggested that customers evaluate an organisation's service quality by comparing service performance with expectations of what they think the performance should be and that four factors and five service quality dimensions shape customer expectations. The four factors influencing expectations of a service provision were: (a) word-of-mouth; (b) personal needs; (c) past experience; and (d) external communication.

The same research revealed that the five service dimensions, which are detailed in Table 10.1, were the most appropriate attributes for assessing quality in a broad variety of services.

From the research, a measurement instrument SERVQUAL was designed in the form of a questionnaire to evaluate service quality and service quality gaps as perceived by customers and managers. Service quality gaps occur when customer and manager perceptions

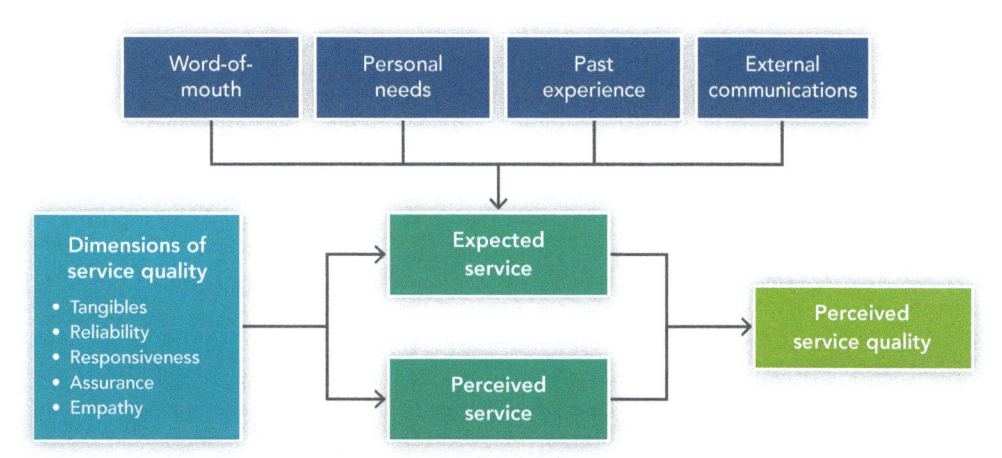

Figure 10.3 Service quality model (SERVQUAL)

Source: Parasuraman et al., 1988

Table 10.1 The dimensions and definitions of service quality

Dimension	Definition
Tangibles	Appearance of physical facilities, equipment, personnel and communication materials
Reliability	Ability to perform the promised service dependably and accurately
Responsiveness	Willingness to help customers and provide prompt service
Assurance	Knowledge and courtesy of employees and their ability to convey trust and confidence
Empathy	Caring, individualised attention the firm provides to its customers

Source: adapted from Parasuraman et al., 1988

do not meet their expectations. The SERVQUAL instrument is a quantitative, diagnostic instrument, which, if used properly, enables managers to identify systematic service quality shortfalls or what has been termed the 'gap analysis'.

There has been extensive debate on the role of expectations in service quality and how expectations are acquired. General works on customer expectations define it as beliefs about product characteristics or attributes. Olsen and Dover (1979) suggest that beliefs are defined as links between an object and attributes and customer expectation can, in this context, be viewed as a belief about a future event based on information gathered by the customer. Carman (1990) defines expectations as attitudes, which customers carry with them when assessing service encounters. Oliver (1980) developed the concept of a 'disconfirmation paradigm' based on the premise that customers carry certain expectations. If expectations are confirmed during the service encounter, the result is either acceptable quality or customer satisfaction. Alternatively, if there is a positive or negative 'gap' between expectations and perceptions, i.e. disconfirmation, the result is either perceived good or bad quality and customer satisfaction or dissatisfaction. The disconfirmation theory tries to distinguish between service quality and customer satisfaction as there are schools of thought that these are related but different constructs (Cronin and Taylor, 1992). Oliver (1993) contests that service quality can be 'perceived', i.e. a high-end clothes boutique can be regarded as being of high quality even if the customer has not visited it but customer satisfaction is purely experiential in that you cannot be satisfied unless you have experienced a service or product; that is, you have visited the boutique yourself.

CUSTOMER SERVICE AT JOHN LEWIS

John Lewis Department Stores is a retail chain operating throughout the UK. The first John Lewis store was opened in 1864 in Oxford Street London and the company is owned by the John Lewis Partnership, a structure which incentivises all employees to deliver service quality across every aspect of its customer offer. The chain is known for its policy of 'Never Knowingly Undersold', which has been in use since 1925 and which commits to match competitor prices on the same goods. John Lewis meets and often exceeds customer expectations through its long-established reputation for offering a wide selection of high-quality goods and services, positive word-of-mouth recommendations from customer to customer and by using engaging advertising and communication messages (see photo opposite of Managing Director Andy Street). It meets customer perceptions of the shopping experience through clean, well-organised stores and smartly attired service staff (tangibles), through the consistent standard of its goods and service delivery (reliability), through its well-staffed

Source: with permission from Paul Grover/Rex Features

customer service points and next-day delivery internet sales orders (responsiveness) by employing a high level of knowledgeable staff particularly for technology and electrical goods (assurance) and ensuring the staff deliver friendly and courteous service staff (empathy). John Lewis Department Stores are currently performing well in a depressed retail market but the challenge for the company is to continue to outperform retailing as a whole and to maintain their service quality delivery.

A traditional means of delivering service for retail organisations has been through the interaction of their service staff with their customers. However, realising full service potential within retail settings can be problematic since this is a highly complex environment that relies on a mix of factors including goods, price and service (Mehta et al., 2000). Customer evaluation of retail organisation performance may depend on goods quality and process quality, which encapsulates service and imagery (Burton et al., 2001). Traditionally, services are highly participative and high-street retailers especially, can be generically characterised by its relatively high level of customer/employee interaction known as the service encounter.

The service encounter

A service encounter can be defined as 'face-to-face interactions between a buyer and a seller in a service setting' (Solomon *et al.*, 1985). What takes place in these encounters is communication and exchange of information and knowledge, usually but not exclusively, with a human being. The service encounter will usually involve customer participation in the process and the information the customer provides to the service provider can influence the quality of service the client may receive. This information can be delivered in a physical form as well as through a verbal exchange. Service encounters are also shaped by customer perceptions of the service providers and what occurs during these encounters is central to total service delivery perceptions. They are, effectively, the bridge between buyer and seller, and embody relations with service employees, interaction with other customers and reactions to the retail environment (Harris and Baron, 2004). From an employee perspective, service encounter quality can be assessed across a range of factors including competence, listening skills, dedication level and personal communication including exchange of information and knowledge. Studies suggest that service encounter quality works on a relational basis whereby the various dimensions of the interaction evolve into a consistent pattern of performance, perceptions and attitudes that ultimately represent the 'personality' of the relationship (Svensson, 2006) and customers have come to expect a conversational context from a service encounter that will involve retail service staff. The quality of customer service staff's performance is assessed by certain retailers by employing 'mystery shoppers' who shop anonymously to test the service quality offered in stores (see Mystery shopping vignette below).

The physical appearance of service staff also plays a key role. Good service encounter quality is achieved by employing customer-facing staff who are extrovert, have agreeable personalities and have a high level of customer empathy (Hurley, 1998). Good social skills such as 'smiles easily' and 'is naturally enthusiastic'; good communication skills, in particular the ability to listen well and interpret information are essential combined with a high level of self-esteem in terms of appearance and confidence. Further studies suggest that perceptions and attitude reflect the level of competence by which the service encounter is delivered (Wong and Sohal, 2003). Service heterogeneity, however, means that customers will experience differently constituted encounters on different occasions, and the inseparable nature of service suggests that a poor service encounter will substantially influence perceptions of the total service experience, both in the present and the future (Baron *et al.*, 2008). The way in which the service encounter is perceived, and the impact this has upon customer perspectives on store image and service quality, can also be indirectly impacted by the nature of goods on offer, the price at which those goods are sold and the economic and social climate pertaining at the time. Case study 1 at the end of the chapter poses some questions around these different attributes.

MYSTERY SHOPPING

The role of the mystery shopper offers some insights into retailers' requirements of their customer-facing staff. Michelle Sutton has been employed by various companies as a mystery shopper, to assess the quality of service provided by retailers. She has worked in this role on a part-time basis for 18 years, and has found that it fitted in effectively alongside bringing up her three children. Michelle started her career as an accounts administrator before being recruited by a market research agency and being trained by QRS Market Research. Mystery shoppers are usually employed on an ad hoc basis, with a fee for each job plus expenses and are not required to be graduates. People of all ages and socio-economic groups are required, e.g. an agency could be looking for a woman aged 40 to 50 who needs a car servicing, so they'll seek someone who fits into these criteria.

Michelle's responsibilities can vary, with retailers setting different criteria depending on what they wish to investigate. Mystery shopper visits are usually arranged to enable the retailer to evaluate the level of customer service, but they can also be used for other purposes, such as to gauge customer perceptions of the store environment or product quality. Michelle normally works with a supervisor from a Market Research agency, commissioned by the retailer she is asked to visit, to enable the store to receive an independent, objective opinion. However, Michelle has also worked directly with a supermarket for four years on a specific project. Her job is currently limited to one county, but she is considering working further afield as a mystery shopper for hotels now that her children have grown up.

Michelle visits a wide range of retailers in her role, from pharmacists to supermarkets and restaurants. For example, for one job she was asked to eat in at a fast-food restaurant, then buy a drive-through meal at the same branch to check that the food was of the same quality and temperature. On another occasion she had to bandage her hand before going to a supermarket with her son in a pushchair and ask for assistance, to check that the staff helped her with her packing and leaving the store. She was asked to assess whether staff behaved in a caring way without being patronising. She has also had to check whether staff in a hardware store were willing to sell knives to underage customers, as this is illegal and would result in the retailer being fined. Also, she was once given the task of visiting three garages in a day to assess how they treated a woman buying a car by herself. Michelle explains here what she looks for when assessing customer service quality:

> All of my paperwork starts with 'did they make eye contact' so that seems to be what employers want from their staff. Undivided attention has to be something I look for and they have to interact and be interested in you as a customer. When they say 'Do you need any help with your packing?' some people say it so uniformly, whereas it's better to tailor it to the client who's in front of them. Sometimes it's almost as though people have been practising all week before I visit, such as being able to reel off all the calories or additives for meals in a restaurant. I've never had anyone being awful while mystery shopping which makes me think they're really on their toes at the time you're going in. I've been into the same shop a week later though and the same person could be chatting to their friends and making you wait.

As well as buying products, Michelle's role involves assessing customer service when returning items, e.g. by taking goods back without a receipt to check whether staff did this without quibbling (this may depend on the store's returns policy). She explains: 'I assess both sides, so it covers the whole process, to see how the returns procedure works. You want it to be quite a nice experience because it still falls within the retail umbrella, so it gives people an opinion.'

Michelle says that the main criteria required for a mystery shopper are to meet targets, read the brief thoroughly and return the information on time. A good knowledge of the local area and a driving licence are also necessary. Michelle considers communication, self-motivation, organisational and creative skills to be important in her role, as well as using computers to receive and input information. She says 'you need to act out a scenario and this can sometimes be uncomfortable, but you become a bit of an actress. If you're ever found out, you just need to walk away, although this has never happened to me'. She recommends that mystery shoppers shouldn't be too selective about which projects to accept, otherwise the agency may not offer them as much work in the future. Mystery shopping is a role which can potentially fit alongside being a student or looking after a family. If you are interested in being recruited for this role, you could either approach a market research agency or large retailers as they sometimes employ mystery shoppers directly.

Electronic service delivery

Many retail goods and services are now being delivered electronically as multichannel retailing becomes ever more popular and challenges the concept of person-to-person customer service. Multichannel retailing by which shoppers can purchase across a number of different retail channels, which are typically online or through a physical store, is reshaping the traditional retail experience (Dugal *et al.*, 2012). Amazon is seen as the model of best practice but John Lewis, Debenhams and Burberry are also good examples.

The move away from the traditional face-to-face retail customer service delivery means that customer service is increasingly being delivered remotely or electronically, typically through call centres. In the UK the first call centre opened in 1985 and it is estimated that there are now over 6000. Call centres are essentially a work environment in which the main business is mediated by computer and telephone-based technologies that enable the efficient functioning of incoming (and outgoing) calls. They are structured to allow increased and better access to services for customers (inbound); provide more efficiency for organisations, deliver more of a service provision potential, both for customers and organisations and enhance sales opportunities for organisations (outbound).

Call centres work through a number of systems and technologies, which produce reliable, rapid, and low-cost service results with volume of contact transactions often a key requirement. The increase of retail products and services through the internet has seen the balance of business generated through call centres changing and moving away from phone-based contact towards email and internet, as shown in Figure 10.4.

Staffing call centres in order to deliver good customer service is challenging as they are typically staffed by temporary or part-time workers. The interface with the customer can often be transactional rather than relational, which together with an emphasis on the pressure to deliver a fast customer interface can result in conflict, boredom and depletion of emotional resource which can lead to high churn, stress-related absence, and withdrawal (Chung and Schneider, 2002). Call centres need to address how they wish to progress and decide whether they want to foster a willingness to engage with customers or just develop capacity. They also need to ask themselves whether they wish to focus on quality or quantity and to deliver more service or better service. As more people shop via the internet, organisations will have to face these issues and resolve what can be termed the 'paradox of consequences'.

As part of the technological customer service development, there is also the increasing use of automated self-checkout systems in retail stores and other retail services that enable the customer to complete the purchase themselves and which reduces the need to encounter service staff or engage in a personal service interaction. Customers are now enabled to engage in an electronic retailing process through the application of self-service technologies (SSTs) characterised as support processes that allow customers to deliver or facilitate, services themselves, and which typically involve some aspect of electronically enhanced mechanisation (Beatson et al., 2006). The development of SST technology enables organisations to change processes and provide new functional benefits for customers. SSTs appear in different forms; typical examples are booking and buying over the internet, use of automatic teller machines and self-scanning checkout and payment systems and these types of technologies are changing the traditional retail services landscape, which has relied, historically, on personal interactions between customers and service providers.

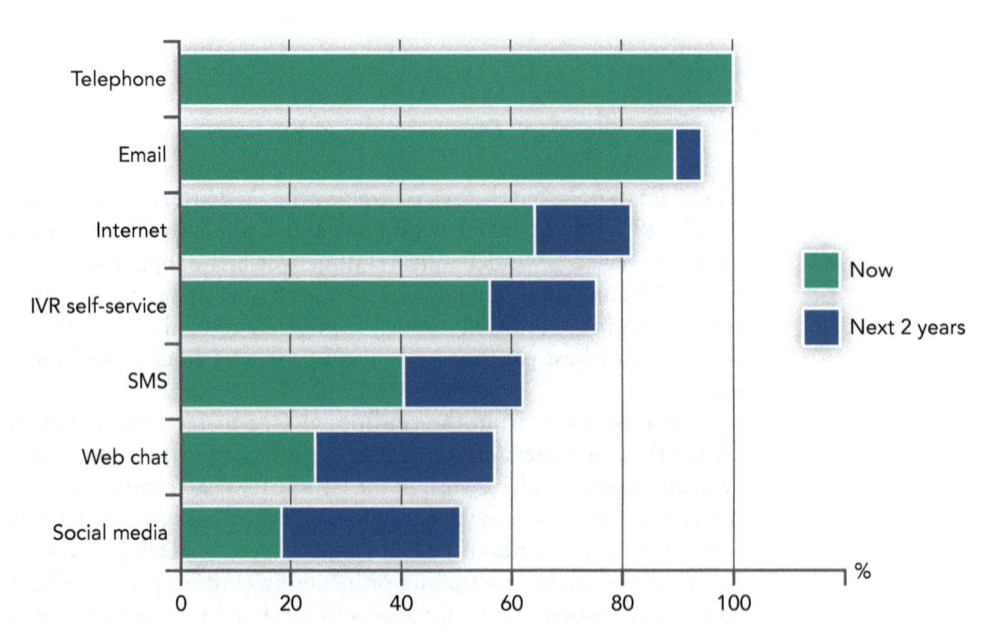

Figure 10.4 Channel use within the contact centre
Source: Dimension Data, 2011

Within the retail sector, grocery outlets were the early adopters of self-scanning checkouts but this technology has now spread to populate a wider range of retail stores including those that have established their competitive advantage via face-to-face customer service interaction. The introduction of SSTs has not been without service issues with common problems ranging from customers failing to bag items correctly to difficulties in recording items such as vegetables and bakery goods, but despite these issues, a growing number of large retailers now offer a self-service checkout option.

Good customer service does not just happen but occurs as a result of a determination by an organisation's leaders that everyone in the company should be responsible for serving the customer. This concept can only be enabled through the promulgation of an organisational service culture.

Service culture

A service culture is a necessary requirement for a retail organisation committed to the concept of delivering a high level of customer service. The term 'culture' can be used to describe the system of assumptions shared by members of the organisation, which then define its values and influences the members' perception of the correct way in which to think and behave. Culture is especially important in retail organisations because the retail service staff creates the service and if they are not service orientated some level of failure is inevitable. Service culture has been described by Albrecht (1988) as that which 'influences people to behave and relate in service-orientated ways, or customer-first ways'.

A retail service culture can evolve or there may be concerted efforts to establish a climate supportive of service through leadership, rewards and recognition processes communication, structure and language. Some characteristics of a retail service culture are outlined below.

- Managers involve customers to determine their needs through customer feedback processes.
- Customers are seen as the top priority and employees take pride in their jobs and in providing superior customer service.
- Error is perceived as an opportunity for learning and people work together to fix a problem rather than attribute blame.
- Managers lead others to assume responsibility for improvement.
- The root causes of problems are discovered and preventative measures found.
- Service staff understand the service vision and are empowered to make the vision real.
- Decisions are based on long-term strategic objectives.
- Rewards and recognition are aligned with customer needs and are frequently not financial.

Retail organisations use a number of vehicles by which to communicate the service culture. A service mission statement is often drawn up and displayed in staff rooms and in training materials. Training courses focus on the customer service ethos and customer satisfaction surveys are used to evaluate overall customer satisfaction levels and identify service staff that have shown exemplary service skills. Such staff are then recognised and rewarded. Despite an organisation's best efforts and focus on customer service delivery, service failure will, at times, occur. However, it is the ability to address the service shortfall and recover the failure that will distinguish the retailers who truly understand customer service.

HAPPYORNOT CUSTOMER SERVICE RATING SYSTEM

The HappyOrNot device helps companies to improve their service image and service performance by allowing customers to rate service at the touch of a button in store. The device aims to enhance service levels, customer satisfaction and loyalty, motivating personnel to achieve their objectives and improve their performance. The system supplies enterprise-wide service quality data quickly to support customer-focused decision-making by retailers and other services. The co-founders, Heikki Väänänen and Ville Levaniemi established the company in Finland in 2009, after they had both worked in the mobile gaming and software businesses. This shared background and business experience helped them to combine the vision of ease of usability (for end customers and clients) and added value for the retail chain, in order to make it desirable for companies to invest in the system. By the end of 2013, HappyOrNot's sales channels and customers had spread to 30 countries.

Heikki invented the HappyOrNot device, inspired by his experience as a teenager of receiving continuously poor service from a sales assistant at a computer store. This gave him the idea for an easy, direct, but anonymous feedback method to report customer service problems directly to the senior management of the whole chain, rather than just a single store, via a hotline button. Approximately 15 years later, Heikki revisited the concept, but this time with a more serious intent. His background in the gaming business along with the business network he had already established, helped the company to take off quickly in Finland. The first clients were acquired in 2009, a leading Finnish retail chain and one of the leading Finnish banks. From the 'panic button' concept, it evolved into a service providing a continuous, measurable Key Performance Indicator for retail and service chains.

The business now has over 300 retail and service chain companies as customers, including Carrefour

Source: with permission from HappyOrNot

(the world's second largest retail corporation, based in France); Delhaize (the leading supermarket chain in Benelux countries); Dixon's Retail (Europe's leading consumer electronics retailer) in seven countries in six different store chains; Decathlon (French consumer sports equipment and clothing chain); Migros (Swiss retail chain) and IKEA (in the Swedish retailer's Danish stores). HappyOrNot receives feedback about its system from clients via such channels as social media, trade events and news publications. One of the company's clients, Bent Wulff Jakobsen, Medical Director of Scandinavian Healthcare firm Aleris, says:

> The HappyOrNot device and service makes it easy for our visitors to instantly give feedback on our performance. With a simple click on a smiley button, you answer the survey question. Reports are automatically generated and delivered to our organisation to evaluate, develop, and make our performance be even better.

An advantage of the HappyOrNot device is that it uses communication methods which can be understood globally. The system is easy to use and the company has developed the software to make sure that the results are reliable, even if children play with the device, as it registers feedback only when it is in normal use. HappyOrNot concentrates on the Customer Experience Market (CEM) and its target is to be the best-known company in this industry, with plans to introduce a larger service portfolio for retailers in the longer term.

www.happy-or-not.com; https://twitter.com/happyornotcom; https://www.facebook.com/pages/HappyOrNot-Ltd/414273172016829

Service recovery

Service recovery means making an effort to return things to a normal state; to regain control or to regain something lost when things go wrong. Customer problems handled at the first point of contact can often be resolved satisfactorily with little effort or cost. Customer problems that are not given sufficient time and attention and which are left unresolved can gather momentum and grow out of all proportion and result in considerable and expense and a lost service recovery opportunity. According to Hart *et al.* (1990) the most effective way to recover from service mishaps is for workers on the front line to identify and solve the customer's problems even if doing so requires individual decision making and rule breaking. Bitner *et al.* (1990) identified service failures are falling into three main categories:

- service delivery failure, which accounted for around 43 per cent of complaints;
- unsatisfactory responses to customer needs and requests, which was estimated at 16 per cent of complaints;
- unprompted/unsolicited/unacceptable employee actions, which were around 42 per cent of complaints.

Customer responses to service failure can work on a number of levels and Buttle and Burton (2002) identified a number of differing customer responses. At the fundamental level failure is perceived as a betrayal of trust and results in the customer placing more intense focus on service delivery from the service provider. Repeated service failures contribute to a reduction in perceived value of the organisation and the customer is then faced with different causes of action. They can do nothing and carry on buying; they can practise 'negative word-of-mouth' in that they tell friends and family about their poor service experience. Alternatively, they may complain to a third party, e.g. a consumer group, or they could 'vote with their feet' and just defect to another service provider.

A study by Keaveney (1995) of 500 customers suggested that 'service failure' was implicated in 59 per cent of defections and of the sample service failure was the only reason for 45 per cent of defection. Some 75 per cent of the sample had 'complained' to friends or acquaintances but only 7 per cent had complained to the organisation. Customers frequently do not complain even if they experienced an unsatisfactory service issue because they feel it is not worth the time and trouble and will not do any good; it is perceived

Table 10.2 Percentage of critical incidents contributing to defection

Reason for service failure	%
Core service failure	44.3
Service encounter failure	34.1
Pricing	29.9
Inconvenience	20.7
Poor response to service failure	17.3
Competition	10.2
Ethical problems	7.5
Involuntary switching	6.2
Other	8.6

Source: Keaveney, 1995

as being difficult and will expose them to embarrassment and they may be made to feel responsible for the service failure. Table 10.2 details the percentages of critical incidents contributing to defection.

There are significant implications for retailers and retail services in not addressing customer complaints effectively. Increasingly consumers frame their 'corporate betrayal' to demonstrate their power, influence others and gain revenge and technology is allowing customers to communicate their dissatisfaction to a wide audience. The internet is also facilitating the growth of 'anti-brand communities' (Hollenbeck and Zinkhan, 2006) with the damage to firms as a result of negative word-of-mouth via 'high-tech' channels potentially huge. Retail organisations must establish a series of objectives for successful complaint management of which some should be as identified as:

- stabilisation of customer relationships;
- increase in purchase intensity and frequency;
- implementation of a customer-oriented strategy;
- positive word-of-mouth promotion;
- improvement of products and services;
- avoidance of switching costs;
- avoidance of the cost of disagreements;
- avoidance of other internal/external failure costs.

Service failure at some stage is inevitable but having a recovery process in place can retain customer satisfaction and loyalty. Customers need four main courses of action from a service failure. Firstly, they can be offered a 'fair fix' by which their product is replaced or refunded. Secondly, they can be treated in a caring and responsive way and for their complaint to be treated seriously. Thirdly, they can be offered value-added atonement, which could be some level of compensation for the customer's time and effort in reporting the complaint. For example, some supermarkets will offer a double refund on returned food products to reflect the time and travel costs required to return the product. Finally, customers want organisations to keep their promises.

Retailers need to anticipate that service failure is inevitable and put in place processes to manage complaints. Managing customer expectations for return or exchange of goods through a well communicated returns policy is commonplace amongst most retail organisations. This is often facilitated by a well signposted customer service desk staffed by trained staff. Other ways for organisations to communicate their willingness to address complaints are through information on websites, phone numbers for contact centres on the reverse on till receipts, customer feedback cards and posting boxes located in highly visible places. When service fails there is a need to act fast and not 'sit' on complaints in the hope the customer will go away, so training frontline employees to deal with customer complaints is key, particularly as face-to-face customer contact is often the best method of dealing with irate or angry customers. Where possible retailers should try and resolve the complaints on the first contact then close the customer feedback loop by ensuring relevant departments are made aware of faulty products or other service complaints so that similar mistakes can be prevented in the future. Technology is key to tracking complaints and finally measures the cost of effective service recovery. It should not be measured in just financial terms but in potential costs to reputation.

CHAPTER SUMMARY

Retail is currently experiencing some of the most wide-reaching changes in its history. The traditional 'bricks-and-mortar' model of stores and shops is making way for technologically driven retail offerings. Internet shopping now accounts for around 10 per cent of all retail purchases and is expected to double over the next decade. Multichannel retailing is rapidly evolving allowing retailers to respond to consumer demand across all customer contact points in a streamlined, integrated and cost-effective manner. Consumer power has been enhanced by the internet, which enables ready access to greater information, price comparisons and other consumers' recommendations. New mobile platforms, including smartphones and tablets, are being adopted by consumers and are leading retail into new territory. As a result, customers will demand a different type of customer service delivery since customers will increasingly be able to access goods and services through a range of channels, which also allows them to communicate to a wide audience when their product and service expectations have not been met. The best retail organisations will recognise this changing service landscape and put in place service strategies to ensure that delivering good customer service remains a competitive advantage.

EXERCISES AND QUESTIONS

1. What are the key advantages for retailers of using the SERVQUAL model? Consider whether the model has any disadvantages.
2. Compare SERVQUAL with the model in Figure 10.2. Which model do you believe is most appropriate to online retailing, explaining your reasoning.
3. Considering different types of retailer – fashion, food, electricals, home interiors etc. – discuss how each of these types of retailer could create a social shopping experience that increases their value to the community and customers. Explore how that can increase consumer engagement in terms of attraction, conversion (i.e. from taking interest in a product to purchasing it) and retention, to ultimately increase profitability.
4. Inspired by the HappyOrNot device in the case study in this chapter, working in small groups carry out a brainstorming session to develop some creative ideas for assessing customer service quality. Select the most viable idea and describe how a retailer could implement it in practice.

5   What are the main methods of effecting a service recovery? Consider examples of occasions when you've received poor service from retailers. Who did you tell about it? Suggest how the retailers could have made a better service recovery in such cases.

6   How do customer service techniques differ between online and bricks-and-mortar retailers?

7   List three retailers which you consider to offer good customer service and three examples of retailers with poor customer service. What customer service techniques do you believe that the second group could learn from the first group on your list?

REFERENCES

Albrecht, K. (1988) *At America's Service: How Corporations Can Revolutionize the Way They Treat Their Customers*, Homewood, IL: Dow Jones.

Baron, S., Harris, K. and Hilton, T. (2008) *Services Marketing: Text and Cases*, 3rd edn, Basingstoke: Palgrave.

Beatson, A., Coote, L.V. and Rudd, J.M. (2006) Determining consumer satisfaction and commitment through self-service technology and personal service usage, *Journal of Marketing Management*, 22, 853–882.

Bitner, M.J., Booms, B.H. and Tetreault, M.S. (1990). The service encounter: diagnosing failure and unfavourable incident, *Journal of Marketing*, 54 (Jan), 71–84.

Burton, J., Easingwood, C. and Murphy, J. (2001) Using qualitative research to refine service quality models, *Qualitative Market Research: An International Journal*, 4(4), 217–223.

Buttle, F. and Burton, J. (2002) Does customer service failure influence customer loyalty? *Journal of Consumer Behaviour*, 1(3), 217–227.

Carman, J.M. (1990) Consumer perceptions of service quality: an assessment of the SERVQUAL dimensions, *Journal of Marketing*, 66, 33–55.

Chung, B.G. and Schneider, B. (2002) Serving multiple masters: role conflict experienced by service employees, *Journal of Services Marketing*, 16(1), 70–87.

Clow, K.E and Vorhies, D.W. (1993) Building a competitive advantage for service firms, *Journal of Services Marketing*, 7(1), 722–32.

Cronin, J.J. and Taylor, S.A. (1992) Measuring service quality: a re-examination and extension, *Journal of Marketing*, 56(3), 55–68.

Dabholkar, P.A., Thorpe, D.L. and Rentz, J.O. (1996) A measure of service quality for retail stores: scale development and validation, *Journal of the Academy of Marketing Science*, 24(1), 3–16.

Dugal, L.F., Kahn, I. and Klein, R (2012) Understanding how multichannel shoppers are reshaping the retail experience, *Apparel Magazine*, April, 53(8), 4.

Grönroos, C. (1984) A service quality model and its marketing implications, *European Journal of Marketing*, 18(4), 36–44.

Harris, K. and Baron, S. (2004) Consumer-to-consumer conversations in service settings, *Journal of Service Research*, 6(3), 287–303.

Hart, C., Heskett, J.L. and Sasser, W.E. Jr (1990). The profitable art of service recovery, *Harvard Business Review*, July–August, 148–156.

Hollenbeck, C.R. and Zinkhan, G.M. (2006) Consumer activism on the internet: the role of anti-brand communities, *Advances in Consumer Research*, 33, 479–485.

Hurley, R. (1998) Customer service behaviour in retail settings: a study of the effect of service provider personality, *Journal of Academy of Marketing Science*, 26(2), 115–127.

Keaveney, S. (1995). Customer switching behaviour in service industries: an exploratory study, *Journal of Marketing*, 59(April), 71–82.

Kotler, P. (1991) *Marketing Management. Analysis, Planning, Implementation and Control*. New Jersey: Prentice-Hall.

Lindquist, J. (1974) Meaning of image: a survey of empirical and hypothetical evidence, *Journal of Retailing*, 50(4), 29–38.

Mehta, S.C., Lalwani, A.K. and Han, S.L. (2000) Service quality in retailing: relative efficiency of alternative measurement scales for different product-service environments, *International Journal of Retail & Distribution Management*, 28(2), 62–72.

Oliver, R.L. (1980) A cognitive model of the antecedents and consequences of satisfaction decisions, *Journal of Marketing Research*, 17, 460–469.

Oliver, R.L. (1993) A conceptual model of service quality and service satisfaction, *Advances in Services Marketing and Management*, 2, 65–85.

Olsen, J. and Dover, P. (1979) Disconfirmation of consumer expectations through product trial, *Journal of Applied Psychology*, 64, 179–89.

Parasuraman, A., Zeithaml, V.A. and Berry, L.L. (1985) A conceptual model of service quality and its implications for future research, *Journal of Marketing*, 49 (Fall), 41–50.

Parasuraman, A., Zeithaml, V.A. and Berry, L.L. (1988) A multi-item scale for measuring consumer perceptions of service, *Journal of Retailing*, 64(1), 12–37.

Solomon, M.R., Surprenant, C., Czepiel, J.A. and Gutman, E.G. (1985) A role theory perspective on dyadic interactions: the service encounter, *Journal of Marketing Management*, 49, 99–111.

Svensson, G. (2006) The interactive interface of service quality, *European Business Review*, 18(3), 243–257.

Wong, A. and Sohal, A. (2003) A critical approach to the examination of customer relationship management in a retail chain: an exploratory study, *Qualitative Market Research: An International Journal*, 6(4), 248–262.

Zeithaml, V.A., Parasuraman, A. and Berry, L.L. (1990) *Delivering Quality Service, Balancing Customer Perceptions and Expectations*, New York: The Free Press.

FURTHER READING

Profile of John Lewis customer services advisor: http://www.jlpjobs.com/your-career/partner-profiles-vi.htm.

Cronin, J.J., Brady, M.K. and Hult, G.T.M. (2000) Assessing the effects of quality, value, and customer satisfaction on consumer behavioral intentions in service environments, *Journal of Retailing*, 76(2), 193–218. (This was the most downloaded article ever in the *Journal of Retailing* at time of writing.)

Jayawardhena, C. and Farrell, A.M. (2011) Effects of retail employees' behaviours on customers' service evaluation, *International Journal of Retail & Distribution Management*, 39(3), 203–217.

Piercy, N. (2014) Online service quality: content and process of analysis, *Journal of Marketing Management*, 30(7–8), 747–785.

Yua, W. and Ramanathan, R. (2012) Retail service quality, corporate image and behavioural intentions: the mediating effects of customer satisfaction, *International Review of Retail, Distribution and Consumer Research*, 2(5), 485–505.

Case study 1

Customer service at Boots UK

Boots UK is a leading pharmacy-led health and beauty retailer with an ongoing policy of employing knowledgeable, well trained staff and for providing a high standard of customer care and personal service. It has substantial market share in healthcare, cosmetics and toiletries. While particular staff members are trained in very specific customer service skills such as healthcare and cosmetics all employees are required to provide a friendly/personalised service. The nature of health and beauty is also such that a relatively high proportion of business requires sales staff to interact with customers to help explain, for example, product usage and benefits. Boots UK was voted 20th in the *Sunday Times* 2013 rankings for the top 25 Best Big Companies to Work For, demonstrating the retailer's emphasis on its staff.

In addition to an emphasis on high quality customer service, the retailer differentiates itself through its loyalty card launched in 1997. This offers points for money spent which can be redeemed against product purchases. The card has 17.8 million members and is one of the largest UK loyalty card schemes. Price discounting of health and beauty products is becoming commonplace as more retailers such as grocery stores offer wide ranges of these lines in particular products such as shampoos, toothpaste and bath products. Grocery stores are typically situated in out of town locations making it easy for customers to include the purchase of toiletries as part of their weekly food shop. In recent years, Boots UK, which has stores situated in city centres, local high streets and in edge of town retail park locations, has had to compete harder with grocers on key product sectors such as hair care, bath and dental products. It maintains its leading reputation in cosmetics and healthcare categories and through its expanding customer service offerings in pharmacy and healthcare.

DISCUSSION QUESTIONS

1 What could Boots UK do to counteract the grocers' price discounting?
2 What additional customer service could Boots UK offer?
3 Should Boots UK continue to offer their current levels of high quality customer service? Explain the reasons for your answer.

Source: with permission from Boots UK

Case study 2

Self-scan checkouts

Tesco impacted upon the future job security of checkout workers after opening Britain's first entirely self-service shop in 2010. The Tesco Express in Kingsley, Northampton has a total of five self-scan tills overseen by a single member of staff but no manned checkouts. It is described by the company as an 'assisted service store' designed to increase efficiency and speed up the shopping process but critics warn that the move marks the end of basic human interaction during weekly shopping trips and could eventually cost thousands of jobs. The major supermarkets employ around 750,000 workers in Britain and Tesco has the biggest workforce at around 221,000. The retail giant says customer feedback had been positive as the new system removed the need for queuing. A spokesman said: 'Customers like the fact there are always five checkouts available. Before you could have four manned checkouts but only one person working the till.' The spokesperson then added: 'It's a lot quicker but some people have never used them before so a member of staff is there to assist. If needs be there can be five members of staff assisting customers. We have had no negative feedback so far.'

DISCUSSION QUESTIONS

1. What are the problems for the customer with this one self-service option?
2. What are the main issues Tesco could face by offering only this one self-service option?
3. Do you think Tesco should open more of these stores? Explain your answer.

Source: © British Retail Photography/Alamy Images

CHAPTER 11

Multichannel retailing

Anthony Kent, School of Art and Design, Nottingham Trent University

Learning objectives

The objectives of this chapter are to:

- explain the dynamics of online retailing;
- assess the development and advantages of multichannel retailing;
- identify the key developments in mail order;
- discuss other forms of non-store retailing.

Introduction

Non-store retailing requires marketing strategies that do not use physical stores to reach consumers and complete transactions (Berman and Evans, 2010). While different terms are used to describe this process, 'home shopping' is commonly used to define different media and formats to distribute goods and services.

- *Online retailing by internet retailers*: also referred to as 'pureplay' retailers, and retailers who use both stores and the internet to communicate with, and sell to, customers.
- *Mail order*: this element comprises traditional catalogue retailers, but also store-based retailers with catalogues, such as French Connection and Tesco Direct. Catalogue sales can be made through a number of channels including the internet, interactive TV, by telephone and agents.
- *Direct marketing*: a form of retailing that uses impersonal techniques, notably TV shopping, newspaper, magazine and computer-based advertisements. **Direct selling** requires person-to-person contact, typically door-to-door salesmen, and party plan selling, where agents sell to groups of customers at home.

Home shopping is a dynamic market, characterised by rapid change in technologies and their adoption by consumers. Mail order used to be dominated by printed catalogues but online has become the dominant marketing and sales channel by which successful retailers integrate their online and offline operations and where the dividing line between the two is increasingly ill-defined. The variety and sophistication of personal computing devices and their software, such as smartphones, and new media channels offer more possibilities for consumption. Consequently the market has become more complex and unpredictable. The challenge for marketers is to provide a seamless experience of the brand from retail store to mobile device.

Multichannel defines more than one way to distribute or mediate goods and services to markets. Retail stores combined with an online website typically create a multiple channel rather than single channel to market. Websites are increasingly accessed through a variety of devices; in the past, a home PC provided the main point of access but consumers are more frequently turning to internet-enabled laptops, tablets, and smartphones for search and ordering activities.

The uptake of multichannel retailing is not uniform and has a distinct regional variation. Home shopping has been far more successful in Northern Europe than in the South, owing to variations in the climate, differing qualities of postal services and diversity of shopping habits and retail industry structures. Online access has created new leaders in home shopping where Amazon and Otto dominate the European market. Amazon is the dominant home shopping business across Europe.

This chapter explains the development of non-store-based retailing through mail order, and enables you to assess the problems of adaptability by companies in the UK and their failure to exploit the new opportunities arising through the internet. Secondly, it evaluates the variety of online retail strategies to enter the market and the range of marketing elements required to plan entry into the online market. Finally it examines how multichannel retailing has become a dominant consideration for retailers and the main drivers for successful development. It will provide you with an overview of changes in the market that enable retailers to engage with consumers.

Mail order

Mail order originated in the USA in the nineteenth century where it proved an ideal method of selling to scattered communities and consumers. In the UK it went through a series of distinct phases starting with watch clubs, which enabled working men to buy a useful item they could not otherwise afford. Later, companies entered the market to provide a wider range of goods, and club and credit-based agencies continued until 1950s. During this period mail order recorded its highest growth with a steadily increasing share of the retail market, as rising purchasing power accompanied by low food price increases created new levels of consumer affluence. Sales were achieved through catalogues and these claim a number of competitive advantages compared to store-based retailers:

- *Reduced start-up costs*: mail order avoids the need for physical stores, fixtures and fittings, local stockholding and retail employees. Typically, companies in the UK used a network of part-time agents to sell their goods.
- *Credit terms*: often to customers who were otherwise unable to afford them. Products were offered through catalogues, and orders and deliveries were made by agents working in the nearby, often working-class neighbourhoods who also collected and administered weekly payment schedules.
- *Operational efficiency*: mail order companies undertake wholesaling, stocking large quantities of products and breaking bulk, and retailing functions, supplying customers from a central warehouse. From an operational perspective, companies can locate in low-cost areas acquiring additional warehouse space and office capacity to keep pace with demand. These were initially supported by a reasonably reliable delivery infrastructure that used the Post Office and railway network. From the 1970s, companies introduced their own delivery fleets and depots, which allowed them to distribute goods to regional drop-off points where they could be delivered locally by van. This enabled them to take control of their supply chains.
- *Prices can be lower than shop prices due to reduced costs*: although in practice, prices tend to be the same as or more expensive. Targeted mail order 'specalogues' and more focused mail order companies can create more flexibility with prices through their market positioning and product assortment.
- *Additional non-price features*: include convenience, friendliness, variety and quality of goods. Convenience has been important where all family members are employed, local retail outlets provide a limited offer and larger shopping centres are not easily accessed.
- *Large catalogues encourage impulse buying*: development of catalogues became a significant investment for companies. By the early 1960s, they were produced twice yearly, consisted of 500–700 pages rising to some 1000 pages later on, and carried 11,000–12,000 items. They came to be extremely well produced and attractive, well-designed catalogues contributed to competitive success. Celebrities from television were increasingly used to endorse products, and the development of branded goods ranges led to 'exclusive' clothes by well-known designers or endorsed by others (Coopey *et al.*, 2005).

Mail order's reliance on part-time agents, mostly women, was an important part of the business. Agents showed catalogues to customers, took their orders, collected their payments and sent them on to the company. Agents accepted orders and passed them on to the customer, and processed the return of goods. Some presentational skills were necessary as well as social confidence, and good judgement about the reliability of the customer. Agents could provide credit references, through a relatively informal process, which allowed catalogue sales to be financed by 'free' credit instalments for weekly paid workers when credit was difficult. At its height in the early 1980s, the mail order industry employed some five million agents, drawn from socio-economic groups C2, D and E but predominantly from skilled employees, C2 (see Chapter 3 Retail consumer behaviour and market segmentation).

Market development

Over time more attention was paid to design and marketing as companies focused on attractive lifestyle market segments, and the creation of 'specialogues'. Customer databases that track spending patterns, changes in behaviour and general sales trends, provide opportunities for targeting high spending and frequent customers with personalised offers.

Increasingly sophisticated segmentation and targeting techniques have enabled shorter but more specific catalogues to be mailed out to selected customers. Fashion and sports retailing, for example, have seen an increasing interest in specialised mail order in the UK. Accompanying this development has been a trend away from agency mail order to direct mail order. The Next Directory was a major departure in this field. Launched in 1987, it specifically targeted new catalogue users, dispensing with agents in favour of more convenient phone and credit card-based ordering and sales. Although the company acquired a chain of newsagents with some intention to use the shops as collection points, deliveries were made direct to the respondent's home. The use of technology and higher quality products resulted in a transformation of image for the mail order sector (Kent and Omar, 2003).

Developments in the traditional mail order system

Changes in the retail market, combined with retailers and banks offering credit terms to a wider range of customers, led to the long-term decline of the agency system. The total number of customers per agent reduced, as agents increasingly limited their business to themselves and their families and by the mid-1990s the number of agents in the A, B and C1 classes reflected the arrival of the personal shopper, or agent-customers. The arrival of computer-based credit scoring placed less emphasis on local agent's knowledge. Ordering by mail was replaced by phone, which enabled faster order processing and a reduction in returns (Coopey *et al.*, 2005). Online ordering later supplemented or replaced the phone as companies switched to online catalogues.

An ongoing feature of mail order since the 1990s has been the consolidation of both internal organisational structures and the external competitive environment. Operational rationalisation, to reduce costs, led to larger fulfilment centres, and faster order processing resulted in new call centres linked to central computers recording real time stock levels.

With lower profits in mail order, the number of competitors also started to rationalise. The John Myers catalogue became part of GUS's BMOC and Freemans was acquired by Sears. The 1990s saw Grattan taken over by the German mail order specialist, Otto Versand, and Empire by the French company, Pinault-Printemps – Redoute (PPR). The appeal of these companies to their new owners was their potential for entry into the expanding direct mail order market. They responded to new challenges, moving from mass mailings to targeted campaigns aimed at more fashion conscious customers, for example Empire's catalogue offered French brand status without the expense.

Mail order and the internet

As e-commerce expanded rapidly in the late 1990s, there was an assumption that catalogue retailers, being in 'a similar sort of business' in terms of orders and stock, would be at an advantage. Agency mail order catalogues, effectively home shopping department stores, had the infrastructure and led the way in home shopping fulfilment expertise.

However, the progression to e-retail was by no means simple. Phan *et al.* (2005) note that at the beginning of the e-commerce evolution, the negative effects of bad management decisions were masked by distorted market signals and the rapid and unpredictable early development of the e-commerce industry. Lack of knowledge in e-commerce and underinvestment in initial IT to support its new e-commerce strategies were the major causes for the unexpected failure (Strategic Direction, 2006). For agency mail order companies, the root cause was that the key to those businesses was not their retail offer, but their provision of credit. Even a business like Shop Direct, which now offers different catalogues with different price structures, has not managed it. So, in effect, these businesses had to start again from scratch and they have not managed it.

In recent years there has been an increase in the importance of e-commerce or internet-based mail-order selling (see Figure 11.1). Traditional mail order businesses were slow to respond to the internet although mail order now uses a variety of distribution strategies, and in 2007 accounted for 41 per cent of their sales, and in some cases more, Next with 50 per cent and Boden with 60 per cent. In the US, LL Bean and Lands End Inc. have both been more successful in leveraging their mail order operations for online retailing.

Rising competition, particularly online changing company structures, demographic changes and the economic recession have provided significant challenges and flexibility and responsiveness have become ever more critical elements of online trading. While the mail order market continues to decline as a percentage of total retail, it is possible that the rate of decline in sales will slacken as customers increasingly comprise those who have always used agents and are unable to access credit elsewhere.

The retail environment has dramatically changed since the advent of the internet, creating interactive online interfaces. The tablet catalogue is a new development in the field of e-commerce and catalogue shopping. Tablet catalogue pages look identical to those in print catalogues. It is noteworthy, however, that tablet catalogue retailers have built in many additional features not offered in traditional print catalogues to upgrade consumer shopping experiences and assist in the decision-making process.

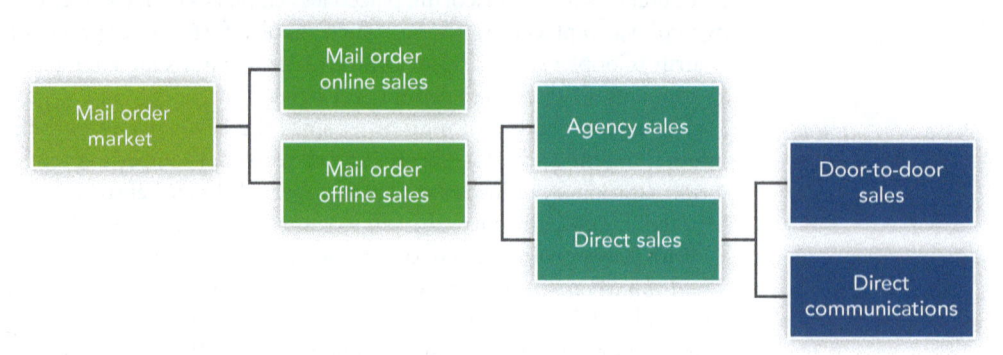

Figure 11.1 Mail order shopping channels

MINI CASE STUDY
Grattan and Otto UK

The problems facing a traditional agency mail order business, Grattan, can be traced back to changes that took place from the 1990s and the relentless increase in e-commerce. From 2005 online sales took off while catalogue sales throughout the industry declined by £273m. One area of expansion for the company was Parcelnet, its distribution network, which benefited from increased home delivery business from other companies' online orders. A further review completed in 2009, resulted in the restructuring of the company into Freeman Grattan Holdings (FGH) that brought all home shopping brands together. Freeman's offices and warehouse closed, with distribution being centralised in Bradford and the company's call centre in Sheffield. The two big agency catalogues were now planned as home shopping destinations to combine a range of exciting retail brands in a virtual online shopping mall. This concept emulated the re-invention of department stores as mini-shopping malls filled with retail brands in the 1990s.

With this online initiative FGH launched four new offers to the UK: Bon Prix, Curvissa, Swimwear 365 and Witt UK and continued to develop the established brands of Kaleidoscope and Look Again. It changed the design of the two main catalogues to offer more specialisation: Grattan increased its range through a number of distinctive 'shops' including Oli and Arizona. One problem will be to continue to cultivate these offers – and ensure that they do not start to bleed into one another – to drive future growth. Each brand was managed by its own team and set individual targets, which created a high level of morale. Internal competition and collaboration between brands allowed the organisation as a whole to prosper. The traditional catalogue continued to have a place, prompting customers to visit the website and traditional marketing methods were used alongside social media, including Facebook and Twitter.

Home shopping used to be a social business with a catalogue shared with friends and family. Curvissa and Bon Prix give customers the same opportunity. Getting customers to look at the page, the 'shop window', is aligned with getting best products at the best prices and every page has to pay its way. Consequently products are increasingly photographed against plain backdrops to reduce costs. By 2012 customer service had become more important than ever. New premises in Bradford facilitated a new Customer Service initiative, 'CSI: Yorkshire', with four objectives for its IT capability: keeping any promises made to customers, letting them know what is happening at every stage of the process, giving customers power to manage own accounts, responding immediately and positively to any issues (Ward, 2012).

QUESTIONS

1 How successfully did Otto handle the acquisition of Grattan?

2 Was the decline of traditional mail order inevitable?

3 To what extent does FGH's portfolio of brands create a successful competitive position?

Direct marketing

Direct marketing offers more focused communication and sales opportunities than mail order (see Table 11.1). It is defined by the US Direct Marketing Association as 'an interactive system of marketing which uses one or more advertising media to effect a measurable response/and or transaction at any location'.

Effectively to be classed as direct marketing your activity must involve response, it is often two-way communication, developing a relationship between supplier and customer. Response is carefully measured in an attempt to take the waste out of marketing and should be part of your long-term strategy. Activity through virtually any media can be classed as direct marketing, including telemarketing, and it is one of the fastest growing marketing disciplines in the UK. Media selection is important as the key criteria are costs of print and online set-up, lead times to create offline and online materials, distribution efficiencies, data collection and flexibility to changing market conditions. The development of direct marketing campaigns increasingly demands attention to how it relates to other marketing initiatives.

Table 11.1 Direct marketing media

Printed catalogues	Mass media: newspaper, magazine, TV and radio
Flyers	Inserts
Online media	E-kiosks
Door drops	

- *Integration*: how the campaign fits with other channels, in particular TV and online.
- *Content*: marketers must consider the impact on the consumer, and the real value of the medium compared to perceptions of junk content.
- *Frequency*: it is important to consider what the appropriate timing between campaigns should be.
- *Measurement*: the effectiveness of the marking campaign should be measured in each medium.

TV shopping consists of two elements, shopping channels dedicated to retailing, and more commonly found in the USA, Direct Response TV or infomercial. The infomercial is a longer length advertisement from 10 to 120 minutes aired at non-peak times which contains phone numbers or other contact points with the retailer. It experienced very strong growth in the UK in the years up to 2006 as the emergence of digital TV provided a significant boost to the market, increasing these programmes' exposure. Since then, TV shopping has declined as the digital effect recedes and the medium is impacted by a greater proportion of sales going online as operators enhance their multichannel credentials. Examples of this include stations streaming their programming online and QVC Active where orders can be placed via interactive TV. Spending tends to be on discretionary areas and comparison shopping.

Direct selling is a niche business that has proved resilient but limited by its methods of operation and is unlikely to increase its share of the home shopping market in face of online retailing. This channel has grown largely at the expense of agency mail order, as the items sold are smaller and less impacted by economic downturns. Also, representatives are more easily recruited in an economic recession as they look to supplement their income, customers have also been more cautious with their spending, cutting back in discretionary areas such as homeware, leading to a lower average order size. Direct selling is coming under greater threat from discount supermarkets and high-street retailers, like pound shops, leading to a longer term decline.

The development of the internet has seen the development of new direct marketing media. These have a range of communication functions, from the provision of generic information to specific information about the organisation (Molenaar, 2012). Increasingly they enable personal and interactive communication with consumers either individually or through social media.

Webcam and chat

- *Twitter*: immediate and personal response to messages or passive, following other tweeters to read their messages. Direct messaging enables personal responses, alternatively a public response can be achieved and retweeting allows users to forward a message publicly. These can be used to create and focus interest in a specific theme.
- *Emails and newsletters*: email, opt-in system use for bulk distribution of emails of text messages. Every receiver has to give prior permission for the email or text message to be sent to them. These are commonly used for all sort of applications, such as announcements, newsletters, ezines, and marketing communications of business.
- *Newsletters*: these can include a variety of e-forms of newspaper. Blogs provide important insights into news and opinion, and more critically new ideas from fashion designers.

The key to engagement is relevance as consumers lose interest in the very large number of irrelevant special offers which are likely to be dismissed as spam or junk mail. Personalised e-communications can provide customers with product and service offers that consumers are actually interested in receiving.

Online retailing

Generally, e-business has been defined as a range of business activities taking place via internet applications, and including etailing, and also messaging, blogs, podcasts and other web-enabled communication tools (Kurtz and Boone, 2010). Adoption of online *retailing* refers to companies which establish electronic product/service transactions through the internet, providing direct-to-consumer channels which involve material, information and cash exchanges between the participants (Doherty and Ellis-Chadwick, 2009). Multichannel retailing looks at using more than one channel or medium to manage customers in a consistent and coordinated way across all media channels (Liu and Tsai, 2010; Stone *et al.*, 2002).

As the internet developed in 1990s new competences for online retailing began to emerge. While the technologies rapidly evolved, knowledge of website construction and opportunities for increased consumer interaction became important. Initially the internet provided information about retailers but with the development of credit and payment systems financial transactions became possible. These saw a need for trust in the systems operations and their security, and the need to the develop encryption software and secure delivery services.

Generic online retail strategies

The arrival of the internet saw the development of two types of retailer: retailers who only sell online described as 'pureplay' retailers and those who also trade from physical stores, originally termed **bricks and clicks**. New concepts evolved which replicated the real retail world in online shopping malls, but also created new forms of trading as portals, points of entry to other online sites, auction and aggregation sites. As online retailing becomes more dominant so it will influence the conceptualisation and design of physical stores inspired by interactive online experiences. More confident and knowledgeable consumers may lead to other stores taking on a different role, as showrooms and showcases to view or sample products, and as convenient points for collection and return of goods bought online.

Pureplays

The internet provided opportunities for new retailers to operate without physical stores; these were known as pureplay online retailers. E-commerce attracted considerable funding for new companies with business plans based on the potential advantages of a low-cost online environment. Many failed to build significant market share due to flaws in their business models concerning market growth, acceptance by consumers of online transactions and problems with fulfilment and delivery.

One of the most successful sites is Amazon, which has managed to establish itself as the generic home shopping site from its origins in book retailing. Working with partners Amazon has extended its product range into many other sectors, continually expanding its customer advice and delivery services.

'Bricks and clicks'

This model developed as a hybrid of physical stores and online website as established retailers created a web presence, initially providing information but later selling and providing a more engaging point of communication with its customers. Virtual malls and portals emerged, to help unfamiliar users of the internet search and create a sense of security.

The typical entry strategy for retailers, a 'silo' approach, maintains a distinction between the channels with an online team of practitioners managing the new business separately from in-store retail team. The online business can be overshadowed in these early stages, as traditional retail activities dominate the organisation's attention.

Table 11.2 Advantages of online and offline retailing

Online retail sites	Physical/offline retail stores
Consumer data	Feel and try
User feedback and reviews	Edited choices
Information and expert advice	Instant delivery
Global availability: same products available everywhere	Simple returns
Broad and deep product and service assortments	Real people
Low prices	Social opportunities
Accessibility: at any time/day	Immersive experiences

Therefore the aim of the strategy is to nurture and grow the business with the appropriate and required level of attention, and allow for an initial high level of concentration and the investment of time and resources (see Table 11.2).

The reverse process is also evident as online businesses move into physical stores; successful online companies use their statistical and demographic data to target retail locations. However, their distinctive online branding and communications must be integrated into the physical store experience, for it to remain truly differentiated from its competitors.

Shops as showrooms

Consumers use stores to gather details about the physical product and later compare prices to buy online. With high fixed costs, this will place greater pressure on store profitability leading to more closures. To offset these problems stores could be used to expand click-and-collect services where consumers can try out, pick and return products bought online at their convenience.

New retailing models

Auction sites provide opportunities for consumers and companies to trade their own goods online and quickly became enormously popular. eBay has been particularly successful in attracting small retailers to its sites and became a portal for small retailers and the clearance activity of major retailers (Mintel, 2012).

Services

Services do not require any physical delivery to take place, and in that respect easily migrate to online environments. They have seen major growth and now dominate the travel, financial services and entertainment sectors.

OAK FURNITURE LAND: FROM ONLINE TO PHYSICAL STORES

Oak Furniture Land began selling hardwood furniture online in 2004, and by the end of 2006, had become the biggest eBay retailer in the UK with £2.7m of annual sales. However, the company decided to set up a separate website, Oakfurnitureland.co.uk, which opened after Christmas in 2006. As the website continued to flourish and eBay moved away from auctions and towards a more conventional sales business model, the volume of people viewing the company's furniture dropped and it eventually left eBay altogether.

Oak Furniture Land opened its first offline showroom in 2009. This was located in the empty offices at the entrance to its large warehouse on a rural airfield site, which provided enough space for the experiment. At the time this was a questionable strategy as the economic recession was taking its toll on physical retailers, and the company was continuing to expand its business online. Nevertheless the company explained that its online business was not without cost, which included paying over £250,000 each month to Google to maintain its search ranking. With a turnover of £150m, it would make a higher profit through online sales rather than physical stores, but as the company observed, there were still plenty of people who wanted to buy furniture in shops and the availability of shop sites at manageable rents as a result of the recession, provided good opportunities to expand the business.

The shop proved to be an immediate success, with sales of £5m in its first year, proving that customers wanted to see and feel the furniture. Initially there were concerns that the shop would cannibalise online sales but in fact both channels continued to grow. One year later Oak Furniture Land opened a bespoke showroom in the nearby town of Cheltenham and by 2013 had expanded to 43 stores in out-of-town locations. The hardwood furniture specialist had transformed itself from a pureplay etailer to operating a physical store network, which was focused on rapidly increasing its profits from both its stores and online.

Sources: The Virtual PR Agency, 30.12.2011; Lawson, A. (2013) Oak Furniture Land reports record sales and profits, *Retail Week*, 31 January 2013; City AM, 18.2.2013, Wilson, A. (2013) Oak Furniture Land: From eBay trader to retail mogul, *Daily Telegraph*, 4 February 2013; oakfurnitureland.co.uk.

Consumer engagement

The internet environment influences consumer behaviour in different ways. Technology and connectivity enable people to create new ways of working and behaving, and to re-invent the rules of interaction with retailers. Sustainability is enhanced through new design techniques and opportunities to create, personalise and share products. It enables people to place more importance on creativity and culture, to be creators as well as observers, providing opportunities for retailers to embrace story-telling, and interactions with the cultural heritage of the brand. The internet provides more scope for autonomy, personal choices and in flexible working patterns.

Three fundamental elements, mass customisation, interactivity and interest-driving, of the internet demonstrate the significance of consumer engagement in online retailing (Dann and Dann, 2011). Customers evaluate the service interface in a more holistic way and since they participate more actively in the service encounter, the service must be designed to enable them to engage with the retailer (Cassab and MacLachlan, 2009).

Distinctively, the online channel can form an entry hub to other touchpoints, and multiple touchpoints will shape the service interface (Peterson *et al.*, 2010). Therefore retailers will need to work hard to ensure that their websites provide consumers with an enjoyable and reliable shopping experience (Doherty and Ellis-Chadwick, 2009). Design of a customer engagement strategy depends on understanding exactly how people interact with a company throughout the decision journey: with the product itself, or with sales, service, marketing, PR or other elements of the business. As consultancy firm McKinsey explain, companies need to think as customers do, so that 'engagement' is a set of related interactions that added together make up the customer experience (*McKinsey Quarterly*, 2011).

Long tail effect

The long tail describes the demand curve that demonstrates the move from high sales concentrated in a relatively small number of high-selling products to a 'long tail' of low sales across a wide range of goods. In contrast to the Pareto 80:20 rule, which explains that most sales will be derived from a relatively small number of products, the long tail effect demonstrates that consumers continue to buy small quantities of products for a long time after their initial launch. The theory was initially proposed by Anderson (2004) concerning online entertainment where narrowly targeted goods and services could be sold to niche markets, making them as profitable as mass-markets. Amazon holds a vast inventory but in not much depth compared to specialised or limited-line strategy retailers focusing on a few big-selling items (Sheehan, 2010).

For online retailers, the cost of stocking goods is lower as they can be held in large, low-cost distribution centres rather than distributed around more expensive stores. Digital processes themselves reduce production costs, promotion and distribution. The benefits of the internet include opportunities for retailers to aggregate national or international markets; unlike bricks-and-mortar retailers they are not dependent on local sales. The depth of the product ranges will change the types of products that are profitable, enabling smaller suppliers and new entrants to gain exposure to the market. However, with so many products and services in the long tail, it is important that retailers provide search tools for consumers to find them (Brynjolfsson and Hu, 2011).

New technology

Technological advances have presented online retailers with new ways to gain competitive advantage. Typically this is through experimentation with new developments followed by the exploitation of viable opportunities. However, in such a dynamic market, there are significant risks associated with identifying new trends, some of which will be 'game changers' in each of hardware, software and media, and translating them into marketing opportunities.

Online marketing, and the early years of internet retailing, is fundamentally about improving the supply of information and reducing the significance of price-oriented strategies. Many researchers of e-commerce indicate that with a technology-mediated customer interface, a retailer delivers services through available information which refers to the attributes (features and functions) provided on the computer interface. An example of this is the increasing use of touchscreens, which encourages consumer engagement with content and ownership (Tun-Min and Tung, 2013).

One significant element of online interaction is to elevate the role of customer insights, and generating rich customer insights is both challenging and important. Companies must constantly communicate with consumers, analyse and explain patterns from their behaviour, and respond quickly to signs of changing needs. Online retailing puts a premium on problem-solving and strategic-marketing skills supported by market research capabilities. These have implications for retailers' investment in IT capacity in relationship technologies, and specifically Customer Relationship Management (CRM) and Supply Chain Management, and real-time data capture and processing both online and offline.

The analysis of data from personal browsing and buying behaviour can be combined with product metadata to predict and prompt future consumer demand. However, in this seamless environment customers can often know more about products than sales assistants, resulting in poor customer satisfaction. Technology can be used in-store in a different way, to help assistants with mobile devices that provide product information from the retailer's enterprise resource management and CRM systems and also detailed information about the customer from social media (Bird, 2013).

While information gathering and communication are fundamental to the online interface, the replication of in-store experiences provides another important technological objective. Human–computer interaction is a key consideration in new experiential technology, with interactive videos, holograms and 3D modelling being used to influence the ways people shop. These online facilities bring consumers closer to the physical, sensory experience of garments, their tactile qualities and fit achieved in store.

At an individual level technologies enhance the processes of online shopping with a range of functions. **Mobile commerce (m-commerce)** is based on smartphone connectivity and provides more convenient browsing and payment systems, but also through geopositioning and locator applications, retailers can locate potential consumers and connect them to personalised, store offers and information.

Website design

Information stimulates purchases, generates new businesses and builds relationships using a website and other e-communications media. They support a brand through an online experience and provide gateways to information and services through search engines, directories and services such as personalised news.

Website attractiveness is achieved through a number of dimensions, outlined below.

- A high rank on search engines, selling site or marketplaces.
- Affiliate marketing, specific services such as comparison sites and a good domain name.
- Information sites.
- Generic applications: the development of more powerful processors and devices, and opportunities to facilitate, from Web 1 to Web 3 and beyond.
- Mobile interaction with consumers.
- Facilitation: through to the central role of the user.
- Decision-making processes, guided choice, triggers, buying process, no purchase without comparison.
- Research/ information: analyses where do visitors come from, improving pages on the site, web stats, measuring success, cost per click, cost per order, average order value, click through rate, return value and basket value.

For fashion clothing retailers, the primacy of product design and price is evident in the organisation of their online business. New managerial responsibilities are required in the design and visualisation of the online site, and increasingly, online imagery needs to match the reality of the product. In addition, the content of each page must attractively convey the product characteristics and their sensory qualities with the aim of increasing customer dwell-time at the site.

RETAIL MARKETING CAREERS
Jessica Goudkuil, etailer owner/manager

Jessica is the owner/manager of Bead Boutique, an etailer selling beads and jewellery components. Jessica gained a Higher National Diploma (HND) in Business Management and Marketing at Harper Adams University before beginning her marketing career in a pharmaceutical company, then moving to an insulation firm, where she gained marketing experience including e-commerce and advertising. In her spare time, Jessica joined a silversmithing group and while looking for less expensive ways to make jewellery she investigated buying her own materials. This inspired her to launch Bead Boutique in 2010, in a shop that she describes as 'the size of a small dining room' on the main street of Long Melford in rural Suffolk. The shop created a lot of interest and after six months she moved to a slightly larger outlet nearby. She also set up a website, initially

Jessica Goudkuil

to promote the store and then began selling online. Bead Boutique moved to a larger store the following year, with a well-lit, spacious upper floor for holding jewellery-making classes. However, these premises were further away from the village's main shopping area and supermarket, so footfall was reduced and the extra space doubled the overheads, making the store less financially viable.

Being a niche retailer, in that it has a narrowly focused product range with a wide assortment, Bead Boutique was more suited to continuing as a purely online retailer, to appeal to customers in a wider geographical area. Jessica explains how she made this decision:

> We got to the point where people from the next town were buying online from us and it became apparent that shopping online was becoming far easier than buying from the shop because of opening hours. Customers were buying online in the evening after work and it appeared that the shop could become redundant. Setting up the website was costly at first but for any business now, regardless of what you do, people will always look you up on the net and if it doesn't come up you might have lost that lead.

Jessica feels that having a website with a good aesthetic standard makes customers more confident about making payments on it. She also considers that an advantage of selling solely online is that the timing of her work is more flexible, without the commitment of opening a shop six days a week. Since the business moved online, Jessica has continued to run beading parties and workshops at people's houses or in hired premises around Suffolk. Her target customers are women in a wide variety of age groups, starting with 'little beaders' children's birthday parties. Her classes are also popular for hen parties where she teaches them to make pearl jewellery, teaming up with another company that puts on vintage tea parties. 'Retired ladies' also form part of Bead Boutique's target market. Jessica caters for teenagers by supplying jewellery-making kits with step-by-step guides that are often bought as presents. She also offers free jewellery-making project guides on the website and YouTube.

Bead Boutique uses several methods of promotion, including digital marketing communications. Jessica pays for SEO from the company who built the website, to achieve a high position on search engines. She's also registered on business guide Yelp and uses Google Analytics to assess where customers come from. Bead Boutique has a database of around 600 customers that can be used very effectively for direct marketing, as a single email offering a discount recently generated £1000 in additional turnover. Jessica has found that 34 per cent of the customers on her database read emails from Bead Boutique, which she has been told is higher than average. She can also communicate with customers through her blog and reply directly to queries via Twitter or phone, to replace some of the interaction she gave in person in the shop. Free postage is offered by Bead Boutique above a specific order value and at certain times on all orders, to help increase sales. In terms of traditional media, the company advertises in local glossy magazines such as Suffolk Life, as well as featuring in editorial content, which Jessica considers portray a better quality image than newspaper adverts. She also advertises in specialist magazines such as *Make & Sell Jewellery* and *Crafts Beautiful*.

Jessica requires a variety of skills to run an online business. She needs creative and technical abilities to make jewellery and loves making new products but says that she has to be prepared for ideas to not work sometimes. She uses YouTube and Pinterest to pick up new ideas for jewellery-making. Jessica puts her marketing knowledge into practice when writing a SWOT Analysis for the business, maintaining an awareness of her competitors and planning marketing communications. She uses communication skills in many ways to deal with her customers and suppliers, which include wholesalers, printers, web designers and advertising companies. She also uses negotiation skills, e.g. when approaching her suppliers to request lower minimum order quantities. She uses her planning and organisational skills, as well as self-motivation, for administration and keeping stock levels up-to-date, packing and posting. Jessica likes the flexibility and independence of running her own business, but she says this also creates a lot of responsibility:

> You're not having anyone to tell you what to do every day, although sometimes it would be quite nice. You're your own boss and if you make a mistake you haven't got anyone to blame except yourself, which can be quite tough really, so setting up the business was quite a gamble at the start. I enjoy teaching and having appointments with people but meeting people every day in the shop was taking its toll a little bit.

Jessica offers the following advice for anyone planning to set up a small independent retailer:

Work out your daily calculations as to how much it costs to run a shop before you even put the key in

Source: photograph © Katie Drouet

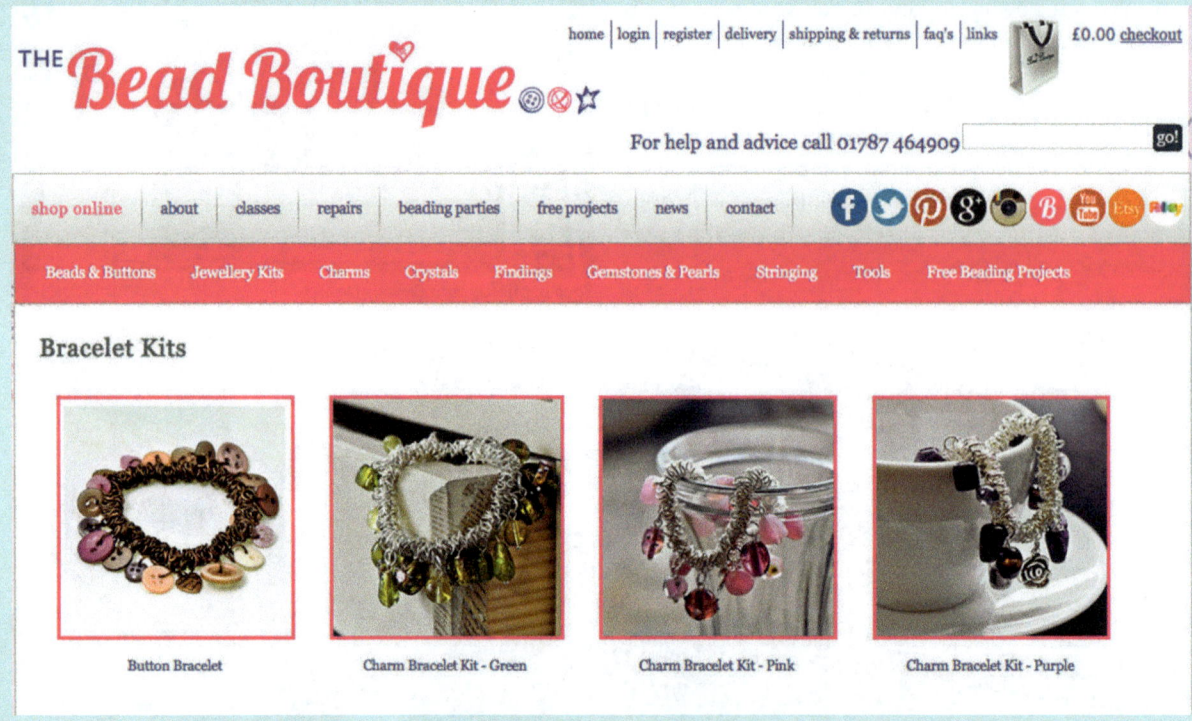

Bead Boutique's store and website
Source: photographs Jessica Goudkuil

the door, so you know what you need to take in the till. Mine was £69 per day. Also, when developing branding get a few different concepts first because it's your front-of-house and it needs to be kept updated and adapted across all sorts of media. If you've got a USP you need to put that on your business card. Finally, build good relationships with advertisers and suppliers and get them on your side, because this will be to your benefit.

www.thebeadboutique.co.uk; www.youtube.com/channel/UC7_7C6MJaxMMtcGplunfJmg; http://thebeadboutiquelongmelford.blogspot.co.uk/; Twitter:@beadboutiqu

Online communications

Traditional concepts of advertising as a one-way process, pushing a message to the consumer, and mass media in general will play a less important role in the future. More pervasive marketing needs the entire organisation to engage customers whenever and wherever they interact with a company, in a store, on the phone, responding to email, a blog post, or an online review.

The online promotional mix consists of eight different forms (Dann and Dann, 2011).

- *Advertising*: banner advertising, creates small advertising placements using the same techniques as offline promotion which are live pointers to another point on the internet.
- *Email*: internet is about relationship-based direct marketing, with an empowered consumer.
- *Direct marketing*.
- *Personal selling*.
- *Point-of-sale and point-of-purchase displays*: navigating to the payment page, through special offers, may also occur on checkout page or shopping cart with recommendations.
- *PR*: search engine optimisation.
- *Sales promotion*: user-generated content, an offshoot of word-of-mouth plus self-generated content to form a community with other fans.
- *User-generated content*.

Channel synergy requires retailers to leverage the brand and marketing mix consistently across all channels. Allocating responsibility for building touchpoints is increasingly important because of the degree to which web-based engagement is requiring companies to create 'broadcast' media; for example, some retailers have created publishing divisions to feed ever-increasing demand for content required by their websites, social media, internal and external publications, multimedia sites and coupons and other promotions. Editorial teams 'socialise' their brands – transforming customer relationships by producing blogs, digital magazines, and other content for frequency and depth of interactions. In this market, the customer demands an ever-increasing need for timely, relevant and compelling content across a variety of media.

In the fashion sector, communications typically embrace blogs and magazines. With the latest stories about trends, coolhunting and celebrities, and designer insights into their own work, these media blur the boundaries between online and offline and retail and magazine. The brand experience is extended across channels, and is specifically used by luxury brands to explain and reinforce the exclusive heritage of the brand.

Fulfilment and delivery systems

Online retailing requires both speedy execution of orders and reliable delivery, as companies aim to satisfy customers with shorter delivery lead times. Options include same-day deliveries and tracking the real-time status of the order through invoice and individual order numbering systems.

The integration of store and online operations is evident in 'click and collect', which enables customers to order goods online and picked up in-store or collected from a third party. Its main advantage is convenience; for the customer it avoids both the need for home delivery with unpredictable delivery timetables and 'slots' and the risk of arriving at the store and finding that the goods, for example a clothing size, is unavailable. For the consumer it could be said to be a win–win situation and for the store-based retailer it creates a clear advantage over pureplay online retailers. Increasingly, in practice, this

MINI CASE STUDY
Zappos shoes: a service-led business model

Zappos started out selling shoes online in 1999 at the end of the dotcom boom. To compete against existing mail order and home shopping companies the US-based company had to revolutionise its business model around excellent customer service, to craft an engaging culture and develop unique operational features. Three organisational components turned out to be critical: creating a team with diverse strengths, to have the courage to follow their convictions, what employees think is 'right', and a passionate approach to work. The highly competitive online market meant that the company had to demonstrate its flexibility to adapt and rapidly learn from its mistakes.

Online retailers can focus their resources on marketing and creating easy user experiences that make their websites more appealing to customers. Zappos' success has typically involved a trial and error approach to improving processes and maximising its customer service. In taking over their Fulfilment Centre and responsibility for the distribution of the product ranges, the company demonstrated its customer-centric practices to deliver products and services as efficiently as possible. For customers this means free returns, sending out a replacement order before the return comes back, honouring returns up to 365 days from date of purchase and other customer-focused activity. The company found that some its values were known when it started out but others have been discovered on the way: they are both implicit and explicitly stated and employees are not restricted by scripts and rules. The 'Zappos experience' replaces selling with an adherence to business precepts: serve a perfect fit, make it effortlessly swift, and play to win (Michelli, 2012).

---

necessitates retailers re-designing existing IT and logistics infrastructure to use 'click and collect'. In other respects too, internet and catalogue channels have different requirements. Packaging and labelling must accommodate the delivery of individual items to customers, compared to physical store channels where products are packed in multiple units and delivered in outer cartons (Zhang et al., 2010).

Multichannel retailing

The fundamental impact of the internet and new communication technologies has led to the development of a multichannel strategy. A multichannel *marketing* strategy describes the diversification from online and offline to embrace multiple platforms (Harris and Dennis, 2008). The term can cover a range of marketing functions, including providing customers with transactional options, advisory customer services and alternative communication channels for promotions. The strategy enables the implantation of detailed analytics, measured through website traffic counts, click-through rates, conversion rates, profitability and research studies (Pookulangara et al., 2011). In these ways a multichannel marketing strategy can be distinguished from inter-channel and cross-channel marketing strategies, which define more limited use of one or more communication channels.

For retailers a multichannel strategy requires the integration of online sites and physical stores, but can also include catalogues and telephone sales, with the aim of optimising consumer shopping experiences. In this way the distinction between home shopping, online and physical retailing is increasingly blurred. However, the growth of multichannel retailing has been variable, from strategies that embrace innovative and comprehensive websites, to small-scale, experimental applications (Doherty and Ellis-Chadwick, 2006). Hernandez et al. (2010) specifically demonstrate how the 'winning-over' stages must focus on informing the potential e-customers of the advantages and properties of e-commerce in general and later concentrate on how to maintain favourable and long-lasting relationships with e-customers.

Channel integration is the extent to which channels share common organisational resources, including departments such as marketing, finance and logistics. Channel integration leads to channel synergy, which Pentina and Hasty (2009: 361) define as '. . . using . . . channels in a manner that increases the effectiveness of each separate channel in providing a seamless shopping experience for the customer'. Consequently, channel integration and channel synergy are antecedents of implementing an integrated, seamless multichannel offer to the customer. Andreini (2008) categorises multichannel integration at three levels, the informational supporting model, independent channels model, characterised by low interaction and connection between the two channels and the fully integrated channels model where retailers create an online store as if it is an offline store offering inventory check, reserving/ordering and picking/returning. Synergies between the channels help firms reduce inventory, post-sales and pre-sales costs and enhance profit maximisation more effectively than using a single channel (Kumar and Venkatesan, 2005).

The total integration of channels is defined as **omnichannel**. The consumer is understood to engage with all channels without necessarily favouring any particular one. Retailers need to implement their strategy using three guiding principles, seamless customer experience, a single view of inventory and a single view of the retailers' customers (*Retail Week*, 2013). Omnichannel encompasses all brand touchpoints and channels including mobile platforms and social networks to provide a consistent experience (Bain and Co., 2011).

Enabling customers to shop seamlessly across multiple channels involves them being able to buy a product in one channel and collect it in another (Berman and Thelan, 2004). The 'click and collect' function is re-defining stores, as it enables customers to order goods online and pick them up in-store or collect from a third party. As competition for market share increases, so effective integration of multichannel operations enables retailers to improve customer service, build loyalty and attract new consumers. To implement this strategy requires an organisation-wide focus on maintaining a coherent position across all channels. Management support and strategic fit are found to be of primary importance and require retailers to deploy a portfolio of appropriate resources and capabilities in support of their online operations (Doherty and Ellis-Chadwick, 2009).

An integrative customer model requires both a strong understanding of customer preferences and behaviours and a robust Information Technology (IT) architecture that supports an overarching customer relationship management strategy (Peterson *et al.*, 2010). Powerful databases are used to increasingly target a wider range of channels to provide offers of customers. To achieve these objectives requires retailers to invest in and update the necessary IT and logistics infrastructure. Significant financial resources are required to replace older, legacy systems that have to be re-designed. Some new technologies facilitate multichannel consumer interactions; these include interactive product media screens, digital shopping assistants and stock availability checks.

Companies need to create internal alignment among their organisational factors to 'fit' the conditions in the external environment (Raddats and Burton, 2011). Good organisational design enables effective business decisions to be made with a high degree of consistency, recognising that different strategies require different organisational forms (Galbraith, 1995). In traditional retail businesses, organisational structures should be sufficiently flexible to allow the coexistence of multichannel business operations under the same roof (Tangpong *et al.*, 2009).

At the other extreme from mass marketing, luxury brands have found multichannel integration particularly difficult. Luxury is typified by the exclusive quality of products and services, and their challenge is to manage these fundamental attributes through new and more accessible media. Their online sites typically demonstrate high-quality photography and film, detailing the product features, social media and the tremendous impact of the internet and new technologies has resulted in retailers embracing a multichannel marketing strategy by linking e-commerce, catalogues and bricks-and-mortar stores together to optimise consumer shopping experiences.

The success of multichannel retailing is immediately obvious and highlights the artificial nature of any distinction between home shopping and store shopping. As store-based retailers have increasingly extended their online trading, the distinction between home shopping and store-based retailing is becoming ever more blurred (Mintel, 2012).

Virtual grocery store

Virtually all mobile phones in Europe in the future are expected to be smartphones, capable of accessing the internet. Tesco sees new opportunities to sell to customers using smartphones on the go, and rather than moving customers from one channel to another seeks to bring in additional new business. The company which piloted free WiFi access in its stores, is also experimenting with ideas such as virtual shopping using 3D technology. One example was its trial of the UK's first interactive virtual grocery store at London's Gatwick airport, which the supermarket group indicated a way forward in "the future of shopping". Holidaymakers in the departure lounge browsed 80 core products, from milk and bread to toilet paper, displayed on 10 large refrigerator-sized touch screens. They could scan bar codes underneath these products with a smartphone to place them in a Tesco.com online shopping basket, and arrange for the shopping to be delivered home when they returned from their holiday. The trial follows Tesco's successful launch of virtual stores in South Korea in 2011, which allowed commuters to shop for groceries by pointing their mobile phones at billboards in subway stations and at bus stops.

Source: adapted from *Financial Times*, 6 August 2012. © The Financial Times Limited 2012. All rights reserved. Pearson Education is responsible for providing this adaptation of the original article.

CHAPTER SUMMARY

This chapter introduced forms of non-store retailing and explained the development and characteristics of mail order, direct mail and online retailing for home shopping. Mail order uses a catalogue to reach its customers. In the UK companies successfully used an agency system to distribute their catalogues, to offer credit terms and collect payment. However, in the later twentieth century the system declined and mail order companies failed to use their assets to use the internet. Newer forms of catalogue distribution included direct mail and specalogues that targeted specific customer groups.

Online retailing emerged in the 1990s as the web enabled companies and consumers to interact firstly through the communication of information and later to interact and sell products and services. Online retailing can take a number of forms including pureplay, hybrid bricks-and-clicks, where store-based retailers open up online sites, and online retailers, physical stores, auctions and portals. Stores themselves may take on a showroom function. Online retailers need to take decisions about their market position, defining their product and service assortment, resources, website design and communications. Consumer engagement and interactivity is an important aspect of online retail planning. Multichannel retailing has become a dominant form as retailers seek to maximise the opportunities to engage with consumers. Channel integration needs to be carefully managed so that the customer experience is replicated seamlessly across each channel. Consequently retailers need to co-ordinate communications, inventory and customer data both in store and across an increasingly complex range of online media.

EXERCISES AND QUESTIONS

1. Online retailing has overtaken the traditional mail order channel. Debate whether you think printed catalogues will become obsolete or if there will still be a place for them in ten years' time.

2. Discuss the advantages and disadvantages of customers being able to 'click and collect'. Consider ways in which online and bricks-and-mortar channels could become more integrated in the future.

3. Research into the newest innovations in online retailing via the trade and technology magazines. Present details of two of the key innovations to your fellow students, assessing the viability of their use by online retailers.

4. As seen in the cases in this chapter, Oak Furnitureland has expanded from being an etailer to buying bricks-and-mortar stores, yet Bead Boutique has moved from being a physical store to become an etailer. Discuss the reasons why the retailers made these moves and the possible impact that the types of product they sell could have had on their choice of distribution channels.

REFERENCES

Anderson, C. (2004) The Long Tail, *Wired Magazine*, 12 October,.

Andreini, D. (2008) Multi-channel integration strategies and environmental aspects. A conceptual framework in retailing. 8th International Conference on Business and Economics, Florence, 18–19 October, ISBN: 9780974211459, www.gcbe.us/8th_GCBE/data/Daniela%20Andreini.doc (accessed 10 March 2012).

Bain and Co. (2011) Omnichannel retailing, Report, 22 November 2011, http://www.bain.com/Images/Bain%202011%20Holiday%20Series_Issue%233.pdf, accessed on 10 December 2011.

Berman, B. and Evans, J.R. (2010) *Retailing Management: A Strategic Approach*, 11th edn, Upper Saddle River, NJ: Pearson.

Berman, B. and Thelan, S. (2004) A guide to developing and managing a well-integrated multi-channel retail strategy, *International Journal of Retail & Distribution Management*, 32(3), 147–156.

Bird, J. (2013) Putting service back into retail, *Financial Times*, 30 July.

Brynjolfsson, E. and Hu, Y. (2011) Goodbye Pareto principle, hello long tail: the effect of search costs on the concentration of product sales. *Marketing Science*, 57(8), 1373–1386.

Cassab, H. and MacLachlan, D.L. (2009) A consumer-based view of multi-channel service, *Journal of Service Management*, 20(1), 52–75.

Coopey, R., O'Connell, S. and Porter, D. (2005) *Mail Order Retailing in Britain*, Oxford: Oxford University Press.

Dann, S. and Dann, S. (2011) *E-Marketing, Theory and Application*, Basingstoke: Palgrave Macmillan.

Doherty, N.F. and Ellis-Chadwick, F. (2006) New perspectives in internet retailing: a review and strategic critique of the field, *International Journal of Retail & Distribution Management*, 34(4/5), 411–428.

Doherty, N.F. and Ellis-Chadwick, F. (2009) Exploring the drivers, scope and perceived success of e-commerce strategies in the UK retail sector, *European Journal of Marketing*, 43, 10/11), 1246–1262.

Galbraith, J. (1995) *Designing Organizations: An Executive Briefing on Strategy, Structure and Process*, San Francisco: Jossey Bass.

Harris, L. and Dennis, C. (2008) *Marketing the e-business*, 2nd edn, Abingdon: Routledge.

Hernandez, B., Jimenez, J. and Martin, M.J. (2010) Customer behaviour in electronic commerce: the moderating effects of e-purchasing experience, *Journal of Business Research*, 63(9–10), 964–971.

Kent, A.M. and Omar, O.E. (2003) *Retailing*, Basingstoke: Palgrave.

Kumar, V. and Venkatesan, R. (2005) Who are the multichannel shoppers and how do they perform? Correlates of multichannel shopping behaviour, *Journal of Interactive Marketing*, 19(2), pp. 44–62.

Kurtz, D.L. and Boone, L.E. (2010) *Principles of Contemporary Marketing*, 15th edn, London: South-Western Cengage Learning.

Liu, C. and Tsai, W. (2010) The effects of service quality and lifestyle on consumer choice of channel types: the health food industry as an example, *African Journal of Business Management*, 46(6), 1023–1039. Available from www.academicjournals.org/article1380722327_Liu%20and%20Tsai.pdf

Mintel (2012) *Home Shopping Europe*, July.

McKinsey Quarterly (2011) The Future of Marketing, Issue no. 3.

Michelli, J.A. (2012) *The Zappos Experience*, New York: McGraw-Hill.

Molenaar, C. (2012) *E-Marketing: Applications of Information Technology and the Internet within Marketing*, Abingdon: Routledge.

Pentina, I. and Hasty, R.W. (2009) Effects of multichannel coordination and e-commerce outsourcing on online retail performance, *Journal of Marketing Channels*, 16, 359–374.

Peterson, M., Grone, F., Kammer, K. and Kirscheneder, J. (2010) Multi-channel customer management: delighting consumers and driving efficiency, *Journal of Direct, Data and Digital Marketing Practice*, 12(1), 10–15.

Phan, D.D., Chen, J.Q. and Ahmad, S. (2005) Lessons learned from an initial e-commerce failure by a catalog retailer, *Information Systems Management*, 22(3), 7–13.

Pookulangara, S., Hawley, J. and Xiao, G. (2011) Explaining multi-channel consumer's channel-migration intention using theory of reasoned action, *International Journal of Retail & Distribution Management*, 39(3), 183–202.

Raddats, C. and Burton, J. (2011) Strategy and structure configurations for services within product-centric businesses, *Journal of Service Management*, 22(4), 1–25.

Retail Week (2013) Multichannel Now, Report. London. Available online at: www.retail-week.com.

Sheehan, B. (2010) *Online Marketing*, Lausanne: AVA.

Stone, M., Hobbs, M. and Khaleeli, M. (2002) Multichannel customer management: the benefits and challenges, *Journal of Database Marketing*, 10(1), 39–52.

Strategic Direction (2006) Tesco drives e-retail message home: but 'bricks and mortar' stores continue to thrive, *Strategic Direction*, 22(3), 21–24.

Tangpong, C., Islam, M. and Lertpittayapoom, N. (2009) The emergence of business-to-consumer E-commerce: new niche formation, creative destruction, and contingency perspectives, *Journal of Leadership & Organizational Studies*, 16(2), 131–140.

Tun-Min, J. and Tung, T. (2013) *Predictors of consumer intention to adopt apparel tablet catalog applications*, Proceedings of the European Association for Education and Research in Consumer Distribution conference, University of Valencia, 3–5 July.

Ward, C. (2012) *Grattan: Home Shopping for 100 Years,* Bradford: History Writer.

Zhang, J., Farris, P., Kushwaha, T., Irvin, J., Steenburgh, T. and Weitz, B. (2010) Crafting integrated multichannel retailing strategies, *Journal of Interactive Marketing,* 24(2), 168–180.

FURTHER READING

Coopey, R., O'Connell, S. and Porter, D. (1999) Mail order in the United Kingdom, 1880–1960: how mail order competed with other forms of retailing, *International Review of Retail, Distribution and Consumer Research,* 9(3), 261–273.

Neville, S. (2014) Most retail chiefs still 'too slow' to embrace the internet, *The Independent,* 15 June (available online at: http://www.independent.co.uk/news/business/news/most-retail-chiefs-still-too-slow-to-embrace-internet-9538867.html?origin=internalSearch).

Qu, Z., Wang, Y., Wang, S. and Zhang, Y. (2013) Implications of online social activities for e-tailers' business performance, *European Journal of Marketing,* 47(8), 1190–1212.

Rose, S., Clark, M., Samouel, P. and Hair, N. (2012) Online customer experience in e-retailing: an empirical model of antecedents and outcomes, *Journal of Retailing,* 88(2), 308–322.

Spiller, L. and Baier, M. (2012) *Contemporary Direct and Interactive Marketing*, 3rd edn, Chicago IL: Racom Communications.

Case study

Asos

Asos is a pureplay retailer launched in 2000, that offers more than 50,000 branded and own-label product lines across womenswear, accessories, beauty, jewellery, footwear and menswear. With over 6 million active customers it is the UK's largest independent fashion and beauty retailer. The company is aimed at fashion-forward 16–34-year-olds and is seen as a trend setter by this age group. UK sales have benefited from refocusing on its domestic market with improved delivery, reduced prices and increasing digital marketing. After years of consistently high sales growth, 2012 saw a slowdown. Subsequently the introduction of low-cost Primark merchandise proved to be a particularly successful initiative.

The company has seen considerable success in selected international markets; spreading its fashion forward offer internationally and through new channels. Having launched a US website, followed by French and German language websites in 2010, Asos launched dedicated sites in Australia, Italy and Spain. These were supported by concerted marketing investment in each country. Overall, the company distributes to more than 190 other countries from its central distribution centre in the UK, though the retailer has stated that its long-term goal is to tailor ranges to local customers and reduce the cost of delivery and returns by developing warehousing facilities abroad.

Asos attributes its continued international growth to its innovative approach, focusing on offering its customers new styles and reacting quickly to fashion trends. Offers such as free next-day delivery have also had a strong appeal. However, their international management structure, with local management teams in the USA, France, Germany and Australia also contribute to strong sales growth.

In 2011 Asos rationalised its distribution and order fulfilment processes into a 49,000 square metre facility at Barnsley in the north of England. This new site is operated by a third party company, Unipart Logistics, and will replace the retailer's four distribution centres in Hemel Hempstead, near London. The total cost of the move, including the site acquisition and transfer costs, was estimated to be in £19m, which impacted on operating profits in 2011, which were reduced to £16m, but which recovered to £32m the following year. In common with many other online retailers the company offers a click-and-collect service, through Collect+ a network of 4500 stores that offer long opening hours, convenient, neighbourhood locations and secure storage facilities.

Asos Fashion Finder was launched in March 2011 which is an interactive forum that presents customers with latest fashion trends, product recommendations and the ability to upload outfits and items they like. When showing customers where to buy products from, Fashion Finder does not necessarily direct them to goods sold by Asos, helping the service to establish trust and credibility. The aim is to drive site traffic and build Asos' credentials as a fashion destination (as opposed to a retail destination).

While its advertising expenditure decreased in 2012 the company has been active in developing its online media links. Asos 'on the go' provides apps for mobile connectivity for search and order functions as style guidance. But the company also works with other sites, launching Europe's first fashion transactional Facebook site which stocks Asos's entire range and allows customers to purchase, leave comments, 'like' products, and link their opinions on Asos items to their Facebook profiles. The retailer anticipates that easy access to its ranges will result in improved levels of sales conversion. Conventionally it has sites on Twitter and You Tube, but more recently it created a digital campaign with Pinterest.

Offline, the company has entered into collaborative promotions to extend its exposure to its target market. These have included an interactive campaign with toiletries market-leader Nivea and Pernod Ricard to promote its Malibu and Jacob's Creek brands and offer fashion advice in pop-up bars in four major UK cities.

DISCUSSION QUESTIONS

1. How does Asos differentiate itself as an online retailer?
2. What are the key issues facing the internationalisation of fashion retailers?
3. To what extent does Asos have the capability to become a multichannel retailer?

CHAPTER 12

Legislation and ethics in retailing

Learning outcomes

After completing this chapter you should be able to:

- understand how legislation affects products and retail prices;
- explain the impact of legislation on promotional activities;
- recognise the effect of legislation on retailers' locations;
- examine a variety of ethical issues which impact upon retail marketing;
- appreciate the significance of the 'triple bottom line': environmental, social and financial sustainability;
- evaluate the importance of Corporate Social Responsibility for retailers.

Introduction

This section addresses legal and ethical issues that affect the ways in which retailers operate, based upon the framework of the retail marketing mix. There are many such issues and these can vary from one country to another, so we draw attention to some of the key legislation and ethical aspects which impact upon retailers in different regions. Clearly, retailers have to abide by the law, but in addition they can adopt an ethical stance to minimise their negative impacts and to encourage positive impacts on society and the environment. An ethical stance is guided by moral principles that influence the decision-making and behaviour of the retailer's employees, as explained here by Berman and Evans (2010: 46):

> In dealing with their constituencies (customers, the general public, employees, suppliers, competitors, and others), retailers have a moral obligation to act ethically . . . When a retailer has a sense of ethics, it acts in a trustworthy, fair, honest, and respectful manner with each of its constituencies . . . The best way to avoid unethical acts is for firms to have written ethics codes, to distribute them to employees and channel partners, to monitor behaviour, and to punish poor behaviour – and for top managers to be highly ethical in their own conduct.

In addition to lessening their own sustainability impacts, retailers have the ability to encourage sustainable behaviour in others by:

- influencing suppliers;
- educating consumers;
- taking back recyclables (Martin and Schouten, 2012).

All types of business can address sustainability but retailers are possibly the type that have the most potential to impact upon consumers and suppliers, due to their direct interaction with them. The many facets of retailing that have legal considerations or potential ethical issues are listed in Figure 12.1.

Legislation and regulations affecting retailing

By Helen Goworek and Mercedes Malloy

It is important for retailers to be aware of all of the legislation that pertains to retailing, to ensure that no laws are infringed. Although some of the laws described here and in the textbook may not be compulsory in your own region, they can provide examples of good practice for retailers in other locations. Also, it may be useful to be aware of these laws if you work for a company which exports products to the country to which they apply. The official website which contains historical and newly enacted legislation for the UK can be found at: http://www.legislation.gov.uk/. Countries within the European Union (EU) are also governed by EU laws (see: http://ec.europa.eu/eu_law/index_en.htm). All aspects of the retail marketing mix are subject to legislation, some of which is discussed below (see Table 12.1).

Potential ethical issues	Retailing facets	Legal considerations
Effects on existing traders Impacts on consumer welfare Needs of vulnerable segments	Competitive strategy	Monopolies /competition regulations Corporate taxation Labour laws
Environmental impacts: sensitive areas Traffic flows, environmental impacts Effects on local traders and centres	Location	Planning consents and appeals Local zoning regulations Building regulations
Environmental impacts of logistics 'Food miles' and product quality Ethical international sourcing	Supply chain	Regulations on drivers' hours Restrictions on vehicle sizes/emissions Duty and taxation on some imports
Maintaining real choice for customers Potential impacts on smaller suppliers Avoidance of 'sweatshop' supplies	Retail buying	Restrictions on use of buying power Laws pertaining to bribery/corruption Regulations on some imports
Safe and healthy products 'Green' manufacturing and transport Clarity in labelling	Products and labels	Labelling regulations Weights and measures regulations Safety and fitness for purpose
Clarity of price labels Integrity of price comparisons Predatory pricing and competition	Pricing	Price marking regulations Unit pricing requirements Inclusion or display of relevant taxes
Complex offers – consumer confusion Small print and excessive limitations Promoting unhealthy products	Promotions and special offers	Trades descriptions regulations Bargain offer regulations Restrictions on seasonal sales
Deceptive advertising Invasive advertising esp. online Copy-cat branding	Advertising and branding	Trades descriptions regulations Copyright/patents/trademark laws 'Passing off' regulations
Consumer confusion in some layouts Displays offensive to some groups Tempting children or the vulnerable	Store environments	Duty of care for customers and staff Accessibility for disabled people Restrictions on displays, e.g., tobacco
Respect for customers' time, welfare Hard-selling disguised as service Protection of staff welfare	Customer service	Staff entitlements to breaks/holidays Limits on trading hours Safety of (self) service technologies
Degradation of traditional channels Less accessible to disadvantaged More delivery congestion/pollution	Non-store retailing	Consumer rights to inspect and return Protections against hidden charges Cooling-off periods
Impacts on indigenous retailers Workers' rights Environmental impacts of logistics	International retailing	Tariffs and embargoes Ownership and development laws Other country-specific regulations

Figure 12.1 Examples of legal and ethical considerations in retailing
Source: Peter McGoldrick

Table 12.1 Key legislation affecting the marketing mix

Marketing mix element	Relevant UK legislation and regulation
Pricing	Sale of Goods Act; Price Marking Order
Promotion	Trade Descriptions Act; Advertising standards; Trademarks
Product	Sale of Goods Act; Intellectual property: copyrights, patents and trademarks; Health and Safety laws; General Product Safety Regulations; WEEE Directive; REACH Regulation
Place (location)	Health and Safety laws; Planning regulations

Pricing

Laws on pricing may have different names in different countries but many cover similar principles. The price is part of the contract of sale between the buyer and seller and this is governed in the UK by the Sale of Goods Act (1979). The marking of retail prices so that they are made clear to customers is governed by the Price Marking Order (2004). Price fixing via agreements between firms to keep prices artificially high is disadvantageous to consumers and is therefore illegal in the US under the Sherman Antitrust Act (Lusch *et al.*, 2011). One of the major ethical issues in relation to pricing is Fairtrade. A premium is paid to the producers of Fairtrade products along with fair working conditions and local sustainability (Fairtrade Foundation, 2012). FINE, an international alliance of **Fairtrade** organisations, offers the following definition:

> Fair Trade is a trading partnership, based on dialogue, transparency and respect, that seeks greater equity in international trade. It contributes to sustainable development by offering better trading conditions to, and securing the rights of, marginalized producers and workers – especially in the South (FINE, 2001: 1).

Fairtrade products have grown in market share in recent years, initially from staple items such as coffee and bananas, to achieve mainstream acceptance in some product brands, e.g. Cadbury's chocolate now carries the Fairtrade logo. This market growth is demonstrated by the fact that UK consumers bought more than ten times as much Fairtrade coffee by value in 2011 than in 2001 (Fairtrade Foundation, 2012). McGoldrick and Freestone (2008) found that consumers were willing to pay the price premium associated with ethical products, as long as they were convinced that the goods had genuine ethical credentials and the Fairtrade mark appears to be an effective form of branding which can offer the reassurance that they seek.

Promotion

Legal and ethical decisions about promotion can vary from one country to another. For example, contrasting decisions have been made by courts in the US and France about eBay selling counterfeit goods, demonstrating the differences between legislation (Lusch *et al.*, 2011). The Trade Descriptions Act (UK Legislation, 1968) prohibits false descriptions of products and it is therefore essential for UK retailers to be aware of its contents when promoting and selling goods. This legislation can relate to quantity, size, method and place of manufacture, composition and fitness for purpose of goods, amongst other characteristics.

Many ethical issues can be debated in relation to promotion. For example, photographs can easily be manipulated to make products and models appear more attractive. Cosmetics brand L'Oreal has recently been taken to task for manipulating photographs of the actress Rachel Weisz to make her appear younger, leading to the cancellation of this advertising campaign in the UK (Burrell, 2012). Advertising to children has been another key area of debate in recent years, especially when this encourages them to eat unhealthy foods. This has resulted in a ban in the UK on advertising 'junk foods' during TV programmes which appeal to children (Sweney, 2006).

In addition to legal constraints on retailers' promotional activities, there are numerous ethical issues to be considered. In the UK, the Advertising Standards Authority (ASA) is the regulatory body that compiles codes of practice and regulates advertising with the aim of making it 'legal, decent, honest and truthful'. Every year the ASA receives thousands of complaints about the ethics of adverts. They assess complainants' concerns and investigate whether or not these adverts breached their rules. Consequently, in 2010 more than

2000 advertising campaigns were either changed or withdrawn (ASA, 2012). Another ethically dubious practice is the use of so-called 'bait-and-switch' tactics, where exceptionally low-priced products are advertised to entice people into stores, but sales staff then persuade customers to switch to buying higher-priced alternatives. This deceptive technique is understandably forbidden by US federal regulations which state that retailers must be willing to show or sell products that they have offered through advertisements (Levy and Weitz, 2012).

Product

The Sale of Goods Act (UK Legislation, 1979) states that goods need to be of 'merchantable quality' and this is one of the key pieces of legislation governing product sales in the UK. The Trade Descriptions Act (UK Legislation, 1968) is also significant as it seeks to ensure that the goods supplied are described accurately and therefore meet the purchaser's expectations. Trading Standards Officers are employed to enforce this and other relevant legislation in order to protect standards (Trading Standards, 2012). Although legal constraints on the products sold by retailers focus mainly on product safety, description, liability and warranties (Lusch *et al.*, 2011), there are also many more laws and ethical issues pertaining to products. For example, in the EU a law known as the Waste Electrical & Electronic Equipment (WEEE) Directive was introduced in 2007 to lessen the environmental impacts of the disposal of products. This directive encourages 'closed-loop recycling' by retailers, meaning that they are responsible not only for selling the products, but also for arranging for their disposal after use. According to the Environment Agency (2012):

> The WEEE Directive aims to both reduce the amount of electrical and electronic equipment being produced and to encourage everyone to reuse, recycle and recover it. The WEEE Directive also aims to improve the environmental performance of businesses that manufacture, supply, use, recycle and recover electrical and electronic equipment.

The WEEE Directive affects retailers and other distributors who sell electrical and electronic equipment to the public, because they must ensure that their customers can return their waste equipment of a similar type and function free of charge. Computer retailer PC World has responded to this directive by placing containers in its stores to collect used electrical goods for recycling. It is not currently compulsory for clothing retailers to do the same. However, in 2012 M&S launched an initiative to collect used clothes in its stores for distribution to charity (Luu, 2012). This type of good practice by retailers can help towards reducing the 5.8 million tonnes of textiles which are estimated to be sent to landfill per year in the European Union (Gould, 2014).

Another recent European Community Regulation law relating to the impact of products on the environment is the Registration, Evaluation, Authorisation and Restriction of Chemical substances (REACH), which deals with the safe use of chemicals. Certain allergies and illnesses in Europe are rising and the use of chemicals is suspected to have contributed to this. The REACH Regulation gives greater responsibility to industry to manage the risks from chemicals and to provide safety information on substances used. Producers and importers of chemicals need to register them and provide information for their safe use (European Commission, 2012).

Counterfeiting goods and 'passing off' (when one company uses another's trademark without permission) pose legal problems for many retailers and brands, relating to both the 'product' and 'promotion' elements of the marketing mix. In the UK these issues are covered by intellectual property laws (Intellectual Property Office, 2012), which cover copyright, trademarks and patents. Copyright protection covers creative works such as written, visual, musical and artistic works and is an automatic right, so it is not necessary to apply for it. Since intellectual property laws are often violated, large retailers can employ lawyers specialising in intellectual property to deal with copyright and trademark infringements. The importation of goods into a country to be sold by retailers is governed by customs regulations, so medium and large-sized retailers can also employ specialist staff to deal with importing merchandise.

Consumers have a legal right to return products to a retailer in the UK for a refund if they are faulty, or in legal terms they are not 'fit for purpose'. However, some retailers offer a better deal to customers beyond their statutory rights. Many UK clothing retailers now allow customers the option to return unused products for a refund within 28 days, even if the goods are not faulty. Similarly, multichannel retailer Argos offers a 30-day money-back guarantee to customers who change their minds after buying its products, as long as they are unopened and the customer has retained the receipt. This system can make consumers more inclined to buy products from these retailers, since less risk than usual is involved in the purchase decision. UK retailers have an obligation to comply with the UK Legislation (2005) by ensuring that they do not sell products that they consider or know to be unsafe. In such circumstances they are required to issue a recall notice as specified in the regulations to arrange for consumers to return the product. This may involve the retailer contacting the consumers concerned directly, where practicable, or publishing notices in newspapers and stores to inform customers of the recall.

Increasingly, consumers are becoming concerned with ethical issues relating to the products and services that they purchase. Megicks *et al.* (2010) investigated influences on ethical and socially responsible consumption within the grocery sector and identified four main areas of concern for shoppers: global and local sourcing; product heritage; animal and human rights and marketing communications. These issues are of relevance to retailers in general, as they can also relate to other product areas in addition to groceries.

Retailers are not permitted to monopolise a specific retail product sector and this aspect of UK legislation is overseen by the Competition and Markets Authority (CMA), a body established in 2014 by the merger of the Competition Commission and the Office of Fair Trading, to ensure healthy competition between businesses and to avoid restrictive practices. If mergers between retailers mean that a single company takes a disproportionately high market share the CMA will investigate the situation.

Place (location)

Legislation relating to location is crucial for retailers and the laws which impact upon location are planning regulations, as discussed here by McGoldrick (2002: 274):

> In most countries, retail locations are constrained to a greater or lesser degree by government regulations and planning restrictions. In Britain, the local authority is responsible initially for granting or refusing planning permissions, although appeal inquiries are administered through central government.

Planning regulations impose restrictions on the location and architectural style of stores in the UK. Retailers need to submit planning applications to local authorities to build new premises or sometimes even to change the use of an existing building. Public inquiries can be conducted to acquire the views of local people before the building of a new retail site is approved (McGoldrick, 2002). This is mainly because a large new store can affect the nearby community by increasing traffic pollution and noise, as well as adversely affecting the business of existing shops. This can particularly affect small retailers who can struggle to compete with large retailers' prices. Out-of-town shopping has also been criticised for drawing customers away from traditional town/city centre shopping areas. There has been a severe decline in small independent, non-affiliated shops in the UK in recent years, as out-of-town shopping has increased. Blythman (2004: 5) comments that 'statistics on small shops read like casualties of a curiously uneven war', supported by figures which show that the number of grocers in the UK fell from 116,000 in 1961 to 20,900 in 1997. This situation is also happening in other countries such as Spain, albeit at a different pace (Coca-Stefaniak *et al.*, 2004). One of the negative social consequences of the closure of small shops is the emergence of 'food deserts', which have been defined by geographers Russell and Heidkamp (2011: 1197) as 'an urban or rural area with significantly limited access to retail sources of healthy and affordable food, due to a combination of socioeconomic disadvantages and physical distance'. The closure of small stores can have adverse social effects since this can reduce employment and food deserts have been found to impact mostly upon economically disadvantaged members of society (*ibid.*).

Friends of the Earth (2006) and other pressure groups have campaigned against the expansion of large retailers. The UK grocery sector was referred to the Competition Commission in 2006 owing to concerns about the powers of major retailers in some areas. Certain retailers had been accused of ignoring planning regulations, e.g. a Tesco store built in Stockport in 2004 exceeded the size requested in its planning application by 20 per cent (BBC, 2006). The Competition Commission has developed a 'competition test' to be applied to firms with a 'strong presence' in a locality, to prevent them from opening additional outlets or extending stores in that neighbourhood (Competition Commission, 2008). Under this test, the Office of Fair Trading (OFT) provides advice to the planning authorities on the potential impact of retail sites. Retailers may be permitted to open new stores if they are new to an area or if there are four or more competitors within a 10-minute drive of the proposed site. There are similar laws in Japan that constrain the development of larger stores, thus limiting the attractiveness of this market for overseas retailers (Davies and Itoh, 2001; Economist Intelligence Unit, 2012). It should be borne in mind that planning regulations in other countries may be less stringent than the exacting rules which have been described here.

Legislation and ethics within the extended marketing mix

The earlier part of this chapter focuses on the standard '4Ps' marketing mix. As retailing is a service, it is also appropriate to consider ethics within the context of the extended marketing mix, i.e. the '7Ps'. Health and safety laws and guidelines are particularly relevant to the extra three elements of 'people', 'process' and 'physical evidence'. Employment law and ethical working conditions apply specifically to the 'people' element of the 7Ps. Another legal issue relating to people is retail theft, often referred to as **shrinkage**. We may have the impression that this is attributable solely to customers furtively 'shoplifting' goods, yet unethical consumer behaviour can also take forms such as passively benefitting from shop staff's errors (Mitchell *et al.*, 2009). Furthermore, it has been found that over 40 per cent of retail theft is carried out by retailers' staff, with more than 50 per cent of those staff being employed at management level (Gilbert, 2003). This can be described as 'white collar crime', defined by Johnstone (1999: 124) as 'those acts committed by a fraud or theft by members of the business community who have used their position of trust or responsibility to achieve the criminal objective' and described by Tonglet (2002) as 'consumer misbehaviour' (see Chapter 3 Retail consumer behaviour and market segmentation). These research results have serious implications for the owners of retailers and the monitoring of their staff and customers.

Sustainability and corporate social responsibility

As you are no doubt aware, sustainability is a major global issue, with climate change being the main element that receives frequent publicity in the media. The average global temperature has been found to be rising, and most experts believe that carbon dioxide (CO_2) emissions from burning fossil fuels have contributed to this rise, since emissions increased by 29 per cent between 2000 and 2008, according to the Global Carbon Project (BBC News, 2009). Population growth is another major concern as the world's population was estimated to have reached seven billion in 2011 (*China Daily*, 2011) with diminishing resources available to sustain the planet's inhabitants. The term **triple bottom line (TBL)** was coined by Elkington (2004: 3) who states: 'In the simplest terms, the TBL agenda focuses corporations not just on the economic value that they add, but also on the environmental and social value that they add – or destroy.' At the corporate level, sustainability can be addressed by businesses to a certain extent through the implementation of a Corporate Social Responsibility (CSR) policy. According to Martin and Schouten (2012: 167):

> . . . retailers can reduce many of the barriers to living more sustainably. They can increase consumers' access, in terms of price and assortment, to products that are more sustainable. They can help consumers understand the importance and the increased value of more sustainable living. And they can help provide the infrastructure or systems that make it easier for consumers to make more sustainable choices.

Drivers behind the increased emphasis on sustainability issues in business are summed up as legislation, cost reduction, social responsibility and market pressure. Pressure groups including NGOs such as Greenpeace and Labour Behind the Label, climate change, ethical consumerism and government initiatives are some of the influencing factors that have encouraged retailers to adopt more sustainable practices. Consequently, in recent years it has become standard practice for retailers to publish CSR policies or codes of conduct but more importantly, such policies need to be embedded within the corporate culture in order for them to be effective (Webley and Werner, 2008). The implementation of CSR policies can have the added benefits of contributing towards a retailer's brand image and competitive advantage (Hu and Wang, 2009) as well as potentially saving costs. According to the Sustainable Business Institute (2015):

> Corporate sustainability is the business practice of improving profitability, competitiveness, and market share while preserving natural resources and ensuring the well-being of all life on this planet . . . The bottom line is that sustainable business practices make good business sense – good for the environment, good for business because corporate sustainability offers a compelling return on investment by driving innovation, managing risk, and improving stakeholder relations.

There were 284,490 retail outlets in the UK in 2011 and more than 2.8 million people were employed in the retail sector in 2009, forming 11 per cent of the total UK workforce (BRC, 2012). The retail industry and its staff therefore have a significant impact upon environmental and social sustainability in this country, as well as in many others. UK retailer Marks & Spencer (M&S) integrated environmental and social sustainability within its marketing strategy in 2007 by introducing its 'Plan A' policy covering a variety of relevant issues (Marks & Spencer, 2007). Plan A includes the target of making M&S a carbon-neutral business, meaning that its net carbon output will be zero. M&S's plan started a trend for addressing sustainability impacts which other UK retailers have since followed. The sector's main industry body, the British Retail Consortium (BRC), developed its own sustainability strategy 'A Better Retailing Climate' in 2008, backed by companies accounting for more than half of the retail market by value with the aim of disseminating strategies for sustainability throughout the retail sector (BRC, 2008).

RETAIL MARKETING CAREERS
Christian Smith, Corporate Responsibility Manager

Christian Smith runs his own agency, Inclusi, which specialises in CSR and sustainability. Prior to this he worked as Corporate Responsibility Manager for etailer Asos for three years. Christian was born in London and moved to Sierra Leone with his family for several years during his childhood before returning to the UK. He studied BA (Hons) Modern Languages, specialising in French and German, spending time in both of these countries during his studies. After graduating and working in various jobs, Christian became a language teacher in Japan, where he lived for three years. He then returned to Europe to take a job as a European Researcher for the Tokyo Electric Power Company, focusing on France and Germany. His interest in sustainable clothing was inspired by his next move, when he moved to Brazil, living in Brasilia for a year where he studied Energy and Sustainable Development. He returned to the UK to study for an MSc in Environment and Sustainable Development at University College, London (UCL) whilst working as a recruiter and market researcher for a fashion headhunting agency, Fusion Associates, and 24 Seven Inc. He consequently researched into sustainable fashion for his dissertation.

Christian launched Inclusi in 2013, targeting a mix of clients from his existing contacts and companies that have approached him. He has aimed to maintain a high profile since leaving Asos by attending relevant events and using social media. He has also been talking to venture capitalists about the new paradigm of sustainable production, to encourage them to invest in this area. Christian believes that:

> We have a duty to look at the supply chain as well as our customers to provide an opportunity for a better product, and that means better in terms of quality and the raw materials that go into that product. It's not product then sustainability, it's both at the same time.

During his time at Asos, Christian was involved in liaising with colleagues internally, in addition to dealing with external organisations. Internally, he provided advice on CSR strategy including energy, waste, water, warehouse efficiencies, and material sourcing in the areas of logistics, procurement, supply chain and design. He was responsible for writing and implementing the Asos environmental policy, aligned with the UN Global Compact. He also established an internal CSR communications programme, organising external speakers to give presentations on relevant topics at Asos Head Office. Christian collaborated mostly with Asos's creative, marketing and IT teams, particularly relating to marketing communications for the etailer's sustainable clothing section 'The Green Room'. They redesigned the content and strategy of the web pages together, communicating the stories behind the brands to raise the profile of sustainability activities and Christian also managed the Green Room Twitter account. Another part of his role was to oversee the company's adherence to government policies and regulations by creating reporting mechanisms for WEEE and waste packaging, as well as measuring greenhouse gas emissions data for CarbonNeutral certification using the WRI/WBCSD GHG Protocol. Christian represented Asos in liaising with external bodies such as the British

Source: with permission from Christian Smith

Retail Consortium, WRAP's Sustainable Clothing Action Plan (SCAP) and community engagement programmes including projects with the Prince's Trust.

Christian considers honesty, understanding, empathy and persistence to be the key characteristics for CSR practitioners, combined with the ability to take in complex information about sustainability and supply chains. Here he describes some of the challenges of working in a CSR role:

> How do you take these messages out and really get people engaged and change the way they behave? How do you address these issues in a way that's friendly, engaging and exciting without alienating and making people feel guilty about things? Students now are a lot more social media-savvy and they can find really interesting ways to start sharing these messages. I had the opportunity to go back to UCL and give some lectures about sustainability in practice and students asked me questions my colleagues would never dream of asking. It's about having a target to alleviating human suffering and to cause less damage to people and the planet. We live in a consumerist world and it's hard to get people to think about products in different ways. They need to understand that the products come from somewhere and what that journey is. We have a responsibility. I've been very influenced by the systems thinking course I did at UCL; we can't just think about one area of things. The moment you start talking about fashion you're touching on fifteen or more other areas, such as how you provide for the transportation systems that allow you to be productive in society. It's not just about making money all the time; it's environmental impact, not just economic impact. What is really important is finding a new mantra. Something that alludes to something exciting, innovative and creative. What I want people to think about and act upon is to leave the world in a better shape than when they arrive.

Christian enjoys the research aspect of his role to such an extent that he says 'you find some incredible things, so I don't even feel like it's part of my job because I love it so much and it's something I'm permanently doing'. He is particularly interested in the potential for 3D printing (see Chapter 2 Retail marketing strategy) to make manufacturing more sustainable. Christian offers the following advice to anyone wanting to follow a career involving CSR:

> There aren't that many CSR jobs out there but there are many jobs that if you put your CSR hat on whilst you're doing that job you might be able to have a lot more influence over the companies you work for than you'd think. If you want to go into marketing, go into it but put CSR at the forefront of what you do and challenge your clients and customers to come on that journey with you. Think about brand building, brand stickiness, brand value. If you're a Supply Chain specialist then focus on reducing the company's carbon footprint, transporting more goods by ship than airfreight, because you know it's going to be better for the environment.

Christian also recommends that designers should find out how to design more sustainably, acquainting themselves with techniques that reduce waste, which can inspire the way they design, rather than simply following trends. He cites as examples of good practice the use of an innovative fabric that is created from a combination of milk and cotton, as well as products from the French footwear brand Veja. He considers there to be sufficient people working in CSR roles already and offers the following advice to academics and students:

> It's not just about going into CSR, what we need are everyday people to understand they affect the world, to go into the jobs they would have done anyway and to use their own knowledge to make a difference. To do this, we should integrate CSR into everyday courses.

inclusi.co; Twitter:@inclusi

Social sustainability

Some of the key issues in relation to social sustainability are child labour, poverty and disease in developing countries. These are obviously major problems which need to be addressed by society in general. Nevertheless, retailers can contribute to improving social sustainability through paying fair wages; conducting thorough audits of suppliers to avoid child labour, to respect workers' employment rights and to address health and safety issues; providing benefits such as education and healthcare for workers and their families; and funding projects for communities local to the retailer and its suppliers.

SOCIAL SUSTAINABILITY 299

Sponsoring community projects was mentioned previously in relation to retailers' promotional strategies. However, if the retailer seeks to profit from its support of a community project, this could be viewed negatively by the media or by customers. Certain retailers prefer to keep a low profile about such activities, perhaps to avoid criticism, or possibly because they genuinely believe in the importance of helping the causes which they support. An example of a local community project run by a retailer is Sainsbury's supermarkets' 'Active Kids' programme (Sainsbury's, 2012). Alternatively, retailers can support communities in the localities where their suppliers are based. Ethical fashion retailer 'People Tree', which sells clothing in the UK and Japan, funds schools for the children of staff working for its suppliers in Kathmandu, Nepal (People Tree, 2012).

As part of their CSR strategies, retailers also have the option to buy from suppliers and brands which have strong social sustainability policies. For example, various footwear retailers sell shoes from 'TOMS', a brand which donates a free pair of shoes to a child in a developing country for every pair sold (TOMS, 2012). An organisation which encourages retailers to purchase more socially sustainable products is the Ethical Trading Initiative (ETI), an organisation which aims to promote respect for workers globally (ETI, 2014). The ETI is an alliance of retailers, brands, trade unions and NGOs which can support member organisations with advice on adopting a code of labour practice to enable then to source products that are socially sustainable. The ETI currently has over 60 members, most of whom are retailers, in diverse product sectors and price brackets, from Sainsbury's to Burberry.

LUSH CHARITY POTS

Fresh, handmade cosmetics retailer, Lush, addresses both social and environmental sustainability by selling pots of a hand and body moisturiser called 'Charity Pot' in its stores (see Figure 12.2). Lush donates the whole selling price to charity, apart from Value Added Tax (VAT), which is a compulsory payment. The lotion is both environmentally sustainable, in that it contains organic cocoa butter, and socially sustainable through the projects it sponsors. The retailer seeks to fund small 'grassroots' groups in the UK and overseas that aim for long-term positive change to human rights, the environment and animal protection with average grants of around £4000, from the proceeds of this product. Some of the charities can benefit further by being featured on the pots. Charity Pot, along with all other Lush products, are regularly also donated to

Figure 12.2 Examples of Lush charity pots and Lush staff Mark Deeley and Laura Read selling charity pots in the Nottingham branch
Sources: author's own photograph; Lush, with permission from Lush

organisations by Lush to assist in fund-raising such as raffles, or for their patients/clients to use.

The black plastic Charity Pots themselves are 100 per cent recycled and are also recyclable. Lush is based in Dorset in the south of England and the pots are produced in the UK to minimise carbon emissions during their transport. 10g trial pots situated at the cash desks encourage high numbers of customers to try the product before buying the full-size pot. Lush offers customers an incentive to recycle the pots in store by offering a free fresh face mask for every five full-size pots or tubes of any of their products that are returned to their outlets. Globally, Charity Pot is sold in 21 countries and in 2013 over £2.3 million was raised for grassroots campaigns around the world through sales. Total global charitable giving in 2013 was £3.1 million. Other aspects of CSR used by Lush are the sale of limited edition charity products and a self-imposed carbon tax on flights where money is donated to environmental organisations.

For further information, visit www.lushcharitypot.com.

Source: Lush, 2014, with contributions from Stephanie Boyd

Environmental sustainability

As well as climate change/global warming and CO_2 emissions other major concerns about environmental sustainability are pollution, disposal of waste, the removal of forests (deforestation) and the transformation of land into desert (desertification). Again, these are significant issues which need to be dealt with by society on a large scale. However, retailers have the ability to contribute to lessening environmental sustainability impacts through, for example:

- reducing CO_2 emissions (carbon footprint) by lowering fuel and energy usage;
- using renewable resources and avoiding unsustainable sources;
- selling organic products (grown without the use of pesticides or genetic modification);
- recycling;
- reducing packaging and using sustainable packaging;
- reducing the amount of waste to landfill;
- avoiding the use of hazardous chemicals.

Retailers have many opportunities for lowering their energy usage, for example by reducing the amount of lighting and heating they use in stores and offices. Fuel usage can be minimised during the transportation of products by packing goods carefully to maximise space, using streamlined, fuel-efficient lorries and avoiding deliveries by air freight. Additionally, packaging can be reduced in size and made from recyclable materials. Merchandise itself can be made from recycled materials such as 'Freitag' bags, which are made of recycled lorry tarpaulins (Freitag, 2012). Retailers can encourage responsible forest management by avoiding the use of wood from endangered forests (Forest Stewardship Council, 2012). The use of pesticides can be reduced or eliminated in fabrics, fruit and vegetables, e.g. by retailers selling organic cotton products and organic food.

The factors involved in retailers behaving in a more environmentally friendly manner can sometimes be more complex than they initially appear. For example, less packaging can be used for products in stores, but more packaging may consequently be needed in transit to ensure the products arrive unharmed. It may seem more environmentally sustainable for a UK-based retailer to offer locally sourced fruit and vegetables instead of importing them. Though this saves fuel from transportation costs, more energy may be expended through the heating required to grow the produce in the UK. Additionally, consumers may expect paper bags to be more environmentally friendly than plastic bags, since the wood from which they are made can be replaced by planting more trees and the bags can easily be recycled. On the other hand, although plastic bags are made from fossil-fuel derivatives and this source is not renewable, the lighter weight of the bags means that more of them can be fitted into a delivery than paper bags, thus saving fuel during transport. Many supermarkets in the UK offer recycling facilities for plastic carrier bags in store or with home deliveries. The Irish Government took this a step further in 2002 by imposing a levy on plastic carrier bags, resulting in an immediate reduction in the amount being issued by retailers of over 90 per cent (Environment, Community and Local Government, 2012) and in 2014 the Scottish government introduced a 5p charge on plastic carrier bags. A ban on free plastic bags in China in 2008 also had a positive effect, resulting in a reduction in their use of approximately two-thirds (Xing, 2009). These examples demonstrate the powerful effect that legislation can have on both the environment and consumer behaviour.

ETHICAL CONSUMERS
By Jeff Bray, Waitrose Fellow of Retailing, Bournemouth University

While most of this chapter focuses on the actions of retailers, it is widely acknowledged that their customers often take a keen interest in ethical considerations. In some cases customers will direct their purchasing towards those product brands and retailers that are believed to operate in the most ethical manner, and in other cases customers actively avoid (boycott) brands that are thought to behave in an unethical manner.

Since 1999, the Co-operative bank has conducted a significant annual audit of ethical consumer spending in the UK. The resulting reports highlight very clearly how consumer interest in ethical concerns is steadily growing as highlighted in Figure 12.3. Based on this data it is clear that retailers not only have a moral obligation to act responsibly, but that it is also increasingly likely to be in their commercial interest garnering greater support from customers.

The 'ethical consumer' is one who considers the working conditions of producers and suppliers, and is mindful of the environmental impacts of purchases. Their purchasing decisions can be positive in specifically selecting to purchase through a retailer that is believed to uphold high ethical standards, or purchase products that are specifically denoted as 'fair trade' or 'organic', both recognised standards that assure the fair treatment of workers and environmental consideration in the sourcing and processing of products; or negative through the 'boycotting' of specific brands or retailers due to their perceived negative ethical stance. In the UK it is clear that all of these behaviours are growing in importance with sales of fair trade items increasing from £33m in 2000 to £1.3bn in 2011; sales of organic products increasing from £605m in 2000 to £1.5bn in 2011, and the effect of boycotting increasing from £773m in 2000 to £1.7bn in 2011 (Co-operative Bank, 2012).

In spite of these rather convincing growth statistics, it is clear that not all consumers are equally concerned

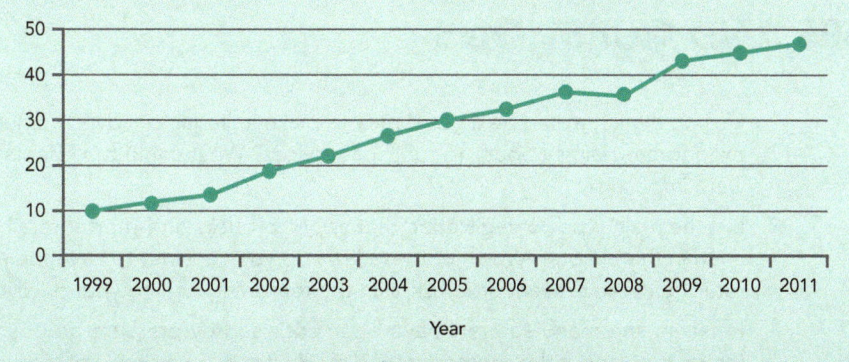

Figure 12.3 Ethical spending in the UK 1999–2011, £bn
Source: compiled from: Co-operative Bank Ethical Consumerism Reports available from http://www.goodwithmoney.co.uk/ethicalconsumerismreport/

about ethical considerations. Significant academic attention has been devoted to trying to understand which consumers are most likely to select ethical products, however different studies often produce conflicting results such that we still lack a clear understanding of consumer behaviour in this regard. What is clear however is that many more customers claim to care about ethical issues than actually purchase according to these principles. This has become known as the 30:3 phenomenon in which roughly 30 per cent of all consumers claim to care about the kind of ethical issues relevant to product purchase, and yet in most cases ethical products have failed to achieve market shares in excess of 3 per cent (Cowe and Williams 2000). A number of studies have examined why these 'conscientious' consumers are not translating their good intentions into purchasing actions and have found that price constraints, lack of choice and a lack of information are all impeding sales (Bray et al., 2011) suggesting that there are significant further opportunities for market growth in this area as retailers develop their strategies.

CHAPTER SUMMARY

This chapter has covered some of the key issues affecting retailers in terms of legislation and ethics, based on a framework of how such factors affect the elements of the marketing mix.

- Pricing needs to conform to legislation, being marked accurately. Fairtrade products pay a premium to the grower of raw materials or the manufacturer.
- Promotion needs to describe products or services accurately and conform to advertising standards set by the ASA.
- Products need to conform to intellectual property law, taking into account product safety as well as sustainability.
- Retail locations need to conform to planning regulations and health and safety laws.
- The services marketing mix contains the additional '3ps' of physical environment, process and people, who are covered by employment law.
- Social and environmental sustainability can be incorporated into retailers' practice and are usually directed by the development and implementation of CSR policies.
- Retailers are uniquely positioned to significantly affect sustainability impacts through their sourcing and selling activities, due to their influence on the supply chain and consumers.

EXERCISES AND QUESTIONS

1. Do you think it would be a good idea to make it illegal for advertisements to 'gloss' or exaggerate claims about products or services? What could the effects be if such laws were imposed?
2. List the main types of legislation that apply to bricks-and-mortar retail outlets, as outlined in this chapter. Which of these laws do you consider to have the most impact on retailing at the present time? Explain the reasoning behind your decision.
3. Retailers and manufacturers have been criticised by pressure groups for not making information about the sources of their products and conditions of the workers transparent to consumers. Do you believe they should be forced by law to do so? If they did so, what effects might this have on the pricing of retailers' products?

4 Intellectual property legislation includes copyright protection that covers creative content such as written, visual, musical and artistic works and is an automatic right, as explained above. Taking this quiz will enable you to check your knowledge of UK copyright law: http://www.ipo.gov.uk/types/copy/c-quiz.htm.

5 UK legislation is constantly being updated and laws obviously differ between countries. Investigate whether there has been any more recent legislation enacted in the UK or your own country since this book was published.

6 Consider the legal and ethical issues that would affect a retailer selling children's toys in your country. Your considerations should include the social implications of promoting and selling products to children and the environmental impact of the merchandise, amongst other points. You should write down what you believe to be the key ethical and legal concerns in order of priority.

7 Search for an official website or publication which includes legislation relating to the country in which you live. Make a note of at least three laws with which retailers in your area would need to comply, e.g. the equivalent of the Sale of Goods Act or price fixing laws. Compare these to some of the laws mentioned in this chapter, noting any differences.

8 Visit one of your favourite stores, taking time to consider the aspects of legislation and ethics that affect your experience there as a consumer, e.g. sales legislation; planning legislation; intellectual property laws and environmental sustainability. Discuss the potential difficulties that could arise for consumers if the retailer did not have to fulfil any of these legal and ethical obligations.

REFERENCES

ASA (2012) *Welcome to the ASA* (available online at: http://www.asa.org.uk/).

BBC (2006) *Tesco planning permission refused*, BBC News, 13 September (available online at: news.bbc.co.uk/1/hi/england/manchester/5342914.stm).

BBC (2009) *Earth 'heading for 6C' of warming*, BBC News, 17 November (available online at: http://news.bbc.co.uk/1/hi/sci/tech/8364926.stm).

Berman, B. and Evans, J.R. (2010) *Retailing Management: A Strategic Approach*, 11th edn, Upper Saddle River, NJ: Pearson.

Blythman, J. (2004) *Shopped: The Shocking Power of the British Supermarkets*, London: Harper Collins.

Bray, J., Johns, N. and Kilburn, D. (2011) An exploratory study into the factors impeding ethical consumption, *Journal of Business Ethics*, 98, 597–608.

BRC (2008) *A Better Retailing Climate* (available online at: www.brc.org.uk/Downloads/A%20Better%20Retailing%20Climate.pdf).

BRC (2012) *2009 employment figures* (available online at: http://www.brc.org.uk/brc_home.asp)

Burrell, I. (2012) Rachel Weisz L'Oréal advert censured for altering image, *The Independent*, 1 February (available online at: http://www.independent.co.uk/news/media/advertising/rachel-weisz-loral-advert-censured-for-altering-image-6297708.html).

China Daily (2011) World population hits 7 billion, 31 October (available online at: http://www.chinadaily.com.cn/world/2011-10/31/content_14010260.htm).

Coca-Stefaniak, A., Hallsworth, A.G., Parkera, C., Bainbridge, S. and Yuste, R. (2004) Decline in the British small shop independent retail sector: exploring European parallels, *Journal of Retailing and Consumer Services*, 12, 357–371.

Competition Commission (2008) *Groceries Market Final Report*, press release issued 30 April 2008 (available online at: www.competition-commission.org.uk/press_rel/2008/. . ./14–08.pdf).

Co-operative Bank, The (2012) *Ethical Consumerism Reports* (available online at: http://www.goodwithmoney.co.uk/ethicalconsumerismreport/).

Cowe, R. and Williams, S. (2000) *Who are the Ethical Consumers?* (available online at: http://www.goodwithmoney.co.uk/ethical-consumerism-report-9/).

Davies, G. and Itoh, H. (2001) Legislation and retail structure: the Japanese example, *International Review of Retail, Distribution and Consumer Research*, 11(1), 83–95.

Economist Intelligence Unit, The (2012) Japan: Consumer Goods and Retail Report, in *Economist Intelligence Unit*, 6 February (available online at: http://www.eiu.com/index.asp?layout=ib3Article&pubtypeid=1122462497&article_id=1588795143&rf=0).

Elkington, J. (2004) Enter the triple bottom line, in Henriques, A. and Richardson, J. (eds) *The Triple Bottom Line: Does it All Add Up?* London: Earthscan.

Environment Agency (2012) Waste electrical and electronic equipment (available online at: www.environment-agency.gov.uk/business/topics/waste/32084.aspx).

Environment, Community and Local Government (2012) *Plastic Bags* (available online at http://www.environ.ie/en/Environment/Waste/PlasticBags/).

ETI (2014) *About ETI* (available online at: http://www.ethicaltrade.org/about-eti).

European Commission (2012) *REACH* (available online at: http://ec.europa.eu/environment/chemicals/reach/reach_intro.htm).

Fairtrade Foundation (2012) *What is Fairtrade?* (available online at: http://www.fairtrade.org.uk/what_is_fairtrade/faqs.aspx).

FINE (2001) Fair Trade Definition and Principles (available online at: www.befair.be/site/download.cfm?SAVE=1314&LG=1–FINEdefinition, accessed 26 August 2009).

Forest Stewardship Council (2012) *About FSC* (available online at: http://www.fsc.org/about-fsc.html).

Freitag (2012) *Freitag Facts and Figures* (available online at: http://www.freitag.ch/about/factsandfigures).

Friends of the Earth (2006) *Supermarket heavyweights trample planning system*, press release 16 January 2006 (available online at: http://www.foe.co.uk/resource/press_releases/supermarket_heavyweights_t_16012006.htm).

Gilbert, D. (2003) *Retail Marketing Management*, Harlow: Financial Times/Prentice Hall.

Gould, H. (2014) Upcycling: turning unwanted materials into desirable fashion, *The Guardian*, 21 January 2014 (available online at: http://www.theguardian.com/sustainable-business/sustainable-fashion-blog/upcyling-materials-fashion-live-chat).

Hu, Y.C. and Wang, C.C.F. (2009) Collectivism, corporate social responsibility, and resource advantages in retailing, *Journal of Business Ethics*, 86, 1–13.

Intellectual Property Office (2012) *Types of IP* (available online at: http://www.ipo.gov.uk/types.htm).

Johnstone, P. (1999) Serious white collar fraud: historical and contemporary perspectives, *Crime, Law and Social Change*, 30, 107–130.

Levy, M. and Weitz, B.A. (2012) *Retailing Management*, 8th edn, New York: McGraw-Hill Irwin.

Lusch, R.F., Dunne, P.M. and Carver, J.R. (2011) *Introduction to Retailing*, International/7th edn, Stamford, CT: South-Western Cengage Learning.

Lush (2014) *Charity Support* (available online at: https://www.lush.co.uk/our-values/charity-support).

Luu, P. (2012) Joanna Lumley launches Marks & Spencer's Shwopping campaign, *The Telegraph*, 26 April (available online at: http://fashion.telegraph.co.uk/columns/phong-luu/TMG9228252/Joanna-Lumley-launches-Marks-and-Spencers-Shwopping-campaign.html)

Marks & Spencer (2007) *Plan A* (available online at: http://plana.marksandspencer.com/).

Martin, D. and Schouten, J. (2012) *Sustainable Marketing*, Upper Saddle River, NJ: Pearson.

McGoldrick, P.J. (2002) *Retail Marketing*, Maidenhead: McGraw-Hill.

McGoldrick, P. J. and Freestone, O.M. (2008) Ethical product premiums: antecedents and extent of consumers' willingness to pay, *International Review of Retail, Distribution and Consumer Research*, 18(2), 185–201.

Megicks, P., Memery, J. and Williams, J. (2010) Influences on ethical and socially responsible shopping: evidence from the UK grocery sector, *Journal of Marketing Management*, 24(5), 637–659.

Mitchell, V.W., Balabanis, G., Schlegelmilch, B.D. and Cornwell, T.B. (2009) Measuring unethical consumer behavior across four countries, *Journal of Business Ethics*, 88, 395–412.

Ord, K. (2008) The drivers behind the increased emphasis on green issues in business, in Mangan, J., Lalwani, C. and Butcher, C. (eds) *Global Logistics and Supply Chain Management*, Chichester: John Wiley & Sons.

People Tree (2012) *How People Tree Does Fair Trade* (available online at: http://www.peopletree.co.uk/content/27/fair-trade).

Russell, S.E. and Heidkamp, P.C. (2011) 'Food desertification': the loss of a major supermarket in New Haven, Connecticut, *Applied Geography*, 31, 1197–1209.

Sainsbury's (2012) *Active Kids* (available online at: http://www2.sainsburys.co.uk/activekids/).

Sustainable Business Institute (2015) *What is Corporate Sustainability?* (available online at: http://www.sustainablebusiness.org/2.html).

Sweney, M. (2006) Total ban for junk food ads around kids' shows, *The Guardian*, 17 November (available online at: http://www.guardian.co.uk/society/2006/nov/17/health.food).

TOMS (2012) *One for One* (available online at: http://www.toms.co.uk/one-for-one).

Tonglet, M. (2002) Consumer misbehaviour: an exploratory study of shoplifting, *Journal of Consumer Behaviour*, 1(4), 336–354.

Trading Standards (2012) *Policy* (available online at: http://www.tradingstandards.gov.uk/policy/index.cfm).

UK Legislation (1968) *Trade Descriptions Act* (available online at: http://www.legislation.gov.uk/ukpga/1968/29/contents).

UK Legislation (1979) *Sale of Goods Act* (available online at: http://www.legislation.gov.uk/ukpga/1979/54).

UK Legislation (2005) *The General Product Safety Regulations 2005* (available online at: http://www.legislation.gov.uk/uksi/2005/1803/part/3/made).

Webley, S. and Werner, A. (2008) Corporate codes of ethics: necessary but not sufficient, *Business Ethics: A European Review*, 17(4), 405–416.

Xing, X. (2009) Study on the ban on free plastic bags in China, *Journal of Sustainable Development*, 2(1), 156–158 (available online at: http://www.ccsenet.org/journal/index.php/jsd/article/viewFile/299/267).

FURTHER READING

CarbonNeutral Company: http://www.carbonneutral.com/our-services/carbonneutral-certifications

Carrigan, M. and Attalla, A. (2001) The myth of the ethical consumer: do ethics matter in purchase behaviour?, *Journal of Consumer Marketing*, 18(7), 560–578.

Ethical Trading Initiative: http://www.ethicaltrade.org/get-involved

Goworek, H. (2014) Sustainable marketing, in Molthan-Hill, P. (ed.) *The Business Student's Guide to Sustainable Management*, Greenleaf Publishing.

Greenpeace Sustainable Tuna League Table: http://www.greenpeace.org.uk/blog/oceans/win-bin-our-2014-tuna-league-table-20140228

Griffith, R. and Harmgart, H. (2012) Supermarkets competition in England and planning regulation, *International Review of Retail, Distribution and Consumer Research*, 22(1), 1–25.

Newholm, T. and Shaw, D. (2007) Studying the ethical consumer: a review of research. *Journal of Consumer Behaviour*, 6, 253–270.

Price Marking Order: http://www.legislation.gov.uk/uksi/2004/102/introduction/made

Regulations on the disposal of used electrical and electronic equipment in the UK: http://www.environment-agency.gov.uk/business/topics/waste/139283.aspx

Rettie, R., Burchell, K. and Barnham, C. (2014) Social normalisation: using marketing to make green normal, *Journal of Consumer Behaviour*, 13, 9–17.

Case study

Some challenges in product sourcing in global retail supply chains

By Nick Ellis, Head of Department of Marketing, University of Durham

Setting the scene

This case study looks at the management of the inter-firm relationships between several European retailers and one of their key Indian suppliers. It does so in the context of concerns regarding the treatment of stakeholders too often forgotten in the making of strategic supply chain decisions: the manufacturer's local employees.

Some of Europe's largest clothing retailers source significant quantities of garments manufactured in India. The huge buying power of these European companies allows them to negotiate extremely low wholesale prices and very short production timescales. While this is commercially beneficial for the retailer, it effectively helps to determine the environment and labour conditions for the workers who are making the clothes. Research by local NGOs in Tirupur, India has exposed some highly questionable working conditions in Tirupur's textile and garment factories that manufacture clothing for big European fashion retailers, according to the European Coalition for Corporate Justice (ECCJ, 2011). It appears that the employment practices of some Indian companies in the global supply chain create poor social and economic conditions for Indian workers and their local communities.

The ECCJ is a non-profit organisation that promotes corporate accountability by representing NGOs, trade unions, consumer groups and academic institutions from all over Europe, including national chapters of Oxfam, Greenpeace, Amnesty International and Friends of the Earth. Some of the information collated by the ECCJ in their investigation into the global retail supply chain was provided by the Campaign Against Sumangali Scheme. This is a coalition of organisations in India that works to raise awareness about the so-called 'Sumangali Scheme' and calls for an end to this system of recruitment (see below).

India is the second largest producer of textiles and garments in the world and one of the few countries that covers the whole value chain, from the production of cotton to the last stitching in a piece of apparel. India, together with China, Bangladesh and Vietnam, is a major exporter of finished garments to the US and EU. In 2009 India exported garments worth 4.06 billion Euros to the EU, accounting for 55 per cent of the country's total garment exports (Apparel Export Promotion Council, 2010). Textiles and garments thus play a key role in the Indian economy. In order to attract foreign investment the Indian government attempts to create a business-friendly environment. For instance, special economic zones have been set up where firms are offered various financial incentives. At the same time, implementation and enforcement of labour laws can be slow. This is partly because the textiles and garment value chain is long and complex, with a high incidence of subcontracting.

Investigating an Indian manufacturer

Located in the state of Tamil Nadu, KPR Mill Limited is a leading textile producer and garment exporter. It has integrated the whole value-adding process, from yarn manufacturing to clothing production. The company employs more than 10,000 workers, of which about 90 per cent are female. In the fiscal year 2010, the listed company made net profits of 8.21 million Euros. In 2009, KPR Mill produced 9.029 metric tonnes of fabric and 20.5 million pieces of clothing (ECCJ, 2011). All the clothing the company produces is intended for export, mainly for the European market, where 90 per cent of its exports are sent. According to the firm's own website, buyers from a number of well-known European retailers (or global firms with outlets in Europe) have sourced from this supplier, such as H&M from Sweden, Decathlon, Kiabi and Carrefour from France, C&A from Belgium/Germany and Gap from the US (KPR Mill 2010a).

KPR Mill states that it has 'one of the lowest employee cost of the industry . . . At 3.3% of sales, against an industry average of 8.3%' (KPR Mill, 2010b). Contributing to its low labour cost is the fact that the company employs mainly young women. While factory management claims to only employ girls aged 18 years or older, ECCJ located girls aged as young as 13 working at one of the company's spinning mills. While the benefits of having as many members of the family in employment as possible should not be discounted by those of us blessed with a Western sense of relative economic security, the employment of child labourers is a violation of India's Child Labour (Prohibition and Abolition) Act 1986 and a breach of the International Labour Organization's Convention Prohibiting Child Labour.

In fact, the company specifically targets young, unmarried girls mostly coming from socially and economically marginalised indigenous communities. These girls are offered a relatively large amount of money, Rs. 30.000 to Rs. 40.000 (approximately €500 to €650), after three years of employment, which can be used to pay for their dowry. Although legally prohibited, the payment of a dowry is still commonplace in India, where a girl often cannot get married without her family providing money to the groom. This labour recruitment system has, rather ironically, come to be known as the 'Sumangali scheme', where 'Sumangali' refers to a happy and contented married woman in Tamil.

Moreover, KPR Mill prohibits the formation of a trade union even though this contradicts Indian law and international treaties. According to the factory management, workers earn above the legally set minimum wage. Statements of workers and ex-workers, however, indicate that workers are paid less than this. A considerable amount is deducted from the workers' wages to pay for factory-provided meals and to save for the dowry. In addition to low wages, women have been subjected to excessive working hours: workers and ex-workers told ECCJ they have to work 12-hour shifts several times a week. The working week consists of six working days so, unsurprisingly, the workers are frequently exhausted. There are also many complaints of poor food quality. In March 2009, 24 girls working were admitted to hospital with food poisoning, and three later died (*Kalai Kathir*, 2009). The workers' health is furthermore compromised by work floor conditions. In the spinning area, humidity, heat and swirling cotton fibres all contribute to ill-health and breathing difficulties.

Although India may have laws in place against these types of malpractice, ECCJ could not identify that any action had been taken against the manufacturer by the Indian Labour Department. For the parents of the girls working in the garment factory, most of whom are financially vulnerable and have not had access to education, allowing their daughters to continue to work for KPR Mill means they will at least be given meals three times a day. Thus local communities affected by the impacts of this supplier to European retailers tend to feel powerless and largely remain silent.

Responses from EU retailers

In 2010, after a fact-finding mission by journalists organised by the ECCJ, various newspapers reported on labour conditions at KPR Mill. Following these media articles, some of these retail brands announced they have ended their trade with the supplier or that they are considering terminating the relationship. Before publishing its findings, ECCJ sent their draft report to those companies mentioned in it. The responses of these retailers are summarised below.

- H&M responded that, following several audits, it has decided to end its business relationship with KPR Mill's garment division. H&M states that it did not have 'the needed trust for a continued relationship and has therefore decided to terminate the business relationship.' H&M informed ECCJ that it works with other buying companies in the Brands Ethical Working Group. This group is discussing how buyers can work together to prevent the Sumangali scheme among spinning mills. H&M has also addressed the issue with the Apparel Export Promotion Council in India and the Indian Minister of Textiles.

- Carrefour explained that it has taken the decision to end its relationship with KPR Mill. It said no discussion had been possible with KPR Mill about their use of the Sumangali scheme. More broadly, Carrefour had teamed up with a local NGO, 'to identify possible cases of Sumangali scheme in its supply chain and avoid starting to work with suppliers using this scheme'.

- C&A claimed to have already ended its cooperation with KPR Mill in 2007 when it discovered the use of the Sumangali scheme. It subsequently placed a test order with a KPR subsidiary in 2010, not knowing that in fact it was dealing with KPR Mill. When this was discovered, C&A stated that the order was pulled. C&A informed ECCJ that it is currently conducting extensive auditing of its Tirupur supply base in order to be certain that similar practices do not occur in its supply chain.

- Decathlon (now Oxylane) conducted an audit at KPR Mill following the press reports. During this audit some critical non-conformances with Decathlon's code of practice were identified. Decathlon subsequently suspended its production, and KPR Mill was given the time to set up and implement a corrective action plan. Decathlon states that recent audits have confirmed a strong improvement. It has therefore decided to re-launch its production at KPR Mill.

- Gap denied having any business relationship with KPR Mill.
- Kiabi did not respond to ECCJ's draft report at all.

Discussion

So what may we conclude about retailers' decision-making processes from this case study? The ECCJ believes that EU companies have a duty of care to ensure that human rights and environment are respected throughout their operations, including their supply chain. In order to be effective and increase leverage to address these problems, it asserts coordination amongst retail buyers is crucial; for instance by mutual agreement, such as the Brands Ethical Working Group supported by H&M above, not to purchase goods from supply chains where questionable practice exist.

Admittedly, while some of the retailers in this case only appear to have responded following media revelations, there does seem to be a shift towards much closer examination of inter-firm relationships and the practices of partner firms within the retail supply chain. Moreover, in addition to retailers imposing their own codes of practice 'vertically' within the supply network, they are starting to collaborate 'horizontally' between themselves. This sort of agreement may be difficult to achieve across the sector, however, if retailers are caught in a 'race to the bottom' to lower their production costs – after all, what better way to gain a competitive advantage over your main high-street rival than to be able to source your products more cheaply than they can?

The functional separation of departments (such as marketing and purchasing) inside retail companies may also have had some impact on buying decisions. Simply signing a contract to produce a new style of clothing in an export processing zone does not require an individual to think in great detail about the ramifications of this simple action (signing the form). A manager may have done what was expected from someone in a purchasing role by having sought out a low cost manufacturer. Indeed, despite the claims by several of the EU retailers regarding their Indian sourcing practices in this instance, in many day-to-day activities the 'consideration of ethics . . . is somewhat forgotten in the . . . quest to achieve economic and financial goals' (Laczniak and Murphy, 2006: 155).

Taking this point even further, we might ponder the fact that criticisms of firms like Nike, Walmart and other major companies accused of using 'sweatshop' labour (Knight and Greenberg, 2002) have kept supply chain sourcing issues in the news for some years. But, in all honesty, should a retailer or clothing manufacturer care about those producing its goods? Does such controversy surrounding the way garments are produced have much impact on total sales? Some of the retailers highlighted in ECCJ's report may have been concerned about their reputations, but what do consumers actually think? Is it the case that, as Holt et al. (2004: 72) propose: 'consumers vote with their checkbooks if they feel that transnational companies aren't acting as stewards of public health, worker rights, and the environment'? This seems rather a very strong assumption to make about the buying behaviours exhibited by consumers. A hard-pressed retailer might not consider it a very compelling economic argument, regardless of its moral validity.

References

Apparel Export Promotion Council (2010) AEPC News: India-EU FTA to garner extra garment exports worth $3 billion, http://www.aepcindia.com/news.asp?id=319&yr=2010 (accessed on 4 October 2010).

European Coalition for Corporate Justice (2011) Trapped in Chains: Exploitative working conditions in European fashion retailers' supply chain, Brussels, Belgium: ECCJ.

Holt, D.B., Quelch, J.A. and Taylor, E.L. (2004) How global brands compete, *Harvard Business Review*, September, 68–75.

Kalai Kathir [Tamil newspaper] (2009), Erode edition, 19 March.

Knight, G. and Greenberg, J. (2002) Promotionalism and subpolitics: Nike and its labor critics, *Management Communication Quarterly*, 15(4), 541–570.

KPR Mill (2010a) Clientele http://www.kprmilllimited.com/client.php (accessed on 7 October 2010).

KPR Mill (2010b) People http://www.kprmilllimited.com/people/php (accessed: 14 September 2010) – KPR Mill has recently deleted this statement from its website.

Laczniak, G.R. and Murphy, P.E. (2006b) Normative perspectives for ethical and socially responsible marketing, *Journal of Macromarketing*, 26(2), 154–177.

DISCUSSION QUESTIONS

1 As is normally the case in the Western hemisphere, the retailers here are not vertical companies in that they do not own the factories where their clothing is produced. Despite this, do you consider them to have some responsibility for the conditions in which their products are manufactured? If so, can you suggest any other actions that they could have taken to avoid or address the issues involved in this case study?

2 What can consumers do to help avoid this type of unethical practice taking place?

3 What national or international regulations or laws would you suggest could be implemented to improve working conditions in factories in developing countries?

CHAPTER 13

International retail marketing and emerging markets

Lisa Qixun Siebers, Nottingham Business School

Learning objectives

The objectives of this chapter are to:

- explain the concept and general practices of international retailing;
- discuss the major steps of the retail internationalisation process;
- identify key theories of retail internationalisation;
- explicate significant factors that have impact on international retailing in an emerging market retail environment;
- explain retail internationalisation strategies implemented by large retail organisations in an emerging market, particularly in China.

Introduction

This chapter provides both theoretical and practical bases for readers to understand the fundamental and recent frameworks on the retail internationalisation process. It aims to provide guidance for explaining contemporary international retail phenomena, tackling real-world retail business issues and raising future questions for consideration in a retail context.

International retailing is a relatively recent phenomenon that was first being studied in the 1960s in the USA, where it was claimed to have had the special advantages in its retail model compared to other less developed markets (Hollander, 1970; Wood and Keyser, 1953; Yoshino, 1966). These authors identified the main factors that influence the expansion of international retailers in a foreign market, including political and economic conditions, social and cultural issues, and the local retail structure, such as the distribution system, supplier development, and local management issues. These ideas have been used by scholars to further analyse how and why international retailing took place in the late 1970s. For example, Waldman (1978) identified significant factors in multinational marketing management in mass retailing firms based in Europe, particularly English and French-speaking countries. Throughout the 1980s and 1990s, relevant research moved on not only to identify but to analyse how and why international retailing activities happened. For instance, Kacker (1985) assessed the prevailing trends in international retailing based on an analysis of European investments in the US retail market. Other authors found that the increase in international activities stimulated European retailers to invest in the US market (Eckstein and Weitzman, 1991).

From the mid-1990s, the growth of the developing markets attracted a great deal of research to identify what can be most attractive in an emerging global-regional market with high potential for the internationalisation of retail firms (Chen and Sternquist, 1995; Forsythe et al., 1996; Runyan and Sternquist, 1994; Treadgold, 1995; Yang and Keung, 1996). Internationalising retailers have made significant learning progress since and multinational retailers have learnt more than global ones (Sternquist, 1997).

The new century has seen retailing as an international activity in the sourcing of goods for resale, the operation of shops, and the usage of foreign labour, ideas and capital (Dawson and Mukoyama, 2006; Dawson, 2007). Sternquist (1997) classifies retailers as multinational retailers and global retailers. She claims that the former learns more about the host market because they need to be more localised and these retailers normally adopt joint venture or acquisition entry mode such as Walmart and Tesco; the latter group of retailers mainly adopt a global approach, by which they operate homogeneously in the international market by franchising or licensing such as McDonald's and Body Shop. Given these examples are largely successful retailers, one cannot generalise which approach is the best, but a suitable one needs to be considered for the type of retail business (products and services on offer), the economy of scale of the retailer, its financial capacity and international experience.

Defining international retailing

International retailing has been re-defined over the past two decades with such activities increasing around the world. International retailing is normally assumed to concern retail operations, owned by a single company, in more than one country: 'International retail operations may be defined as the operation, by a single firm, of shops, or other forms of retail distribution, in more than one country', according to Dawson (1993: 11). This definition is insufficient to describe the multi-faceted nature of international retailing in the current global retail environment. According to Alexander (1997), international retailing is the management of retail operations in markets which are different from each other in their regulation, economic development, social conditions, cultural environment, and retail structures. Further, international retailers transfer the total culture of the firm, the capability to adapt to the market, techniques of retailing, and consumer values and expectations to the new market (Dawson, 2007). However, international retailing is a more complex phenomenon because the total culture of a firm may not be capable for transferring to a new market in most cases. This chapter refers to international retailing as cross-border retail operations in a geographically different market coupled with cultural and business differences in the new market.

The rise in importance of international retailing in emerging markets continues in the 21st century. With the recent dramatic changes in China's retail environment, particularly after its entry into the World Trade Organization (WTO) in late 2001 and the changing policies towards foreign direct investment (FDI) in the retail sector in the past decade. Empirical research on the Chinese retail sector has become urgently required. Siebers (2011) explains the factors influencing retailer internationalisation in China's market. Overall, most of empirical data in the international retailing context have been obtained from developed markets and there are further needs to understand the retail internationalisation process into and from emerging markets. The key topics of this chapter include:

- defining international retailing;
- the development of international retailing;
- the international retail environment;
- the retail internationalisation process;
- retail internationalisation strategies;
- the case of China.

WALMART IN CHINA

Walmart was founded in 1962 by Sam Walton. It is the largest retailer worldwide, operating 5000 units in 10 countries by the end of 2005. Walmart entered China in 1996. They spent two years investigating the market from their headquarters in South China before finally deciding where to open their first store. Walmart was not permitted to open a store in Shanghai due to local governmental policies. They finally opened their first store in Shenzhen through a joint venture agreement with the support of the local government. In 2004, Walmart topped the China Business Competitiveness Index among commercial and trade firms. It has also established a good reputation in China; partly because it procures over 95 per cent of local products wherever a store is opened. It was ranked No. 1 under 'Good Credibility and Accurate and Prompt Payment' for several years by China Chain Store and Franchising Association (CCFA). In addition, through its Global Procurement Centre in Shenzhen, the company purchases a high volume of merchandise in China to export to the rest of the world. At present, Walmart operates a number of formats in China including Supercenters, Sam's Clubs, and Neighbourhood Markets. Walmart has expanded rapidly in China's market. The number of Walmart's outlets in China increased from 47 in 2005 to 100 in 2012, creating more than 18,000 new job opportunities.

In late 2012, Walmart China announced a new strategic optimisation plan, aiming to better meet the needs of Chinese consumers. The optimisation plan consists of five key long-term strategies: to regain price leadership; to grow with a focus on business fundamentals, to simplify the business, to invest in supply chain and technology, and to develop energised associates. These strategies illustrate the company's continued commitment to growth in China. However, whether the fast expansion strategy is appropriate in a dynamic emerging market environment shall always be questions. The future of Walmart's operations may help to deliver the answer.

Source: Siebers, 2011; www.wal-martchina.com

International retailing and its development

Retailing activities initially resulted from the development of distribution systems via a number of steps. First of all, the growth of large manufacturers led to increases in the production of consumer goods, stimulating the development of distribution systems and the growth of large retail organisations. These companies initially developed in urbanised and industrialised societies and retail structures vary across markets with similar economic and social conditions. Large retail organisations dominate in some markets such as in the USA, whereas small, local retailers retain considerable market share in other markets such as Greece.

Stages of development

The stages of development of traditional distribution channels experienced three phases. The first phase was in the 1950s, when manufacturing operations dominated in North America and Western Europe, large manufacturers sold their products to intermediaries/wholesalers, who then sold the products onto retailers. The second phase appeared in the 1960s, when large retail companies emerged and the traditional pattern of distribution broke down in some markets. Empowered retail operations began to buy directly from the manufacturers and removed the costs of dealing with the middle-man. The third stage took place by the 1980s, when the retailer had taken the control of the distribution system and was in a strong position to have an impact on manufacturers (Alexander, 1997). Retailers have become dominant in the international market since the 1990s. Before 1993, there was no retailer on the list of top 100 transnational corporations (TNCs). However, there were four by 1999, namely Royal Ahold (The Netherlands), Metro (Germany), Carrefour (France) and Walmart (USA) and no less than 14 by 2003 (Wrigley et al., 2005). Except for IKEA, the global furniture retailer, they are mainly food and general merchandise retailers (Tacconelli and Wrigley, 2009). These large retail multinational enterprises (MNEs) started to expand into the emerging markets in the mid to the late 1990s (Siebers, 2011).

The periodisation of distribution channel development can also be divided into three stages by the development of national and international distribution processes in which the manufacturer, consumer and trade have been pre-eminent according to Pommering (1979). The first stage was after World War II when the manufacturer emerged as the dominant force. The decade of the 1950s is therefore seen as the period of manufacturing dominance. The second stage occurred with the increase in wealth in Western society and supply of goods available to consumers, as well as a move to a marketing rather than sales-based approach to product distribution. The decade of the 1960s is seen as the consumer-dominated period. The third stage took place in 1970s with the emergence of large retail enterprises and the focus of market power in the retail sector (i.e. retail dominance), and the retail trade began to assume additional functions.

International retailers' expansion emerged significantly in markets with developed and efficient distribution systems in urbanised and industrialised countries. Many retailers that operate in the international market have developed a large chain operation at home across various regions through which they have accumulated abundant preparation to gain international experience, because international retailers' domestic markets provide them with a basis on which they can develop their operations into other markets. Thus, with experienced retailers' operations, these domestic markets and their consumers became mature in particular with the acceptance of certain retail format, products, services and so forth on offer, and they started to attract more international operators. By the 1990s, international retailing activities focused primarily on Australasia, EU, Japan, and North America regions. In the 21st century, due to the saturation of markets in the developed world, and the opening up of many developing markets, e.g. the relaxation of foreign investment rules and regulations, and the improvement of living standards and infrastructure in these markets, the focus of international retailing shifted to major developing countries, such as China and India (also see Siebers, 2011).

The retail internationalisation process

Motivation

International retailing often first takes place between markets where there are comparable or similar socio-economic conditions. They then expand into less developed markets such as colonial or former colonial territories and geographically proximate markets (Sternquist, 1998). With saturation of the above markets, international retailers have started their expansion into markets with psychic distance such as China (Siebers, 2011). Psychic distance refers to the distance derived from the perception and understanding of cultural and business differences between home markets and foreign markets, such as legal, political and economic environment, business practices, languages, industry structure, and so forth (Evans *et al.*, 2000). This concept will be further explained in the next section.

International investments together with choices of a specific location in the global market and the choices of a location as the first entry point in a particular international market are crucial factors in the process of retail internationalisation. These are related to push and pull factors (see Figure 13.1). Push factors refer to the factors in mature domestic markets that push a retailer to expand into a foreign market, considering negative market development limitations in a retailer's home country such as a high level of competition, retail format saturation and constrained regulatory conditions (Treadgold and Davies, 1988). Consequently, the reaction of domestic retailers to limited opportunities in their home market pushes retail organisations to move towards international markets. From the 1990s, retailers started to take a more spontaneous approach for international expansion by pull factors. According to Williams (1992), a drive to achieve greater economies of scale, stable politics, growing economies, freer trade, and large populations are pull factors which attracted retailers to internationalisation. These factors in a foreign market pull a retailer to expand into it, considering positive market growth potential in the proposed host country such as a lower level of competition, unique retail format offering, and supportive regulatory conditions as well as large population. Moreover, retailers' know-how and techniques transfer from domestic markets, helping them to establish effective international distribution systems and supply chains to stimulate further international expansion.

Push factors
Strong competition
Maturing formats
Market saturation
Trading restrictions
Economic conditions
Adverse demography

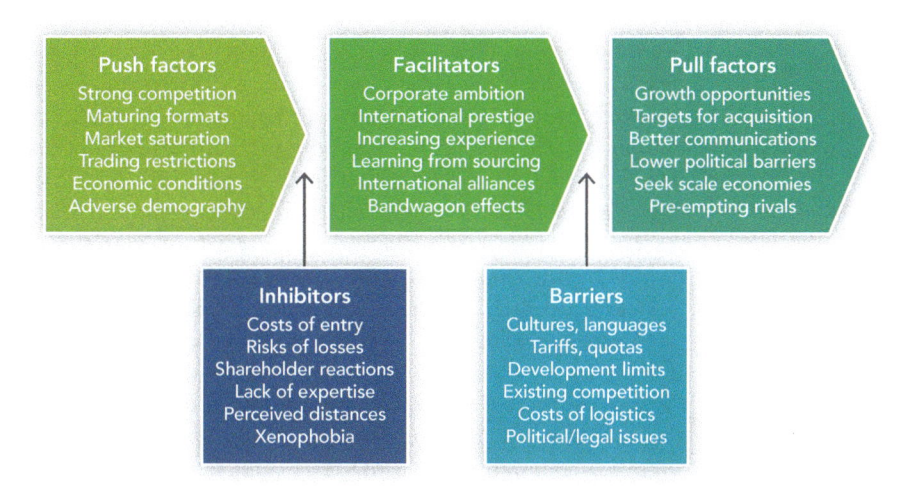

Facilitators
Corporate ambition
International prestige
Increasing experience
Learning from sourcing
International alliances
Bandwagon effects

Pull factors
Growth opportunities
Targets for acquisition
Better communications
Lower political barriers
Seek scale economies
Pre-empting rivals

Inhibitors
Costs of entry
Risks of losses
Shareholder reactions
Lack of expertise
Perceived distances
Xenophobia

Barriers
Cultures, languages
Tariffs, quotas
Development limits
Existing competition
Costs of logistics
Political/legal issues

Figure 13.1 Drivers of retail internationalisation
Source: adapted from McGoldrick, 1995

The process

The retail internationalisation process is a combination of transfer of knowledge, management practices, corporate culture and technology of a retailer from its home market to a host market, where the retailer operates in a different political, legal, economic, social-cultural, and technological environment. This process is normally divided into five main stages: pre-entry, entry, post-entry, assimilation, and exit stages according to Dawson and Mukoyama (2006). Retailers undertake various business activities at these different stages, forming the process of retail internationalisation. At the pre-entry stage, retailers' key activities include knowledge review of a potential market, local market research and investigation, decisions on extent of earlier operations, and strategy evolution. Retailers need a strong business formula in the domestic market and perceived added value in the international market, and the size of the particular segmentation of the host market is significant (Dupuis and Fournioux, 2006). At the entry stage retailers' key activities involve formula design, market choice for entry, timing of entry, entry method, and establishment of relations with suppliers. Each of these elements is worth in-depth discussion. For instance, a market choice for entry requires a thorough business environment scanning and a choice of entry mode may result in various levels of control, risks, and returns, e.g. franchising has less control compared to a joint venture entry mode, therefore less risks and less returns; but compared to export entry mode, franchising has more control, therefore, taking more risks and obtaining more returns. At this stage, adaptation to the host market may be necessary.

At the post-entry stage retailers focus on enhancement of their retail brand development, knowledge transfer to head office, network development, increase their rate of expansion, and improve their management of cost structure. During this process, retailers have had operational experience in the host market and they may have established their capacity to be a leader in that market, therefore, their business formation may be ready for change. For example, they may re-evaluate their franchising strategic alliances, increase network density in their joint ventures, establish strong relationships with suppliers and adjust their initial entry mode to acquire more stake in acquisition. Some retailers also gradually reduce their host market presence. Overall, effective learning is crucial for retailers at this stage. At the assimilation stage retailers develop their social integration of firms, triggering the establishment of an independent firm, i.e. the creation of a subsidiary company. They have the capacity to reshape the business formula or develop a multi-structure strategy in their format and business channels for repositioning (Dupuis and Fournioux, 2006). Some retailers form wholly owned business ventures at the post-entry stage of market expansion. When retailers choose to exit from a market due to mainly poor operations, they may have sales unit closures and sales of operations to other retailers. These key issues include the failure of transferring of management practices from one market to another such as OBI's exit from China in 2009, selling all its stores to B&Q in China; and the lack of understanding of local consumers in the new market, such as the Home Depot's exit from China in 2012 due to the fact that Chinese consumers do not adapt to the DIY (do-it-yourself) style of home improvement.

Time is an important factor in the retail internationalisation process. Retail firms take different amounts of time at each stage in different markets, and their managerial activities are also different at each stage. Some retailers became involved in international activities over a long period in a certain market, such as Walmart in China (from 1995). For others, such as Tesco (from 2004), their retail activities in China are relatively recent. Therefore, there is clearly a temporal dimension in foreign retail firms' corporate learning activities (Currah and Wrigley, 2004). For example, Carrefour had already spent a significant amount of time on the learning curve because of their abundant international experience, gained by having previously entered several foreign markets. From this experience, Carrefour learned how to quickly identify the potential for future growth in China and expanded very quickly there, to become the biggest foreign retailer in the country by 2005 (Siebers, 2012). Carrefour also had the experience to quickly decide when to withdraw from markets: their decisions to withdraw from the US, the UK, Germany, and Japan were all very rapid (Dupuis and Prime, 1996).

Peter Agnefjäll, Ikea chief

By Richard Milne

In 2013, Peter Agnefjäll officially became the Swedish company's fifth chief executive in its 70-year history. Mr Agnefjäll's appointment reasserts the trend of Ikea chief executives having been an assistant to its still influential founder, Ingvar Kamprad. Discussing his priorities as chief executive of the world's leading furniture retailer, which recorded sales of €27bn last year, he adopts an approach that goes against the grain of his predecessor Mikhal Ohlsson's planned store openings of 20–25 a year up to 2020, which had caused Mr Kamprad to break his normal silence to express his disagreement. Mr Agnefjäll, who was assistant to Mr Kamprad as well as to former chief executive Anders Dahlvig and to Mr Ohlsson in 2008 and 2009, agrees with the founder, saying he does not recognise the 20–25 target and that the emphasis should be on improving Ikea's 300 or so existing stores.

He may be close to Mr Kamprad but retailing was in his blood. Mr Agnefjäll's father ran several supermarkets in the southern Swedish city of Malmö and was helped out by his son at weekends. It taught Mr Agnefjäll some crucial lessons: 'You realise that maybe the customer is the important person. Yes, in a way it's not rocket science. It is about having the right products at the right prices when the customer wants it'. The quote is typical of Mr Agnefjäll as well as of Ikea: simple almost to a fault with some homespun wisdom thrown in. Much of Ikea's philosophy is still based on The Testament of a Furniture Dealer, a series of pithy and homely statements on business principles written by Mr Kamprad in 1976. However, Mr Agnefjäll took a different course and studied business at the Linköping University in central Sweden. He soon realised that his heart was in retailing even if he didn't want to work in his father's supermarkets. Instead he started out at Ikea as a trainee in 1995. A year later, his first proper role came in the children's department at the stores in Malmö and Älmhult, about 90 minutes away.

Mr Agnefjäll remembers it as an exciting time as Ikea had just started taking the section seriously. 'We sold furniture, we sold quilt covers, like a miniature Ikea you could say. For me, it was a fabulous learning place because you got to know a little bit about all kinds of products, all kinds of materials, different questions that customers were asking on a bed and on a quilt cover', he says. There followed a stint at Ikea of Sweden, a separate company that is responsible for developing the global product range. Once, when Mr Agnefjäll was looking after purchasing for the children's department, Ikea had to stop selling a teddy bear because there was a danger its eyes could fall off. Instead of cutting links with the supplier at the cost of 600 jobs, he sent a designer to the factory and she came up with the Famnig cushion, a red heart with arms attached to it. It became a best-seller and the supplier had to double its workforce. 'Many companies at that stage would have abandoned the supplier, but ... abandoning them would have put many, many people in a difficult situation. So we developed a new set of products but without these important details that became hazardous', he says.

Next, however, came a dramatic break for a future Ikea chief executive: Mr Agnefjäll left the company.

Peter Agnefjäll, Ikea chief executive
Source: © epa european pressphoto agency b.v./Alamy Images

He insists that he joined Golfstore, a Malmö-based golf retailer, as marketing manager because of homesickness, not any frustration with the furniture retailer, but he soon realised he preferred Ikea. So, he was soon back at the furniture company, first working on the product range and then perhaps in his toughest assignment: store manager in Padua, Italy – without speaking a word of Italian. His first act was to get rid of the manager's separate office; it was turned into a meeting room and instead he sat with the rest of his staff. 'People were looking at me. They felt that was very strange but from a Swedish perspective you want to be close to your team, and close to people, so for me that was very natural', he says. There were also the small differences: 'The Italians, they bought their coffee cups in children's Ikea, because they were more suited for espresso'. Mr Agnefjäll concedes the language was a barrier but that he learnt to be direct in his communication and was soon hired as Mr Dahlvig's and Mr Kamprad's assistant.

Mr Agnefjäll spent the year prior to his appointment as CEO shadowing Mr Ohlsson and preparing to lead Ikea's 139,000 workers. The new chief executive's priority is to double its sales to €50bn by 2020 while ensuring that Ikea's values-based culture survives further expansion into China and, it hopes, India. Mr Agnefjäll has moved with his family to the group's headquarters in the Netherlands but he admits that not all his furniture is from Ikea. Some items are antiques, he says, before adding: 'I'd say that the absolute majority of the products in our home are Ikea furniture'.

FT *Source:* adapted from Milne, R., *Financial Times*, 1 September 2013. © The Financial Times Limited 2013. All Rights Reserved. Pearson Education is responsible for providing this adaptation of the original article.

Ikea hails recovery in consumer sentiment

By Richard Milne

Mr Agnefjäll hailed a broad-based recovery in consumer sentiment around the world as the Swedish flat-pack furniture retailer sought to put a 'challenging year' behind it. The world's biggest seller of furniture reported a rise of just 3.1 per cent in both net profit and sales in the year to the end of August 2013, well below the average 10 per cent revenue growth it is targeting this decade. But Mr Agnefjäll told the Financial Times: 'Consumer spending is improving . . . Last year we had a turnaround in the UK and it is continuing in a good way . . . Some of the markets that have been more challenging – which has been basically the Mediterranean countries – we see positive signs of activity'.

Ikea's performance in 2013 caused some, including its chairman, to doubt whether the retailer can meet its own target of doubling sales. The privately owned Swedish group thinks it can reach this by 5 per cent growth in sales in existing stores each year and a 5 per cent increase coming from new stores. In 2012–13 revenues grew 3.1 per cent to €27.9bn while net profit rose to €3.3bn. Ikea opened just five stores, the lowest number in decades. But Mr Agnefjäll said that in 2014 it should open 'more than 10' as it increases its investments by more than a quarter to €2.5bn. The countries with the fastest growth were China – where Ikea is opening three stores a year – and Russia, but Mr Agnefjäll praised the performance of the US, where its sales grew 6–7 per cent: 'The US is remarkable . . . We see two things: the unemployment rate is the lowest since 2008, and secondly the housing market is picking up and people are starting to move again and that is an important factor for the growth of Ikea'. For the first time in six years, Ikea will pay a dividend – of €3bn – to its owner, the Dutch-registered Stichting Ingka Foundation, which is only allowed to spend the money on investing in the retailer or charitable donations. It still has €16bn of gross cash on its balance sheet.

Ikea has only revealed its profit figures since 2009 and so they are eagerly pored over by retail experts. It increased its gross margin – a crucial profit indicator for retailers – by 1.5 percentage points to 43.3 per cent, despite decreasing prices by 0.2 per cent. However, its performance lagged behind one of its biggest rivals, South Africa's Stenhoff International, which owns the French brand Conforama. Stenhoff's international retail business increased sales by 10 per cent and operating profit 23 per cent in the year until the end of June 2013.

FT *Source:* adapted from Milne, R., *Financial Times*, 29 January 2014. © The Financial Times Limited 2014. All Rights Reserved. Pearson Education is responsible for providing this adaptation of the original article.

The international retail environment: an emerging market perspective

Macro- and micro- environment

Both the macro-environment at the international level from a global perspective and at the national level from a local market perspective, as well as the micro-environment at the industrial level of the business environment, influence retailers' international expansion process. An attractive retail environment provides opportunities for retailers to enter or expand in an international market. However, the uncertainty and unpredictability of the external environment is an important factor influencing the decision-making on international operations (Anderson and Gatignon, 1986). Country risk factors such as political instability, and economic and foreign exchange fluctuations are important factors to be considered by foreign firms (Herring, 1983). In this regard, such factors as international political relationships between home and host countries, GDP growth of the host country and foreign currency exchange require in-depth analysis. Moreover, emerging markets see distinctive characteristics and political, economic, social-cultural and technological dynamics in their retail environment. Therefore, the focus on retail business environment analysis shall be given to emergent phenomena such as deregulation and opening of the market; policies and their changes of both central and local governments, particularly on foreign retail investments.

Deregulation

Retailers are attracted by economic development, that is to say, both a high level of development and low level of growth in less saturated markets contribute to market attraction. On the one hand, international operations may be encouraged to develop where markets have high-spending consumers, such as the cosmopolitan markets of the New York–London–Paris axis (Hollander, 1970). On the other hand, trading organisations are attracted by the underdeveloped markets to grow retail operations in the transitional economies where there is the growing retail market demand. More than half of the developing countries are participating in globalisation by increasing their involvement in international trade and decreasing their tariffs in order to catch up with developed countries (Winters, 2004). Deregulation such as entry into the World Trade Organization, a body that seeks to promote trade between nations through the lowering or abolition of international trade tariffs and quotas (e.g. China's relaxation on laws and regulations in the retail sector in 2001), releases restrictions on foreign business expansion and results in raised living standards. Trade liberalisation and the increase of income and number of middle income consumers directly influence retail consumption, from which foreign retailers are able to benefit (also see Siebers, 2011).

Government policies

The changes in government policies regarding the commitment to systemic transformation, macroeconomic stability, infrastructural development, and establishing a market-oriented legal framework in transitional economics attracted FDI (Meyer, 1998). Government policies determine regulatory conditions, influenced by cultural assumptions, economic development and social conditions, which further influence retail development of both domestic and foreign retailers. A more ideal retail environment is reliant on a comprehensive set of legal rules that provide protection for foreign investors, the ability to govern the operation of corporations and the securities in the market. Due to the retail nature of land use, laws on private property rights are influential for the location choices of foreign retail businesses in a particular city or country; and ownership status of a country's enterprises impacts on the protection for large private investors (Kato and Long, 2006), considering most of the multinational retailers are privately owned listed companies.

Relaxation of the regulatory environment comprises one of the pull factors for retail expansion. For example, all the regulatory changes in China have had a direct influence on the expansion process of foreign retailers, particularly from 1992 when China opened its retail sector through to 2001 when China entered the WTO and continuing to 2004 when all remaining restrictions were released in China's retail sector. Although the foreign retail growth sees a decreasing trend, the majority of large retail giants remain ambitious for further expansion in the country.

Since large countries, in particular emerging markets such as the BRICS group, referring to the fastest growing emerging markets including Brazil, Russia, Indian, China and South Africa, may have many different administrative divisions and cities, it is important to analyse the influence of both central government and local government policies on the expansion process of foreign retailers. Especially, local governments have important regulatory authority in some states, e.g. China, where they exercise discretion in setting tax, specify entry barriers, and create administrative red tape for businesses operating within their jurisdiction. Some local governments protect companies they own from those they do not own (Law *et al.*, 2003). It is therefore vital to identify and explain the roles of central and local government policies in the process of retail internationalisation in a host market.

Psychic distance

The concept of **psychic distance** has been given attention in recent studies of firm internationalisation (see Evans *et al.*, 2000) as well as retail internationalisation (see Siebers, 2012). Psychic, derived from the word psyche, refers to the mind or soul; distance is related to similarities or differences regarding the degree or amount of separation between two points (Sykes, 1987). Based on the above concepts and previous literature, Evans *et al.* (2000) believe that psychic distance is not the simple presence of an external environmental factor but it is the way the mind processes the perception and understanding of cultural and business differences that forms the foundation of psychic distance. Evans *et al.* (2000: 377) define psychic distance in a more holistic way: 'the distance between the home market and foreign market resulting from the perception and understanding of cultural and business difference'. Obviously, this definition is considered as the combination of cultural distance and business distance, and emphasises both 'psychic' and 'distance' to analyse how international retailers' performance is influenced by psychic distance and other relevant factors from a holistic view.

Psychic distance is linked to cultural distance (Hofstede, 1983; Lindsay *et al.*, 2003) and business distance (Dupuis and Prime, 1996). Cultural distance is often referred to different national cultures of foreign markets in which international firms operate (Hofstede, 1983, 1991). The influence of cultural distance on retail internationalisation has been considered to be particularly important (Dupuis and Prime, 1996). Tordjman (1988) refers to the cultural proximity of a target country for an internationalising retailer. The concept of business distance was developed in the field of international business at the Uppsala Business School in Sweden (Carlson, 1975). Dupuis and Prime (1996) define business distance as the perceived gap between the domestic and host country in terms of each of the core dimensions determining competitiveness, such as consumers, outlets, networks and environment. The Uppsala studies found that firms tend to expand into markets in which the business distance is relatively short in terms of political, economic, legal, geographic and cultural distance.

However, it has been noted that the existence of psychic distance between home and host country does not necessary lead to poor performance, but perceived psychic distance is crucial. That is, perceived similarity between home and host countries may lead to poor operating performance and perceived greater psychic distance may contribute to better performance, as seen, for example, in Carrefour's failure in the USA and success in Taiwan (O'Grady and Lane, 1996) and in China. Thus, the responses to psychic distance are significant for retailers' performance (Evans *et al.*, 2000). In this regard, organisational change, leadership and innovative ideas may play important roles in retail internationalisation, which is directly related to the learning experiences of retail operations. There is clearly a temporal dimension in foreign retailers' corporate learning activities (Currah and Wrigley, 2004). The different stages of learning process can influence the process of internationalisation. It can be argued that the ideal markets for internationalising retailers should be those with close geographical proximity, close cultural associations, and similar economic conditions to domestic markets. Where, however, the retail structure undergoes a modernisation process (when the familiar and close markets are saturated), retailers tend to assess their competencies and expand into international markets with greater cultural differences and geographical distance because they are attracted by the economic and commercial opportunities in these countries' markets.

Indeed, having a big cultural or business distance may not be the main factor to explain retailers' failure in a foreign market. The degree of adaptation to the local market can contribute to retailers' success or failure in the foreign market. Dupuis and Prime (1996) found that Carrefour's failure in the US was attributable to the lack of adaptation to US consumer tastes for the one-stop shopping concept. In contrast, the success of Carrefour in Taiwan has been partially attributed to its adaptation of concept to the local market. On the basis of the implied assumption of the internationalisation process, it would be expected that Carrefour would not be so successful in Taiwan because of the bigger cultural and business differences between Taiwan and its domestic market, France (Dupuis and Prime, 1996). The perception of cultural and business differences enhances performance if retailers can make appropriate adaptation to the market (Evans *et al.*, 2000). Overall, cultural differences in the host country add complexity to the environment of foreign market operation (Lindsay *et al.*, 2003). Therefore, to consider psychic distance when analysing factors influencing the expansion process of foreign retailers is essential.

Infrastructure and distribution in emerging markets

The efficiency of distribution is important for international retail business (Yoshino, 1966). For example, China's current infrastructure has limited the spread of a foreign retailers' distribution system. Walmart's advanced distribution management system in China becomes ineffective due in part to varying conditions of the motorways, which means that goods cannot be distributed efficiently. The distribution structure directly influences competitive strategies of international retailers in China (also see Cao and Dupuis, 2010), and is likely to be applied to other emerging markets.

Transportation is also a challenge for 'big-box' retailing in emerging markets. Transportation of goods from stores to consumers' homes has an important influence on the process of foreign retailers' expansion (Dupuis and Prime, 1996). In order to respond to its unbalanced transportation systems, retail transnational corporations choose locations near their previous stores to expand into, so that they can utilise established distribution systems. However, good opportunities are ahead because transportation is improving given the fast-growing emerging economy such as the increase of the number of cars per 100 households in China and India. Increased predominance of private automobiles may require new location strategies of international retailers. In addition, urbanisation has generated changes in consumer's lifestyles, increasing demand for modern retail formats. Large superstores in suburbanised areas and local expresses in urban cities may soon be demanded by emerging markets such as BRICS countries.

Russia customs rules hit online retailers

By Kathrin Hille and Robert Wright

Customs rules can have a major impact on retailers' ability to export clothing to international markets. For example, Western online retailers are hitting a fresh roadblock in their push into Russia, one of the world's fastest-growing ecommerce markets, as new customs regulations hinder courier deliveries to private customers in the country. In 2014, DHL and FedEx said they had suspended express deliveries from abroad to individuals in Russia because of stricter customs procedures that require lots of extra paperwork on all parcels for personal use except for documents, regardless of the shipment value. 'This impacts mostly shipments for business-to-consumer ecommerce for customers such as Amazon and Net-A-Porter', said Daniel McGrath, spokesman for DHL Express. 'That is a minor part of our business, but it is a fast-growing market'. UPS has not suspended services yet but said: 'We have told our customers that we've experienced significant delays in clearance and deliveries as a result of the change in customs procedures'.

With close to 70 m internet users, roughly half of its population, Russia is Europe's largest internet market by users. Currently just 2 per cent of Russian retail sales are conducted online, but that is expected to rise to 5 per cent, more than tripling the size of the online retail market by 2015, according to Morgan Stanley. That has driven several foreign ecommerce companies to try to break domestic players' near-total dominance of the market. Both Ebay and AliExpress, an arm of China's Alibaba, set up Russian-language sites last year. Some boutique outlets such as the London-based online fashion retailer Net-A-Porter have also expanded in the country. Amazon offers shipping for some of its articles to Russia, but not books.

The foreign online retailers are up against Ozon, the market leader, whose business model resembles Amazon, as well as smaller and more specialised Russian companies. Shipping and payment are cited as the most common hurdles to market entry. DHL said it had suspended express delivery services to individual customers in Russia in 2010 when customs first introduced tighter restrictions, but later resumed services for some ecommerce customers. But the latest changes require the submission of some original documents and credit card payment records at customs. 'Those services we just can't provide', Mr McGrath said. Investors frequently cite cumbersome customs clearance as one of the most serious hurdles to doing business in Russia, and the government has been focusing on simplifying procedures. The latest changes are believed to be aimed at preventing consumers from dodging import tax by underreporting the value of goods for personal use. Ecommerce industry executives fear that this push could eventually lead to a lowering of the tax-free threshold, a move that would hurt foreign online retailers even more.

Source: adapted from Hille, K. and Wright, R., Russia customs rules hit online retailers, *Financial Times*, 24 January 2014 © 2014 The Financial Times Limited. All Rights Reserved. Pearson Education is responsible for providing this adaptation of the original article.

Retail internationalisation strategies

Globalisation versus localisation

The concept of localisation was introduced by James Watson from Harvard University (Berger, 2002), and has attracted considerable interest in the past decade. There has not been a universal definition of localisation and it has been studied conceptually in the disciplines of political economy, anthropology, sociology and international relations (Coca-Stefaniak *et al.*, 2010). Hansen (2002: 15) defines localisation as 'a set of processes through which the forces of globalisation are accommodated, resisted and absorbed, and given expression in any particular context'. Localisation is regarded as a process which reverses the trend of globalisation by discriminating in favour of the local (Hines, 2000) and 'ideological antithesis of globalisation' (Hines, 2000: 256). Effective marketing strategies result from the combination of national and local conditions that fosters competitive advantage (Porter, 1990).

Local dependent firms tend to maintain healthy and close relations to their local environment, seeking survival in a particular local economy (Cox and Mair, 1991). Internationalising retailers have applied various localisation strategies for market growth, such as the key strategies grocery retailers Walmart and Tesco use in their overseas markets.

A localisation strategy that responds to the cultural differences in the host market is adaptation to local management practices and processes (Dawson, 1994). Some retailers such as Seven Eleven Group's in the US and China (Yahagi and Kar, 2009) were successful globally by applying localisation strategies; but others applying localisation strategies had success locally despite having a negative impact on overall performance, such as Nestlé (Will *et al*., 1991). Previous literature acknowledges the important role played by local factors in achieving national retail success (e.g. Vyt, 2008), and reports that localisation can help firms to gain a certain element of competitive advantage, but found that drawbacks exist if localisation is used as key element for differentiation (Coca-Stefaniak *et al*., 2010).

A major milestone in the studies of localisation was the point at which the concept of localisation was embraced in a globalisation context and the word 'glocalisation' was created (see Schiller, 1971). The main idea of glocalisation is to challenge the model of Western cultural imperialism and respond to the interface of global and local (de Nuve, 2007) and the dynamics homogenisation and heterogenisation (Eric, 2007). A company's global corporate culture, ideas, product and service may be questioned and challenged by specific local market characteristics and consumer demand. Over time, the concept of localisation, derived from globalisation, has been evolved to glocalisation (Robertson, 1994) and globalisation (Ritzer, 2004). As a result, a localisation approach has been adopted by many global firms because they are facing difficulties in obtaining competitive advantage by a global approach in a specific local market. Consequently, the importance of interaction between global and local has been addressed. For example, Matusitz (2011) discusses Disney's success in Hong Kong by adaptation to the local market, reversing its failure position to success by switching from a global to a local perspective.

Overall, as a viable alternative business strategy, localisation has received relatively low consideration because of its comparative novelty (Coca-Stefaniak *et al*., 2010). The fact that large multinational retailers are not only internationalising but are also localising has been neglected. The paucity in understanding of local factors had led to many failures of multinational companies in developing economies (Bhattacharya and Michael, 2008), such as the previous examples of OBI and the Home Depot's exit from China. There is not a strategy that fits all the markets at all times. In the context of business innovation, hybridisation management practices that combine local and global management approaches have been advocated, including hybrid human resource management (HRM) systems (Chen and Wilson, 2003), a hybrid way of adaptation to the local culture and maintaining corporate culture in establishment of effective local networks, as well as provision of customised products and services and introduction of new market ideology (Siebers, 2013). Retail internationalisation activities in emerging markets remain recent and dynamic, because most of emerging markets are still in the process of opening their doors (or in a position to) to foreign businesses, and currently the most exuberant potential market is India after China's retail market is towards saturation of retail businesses. New business model innovations are in demand to create long-term and sustainable growth in an international market.

Entry mode and operational structure

Entry mode selection has impacts on retailers' decisions on the geographical dispersion of firms' international activities (Erramilli, 1991). In most cases, a foreign retailer's entry mode into a new market needs to first consider laws and regulations in the host market. Similar to any other internationalising firms, companies in the retail industry choose export, import, licensing, franchising, joint ventures, acquisition and strategic alliances to expand into a host market (see Table 13.1). However, there are specific factors that influence a retailer's entry mode selection including psychic distance, internal competencies, firm-specific factors, country-specific factors and external environment.

Psychic distance has been explained earlier as the distance between the home market and the host market resulting from the perception and understanding of cultural and

Table 13.1 Market-entry methods

Market-entry method	Example of advantages	Example of disadvantages
Acquisition	Fast substantial market presence	High cost and risk
Joint venture	Each brings own skills, e.g. market knowledge and format experience	Need suitable partner, can be clash of company cultures
Organic growth	Incremental process, can learn and adapt as you go	Slow growth, delay before returns against investment
Shareholding	Reduces risk, can learn about company from the inside and decide whether to invest further	Culture clash between teams of management
Franchise	Very fast and low-cost way to roll out stores	Limited control, need suitable franchisees

Source: Gilbert, 2003

business difference (Evans *et al.*, 2000). Internal competencies refer to a firm's characteristics, e.g. resource commitment, differential advantages and international experience, and decision-makers' characteristics, e.g. perception and attitude towards expansion, work experience particularly in a foreign market, leadership delegation and empowerment and education level. Firm-specific factors refer to firms' internal commercial agreements, business networking, investigation and research, localised management team and degree of localisation. Country-specific factors include distribution system, competition-driven suburbanisation, and transportation and urbanisation (also see Siebers, 2011).

The existence of psychic distance between home and host country does not necessarily lead to poor performance, but perceived psychic distance is crucial. That is, perceived similarity between home and host countries may lead to a wholly owned entry mode and perhaps poor operating structure and performance due to lack of knowledge of the local market. In contrast, perceived greater psychic distance may contribute to a more collaborative entry mode, such as joint ventures and better performance. Thus, the responses to psychic distance based on firm-characteristics and firm-specific factors directly impact on retailers' interpretation to country-specific factors and its external environment. As a result, perceived psychic distance is significant for foreign retailers' entry mode selection. In most cases, perceived greater psychic distance results in a joint venture entry mode and corresponding operational structure, with considerations of local laws and regulations, e.g. foreign retailers do in an emerging market such as China. In comparison, perceived smaller psychic distance may lead to a wholly owned entry mode, because the retailer recognises its strong potential competencies of operations in the new market. Responses to psychic distance are also related to the retailers' learning experiences from their retail operations, which differ strategically from one retailer to another. During the learning process, psychic distance is expected to reduce since retailers become more localised.

CHAPTER SUMMARY

This chapter aimed to help understand the concept and development of international retailing, in addition to the retail internationalisation process and some of the key strategies. Key theories in the relevant field have been used to support the discussion on motivation of retail internationalisation, the retail business environment analysis, the cultural considerations, entry modes and strategies in international retailing. For the motivation and the retail business environment, push and pull factors that influence international activities of retailers in both retailers' home and host market have been emphasised, by indicating the importance of the multi-level analysis to understand the international retail environment, including the international level, the national level and the industrial level of macro and micro business environment scanning. During the internationalisation process retailers also need familiarity with laws and regulations of a foreign market. In particular, business and culture differences are the key issues for retail operations in a new market. Expansion into an emerging market also requires effective infrastructure such as distribution system. From a strategic perspective, globalisation and localisation are two controversial internationalisation strategies of retailers and the newer concept of glocalisation have been created. Here, hybrid management practices in retail organisations such as Walmart and Carrefour in China have shown successful stories. Retailers' entry mode and operational structure are influenced by a number of factors including psychic distance, internal competencies, firm-specific factors, country-specific factors and external environment, among which perceived psychic distance is the start point to help to determine what type of retailers' international activities shall take place in a foreign market, based on factors such as the retailers' interpretation to the external environment and their chosen entry mode.

EXERCISES AND QUESTIONS

In order to further understand the content of this chapter, please consider the following questions.

1 What are the main drivers for retailers to internationalise?
2 What important factors do retailers need to consider before expanding into a new market?
3 What factors do managers of retail organisations need to consider to make effective internationalisation strategies?
4 What is psychic distance and how is it important for retail strategies in a foreign market?
5 What are the potential impacts on social and environmental sustainability when retailers move into overseas markets? Watch or read the information at the following link to help you consider some of the key issues: http://www.bbc.co.uk/news/world-asia-india-19606503.

REFERENCES

Alexander, N. (1997) *International Retailing*, Oxford: Blackwell Publishing.

Anderson, E. and Gatignon, H. (1986) A transaction cost analysis and propositions, *Journal of International Business Studies*, 17, 1–26.

Berger, D. (2002) *Die Schule der Kenlas: Die Aufgabe*, BoD (Books on Demand).

Bhattacharya, A.K. and Michael, D.C. (2008) How local companies keep multinationals at bay, *Harvard Business Review*, March, 85–95.

Cao, L. and Dupuis, M. (2010) Strategy and sustainable competitive advantage of international retailers in China, *Journal of Asia-Pacific Business*, 11(1), 6–27.

Carlson, S. (1975) How foreign is foreign trade? A problem in international business research, *Studia Oeconomiae Negotiorum*, Uppsala.

Chen, S.H. and Wilson, M. (2003) Standardisation and localisation of human resource management in sino-foreign joint ventures, *Asia Pacific Journal of Management*, 20, 397–408.

Chen, Y.F. and Sternquist, B. (1995) Differences between international and domestic Japanese retailers, *Service Industries Journal*, 15(4), 118–133.

Coca-Stefaniak, J.A., Parker, C. and Rees, C. (2010) Localisation as a marketing strategy for small retailers, *International Journal of Retail & Distribution Management*, 38(9), 677–697.

Cox, K.R. and Mair, A. (1991) From localised social structures to localities as agents, *Environment & Planning Annals*, 23, 197–213.

Currah, A. and Wrigley, N. (2004) Network of organizational learning and adaptation in retail TNCs, *Global Networks*, 4, 1–23.

Dawson, J. (1993) *The internationalisation of retailing*, Department of Business Studies, University of Edinburgh working paper, 93/2.

Dawson, J. (1994) The internationalization of retailing operations, *Journal of Marketing Management*, 10267–1268.

Dawson, J. (2007) Scoping and conceptualising retailer internationalisation, *Journal of Economic Geography*, 7, 373–397.

Dawson, J. and Mukoyama, M. (2006) Retail internationalization as a process, in *Strategic Issues in International Retailing: The Internationalisation of Retailing*, in Dawson, J., Larke, R. and Mukoyama, M. (eds), London and New York: Routledge.

De Nuve, T. (2007) The glocal and the singuniversal, *Third Text*, 21(6), 681–688.

Dupuis, M. and Fournioux, J. (2006) Building an international retail strategy, in *Strategic Issues in International Retailing: The Internationalisation of Retailing*, Dawson, J., Larke, R. and Mukoyama, M. (eds), London and New York: Routledge.

Dupuis, M. and Prime, N. (1996) Business distance and global retailing: a model for analysis of key success/failure factors, *International Journal of Retail & Distribution Management*, 24(11), 30–38.

Eckstein, M.B. and Weitzman, F.I. (1991) Foreign investment in US retailing: an optimistic overview, *Retail Control*, January, 9–14.

Eric, Z. (2007) Glocalisation, art exhibitions and the Balkans, *Third Text*, 21(2), 207–210.

Erramilli, M.K. (1991) The Experience Factor in foreign market entry behaviour of service firms, *Journal of International Business Studies*, 22, 479–501.

Evans, J., Treadgold, A. and Mavondo, F.T. (2000) Psychic distance and the performance of international retailers: a suggested theoretical framework, *International Marketing Review*, 17, 373–91.

Forsythe, S., Cavender, D. and Gu, Z. (1996) Positioning U.S. retailers for growth opportunities in China: identifying and responding to consumer needs, *Proceedings, Recent Advances in Retailing and Services Science*, Vienna, Austria.

Gilbert, D. (2003) *Retail Marketing Management*, 2nd edn, Harlow: Pearson Education.

Hansen, G.E. (2002) *The Culture of Strangers – Globalization, Localization and the Phenomenon of Exchange*, New York, University Press of America.

Herring, R.J. (1983) *Managing International Risk*, Cambridge: Cambridge University Press.

Hines, C. (2000) *Localization: A Global Manifesto*, London: Earthscan.

Hofstede, G. (1983) National cultures in four dimensions: a research-based theory of cultural differences among nations, *International Studies of Management and Organisation*, 7, 46–74.

Hofstede, G. (1991) *Cultures and Organisations: Software of the Mind*, Maidenhead: McGraw-Hill.

Hollander, S. (1970) *Multinational Retailing*, East Lansing, MI: Michigan State University Press.

Kacker, M.F. (1985), *Transatlantic Trends in Retailing: Takeovers and Flow of Know-how*, Connecticut: Quorum Books.

Kato, T. and Long, C. (2006) CEO turnover, firm performance, and enterprise reform in China: evidence from micro data, *Journal of Comparative Economics*, 34, 796–817.

Law, K.S., Tse, D.K. and Zhou, N. (2003) Does HRM matter in a transitional economy? *Journal of International Business Studies*, 34, 255–265.

Lindsay, V., Chadee, D., Mattsson, J., Johnston, R. and Millet, B. (2003) Relationships, the role of individuals and knowledge flows in the internationalisation of service firms, *International Journal of Service Industry Management*, 14, 7–35.

Matusitz, J. (2011) Disney's successful adaptation in Hong Kong: a glocalization perspective, *Asia Pacific Journal of Management*, 28, 667–681.

McGoldrick. P. (1995) Introduction to international retailing in *International Retailing: Trends and Strategies*, P.J. McGoldrick and G. Davies (eds), London: Pitman.

Meyer, K. (1998) *Direct Investment in Economics in Transition*, Northampton, MA: Edward Elgar.

O'Grady, S. and Lane, H.W. (1996) The psychic distance paradox, *Journal of International Business Studies*, 27, 309–333.

Pommering, D. (1979) Brand marketing: fresh thinking needed, *Marketing Trends*, 1, 7–9.

Porter, M.E. (1990) *The Competitive Advantage of Nations*, New York: The Free Press.

Ritzer, G. (2004) *The Globalization of Nothing*, Thousand Oaks, CA: Pine Forge.

Robertson, R. (1994) Globalization or glocalisation, *Journal of International Communication*, 1, 33–52.

Runyan, R.C. and Sternquist, B. (1994) Negotiations in retailer-supplier channel relations, *Proceedings: Academy of Marketing Science*, 8, 73–74.

Schiller, H. (1971) *Mass Communication and the American Empire*, Boston: Beacon.

Siebers, L.Q. (2011) *Retail Internationalisation in China: Expansion of Foreign Retailers*, Basingstoke, UK: Palgrave MacMillan.

Siebers, L.Q. (2012) Foreign retailers in China: the first ten years, *Journal of Business Strategy*, 33, 27–38.

Siebers, L.Q. (2013) Hybridisation management practices in business model innovation: a case of China's retail sector. The 6th International Society for Professional Innovation Management (ISPIM), Innovation Symposium – Innovation in the Asian Century, 8–11 December, Melbourne, Australia.

Sternquist, B. (1997) International expansion of US retailers, *International Journal of Retail & Distribution Management*, 25, 262–268.

Sternquist, B. (1998), *International Retailing*, Fairchild Books.

Sykes, J.B. (1987)*The Australian Concise Oxford Dictionary*, 7th edn Melbourne: Oxford University Press.

Tacconelli, W. and Wrigley, N. (2009) Organizational challenges and strategic responses of retail TNCs in post-WTO-entry China, *Economic Geography*, 85(1), 49–73.

Tordjman, A. (1988) The French hypermarket: could it be developed in the states?, *Retail and Distribution Management*, July–August, 14–16.

Treadgold, A. (1995) *Structural trends and developments in food retailing and distribution in South East Asia*, 2nd Recent Advances in Retailing and Services Science Conference, 11–14 July, Brisbane, Australia, p. 97.

Treadgold, A.D. and Davies, R.L. (1988) *The Internationalisation of Retailing*, Harlow: Longman.

Vyt, D. (2008) Retail network performance evaluation: a DEA approach considering retailers' geomarketing, *International Review of Retail, Distribution and Consumer Research*, 18, 235–253.

Waldman, C. (1978) *Strategies of International Mass Retailers*, New York: Praeger.

Will, J., Samli, C.A. and Jacobs, L. (1991) Developing global products and marketing strategies: a construct and a research agenda, *Journal of the Academy of Marketing Science*, 19, 1–10.

Williams, D. (1992) Motives for retailer internationalization: their impact, structure, and implications, *Journal of Marketing Management*, 8, 269–285.

Winters, L.A. (2004) Trade liberalisation and economic performance: an overview, *Economic Journal*, 144, F4–F21.

Wood, R. and Keyser, V. (1953) *United States Business Performance Abroad: The Case of Sears, Roebuck, Mexico, S.A.*, Washington D.C.: National Planning Association.

Wrigley, N., Coe, M.N. and Currah, A. (2005) Globalizing retail: conceptualizing the distribution-based transnational corporation (TNC), *Progress in Human Geography*, 29(4), 437–457.

Yahagi, T. and Kar, M. (2009) The process of international business model transfer in the Seven-Eleven Group: US-Japan-China, *Asia Pacific Business Review*, 26, 68–77

Yang, O. and Keung, R. (1996) *Distribution reforms in China and its implications: a government official's perspective*, 3rd Recent Advances in Retailing and Services Science Conference, 22–25 June, Telfs/Buchen, p. 211.

Yoshino, S. (1966) International opportunities for American retailers, *Journal of Retailing*, 43(3), 1–10.

FURTHER READING

Dawson, J., Larke, R. and Mukoyama, M. (2006) *Strategic Issues in International Retailing, The Internationalisation of Retailing*, London and New York: Routledge.

Dimitrova, B.V., Rosenbloom, B. and Larsen Andras, T. (2014) Does the degree of retailer international involvement affect retailer performance?, *International Review of Retail, Distribution and Consumer Research*, 24(3), 243–277.

Edger, C. (2013) *International Multi-Unit Leadership – Developing Local Leaders in International Multi-Site Operations*, Surrey: Gower.

Evans, J., Treadgold, A. and Mavondo, F.T. (2000) Psychic distance and the performance of international retailers: a suggested theoretical framework, *International Marketing Review*, 17, 373–91.

Matusitz, J. (2011) Disney's successful adaptation in Hong Kong: a glocalization perspective, *Asia Pacific Journal of Management*, 28, 667–681.

Robinson, D. (2014) Web shopping – online stores think local to grow global, *Financial Times*, 25 January 2014 (available online at: http://www.ft.com/cms/s/0/6d338714–84f0–11e3–8968–00144feab7de.html#axzz2ufYYSfur).

Siebers, L.Q. (2011) *Retail Internationalisation in China: Expansion of Foreign Retailers*. Basingstoke, UK: Palgrave MacMillan.

Case study

Indonesia's ecommerce industry awakens

By Ben Bland

Like other executives running fast-growing internet businesses in Indonesia, Rio Inaba, chief executive of the Indonesian division of Rakuten, the fast-expanding Japanese ecommerce group, has profited from the lackadaisical office culture in Southeast Asia's biggest economy.

With home internet access slow and expensive, the peak time for online shopping in this nation of 250 million people is during office hours, when an increasing number of white-collar workers while away the day buying clothes, gadgets and airline tickets on their company PC.

'Our busiest time is still about 11 a.m. before traffic dips at lunchtime and then picks up again when people get back to their desks', says Mr Inaba, chief executive of Rakuten, the fast-expanding Japanese ecommerce group.

But the rise of cheap smartphones and tablets that sell for less than $100 is rapidly broadening access to the internet and pushing the nascent ecommerce market towards a 'take off' point in terms of scale and profitability, in spite of significant challenges because of poor infrastructure and payment systems.

'We're seeing phenomenal growth in mobile transactions', says Mr Inaba, adding that order volume and revenue from Rakuten's online marketplace in Indonesia are more than doubling every year, led by demand for gadgets, fashion accessories and toys.

Ellyana Fuad, the Indonesia chief executive for Visa, the credit card company, believes that the world's fourth most populous nation is approaching a 'big bang' for ecommerce as the number of internet users doubles to 125 million by 2017 and smartphone ownership rises from 20 per cent to 52 per cent in the same period, according to Redwing, an advisory group.

Although the ecommerce market is still small and fragmented and there are no hard statistics, industry executives estimate that annual sales could grow from $1bn–$3bn now to $10bn by the end of 2015.

Competition is heating up. A wide range of companies have entered the market in the past few years, from international market leaders such as Rakuten, eBay and Sumitomo to local start-ups, state-owned utility companies and the Hartonos – Indonesia's wealthiest family and owners of classified website Kaskus.

'The market is growing faster than the industry', says Natali Ardianto, the co-founder and chief technology officer of Tiket.com, which sells airline and rail tickets.

. . . Set up by seven young technology entrepreneurs fifteen months ago, Tiket.com has since taken on 89 staff and, with 3000 transactions per day, recently turned its first profit.

But Mr Ardianto warns that it is not easy to succeed in ecommerce in Indonesia given the poor physical infrastructure and the lack of smooth payments systems.

Indonesia's woeful transport connections make online retail more attractive both for big-city dwellers who want to avoid incessant traffic jams and for residents in more remote places that are far from the nearest shopping mall.

But getting the goods to the customer is tough, particularly when it comes to the 'last mile', owing to a lack of detailed maps, unclear addresses, and courier companies not offering timed deliveries.

As a result, companies from fashion retailer Zalora to Sukamart.com, a grocery retailer owned by Japanese trading house Sumitomo, have been forced to set up their own delivery services in greater Jakarta, one of the world's biggest and most chaotic metropolitan areas.

'In China and Japan the quality of courier services is quite good', says Taketo Kokubo, Sukamart.com chief executive. 'We tried to use local companies [in Indonesia] but we had problems so we're starting our own delivery team'.

Payments are also a headache with low banking and credit card penetration and online payment systems still in the developmental stage.

Tiket.com has to offer 14 different payment methods from bank transfers to various internet banking platforms to credit cards, the use of which is rising rapidly from a low base.

. . . 'We have to find a way to lower the hurdles for new customers to try internet shopping', says Rakuten's Mr Inaba.

With many consumers forced to go to the bank to pay for online orders and companies required to build their own delivery networks, ecommerce in Indonesia still resembles the bricks-and-mortar retail industry in some important respects.

'In a complex market like Southeast Asia, you need a presence in each country . . . countries have different tastes and customs regulations and you need your own warehouse, local buyers and marketing department', says Magnus Grimeland, the Indonesia managing director for Zalora, which is backed by German ecommerce group Rocket Internet.

Rakuten, Sukamart and Zalora have successfully negotiated Indonesia's regulatory minefield and set up as foreign-owned companies. But industry executives believe the government is working on plans to restrict future foreign investment in the sector as part of a wider protectionist push that has already hit the bricks-and-mortar retail sector.

As with many aspects of the Indonesian economy, it will be tough to achieve the huge potential for growth in the long term without better infrastructure.

'No matter how many people want to buy a handbag online, the logistical and payment infrastructure is still not good, the mobile internet speed is not great and the fixed-line internet connections are slow and expensive', says Mr Inaba.

Additionally, online shoppers in Indonesia often require hand-holding. While the average European fashion website receives customer queries on only 5 per cent of orders, Zalora receives an average of one phone call or message per order from concerned customers confirming their request has been received. But the company says that is a decline from two queries per order when it launched two years ago, as Indonesians become more accustomed to shopping online.

Although the capital city drove initial growth in the ecommerce market, both Rakuten and Zalora say that 70 per cent of their orders now come from outside Jakarta. Indonesia's second- and third-tier cities are growing fast but many still lack shopping malls, presenting a big opportunity for companies that can deliver their products to these places. 'We see a lot of demand for toys and musical instruments from outside Jakarta, where people can't find these things', says Rakuten's Mr Inaba.

There are tens of millions of potential online shoppers in Indonesia, but the most successful sites are selling products with a value of less than Rp200,000 ($17), says Mr Ardianto of Tiket.com. Sukamart says that its average basket size is Rp300,000-Rp500,00. This compares with an average basket size of about £60 ($100) at Asos, the UK online clothing retailer. Rakuten, Sukamart and Zalora have successfully negotiated Indonesia's regulatory minefield and set up as foreign-owned companies. But industry executives believe the government is working on plans to restrict future foreign investment in the sector as part of a wider protectionist push that has already hit the bricks-and-mortar retail sector.

Source: adapted from Bland, B. (2014) Indonesia's ecommerce industry awakens, *Financial Times*, 21 February.
© The Financial Times Limited 2014. All Rights Reserved. Pearson Education is responsible for providing this adaptation of the original article.

DISCUSSION QUESTIONS

1 What are the main potential problems that should be anticipated by online retailers intending to expand into the Indonesian market?

2 Despite such problems, what are the potential advantages for a retailer in trading online in Indonesia?

3 Based on the case, what advice would you give to the following etailers intending to launch in Indonesia, to help them overcome some of the current difficulties in trading there:

   a An electronics etailer.
   b A musical instruments etailer.

Glossary

4Ps is the term used to describe the four elements of the traditional marketing mix: product, price, promotion and place

7Ps is the term used for the seven elements of the extended (services) marketing mix, which could be said to be more suited to the retail sector than the traditional 4 Ps

advertising is promotional communication from organisations to the public in paid-for media outlets such as TV channels, newspapers and online banner adverts

ambient media refers to promotion via non-traditional forms of advertising media in the consumers' surroundings, which is often humorous or surreal

backward pricing is achieved by establishing the retailer's desired selling price, based on how much the retailer expects customers to be willing to pay for a product or service

behavioural segmentation is a method of segmenting customers into groups relating to their consumption or usage of a product, e.g. they may be highly loyal, regular or infrequent users of a product or service

boutique layout is a style of store layout where some of the goods are displayed centrally and other products are typically stacked on shelves by the walls, with customers usually travelling in one direction in a clear pathway around the central area (hence its alternative name of 'racetrack' layout)

brand commitment assesses the extent to which customers are loyal to a particular brand, usually by repurchasing the brand's products (also known as 'internal brand commitment' when applied to employees' loyalty towards the brand)

brand equity is the value of a brand to a company and its stakeholders, going beyond financial assets and profitability to incorporate the loyalty and recognition that the brand engenders

brand extensions give companies the opportunity to exploit the brand equity in their existing products by applying the same brand name to a new product category, thereby achieving growth for the brand by providing more goods to existing customers or by reaching new customers

brand identity reflects the core value of a brand and is communicated to consumers via the various elements of the marketing mix

brand image refers to consumers' interpretations of a brand, based on the brand identity projected by the company, as well as other sources such as fellow consumers and the media

brand positioning aims to locate a brand in a particular place in comparison to its competitors, in the mind of the consumer

brand recall occurs when consumers can remember the name of a brand without being prompted

brand recognition occurs when consumers can recall the name of a brand when prompted

branded products carry another company's brand name, rather than that of the retailer, and though they are frequently referred to as 'manufacturer brands', such brands tend to concentrate on design, sales and promotion/advertising, sub-contracting the manufacturing to other companies

bricks and clicks refers to companies that sell from physical stores (i.e. 'bricks-and-mortar') as well as selling online

B2B (business-to-business) refers to businesses making transactions directly with other businesses, rather than with consumers

B2C (business-to-consumer) refers to companies such as retailers selling their goods and services directly to consumers, rather than to other businesses

buying cycle is the term used by many UK retailers for the key events and processes that the buyers carry out in order to select a suitable product range to meet customers' requirements

category management involves the selection and management of a group of related products, by a category manager employed either by a brand or by a retailer

centralised buying takes place in larger retail chains where it is standard practice for buying and merchandising teams to be centralised in a department based at the retailer's Head Office (when products are selected by individual stores within the same company, this is called decentralised buying)

chain stores/multiples are retailers with two or more outlets under the same name and the main business functions are usually centralised at Head Office

comparative shopping trips are undertaken by buyers, merchandisers and other retail employees to observe comparable merchandise sold in the outlets of competing retailers, to assist in the product development process and gain a more in-depth knowledge of the market for a specific product category (also known as 'comp shopping')

competition-orientated pricing refers to setting selling prices which are comparable to that of similar products sold by competitors

concessions are relatively small retail outlets that have an agreement to trade within a larger retailer's store

consumer neuroscience is a relatively recent innovation in marketing research that uses technology to track customers' brain responses to shopping

C2C (consumer-to-consumer) refers to a business model which enables consumers to sell directly to other consumers, particularly via online platforms

co-operative promotion uses techniques to promote both a retailer and brand jointly

corporate branding aims to promote a complete organisation such as a parent company, rather than the individual brands, products or services that it sells, usually with the intention of portraying a positive image to stakeholders such as shareholders and employees

Corporate Social Responsibility (CSR) is addressed by companies when they acknowledge responsibility for the social and ethical impact of their operations and investments, resulting in the compilation and implementation of CSR policies by many retailers

cost-orientated pricing is price-setting based on the cost of buying the products from suppliers marked up by a standard percentage, then rounded off to the nearest price point

critical path is a term used to describe the key dates in the production and distribution processes that need to be adhered to in order for merchandise to meet deadlines for delivery to stores

CRM (customer relationship management) involves an organisation's direct communications with its customers to encourage repeat purchasing

customer profiles are written or visual compilations of details describing the lifestyle of typical 'target customers' at whom the retailer's products or services are aimed (also known as a 'pen portrait')

customer service is the term used within retail organisations to describe the interface between the customer and the organisation that provides the service, but it is also used to describe a department which is responsible for providing assistance to customers with problems or complaints

demand-orientated pricing methods of setting prices by estimating the amount that customers will be prepared to pay for a product or service

demographic segmentation uses measurable aspects of the population, such as age and income, to segment consumers into groups

direct mail is a form of direct marketing where communication is sent directly from retailers to consumers and is often customised for the respondents, e.g. via post, email or text message

direct marketing involves communicating directly with existing or potential customers to promote or sell products or services

direct selling/direct retailing is a form of home shopping where the customer can purchase goods directly from a salesperson visiting the home or an advert, thereby merging a distribution channel with a communication channel

directional shopping is the term used for travelling to appropriate locations to gain an awareness of future trends for a specific type of merchandise, mainly by viewing products from more expensive, influential stores

ecommerce refers to conducting business via the internet

electronic point-of-sale (EPoS) technology is used to record sales transaction information in stores which can be sent directly to Head Office for analysis

etailing is a form of retailing where businesses sell goods to consumers online (also known as e-retailing)

ethnography is a research technique involving in-depth observations of consumers to reveal detailed aspects of their shopping behaviour and product consumption

everyday low pricing (EDLP) refers to charging consistently low prices throughout the year, with relatively few price promotions and markdowns

experiential consumer behaviour views purchasing as an enjoyable experience, based on hedonistic, emotional values rather than rational thinking

extended marketing mix is the term for the '7Ps' which adds people, physical evidence and process to the four elements of the traditional marketing mix (also known as the services marketing mix)

Fair Trade is a respectful trading partnership between a buyer and supplier, where a premium is paid to the producers and fair working conditions are ensured

final selection is the key meeting for the retail buying function when decisions are made about which specific products are to be sold by the retailer, with the approval of senior managers

focus groups are a qualitative method of primary research (i.e. not based on statistics) where selected respondents participate in a discussion to enable an organisation to discover their views on a specified issue

franchise is the term used when a dealer (the franchisee) runs a business under a contractual arrangement to sell a specific company's (the franchisor's) goods or services, under the name of the franchisor's company

freeform layout is a style of store layout where merchandise is grouped into clusters in the shop, so that customers can wander around and gain a good view of the products

geographic segmentation groups consumers by country or region and when combined with demographic factors it is known as geodemographic segmentation

geographical information system (GIS) refers to a digital method of analysing geographic data about a location, which is often used in the retail sector to identify suitable locations for stores

geographical pricing this price-setting method refers to varying prices for the same product in branches of a single retail chain, depending on the retail outlet's location.

gondolas are merchandise display units used within shops in the central area of the sales floor, usually containing shelves or slats

grey market is the term used when branded products are sold at relatively low prices by unauthorised retailers, without the approval of the brand

grid layout is the term used for a shop layout with rows of aisles, as favoured by supermarkets

gross margin is the percentage of the selling price of a product that remains after subtracting the cost price, before the retailer's costs have been taken into account

home shopping refers to non-store based retailing that distributes goods and services directly to consumers' homes via different media and formats, including etailing, mail order and direct marketing

independent stores are individual stores or small retail chains which operate independently and are not owned by another company

integrated marketing communications (IMC) is a term used to emphasise that different communication strategies need to be complementary and well blended

macro-environment refers to the relevant external issues that can be analysed in relation to an organisation's external marketing audit that are often referred to as 'PESTEL' factors (Political; Economic; Societal; Technological; Ethical and Legal)

mark-up is the difference between the retail selling price and the supplier's cost price, that is retained by the retailer to pay for its outgoings

markdown prices are discounted to reduce the volume of stock, e.g. because products are perishable or to match competitors' prices

market segmentation is used to divide consumers with similar characteristics or behaviour into segments, with the aim of meeting their needs effectively, thus helping to improve an organisation's profitability (see also: demographic, geographic, psychographic and behavioural segmentation)

marketing mix is the term used to describe the framework of four key elements of marketing (product, price, promotion and place) that should each be managed effectively in order to meet customer needs

merchandising is carried out by retail merchandisers to arrange for the products selected by the buying team to be produced by suppliers on time and in the right quantities and distributed via the retailer's distribution channels (please note that visual merchandising is a different job role)

micro-environment is the term that describes internal factors which are closely connected to the company, particularly within the retailer, its customers and direct competitors, to help in assessing its existing strategies, objectives, resources and performance, to facilitate future strategic planning

mission statements sum up the company's values, reflecting the interests of stakeholders in the organisation and may be composed or revised as the first stage in strategic planning

mobile commerce (m-commerce) is business that is undertaken via smartphone connectivity, providing convenient browsing and payment systems, as well as allowing retailers to locate potential consumers and connect them to personalised, store offers and information through the use of geopositioning and locator apps

mobile-device retailing (m-tailing) has developed as internet-enabled smartphone and tablet PC usage increase, enabling consumers to have more frequent access to social media and to use retailers' apps to receive information from retailers and buy products whilst they are on the move, thereby blurring the boundaries between promotion and distribution

multichannel retailing refers to selling products or services to customers via more than one platform, e.g. stores, websites and catalogues

multiple-unit pricing aims to sell products in large volumes within a relatively short period of time by encouraging customers to buy more than one of an item

mystery shopping is used by retailers to assess customer service staff's performance by employing anonymous shoppers

net profit margin is net profit (the amount of money that the company retains from its sales revenue after paying for products from suppliers and operating expenses) divided by sales revenue, which is then expressed as a percentage

odd pricing is when prices of products or services end in odd figures such as .99 or .95, with the intention that the customer will perceive them as being cheaper

omnichannel retailing refers to the integration of a retailer's various distribution channels to provide a seamless service, e.g. promotion via social media with a link to purchase online and delivery to a local store ('click-and-collect')

open-to-buy is a portion of the retailer's budget retained for selecting products shortly before or during the trading season, to respond more quickly to constantly changing product trends and customer needs

organisational buyer behaviour (OBB) is the purchase of goods to be used within a company, which usually takes place in B2B markets

outlet stores sell discounted merchandise, usually from previous seasons, and are usually grouped together in an outlet village

own-label merchandise is developed through collaboration between a retailer's in-house staff and suppliers and is normally sold exclusively in the retailer's outlets (also known as private brands in the US)

perceptual maps assess consumers' perceptions of retailers, products or brands by positioning the companies on a diagram in relation to two separate attributes, such as price and quality

personal selling is when sales staff communicate directly with customers to persuade customers to buy products or services and may offer after-sales service

planograms demonstrate the in-store presentation of products and can be drawn either manually or using software, forming the intersection between in-store display and merchandising as they incorporate both layout and space allocation

point-of-purchase promotion (POP) takes place in stores, to influence customers at the time of purchase decision-making and often takes the form of free-standing displays supplied by the product manufacturer (also known as point-of-sale)

predatory pricing can be used by large retailers to set prices below those of competitors, with the aim of driving competitors out of business

price architecture means offering more than one price level in order to appeal to different types of customer or occasion, e.g. a policy of three different price levels: 'good, better, best'

price elasticity is the degree to which changes in price affect the quantities of products purchased by customers.

price lining means adopting a specific selection of price points, to meet customers' expectations and to avoid random, less memorable prices

pricing skimming occurs when a high price is charged to maximise profits whilst the product is viewed as new and exclusive, before competitors have chance to offer similar merchandise (also known as market skimming)

primary research is conducted for a specific organisation or project either by a retailer's own marketing team or a specialist market research agency, typically using either a quantitative (e.g. questionnaires) or qualitative method (e.g. focus groups)

product assortment refers to the extent of different product types offered by a retailer, which is usually either 'narrow and deep' or 'broad and shallow'

product development refers to the process through which products are designed, prepared and produced prior to becoming commercially available to customers (also known as 'new product development' or 'NPD')

product technologists are employed by retailers or suppliers to manage aspects of the quality and manufacture of products that are sold by retailers

psychic distance refers to perceptions of differences between cultures in an international business context

psychographic segmentation is used to divide consumers into groups based on lifestyle characteristics, personality and attitudes and it is therefore well suited to retailers, since consumers generally purchase items to enable them to pursue their chosen lifestyles

psychological pricing is used when products and services are priced so that customers may perceive the cost as being cheaper, e.g. when it ends in a figure such as .99

public relations (PR) is promotional publicity in which the medium that features the product or service is not paid directly for this

pure players are retailers that only sell products or services online, without bricks-and-mortar stores

quality control (QC) refers to the process and the job role associated with ensuring that the retailer's merchandise is manufactured to an acceptable standard (the job role may also be referred to as a **product technologist**)

range planning involves compiling a collection of products within financial and design parameters, suitable for the target customer's taste and lifestyle

range review is the term used for a meeting where retail merchandisers present the key findings about the performance of a product range from a previous season, typically attended by their colleagues in buying, design, technology and senior management

rationalisation is the process of reorganising a company, especially when reducing certain elements of a business to minimise costs, e.g. by closing down a number of unprofitable retail branches

relationship marketing (RM) takes into account the lifetime value of the customer to the retailer, rather than a series of individual transactions, thereby aiming to meet the needs of both parties in the relationship and helping to build long-term relationships

retail atmosphere refers to the sensory impact of the retail environment, which affects consumers' visual, aural, olfactory and tactile senses, thus playing a part in retailers' brand image

retail buying is a form of organisational buying where professional buyers select appropriate merchandise to sell to the retailer's target customers

retail co-operative refers to a retailer that is owned by its members and which usually has centralised buying to take advantage of economies of scale

retail operations refers to the management of the work needed to run retail distribution channels on a day-to-day basis

retrobranding means offering new products that have been inspired by a previous era but which have modern functionality

return on investment (ROI) is a method of measuring the performance of a financial investment by calculating the amount gained from the investment minus its cost, divided by the cost of the investment, usually expressed as a percentage

reverse auctions take place when a retailer sets a specification for a product and suppliers tender for the business by each proposing a cost price

sales promotion customers are provided with incentives to purchase particular products for a limited timescale, e.g. by offering a discount or free gift

scrambled assortment refers to retailers offering a selection of unrelated types of merchandise

search engine optimisation (SEO) is a process which aims to put companies' websites high on the list of answers on internet search engines

secondary research refers to market information that has previously been published, usually in print or digital form, and is generally more economical than the cost of a company commissioning the research themselves (also known as 'desk research')

segmented pricing refers to retailers selling products or services at different prices depending on the market segment that purchases them, e.g. children or students

service delivery refers to interactions where customers receive services from service providers, in person, by phone or via electronic media

service dominant logic (S-D Logic) is a theory devised by Vargo and Lusch (2004) that all organisations and markets are fundamentally involved in the exchange of services and therefore service takes priority over product manufacture

service recovery means aiming to return the relationship between a service provider and a customer to a normal state by regaining control when a problem occurs or by retrieving something lost

services marketing mix refers to the 7Ps (product, price, promotion, place, people, physical evidence and process) that should be managed in order for services to function effectively (also known as the extended marketing mix)

shrinkage refers to the unplanned reduction of the amount of stock within a retailer, e.g. due to shoplifting or damage

situation analysis investigates an organisation's current position and establishes its potential future direction, by analysing key internal and external factors that affect the company

socio-economic groups are used to categorise customers into six key groups (A, B, C1, C2, D and E), based around their income bracket and occupation

sponsorship is a promotional strategy that offers the opportunity to place company logos or messages on sites associated with events that the sponsors have paid towards, to gain exposure of the brand name that contributes towards its brand identity

stock control refers to the management of a retailer's stock of products to ensure delivery and distribution to stores are on time and in the right quantities

stock-keeping-unit (SKU) refers to the reference code for a specific item of merchandise stocked by a retailer

stockout is the term used when a retailer runs out of stock of a specific product earlier than anticipated and therefore cannot fulfil demand from customers

strategic objectives are the overall goals of the organisation which are usually instigated by senior management and reviewed on a regular basis

supply chain management (SCM) is necessary since retailers do not usually manufacture the products they sell and they therefore need to manage their suppliers to ensure that they deliver suitable products by the agreed delivery date

sustainability refers to development that meets human needs currently as well as in the future, in relation to both society and the environment

SWOT analysis can be undertaken as part of the business situation analysis to identify the retailer's key strengths, weaknesses, opportunities and threats, to assist in specifying key issues that impact upon the organisation

trading involves managing stock during the period in which it is available for sale to the public

triple bottom line (TBL or 3BL) is a term used by Elkington (1994) to encourage organisations to aim not only for financial sustainability, but to also take into account environmental and social sustainability (sometimes referred to as 'people, planet, profit')

user-generated content (UGC) refers to information posted online publicly, such as reviews of products or services, which enables consumers to make more informed purchase decisions

variety chain refers to a type of retailer selling a variety of product lines which are mostly under the store's own label

visual merchandising (VM) involves enticing target customers into stores (or onto transactional websites) through effective displays and encouraging them to purchase through the skilful and attractive layout of products

wholesalers are intermediary organisations that 'break bulk' by buying in large quantities and selling in smaller quantities at a slightly higher price to make it financially viable to offer this service to small retailers

word-of-mouth (WoM) refers to consumers informing each other about products, brands and retailers, making recommendations or criticisms, which they may view as being more objective and authentic than marketing communications from companies

Index

Note: Glossary page numbers appear in **bold**

& Other Stories 96
€uro 50 Stores 143–4
4Ps 9, **331**
　see also marketing mix
7Ps 9, 295, **331**
30:3 phenomenon 302
99p Stores 20, 143–4

Aaker, D.A. 93
Abercrombie & Fitch (A&F) 237–8
Abimarvel 173
above-the-line promotion 162–3
　see also advertising
AC Nielsen 126
Accessorize 199
ACORN classification 69
acquisitions *see* mergers and acquisitions
Adel Rootstein 227
Adidas 200
advertising 9, 162–71, **331**
　Asos 288
　Bead Boutique 278
　brand image 9
　branded merchandise 99
　consumer decision-making 59
　consumer neuroscience 64
　history and development 5
　infomercials 13, 166, 272
　legislation and ethics 292–3
　location 198
　market segmentation 69, 70–1
　online 166, 167, 168, 177, 178, 281
　and pricing 151–2
　Product Life Cycle 87
　TK Maxx 168
Advertising Standards Authority (ASA) 175, 292
advertorials 168
adzines 168
affiliate advertising 178
age, segmentation by 68
ageing of population 18, 44, 68
Agnefjäll, Peter 317–18
Åhléns 113
Ahold/Royal Ahold 214, 314
AIDA model 163
Albrecht, K. 257
Aldi 16, 18, 107, 147, 159, 168, 177, 194, 197–8, 214, 227
Ale-Hop 91

Aleris 259
Alexander, N. 312
Alibaba/AliExpress 322
All Saints 219, 240
allocators 128
Amazon 14, 17, 38, 106–7, 249, 255, 267, 273, 276, 322
ambient media 167, 170, **331**
American Sugar Refining 95
Amnesty International 307
AMS 214
Amway 13
anchor tenants 200
Anderson, C. 276
André, E. 67
Andreini, D. 283
Ann Summers 13
Ansoff's product–market matrix 48–9
Anthropologie 244–5
anti-brand communities 260
Antler 200
Apparel Export Promotion Council, India 308
Apple 26, 90, 195, 221
apps 180, 188, 237
Arcadia 20, 73, 133, 195
Ardianto, Natali 329, 330
Arens, W.F. 170
Argos 39, 192, 197, 294
Ariel 94
Arizona 271
Arnold, M.J. 71
aroma, and retail atmosphere 235–6
Asda 7, 20, 45, 47, 99, 111, 211, 226
　George at Asda 94, 191, 226
　pricing 137, 147, 159
Asos 94, 188, 288, 297–8, 330
aspirational/occasional category 124, 125
Associated Independent Stores (AIS) 111
atmosphere, retail 234–8, **335**
Au Printemps 218
auctions 146, 274
　reverse 145, **335**
audits, marketing 43–7, 48
aural components, retail atmosphere 234–5, 236
Australasia 314
Australia 121–2, 169
Austria 188
avatars 237
Avon 13

B&M (buying and merchandising) *see* buying and merchandising
B&M (retailer) 206
B&Q 94, 152, 316
B2B (business-to-business) 110, 112, 113, **331**
B2C (business-to-consumer) 2, 182, **331**
Babin, B.J. 73
backward pricing 144, **331**
bait-and-switch tactics 293
Bakewell, C. 62
balanced scorecard 23
Bangladesh 307
banner adverts 178
BARB (Broadcasters' Audience Research Board) 166
bargaining power 47
barriers to entry 47, 320, 322
Bata 175
Bead Boutique 277–80
Beckham, David 188
behavioural segmentation 68, 71–2, **331**
Bekkedahl, Carol 81
Bell, E. 75
Bellizzi, J.A. 235
below-the-line promotion 163
Bench 187
Bennison, D. 191
Benson, J. 6
Berlin 206–8
Berman, B. 34, 38, 127, 172, 173, 228, 234, 290
bespoke merchandise 139
Bic 81
Bicester Village 61, 154, 187
billboards, advertising 167, 168, 169
Bitner, M.J. 259
Black Friday 153, 164
Blackwell, R.D. 57, 67
blogs/bloggers 19, 173, 272, 278, 281
　marketing communications 177, 178, 179, 188
　opinion leaders 62, 65
Bluewater Regional Shopping Centre 200, 202
Blythe, J. 5, 61
Blythman, J. 295
BMOC 269
Boden 270
Body Shop 226, 312
BOGOF offers 145, 176

Boland, Richard 10
Bon Prix 271
Bone, P.F. 235
boo.com 19
Booker 214
BOON 236
Booths 194
Boots 96, 168, 175, 195, 199, 248, 264
Boston Consulting Group (BCG) matrix 42, 49
boutique layout 224, 227, **331**
Brahma 106
Braithwaite, Alan 133, 134
brand citizenship behaviour 100
brand commitment 99–101, **331**
brand design consultants 221–3
brand equity 95, 177, **331**
brand extensions 95–6, 187, 188, **331**
brand heritage 8
brand identity 6, 93, 95, **331**
brand image 9, 47, 95, 151, 175, 296, **331**
    designer/luxury brands 115, 153, 154
    retail design and layout 217, 221, 229, 231, 240
brand loyalty 66, 125
brand management 83–4, 93–108
    brand equity 95
    brand extensions 95–6
    brand identity and brand image 95
    brand names 94
    brand positioning 96–8
    branded and own-label merchandise 98–9
    careers 101–2
    global brands 106–8
    internal brand commitment 99–101
    rebranding 98
brand names 94
brand personality 95
brand positioning 96–8, **331**
brand recall 93, **331**
brand recognition 93, **331**
brand stretching 96
branded products 6, **331**
    99p Stores 144
    buying and merchandising 113–15, 116, 118, 120
    Family Shopper 214
    grey market 154
    mail order 268
    pricing strategies 140, 144
Brands Ethical Working Group 308, 309
BrandZ 106, 107–8
Brazil 20, 320
BRIC/BRICS groups 20, 320
bricks and clicks 273–4, **331**
British Home Stores (BHS) 94
British Independent Retailers' Association 10
British Retail Consortium (BRC) 10, 296

broadcast media 164, 166, 167, 170
Brooke-Smith, Tamsin 173–4
Brown, J. 168
Brown, S. 16, 18, 62, 89
Browne, S. 204, 206
Bryman, A. 75
budget planning 129
build strategy 49–50
Burberry 106, 124, 125, 237, 255, 299
Burt, S. 27, 116, 191
Burton, J. 259
Burton Group 6, 73
business distance 320, 321, 324
Business History 27
business intelligence (BI) 22–4
business-to-business (B2B) 110, 112, 113, **331**
business-to-consumer (B2C) 2, 182, **331**
Butler, Sarah 133
Buttle, F. 259
Buy One Get One Free (BOGOF) offers 145, 176
buying and merchandising (B&M) 109–35
    branded and 'designer' merchandise 113–15
    careers 121–3, 126, 149–50
    category management 124–6
    centralised and decentralised buying 111–12
    online and mail order companies 123–4
    organisational buying theories 112–13
    own-label merchandise 115–16
    pricing 137
    retail buying cycle 116–23
    retail sales forecasting and budget planning 129
    retail space planning and allocation 128
    roles 110–11
    supply chain management and stock control by retailers 127–8
    supply chains 133–5
buying cycle 112–13, **331**
buying power 20

C&A 307, 308
C2C (consumer-to-consumer) 2, 6, 13, 146, **332**
Cadbury's 144, 292
Caffè Nero 15
call centres 255–6, 269
Calvert, Kate 54
Calvin Klein 106
Campaign Against Sumangali Scheme 307
Cancer Research (CR) 168, 222–3
Capital FM 169
car parking 199, 200, 204

carbon dioxide emissions 296, 300
Carman, J.M. 252
Carphone Warehouse 94, 199
Carrefour 258–9, 307, 308, 314, 316–17, 321
cash cows (BCG Portfolio Analysis) matrix 49
catalogue shopping 11, 193, 238, 240, 267–71
    see also mail order
catalogue stores 11
catchment areas 203, 204
category management 124–6, 127, **331**
Catwalk Cakes 231, 233–4
CAVIAR (Cinema and Video Industry Audience Research) 166
celebrities 173, 188, 268
centralised buying 111, **331–2**
Centre for the History of Retailing and Distribution (CHORD) 6
chain stores/multiples 11–12, **332**
    buying and merchandising 99, 111, 115
    future of retailing 26
    history and development 7
    location 204
    market levels 137–8
    retail hierarchy 195
Chang, H.J. 61
changing rooms 237
channel integration 283
channel synergy 283
Chaplin's butcher's shop, Groby, Leicestershire 7–8
Cheap Monday 96
Chelsea Girl 98
Cheshire Oaks 154, 200
Chetochine, Georges 228
child labour 308
China
    BRIC/BRICS groups 20, 320
    deregulation 319, 320
    infrastructure 321
    international retailing 313, 316, 318, 321, 323
        courier services 329
        designer outlet villages 154
        development 315, 316–17
        operational structure 324
        Walmart 313, 316, 321
    local governments 320
    plastic bags ban 301
    supply chains 133, 187, 307
China Daily 74
Chinese consumers 61, 62, 154
choice criteria 60
city centres 199
City Dressing 19
CK 94
Claire's Accessories 173

Clark, James 149–50
Clarke, Andy 159
Clarke, I. 191, 193, 198, 204
Clarke, Steve 53, 54
Classic FM 169
Clear Channel 169
click and collect 192, 194, 274, 281–2, 283, 288
closure of stores 195–8
Clow, K.E. 250
Coca-Cola 106
cognitive dissonance 60
cold chain 194
Collaborative Independent Retail Networks (CIRNs) 99–101
colour, and retail atmosphere 235, 236
Comic Relief 168
Comme des Garçons 237
commercialisation (product development) 85
communication 161–89
   Bead Boutique 278, 279
   careers 171–2, 173–4
   digital and social media 177–81
   direct marketing 177
   multichannel retailing 276, 281
   personal selling 181–2
   public relations 172–4
   relationship marketing 182
   sales promotions 175–6
   sponsorship 175
   strategies 162
   Superdry 187–9
   word-of-mouth 181
   see also advertising
community projects 299
comparative shopping 86, **332**
comparethemarket.com 59
comparison goods 195, 199
competition
   location 199, 205, 206
   mail order 269, 270
   market attractiveness 47
   pricing 137, 147
   see also competitive advantage
Competition and Markets Authority (CMA) 294
Competition Commission 294, 295
competition-orientated pricing 140, 141, **332**
competition test 295
competitions 176, 177, 188
competitive advantage
   Corporate Social Responsibility 296
   customer service 251
   global supply chains 309
   international retail marketing 322, 323
   multichannel retailing 268, 276
   relationship marketing 182
   sources 47, 48

competitive marketing objectives 49–50
competitor shopping 86
complaints 259–60, 261
compulsive shopping 67
concessions 11, **332**
conflict theory 18
Conforama 318
conforming store format 197–8
Conran, Jasper 96
Conran shop 92
Consortium, The 22
consumer behaviour 55–82
   careers 63–5
   decision-making 58–61
   definition 55
   ethical 301–2
   experiential 61
   influences 61–6
   loyalty 66–7
   market segmentation 67–72
   marketing research 73–5
   motivation and needs 57–8
   negative 67, 295
   profiles 72–3
   targeting the female consumer 81–2
consumer culture 55
consumer loyalty 66–7
   brand equity 95
   everyday low pricing 147
   market segmentation 71
   multichannel retailing 283
   post-consumption evaluation 60
   relationship marketing 182
   service recovery 260
   social media 106
   see also loyalty schemes
consumer neuroscience 55, 63–5, **332**
consumer rage 67
consumer-to-consumer (C2C) 2, 6, 13, 146, **332**
consumers
   core 39
   decision-making 58–61
   engagement 249–50, 275
   feedback/product reviews websites 20
   identification of 39
   legal rights 46
   motivation 57, 61
   needs 57–9
   personality 61
   power 20
   roles 57
contagious expansion 194–5, 198
Context, Power of 90
convenience/staple category 125
convenience stores 7, 11
Converse 93
coolhunting 65
Co-operative 7, 197, 301

co-operative, retail 11, 12, **335**
co-operative promotion 175, 176, **332**
copycat strategies 95
copyright protection 294
core customer 39
corporate branding 94, **332**
Corporate Social Responsibility (CSR) 2, 7, 20, 46, 66, 296–9, 300, **332**
Cos 96
cost leadership strategy 47, 48
cost-orientated pricing 140–1, **332**
cost-plus pricing 140
cost price 137
Costiff, Michael 237
Cottage Homes 10
counterfeit goods 95, 292, 293–4
couture merchandise 139
Cow 168
Craven, J. 187
Crayola 93
credit 67, 268, 269, 270
Creston 63
critical path 117, 120, **332**
Cult Clothing 187, 188
cultural distance 320, 321, 323–4
cultural factors, consumer behaviour 61
Currys 26
Curvissa 271
customer magazines 168
customer profiles 66, 72–3, **332**
Customer Relationship Management (CRM) 41, 66–7, 182, 276, **332**
customer service 246–65, **332**
   Boots 264
   characteristics of services 248–50
   electronic service delivery 255–7
   HappyOrNot device 258–9
   John Lewis 252–3
   multichannel retailing 283
   mystery shopping 254–5
   personal selling 181
   retail life cycle 14
   self-scan checkouts 265
   service culture 257–9
   service encounter 253–5
   service quality models 250–2
   service recovery 259–61
   signage 230
   Skandium 92
customers *see* consumers
customs rules, Russian 322
Cut & Dried 94
Cyber Monday 153, 164

Dahlvig, Anders 317, 318
Dalston 237
Darwinian theory of natural selection 34, 35
data architecture 23
data mining 75

Datamonitor 18, 37, 74
Davies, George 191, 221
Davies, J. 191
Davies, M. 198
Dawson, J. 312, 316
de Balanzó, Cristina 63–5
De Chernatony, L. 66
Deacon, Sarah 121–3
Debenhams 96, 113, 153, 200, 237, 255
Decathlon 259, 307, 308–9
decentralised buying 111, **332**
deciders 113
Decision Making Unit (DMU) 113
decline stage, Product Life Cycle 87–9
Defra 72
Deichmann Shoes 199
del Rey, Lana 62
Delhaize 259
delivery systems, multichannel retailing 281–2
demand and price, relationship between 148–51
demand-based pricing strategies 141–7
demand-orientated pricing 140, 141, **332**
demographic segmentation 68–70, **332**
demographics 68
   consumers/potential consumers
      Anthropologie 245
      behaviour 62
      future of retailing 26
      identification 39
      location decision-making 205, 206
      loyal 66
      mail order 270
      Superdry 188
   employees 10
   trends 18, 44
department stores 6, 11, 98, 113, 115
deregulation 319
design, sustainable 298
design agencies 101–2
design and layout 128, 216–45
   Anthropologie 244–5
   careers 221–3
   exterior store design 217–21
   interior store design 224
   non-store selling environment 238–40
   retail atmosphere 234–8
   security 67
   store layout 224–8
   visual merchandising 228–34
designer merchandise *see* luxury market
designer outlets *see* outlet stores/villages
designers 116
desk research *see* secondary research
Dewsnap, B. 124
DFS 164
DHL 322
di Caprio, Leonardo 188
Diesel 93

differentiation strategy 47, 48
diffusion of innovation 62–6, 89–90
digital media 177–81
   advertising 166, 167, 168, 177, 178
   signage 230
Dior 154
direct mail 13, **332**
direct marketing 41, 177, 182, 267, 271–2, 278, 281, **332**
Direct Response TV 272
direct selling/direct retailing 177, 267, 272, **332**
directional shopping 86, 116, **332**
disabled access 218
disconfirmation paradigm 252
discount cards/vouchers/coupons 154, 175, 176
discount stores 11, 138, 159, 214–15
Disney 106, 323
disposal of products 293
distribution 194, 198, 268, 270, 314, 321
Distribution Centres 128
diversification 39, 48
divestment 50, 61
Dixon's Retail 259
DKNY 94
dogs (BCG Portfolio Analysis) matrix 49
Dolcis 7
Dollar Tree 142
Dollar$tore 142, 143
door entrances 218
door-to-door selling 13
dotcom boom 19
Dove 82
Dover, P. 252
Dover Street Market 237
downsizing 32, 39
Dr Martens 93
Drapers 37, 74
Dunkerton, Julian 187
Dunn, Daniel 171–2
Dunne, Mark 228
Dunnes 199
dunnhumby 126, 171–2
Dupuis, M. 320, 321

EA 23
early adopters (diffusion of innovation) 65, 66, 89, 90, 178
early majority (diffusion of innovation) 65, 66, 89, 90
eBay 2, 6, 13, 106, 146, 187, 274, 292, 322, 329
ecommerce **332**
   international retail marketing 322, 329–30
   see also etailing; multichannel retailing
economic factors (PESTEL analysis) 44
economies of scale
   brand extensions 96

centralised buying 111
cost leadership strategy 48
globalisation 20
internationalisation 315
market attractiveness 47
mass market 138
price and value, relationship between 152
wheel of retailing 16
Egypt 35
EKB model 58
elastic demand 150
electroencephalography (EEG) 55, 64
electronic point-of-sale (EPoS) 6, 18, 120, **332**
electronic service delivery 255–7
electronic word-of-mouth (eWOM) 177
Elkington, J. 296
Ellen, P.S. 235
email 272, 281
emerging markets 312, 319–22
   Indonesia's ecommerce industry 329–30
   infrastructure and distribution 321–2
   psychic distance 320–1
Empire 269
employees
   consumer rage 67
   customer service 247–8, 253–4, 255, 257, 259, 261, 264
   demographics 10
   feedback to buyers 120
   HRM 50, 323
   internal branding 94
   legislation and ethics 46, 295
   location 198, 210, 211
   mail order companies 268
   manufacturing 307–9
   personal selling 181–2
   retail marketing planning 35
   retail marketing strategy 42
   self-scan checkouts as threat to jobs 265
   Skandium 92
   students as 10
   theft by 67, 295
   Walmart 2
   see also Human Resources Management
employer branding 94
employment levels 44
empty premises 19
energy usage 300
entrances to stores 218
entry barriers 47, 320, 322
entry mode, international retail marketing 316, 323–4
Environment Agency 293
environmental behaviours framework 72
environmental scanning 43

environmental sustainability 20, 45, 221, 300–1
Envirosell 75
etailing (e-retailing) 13, 273–5, **332**
    Bead Boutique 278–80
    downsizing strategy 39
    fulfilment and delivery systems 281–2
    global brands 106–7
    history and development 7
    impact on retail environment 19
    long tail effect 276
    mail order companies 269–71
    market share 19
    marketing mix 9
    personal selling 182
    retail accordion 17
    retail buying for 123–4
    selling environment 238–40
    technological developments 276
    see also ecommerce; multichannel retailing
ethical factors (PESTEL analysis) 45–6
ethical issues 289–310
    careers 297–8
    consumer behaviour 301–2
    corporate social responsibility 296–8
    extended marketing mix 295
    global retail supply chains 307–10
    impulse purchases 226–7
    place 294–5
    predatory pricing 147
    pricing 292
    product 293–4
    promotion 292–3
    sustainability 296
        environmental 300–1
        social 298–300
Ethical Trading Initiative (ETI) 299
ethnicity 45
ethnography 61, 75, **332**
Euroland 142
Euromonitor 37
Euronics 111
Europe
    buying and merchandising 127
    designer outlet villages 154
    international retailing 20, 312, 314
    Superdry 188
    supply chains 133, 134
    wheel of retailing 16
European Coalition for Corporate Justice (ECCJ) 307, 308, 309
European Journal of Marketing 74
European Sign Expo 230
European Union (EU)
    disposal of goods 61
    geographical pricing 146–7
    global supply chains 307, 308–9
    international retailing 314
    legislation 290, 293

Evans, J.R. 11, 28, 34, 38, 127, 172, 173, 228, 234, 290, 320
everyday low pricing (EDLP) 141, 144, 147, **332**
evolutionary strategy 36
evolutionary theory 34, 36
expansion
    contagious 194–5, 198
    hierarchical 195
    location 192, 194–5
    see also international retail marketing
expectations, and service quality 250–1, 252
Experian 204
experiential consumer behaviour 61, **332**
extended marketing mix 9, 295, **333**
extended problem-solving 59
extension category 124–5
exterior store design 217–21
Eye 169
eye-tracking 64, 75, 228

Facebook 19, 75, 168, 178, 179, 188, 237, 271, 288
Fahy, Helen 111
Fahy, J. 55
Fair Trade 292, 301, **333**
Fairhurst, A.E. 110
family lifecycle (FLC) 68
Family Shopper 214
Farm Foods 214
fascia 197, 217
Fat Face 199
Federal Express 322
feedback
    to buyers 120
    from loyal customers 66
    websites 20
Fenwick 111, 112
Fernandez, Luis 95
Ferrell, O.C. 35, 36, 84, 95, 151
Few, Law of the 90
Fiat 82
film advertising 166, 167
final selection 119–20, **333**
finance strategy 50
financial objectives 50
financial performance 39
Financial Times 74
FINE 292
Finland 258
Fiorito, S.S. 110
Fitch Ratings 159
fittings 224, 225–6
Five Forces model 47
Flannels 225
Fleetwood Freeport 200
flyers 167, 168, 175, 177
focus groups 61, 71, 74, 85, **333**
focus strategy 48

food deserts 295
Foot Locker 12
foreign direct investment (FDI) 313, 319
forests 300
France 292, 321
franchise 11, **333**
    international expansion 312, 316, 324
Fred Perry 93
freeform layout 224, 227, **333**
freehold 194, 198
Freeman Grattan Holdings (FGH) 270–1
Freemans 269
Freestone, O.M. 292
Freitag bags 300
French Connection 267
Friends of the Earth 295, 307
Fuad, Ellyana 329
fuel prices/usage 44, 300, 301
fulfilment systems, multichannel retailing 281–2
functional magnetic resonance imaging (fMRI) 55
functional quality 250–1
funnel entrances 218, 219
future of retailing 26, 32

Game 22, 23–4
Gap 14, 96, 200, 307, 308
gap analysis 252
Garcia Escuela, Gisela 244, 245
gatekeepers, organisational buying decision 113
Gauzente, C. 178
Gehry, Frank 217
gender *see* men; women
geodemographic segmentation 68–9, **333**
geographic segmentation 68–70, **333**
geographical information system (GIS) 204, **333**
geographical pricing 146–7, **333**
George at Asda 94, 191, 226
Germany 188, 317
gifting 173, 188
Gilbert, D. 2, 35, 66, 94, 137, 162, 163
Gilly Hicks 237
Giourouki, Lito 126
Gladwell, M. 90
global brands 106–8
global economic crisis 2, 20, 44
    consumer credit 67
    downsizing strategy 39
    pricing 137
    retail marketing strategy 34
global retail market, value of 2, 18
global retailers 3, 312
globalisation 6, 20, 319, 322–3
glocalisation 323
goals *see* objectives
Gonalston Farm Shop 231

gondolas 224, 226, **333**
Google 178, 181, 275
Gordon, Garry 134
Goudkuil, Jessica 277–80
government policies 319–20
graffiti 170
graphics 229–30
Grattan 123, 269, 270–1
Graze 177
Greece 35, 314
Greenpeace 296, 307
grey market 154, **333**
grid layout 224, 227, **333**
Grimeland, Magnus 330
Grocer, The 37, 74
Grönroos, Christian 182, 250
gross margin 43, 147, 150, **333**
Groupon 177
growth cycle, potential 20, 22
growth stage, Product Life Cycle 87
G-Star 188
Guardian, The 74
Gubar, G. 68
Gucci 106, 154
guerrilla marketing 170
GUS 269

H&M 20, 62, 96, 117, 229, 307, 308, 309
Habitat 92, 244, 245
habitual decisions 59
Hadida, Armand 237
Haenlein, M. 178
Handmade Burger Co. 38
Hansen, G.E. 322
Hansen, Janice 231
HappyOrNot device 258–9
Hardie, C. 62
Harrods 96
Hart, C.A. 91, 124, 259
Hartline, M.D. 35, 36, 84, 95, 151
Hartonos 329
harvesting 50, 87
Hasty, R.W. 283
Hatchards 218
Head Office 24–5, 111
Headlee, Robin 106
hedonic needs 57–8
Heidkamp, P.C. 295
Heineken 63
Heinz ketchup 86
Hepworth 6
Hermès 217
Hernandez, B. 282
hierarchical expansion 195
hierarchy of needs 57
Higham, W. 90
Hillards 194
Hines, C. 322
hire purchase 6
hold strategy 49

Holder, James 187
Holition 224
Hollander, S. 16, 35, 36, 38, 40
Hollister 237–8
Holt, D.B. 309
home delivery 7
Home Depot 316, 323
home shopping 13, 267, **333**
  retail buying for 123–4
  and store shopping, blurred distinction between 284
  supply chains 133
  see also catalogue shopping; etailing; mail order; multichannel retailing
Hondos Center 38
Hong Kong 323
Hopkinson, Matthew 205
hotspots 226–7
House of Fraser 73, 98, 149, 172, 192, 200
Human Resources Management (HRM) 50, 323
hypermarkets 11

Iceland 142
iconic category 124, 125
idea generation (product development) 84
IKEA 165, 191, 199, 203, 218, 259, 314, 317–18
impulse buying
  category management 125
  experiential consumer behaviour 61
  mail order 268
  as negative consumer behaviour 67
  point-of-purchase promotions 175
  store layout 226
IMRG 10
Inaba, Rio 329, 330
Inclusi 297
Independent, The 74
independent stores 11, 12, **333**
  branded merchandise 98, 113–14
  buying and merchandising 113–14, 127
  consumer engagement 249–50
  decline 295
  future of retailing 26
  relationship marketing 182
  retail hierarchy 195
India 20, 320
  global supply chains 187, 307–9
  infrastructure 321
  international retailing 315, 318, 323
Inditex 96
Indonesia 169, 329–30
Industrial Revolution 5
inelastic demand 150
influencers 113

infomercials 13, 166, 272
information search 59
infrastructure in emerging markets 321, 329
initiators 113
innovation, diffusion of 62–6, 89–90
innovators (diffusion of innovations theory) 65, 66, 88, 89, 178
insight reporting 23
in-store displays 231–4, 244
integrated marketing communications (IMC) 162, 181, **333**
intellectual property 47, 293–4
interest rates 44
interior store design 224–7
internal brand commitment 99–101, **331**
internal branding 94
International Journal of Retail and Distribution Management 74
International Labour Organization, Convention Prohibiting Child Labour 308
international retail marketing 20, 311–30
  defining 312–13
  development 314–18
  emerging markets 319–20
    Indonesia's ecommerce industry 329–30
    infrastructure and distribution 321–2
    psychic distance 320–1
  IKEA 317–18
  retail marketing strategy 35
  Russian customs rules 322
  strategies 322–4
  Walmart in China 313
International Review of Retail, Distribution and Consumer Research 74
internet
  anti-brand communities 260
  communication 281
  consumer decision-making 59, 60
  consumer engagement 275
  consumer-to-consumer market 2, 6, 13
  Cyber Monday 153
  diffusion of innovation 90
  direct marketing 272–3
  discount coupons 154
  discount designer websites 153
  electronic service delivery 256
  experiential consumer behaviour 61
  future of retailing 26, 32
  history and development of retail marketing 6, 7
  home shopping 13
  impact on retail environment 19–20
  Indonesia 329, 330
  long tail effect 276

mail order 269–71
marketing communications 177–81
　advertising 166, 167, 168, 177
netnography 75
retail locations 192, 197, 204
supply chain 6
user reviews 59, 60
see also ecommerce; etailing; multi-channel retailing; social media; websites
interviews, marketing research 74
introduction stage, Product Life Cycle 87, 88
iPod 90
Ireland, Republic of 99–100, 301
Issey Miyake 217
Italy 116, 318

Jack Wills 94, 177
Jackson, Betty 96
Jakobsen, Bent Wulff 259
Jamie's Italian 94
Japan 12, 187, 295, 314, 317, 329
JC Decaux 169
JD Sports 94
Jobber, D. 36, 55
Johansson, J. 116
John Frieda 82
John Lewis 41, 141, 166, 168, 192, 199, 200
　customer service 248, 252–3, 255
　location 199, 200, 203
John Myers 269
Johnstone, P. 295
joint ventures 312, 313, 316, 324
Jones, K. 191
Journal of Interactive Marketing 180
Journal of Marketing 27
Journal of Retailing 18, 27, 74
Journal of Services Marketing 74
journalists 62, 172, 174, 188
joyofsocks.com 17
JRA Research 74

Kacker, M.F. 312
Kaleidoscope 271
Kamprad, Ingvar 317, 318
Kanji, Sunita and Suresh 214
Kantar 126, 159
Kapferer, J.N. 95
Kaplan, A.M. 178
Kaskus 329
Kawakubo, Rei 237
Keaveney, S. 259–60
Kelkoo 141, 178
Kent, A.M. 235
Kentucky Fried Chicken 63, 98
Key Note 37, 74
KFC 63, 98
Kiabi 307, 308

King, Justin 159
Kingfisher 6
Kline, B. 110
KMart 197
Knox, Martin 26, 221–3
Kokubo, Taketo 329
Koolhaas, Rem 217
Kozinets, R.V. 75
KPR Mill 307–9

L'Eclaireur 237
L'Occitane 106
L'Oréal 93, 292
La Patisserie des Rêves, London 21
Labour Behind the Label 296
Lacoste 200
Laczniak, G.R. 309
laggards (diffusion of innovation) 65, 66, 89
Lakeside Regional Shopping Centre 201
Lalani family 143, 144
Lancôme 93
Lands End 270
late majority (diffusion of innovation) 65, 66, 89, 90
Lau, Susie 65
Law of the Few 90
layout of stores *see* design and layout
Leahy, Sir Terry 191
Lear, K. 175
learning process in internationalisation 321
leasehold 194, 198
legal factors (PESTEL analysis) 46
legislation and regulations 289–95, 302–6
　disabled access 218
　environmental sustainability 301
　extended marketing mix 295
　grey market 154
　guerrilla marketing 170
　India 308
　international retail marketing 319–20, 322, 323, 324, 330
　markdowns 152
　place 294–5
　pricing 292
　product 293–4
　promotion 292–3
　user-generated content 178
Lena Hoschek 207, 208
Levaniemi, Ville 258
Levi's jeans 86
Levy, M. 98
Li, Y. 204
licensing 312
Lidl 137, 151, 159, 197, 214
lighting 223, 224–5, 235, 236
limited problem-solving 59
line extensions 96

Liu, L. 204
LL Bean 270
LN-CC 237
Local Data Company (LDC) 204, 205
Local Planning Authority (LPA) 209–10
local search-engine optimisation 180–1
localisation vs globalisation 322–3
location 190–215
　Aldi 198
　B&M 206
　Berlin 206–8
　careers 205
　decision-making
　　framework 193–8
　　process 203–4
　importance 192–3
　legislation and ethics 291, 294–5
　local discount stores 214–15
　M&S 200
　planning system 209–11
　pricing 137
　site-specific issues 206
　types 198–202
locational management options 195, 197
Londis 111
long tail effect 275–6
Look Again 271
lovemarks 93
loyalty *see* consumer loyalty
loyalty schemes 66
　Boots 264
　data mining 75
　direct marketing 177
　Relationship Marketing 182
Lury, C. 55
Lusch, R.F. 2, 35
Lush 299–300
luxury market 138–9
　buying and merchandising 113–15
　designer outlet villages 152–3, 154
　grey market 154
　multichannel retailing 283–4
　price and value, relationship between 151

M&S *see* Marks & Spencer
Mac 93
Mace 111
macro-environment 39, 43, 44–6, 319, **333**
Madonna 62
Madsen, Henrik 154
magazines
　advertising 167, 168–9
　customer magazines 168
　online communication 281
mail order 6, 13, 19, 123–4, 267–71
　see also catalogue shopping
Malmö 2014 festival 170
Manchester City Council's retail planning policies 210

mannequins 224, 227
manufacturers
    advertising 166
    distribution channel development 314
    employees 307–9
    pricing strategies 140–1
    history and development 5, 6
markdown 50, 120, 149, 152–4, **333**
market attractiveness 47
market development 48
market levels 137–9
market mavens 62
market penetration 48, 87
    pricing 142
market research 73–5
    careers 26, 41
    consumer behaviour 61, 72
        neuroscience 55, 63–5, **332**
    consumer needs 59
    SWOT analysis 37
    value chain 48
market segmentation 67–72, **333**
    customer loyalty 66
    history and development of retail marketing 6
    mail order 269
    Superdry 188
market skimming (pricing skimming) 87, 142, **334**
market stalls 238
market traders 11
marketing, history and development 4, 5
marketing audits 43–7`, 48
marketing communications (marcomms) *see* communication
Marketing Magazine 74
marketing mix 9, **333**
    brand identity 95
    DFS 164
    differentiation strategy 48
    legislation and ethics 290–5
    location 191
    online communication 281
    pricing 137
    Product Life Cycle 86, 87
    retail design and layout 217, 221, 238
    retail marketing strategy 35
    value 151
    websites 240
    word-of-mouth 181
marketing plans 40–2
marketing research *see* market research
Marketing Sciences Unlimited 63
Marketing Week 74
Marks, Michael 16
Marks & Spencer (M&S)
    advertising 164
    as anchor tenant 200
    brand names 94
    Corporate Social Responsibility 7, 296

Head Office departments 25
history and development of retail marketing 7
location 194, 199, 200, 203
middle market 138
own-label merchandise 99
Per Una 94, 191, 229
recycling of clothing 293
refits 197
retail hierarchy 195
Simply Food stores 192
stores as collection points 192
UK sourcing 134
visual merchandising 229
wheel of retailing 16
Your M&S magazine 168
mark-up 137, 147, 148, **333**
    backward pricing 144
    price elasticity 150–1
marquee *see* fascia
marrying margins 148
Martin, D. 296
Maslow, Abraham 57
mass market 137–9
Massimo Dutti 96
Matalan 99, 147, 151
maturity stage, Product Life Cycle 87
Matusitz, J. 323
Maverick Sabre 168
McArthurGlen Group 154
McCann 165
McCarthy, Dave 159
McCartney, Stella 168
m-commerce *see* mobile commerce
McDonald, M. 66
McDonald's 175, 312
McGoldrick, P.J. 48, 67, 110, 203, 234, 292, 294
McGrath, Daniel 322
McKinsey 275
McLean, Andrew 244, 245
media buyers 171
Megicks, P. 294
men 62
merchandising **333**
    see also buying and merchandising
mergers and acquisitions
    history and development of retail marketing 6, 7
    international retailing 312, 324
    legislation 294
    location 194, 197, 211
    rebranding 98
    strategy 39
Metro 314
MFI 7
micro-environment 43, 46–7, 319, **333**
Microsoft 23, 96
middle market 138–9
Migato 35

Migros 259
Millers 121–3
Millward Brown Optimor 107
Minney, Safia 172
Mintel 27, 37, 73, 74
mirrors 224
MIRSA Analogue-Finder system 204
Miss Selfridge 73
mission-based shopping 228
mission statements 38, **333**
    balanced scorecard 23
    service culture 257
    strategic planning 36
Mitchell, V.W. 62
Miu Miu 237
mobile commerce (m-commerce) 277, 283, **334**
mobile device retailing (m-tailing) **334**
    advertising 178
    consumer decision-making 60
    global brands 106
    marketing communications 180
    pricing strategies 141
Modish 238, 239
Modulor 207–8
Molson, Kelly 26, 101–2
Monoprix 94
Monsoon Accessorize 197
moral principles *see* ethical issues
Morocco 133
Morrisons 7, 20, 94, 111, 159, 170, 192, 194, 197
Mosaic 69
Mothercare 199
motivation
    consumer behaviour 71
    international retailing 315
m-tailing *see* mobile device retailing
Mukoyama, M. 316
multichannel retailing 2, 247, 266–88, **334**
    Asos 288
    buying and merchandising 123
    careers 277–80
    consumer engagement 275
    direct marketing 271–2
    downsizing 39
    electronic service delivery 255
    fulfilment and delivery systems 281–2
    future 32
    long tail effect 275–6
    mail order 267–71
    new technology 276–7
    non-store retail selling environment 238–40
    online communications 281
    website design 277
    see also ecommerce; etailing; home shopping
multinational corporations (MNCs) 312, 314, 323

multiple-unit pricing 144, 145, **334**
multiples *see* chain stores/multiples
Murphy, P.E. 309
music, and retail atmosphere 235
mystery shopping 254–5, **334**

N Brown 133, 134, 193
nation branding 94
National Farmers' Retail and Markets Association 10
National Health Service (NHS) 41
National Readership Survey (NRS) 69, 166
National Retail Federation 111
National Statistics Socio-Economic Classification (NS-SEC) 70
Neal's Yard Remedies 138
Neff, J. 59
Nepal 299
Nestlé 323
Net-A-Porter 180, 322
net profit margin 39, 43, **334**
net promoter score 67
netnography 75
neuro-marketing 55
Neuromarketing Science and Business Association 64–5
neuroscience, consumer 55, 63–5, **332**
New Look 134
new product development (NPD) *see* product development
New Zealand 169
newsletters 272
newspaper advertising 167, 168
Newton-Jones, Mark 133
Next 6, 164, 188, 191–2, 194, 196, 200, 210, 221–2, 269, 270
niche retailers 17
Nike 106, 221, 309
Nintendo Wii 96
Nivea 288
non-store-based retailing 238–40
   see also home shopping; multichannel retailing
Nordea Bank 38
Nordstrom 248
North America 314
North Face 219
not-for-profit sector 50
Numark 111
Nutella 93

Oak Furniture Land 94, 274–5
obesity 44
OBI 316, 323
objectives
   communication 162
   competitive marketing 49–50
   financial 50
   pricing 137, 139–41

setting 38–9
strategic 49, **336**
observational research 75
odd pricing 142, **334**
Office of Fair Trading (OFT) 294, 295
offshore sourcing 20
Ohlsson, Mikhal 317, 318
Olay 82
olfactory components, retail atmosphere 234–6
Oli 271
Oliver, Jamie 188
Oliver, R.L. 252
Olsen, J. 252
omnichannel retailing 26, 283, **334**
One Direction 173
online consumer reviews 177, 178
online retailing *see* etailing
OpCapita 24
open store entrances 218
open-to-buy 129, **334**
opening times 7, 8
operational efficiency, mail order companies 268
opinion leaders 62–6, 90, 173
Oracle 151
organic international expansion 324
organic products 301
organisational buyer behaviour (OBB) 110, 112–13, **334**
organisational buyer decision-making (OBDM) 112–13
Original Factory Shops 197
Otto Versand 267, 269, 270–1
out-of-home (OOH) media 169–70
outdoor advertising channels 169–70
outlet stores/villages 11, 61, 153, 154, 187, 201, **334**
own-label merchandise 98–9, **334**
   99p Stores 144
   brand equity 95
   buying and merchandising 110, 111, 115–16, 118, 120
   Family Shopper 214
   history and development of retail marketing 6, 7
   product development 85
   symbol groups 111
Oxfam 307
Oxylane 308
Ozon 322

packaging 300
Paperchase 199
parallel market *see* grey market
Parasuraman, A. 248, 251
Parcelnet 270
Pareto 80:20 rule 275
Parsons, A.G. 235
party plan selling 13, 267

passing off 293–4
Pasta Hut 98
patents 294
Paul Smith 92
Pavegen floor tiles 218–21
PC World 60, 293
peer group pressure 57
Pegler, M.J. 228
pen portrait *see* customer profiles
Pentina, I. 283
People Tree 172, 299
perceptions
   consumer behaviour 57
   service quality 250–1, 252
perceptual maps 96–8, **334**
performance evaluation 120–3
Pernod Ricard 288
personal branding 94
personal selling 13, 181–2, **334**
   online 281
PESTEL analysis 42, 44–6, 141
pesticides 300
petrol prices 44
Phan, D.D. 269
Philips, Dalton 159
Piano, Renzo 217
Pinault-Printemps – Redoute (PPR) 269
Pinterest 75, 179, 279, 288
Pizza Hut 98
place *see* location
place branding 94
Planned Behaviour, Theory of 56
planning
   policy 294–5
   retail marketing 35–6
   strategic *see* strategic planning
   system 209–11
Planogram Builder 232
planograms 128, 231, 232, **334**
point-of-purchase (POP) 31, 281
point-of-purchase promotion (POP) 175, 176, **334**
political factors (PESTEL analysis) 44
Polo Ralph Lauren 200
Pommering, D. 314
pop-up shops 12–13
POPAI 175
population growth 296
Porter, M.E. 47–8
portfolio analysis 49
positioning maps 96–8
post-consumption evaluation 60
Post Office 44, 230, 268
posters
   advertising 167, 168, 169, 170
   in-store 188
Poundland 95, 144, 159
Poundstretcher 20
Poundworld 95, 144

power
  bargaining 47
  buying 20
  consumer 20
  retailer 14, 47, 127
  supplier 47, 127
Power of Context 90
Prada 106, 154, 217
predatory pricing 147, **334**
Premier Inn/Premier Travel Inn/Premier Lodge 98
Premium and Green Showroom 114
pre-purchase evaluation of alternatives 60
pre-selection stage, retail buying cycle 118–19
press releases 172
Pret A Manger 92
price architecture 139, 142, **334**
price bundling 145
price comparison websites 20, 59, 141, 178
price elasticity 148–51, **334**
price lining 142, **334**
Price Marking Order (2004) 292
price-matching schemes 159
price reductions *see* markdown
Price Runner 141
price sensitivity 151
price wars 137, 142, 159–60
pricing 136–60
  99p stores 143–4
  branded vs own-label merchandise 99
  calculating retail prices 147–8
  careers 149–50
  designer outlet villages 154
  elasticity 148–51
  facets 138
  legislation and ethics 291, 292
  mail order 268, 270
  markdowns 152–4
  market levels 137–9
  objectives and strategies 139–41
  Product Life Cycle 87
  retail buying cycle 119–20
  skimming 87, 142, **334**
  strategy implementation 141–7
  subbrands 94
  supermarket price wars 159–60
  and value, relationship between 151–2
  visual merchandising 231
pricing skimming 87, 142, **334**
Primark 288
primary research 73, 74–5, **334**
Prime, N. 320, 321
print advertising 164, 166, 167, 168–9, 170
private brands *see* own-label merchandise
problem-solving 59

Procter & Gamble 9, 164, 171
procurement departments 113
product, legislation and ethics 291, 293–4
product assortment 91–2, 137, 268, **334**
product development 6, 48, 84–6, **334–5**
  buying and merchandising 111, 115–16, 127
  own-label merchandise 99, 115–16
  Product Life Cycle 87
product life cycle (PLC) 14, 15, 49, 86–9
product management 83–93, 102–5
  new product development 84–6
  product life cycle 86–9
  product/service continuum 92–3
  product trends and diffusion of innovation 89–90
  retail product assortment 91–2
  Skandium 91–2
product placement 166
product reviews websites 20
product/service continuum 92–3
product technologists **335**
production orientation 5
profit margin 147–8
profitability
  Asos 288
  assessment 39
  backward pricing 144
  brand extensions 96
  branded vs own-label merchandise 99
  buying and merchandising
    procurement department 113
    retail buying cycle 119, 120
    retail space planning and allocation 128
    stock control 128
  geographical pricing 147
  margin 147–8
    gross 43, 147, 150, **333**
    net 39, 43, **334**
  objectives 50
  price and value, relationship between 151
  pricing strategies 140
  supply chains 133
  time spent in stores 75
promotion
  legislation and ethics 291, 292–3
  online 281
  see also advertising
promotional pricing 141
psychic distance 315, 320–1, 323–4, **335**
psychographic segmentation 68, 70–1, **335**
psychological pricing 137, 141–2, **335**
public relations (PR) 172–4, **335**
  careers 173–4
  digital media 177

online 281
Superdry 188
Publicis 170
Pull & Bear 96
pull factors, internationalisation 315, 320
pull strategy, marketing communication 162
Puma 62–5
purchase, consumer decision-making 60
pure players 13, 267, 273, **335**
push factors, internationalisation 315
push strategy, marketing communication 162

QR codes 19, 60, 230
QRS Research 74
qualitative market research 74–5
quality control (QC) 120, 127–8, **335**
quantitative market research 74–5
question marks (BCG Portfolio Analysis) matrix 49
quick response (QR) codes 19, 60, 230
QVC 13, 166, 272

racetrack layout *see* boutique layout
radio advertising 166, 167, 169
Radio Frequency Identification (RFID) 20
Rafiq, M. 91
RAJAR (Radio Joint Audience Research) 166
Rakuten 329, 330
Ralph Lauren 154
Range, The 91
range planning 118, 119, 124, **335**
range review 118, 123, **335**
rationalisation 195–8, **335**
Rayner, Clare 26, 249–50
REACH (Registration, Evaluation, Authorisation and Restriction of Chemical substances) Regulation 293
rebranding 98
recession 34, 144, 270, 275
  see also global economic crisis
recycling 293, 300, 301
Redken 93
refascia 197
reference groups 61, 62
refits 197
refund vouchers 176
regulations *see* legislation and regulations
reintroduction of products 88–9
relationship marketing (RM) 9, 66, 162, 182, **335**
relocation 197
remerchandising 197
rental arrangements 6

repeat orders 120
replenishment 128
Resale Price Maintenance Act 6
research and development 47
Resolution Interiors 223
retail accordion 16–17
retail analysts 26
retail atmosphere 234–8, **335**
Retail Bulletin 37, 74
retail buying **335**
    cycle 116–23
    see also buying and merchandising
retail concepts 13
retail co-operative 11, 12, **335**
Retail Gazette 37, 74
retail industry associations 10
retail life cycle (RLC) 14–15, 86
retail marketing
    defined 9
    development 4–7, 9–10
    history 4–7
    scope 9–10
    planning 35–6
    strategy *see* retail marketing strategy
retail marketing strategy 33–54
    careers 41–3
    communication 162, 163
    competitive advantage, sources of 48
    competitive marketing objectives 49–50
    definition 35
    developing 39–40
    HRM and finance strategy 50
    identifying consumers 39
    implementing the marketing plan 40
    internal and external marketing audits 43–7
    market attractiveness 47
    market penetration and diversification 48–9
    mission statements 38
    planning 35–6
    portfolio analysis 49
    setting goals and objectives 38–9
    situation analysis 36
    SWOT analysis 36–7
    value chain 47–8
    WH Smith 53–4
retail operations 25, **335**
retail parks 6, 199, 210
retail theories 13–18
Retail Trust 10
Retail Week 27, 37, 74
retailCORe 10
retailer business formats 11–13
retailer categories 11
retailer power 14, 47, 127
retailing, definitions 2
retailing management 24–6
Retailmap 37, 96
retailRIGHT 10

retrobranding 88–9, **335**
return on investment (ROI) 41, 43, **335**
returns procedure 255, 260–1, 294
reverse auctions 145, **335**
reverse graffiti 170
Reynolds, K.E. 71
Rhodes, Zandra 172
Ries, A. 173
Ries, L. 173
Rihanna 62
risk
    consumer decision-making 59, 60
    international expansion 319
    returns policy 294
River Island 62, 96, 98, 111, 134
Roberts, Kevin 93
Rocha, John 96
Rocket Internet 330
Rogers, E.M. 65
Rogers, M.R. 89, 90
Roig-Tierno, N. 206
roll out 194, 197
Ronson, Mark 188
Rose Bakery 237
round pricing 142
routine decisions 59
Royal Ahold 214, 314
Royal Mail 44
Rubber Cheese 101–2, 238
Rucker, Jeremy 19
Russell, S.E. 295
Russia 20, 318, 320, 322

Safeway 194, 197
Sainsbury's 7, 47, 99, 173–4, 192, 299
    location 192, 199, 210
    pricing 139, 159
    Sainsbury's magazine 168, 169
Sale of Goods Act (1979) 292, 293
sales events 153, 164
sales forecasting 129
sales promotion 175–6, **335**
sales taxes (VAT) 147, 152, 154
sample products 176
Samsonite 106
SAP 151
Saxa 95
scale economies *see* economies of scale
Scamell-Katz, Siemon 228
scent, and retail atmosphere 235–6
Schmidt, Christina 91–2
Schouten, J. 296
Schuh 224
scrambled assortment 91, **335**
screening and evaluation (product development) 85
search engine marketing (SEM) 177, 178, 180
search engine optimisation (SEO) 102, 178, 180–1, 275, 281, **335**

search engine results pages (SERPs) 178, 180
Sears 269
seasonal sales 153, 176
second-hand goods 146
secondary research 73–4, **335**
security 67
Segmentation, Targeting and Positioning (STP) 39, 68
segmented pricing 145–6, **335**
self-scan checkouts 247, 256, 257, 265
self-service technologies (SSTs) 256–7
    see also self-scan checkouts
Selfridges 218, 230
semi-open store entrances 218, 219
service culture 257–9
service delivery 247, **335**
service dominant logic (S-D Logic) 9, **335**
service encounter 249, 253–5
service quality models 250–2
service recovery 249, 259–61, **335**
service sector 274
services, characteristics of 248–50
services marketing mix 50, **336**
    see also extended marketing mix
SERVQUAL instrument 251–2
Seven and i Holdings 20
Seven Eleven Group 323
Shanghai Tang 38
shareholding, and international expansion 324
shelving 224, 225
Shepherdson, Jane 111
Sherman Antitrust Act 292
Shop Direct 133, 134, 270
shoplifting 67, 295
Shoppercentric 62
shopping centres 200
shopping channels 272
Short, Paul 133, 134
showrooming 249
showrooms 274
shrinkage 295, **336**
Siebers, L.Q. 313
signage 229–30
Simmons, J. 191
site assessment 206
situation analysis 36, **336**
Skandium 91–2
small-to-medium enterprises (SMEs) 2, 26
smartphones 60, 180, 283, 329
    see also mobile commerce; mobile device retailing
smell, and retail atmosphere 235–6
Smith, Christian 297–8
Smith, William Henry 54
Sneddon, Alastair 22–4, 26
social, local and mobile aspects of shopping (So-Lo-Mo) 26

social media
  global brands 106
  impact on retail environment 19–20
  mail order 271
  marketing communications 166, 168, 177–80, 188
  multichannel retailing 276
  netnography 75
  opinion leaders 65
  PR 173
  see also Facebook; Pinterest; Twitter; YouTube
social sustainability 20, 45, 298–300
societal factors (PESTEL analysis) 44–5
socio-economic groups 69–70, **336**
Solomon, G.W. 139
Solomon, Jonathan 41–3
Solomon, M.R. 55, 68, 253
Somerfield 197
Sony PlayStation 96
Sorensen, Herb 228
sound, and retail atmosphere 235, 236
sourcing 118
South Africa 320
South Korea 283
Spain 188, 295
Spar 111
spatial interaction models 204
specialist stores 11–12
specialogues 268, 269
Specsavers 165, 178
sponsorship 175, 299, **336**
sports sponsorship 175
stallholders 11
Staples 199
Starbucks 15
stars (BCG Portfolio Analysis) matrix 49
start-up costs, mail order companies 268
status, and retailer power 14
Stefani, Jamie 188
Stenhoff International 318
stereotypes 71, 81
Sternquist, B. 312
Stevenson, John 54
Stichting Ingka Foundation 318
Stickiness Factor 90
stock control 115, 127–8, **336**
stock-keeping units (SKUs) 128, **336**
stockout 128, **336**
store cards 66
  see also loyalty schemes
store layout *see* design and layout
store loyalty 66
Storehouse 6
Stratasys 85
strategic analysis 34
strategic business units (SBUs) 49
strategic objectives 49, **336**
strategic planning 35–6
  benefits 34

mission statements 38
situation analysis 38
Vision Express 42
strategic retail growth 40
strategy
  multichannel 282–3
  pricing 139–41
  retail marketing *see* retail marketing strategy
Street, Andy 203, 252
strike action 44
students
  as employees 10
  lock-ins 145–6
  socio-economic grouping 69–70
studying retail marketing 27
stylebubble 179
subbrands 94, 99, 139
subcultures 45, 61, 62
substitute products 47
Subway 94
Sukamart.com 329, 330
Sumangali scheme 307, 308
Sumitomo 329
Sunday opening 7
Superdrug 195
Superdry 187–9, 197
SuperGroup 188
supermarkets 11
  BOGOF offers 145
  branded and own-label merchandise 99
  buying and merchandising 111, 127
  competition from pound shops 144
  conflict theory 18
  environmental sustainability 301
  history and development 5, 6, 7, 8
  maturity stage of retail life cycle 15
  negative consumer behaviour 67
  pricing 139, 147, 152, 159–60
superstores 11
supplements, advertising 167, 168
suppliers
  buying and merchandising 122, 127
    organisational buying decision 113
    own-label merchandise 116
    Quality Control 128
    retail buying cycle 118, 120
    roles 111
  market attractiveness 47
  power 47, 127
  pricing 137, 140
    predatory 147
    retail price calculation 147, 148
  retail marketing planning 35
supply chain 133–5
  Corporate Social Responsibility 297, 298
  global 307–10
  history and development 5–6
  mail order companies 268

supply chain management (SCM) 127–8, 276, **336**
surveys, market research 74
sustainability 296, **336**
  environmental 20, 45, 221, 300–1
  history and development of retail marketing 7
  social 20, 45, 298–300
Sustainable Business Institute 296
Sutton, Michelle 254–5
Swann, Kate 53
sweatshop labour 309
Sweden 116
Swimwear 365: 271
Swindley, D.G. 110, 111
SWOT analysis 36–7, 42, **336**
symbol groups 111

T.M. Lewin 199
T&S 194, 211
tablet catalogues 270
tactile components, retail atmosphere 235, 237
Tai, S.H.C. 62
Taiwan 321
Tasker, A. 192, 203
taste, and retail atmosphere 235, 236
Tate & Lyle 95
Taylor Nelson Sofres (TNS) 63, 75, 228
technical quality 250–1
technological developments
  advertising 169–70
  future of retailing 26
  impact on retail environment 18–19, 20
  multichannel retailing 276–7
  PESTEL analysis 45
Ted Baker 94, 195, 197
Telegraph, The 74
telemarketing 271
television
  advertising 164, 166, 167, 170
  sales promotions 175
  shopping 13, 272
Tempah, Tinie 188
temporary shops 12–13
Tesco
  acquisitions 194, 211
  advertising 9
  category management 126
  Clubcard 171
  conflict theory 18
  expansion 192, 194–5
  history and development of retail marketing 7
  international retailing 312, 316, 322
  location 191, 194, 210, 211
  m-commerce 283
  planning regulations violation 295
  price wars 159

self-scan checkouts 265
Tesco Direct 267
Tesco Express 197, 211, 265
Tesco Extra 197
Tesco Metro 197
wheel of retailing 16
test marketing (product development) 85
theft 295
This Year/Last Year (TYLY) 123, 129
Thompson, V. 75
Thornton's 200
thresholds 203
Tiket.com 329, 330
Times, The 74
Tin Fish 114
tipping point 90
TK Maxx 153, 168, 199
TNS Magasin 75
TOMS 299
Tonglet, M. 67, 295
Toni & Guy 38
top of the mind recall 93–4
Topshop 111
Tordjman, A. 320
Total Students Ltd 145
touchpoints 275, 281
touchscreens 276
town centres 199
Trade Descriptions Act (1968) 46, 292, 293
trade fairs/exhibitions
   buying and merchandising 114, 115, 127
   product development 86
   retail design and layout 222, 230
trademarks 95, 154, 294
trading 120, **336**
transnational corporations (TNCs) 314, 321
transport
   advertising 167, 169–70
   in emerging markets 321, 329
   fuel 44, 300, 301
   history and development of retail marketing 5, 6
   hubs as retail locations 198–9
   supply chains 134
Travel Inn 98
trends, product 89–90
trial runs (product development) 85
TripAdvisor 178
triple bottom line (TBL, 3BL) 296, **336**
Tupperware 13
Turkey 133, 134, 187
TV *see* television
Twitter 19, 54, 178, 179, 181, 188, 271, 272, 278, 288

Ubisoft 23
Ugolini, L. 6

Underhill, Paco 75, 228, 237
Unilever 164
Unipart Logistics 288
Uniqlo 14, 175, 224
unique selling proposition 14, 229
United Kingdom
   advertising 164, 166, 169, 178
   ageing of population 44, 68
   BBC radio stations 169
   buying and merchandising 111, 116, 122, 127, 128
   call centres 255
   Carrefour's exit 317
   demographics 68, 69
   direct marketing 271
   environmental sustainability 300–1
   ethical consumer behaviour 301
   food wastage 145
   geographical pricing 147
   global economic crisis 20
   grocery industry, competition 47
   history and development of retail marketing 4, 6–8
   independent shops, decline of 295
   legislation 290, 292, 293–5
   mail order 267–8, 269
   markdowns 152, 153
   market levels 138
   Migato 35
   m-tailing 180
   petrol prices 44
   planning system 209–11, 294–5
   product assortment 91
   psychological pricing 142
   recession 44
   retail hierarchy 195, 196
   retail life cycle 15
   retail premises vacancies 19
   service sector 248
   shoplifting 67
   size of retail sector 247, 296
   socio-economic groups 69, 70
   Superdry 187
   supply chains 133–5
   symbol groups 111
   television shopping 272
   trade fairs 115
   VAT 147, 152, 154
United Nations (UN) Global Compact 297
United States of America
   advertising 169, 178
   buying and merchandising 110, 111, 127
   diffusion of innovations theory 65
   domination of large retailers 314
   eye tracking 228
   global economic crisis 20
   international retailing 20, 194–5, 307, 312, 314, 317, 318, 321, 323

   legislation 292, 293
   mail order 267, 270
   mission-based shopping 228
   retail accordion 17
   sales events 153, 164
   shopping villages 200
   television shopping 272
   wheel of retailing 16
UPS 322
Urban Outfitters 244, 245
urbanisation 321
URBN Inc. 244
user-generated content (UGC) 178, 281, **336**
users (organisational buying decision) 113
utilitarian needs 57–8

Väänänen, Heikki 258
vacant premises 19
Value Added Tax (VAT) 147, 152, 154
value and price, relationship between 151–2
value chain 47–8
Value Retail 154
value retailers 7, 20, 151
Van der Vorst, J. 124
variety chain 11, **336**
Varley R. 128, 217
VAT (Value Added Tax) 147, 152, 154
Veja 298
Vejlgaard, H. 89, 90
Victoria's Secret 48, 237
Vietnam 228, 307
viral marketing 170, 177–8
Virgin 96
Vision Express 41–3, 240
visual components, retail atmosphere 234–5, 236
visual merchandising (VM) 57, 228–34, 240, **336**
Vivista 22
Vlachos, P.A. 66
Von Oech, R. 170
Vorhies, D.W. 250
Vrechopoulos, A.P. 66

Wagner, J. 110
Waitrose 16, 62, 140, 192, 194
Waldman, C. 312
Walkers crisps 144
Wall Street Journal, The 74
Walmart 2, 7, 16, 47, 106, 107, 178, 309
   international retailing 312, 314, 322
   China 313, 316, 321
Walnut Unlimited 63–5
Walsh, K. 154
Walshe, Peter 106
Walters, D. 191
Walton, Sam 313

wastage 145
Waste Electrical & Electronic Equipment (WEEE) Directive 293
Watson, James 322
wearable technology 26
weather, and sales forecasting 129
Web 2.0 19, 178
webcam 272
websites
  access 267
  consumer engagement 275
  consumer reviews 177, 178
  design 277
  marketing communications 177, 178, 179, 181, 188
  selling environment 238, 240
  see also etailing; internet
Webster, F.E. 112, 113
Weekly Sales, Stock and Intake Plan (WSSI, 'Wizzy') 128
Weitz, B.A. 98
Wells, W. 68
Westfield London 245
Westfield Stratford 218–21

WH Smith 53–4, 175, 177, 195
wheel of retailing 15–16
Which? 59
Whistle Stop 143
Whistles 111
white collar crime 295
Whitman, Meg 81
Whittington, R. 36
wholesalers 5, 8, 140, **336**
Wilkinson, Steve 106
Williams, D. 315
Williamson, Matthew 96
Wilson, Charles 214
Wind, Y. 112, 113
window displays 217–18, 220, 229, 230
window shopping 59
Witt UK 271
Wm Low 194
women
  consumer behaviour 62, 67
  global supply chains 307–8
  lifestyle changes 7–8
  targeting 81–2
Wood, S. 192, 203, 204, 206

Woolworth 7, 15, 143
word-of-mouth (WoM) 181, **336**
  brand loyalty 66
  consumer decision-making 59, 60
  electronic (eWOM) 177
  negative 259, 260
  opinion leaders 62
World 237
World Trade Organization (WTO) 313, 319, 320
WPP 170
Wright, Paul 101, 102

Yahoo 178
yoox.com 153
YouTube 166, 168, 178, 278, 279, 288

Zalora 329, 330
Zappos 282
Zara 96, 106, 117, 128, 166, 220, 221
Zeithaml, V.A. 251
Zikmund, W.G. 73